CASES IN

OPERATIONS MANAGEMENT

CASES IN
OPERATIONS MANAGEMENT

SECOND EDITION

Robert Johnston
Warwick Business School, University of Warwick

Stuart Chambers
Warwick Business School, University of Warwick

Christine Harland
School of Management, University of Bath

Alan Harrison
Cranfield School of Management, Cranfield University

Nigel Slack
Warwick Business School, University of Warwick

FINANCIAL TIMES
PITMAN PUBLISHING

FINANCIAL TIMES MANAGEMENT
128 Long Acre, London WC2E 9AN
Tel: +44 (0)171 447 2000
Fax: +44 (0)171 240 5771
Website: www.ftmanagement.com

An imprint of Pearson Education Limited

First published in Great Britain in 1993
Second edition 1997

ISBN 0 273 62496 2

British Library Cataloguing in Publication Data
A CIP catalogue record for this book can be obtained from the British Library

7 9 10 8 6

Typeset by Tek-Art, Croydon, Surrey
Printed and bound in Great Britain by
Redwood Books, Trowbridge, Wiltshire

*The Publishers' policy is to use paper manufactured
from sustainable forests.*

Contents

Part 3
PLANNING AND CONTROL

Part 4
IMPROVEMENT

Part 5
THE OPERATIONS CHALLENGE

Contributors

AUTHORS

Robert Johnston	Reader in Operations Management, Warwick Business School, Warwick University
Stuart Chambers	Lecturer in Operations Management, Warwick Business School, Warwick University
Christine Harland	Senior Research Fellow, Centre for Research in Strategic Purchasing and Supply (CRiSPS), School of Management, University of Bath
Alan Harrison	EXEL Fellow in Automotive Logistics, Cranfield School of Management, Cranfield University
Nigel Slack	Professor of Manufacturing Policy and Strategy, Warwick Business School, Warwick University

ASSOCIATE CONTRIBUTORS

Adam Bates	Strategic Development Executive, British Tourist Authority
John Bicheno	Reader in Operations Management, University of Buckingham
Robert Craven	Independent Consultant
Jim Crew	Managing Director, Eurocamp Travel Ltd
Michael Eavis	Managing Director, Glastonbury Festivals Ltd
Tang Kam Hung	Former MBA student, Warwick Business School
Tammy Helander	Independent Consultant
Rob Lummis	Personnel Director, Land Rover Vehicles
Stephen Mottram	Factory Manager, Jeyes Group plc
Sara Mountney	Research Associate, Warwick Business School
Alistair Nicholson	Professor, London Business School
Mark Robinson	Director, Wates Estates Agency Services, London
Kevan Scholes	Professor and Director, Sheffield Business School
Karen Turner	Manager, The Hillingdon Hospital
Christopher Voss	BT Professor of TQM, London Business School
Adrian Watt	Independent Consultant
Angela Watts	Finance Officer, Glastonbury Festivals Ltd
Graham Whittington	Marketing Specialist, Lancashire Enterprises plc
David Woodgate	Manager, National Westminster Bank
Kenneth Work	I.S. Consultant, Logica UK
Iain Young	Independent Consultant

Preface

The teaching of operations management is now, more than ever, reliant upon the use of case studies. A basic problem faced by teachers devising such courses, however, has been the limited availability of suitable operations management case material, based on European companies, that is readily available for classroom use. We hope that this collection of cases will provide much needed support for teachers of operations management as the cases cover a wide variety of operations management issues in many different settings. We also believe that the cases can be successfully incorporated into operations management teaching programmes at undergraduate and postgraduate levels and also in executive programmes.

This second edition of our casebook contains an expanded and updated collection of 43 cases which we have used, and continue to use, in our own teaching. This edition has been restructured to follow the themes of, and illustrate the main points contained in, our comprehensive operations management text (Slack, N., Chambers, S., Harland, C., Harrison, A. and Johnston, R., (1998), *Operations Management*, Second Edition, Pitman Publishing). This casebook can be used as a companion to the text. We have also, in this edition, expanded the introductory sections so that the book can also serve as a standalone text for shorter, introductory operations management courses.

The first section of the book (Introduction to Operations Management Case Analysis) deals with some issues concerning how to study operations management using cases and how to analyse case studies. Some students do not always see the value of case studies so this introductory section will hopefully allay their concerns. This section sets out the importance of using case studies in studying operations management and identifies many of the benefits of so doing. It explains the nature of cases – what they are, what they are not – and provides some suggestions for their analysis; it also explains the objectives of the whole book and describes the book's structure.

The main body of the book is structured under the five 'traditional' operations headings which are likely to be covered in most operations management courses: operations management, design, planning and control, improvement, and the operations challenge. We have provided several cases in each part, covering each main topic area, with an introduction at the start of each part which provides an overview of the area and explains how some of the cases fit into that topic. These part introductions also provide some suggestions for further reading.

Each case study is accompanied by a set of questions. The questions are indicative of some of the significant issues found in each case and should guide students in their analysis. It is recognised that teachers may prefer to devise alternative sets of questions which better reflect their favoured teaching schemes and styles of approach to case analysis. Many of the issues and debating points that arise from the cases are considered in the *Lecturer's Guide* which accompanies the casebook.

In most cases the organisations on which the cases are based have been kind enough to allow their names to be used. While all the cases reflect real issues facing the organisations at the time, the cases have been written for the purposes of class discussion and student instruction only and are not designed to illustrate the effective or ineffective management of an organisation.

We hope that you, both teachers and students, will derive as much value and pleasure from these cases as we have in our use of them. We would value any comments and suggestions you might have about the book.

We would like to thank all those organisations, whether named or disguised, for their help with the preparation of the material used in this book. We are most grateful to the managers and staff of these organisations for giving their time and their assistance, without which this book could not have been possible.

We would like to thank our associate contributors for their work in the preparation and development of some of the cases and all our past students who have participated in the discussion, and development, of these cases.

Thanks also to Financial Times Pitman Publishing who have enabled and encouraged us in the preparation of this book, in particular Penelope Woolf and Stuart Hay.

Special thanks go to Mary Walton, the Operations Management Group Secretary at Warwick Business School, for her work, dedication and support.

Robert Johnston
Stuart Chambers
Christine Harland
Alan Harrison
Nigel Slack

Introduction to Operations Management Case Analysis

INTRODUCTION

Operations management (OM) is a practical subject. Trying to learn about OM and the decisions that operations managers take each day in all organisations around us cannot easily be studied by reading texts or listening to lectures alone. Certainly these will give you important and helpful information, but the subject does not come alive until it is practised. You can learn how to fish from a book, but you will never understand the nuances of whirlpools and eddies until you have seen them for yourself; you cannot understand the excitement of playing sport from a book, you have to do it; you can learn recipes for meals from a recipe book but you will not know how good the food tastes, or how difficult it is to cook, until you have tried them out for yourself.

Unfortunately, opening this book will not physically transport you into the office of an operations manager and allow you to take over their job. But it will get you close! It will provide you with information from over 40 different organisations, from several different countries, and will give you some fascinating insights into what operations managers do and how they work, as well as the issues they face. Most importantly this book will give you the opportunity, in a safe environment, to experiment with the situations they face – giving you the chance to assess, analyse and evaluate the situation they are in and make recommendations.

This casebook will provide you with many benefits:

- real information about a real organisation without having to spend large amounts of time and effort interviewing managers, customers and staff or searching through company documents
- the chance to evaluate situations faced by real operations managers
- the ability to 'hold time still', to assess a situation without it changing as it does in real time – to undertake analysis and evaluation without the pressures of managing the operation
- the opportunity, and the information, to debate and discuss the interpretation and use of the data and to undertake meaningful analysis
- the ability to develop and discuss possible solutions and their implications
- you will not be sacked if you get a decision or the recommendations wrong, nor will you be taken to court if you cost the organisation millions of guilders, francs, dollars or pounds!

All of the cases in this book are real cases, based on real situations faced by real operations managers in real organisations. Most include the name of that organisation, others, for various reasons, do not.

Remember though, the case itself cannot tell us everything. The material has been selected to provide us with enough information to help us understand the particular topic. It has also been chosen with a specific topic in mind. Herein lies a problem for studying operations cases. The reality is that any operations problem involves elements of people issues, quality, scheduling, technology, and so on and every operations manager has to bring all their knowledge and experience to bear to deal with the issue at hand, as a whole.

For the purpose of teaching and learning, we have had to spilt up the body of knowledge on operations management into convenient chunks. However, you will find that there are great overlaps when working on the cases. Bear in mind that the cases have been written to illustrate one particular topic but the nature of OM means that you will find, and indeed should look for, links with all the other topics. Through this process of becoming aware of links and interconnections you will start to understand the complexity, and the excitement, of managing operations.

THE AIM OF THIS CASEBOOK

The aim of this book is to demonstrate some of the problems faced by operations managers in various settings, both goods-oriented and service-oriented, through the provision of case studies. Its purpose is to promote discussion as to how operations managers might improve their operations and contribute to corporate objectives, and by so doing equip future and practising managers with the skills and techniques needed to be better able to understand and manage operations.

Analysis of the cases will provide opportunities to apply and test out many of the tools, techniques and concepts of operations management that can be found in many of the excellent production/operations texts that exist, some of which have been referenced at the end of the introductions to each part of the book.

THE NATURE OF OPERATIONS MANAGEMENT CASES

Operations management cases often reflect the nature of operations themselves. They can be complicated. Interacting within any operation there are different pieces of technology, different staff, and different systems and procedures. This makes for a complex decision environment. Although some of the complexity has, of necessity, been taken out in the case writing process you might still find that there are many different things to consider. So you must simplify. Extract what you believe to be important and classify issues, problems and pieces of information. This will give you a clearer picture of the case.

Operations management cases also often involve technology. This does give some people problems. They are reluctant to become too involved in strange technologies because they believe them to be difficult to understand. Yet it is usually not necessary to understand the nature or the workings of the technology itself to analyse the management situation. In the Beaver Engineering Group case (Case 12), for example, you do not need to know how a Computerised Numerical Controlled (CNC) machine works, or even what it looks like! You do need to know basically what CNC machines do, and that information is therefore supplied as a simple explanation in the case.

In essence most technologies *are* quite straightforward. Just ask some simple questions. How big is the technology? How much of the work is done by machines as opposed to human beings? How integrated or connected is the technology? What are the effects on the people who staff the operation? How many different kinds of technology are there in the operation? Is it intended to be used for only one product or service (that is dedicated) or is it adaptable, capable of being 'set-up' for a range of different outputs?

This combination of complexity and technology can mean that you might have to speculate about the precise nature of the operation at some points in your analysis. Don't worry too much about doing this. Provided you are sensible and work from the facts that you do have, and that you do not forget that you are only speculating and you consider the difference it would make to your analysis if your speculation is misplaced, then your analysis will move forward.

THE PROCESS OF CASE ANALYSIS

Case studies can ask you to do a number of things. Usually though they are either asking you to understand a situation and its implications or they are asking you to solve specific problems. Of course, in order to solve problems you first have to understand the situation and its implications. So the difference between these two types of case study is really one of emphasis. In fact one of the most useful ways of approaching case analysis is to treat them as problem-solving opportunities and follow a sequence of activities designed specifically for problem solving.

Figure A.1 shows this sequence of activities. First there is a process of observation, or for case analysis a process of recognising the symptoms of possible problems described in the case. Next there is a process of understanding the overall objectives of the problem-solving process. This will involve understanding the objectives of the operation itself. After this the nature of the problem should be analysed and the interrelationships between different parts of the case established. It is now time to move on to considering the different options which might improve the operation. Eventually it will become necessary to evaluate and choose what you are going to recommend the operation to do. After this your recommended solution will need to be implemented within the operation. Finally, the effectiveness of the implemented solution should be observed and if any further action is needed the whole cycle is started again. (You can, of course, only do this last step in a real situation.)

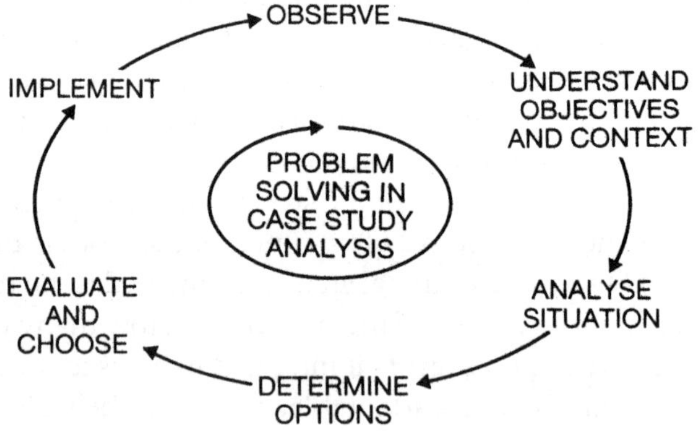

Fig. A.1 The stages of case study analysis

Observe

Reading the facts as laid down in a case study is equivalent to observing an organisation in real life. During this stage be careful of jumping to premature conclusions. Something that seems significant when described in one part of the case study may take on a totally different aspect when placed in the context of information presented later. For this reason some authorities counsel against making notes on the first reading of a case study. Instead read quickly through the case to get a picture of the overall 'story'. Then return to the beginning and work through more thoroughly, either highlighting points or making notes of facts and issues which seem particularly pertinent.

As you are noting what seem to be the key points, be careful to distinguish the strength of the evidence which is cited in the case. Relevant points can be drawn from the following:

- *Facts.* These are the hard pieces of information which are clearly in a precise form and seem unequivocal. For example, 'the turnover of the company is £5 million'. They are the bones of the case around which everything else is built.
- *Inference.* Reported facts are rearranged in such a way as to reach further conclusions. The inferred issue may never be explicitly stated in the case but can nevertheless be drawn from the logic of other statements. For example, if it is stated that the types of product produced by a company doubled over a period of time and if it is also stated that the management of a company invested heavily in more flexible machinery during the same period, it is safe to infer that the managers of the company understood the connection between product variety and operational flexibility.

- *Hearsay*. Many of the cases include statements from managers or other employees. These views are genuinely held and may be based on fact or, at the opposite extreme, they may be emotional responses to the situation. You will have to make judgements about the reliability of this data and weight it accordingly alongside other more 'hard' evidence.
- *Speculation*. In some ways this is a weaker form of inference. Speculation must have a logical base in as much as it must be possible to make a case for the point you are noting. Furthermore, there should be some evidence to support it in the case study, though not to the point where one could in any way logically 'prove' the point.
- *Assumption*. When there is a clear gap or hole in the data in the case study, it may be necessary to make an assumption which, as far as you can tell, seems reasonable in the context being described. For example, we may assume that the behaviour of customers in different countries is sufficiently similar to recommend the same solution for all parts of a multinational's company. The important point is that assumptions must always be seen for what they are: 'best guesses' in the particular circumstances. The important caveat is that you should examine the possible effects if the assumptions you have made prove to be false.

Understand objectives and context

Unless you know what the organisation described in the case study is trying to do, it is difficult to judge the nature of the problems it faces, and, just as important, how the managers in the organisation might view things.

In operations management cases this stage is usually concerned with connecting the overall objectives of an organisation with the specific objectives of the issue or problem described in the case. So, for example, if a case describes the purchase of a particular piece of process technology for an operation, the questions to try to clarify could be as follows:

- What is the history of the organisation in terms of its use of process technology?
- What are the long-term objectives of the operation? Is it primarily a 'for profit' organisation or do other non-financial objectives dominate? What are the implications (if any) for the way it uses process technology?
- How does the organisation serve its customers? Which aspects of what the organisation 'sells' to its customers are the most important to them? Is it:
  - the specification of the product or service?
  - the quality of the product or service?
  - the customer lead time (how long you have to wait) for the product or service?
  - the dependability of delivery of the product or service?
  - the variety, customisation or flexibility of the product or service?
  - the cost of the product or service?

- What aspects of process technology in this particular case (size, cost, capacity, flexibility, etc.) influence the operations objectives?
- How does the way in which the organisation develops its process technology constrain and limit the strategic direction of the organisation?
- Conversely, how does the way in which the organisation develops its process technology enable the organisation to enhance its strategy?

Analyse the situation

Be careful not to skip this stage. It is tempting to do so: the objectives of the organisation have been formulated and the issues already listed from the case study, so why not go straight into thinking of ways of solving whatever problems are described? Even when the decision seems clearly defined, it is worthwhile spending some time analysing the information in the case. Many organisations and individuals have suffered as a result of managers jumping to conclusions without adequate analysis of the situation.

The Concise Oxford Dictionary defines the verb 'to analyse' as to 'ascertain the elements of'. Analysis is the process of breaking down a complex situation into its component parts. This will help you to understand the underlying issues and the relationships between the problems in the case. The most likely outcome is that the nature of the problems in the case can be redefined so as to reveal their root causes.

Many of the cases comprise both narrative and data. It is important that your analysis should review both aspects. If you are dealing with narrative you may need to identify the different products or services provided by the organisation and ask which seem more popular and which are more difficult to provide and why? How are they made or provided, and can you identify the key steps or stages in the operations process? You might ask yourself what different people say about the situation and how good or bad things seem to be. If you are dealing with data you might look for trends and for figures that seem out of line. You may need to calculate averages for comparison, or speeds of queues or of different production processes to identify bottlenecks or delays. Where possible you should identify and tabulate differences, for example between markets, volumes, skill requirements, etc. You may find simple tools like lists, graphs, charts and flow diagrams useful to summarise your findings.

Most questions will be concerned with understanding the nature of the problem and its causes. One useful way of getting to the root causes of the issues described in the case is by using cause–effect listings. This is simply a process of identifying the main symptoms, problems or 'effects' described in the case and then listing all the possible reasons, explanations or 'causes' of these which are described or referred to in the case study. So, for example, if you see an operation as having one major service quality problem which results in errors in the information presented to customers, the cause–effect listing could be as follows.

Effect	*Possible causes*
Errors in information reaching customers	Lack of training? Errors in staffs' information sources? Out-of-date staff information sources? Customers given insufficient guidance on how to request information etc.?

The next step would be to consider the connections and interrelationships between the possible causes based on your analysis of the information.

Determine the options

Having spent some time breaking down the situation into its various elements (analysis) there comes a time to put it all back together (synthesis). This is the creative part of the whole process. It is where you should put forward the various courses of action that could be considered by the organisation in order to 'solve' the problems described in the case, or generally to improve the operation's performance. You will usually find that the questions associated with the case will help you do this. You may be asked to list the range of options, or identify the various ways that an organisation might go about doing something.

This is where the work you did in analysing the information in the case will again pay off. Although at an early stage you may have only thought of one or possibly two 'obvious' solutions, a good piece of analysis is likely to have helped you identify many more possibilities. Furthermore, it is more likely that these options will deal with the 'real' problems and the causes of these, rather than what you may have believed to be the situation on first reading the case.

As in most creative activities, two principles are worth bearing in mind in developing options. First, don't evaluate or criticise potential solutions too early. Go for quantity rather than quality of solutions to begin with. Try to 'brain-storm' all the possible ways of dealing with the situation. Do not reject any options at this stage, however crazy they may seem. Second, organise the solutions in some sets that naturally group together and check for overlaps, gaps and inconsistencies.

Evaluate and choose

Evaluating means determining the value or worth of things. That is exactly what this stage consists of, determining the worth of the options generated in the previous stage and assessing how likely they are to contribute to improving the situation described in the case.

Your ability to evaluate a situation will be a function of the analysis you have already undertaken, though you may find that you have to undertake a little more analysis in order to evaluate all of your options. You should also test out your arguments against the material in the case to ensure that the evidence supports your conclusions.

The process of evaluation is best carried out by considering three questions about each option:

1 *How feasible is each option?* The feasibility of an option indicates the degree of difficulty in adopting it. It takes into account the time, effort and money needed to put it into practice. For example, you could consider whether the organisation has the technical or human skills required to carry out the option, whether it has the funding or cash requirements to invest in the option and generally whether it has the capacity or capability of implementing the option.

2 *How acceptable is each option?* By acceptability of an option we mean how far it takes the operation towards its objectives. In effect it is the 'return' we get for choosing that option. Acceptability is best judged in two ways. First, by assessing the operational impact of the option, that is how is it likely to affect the operational performance of the organisation. For example, does the option increase the likelihood that the product or service of the operation will be closer to what customers want? Second, acceptability ought to be judged in terms of the financial impact of each option. If there is sufficient financial data in the case, it is useful to work out some of the more conventional financial evaluation measures such as return on investment or payback period.

3 *How risky is each option?* Perhaps the most robust way of evaluating the risk inherent in each option is to assess its 'downside risk'. That is in effect asking the question, 'What is the worst outcome that could happen if a particular option is chosen?'. The next obvious questions are: 'What would be the effect on the operation if that worst outcome occurred?', 'Could the operation survive?', and 'Is it worth the operation taking such a risk?'.

Implement

If you are asked to, or choose to, make recommendations as part of your case study analysis then they will be incomplete without some consideration of how they might be put into practice. The analysis of the case study may set the destination, but the implementation stage defines how you get there, which is a more difficult task.

The best way to consider implementation issues is to set an 'implementation agenda' – a set of basic questions whose answers set the basic plan for implementation:

- *When to implement?* Some times are better than others. What is happening in the organisation which could affect the chances of the recommended course of action being a success? Are some times of year quieter or more suitable for launching a change in the operation? It is clearly better to make changes when conditions are right. A word of warning though, there is never a perfect time, only ones that are better than others.

- *How fast to proceed?* Should one implement the recommendations over a short or long period of time? Is there an advantage, for instance, in moving quickly to apply the recommendations throughout the organisation, or should a more gradual dissemination be planned?
- *Where to start?* In which part of the organisation should the recommendations be applied first? There are two schools of thought here:
  1 Start first where you will achieve the most improvement.
  2 Start first where you are sure you will succeed.

The advantage of the first is that the changes will quickly 'pay back' the cost, time and effort invested. The advantage of the second is that the risk of failure is minimised and the people involved in implementation learn the problems associated with the recommendations as they go along without losing credibility.

THE STRUCTURE OF THE BOOK

This casebook has been structured to complement and correspond with its companion text: Slack, N., Chambers, S., Harland, C., Harrison, A. and Johnston, R. (1998), *Operations Management*, Second Edition, Pitman Publishing. Each part concentrates on a different aspect of operations management. Several cases are provided in each part which set out to describe some of the key issues involved and to show some of the difficulties and questions faced by operations managers. Introductions at the start of each part outline some of the key aspects of the topic and explain how the cases in that part fit into the topic area. Some suggestions for further reading are also included.

Part 1 Operations management

This part provides an overview of the nature and tasks of operations management. A framework is provided that encapsulates these and sets out the structure for the rest of the book and for the studying of the subject. It deals with the processing of materials, information and customers, and the creation of goods and services. This part also investigates the role of operations in supporting, implementing and driving corporate strategy.

Part 2 Design

This part and its associated cases demonstrates the processes involved in designing products and services, and also the processes which create and deliver them. It identifies the importance of design and how products and services need to be designed not only to meet customer expectations but also to support the strategic intentions of the organisation. This part outlines the key stages involved in the design of a product or service, from concept to final specification. It also outlines the key activities involved in designing the process of delivery including network design, layout and flow, the use of technology and job design.

Part 3 Planning and control

This part investigates a central and critical operations task. Planning and control is often a large and complex task though it basically involves ensuring that the operation has sufficient resources to be able to meet demand. This part outlines some of the key planning and control activities including the planning and control of capacity, inventory, the overall supply chain (including purchasing and distribution), materials, projects and quality. It also outlines the basic planning and control issues involved in just-in-time. The cases provide coverage of all of these topics.

Part 4 Improvement

This part and its associated cases outlines what is emerging as an important operations task. It covers the importance of performance measurement and identifies several techniques that can be used to improve organisational performance such as flow charts, scatter diagrams, cause–effect diagrams and Pareto diagrams. This part also covers total quality management (TQM), one of the best known improvement philosophies.

Part 5 The operations challenge

The cases in this part provide an opportunity to assess operations management in its wider context. The introductory section outlines the key challenge for operations managers, understanding how operations contributes to the success of the organisation as a whole. As well as discussing the difficulties, it examines the key steps involved in formulating an operations strategy. It also assesses four key challenges operations managers face in the development of an operations strategy: the need to develop ethical operations strategies, to consider the international dimension of operations strategies, to be creative in devising strategies and the ultimate challenge of implementing the chosen strategies.

Further reading

Armistead, C. G. (ed.), (1994), *The Future of Services Management*, Kogan Page.
Berry, L. L. (1985), *On Great Service: A Framework for Action*, Free Press.
Bignell, V. *et al.* (eds), (1985), *Manufacturing Systems*, Blackwell.
Bowen, D. E., Chase, R. B., Cummings, T. G. and Associates, (1990), *Service Management Effectiveness*, Jossey-Bass.

Brunsson, N. (1985), *The Irrational Organisation: Irrationality as a Base for Organisational Action and Change*, Wiley.
Buffa, E. S. (1976), *Operations Management: The Management of Productive Systems*, Wiley.
Chase, R. B. and Aquilano, N. J. (1973), *Production and Operations Management: A Life-Cycle Approach*, Irwin.
Collier, D. A. (1987), *Service Management – Operating Decisions*, Prentice Hall.
Collier, D. A. (1994), *The Service/Quality Solution: Using Service Management to Gain Competitive Advantage*, Irwin and ASQC Quality Press.
Cooke, S. and Slack, N. (1992), *Making Management Decisions* (2nd edn), Prentice Hall.
Easton, G. (1992), *Learning from Case Studies* (2nd edn), Prentice Hall.
Fitzsimmons, J. A. and Fitzsimmons, M. J. (1994), *Service Management for Competitive Advantage*, McGraw-Hill.
Grönroos, C. (1990), *Service Management and Marketing*, Lexington Books.
Harris, N. D. (1989), *Service Operations Management*, Cassell.
Haywood-Farmer, J. and Nollet, J. (1991), *Services Plus: Effective Service Management*, Morin.
Heskett, J. L., Sasser, W. E. and Hart, C. W. L. (1990), *Service Breakthroughs: changing the rules of the game*, The Free Press.
Hill, T. (1993), *Manufacturing Strategy* (2nd edn), Macmillan.
Hill, T. (1991), *Production/Operations Management: Text and Cases* (2nd edn), Prentice Hall.
Jones, P. (ed) (1989), *Management in Service Industries*, Pitman Publishing.
Krajewski, L. J. and Ritzman, L. P. (1993), *Operations Management* (3rd edn), Addison-Wesley.
Lovelock, C. H. (1988), *Managing Services*, Prentice Hall International.
Meredith, J. R. (1992), *The Management of Operations* (4th edn), Wiley.
Murater, K. and Harrison, A. (1991), *How to Make Japanese Management Methods Work in the West*, Gower.
Murdick, R. G., Render B. and Russell R. (1990), *Service Operations Management*, Allyn and Bacon.
Normann, R. (1991), *Service Management* (2nd edn), Wiley.
Reynolds, J. I. (1978), 'There's Method in Cases', *Academy of Management Review*, January: 129–61.
Schroeder, R. G. (1989), *Operations Management*, McGraw-Hill.
Skinner, W. (1985), *Manufacturing: The Formidable Competitive Weapon*, Wiley.
Slack, N. (1991), *The Manufacturing Advantage*, Mercury.
Slack, N., Chambers, S., Harland, C., Harrison, A. and Johnston, R. (1998), *Operations Management* (2nd edn), Pitman Publishing.
Starr, M. K. (1972), *Production Management, Systems and Syntheses*, Prentice Hall.
Wild, R. (1989), *The International Handbook of Production/Operations Management*, Cassell.
Wild, R. (1995), *Production and Operations Management*, Cassell.

Part 1

OPERATIONS MANAGEMENT

Introduction

Operations management is concerned with the design, planning, control and improvement of an organisation's resources and processes to produce goods or services for customers. Whether it is the provision of airport services, greetings cards, plastic buckets, holidays or even pop festivals, operations managers will have been involved in the design, creation and delivery of those products or services (*see* Fig. P1.1).

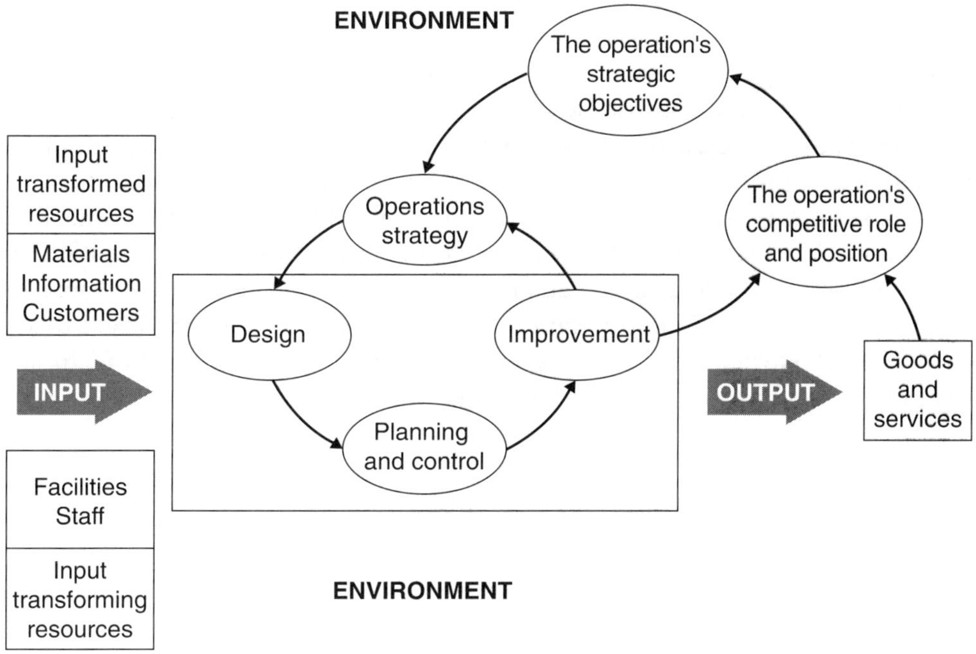

Fig. P1.1 A general model of operations management

Designing products and services

Design is the activity of determining the purpose, physical form, shape and composition of products and services, and also, importantly, designing the processes that will be used to produce them. You will see from the Birmingham International Airport case (Case 1) that each part of the airport – terminals, baggage handling services, aeroplane servicing and catering, for example – has been carefully designed to fulfil not only its current role, but also with the possible demands of the next year and even the next 10 years in mind. In the case of Focus Plastics (Case 4) the fashionable designs of the 'Concept' range have accounted for the rapid growth and profitability of the business. Design is an important activity that will ensure the long-term success of the organisation and is covered in Part 2 of this book.

Planning and controlling the operation

The planning and control of operations is a major task for all operations managers: co-ordinating all the different internal operations to ensure that materials and customers are in the right place at the right time for the right operation. Each part of Birmingham Airport's operation has to be planned so that it has enough staff, enough inventory, enough space, the appropriate passengers, the correct baggage, the right planes, the proper equipment, in the right place at the right time. The staff involved, from the airport, airlines and associated organisations, have to undertake all the tasks they have been given so that the operation works smoothly, and management must then control these operations to ensure that all goes to plan and meets the needs of the customers – today, tomorrow, next week, next month and next year. Planning and control is the activity of deciding what the operations resources should be doing, then making sure that they really are doing it. For Glastonbury Festival (Case 3) the success of the event depends on the planning of all resources so that the festival is ready for service over the long, enjoyable weekend. At Wace Burgess (Case 2) good planning ensures that greetings cards are ready in time for all the festivals and events. It's no good supplying the last batch of Christmas cards in January! This topic is developed in Part 3.

Improving the performance of the operation

When products and services have been designed and the operation's work is being planned and controlled, this is not the end of operations management's direct responsibilities. The continuing responsibility of all operations managers is to improve the performance of their operation. Failure to improve at least as fast as competitors (in for profit organisations) or at the rate of customers' rising expectations (in all organisations) is to condemn the operations function always to fall short of what customers expect and what the organisation as a whole requires from it. Richard Lambert, the Head of Planning and Development at Birmingham International Airport, talks about trying to 'keep up with the game in this rapidly changing world'. It is through constantly looking for ways to improve what the airport does and how it does it that the airport will be helped to maintain and improve its competitive position. Executive Holloware (Case 35) needs to improve the quality of its products or it may well go out of business! Part 4 contains cases concerning how organisations go about the important improvement task.

Operations strategy

Although the operations function is central to the organisation because it produces all the value-added goods and services, it does not exist in isolation. It has to work in conjunction with all the other functions of the organisation: marketing, accounting and finance, product/service development, human resources, purchasing and the engineering/technical functions, for example. Each of these influences, and is influenced by, the activities of the operation. Each of these functions has its own important role to play in the organisation's activities and they are (or should be) bound together, along with operations, by common organisational goals.

The strategic role of an organisation is to co-ordinate the activities of all these functions so that the organisation as a whole coherently and consistently meets not only the needs of the customers, but also fulfils the strategic intentions of the organisation. Operations strategy is concerned with helping the operation contribute to the organisation's competitiveness or strategic direction. This topic is dealt with in more detail later in this introduction and in Part 5.

There is a strategic issue in most of the cases in this book. For example, in Focus Plastics (Case 4) the three markets described must be served in very different ways and so operations must be closely involved in supporting these different requirements if the business is to continue to grow profitably.

THE TRANSFORMATION MODEL

All operations produce their goods or services by a process of transformation (*see* Fig. P1.2).

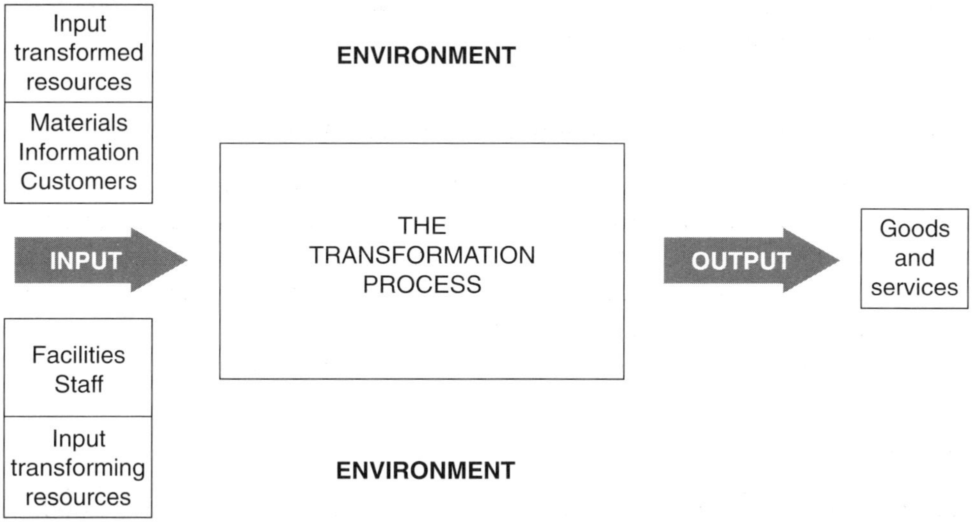

Fig. P1.2 The transformation model

The transformed resources

Operations transform a mixture of customers, materials and information.

Customer processing

Birmingham International Airport, for example, processes *customers* through its termini. Individual passengers are processed into batches of customers ready to board the right planes at the right times. Plane loads of arriving passengers are processed through customs and immigration and reunited with their bags and transport.

Materials processing

The airport also processes *materials* such as baggage, food and aeroplanes. In-bound aircraft, for example, are transformed into clean and re-fuelled out-bound aircraft. Incoming raw food is transformed into meals for staff and passengers.

Information processing

The airport's operation also processes a large amount of *information* – plane schedules, air traffic control (ATC) information and individual requests from passengers. ATC information, for example, is transformed into departure and arrival times on the passenger information screens.

The transforming resources

The materials, customers and information are transformed resources, they are changed in some way during the operation. What transforms them are the transforming resources – the operations facilities and staff. The cleaners, caterers and re-fuellers transform the aircraft; the check-in staff, departure lounges and restaurants transform the passengers.

Customer/materials/information processing operations

Very few operations are exclusively engaged in processing only customers, or materials or information. Yet one usually predominates, for example Birmingham International Airport, like Lunn Poly Travel (Case 5) and Glastonbury Festival (Case 3) predominantly transform customers whereas Wace Burgess (Case 2) and Focus Plastics (Case 4) predominantly transform materials. All of them, however, transform all three – information, customers and materials – to a greater or lesser extent.

Outputs

The outputs of the transformation process are goods and/or services. Goods, like greetings cards and plastic household items are tangible; you can touch them. Goods are usually produced prior to their consumption. Goods can often be stored, at least for a short time after their production, which may ease the planning and control task. There is often little contact between the staff producing the goods and the customer, so customers' perceptions of the quality of the goods is often based solely on the evidence of the goods themselves and not on the process by which they were made.

Services, such as festivals and music, tend to be intangible though they are seen and experienced by the customer. They can be difficult to store; space at a pop festival cannot be 'stored' and kept for use by paying customers a week later. Services are usually produced at the same time as they are consumed and so there is often contact made between the customers and the staff providing the service. As a result the customers' views about the quality of the service will not just be about the 'service' itself, but the way in which it was produced – that is the process.

Most operations produce goods *and* services

As most operations transform information, materials and customers they produce combinations of goods and services. Lunn Poly provides information about holiday destinations and availability, their brochures and tickets are the material evidence that customers may take away. Their service is to help you choose and book an appropriate holiday. Glastonbury Festival has to provide not just the music and

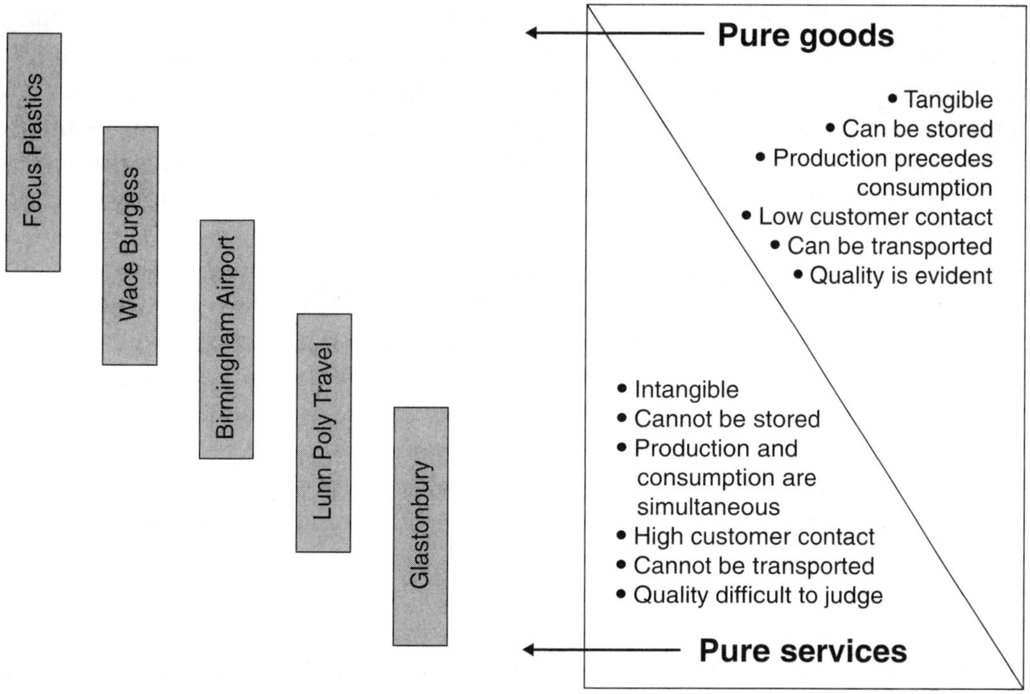

Fig. P1.3 A mix of goods and services

entertainment but also the food and water for the thousands of visitors that spend four or five days there. Wace Burgess does not only produce greetings cards but also provides technical and graphics advice to the designers, allowing them to explore the boundaries of creativity and innovation.

Figure P1.3 shows the relative position of the five organisations in Part 1 of the book in terms of the mix of goods and services that they produce.

Some goods producers, such as computer manufacturers which have lost the ability to differentiate themselves from their competitors through the goods that they offer, are using the provision of services; after-sales support, distribution systems, care and warranty service, for example, to achieve a competitive advantage. Similarly, some service organisations, like airlines, while providing similar levels of service to customers, are forced to compete on their goods; their routes, type of food offered, type of video entertainment system and other on-board services and types of aircraft.

OPERATIONS WITHIN OPERATIONS

Most operations are a complex set of interrelated smaller operations each with a specific function. These sub-operations interact together to provide the main goods and services to customers, each having its own transformation process.

Birmingham Airport, for example, though one large operation, is made up of many interdependent and often autonomous 'internal' operations, or micro-operations – the catering operation, the cleaning operation, the baggage handling operation, runway maintenance, fire service, and security service for example. At Wace Burgess, a manufacturing business, there are a variety of micro, internal, operations including purchasing, customer support, graphics preparation, printing, cutting and folding departments. All these internal operations may be quite different from each other but they all have to be designed, planned, controlled, improved and co-ordinated with each other.

Just as operations have external customers, so all the different micro-operations have internal customers too. The airport's customers are the passengers who are coming to the airport to get on a plane and also the airlines for whom the airport provides passenger facilities, fuel and landing services. These are the 'external' customers – customers who are outside the organisation – who desire and pay for the goods and services it produces. The airport's internal customers include pilots who need ATC information, baggage handlers who need the bags after they have been processed by check-in staff, and airlines requiring their planes to be serviced with fuel and food.

Operations are usually a complex network of micro-operations which form internal customer–supplier relationships, which together provide the goods, services and information to the external customer. If any part of a micro-operation is not properly designed, planned or controlled then the provision of goods or services to the external customer may be jeopardised. This is one of the foundations of total quality management (TQM) which is dealt with in Part 4.

As micro operations act in a similar way to the macro-operation, then most of the ideas relevant to the macro operation are also relevant to the micro-operation. In other words, many of the issues, methods and techniques which we treat in this book as applying to the operations function as a whole also have some meaning for each unit, section, group or individual within the organisation. All parts of an organisation, whether micro-operations such as catering or indeed other functions such as marketing or finance, can be viewed as operations in their own right. Each such operation will provide goods and/or services to internal or external customers, and each will have to design, plan, control and improve its outputs and the processes by which it creates those outputs. The implications of this are important. It means that every manager in every part of an organisation is, to some extent, an operations manager. All managers need to organise their resource inputs effectively so as to produce goods and services.

TYPES OF OPERATIONS

There are four particularly important dimensions which can be used to distinguish between different operations: the *volume* of their output, the *variety* of their output, the *variation* in the demand for their output and the degree of *customer contact* which is involved in producing the output.

The volume dimension

All the cases in Part 1 of this book are high volume operations supplying repetitive or standardised products and services. This allows for repeatability, specialisation and systemisation usually resulting in relatively low unit costs. Operations such as Beaver Engineering (Case 12) and Talleres Auto (Case 34) are examples of lower volume operations where a wide range of options is available, with less predictability and fewer opportunities for repetition and systemisation.

The variety dimension

The greater the variety of products or services produced, the more flexible the operation has to be. Focus Plastics has recently introduced its 'Concept' range which has expanded the range of shapes and colours that it can offer.

The variation dimension

Variation is concerned with the change in patterns of demand for products or services. Little variation in demand allows some organisations easily to plan and control their activities, resulting in a high utilisation of resources. Variation is a real problem for Wace Burgess which has to produce vast quantities of cards for just one big peak period, Christmas. Variation is an issue for many of the other cases in this book where demand is seasonal and/or uncertain, for example, Holly Farm (Case 16) and Sheepbreeder (Case 25).

The customer contact dimension

All operations have some degree of customer contact, but some have much more than others. Focus Plastics is a relatively low contact operation but still gets orders and customer enquiries daily. Lunn Poly and Glastonbury Festival have much greater levels of contact between their customers and the operation.

OPERATIONS STRATEGY

Operations management is a very immediate occupation. It involves hundreds of minute-by-minute decisions throughout the working week. Because of this it is vital that operations managers have a set of general principles which can guide decision making in the direction of the organisation's longer-term goals. This is an operations strategy – the overall set of activities and decisions that creates the role and objectives of the operations so they contribute to and support the organisation's ultimate business strategy.

Operations role

The operation may take three different roles within an organisation, as a *support* to business strategy, as the *implementer* of business strategy, and as the *driver* of business strategy.

Supporting business strategy

One role of the operations part of the business is to *support* strategy. That is, it must develop its resources to provide the capabilities which are needed to enable the organisation to achieve its strategic goals. Lunn Poly decided to sell and support inclusive tour packages only. The operation, therefore, had to adapt itself to support this intention, for example by selling off its commercial division which was dedicated to tailored travel packages.

Implementing business strategy

A strategy is only a statement of intent, it is the operation's role, therefore, to make it happen: the role of operations is to 'operationalise' and *implement* the chosen strategy. Lunn Poly had the strategy of becoming the number one retailer of package holidays. As a result the operation had to increase the number of its shops, change its way of dealing with customers in the shops and train its staff to sell holidays rather than just provide information for example.

Driving business strategy

The third role of the operations part of the business is to *drive* strategy by giving it a long-term competitive edge. Badly chosen staff, inappropriate computer systems or the sale of inferior holidays by Lunn Poly would have seriously undermined its long-term success. Conversely, by getting all these right it succeeded in becoming the number one retailer in a very short space of time.

Operations performance objectives

It is important to realise that even the most original and brilliant strategy can be rendered totally ineffective by an inept operations function. So how does an operation go about ensuring that it contributes effectively to the organisation's strategy? It does so through five basic 'performance objectives': the *quality* of its goods and services; the *speed* with which they are delivered to customers; the *dependability* with which the operation keeps its delivery promises; the *flexibility* of the operation to change what it does; and the *cost* of producing its goods and services. Achieving high performance in any one of these can give competitive advantage to a business. For example:

- The quality advantage. By ensuring that the operation *does things right*, by not making mistakes or creating defective products or poor service, the operation can provide a quality advantage to the organisation.
- The speed advantage. By *doing things fast*, an organisation can minimise the time between a customer asking for goods or services and the customer receiving them in full. In so doing, it increases the availability of its goods and services to customers thereby giving it a speed advantage.
- The dependability advantage. By *doing things on time*, and keeping delivery promises which have been made to customers, the operation can provide the organisation with a dependability advantage.
- The flexibility advantage. By being able to *change what is done*, that is being able to vary or adapt the operation's activities to provide individual treatment to customers or cope with unexpected circumstances, the operation can gain a flexibility advantage.
- The cost advantage. By *doing things cheaply*, that is giving good value to customers while keeping to budget or providing the right level of return for an organisation, the operation can provide a cost advantage.

So by translating organisational strategy into these operations performance objectives and identifying their relative importance, operations can focus on what is important and on doing it well.

A FRAMEWORK FOR UNDERSTANDING OPERATIONS MANAGEMENT

We can now combine the three important themes to provide a unified framework for understanding operations management (*see* Fig. P1.4).

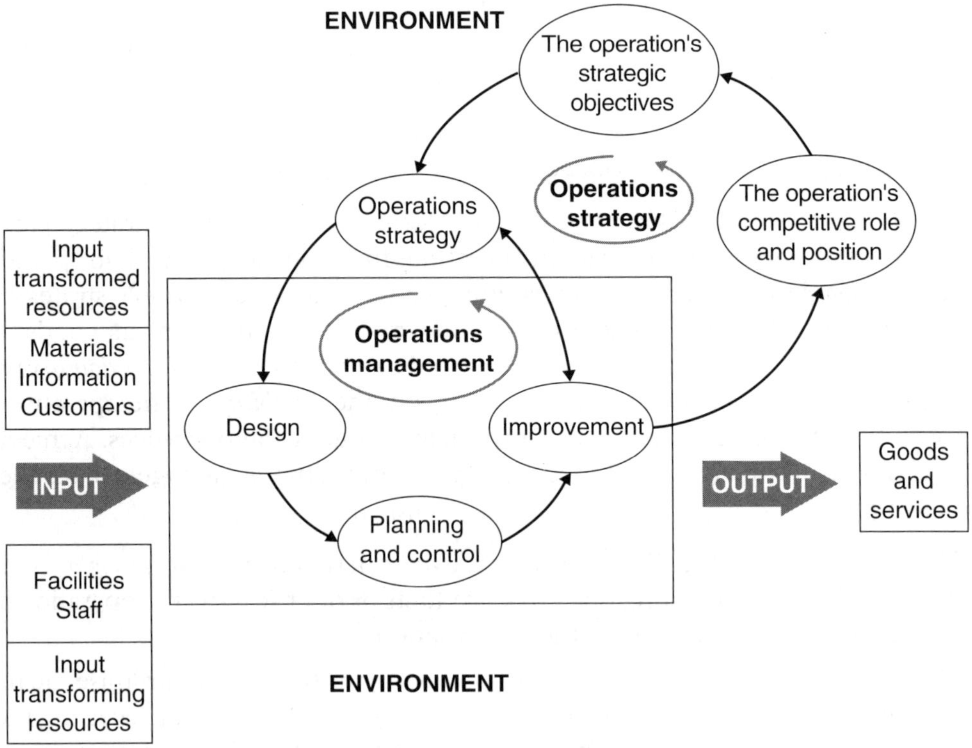

Fig. P1.4 A framework for understanding operations management

The first theme is the key operations management tasks – the design, planning and control, and improvement activities. The framework shows these activities as being connected in, more or less, the chronological order in which they would happen if a totally new operation was being developed. It would first be designed, then operated through planning and control activities and, over time, would be continually improved.

The second theme is the fundamental purpose of operations management: the transformation of input resources, both transformed and transforming, into goods and services as illustrated by the input–transformation–output diagram.

The third area is operations strategy: understanding the organisation's strategic intentions and then translating them into operations performance objectives to guide operations decisions about the design, planning, control and improvement of operations resources and processes.

The model in Fig. P1.4 shows two interconnected loops of activities. The bottom one more or less corresponds to what is usually seen as *operations management*, and the top one to what is seen as *operations strategy*. This book, like its associated textbook, concentrates on the former but tries to cover enough of the latter to allow the reader to make strategic sense of the operations manager's job.

THE COMPLEXITY AND CRITICALITY OF OPERATIONS MANAGEMENT

You should be starting to get a feel of just how complex and critical the operations management task is. It is complex because of all the different and yet interrelated activities, because of the large variety of tasks involved, and the large number of associated tools and techniques. It is critical because if anything goes wrong, not only could it lose a customer or create bad will, it could also undermine the whole competitive strategy of the organisation.

SUMMARY

This part, including Cases 1–5, has aimed to demonstrate the nature of operations management and also to provide a structure for studying the subject in more detail. Operations management deals with the processing of materials, information and customers, and the creation of goods and services. Also considered in this part is the role of operations in supporting, implementing and driving corporate strategy.

Key points

- All organisations have an operations function which produces their goods and services, and all organisations have managers who are responsible for running the operations function.
- The operations function (or 'operation' or 'operations system') is important to the organisation because it directly affects how well the organisation satisfies its customers.
- The most useful method of modelling operations is as an input–transformation–output system. Input resources can be classified as *transforming resources* (the staff and facilities) which act upon the *transformed resources* (materials, information and customers) which are in some way transformed by the operation.
- Outputs from the operation are usually a mixture of goods and services, although some operations are pure goods producers or pure service producers.
- Operations comprise many micro operations; these micro operations form a network of internal customer–supplier relationships within the operation.

- Operations can be classified along four dimensions which indicate their level of volume, variety, variation and customer contact.
- The key tasks of operations managers are the design, planning, control and improvement of operational resources and processes.
- By understanding the strategic intentions of an organisation and translating these into operations performance criteria, operations can support, implement and drive business strategy.
- The effective management of operations is critical to organisational success.

Recommended reading

Slack, N., Chambers, S., Harland, C., Harrison, A. and Johnston, R., (1995), *Operations Management*, Pitman Publishing. Chapters 1, 2 and 3.

Selected further readings

Adams, E. E. and Ebert, R. J. (1992), *Production and Operations Management* (5th edn), Prentice Hall.

Andrews, C. G. (1982), 'The Critical Importance of Production and Operations Management', *Academy of Management Review*, Vol 7, Jan.

Berry, W. L. and Hill, T. (1992), 'Linking Systems to Strategy', *International Journal of Operations and Production Management*, Vol 12, No 10.

Bowen, D. E., Chase, R. B., Cummings, T. G. and Associates (1990), *Service Management Effectiveness*, Jossey-Bass.

Chase, R. and Hayes, R. H. (1991), 'Beefing up Operations in Service Firms', *Sloan Management Review*, Fall: 15–26.

Hayes, R. H. and Wheelwright, S. C. (1984), *Restoring Our Competitive Edge*, Wiley.

Hill, T. (1991), *Production/Operations Management* (2nd edn), Prentice Hall.

Hill, T. (1993), *Manufacturing Strategy* (2nd edn), Macmillan.

Krajewski, L. J. and Ritzman, I. P. (1987), *Operations Management* (3rd edn), Addison-Wesley.

Schonberger, R. (1990), *Building a Chain of Customers*, Hutchinson Business Books.

Slack, N. (1991), *The Manufacturing Advantage*, Mercury Business Books.

Voss, C. A. (1992), *Manufacturing Strategy*, Part 4, Chapman and Hall.

Wild, R. (1989), *Production and Operations Management* (4th edn), Cassell.

CASE 1

Birmingham International Airport

Robert Johnston

Case date 1996

If you stand in the viewing gallery at Birmingham International Airport at around 5 p.m. on a weekday you will see, in the space of an hour and a half, between ten and twenty flights arrive and depart the new Eurohub transfer terminal. At the same time aircraft are arriving at and leaving the Main Terminal next to the Eurohub. Across the runway and acres of tarmac, at the site of the original airport, the overnight freight operation is just beginning to wake up with the arrival of staff and the preparations for the first aircraft from Europe or the USA.

Inside the airport, some of the 4000 staff of the 50 organisations based there see to the needs of their customers. The baggage handling operation is sorting, checking and dispatching bags to the many departing aircraft. The ground crews are loading and unloading aircraft, putting meals on board, filling the fuel tanks and cleaning the aircraft during their brief spell at the airbridge. The airlines' ticketing staff are dealing with lines of passengers, each of whom may have a different final destination. The information desk is fully manned, dealing with the many queries: people wanting to know if their plane is on time, or the location of the bank or hotel, or trying to work out how to get by road or rail to their final destination. Passengers flow through the lounges, passport control and security checks, use toilets, duty free shops, restaurants – all of which have to be kept clean and stocked for their convenience. All of these activities, and more, are designed, managed and controlled by the operations managers of the airport and the associated air travel concerns.

Richard Lambert, Head of Planning and Development summed up the job:

'Basically, the job of operations is to make sure that everything goes smoothly all the time. From making sure all the lights are working on the runways, to keeping the fire crew fully trained and fully alert, to processing our customers through the termini and servicing the planes on the aprons. This is not always easy as staff may not always be available, aircraft may be delayed and air traffic controllers may strike.

'As well as being concerned about today's events, today's planes and passengers, we have to look ahead to tomorrow and beyond. This too is not straightforward as the situation is always changing. You see, if you look at the forecast increase in air traffic over the next 10 years, you will see that we need to keep developing and expanding the

airport if we want to respond to that future demand. We have had major building projects on the site every year for the past decade. Indeed, it has been said that an airport is really a building site where planes occasionally land and take off. However, we have to ensure that we are going to meet the travel needs of our future customers, but without inconveniencing those that are using our airport today.

'Each part of the airport has to be carefully ***designed*** *to fulfil its job today, but with next year and the next 10 years in mind. Each part of the operation has to be* ***planned*** *so that it has enough staff, enough stock, enough space, the appropriate passengers, the correct baggage, the right planes, the proper equipment, in the right place at the right time. The staff involved from the airport, airlines and associated organisations have to undertake all the tasks they have been given so that the operation works smoothly, and management must* ***control*** *these operations to ensure that all goes to plan and meets the needs of the customers – today's customers and tomorrow's. We also have to look to* ***improving*** *what we do and how we do it in order to keep up with the game in this rapidly changing world.'*

Questions

1 List some of the micro operations to be found at Birmingham International Airport. For each micro operation:
   (a) identify the main transforming and transformed resources;
   (b) state which is the predominant transformed resource, i.e. customers, materials or information;
   (c) describe the output of each micro operation and say who you think its customers are.

2 What would you say are the main problems in designing, planning, controlling and improving an airport?

CASE 2

Wace Burgess

Stuart Chambers and Tammy Helander

Case date 1995

BACKGROUND

Wace Burgess is a member of the Wace Group, a company in the pre-press and print technology market, with a mission:

> *'to become a world-class company providing complete production service for corporations, enhancing the perceived values of their products and services by improving the quality and efficiency of the communication process'.*

The Wace Group operates in a wide range of communication-related sectors including imaging networks, advertising, promotional print, corporate literature, academic journals, rigid and flexible packaging, and labels. Wace Burgess, a business employing around 250 people, specialises in the colour printing of greeting cards, gift wrap, posters, calendars, book jackets and folders. Their customers are mainly creative publishers, supplying retailers.

GREETING CARDS

The largest part of the business is the production of cards, which are of three types: Christmas cards, everyday cards (including birthday cards), and special days' cards (Valentine's Day, Mother's Day, Father's Day, Easter, etc.). Although Wace Burgess is the preferred supplier of many publishers, each order is typically quite small, but with many different designs. Until recently the card market mainly comprised specialist publishers who sold to all sizes of retail outlets such as newsagents, gift shops, card shops, etc. However, the situation had begun to change at the beginning of the 1990s. More and more cards were being sold through larger retailers including supermarkets, which had begun to take a greater interest in the highly profitable card market.

Wace Burgess had always been a company that wanted to be at the leading edge of the market and technology developments. If there was a market out there for supplying the larger retailers, they certainly planned to be part of it. Both as a result of their excellent reputation for quality and responsiveness, and as a result of considerable sales effort, it seemed that in the autumn of 1994 they had their first real chance to supply a big retailer – Marks & Spencer (M&S). Vicky Dockety, one of the account managers, had for some time been talking, via a publisher, to M&S and she now seemed to be close to actually getting the first order. She had already outlined the preliminary requirements to some of the technical specialists and several managers within the company.

ORDERS

The vast majority of the orders were for print runs of between 5000 and 10 000 sheets, the average being about 8000. The most popular size of the cards was around 175 × 125 mm (for some typical orders *see* Table 2.1). A sheet was a piece of thick paper printed in the lithographic printing machines, normally with standard sizes

Table 2.1 Some typical card orders received by Wace Burgess in August 1994

Order number	*Customer*	*Description*	*Quantity (sheets)*
CI 164	Creativity Inc.	Birthday humour (8 designs)	5 000
CI 165	Creativity Inc.	Reasons to be happy	12 000
CI 166	Creativity Inc.	Don't forget (B)	15 000
CI 167	Creativity Inc.	Better late than never	10 000
GF 2378	Gordon Fraser	Everyday gift cards:	
		Portrait P56	5 000
		Landscape L78	10 000
		Landscape L83	8 000
		Landscape L98	10 000
		Animal A254	7 000
		Animal A342	6 000
IN 4512	INK Group	Christmas cards:	
		Farside F34	5 000
		Farside F56	5 000
		Mix M87	7 000
		Mix M96	3 000
		Mix M105	8 000
CV 34	Cardivity	Economy Christmas cards:	
		Angels A5	7 000
		Holly	7 000
		Pudding	8 000
DC 75	Descom Cards	Luxury Christmas cards:	
		Bauble, twin pack	4 000
		Mixed pack LP5	5 000
		Father Christmas FC30	5 000
		Sleigh	6 000

of up to 720 × 1020 mm, and with typically 12 to 16 cards printed on it. However M&S had specified a smaller size of sheet, with smaller cards, very carefully arranged so that almost no paper would be wasted. They were asking for just five design variants. The delivery requirements were also unusual in that they would be precisely scheduled over several weeks, in contrast to the single delivery for most normal orders.

If they were to get the order from M&S, it would mean processing a single order of 600 000 sheets, so Vicky was somewhat concerned about their ability to deliver on time and to preserve their excellent reputation in the market. However, she had recently been in a meeting with the management team, where Barry Jackson, the Managing Director had made the case for pursuing the order:

'Our market is changing. We know now that the big retailers and supermarkets will play a larger part in the future of selling cards, as well as the specialist publishers, which have made up our traditional customer base. We must do all *we can in order to be in that market when these changes take place. We don't want to loose our first-place position. I urge you all to ensure that you really have done everything you can to get these new accounts. As you all know we are totally committed and determined for Wace Burgess to grow with the developing market.'*

Barry was, however, aware that Vicky was close to getting the contract with M&S and specifically urged her:

'Come back to me on that order, we could do with this business! If we can prove ourselves this time we might be able to win more of their work in the future. Check with the manufacturing and technical side once again to see that there aren't any issues we've overlooked, and come back to me as soon as possible. Because the prices will be tight, we cannot afford to have any problems with this one!'

THE FACTORY

Although Vicky had been through the factory many times since she joined the company six months earlier, she paid particular attention to what John Wakeling, the Technical Director, had to say about the manufacturing details when they made a factory tour with some customers. They always started in the gallery, where the whole of the huge factory could be viewed from above through glass windows. It was always impressive to see the busy plant with its many separate operations.

They started at the beginning of the process by the printing machines, and walked past the stacks of printed card sheets, being stored before going into the bindery, where they would be cut on the 'guillotines'. While the customers were being shown some details by one of the supervisors, John and Vicky started to discuss the M&S order. John reassured Vicky of their capabilities to handle the order, but admitted that capacity could be a problem:

'Of course there will be a strain on our capacity, because we already have a fairly full order book for the next two months. We work two eight-hour shifts now in the printing, bindery and packing sections. But we can always put on overtime or, if necessary, put on an extra shift on Saturdays and Sundays. We normally print several million cards a day, and most of these are small orders that take around a couple of hours to do. On average we print between 5000 and 6000 sheets per hour.'

'How about the set-up times?', Vicky asked.

'Oh, that is not really a problem, a litho print set-up takes about two hours for normal cards but changing to smaller sheets can take a little longer; perhaps about three hours – but that isn't too much of a problem. So, as for the printing, there is absolutely no need to worry! Set-ups are very fast both for guillotining and folding: around 10 minutes each for a typical job. It is possible to outsource die-cutting as well as the embossing, but it is more difficult with the folding and packaging. We could use home-workers, but it would take some time, and this takes a lot of organising and transport. If outsourced, this must also meet our very specific standards in order to meet the customers' quality demands.'

Die-cutting means that the edges of the cards are not cut straight, but into shapes, and embossing means that the paper surface is pressed between profiled plates to create an interesting surface.

'How about the quality?', asked Vicky. *'Can we hold the standards for such a large order – as that is one of the main reasons we would win the order? I am concerned that if something were to go wrong it might be the last order we will see!'*

John Wakeling was just as concerned, as this order certainly was a big challenge:

'Of course there shouldn't be any problems. Our quality checks are rigorous and are built into the process. After each 500 sheets (about every six minutes) we take a sample and check it against the agreed specification, and we have other checks both at the beginning and the end of the process. On the rare occasions that we have had technical problems, such as in meeting an unusually difficult specification, we have been prepared to completely reprint an order to get the appearance the customers want. Only high quality, on-spec products will be sent out, and it is because of this that the customers trust us with their most demanding work. I am sure that we will be able to satisfy the M&S order without any problem, but we will certainly be extra careful as well!'

While they were continuing through the factory with the customer, they came across Simon Payne, the Planning Manager:

'Vicky, I just wanted to tell you that the special paper you were asking about for the M&S order, has proved easy to get delivered quickly should it be needed. I checked it with the suppliers, and they reassured us that they would be able to make it.'

Later on, Vicky read a memo from one of the production schedulers about capacity. Although John had tried to reassure her, she had been anxious to have some more details. The note read:

Dear Vicky,

Concerning the questions on capacity you asked for, we do have somewhat different capacities on the different machines. The normal output rate for the printers using standard materials is 6000 sheets/hour, for the guillotines 4000 sheets/hour on average, and for the folders 24 000 cards/hour. As you know, we have 5 printing machines, 3 guillotines, and 5 folders – which gives us a lot of capacity, so we shouldn't have any problem with fitting in your job for M&S. Should you need any more details on capacity effects you should ask Simon Payne. He used to do detailed capacity scheduling, before he was put in charge of the reorganisation of the academic publications area.

Best regards, Tim

Vicky would remember to ask Simon during the day, but the scenario did not look too bad, and she trusted the judgement of John, who had been in the company for a long time, and knew everything worth knowing about the printing business and technology. The factory certainly worked very smoothly and was good at keeping delivery promises, producing high quality cards at short notice.

On her way back from the factory she passed the Customer Services and Prepress room. Here the graphics were finalised before being checked by the customers and company specialists, before being made into printing plates. The staff here were among the best in the industry at ensuring that the artistic details in the card designs were reproduced accurately and to the required colour standards – routinely improving the customers' artwork using the latest computer imaging technologies, as well as using the staff's own design skills. Vicky had confidence in these technical skills, but also knew that the customers valued the department's organised approach to getting this work completed quickly. There could be no better supplier for M&S, she was sure of that! She had done absolutely everything to accommodate them, but she clearly understood that, with these huge volumes, the customer could be very particular with regard to quality and delivery performance.

She had earlier asked one of the supervisors about the issue of extra personnel, should they be forced to put on an extra shift. She dialled his internal number again; the reply was, again, positive:

'Yes, I have checked it with personnel as well, and there should be no problems. You know, it is quite easy for us to hire extra people when required, both students and others on a short-term basis; but only for the labour-intensive jobs such as packing. We usually put them in teams of two: one experienced and one new. It usually works out very well.'

THE M&S CHRISTMAS CARDS

The set of cards that M&S had ordered did not really appear so different from many past orders. All the cards were embossed, and the colours were mainly warm reds and greens, with some use of metallic inks and gold foil blocking, which had not often been required on this type of paper. The designs comprised simple eye-catching images including Christmas trees, tartan teddy bears, nostalgic images of children, and a winter rabbit – they were really very charming. The publisher's graphics skills had been used very effectively, and the final designs were to be die-cut to give a more interesting shape. The quality of the special paper gave an unusually matt finish to the sample printing, and so the cards would have a very sophisticated, up-market appearance. Combined with Wace Burgess's manufacturing skills, this design concept would be a winner, and so Vicky felt sure that this would be the beginning of a successful long-term relationship with M&S.

The special paper could be obtained from one of the usual paper suppliers but, for the metallic inks and gold-blocking, they would have to use a relatively new supplier of whom they had little experience. The die-cutting and gold-blocking would be outsourced, as the factory did not have suitable equipment for the job. It seemed that there were no technical problems with the card or any unusual features that would have to be solved. In fact, it was not one of the most difficult cards they had tackled in terms of design or production. But with Christmas approaching, time was getting tight. The order should be received before the beginning of October, for delivery by mid-November – an unusually short lead time considering the size and special requirements of the order.

Questions

1. What are the external performance objectives for the M&S business, and how do these differ from those for existing customers?
2. What are the potential risks and rewards of accepting the order from M&S?
3. Should the company accept the order if they get it?
4. Should management introduce any special or different practices in the factory to handle the M&S order, if it is received?

CASE 3

The Glastonbury Festival

Sara Mountney, Michael Eavis and Angela Watts

Case date 1996

INTRODUCTION

Every summer thousands of people flock to music festivals all over the UK, Europe and the USA. One of the most established is the Glastonbury Festival of Contemporary Performing Arts, which celebrated its twenty-fifth anniversary in 1995.

The first festival was held at a farm in the village of Pilton in Somerset in the UK in September 1970. Fifteen hundred people attended, paying £1 for the weekend event which included Marc Bolan as the headline act, and free milk from the farm. The festival was organised by the farm owners, Michael and Jean Eavis, who had been inspired to have a go themselves after visiting the Bath Blues Festival earlier in the year.

The festival is now a large scale event with over 1000 acts on 17 stages. It is held (more or less annually) on the midsummer weekend in June, at the same farm. Michael leads the organisation, with Jean's support. In 1995, 80 000 people attended. Festival dates and attendances are shown in Table 3.1.

Table 3.1 Festivals and attendance figures

Festival year	*Attendance*	*Festival year*	*Attendance*
1970	1 500	1986	40 000
1971	12 000	1987	40 000
1979	12 000	1989	50 000
1981	18 000	1990	65 000
1982	25 000	1992	70 000
1983	30 000	1993	80 000
1984	35 000	1994	80 000
1985	40 000	1995	80 000

Source: Western Daily Press, 22.06.95.

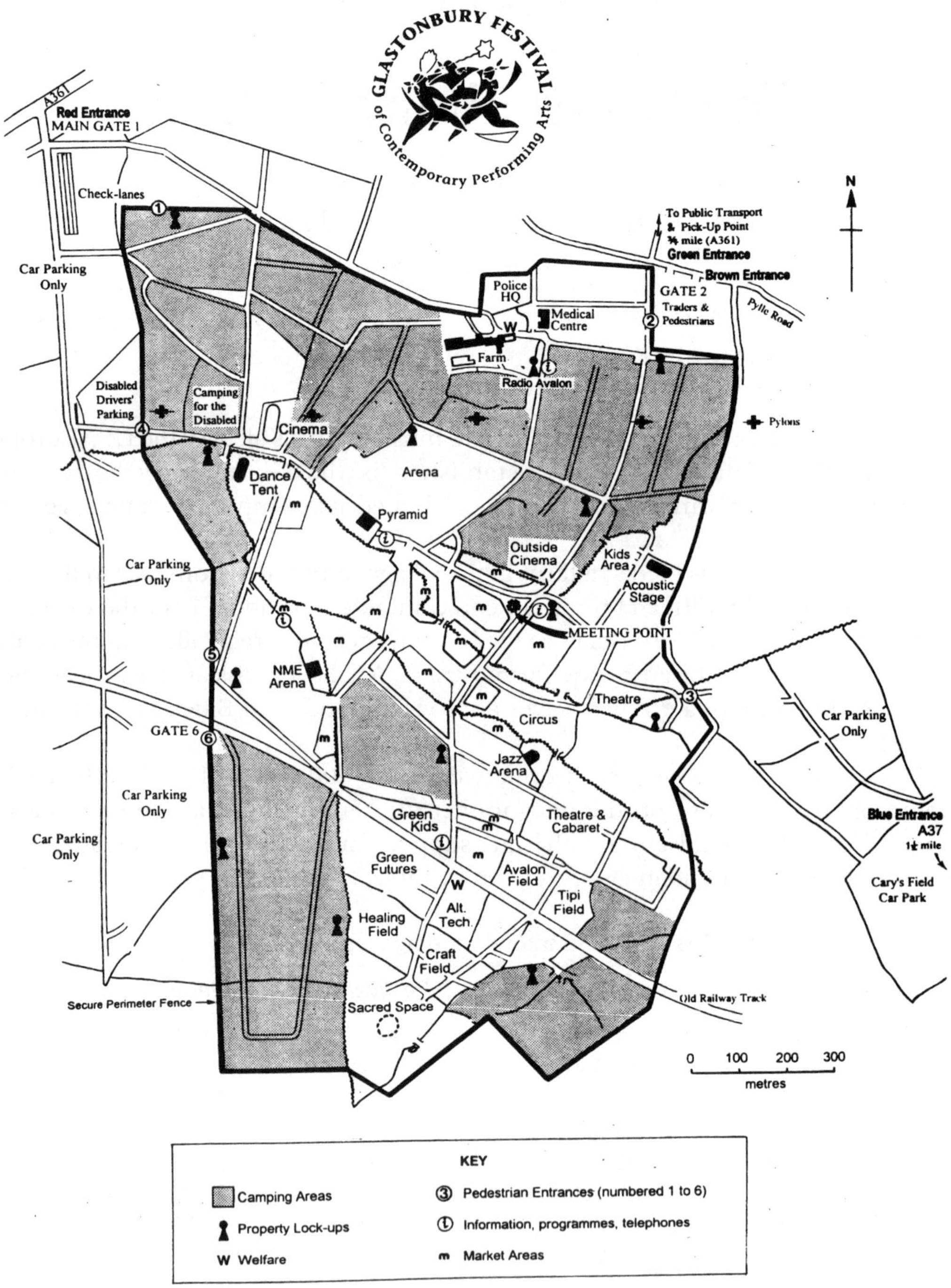

Fig. 3.1 The map of the Glastonbury Festival site in 1995

THE FESTIVAL SITE

A map of the 1995 festival site is shown in Fig. 3.1. Around 189 hectares in area, the site comprises the Eavis's own farm land and that of three neighbouring farms rented for the duration. The main areas of the site are car parks, camp sites (fields set aside for tents), the stages and entertainment venues, an area of market stalls and the 'green field' site, which holds a number of stalls, displays and exhibits to promote environmental and spritual awareness (the town of Glastonbury itself, about six miles away, is the subject of many mystical and mythical traditions).

As the festival site is empty farmland, the festival infrastructure has to be built from nothing every year. A number of structures are built or brought in which literally turn the site into a self-sufficient 'town' for the duration of the festival. Roads have to be relaid, bridges and pipes are installed, fences erected and caravans, Portakabins, marquees and toilet blocks added. A number of utility and personnel services are also required to support the site – electricity, water, telephone cabling, catering, security, police, first aid, welfare, stewards, litter pickers, and so on.

PLANNING THE FESTIVAL

Understandably, an enormous amount of organisation is required behind the scenes in the months leading up to the festival. The main organisation is carried out by a team of around 12 people, led by Michael Eavis. The site is split into geographical areas and delegated to a number of co-ordinators who are largely responsible for the organisation of these areas, although Michael takes a close personal interest in all of the events planned. Two site managers supervise the site layout, contracts and construction. In addition, a number of contractors take on the organisation, construction and running of the services needed on site before, during and after the festival. These are shown in Table 3.2. The contractors are usually specialist companies who deal with large events such as Glastonbury, many of whom have been involved for a number of years. The area co-ordinators are volunteers with 'other jobs' who work on Glastonbury in their spare time for enjoyment and are generally paid a modest amount. They are either involved in similar work or do something completely different, like teaching. Most have been involved in the festival for a number of years, many from the start, and have a detailed inside knowledge of what is required.

Preparation for the festival begins in the preceding December with a licence application to the local district council. This licence lays down the standards that the festival must meet regarding the site plan, vehicles and roadways, attendance and tickets, sanitary facilities, site security and safety, health and safety, emergency co-ordination and site communication, noise and food hygiene. Failure to comply with these restrictions will result in prosecution.

Table 3.2 Co-ordinators and contractors

Area co-ordinators	*Contracted services*
Theatre and circus	Communications
Pyramid stage (main stage)	Site information
NME *(New Musical Express)* stage	Staff catering
Jazz and World Music stage	Green litter
Acoustic stage	Rubbish and hygiene
Cinema	Medical
Kid's area	Welfare
Dance tent	Stewarding
Market manager	Car parking
Green markets	Gate and traffic
Green fields	Fencing
Site management	Water
	Electricity
	Security
	Police
	Toilets
	Fire
	Stage construction
	Sound and PA
	Lighting
	TV and radio broadcasting

In January, with the festival officially announced, the contractors and co-ordinators meet with Michael to discuss the plans for the festival. Each organiser is delegated their specific area and a budget, and their requirements are discussed. Then, from January to March, the market traders are booked, dealing directly with the farm. The booking of bands and acts is an ongoing process and is liable to change right up to the last minute, but it is preferable that bookings are confirmed as early as possible. Due to the sheer popularity of the festival, however, it is not difficult to find bands or replacements – often they approach Michael directly.

As the weeks pass, further meetings and discussions take place until six weeks beforehand, when the co-ordinators start working full-time on the festival. On 1 June, the various contractors move on site and begin construction. From this point on, work is monitored very closely; in the past, some stages have had to be moved because they were built in the wrong place! This part of the organisation presents its own challenges, such as providing accommodation, catering, power and water for the crews – who are resident up to, during and after the festival – constructing, monitoring and dismantling equipment.

RUNNING THE FESTIVAL

The weekend of the festival finally arrives. The main events take place from the Friday to the Sunday evening, but the campsite opens on the preceding Wednesday morning and closes on Monday.

The quotations below describe some of the experiences of 1995 festival-goers:

'Arriving on the Thursday before the festival, we were amongst the first to pitch tents. I didn't realise quite how much that mattered until the Saturday morning, by which time people were fitting tents into gaps barely big enough for the pegs! From the upper perimeter of the site you can see a sea of red, orange, green and blue stretching out before you. An awe-inspiring sight!'

'I was surprised at how crowded the festival can get! I remember being caught in a bottleneck of people trying to cross a bridge over a stream from one field to another. I felt almost as though I could have picked up my feet and still been carried along! The crowd is rarely so bad, but if there are two or more unpopular acts several thousand people suddenly want to be elsewhere!'

Each contractor has on-call crews to monitor the festival and react to problems. These naturally depend on the service itself. Two prime examples are electricity and water:

- *Electricity.* A number of diesel generators are installed around the site which need refuelling twice a day. A refuelling circuit around all the generators takes 12 hours to complete. The generators will use around 40 000 litres of diesel fuel in four days.
- *Water.* The festival requires nearly four million litres of water over five days. This is used for stand pipes and for catering purposes – there are virtually no flush toilets on the Glastonbury site. The water cannot be drawn from mains sources which are designed for the local village only, so it is transported in milk tankers holding 7500–20 000 litres from a reservoir seven miles away. These run for 24 hours a day from two days before the festival to the Monday after the festival closes.

  There is a 100 000 litre storage facility at the farm which is continuously replenished by the tankers and there are five tankers on the site at various locations, each holding 20 000 litres. These tankers are monitored closely and refilled as required. This supply of water is then distributed throughout the site by a 15 kilometre network of temporary pipes. Seven pumps are used at peak times to pump water throughout the pipe network.

  The water itself has to be treated with chlorine and is monitored by Council Environmental Health Officers to ensure that it meets the standards required.

Other organisations, such as emergency services and stewards, need to be able to react to situations quickly, as demonstrated by the report of a 1994 festival-goer:

Table 3.3 Direct employment – 1994

Area	*Number*
Litter pickers	343
Theatre	35
Site	28
Jazz stage	23
Safety	8
Cleaning	8
Market stalls	7
Pyramid stage	6
Catering	8
Green areas	10
Total	476

'In 1994 somebody was shot in a field. The speed at which it was dealt with was impressive. The Police and Ambulance had the place sealed off in minutes.'

In 1994, 476 people were employed directly by Glastonbury Festivals Ltd. The breakdown of areas where they were employed is shown in Table 3.3; this list does not include subcontractors or voluntary workers. For example, 600 volunteers worked as stewards (organised by Oxfam Campaigns) during the 1995 festival.

THE AFTERMATH

Once the festival is over, the site must be cleared and returned as farm land. The service equipment – piping, toilets, generators, wiring, etc., is removed within the week and a litter removal operation takes four weeks. Litter picking is then carried out once a week, all year round, in Pilton; when the leaves fall off the bushes in autumn, previously unnoticed litter has to be cleared from them. The organising team meets to review the festival and any changes which may be made for the following year about a month after the event.

Michael Eavis is keen to reduce the environmental impact of the festival on the surrounding area, both during and after the festival:

- festival-goers are encouraged to use public transport, with the railway and coach networks providing additional services
- a 50m high wind turbine contributes 150kW to the power required for the stage lighting power system
- tin and glass collected by litter pickers are recycled and polystyrene products (e.g. cups and containers) were banned in 1995
- an enormous slurry pit collects and filters the sewage from the toilets, which is then processed and re-used on the land after six months.

A 1995 festival-goer commented on the environmental factors of the festival:

'The environmental aspect of the festival seems to be a little underplayed. The wind generator, vast and impressive up close, soon diminishes to a toy. Greenpeace celebrated the dismantling (rather than the sinking) of the Brent Spar oil rig in 1995, but it hardly became a focal point. The amount of rubbish generated must be phenomenal! It is kept in check by Litter Patrols who can be seen on the back of filthy trucks with oil drums

full of rubbish, and wandering around with rubbish bags, handed to all and sundry 'volunteers'. The legendary toilets live up to their reputation. No matter how often they may be cleaned you can't escape overflowing cubicles!'

FESTIVAL FINANCES

The 1994 budget for the festival stood at around £3.5 million which was raised from ticket sales and traders' fees. Ninety per cent of this budget is spent on festival overheads and the remaining 10 per cent goes to charitable causes, the main beneficiaries being Greenpeace and a large number of local organisations. Income from ticket sales and traders' fees in 1994, for example, was £3 540 000 and was allocated as shown in Table 3.4.

Table 3.4 Breakdown of costs from the 1994 Glastonbury Festival

Area	*Expenditure (£)*
Bands	500 000
Theatre performers	200 000
Green field area	80 000
Staging	100 000
Cinema	15 000
Litter picking and waste disposal	150 000
Children's areas	30 000
Wages	500 000
Police	360 000
Other security	200 000
Land use (neighbours)	75 000
Fire services	45 000
Medical and welfare	30 000
Administration and office costs	65 000
Plant hire	300 000
Electricity	165 000
Water	60 000
Licensing and rates	30 000
Catering	50 000
National Insurance	35 000
Site contractors	100 000
Advertising	50 000
Gate costs	40 000
Communications and telephones	20 000
Car parking	30 000
Charitable donations (at least)	310 000
Total	3 540 000

POPULARITY

Of all the festivals, Glastonbury appears to be the most popular. Tickets invariably sell out, with demand far outstripping supply. Perhaps the reason for the festival's enduring popularity is the fact that it is organised by a group of enthusiasts and volunteers, as opposed to being a commercially-driven operation.

Aspects of festival organisation take place throughout the year – once the festival is over and the site cleared, the financial and administrative issues need to be settled. It is not surprising, then, that every few years the organisational team need a break. Consequently, no festival was held in 1996 to allow them to do this.

Finally, the following extracts from interviews with two festival-goers may explain the popularity of the festival and why they return, year after year. First, Jill Griffiths has been to the 1994 and 1995 Glastonbury Festivals and spoke of her experience:

> *'What makes Glastonbury different is the sheer scale and diversity of the event. It's part concert, part carnival, part comedy festival, part market. You never really know what's going on around you while at the festival, simply because so much is happening. The festival becomes defined by what you missed as much as by what you did. It's the little things that really make the festival for me. I remember standing transfixed, for quarter of an hour, as a fellow festival-goer stood juggling clubs. It was quite amazing watching a non-performer just standing in a field doing his own thing while the world wandered by.*
>
> *'The festival never shuts down over the weekend. There is always somewhere to eat, not to mention somewhere to buy clothes! After the main scheduled acts have finished there are films to watch and several stalls transform themselves into dance venues, where the young, irrepressible or otherwise fuelled can still be seen when the sun comes up.'*

Karl Alldis, the second interviewee, first went to the Glastonbury Festival in the early 1980s:

> *'I've been to around six or seven festivals at least. When I first went, I expected a typical open-air concert, with a big stage and a campsite – fairly basic facilities. The reality was a complete shock! It was huge – the sheer volume of people was overwhelming, but this made it more exciting.*
>
> *'Instead of a simple, open-air concert, I found the festival interesting and intricate. It was obvious that there was a highly complex and organised infrastructure to the festival. It was almost like a town in its own right. I discovered something new and different every day.*
>
> *'It's definitely changed since I started going. Every year it's bigger – now we have to organise ourselves with our own programmes and schedules to make sure we see everything we want to! It's now a lot more structured and organised, but I think that in some ways it's lost some of its charm. It used to be a bit rough and ready – water and toilet breakdowns and so on – but maybe now it's too slick. It seems more of a commercial activity, it's lost a lot of its "naive expectations", it's like a bohemian shopping mall! I*

think maybe now the festival's matured like an adult, it's getting too set in its ways. Perhaps it needs an injection of new ideas.

'I keep going back because it's like going home to a small town. It's the wide range of people that really make it – they're so varied and interesting. It's like a tribal gathering, an extraordinary weekend trip to a more liberal lifestyle. And it's always different each year.

'One of the worst things that happened was a shooting in 1994. That was unprecedented. There is a lot of theft as well, although I've been very lucky. At the time it's a trauma, but usually it's replacable things that go. In fact, it adds to the experience.

'I remember one festival in the 80s when it rained all the time. We had to pitch our tent in thick mud and people were sliding all over the place! But it adds to the sense of adventure – it adds to the stories you can tell people afterwards! One of the worst things that has happened to me personally is losing my tent – I spent the whole day trying to find it. It's very easily done!

'The best thing about Glastonbury is the atmosphere. It's a combination of everything, really – there's a general feel-good factor and then there's the blend of activities. It's a cultural island. And the whole is definitely more that the sum of its parts.'

Questions

1 What is the role of an operations manager such as Michael Eavis at the event? How does this change at different stages of the festival organisation?

2 List the different types of transformation processes involved in the festival activities.

3 What would you say was the competitive advantage of the festival? How would you define the customers' perception of this?

CASE 4

Focus Plastics plc

Stuart Chambers

Case date 1996

INTRODUCTION

> *'Our strategic decision to exit industrial products and to concentrate on the household market has clearly allowed us to build up both our technical expertise and marketing skills; and this is reflected in our impressive results [Table 4.1]. No-one in the industry can come anywhere near our sales margin and RONA (return on nett assets).'*

It was with this confident statement that James Thompson, CEO of Focus Plastics addressed the final board meeting of 1995. His confidence was shared by his colleagues. After all, Focus Plastics was one of the UK's longest-established plastic injection-moulding businesses and is a member of a large industrial group involved in the packaging and engineering industries. Originally founded by two friends who had studied organic chemistry together at university, it had grown quickly into a successful small business supplying specialised high quality small plastic mouldings for a variety of industrial customers, largely in the consumer durable, toy and automotive component industries. During the late 1960s, the company gradually extended their range to include popular household items such as washing-up bowls, pedal bins, baby baths, buckets and dustpans. These were sold under the 'Focus' brand name, mainly through wholesale distributors. By the early 1980s the household business had grown to account for over 75 per cent of turnover which had itself more than doubled in 10 years. New large injection-moulding machines had been purchased to cope with the success of the household products, and the increased capacity provided economies of scale which enabled Focus to compete aggressively in a market where barriers to entry were low. However, competition was increasing, mainly from small competitors who tended to offer very narrow ranges of products (e.g. just buckets or bowls), not least because of the high cost of moulds: a single mould for a bucket could cost £30 000 or more, depending on size and complexity.

Table 4.1 Focus Plastics

Financial Information from 1985–95 (year ended 31 December)

	1983 *£000*	*1985* *£000*	*1987* *£000*	*1989* *£000*	*1991* *£000*	*1993* *£000*	*1995* *£000*
Fixed assets							
Plant etc.	1683	1656	1197	1260	1836	2514	2940
Moulds	306	390	510	540	960	1752	1860
Total	1989	2046	1707	1800	2796	4266	4800
Current assets							
Debtors	1449	2394	2526	2451	3963	2889	4119
Inventory	786	1758	3087	3777	4677	6729	7701
Total	2235	3990	5613	6228	8640	9618	11820
Total assets	4224	6036	7320	8028	11436	13884	16620
Share capital	150	150	150	150	150	150	150
Retained profits	840	1260	1590	1710	2490	5280	7980
Group indebtedness	1350	1590	2460	2640	3360	2370	1470
Total	2340	3000	4200	4500	6000	7800	9600
Current liabilities							
Creditors	1878	1596	1884	3402	5322	5232	5295
Bank	6	1440	1236	126	114	852	1725
Total	1884	3036	3120	3528	5436	6084	7020
Total liabilities	4224	6036	7320	8028	11436	13884	16620
Net sales	7566	8616	12636	13398	15324	16182	24063
Net profit before tax	438	555	822	1086	1686	2124	3150
Sales by market							
Industrial	1510	0	0	0	0	0	0
Focus	6056	8616	9225	8740	7780	6622	6533
Concept	0	0	3411	4658	7544	9560	16210
Concept Office	0	0	0	0	0	0	1320

THE PRODUCTS

By contrast, Focus Plastics offered a full range of items, often in several colours, so it could supply all the plastics needs of the wholesalers. In total, the company produced around 200 stock keeping units (SKUs), yet it also developed a reputation as a reliable source of supply of good quality products. Conversely, the value of industrial products had grown only slowly. Consequently, in 1983, it was decided to exit from the complex and cyclical industrial market in order to concentrate on developing the more profitable household products business. The Managing Director, Jim Thompson, explained:

'We recognised that the industrial market was becoming a distraction to both our production and sales operations. Typically, order sizes and therefore batch sizes, were getting smaller; and we were also losing some larger contracts, such as toy components, as production moved abroad. Similarly, our automotive customers were ordering smaller quantities and higher variety. In the end, we decided that the industrial business did not fit in well and was particularly difficult to plan and control alongside the longer runs of household products. Even in the Sales Office, it was felt that the commercial relationships with household product wholesalers were clearer and under control, whereas business with the industrial customers was unpredictable and unstable. Schedule changes in quantity and delivery date were an everyday occurrence that disrupted the office and caused most internal communication problems. By 1985, all our industrial business had been terminated; the results are for all to see: our profit has risen faster and our reputation for household products has become the benchmark for the industry. But this dedication to one market was recognised as carrying risks, and we were determined to differentiate Focus Plastics from our competitors. We knew that it was quite easy for 'hungry' smaller manufacturers to compete for the volume business by undercutting our prices. Our overheads were higher than theirs for many reasons; we operated from modern premises, and used the latest, precision equipment, which we kept well maintained and safe. We bought the best quality moulds, and generally positioned ourselves as "the professionals" with high quality catalogues, modern computer and telesales equipment and a well-trained salesforce. Lastly, we were recruiting the design and marketing skills needed to keep ahead in the game! Linda Fleet, our Marketing Director, has been in charge of this development, which has taken us into new exciting markets.'

MARKETING

Linda Fleet had joined Focus Plastics in 1986, having previously worked in marketing for a large retail chain of paint and wallpaper retailers.

'My experience in the decorative products industry had taught me the importance of fashion even in mundane products such as paint. Certain premium-priced colours and textures, would become popular for one or two years, supported by professional advertising

and features in lifestyle magazines such as Homes and Gardens. *A year later they would look old-fashioned and people who care about their surroundings would decorate individual rooms or even the whole house. The manufacturers and retailers which created and supported these fashion trends were dramatically more successful than those who simply provided standard ranges. Instinctively, I felt that this must also apply to plastics. In Scandinavia and Germany, the most up-market stores offer a few beautifully-designed household plastics in the latest colours. We decided to develop a whole co-ordinated range of such items, and to open up a new distribution network for them via kitchen equipment and speciality retailers. This was a big investment, but it certainly paid off! As you can imagine, there was a degree of scepticism throughout the company, at every level, but eventually the Board fully supported the idea, and backed it with a major investment in product design and new tooling.*

'Our first new range, which comprised storage jars, mixing bowls, strainers, salad bowls, towel holders, and other kitchen items, was launched in 1987, under the "Concept" *brand name. Within one year, we had over 3000 retail outlets signed up, provided with point-of-sale display facilities, brochures and initial stock. Advertising and articles in suitable magazines and newspapers generated an enormous interest from the public, which was reinforced by the use of our products on several TV cookery programmes. Our salesforce did a tremendous job with the retailers, supporting local promotions. This was undoubtedly the most exciting event in the history of the company. Within 12 months we had developed an entirely new market and were the envy of our competitors.* Concept *now provides over 70 per cent of our revenue and the bulk of our profits. The unit prices we can achieve are on average up to three times higher than for the* Focus *range, so you can see the market appreciates the value inherent in our designs. Although now many of the original designs and colours have been superseded, some older lines remain popular. We quickly learned that the retailers liked the idea of a co-ordinated range of items. Customers could buy a few items to start a "collection" and add to this progressively. Our market research indicated that some customers kept our products "on display" in their kitchens as lifestyle statements rather than putting them away in cupboards. We exploited this idea in our advertising and supported colour preferences with a guarantee to supply any item in any colour for at least five years. We now have the most comprehensive range of "designer" items in the market: five separate ranges of styles, a total of 155 different items, and 15 different colourways. To keep ahead we intend to launch at least one new range every year, and to introduce two new colourways.'*

MANUFACTURING

All manufacturing was carried out in a large, leased modern facility, which was located approximately 20km from the Head Office which housed all non-manufacturing functions. The factory had a process-based layout, with areas for receiving and holding raw materials (bulk plastic granules were stored in tall silos). The moulding area included 24 large injection-moulding machines of various ages.

The most recent had simple robotic devices to remove finished products from the machines and to place them on conveyors which lead to the packing area. Older machines used operators to do this task. Adjacent to the moulding area was a large tool store with a capacity to store about 200 moulds on racks, and a small mould repair section with skilled craftsmen and a range of metal working machinery and handtools.

Products passed by conveyor to the packing hall, where they were inspected and packed in bags or cartons, put on pallets, and stretch-wrapped. These were then taken to an adjacent large, narrow-aisle warehouse with high level pallet racking and special forklift machines. In one corner was a dispatch bay with a platform access to load delivery vehicles. Grant Williams, the manufacturing manager, described the development of these facilities over the preceding 10 years.

> *'The move away from industrial products around 10 years ago allowed us to concentrate our efforts on household items. This had several advantages. First, it allowed us to dispose of most of the older, small injection-moulding machines which had been used to make such things as parts for washing machines and toys. Most of the household items were larger, so we gradually bought more large machines, and where possible used multi-cavity moulds, particularly for smaller items such as salad spoons, cruet sets, and small storage jars and lids. About half the range of items were of this type, and multi-cavity moulds have allowed us to use the large machines very efficiently on all the range. For example, it would have taken the same labour to make three jars (a typical* Concept *product) per minute on the old small machines as 18 jars per minute on the modern large machines with a six cavity mould. That's a 600 per cent increase in productivity! I've been able to visit many other plants around Europe and Asia, and I am convinced that we now achieve the highest productivity and quality in the industry. This has been the result of the hard work of everyone in manufacturing and a consistent drive for best practice. We are proud that we achieve such high dimensional accuracy, excellent surface finish, almost invisible "flash" marks where the mould parts come together, and extreme consistency of colour. It is this excellence which has contributed to the success of the* Concept *ranges. The end product quality is second-to-none! Also, by standardising on the single large machine, any mould can fit any machine. This is an ideal situation from a planning perspective, as we are often asked to make a run of* Concept *products at short notice on the next machine to become available . . . and any one will do!'*

PLANNING AND CONTROL

Sandra White, the Planning Manager, was responsible for the scheduling of all the injection-moulding machines, and for maintaining inventory levels for all the warehoused items. Supported by three other staff, she also prepared performance reports which monitored utilisation of the equipment, output rates for each product, and scrap rates. These figures were also used by her for realistic scheduling, as 'standard times' for production rates of each product were either not always available (particularly for new *Concept* products) or had been overtaken by improvements in efficiency in the production processes.

'We try to establish a preferred sequence of production for each machine and mould. To minimise set-up times we plan for each mould to start on a light colour, and progress through a sequence to the darkest. In this way we can change colours in around 15 minutes, with relatively small amounts of waste material (mixed colour products). Because our moulds are both large and technically complex, mould changes take around three to four hours, so we decided to plan for minimum runs of six shifts (48 hours) production. The factory is usually not scheduled for weekend production, and maintenance is usually performed on Saturday mornings. In the past we would never have run a mould for less than 15 shifts (one week) and the general reduction in batch size has unfortunately brought down average utilisation. But with the wider product range of over 1800 SKUs we really have had little choice.

'Everything would be fine if we were able to stick to schedules, but short-term changes are inevitable in our market. For example, last Friday we had to produce a run of 5000 rain forest green pasta strainers because of unexpected demand levels. This involved complete rescheduling, with one extra mould change, and a long colour change from green to white, with one hour's waste production. Ideally we would like some stability, but the market is dynamic and continual schedule changes affect utilisation, efficiency and *scrap rates. Certainly better forecasts would help, . . . but even our own promotions are sometimes organised at such short notice that we often get caught with stockouts. Although* Focus *products have relatively stable volumes the* Concept *products are much more seasonal, which makes capacity planning and scheduling very difficult at peak times around November (for the Christmas gifts market) and Easter just after the spring trade fair in London. The new* Concept Office *products, introduced in 1995, are relatively constant in volume but seasonal colour promotions have caused us problems in meeting demand from inventory.*

'At the same time, I have to schedule production time for new product mould trials; we normally allow three shifts (24 hours) for the testing of each new mould received, and this has to be done on production machines. From my perspective it is often a difficult choice whether to schedule products that are needed urgently or mould trials for new product launches which are equally urgent.'

NEW PRODUCT DEVELOPMENT

Grant Williams explained the new product development process.

'We receive detailed drawings of the new products from the Design Office, which is managed by Marketing. The Concept *products are often high precision, complicated objects, each of which presents its own technical challenges. However, we pride ourselves on our ability to overcome the technical and quality problems and, when we have decided*

on the basic mould requirements, orders are placed with suitable mould makers. It usually takes around three or four months to get a new mould, which then has to be tested. At the scheduled time, we fix the mould into a machine and undertake trials – adjusting pressures, temperatures of heating and cooling zones, feed rates of plastic and dwell times until we get perfect quality output. These then become the operating parameters and are recorded for future use. This whole process can take up to 24 hours, so we sometimes miss a night's sleep if there is an important trial in progress. Frequently, we have to take the mould out and make minor modifications to the design to get what we want. But in the end, we always achieve the specified quality and optimise the production output rate. The most difficult moulds to get right are the multi-cavity ones; you might have problems with just one cavity, but the technical challenge of solving production problems is what keeps us all going!

'The operators are as keen as we are to get the cycle times as fast as possible, since their bonus payments are based on good output. We make it easy for them by getting the settings right from the outset, but I'm afraid they don't all appreciate that. Sometimes, several operators spend most of a shift involved with normal production set-ups, and argue that they could have made more bonus wages on production. There is always a bit of tension here, but I still believe that we must link wages and output if we are to retain our excellent record of productivity.'

LATEST DEVELOPMENTS

The *Concept Office* brand had been introduced in 1995, and was perceived as a very successful entry into a new market, employing many of the marketing ideas developed with the *Concept* household range. *Concept Office* items comprised filing trays, storage boxes, and a range of desk items – all innovatively styled and in seasonal colours. Users were encouraged to change the colour in use every season to provide variety in drab, open-plan offices. *Concept Office* branded products were sold through a small number of multi-branch office equipment retailers, with bulk deliveries to their central distribution warehouses, supported when necessary by emergency 'top up' deliveries direct to branches that experienced stockouts. High service levels were expected. Premium prices and good margins were achieved through innovative stylish designs and excellent delivery performance. From a manufacturing perspective, the products were, on average, physically larger than *Concept* ones, justifying the use of large machines, but the volumes of the seasonal colours were only sufficient to be produced in the minimum schedule quantities.

Jim Thompson, the Managing Director, summed up his view of the current situation at the latest Board Meeting.

'We continue to trade very profitably but we must now tighten up on working capital and get a bit smarter with the way we develop new products. If we are to continue in the fashion markets we must find ways of shortening the product development cycle. I

also feel that sometimes we give too much time to the Focus *range. We know that the profit margin for this is relatively low, so it should not be given priority over* Concept *or* Concept Office *requirements. To get the manufacturing department under control, I have decided to appoint an Operations Director to take charge of all aspects of manufacturing, warehousing and distribution. He has a much more strategic view of what operations can bring to the business. I hope that you will all give him your fullest support and co-operation.'*

Questions

1 Have Focus Plastics's strategies, since the decision to exit the Industrial Products market, been entirely successful?

2 In what ways have marketing strategies affected manufacturing?

3 What have been the main features of Manufacturing's policies during the period from 1985 to 1995? What operations-based competitive advantages were developed by these approaches?

4 What changes, if any, would you recommend for the business to continue to grow in sales and profit? Do you agree with Jim Thompson's summing up of the current situation (p. 50)?

CASE 5

Lunn Poly Travel

Robert Johnston

Case date 1990

A REVOLUTION IN TRAVEL RETAILING

In 1985 Lunn Poly became a travel agency with a difference. As a result it increased its sales in the inclusive tour (package tour) market by 14 per cent at a time when the market was down by 10 per cent due to the effects of the economic recession in the UK.

Richard Manley, Lunn Poly's Financial Director explained: 'Our goal is to be the number one retailer of overseas holidays by 1989. We want 20 per cent of the inclusive tour (IT) market. That's equivalent to about 1.5 million holidays – about three times as many as we sold last year.'

By December 1985 it looked like the target would be met before 1989. The company had sold 109 000 holidays for summer 1986, compared with 24 000 in the same period last year. The summer market (1 April–14 October) accounts for about three-quarters of the business.

Lunn Poly's sudden appearance in 1986 as the number one retailer of holidays for Thomson, Horizon and Cosmos, and equal first for Intersun, had been the result of the introduction of the Holiday Shop, backed up by huge national advertising campaigns and the £5 holiday offer in 1985 which caused a sensation in national and local press.

The well-conceived and carefully managed Holiday Shop concept sent bookings through the roof. This new concept provided Lunn Poly with a means of focusing on inclusive tour (IT) sales. This, they believed was the market with the best potential for growth with products that were easier to sell and where margins were higher than all other travel agency activities. This resulted in higher productivity and reduced costs in the shops, and improved efficiency at head office. Lunn Poly is now a major force in the industry.

THE HOLIDAY SHOP CONCEPT

Tony Jackson, a General Manager with responsibility for the north-west region explained the Holiday Shop concept:

'Travel agencies are used to service all aspects of the travel trade. You can go to any travel agent and get railway timetable information, a rail ticket, coach tickets, even foreign currency and traveller's cheques. Most travel agencies also operate special accounts for organisations, commercial clients and have to make weird and wonderful travel arrangements for them and also provide them with a credit account. Our concept is different. We don't do any of that. We just concentrate on selling what we are good at – inclusive tour holidays. We have the largest selection of overseas holidays on our racks. This way we keep our eye on the main game and the main profit earner. In this part of the business we make 10 per cent commission and higher, depending on volume of business, and we also sell our own insurance with it. To deal efficiently with all the other trappings of a normal travel agency you need specialised and highly skilled and trained staff and if you are lucky you can make 1½ per cent net. It might take one of my counter staff 30 minutes to work out from the railway timetables the best way of getting to Padstow from Looe on a Saturday morning in May on a cheap weekend return, and if we do manage to sell the ticket we might only make 50 pence. We now only sell IT holidays for home and abroad. Now we can afford to do it better and cheaper than anyone else.'

LUNN POLY TRAVEL LTD

Lunn Poly Travel Ltd was an amalgam of two companies in the 1950s – Henry Lunn, founded in the 1880s, and Polytechnic Travel, founded in the early 1900s. In 1972 it was bought by Thomson Travel which is a subsidiary of ITOL Plc (International Thomson Organisation Limited). In the 1970s, Lunn Poly went through a period of mergers and acquisitions. In the early 1980s the company had a policy of expanding its Commercial Division. In 1984 Lunn Poly purchased two companies, both about the same size and type as itself: Renwick Travel and Ellerman Travel. This takeover added 53 and 66 shops respectively to Lunn Poly's 60. With the great increase in outlets the takeover also brought in some new management with new and challenging ideas, and whose concepts, management and methods were different to those of the old Lunn Poly.

The ITOL group of which Lunn Poly is a part is made up of several holding companies of which Thomson Travel is one, along with Thomson North Sea Oil, the largest profit contributor in the group and several publishing companies. Thomson Travel is the holding company for the travel group which includes Lunn Poly, Portland Holidays, Thomson Holidays and Britannia Airways. John MacNeill is the Managing Director of Lunn Poly Travel, and he also sits on the board of Thomson Travel. The chief executive of Thomson Travel is on the board of ITOL. The major attraction of Lunn Poly to ITOL is not so much its profit contribution, which is relatively small compared to the others in the group, but because for six months of the year it is cash rich when it is holding holiday pre-payments. This cash is invested in Thomson Travel who invest it in Thomson Finance at a base rate of return, where it is used as group funding. Any surpluses are invested in the market.

There is a clear, full and defined financial reporting structure. Each autumn a yearly control budget is prepared for each shop by the General Managers. This is monitored monthly and any variances have to be explained. These are aggregated into a monthly budget by Lunn Poly which is negotiated with Thomson Travel. This has to fulfil certain criteria set by ITOL, including a return on commissions of 15 per cent, a return on managed assets of 40 per cent and 100 per cent cash conversion. These, too, are monitored on a monthly basis, and again variances have to be accounted for. There is also a broader five-year plan.

Richard Manley explained the terms.

'ROC (Return on Capital) is our pre-tax return and is trading profit plus interest. We can make 10 per cent commissions on our holidays and sometimes, because of our higher volumes, we can command override commissions from the tour operators. You see, we are only agents for our suppliers, the tour operators. Their turnover is our sales less the the cost of the holiday, so our turnover is really only the commissions on those sales. The rest of our pre-tax return comes from the profits we generate from interest on our customers' holiday pre-payments in our cash-rich period between January and September. Cash conversion is relatively easy. Because of our positive cash flow all cash is converted into profit. Return on managed assets is not as bad as it sounds. After all, once you have a shop lease, fixtures and fittings, you don't need many other assets.

'We also report our market position and we will be measured by Thomson Travel against our intention to have 20 per cent of the IT market by 1989.'

THE SALE OF THE COMMERCIAL DIVISION

Up until the start of 1986, a good return on commissions had been very difficult to achieve. The Commercial Division, specialising in commercial clients, was detracting from the potential returns that could be made. It was a profitable operation and accounted for a good part of the sales. Lunn Poly's turnover in 1985 totalled £212 million, of which the Commercial Division accounted for £70 million. This was quite low compared to the number one in the field, Hogg Robinson, whose commercial work was around £200 million. So on 8 February 1986 the Commercial Division was sold to Pickford Travel for a significant sum that allowed Lunn Poly to invest in its new strategy.

John MacNeill, Lunn Poly's Managing Director, explained the decision to sell the Commercial Division in *Newsline*, the Lunn Poly staff newspaper, in March 1986:

'There are two reasons. When we looked at the business of the Division and its position in the market the evidence showed that we were dropping behind Thomas Cook

and Hogg Robinson and that Amex (American Express) were coming up fast. We recognised that to get the competitive deals necessary to acquire and keep commercial clients we would need to invest heavily. Our central strategy is to build and strengthen our retail business and we did not want to dilute this effort by diverting funds to Commercial.

'Like many other successful businesses in this very competitive world we are concentrating on what we are good at – selling holidays to the public. Our sister companies, Thomson Holidays and Britannia Airways, are aiming to be the best in their sector of the holiday market and our latest move follows that line. We have therefore taken advantage of a significant offer and have disposed of a good solid business, for which Pickfords have paid an appropriate price.

'We will be able to repay the loans made to us by International Thomson Organisation at the time of the Ellerman and Renwick acquisitions and we are looking to increase quickly the number of shops in our chain.'

LUNN POLY, MARCH 1986

Following the sale of the Commercial Division, which had an anticipated turnover for 1986 of £85 million, Lunn Poly estimated that their turnover would be £160 million for the year. They had 210 shops with an intention to increase the number of shops during the year by about 50.

There were six directors: the Managing Director, the Financial Director (Richard Manley), the Marketing and Development Director, the Personnel Director and two Retail Directors covering the north and the south regions, all of whom were based at the head office in London. The Systems and Accounting Section, under the control of the Financial Director, was based in Leamington Spa. There were about 120 people based in Leamington, 35 in London and a field force of 15 General Managers reporting to the Retail Directors, each General Manager was responsible for about 12 to 15 shops. Each shop has on average four and a half staff. Richard Manley explained:

'Now that the Commercial Division has gone, we have the funds and the time to expand. About a third of my time was involved in commercial work, now it can go on to our current business. We forecast carrying over half a million passengers in 1986 which will be an increase of 40 per cent over 1985. We are looking to open a lot of new shops and we also expect them to be in profit within two years. In the past it used to take three years but now we can do it in two.'

This budgeted increase in volume was being backed by a massive advertising campaign. In 1985 Lunn Poly spent about £1.2 million on marketing – three times the previous year's profits – which resulted in a huge increase in the number of bookings. In 1986 they anticipated spending the same amount.

Richard Manley summed up:

'We are in a high volume, low transaction business. Once we get sales volume to cover overheads, profit comes in easily. Now we can cope with the higher volume, all our systems and people are geared up to it.'

To gain the benefits of national advertising, Lunn Poly was trying to open shops in new areas in order to cover the whole country and, in particular, the company was looking at locations in Lancashire, Yorkshire and East Anglia.

LUNN POLY TRIES HARDER

The reason Lunn Poly was doing better was because it was trying harder. Because of current volumes it was easy to earn override commissions on holidays from its principals – the tour operators – and Lunn Poly was trying to pass some of these on to its customers. The difficulty was that current retail price maintenance agreements mean that they were not allowed to sell holidays at less than brochure price. But, like all their competitors, they were getting round this by providing free insurance or discounting the insurance against the holiday or by providing free transport to airports, etc. Lunn Poly sold their own insurance with their holidays. The margins in insurance could be as high as 40 per cent.

In the words of Financial Director, Richard Manley:

'It's not that we are doing anything different, we are just better at it. We are more productive, our bookings per sales consultant is considerably higher than our competitors' because of our Holiday Shop concept. We only sell quality holidays, our prices are very competitive, we have lots of good shops well designed in good locations, we work hard at dealing well with the customer, we have good staff training and bonus systems, we measure carefully our performance, we use up-to-date technology and we rethink the policies and strategies of the whole organisation every year.'

Quality

Lunn Poly is a bonded travel agent with ABTA, the Association of British Travel Agencies, so that all holidays it sells are underwritten in case of a tour operator's collapse. Lunn Poly does not solely rely on this guarantee but will also only sell holidays if they believe that the operator or the holiday is up to the mark. If they are not, they will not sell them. They give a great deal of exposure to Thomson Holidays, not necessarily because this is a sister company but because Thomson is the market leader.

Richard Manley explained:

'If we didn't push Thomson, we would be cutting our own throats. However, our staff have no more incentive to sell Thomson than any other. They are simply the market leader with 30 per cent of the summer market. We also survey a number of our clients

when they come back from their holiday as to how they rate it. We want to make sure that our holidays are of good quality and are good value for money.'

Price

Many travel agencies seem to be reluctant to enter the high-profile competition war, partly because quality is relatively uniform and all holidays are available to all travel agencies, and partly because margins are relatively tight. However, Lunn Poly believe that some competitors' belief that a customer will walk in just because of who they are is ill-founded. They believed that there is very little customer loyalty and that the average customer is price-sensitive.

Richard Manley explained:

'Discounting is bringing in business, though we are in fact discounting the insurance. We also make sure that our costs are as low as possible so that we can do this, first, by negotiating the best override deals possible and, second, by always looking at overheads to make sure we are lean and mean, especially at the centre. And don't think we get any special favours from Thomson or Britannia, because we don't, they deal with us just like any other agency.'

Location

In 1985 Lunn Poly opened about 20 new shops. Tony Jackson, a General Manager, explained the problem:

'We need a good site with good exposure – success depends on getting the right site. We want prime sites on the major retailing high streets close to the major multiples. If there are other travel agencies close by we don't mind, since we want some of their business. The main problem, once we find a site, is the cost of the lease. In the shopping centres they are usually too high for us, and often are looking for £35 000–£40 000 per annum to rent. We can't cover that on our turnover. However, you can get some excellent sites for a lot less. There is always a lot of competition when a good site comes up, but we are ready.'

Tony had the task of opening 10 new shops in the following nine months to add to his stock of 12.

'There are too few shops in this area. We need better coverage in the north Manchester area. That will allow us to get a better return from our regional TV campaign. Whatever happens, though, we won't open one unless we can expect to make a turnover of £2 million by the second year. With Thomsons being a sister company we can use their figures to see what the competition is doing in the area, that allows us to make reasonable guesses about how the others are doing and so we can get a clear picture of the business.'

Layout

Lunn Poly put all their shops through a refurbishment programme. Tony said:

'On my patch we are about halfway through the shops, though my priority for the fitters is on new shops as soon as they appear. We want to have bright, open-plan, attractive, cheerful shops. We want at least 350 brochure display units, and we don't want counters, we want desks, counters are like a barrier. We want it as open as possible with lots of space around the desks so we can get up, move around and meet people. We can't standardise the layout because the shape of every shop will be different. However we are trying to get a common Lunn Poly set of colours to be used for carpets, wallpaper, lamps, etc. The shop window is a very important asset. We want a large, bright attractive window with lots of offers in it.'

Dealing with the customer

Tony gave his views:

'I don't think we need to spend too much on advertising. I believe we get enough people in our shops already to treble our business. It's a matter of dealing with people properly from the moment when they come into the shop. I don't believe the problem is getting them in here. In my area, I spend less on promotions and marketing than anybody else. There really is no shortage of people coming into the shop. Anyone can wander in, pick up a brochure and go out – which is terrible. They come in because they are thinking about a holiday. What we have to do is to convert that thought into a holiday by helping. What clinches the deal is not the price, though it may help to get them in, nor the product, because everyone else has them, but how we handle the customer. Because of our Holiday Shop concept we have relatively free counters unencumbered with rail and coach ticket sales and enquiries. We have staff who can specialise in IT. What I am trying to do is to improve our conversion rate.

'My philosophy is that if we treat the customer right, understand his or her requirements and match them we will get a sale. It's not that easy, but here's how we do it. My policy is that everyone who walks into the shop must be acknowledged. I am training staff on opening and closing techniques. There are set routines, though I expect every sales consultant to stamp their own personality on it. The welcome in the Salford office might be, "How do? What are you looking for?" and in the Chester office it might be, "Good morning, sir/madam, how may I help you?"

'Once we have started up a conversation we try to get their requirements in detail. We don't lead him/her along, we try to advise, help and sell. At least if they don't buy, they will remember us and come back. We try to find out the type of place, the resort, the type of facilities they want, the type of accommodation, the sort of price range, any preferred airport or flight times or even aircraft, their requirements about the night life

or how quiet or noisy a resort should be, whether they want a disco or a tango, the holiday dates, their numbers and times, etc., etc. We can then advise them on the type of holiday that best suits their requirements. Sometimes it may not be what they had in mind in the first place, but it will suit their requirements.

'It really is important to get this right the first time, because once you have found the holiday that you believe is right they may not say that it is not right or that they are not happy with it but they will allow us to give them an unconditional seven-day option on it and go away and think about it. However, if they are not happy they may be too embarrassed to come back and go through the process again so they go to another travel agent and start all over again from scratch. If you happen to be the lucky one and get it right, you get the booking. I reckon that out of ten options only three come back. It is difficult to get staff to do this completely and carefully and it's a highly skilled job to make sure that you have all the customer's requirements. We also have a process at the end of the booking where we check through all the details of the holiday again. We are doing quite well now in the conversion of those options but we still have a long way to go.'

Training

Because of the Holiday Shop concept, Lunn Poly training was no longer oriented to the technical aspects of dealing with foreign exchange, coach and air tickets, etc., but on selling skills. The main difficulty is the same for all travel agencies. There are four main selling weeks in the year when access to the travel operations booking system via Prestel can be very difficult. However, Lunn Poly tried to spread the workload by off-peak promotions. The Holiday Shop concept also meant that the staff were less tied up with lengthy unproductive sales of non-ITs.

The emphasis was on training how to sell and all the shop managers were sent on a week's training course every year to teach them sales training concepts and also how to be a trainer, because it was their job to train their staff. All shop staff were sales consultants and are expected to read and remember all the travel brochures. The main training here was on product awareness and brochure skills.

Payment and bonus system

Because of the fact that sales consultants no longer need many years of experience and knowledge of the old-style travel agency business, and that what was important were selling skills and up-to-date product awareness, shop managers tend to be younger. Some managers were nearer 25 than the industry norm of 45.

Turnover of staff was high in the industry as a whole, as high as 20 per cent, but because of the Holiday Shop concept this affected Lunn Poly much less than the competition. As Tony said:

'What we need are people with new, youthful enthusiasm, not those in a quiet comfortable rut. We use incentives to try to bring this out. Just as I am motivated to meet my targets, so are all the staff who work in the shops. The pay is normal for the industry, a branch manager might be on £7500–£9000 basic and a sales consultant £4500–£5500, but they are all able to make good bonuses on sales. We have two schemes, an insurance incentive scheme and a profit share scheme. Together they should increase salaries by at least £1500 per person. The insurance scheme can provide 20p–30p per head of insurance sold. The profit share scheme is an end-of-year bonus-based one on profits made on 5 per cent over budget. Most staff in my area are full-time but some people use part-timers and seasonal staff on other rates.'

Budgets

'The budgets are set in a negotiating process,' continued Tony. 'I agree my targets with my Regional Director, Alan Sprong. It's in both our interests to ensure that they are fair, that the overheads are properly stated, that staffing levels are appropriate and that sales targets are fair. I am responsible for setting each of the shop's budgets and then I get comments on them.'

Performance measurement and control

There is a very comprehensive accounting system in Lunn Poly, right down to shop level. All cash sales and overheads are allocated and attributable to each shop. The budgets are based on expected sales turnover and will be influenced by many things, including position, competition, time since opening, marketing effort and local promotions, etc. Each month there is an individual profit and loss account for each shop which shows the performance of each shop compared to budget and each shop's contribution to central costs. These are also discussed each month between the General Manager and the Shop Manager. The financial performance of all the shops in the General Manager's area are also discussed with the Retail Director on a monthly basis.

There are other forms of appraisal as well. Tony explained:

'Besides each shop having to keep to target I would expect every sales consultant to be able to turn over about £2500 worth of business every month. Also I would try to have what we call a development interview with each member of staff every quarter to discuss the figures so far and their contribution. We might also talk about conversion rates, sales techniques – good points, bad points – and set objectives for the future. This might involve a special project like developing youth markets and could involve organising a disco, some local advertising and a window display. I like to provide project opportunities as they develop my staff's skills, increase their sales and also test them out. I try to visit each shop once a week. I don't like the idea of formal meetings but I believe in regular

informal contact. I am very mobile, I have no real base as such and so I don't soak up any overheads. I don't have a secretary and all memos are handwritten and all administrative documents, even those in the shop, are handwritten and self-carbonated to make copying quick and easy. As a General Manager, I too am appraised in the same way and I also get set certain objectives.'

Strategy formulation

Overall financial targets are set by ITOL but Lunn Poly has a fairly free hand in how it achieves them. The board of Lunn Poly debate frequently how those targets might be achieved but also make a policy of involving the General Managers formally, at least once a year, to share and contribute to current thinking. Tony said,

'We are all committed to the Holiday Shop concept and our strategy is to develop and improve it. We all feel we can make a significant input to strategy and it's the way I personally want to work. Once we and the board have agreed the strategy ahead it is our job to sell it to the shop managers and to make it work.'

THE FUTURE

The Holiday Shop concept was an important step for Lunn Poly. It brought about business simplification that would not have been possible before. However, the company does not intend to stand still and has many plans and intentions for the future.

One important area is in new technology. Richard Manley, the Financial Director, explained:

'We have our accounting system based in Leamington Spa. This is primarily used for paying our principals. It's a good recording system, but 10 years old and does not provide the level of management information that we feel we now require. We are now going to scrap it and rewrite it from scratch. It's going to be a big and expensive job. It's very difficult trying to justify the expense, which will be about £1 million, as it is not clearly or directly related to generating profits. That money, you see, could be put into a major advertising campaign. However, this is now under way and the new system should be ready by the end of 1987. We will not be able to expand without it. It's a lot of money to spend, especially as our profits are not many times more than that.

'The second area we are looking at is more automation in the shops. I would like to see each shop with a networked micro that provides all the booking documentation and receipt documentation and at the same time captures financial and management information without anyone here at Leamington Spa or London having to re-enter the data.'

The company has a clear policy of expanding its network of shops and intends opening a further 50. Because of the recent growth, not only through opening new shops but through acquisitions, good communications is seen now to be a very important area. Lunn Poly also sees the need for improvement in staffing and wants to develop better terms and conditions of pay to make sure that they are paying the right people the right rate for doing the right job. By improving the financial package Lunn Poly also hopes to reduce staff turnover.

Richard Manley added:

'In terms of training we have been putting lots of resources into the Commercial Division to the detriment of the Retail Division. Now that Commercial has gone I want to see us really improve the quality of service at the retail end. We have a good "open door" policy for staff that has created an open style of management with local profit centres with clear guidelines, staff involvement in management, lots of briefing sessions, information sharing through many means, manager/staff meetings, working parties and company events. This is a really strong base for future developments.'

Questions

1 What were the significant events in Lunn Poly's history leading up to 1985?

2 What was the 'Holiday Shop concept' and what were the risks associated with it?

3 How would the new concept change the delivery system?

4 What were the implications for the level of customer service and the level of resource utilisation?

5 What were the longer-term issues that need to be addressed?

Part 2

DESIGN

Introduction

The usual image of a designer is of someone who is concerned with the appearance of a product – a fashion designer or a motor car designer, for example. The design activity, however, goes far beyond this narrow aspect of design. In fact, all operations managers are designers. Many of their day-to-day decisions shape the design of the *processes* they manage and in so doing they influence the products and services which they produce. The purchase of every machine or piece of equipment which is bought is a design decision because it affects the physical shape and nature of the operation. Similarly, every time a machine or piece of equipment is moved or a method improved, or a member of staff's responsibility changed, the design of the operation is changed.

Operations managers also have an important influence on the 'technical' design of the *products and services* they produce, by providing much of the information necessary for their design as well as providing the systems which produced them.

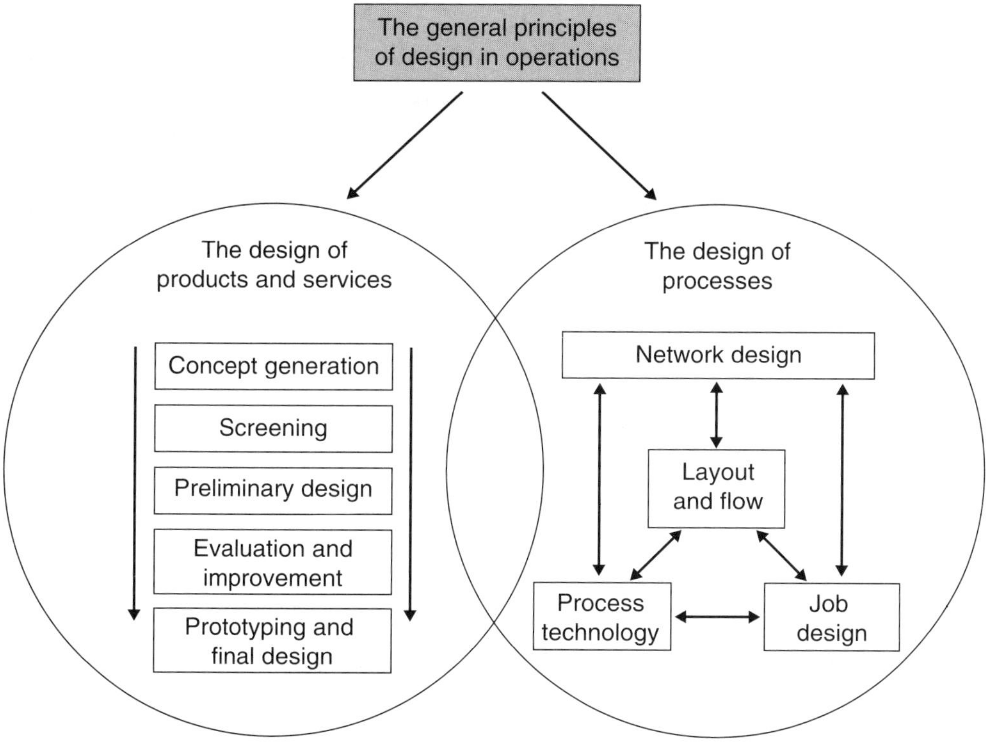

Fig. P2.1 Operations management design activities

This is why operations managers need to understand the basic principles of design, no matter whether it is a product, service or process which is being designed.

Design involves two distinct but closely related tasks: the design of the products and services themselves and the design of the processes for creating those products or services (*see* Fig. P2.1). Each of these will be covered in later sections of this introduction but first let us consider some of the general principles of design in operations.

GENERAL PRINCIPLES OF DESIGN IN OPERATIONS

Design is important

Design is placed early in this book because it is one of the first things that operations managers have to be involved in when setting up an operation. The decisions they make during the design process are important for a number of reasons.

- They involve a lot of money. Most of the decisions described in the two Cadbury World examples (Cases 6 and 7) involve considerable amounts of expenditure. The capital cost involved in purchasing bits of equipment, facilities and technology is rarely going to be very low and often can be exceptionally high. Most operations, especially those with very expensive facilities, cannot afford to get these decisions wrong.
- The decision process happens relatively infrequently. Choosing equipment and people and locating them in the operation is not something that any operations manager would want to do too often. The process is time-consuming and disruptive. The Aylesbury Pressings case (Case 9) is a good example of how the general day-to-day pressures of work make companies reluctant to go through the disruption which redesigning the system entails.
- Design sets the limits of the operation's capability. Once layout decisions are made, they constrain the way in which the operation can be run. For example, in the Cadbury World cases the company chose to locate the attractions in a particular order which then limited the way customers could flow round the whole operation. Any customers trying to go against the flow would cause considerable disruption. Similarly, the way the activities are 'laid out' in the butcher's operation within the McKenzie's supermarket case (Case 8) means that customers pay for the meat before it is cut up for them. This particular design decision limits the degree to which individual customers can change their minds about their purchases.

Design means satisfying the needs of customers

The objective of designing products and services is to satisfy customers by meeting their actual or anticipated needs and expectations (*see*, for example, the National

Westminster Bank, Case 15). Product and service design, therefore, should start and end with the customer. First, the task of marketing is to gather information from customers (and sometimes non-customers) in order to understand and identify their needs and expectations, and also to look for possible market opportunities. Following this, the task of the product and service designers is to take those needs and expectations, as interpreted by marketing, and create a specification for the product or service. The specification will involve three key parts:

- A *concept*, which is the set of expected benefits that the customer is buying.
- A *package* of 'component' products and services that provide those benefits defined in the concept.
- The *process* by which the operation produces the package of 'component' products and services.

Good design provides a competitive edge

Through careful design an organisation can achieve competitive advantage. It can support a quality objective by eliminating weaknesses in products or services, or in the processes to create them. It can develop ways in which products or services can be made quickly, or make each part of the process or the service/product more dependable – which may be critical, for example, as for the Royal Automobile Club (Case 13) in the rescue of stranded motorists. Flexibility can be designed into the products/services and processes to make future changes easier or cheaper than they might otherwise be. Design can also have an important effect on the cost of the product or service. Good design can ensure a high utilisation of resources or could reduce the number of product components or stages in a service.

Product/service design and process design are interrelated

The design of the products/services and the processes of creating them are sometimes undertaken as separate activities, but this seems unwise as the two clearly need to be closely related. Indeed these two activities should be seen as overlapping, as shown in Fig. P2.1. A close relationship between the two can significantly reduce the cost of the overall product or service, and may also reduce 'time-to-market', allowing products and services to be introduced to customers ahead of the competition. Merging the activities of designing products/services and the processes which create them is sometimes called interactive design.

In service operations it is more difficult to see these two activities as being distinct, in fact it is often difficult to separate the process from the service itself. For example, at Warwick Castle (Case 10) the service 'products' are completely intertwined with the process, facilities and interactions experienced by the customers.

The design activity is a transformation process

The design activity is an operation in itself and, therefore, the input–transformation–output process can be applied just like any other operation. The inputs will be market forecasts, market preferences and technical data; together with materials or parts which need to be tested for the suitability of their performance; design staff and equipment, such as computer-aided design (CAD) systems; and development and testing equipment. The output is a definition of the concept, the package and the process (*see* below).

DESIGN OF PRODUCTS AND SERVICES

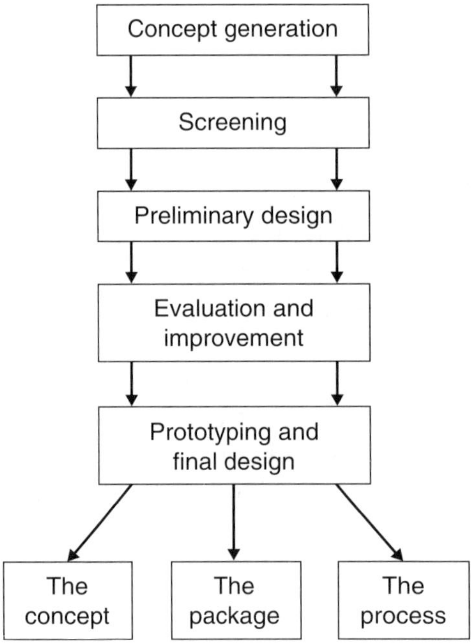

Fig. P2.2 The stages in product/service design

Take the example of Cadbury World (A) (Case 6). The design of their service involved the development of the 'chocolate experience' concept, the idea was checked, or screened, to ensure that it could meet the rates of return required by the company and also deal appropriately with the needs of visitors in their expected numbers. Preliminary designs were developed, not only for the tour but also for the car parks, retail areas and restaurant. In conjunction with leisure consultants, these designs were evaluated and improved until a final design was decided upon. This process of taking an idea for a new product or service and turning it into a final specification is referred to as the design process and involves five stages, *see* Fig. P2.2. Cadbury World is also constantly being redesigned to reflect changes in customer requirements and volumes (*see* Cadbury World (B), Case 7).

Concept generation

Ideas for new product or service concepts may emanate from customers through formal mechanisms like focus groups or questionnaires, or through less formal means such as staff passing on suggestions from customers to the designers. Ideas may also come from other, often competing, organisations or from the organisation's own research and development department.

These roughly formed ideas for new products or services need to be honed into a product or service concept: a clear and simple statement of the overall form, function, purpose and benefits of the idea.

Joc McKenzie (*see* Case 8) was influenced by several things, in particular the Real Meat Consortium, but also the traditional supermarket chains and his internal Business Planning Group. The case ends at the stage of the working party trying to turn this idea into a workable concept.

The concept of the 'Fun Factory' (Cadbury World (B), Case 7) was in response to discussions and other feedback from children who had enjoyed the more tangible aspects of the service and wanted more 'hands-on fun' of this type.

Concept screening

Following on from the end of Case 8, whatever Joc and his team come up with it will have to be tested out against several criteria, including marketing, operations and finance. It will, for example, have to appeal to customers and also differentiate McKenzie from competing retailers to capture and retain customers. It will need to be able to be provided by Joc's resources; he has concerns about whether his car park will be big enough and whether his staff have the right skills for the new ways of working. Joc will also have to evaluate the capital investment required for any new layout and the operating costs of a new operation.

Preliminary design

The next stage for Joc and his team will be to try to develop a preliminary design for the store. They will need to consider an initial specification for the package and the process. The package includes: the range of meats and types of meats (such as organic); the service that will be provided to customers, such as pre-packed and customised cutting; and the environment of the store, its decor and the types of facilities it will need. The process involves the way in which the package of goods and services will be delivered, what will be the flow of materials, the allocation of tasks, how customers will be dealt with, how their orders will be taken and completed and so on. Several techniques are available that might help Joc in this activity, such as process flow charting or creating route sheets. (Several of the cases in this Part provide opportunities to document and evaluate flows such as Cadbury World (A) and (B), Cases 6 and 7; Aylesbury Pressings, Case 9; and National Westminster Bank, Case 15.)

Design evaluation and improvement

The next stage is to take the preliminary design ideas and to test and refine them. Three particularly useful techniques are quality function deployment (QFD), value engineering (VE) and Taguchi methods (for more information, *see* Slack *et al.*, 1995).

Prototyping and final design

The next stage in the design activity is to turn the improved design into a prototype so that it can be tested. Joc McKenzie, for example, may consider making a mock-up of the proposed layout to check the feasibility of the flows or he may just go ahead with the actual implementation of the new service on a trial basis to test customers' reactions to it. In the case of Cadbury World (B) (Case 7), changes were made to the design of flows of customers, but these were not tested or simulated before 'going live'. The managers at Birmingham International Airport created a mock up of the new Eurohub terminal to check the flows of passengers to test out various designs. Some organisations may use much more sophisticated techniques such as the development of computer prototypes using computer aided design (CAD) and simulations. The outcome of this stage is the final specification for the concept, the package and the process of delivery.

Simultaneous development

Although these design stages have been described as sequential, some organisations try to overlap these tasks to reduce time-to-market of their new product or services and to try to overcome potential problems in later stages without the need to halt the process and move back to a previous stage. This is usually referred to as simultaneous or concurrent development (or engineering).

DESIGN OF THE PROCESS

Getting the products and services designed is only part of the design activity. The process of creating the products or services has to be designed. The design of the process involves decisions about the operations network, layout and flow, process technology and the design of jobs.

Network design

This will involve decisions about how the sources of materials and service from suppliers has to be designed. Clearly Cadbury will provide the chocolate, but what about the ingredients for the Inca chocolate drink, the food for the restaurant, and even the materials, models and backdrops for the exhibitions? Network design will also involve decisions about location. In the case of the Cadbury World exhibition the factory had spare land and buildings, but Bournville is not the easiest location to get to, by road or by rail. These issues were weighed up in the location decision. The size of the facility needs to be carefully considered. What are the expected numbers, what happens if the numbers grow rapidly, is there room for expansion? What capacity is the facility to be designed for and how well will it cope with fluctuations in numbers?

Through successive redesigns and modifications, Cadbury World has successfully doubled its capacity (250 000 to 500 000 visitors per year) and simultaneously improved the quality of the experience. Similar improvements in capacity, quality and flexibility were achieved at RAC (Case 13) through the use of new technology.

Layout and flow

Layout concerns decisions about where to put all the facilities, machines, equipment and staff in the operation. This decision will also affect how the materials, information and customers will flow through the operations. This is an important and very visible issue in the design of products and services. There are four 'basic' types of layout: fixed position, process layout, cell layout and product layout.

Layout by fixed position

Although this is called a layout type it is not really a layout as such, since the things to be processed stay where they are and the facilities and/or labour visit them in order to carry out their processing tasks. Usually this type of layout is used where the things being processed are too heavy or too inconvenient to move between facilities. A motorway, for example, is too large to be manufactured and then transported to where it is needed; rather the facilities and labour necessary to manufacture it are moved to where the motorway is to be. Similarly, engineers from a Casgo Centraal's (Case 14) computer servicing operation would generally visit the customer's computer installation in order to service or repair it on site rather than take the computer system away to be repaired. However, off-site repair or servicing might be a possibility for smaller pieces of equipment.

Layout by process

In this kind of layout all similar facilities or people are concentrated together. The material or customers being processed then move between these concentrations of processors as they need them. At Warwick Castle (Case 10), for example, there are various concentrations of similar facilities. The state rooms are all in one place, the armoury in another, the dungeons in another location and the different types of restaurant facilities in their own location. Customers, as they need or want to sample these facilities, flow between them. There is no set order as such, customers being free to move from one to another at will. Similarly, in the Aylesbury Pressings case (Case 9) the original way of laying out the operation puts similar types of press together and similar types of welding machinery together. Different products, because they have different needs, will take different routes through the operation. In both these case studies putting similar facilities together may be convenient, efficient, and allows for specialisation of employees and facilities (or the operation may have no alternative as with the state rooms at Warwick Castle) but it does mean that the flow between the different parts of the operation can be different for every customer or component and thus can also be very complex.

The National Westminster Bank (Case 15) is also configured as a process layout, with nine separate sections for different specialised tasks, but none of these specialised in the process of opening new accounts.

Cell layout

A cell layout is one where the transformed resources entering the operation are preselected (or preselect themselves) to move to one part of the operation (or cell) in which all the transforming resources to meet their immediate processing needs are co-located. The cell itself may be arranged in either a process or product (*see* following section) layout. After being processed in the cell, the transformed resources may go on to another cell. McKenzie's supermarket is a good example of a cell layout where each area can be considered a separate process devoted to selling particular types of goods. The solutions attempted at Aylesbury Pressings also adopted a cell-based approach which took certain 'families' of product and put together all the common facilities needed to process them. This simplified the flow to a certain extent but still retained the ability to be flexible.

Layout by product

Layout by product means putting facilities and people in the order in which they are required to process a particular type of product or service. All materials and customers will then flow in a predetermined and predictable manner from one set of facilities to the next. The Cadbury World exhibition is a classic example of this type of layout. Customers flow in a set route from the ticketing area to the exhibition area, through to a holding area for the Marie Cadbury room, and continue all the way through to the shop and restaurant at the end. It is interesting to note that next door, in the Cadbury chocolate factory itself, chocolate bars are made in exactly the same way. The material moves predictably from the chocolate preparation area through to the moulding area, through to the packing area and so through the rest of the process. In the Brechten Algraphy case (Case 11) the integrated nature of the technology makes any other than a product layout difficult.

Process technology

Whenever operations purchase process technology they have choices to make. Factories need to decide what kind of machines they are going to use, banks need to decide what kind of computers and cashpoints they are going to invest in, and airlines have choices to make between the different kinds of aircraft they will purchase. In examining the choices which operations make, it is useful to think of the technology they are using on three different dimensions:

1 Its degree of automation – how much it still relies on human beings to operate it and how much the technology does without human assistance.
2 The scale of the technology – not its physical size but rather its capacity, that is how much it can process.
3 The degree of integration – how separate pieces of technology are linked with other technologies in the system.

The degree of automation

Process technology varies in terms of the amount of human intervention that it requires. Some of the technology requires little human intervention in its use, for example the CNC machines described in the Beaver Engineering case (Case 12); others require the human to be the brains and eyes of the technology such as the technology described in the RAC study (Case 13). The automation of doors, as described in Cadbury World (B) (Case 7), required no human intervention but did not operate in quite the way conceived by the designers.

The scale of technology

Some operations, such as petrochemical plants, food processing factories or steel making plants, really do benefit from using large scale technologies. They use these technologies because with the high volumes they process they can achieve low costs. But there are also disadvantages to using large capacity pieces of technology. If demand is not very high, they can be left only partly utilised which can increase the operation's costs. The minimum capacity of Brechten Algraphy's technology (Case 11), for example, exposes it to some risk if initial demand for its new product is lower than expected. Also they are generally less flexible than smaller pieces of technology. For example, if an airline chooses to buy only a few very large jumbo jets it will be fine provided it is transporting large numbers of passengers on relatively few routes. On the other hand, if it wants to provide its passengers with a large number of alternative destinations at lower volume then it would be better advised to buy a larger number of smaller aircraft. In other words, it is the volume and variety of its services which will, to a large extent, dictate the mixture of large and small aircraft which an airline buys. This type of decision was also important in the Focus Plastics case (Case 4) where different sizes of injection-moulding machines could be purchased for different volumes and varieties of plastic products. The Brechten Algraphy case also illustrates some of the advantages and risks associated with process integration.

The degree of integration

The integration of technology, or the extent to which it is joined up with other pieces of technology, is also partly dependent on volume. Joining computers up into networks, for example, can make for lower costs and increase convenience, provided the needs and functions required by all the users are broadly similar. However, connecting up all these functions does make the whole process more vulnerable. If the whole computer network goes down everyone is affected. If they were not connected and one individual computer went down, only its user would be inconvenienced.

Job design

For most operations the decision about job design is important, partly because of the large numbers of people usually employed in the operations function and also because the actions of these people – individually and collectively – can have a significant effect on the quality of the goods and services, and the productivity and profitability of the operation as a whole.

Many decisions need to be taken about people's jobs. How many people will be required, what will they have to do, what skills will they need, how should they interface with the technology and the customers? (These are issues in Cadbury World, Cases 6 and 7; RAC, Case 13; Casgo Centraal, Case 14; and National Westminster Bank, Case 15.)

Many tools and techniques exist to help the operations manager design, plan and control the tasks performed by the workforce: work measurement, method study, ergonomics, behaviour approaches to job design – job rotation, enlargement and enrichment, and empowerment. (*See,* for example, Slack et al., 1995.)

Several cases here provide opportunities to determine and evaluate how management might use people to improve operational performance in different work situations. They provide information to allow analysis of the work flows and the work content of many operations tasks. The cases also examine the critical nature of operations personnel – both customer contact and back office support – in providing a high quality, efficient and profitable operation.

The RAC case describes the variety of processes and tasks that have to be co-ordinated in the provision of service to the stranded motorist (Case 13). This organisation recognises that it needs to improve its performance to keep the RAC ahead of the competition. Its use and motivation of staff will be a key element in this strategy.

In 1987 Casgo Centraal moved the focus of its business from manufacturing computers to the maintenance of computer systems (Case 14). Its wide variety of services and associated service levels were causing some problems for its engineers. The case explores the need to harness the involvement of the workforce of technicians in a performance improvement programme.

The critical impact that all staff have upon the customer is demonstrated in the St James's Square Branch of the National Westminster Bank (Case 15). The branch's job of managing and meeting the expectations of its new customers in an increasingly competitive environment was not as successful as the bank had hoped. So, without the injection of additional resources, the branch had the task of becoming more efficient and more quality oriented.

SUMMARY

This Part, including Cases 6–15, has tried to demonstrate the processes involved in designing products and services, and the processes which create and deliver them. Although many operations managers are not directly involved in the process *per se*, they have a major stake in its outcome, the specification of the products, services and processes. As such they need to be aware of the design process and be concerned to take an active part in the process.

Key points

- The overall purpose of the design activity is to meet the needs of customers.
- The design activity is itself a transformation process.
- The design of products and services is a multi-stage process which moves from concept through to a detailed specification.
- Over the last few years, many organisations have been moving away from the sequential approach to product and service design and have been applying interactive design methods. This approach shortens the time-to-market; reduces the number of operations problems, particularly quality problems; reduces development costs; and provides an earlier return on investment.
- The process of creating the products or services has to be designed and it involves decisions about the operations network, layout and flow, process technology and the design of jobs.
- The two activities of product/service design and process design are interrelated and should not be done independently of each other. Bringing them together has many benefits including better designs and faster time-to-market. In the design of services, it is often difficult to separate out the service from the process which produces it.

Recommended reading

Slack, N., Chambers, S., Harland, C., Harrison, A. and Johnston, R. (1998), *Operations Management* (2nd edn), Pitman Publishing. Chapters 4, 5, 6, 7, 8 and 9.

Selected further readings

Abernathy, W. J. (1976), 'Production Process Structure and Technological Change', *Design Sciences*, Vol 7, No 4.

Apple, J. M. (1977), *Plant Layout and Materials Handling*, Wiley.

Bailey, J. (1983), *Job Design and Work Organisation*, Prentice Hall.

Bessant, J. (1991), *Managing Advanced Manufacturing Technology, The Challenge of the Fifth Wave*, NCC, Blackwell.

Bitner, M. J. (1992), Servicescapes: The Impact of Physical Surroundings on Customers, *Journal of Marketing*, Vol 56, April 1992, pp. 57–71.

Charlisle, B. (1983), 'Job design implications for operations managers', *International Journal of Operations and Production Management*, Vol 3, No 2.

Chase, R. B. 'Where does the customer fit in a service operation', *Harvard Business Review*, Vol 56, No 6: 137–42.

Collier, D. A. (1985), *Service management: the automation of services*, Reston Publishing.

Corlett, N., Wilson, J. and Manencia, F. (eds) (1986), *Ergonomics of Working Posture*, Taylor and Francis.

Cross, N. (1984), *Developments in Design Methodology*, Wiley.

Dean, J. H. and Susman, G. I. (1984), 'Organizing for Manufacturable Design', *Harvard Business Review*, Vol 67, No 1: 28–36.

Fox, J. (1993), *Quality Through Design: The Key to Successful Product Delivery*, McGraw-Hill.

Groover, M. P. and Zimmers, E. W. (1984), *CAD/CAM Computer-Aided Design and Manufacturing*, Prentice Hall.

Gunton, T. (1990), *Inside Information Technology, A Practical Guide to Management Issues*, Prentice Hall.

Harrison, M. (1990), *Advanced Manufacturing Technology Management*, Pitman Publishing.

Shostack, G. L. (1984), 'Designing services that deliver', *Harvard Business Review*, Vol 62, No 1: 133–9.

Sparke, P. (1986), *An Introduction to Design and Culture in the Twentieth Century*, Allen and Unwin.

Walker, D. and Cross, N. (1983), *An Introduction to Design*, Open University Press.

Walsh, V., Roy, R., Bruce, M. and Potter, S. (1992), *Winning By Design, Technology, Product Design and International Competitiveness*, Blackwell.

Webb, A. (1994), *Managing Innovative Projects*, Chapman and Hall.

CASE 6

Cadbury World (A)

Mark Robinson and Stuart Chambers

Case date 1981

INTRODUCTION

Cadbury's have been a renowned English manufacturer of chocolate products for more than 100 years. Today, as Cadbury-Schweppes, the firm is a major food products conglomerate, but one with very deep roots. Indeed, the current mission statement of the company echoes the philosophy of John Cadbury, the committed Quaker who founded the company in 1794. Cadbury's mission stresses 'social responsibility' and the desire to be a good neighbour. It also explicitly sets out a commitment to encourage the personal fulfilment of employees. Although such corporate sentiments are not unique to Cadbury, they are rarely so deeply held.

John Cadbury saw his 'drinking cocoa' as a moral alternative to the cheap liquor sold to the working classes in nineteenth-century industrial England. The high quality of Cadbury's products, manufactured in the centre of Birmingham, was rewarded by their commercial success. In 1879, the chocolate factory, by then in his sons' control, was relocated four miles to the south in a rural setting on the River Bourn. The Cadburys' initially purchased 15 acres for the factory, but then bought more and more land. On this holding they developed the first 'model' village to follow a programme of mixed development. This was an environment for all social classes, developed as a balanced mixture of house types. By contrast, earlier 'model' villages were massed collections of a repeated dwelling type: the artisan's cottage. The new site was called 'Bournville' to give Cadbury products a French-sounding origin – at that time French chocolate was considered a world leader. Since then, the products (£1.32 billion sales in 1990), the factory and Bournville itself have all grown. Today, Bournville (now a pleasant suburb of Birmingham) extends to 400 hectares and comprises 6500 dwellings, housing 20 000 people.

CADBURY WORLD

A factory visit to Cadbury's at Bournville has been a highlight for children since the 1920s. Even today, many adults fondly remember their childhood tours and gift of a presentation tin of chocolate. These field trips included the production areas and Bournville village. In 1965 (when 160 000 visitors came), Cadbury decided to stop these tours due to tighter legislation on the hygiene of food production and the possibility of intentional contamination of chocolate by visitors. For years after, however, Cadbury continued to be barraged by requests from educational groups and individuals who were interested in visiting the factory.

In the face of this interest, management decided in the mid-1980s to reintroduce the popular outing to Cadbury. A number of major changes over the intervening 20 years meant that this new 'product' would be different from the old tours. First, rationalisation at the factory had released a large area of land for non-manufacturing uses. Second, the production process itself had become much more automated and enclosed since the 1960s, and was no longer likely to be of such interest to visitors. Finally, the economic climate was more favourable to leisure businesses than had been the case for many years. The new venture was intended to be a contemporary 'leisure experience' but also to have educational value and be guided by the spirit of the old tours. It was this combination of factors that influenced the decision to create Cadbury World.

In the words of the Cadbury World promotional material, 'Cadbury World is a permanent exhibition devoted entirely to chocolate – where it came from, who first drank this mysterious potion, when it became eating chocolate and the part that Cadbury played in this fascinating story.'

The scheme involved building a new 'visitor centre' adjacent to the main production plant, constructing car parks and a play area, and hiring and training 87 staff: at a total cost of around £5 million. Advance estimates by leisure consultants indicated that it would attract 250 000 visitors a year; based on an average ticket price of around £3.50, the return on investment – low for Cadbury – would be just under 10 per cent. After much planning, Cadbury World opened to the public in mid-August 1990.

The 1990 Cadbury-Schweppes Annual Report commented on this new venture: 'Its success as a unique and absorbing leisure experience can be measured by the 185 000 visitors who enjoyed the Cadbury World experience between August and the year end.'

THE EXPERIENCE

Nearly all visitors arrive by car or coach. Parking for cars is arranged in three areas with a total capacity of 484. Separate spaces close to the 'Alternative Exhibition' can accommodate 24 coaches and there is a 'picking up/setting down' area close to the main exhibition. Data suggest that on a representative weekday (during school term time), 15 pre-booked coaches and about 204 cars come to Cadbury World. Typically, there are about 35 visitors per coach and 3 per car.

The site is served by two other means of transport, inheritances from its industrial past: to the rear of the factory are a railway station and a canal pier. Some visitors come by train and there are a few commercial barge operators who run tourist trips from the centre of Birmingham out to Bournville. However, the plant layout means these visitors have about a 10-minute walk around the perimeter of the factory before reaching Cadbury World. This path has been signed as 'The Factory Trail'.

The exhibition's reception area has three tills. Two are for individuals and the other is for the leaders of coach visitor groups. The ticketing system has been the subject of experimentation, the latest being a 'timed ticket'. This prints out a specific time slot on a batch of tickets. However, computer problems meant that this has not been implemented.

Ticket prices and times of opening and entry are set out in Table 6.1.

Table 6.1 Ticket prices and opening times

Opening times	Open every day except Christmas Day Mon.–Sat. 10.00 a.m.–5.30 p.m. Sun. 12.00 noon–6.00 p.m.
Last admissions	Mon.–Sat. 4.00 p.m., Sun. 4.30 p.m.
1991 prices (includes VAT)	Adult £4.00 Child £3.00 (5–15 inclusive) Under fives *FREE* Family rate £12.85 (2 adults and 2 children) Senior Citizen £3.60 (Mon.–Fri. only) Groups (20 or more) must book in advance.

The booking system for groups requires organisers to specify their group's time of arrival and pay a £25 deposit. The maximum size for any single group is set at 60 people. Cadbury World schedules coaches at regular times throughout the day to space the arrival of groups. Because of the difficulty of estimating the duration of road journeys, coaches often arrive late and miss their agreed times. This adds to the queues of visitors at the exhibition's entrance at busy periods.

The entrance to Cadbury World has low barriers funnelling individual visitors toward the tills. Beyond these, the reception area gives access to the exhibition, the shop and the restaurant. Sometimes this area is used for attractions such as a 'honky-tonk' piano player. At other times, a TV continuously plays a four-minute video previewing many of the features visitors will see at Cadbury World. This includes many parts of the interior of the exhibition, the packaging plant, and short extracts of other videos which are running inside Cadbury World. A sketch of the Cadbury World facility is reproduced in Fig. 6.1.

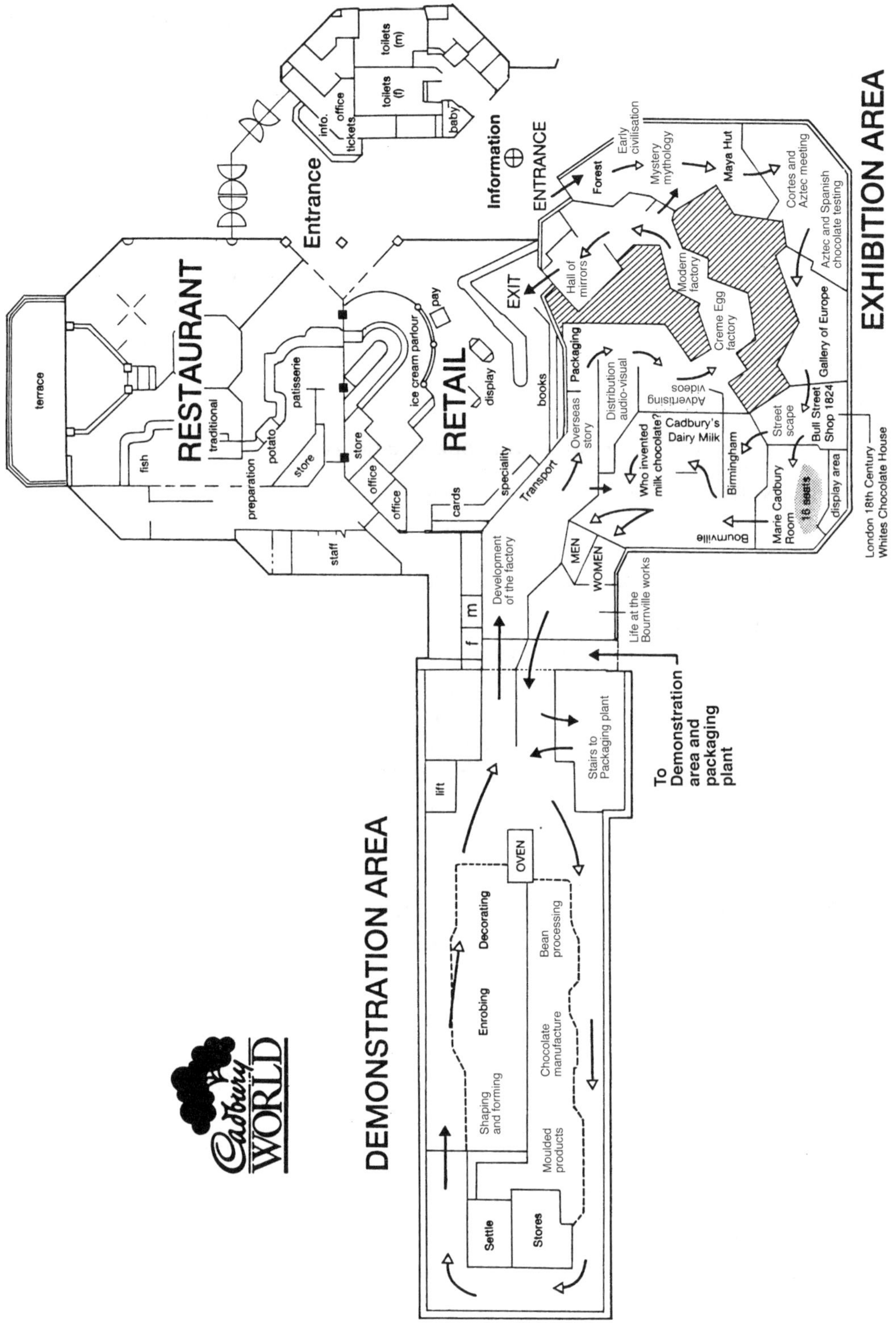

Fig. 6.1 A sketch of the Cadbury World site

The entrance to the exhibition itself is via a pair of unmarked double doors. A ticket collector stationed here controls the number of visitors entering. A judgement of the number of visitors to be admitted at one time is made by the ticket collector, who periodically enters the exhibition and checks the number of visitors before 'Bull Street', which marks the end of the first part of the exhibition. On average, in a busy period 15–20 visitors are let in every two and a half minutes. For most of the exhibition, visitors have no guides.

The first section of the tour describes the ancient origins of chocolate and tries to capture the atmosphere of a South American jungle. Visitors enter a darkened room which has been 'dressed' with artificial trees and lianas. Among these, wax models of South American Indians are shown making and drinking chocolate. The narrative of the story is carried on a variety of short sign-boards and continued, a little further on, by a continuously playing video 'documentary' lasting three minutes. 'Jungle sounds' are played over loudspeakers. Some visitors pass quickly through this section, treating it almost as an antechamber to the exhibition. A family group of visitors was overheard while moving through the jungle:

FATHER: *'I know that smell, what is it?'*

MOTHER: *'Phew, it's nice to get in out of the sun. It's quite cool in here. It'll stop my chocolates from melting. I should have bought them at the end of the tour.'*

FATHER: *'Look at these Indians, they didn't worry about their chocolate melting, they drank it!'*

BOY: *'Mum, come on, I can hear the advert from the TV. The one with the "Man in Black" in it.'*

MOTHER: *'Hold on, you've not seen this yet. There is a video about the Spanish and the Indians. I think it's in the middle, I wonder how long it'll be before it starts again?'*

FATHER: *'Fibreglass! I knew I recognised it.'*

The visitors then pass a scene featuring a representation of Hernando Cortés, the Spanish conqueror of Mexico, beyond which the jungle abruptly ends. This area has a serving hatch and a sign invites visitors to take a small plastic cup of liquid chocolate ('like the Incas used to drink'). A swing-top bin is next to the hatch for the disposal of used cups. This section is generally supervised by a member of staff. An attendant explained: 'We have problems with some of the children. They take five or six of the cups, cover themselves in chocolate and make themselves ill.'

Visitors then pass a pictorial wall-mounted display and move (still at their own pace) into a 'room' describing the introduction of chocolate to Europe. To the rear, the faint sounds of the jungle can still be heard.

Beyond the European Room, visitors enter 'Bull Street' – a replica of a cobbled Georgian street, with contemporary shop windows. An attendant in Bull Street halts the flow of people to form groups outside a door to the next part of the tour.

This next area is the Marie Cadbury room, which has seating for 16 and surrounding standing room. At peak times as many as 70 people are assembled in the room, although it was originally designed for only about one-third of this number.

After the doors close, there is a five-minute automated 'show' which depicts, with taped voices and three static, illuminated scenes, the early days of Cadbury. This programme is operated by the attendant who closes the doors and starts the show with a switch. Completion of the show is indicated to the attendant by an unobtrusive light. This is the prompt to open the doors to allow the next group in. However, the attendant generally waits for a minute or two before opening the doors. In this time, the preceding group, realising that the show is over, begin to look at the wall-mounted exhibits in the room. When the attendant opens the door they begin to make their own way out of a separate exit to the next section of the exhibition. Filling and emptying the Marie Cadbury room takes a total of about four minutes on average, although this does increase for large groups.

The next area comprises pictorial exhibits explaining the history of Cadbury, Bournville village and the social background to the firm. At one end of the room, a video entitled 'Making Chocolate' runs for three minutes. Beyond this is a mock-up of an old factory entrance – with a working 'clock' and 'clocking-in' cards. The entrance has two gates marked 'MEN' and 'WOMEN', as did the original factory. Families are, therefore, separated briefly at this point. This interactive section of the exhibition is often a cause of amusement, with older visitors explaining to children how the 'clock' works.

Throughout the exhibition it appears that different types of visitors spend their time in different ways. Most pensioners like the videos, but skip most of the written material. School groups, however, tend to focus on the notices and narrative material. An educational 'task sheet' available for children from the reception is a way of holding these visitors' attention.

From here, visitors leave the new building and directly enter part of the factory – the East Cocoa Block. The contrast is marked: the experience is typical of a factory built in the 1930s. The floors and stairs are concrete and the walls bare, cream-painted brick. Surprisingly, there is little smell of chocolate.

What the visitor sees next depends on whether the factory itself is running. The factory has scheduled maintenance shut-down periods of about 37 days per year. When the factory is working, visitors see the packaging plant. At other times they miss this out and go directly to the demonstration area. It is clearly indicated in advance that the packaging plant is not guaranteed to be open every day. Nevertheless, a few visitors become quite annoyed if they cannot visit it because of these shut-downs.

THE PACKAGING PLANT

This is located at second-floor level and reached by the original factory stairs. There is a ground-floor waiting area for visitors in wheelchairs who cannot reach the packaging plant, since there is no lift. At the top landing a queue forms in front of a TV playing Cadbury's adverts. The tour comprises a route with three stopping points or 'stations'. A guide collects a group of around 30 people from the landing and leads it to the first station. Here, a short video showing the factory is played with a commentary added by the guide.

Following this halt of about three minutes, the guide leads the group to the next station. On the way, they meet the preceding group returning from the second station. This causes some confusion and delay, as the groups must pass in a narrow walkway. The guide then marshals the group at the second station (about 30 metres from the previous halt) from where the packaging machinery can be seen and heard. The packaging plant itself is a very clean area in which white-coated attendants and engineers monitor the wrapped bars of chocolate rolling off the line. The format here is the same: a brief video which explains the packaging process, with live commentary added by the guide. Visitors may be surprised to see that some guides read their commentary from hand-written prompt cards. After the video has run they follow the preceding group and retrace their steps, meeting the next group on the walkway. Before leaving this area the guide halts, gives another brief explanation and then offers visitors chocolates from a tray. On warm days, visitors are offered paper towels on which to clean their fingers. The packaging plant section of the tour is generally completed in about eight minutes.

THE DEMONSTRATION AREA

This part of the tour is run in guided groups of about 15 people. At peak times, about eight guides are on duty. Guides have the option of addressing their groups with their own voices or, for larger groups, by means of a portable microphone. Visitors are encouraged to ask questions. There are normally several groups on the circuit round the demonstration area (*see* Fig. 6.2).

The demonstration area is on the ground floor and shows a number of production operations carried out by about seven staff on small, 'old technology' machines. These machines have been chosen to enable operations such as the coating of nuts in chocolate to be seen and understood. The visitors are separated from these

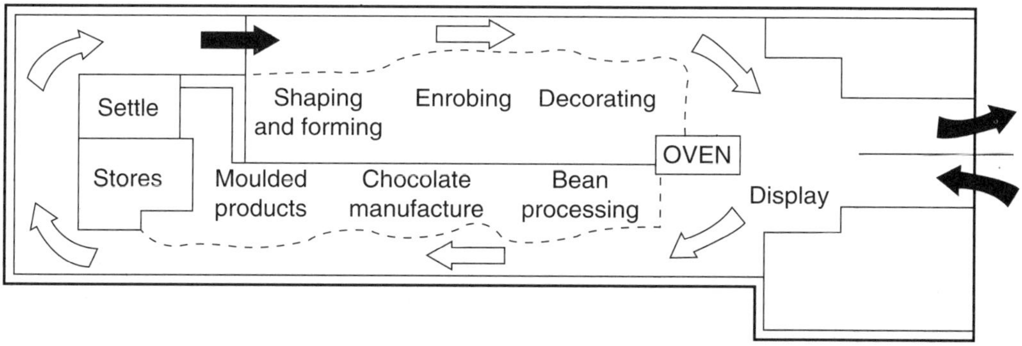

Fig. 6.2 The demonstration area

operations by chest-high perspex screens. The demonstration staff, who have been recruited from the factory, wear white production clothing and have been trained to interact with visitors. After watching an operation (for example vibrating chocolate into moulds or turning out blocks), visitors are offered samples of chocolate. Overhead, a number of hanging photographs show the full-scale production equivalent of each of these machines. This section of the tour continues with a number of demonstrations of the production of luxury, handmade chocolates. As before, staff are behind clear screens; they carry out a number of dipping, ennobling (coating) and finishing operations. After being given more free samples and asking questions, the group moves out of the demonstration area and back into the new building. Although there is not a set number of points of interest, visitors may see up to eight operations in this area.

In the demonstration area, some visitors 'graze', moving from one guide's group to the one ahead, and complete the section in as little as six minutes. By contrast, other visitors take the opportunity to ask many questions, look at all the points of interest and sample all the free chocolate. In this case, they and their guide may take up to 17 minutes to get round. No overtaking of guides by the following guides is allowed. Guides, therefore, need to adjust the length of their explanations in order to match the speed of their group to that of any preceding group – which may include an unusually slow visitor.

Guides have noticed that they find it easier to control their groups when they use the microphones.

EXIT

The remainder of the tour is unaccompanied and focuses on marketing material. This includes a video on the making of a Milk Tray TV advert (the 'Man in Black') and video compilations of advertisements which can be selected by visitors pressing buttons.

The end of the route leads directly into the rear of the shop.

THE SHOP

This sells a wide range of Cadbury products as well as 'branded' mementoes such as tea towels, mugs and T-shirts. Most of the goods are on self-service display and pilferage by children is believed to be a problem. There are three checkouts and most goods are bar-coded. Observations show that, on average, during busy periods a customer can be served at each till every 15 seconds.

While most tour visitors enter the shop through the back entrance (having completed the tour), a number of customers also browse and buy before the beginning of the tour.

THE RESTAURANT

The Centre Services Manager described the restaurant: 'The restaurant is modelled on that of a "Food Court" such as those typically included in modern indoor shopping centres. There is a good choice of foods and there is something for everybody.'

Approached from the reception area via a single entrance, it is a self-service restaurant with five serving points arranged in a row. Four of these are labelled: 'Patisserie', 'Baked Potato', 'Traditional' and 'Seafood'. The fifth is a heavily used point serving tea and coffee. The range of food choice cannot be seen from the entrance to the restaurant. Visitors enter, peruse the various serving points and then make their decision on food type and thus decide which queue to join. This can take a little while, especially in the case of some old people and families. The popularity of the adjacent 'Baked Potato', tea and coffee and 'Traditional' serving points results in knots of customers at busy times. Payment is taken separately at each sales point.

Customers take their selections to the seating area. This is a large airy room providing comfortable surroundings. Fifty-three tables of various sizes provide 169 covers.

Typically, people spend 25 minutes in the restaurant. Tables are promptly cleared and cleaned by pleasant staff based in a 'refuge' in the centre of the seating area. Most visitors to Cadbury World come into the restaurant.

COFFEE AND ICE-CREAM PARLOUR

This small area is approached via the shop and has 46 'covers', comprising stools at the island bar and separate tables around it. The design of the parlour is reminiscent of an American-style diner. The parlour sells coffee, tea and ice-cream. On average, a visitor stays in the parlour for 18 minutes. At any one time, about 25–30 people can be found there.

THE ALTERNATIVE EXHIBITION

This is located close to the coach park, 300 metres from the main exhibition. It is a converted factory building, about 250 square metres in area. In 'feel', it is more like a traditional museum than the rest of Cadbury World. It houses static displays of old machinery, a fire engine and other historic items. More than 95 per cent of visitors to the main exhibition come here. A small 'shuttle bus' is provided to take visitors between the two sites. The Alternative Exhibition is staffed, and visitors (some of whom are retired Cadbury employees) often ask detailed technical questions.

THE UNHAPPY FEW!

Cadbury World receives approximately six letters of complaint per 10 000 visitors. Each one receives a reply. Problems with unhappy visitors in the exhibition are dealt with by staff but, if necessary, the Manager will personally attend to aggrieved parties. Staff are trained to ascertain customers' expectations and why they are disappointed. The objective is to 'send people home happy'. A recent incident involved two pensioners who were upset by the closure of the packaging plant on a day not explicitly specified in the promotional material.

PENSIONERS: *'Your brochure says the packaging plant is closed from tomorrow, not today. This is the second time this has happened. It was closed a month ago when we last came. We want our money back.'*

CADBURY WORLD STAFF: *'I'm sorry the plant is closed, but the factory is preparing for the shut-down today. I know the last time you came it was also closed, but then it was at a clearly scheduled time.'*

After a few more exchanges the Manager saw the customers and gave them vouchers for Cadbury products, which seemed to satisfy them.

MARKETING

The Centre Services Manager explained:

'At present, our only promotion is a limited drop of leaflets to travel agents and Tourist Boards. We also have an arrangement with British Rail for combined, reduced rate travel and Cadbury World tickets.

'We do not see ourselves as being in competition with other attractions in the West Midlands. We have provided a new facility for the local community, and an exciting outing for visitors to the area!

'Our pricing policy was decided after looking at the duration of the "experience". We think it takes a half day: about an hour and a half in the exhibition, half an hour in the Alternative Exhibition and then the restaurant and shop. We then looked at comparable leisure venues such as Warwick Castle and tried to provide value for money for visitors.

'We strive to give the customer a good feeling and believe happy staff create happy customers. To give you an example, recently we were telephoned by an anxious group leader whose coach was coming from a long distance and was delayed. The passengers had not eaten for hours, so we kept the Restaurant open an extra 45 minutes to let them get a meal.'

CUSTOMER INFORMATION

The following gives the breakdown of the relative numbers of visitors in a week in October 1990:

Monday–Friday	60%
Saturday	18%
Sunday	22%

The main categories of Cadbury World visitors are families, pensioners and school parties.

Questions

1. How would you best describe the service concept of Cadbury World? In what ways is the design of the service package compromised by:
   (a) the service concept(s)?
   (b) the limited capital for the project?
   (c) other factors?
2. Draw a process flow chart showing how customers are processed through the operation. What does this suggest about the process design of Cadbury World?
3. Calculate the hourly capacities for each operation in (2) above. How does the Centre Services Manager vary capacity to respond to changes in demand? How could the service be amended to increase bottleneck capacity?
4. Does the low frequency of complaints indicate a high level of customer satisfaction?
5. Is Cadbury World a successful operation?

CASE 7

Cadbury World (B)

Adam Bates and Stuart Chambers

Case date 1995

INTRODUCTION

'Since opening in 1990, Cadbury World has exceeded all of our expectations' explained Jeremy King, Sales and Marketing Manager, to the new Centre Services Manager, Peter Bales. *'Having originally designed the operation for 250 000 visitors annually, current forecasts for the remainder of 1995 are that numbers will top half a million.'*

During Peter's induction into the organisation, Jeremy had suggested that he focus on assessing three major operational issues that had recently been raised. First, automatic doors had been installed at the entrance to the 'Cadbury Room', and Jeremy was concerned that queues were developing in the areas leading up to this part of the exhibition. Second, queuing for the Packaging Plant was extremely lengthy during periods of high demand and he wanted to evaluate whether this had been affected by the new doors at the Cadbury Room. Finally, the tour guides had adopted a 'free-flow' system for the demonstration area. This comprised guides stationed at fixed points giving their commentaries, and allowed visitors to be processed at a faster rate than the conventional guide-led tours. It was not known what effect this new system had had on the quality of the visitors' experience.

CADBURY WORLD IN 1995

Cadbury World has been continuously fine-tuning its visitors' experience over the first five years of operating, altering both the design and layout of the facility, and the flows and processes within it.

The centre provides a permanent exhibition and demonstrations of the manufacturing and packaging processes employed, as well as static exhibition displays of the history and social culture of the company, a museum, a factory shop, children's play area and restaurant.

Demand for the attraction is largely from the leisure market, but the recent inclusion of the study of the Aztecs (who have associations with chocolate) in the National Curriculum for Schools has also generated a reasonably sized educational market.

Originally Cadbury World was open 364 days per year but, in order to reduce its operating costs and in response to known patterns of demand, opening has now been reduced to 294 days, with closures occurring most Mondays, Tuesdays and

Fridays from November through March. The opening times are from 10.00 a.m. to 5.30 p.m., with last admissions at 4.00 p.m. Ticket prices have increased annually, slightly ahead of inflation and 1995 rates are shown in Table 7.1.

Table 7.1 Ticket prices at Cadbury World in 1995

Pricing category	*Admission price (£)*
Adult	4.90
Child (5–15 years)	3.35
Child (under 5)	Free
Family: 2 adults + 2 children	14.00
Family: 2 adults + 3 children	16.85
Senior citizen	4.20
Adult group	4.25
Child group	2.90
School/Senior citizen group	2.90

RESERVATIONS AND TICKETING

Reservations are now required to guarantee entry, and this is clearly marked on all Cadbury World literature. Most visitors' first direct contact with Cadbury World, therefore, now occurs on the telephone, and every effort has been made to ensure that this is as satisfactory, informative and friendly as possible. If the packaging plant is scheduled to be closed, as happens at certain times throughout the year, visitors are informed at this time. The reservation system is free to the visitors and is used to book up to 80 per cent of any day's capacity. After that visitors are told that no more reservations can be taken, thus allowing Cadbury World some slack, and not disappointing too many visitors who may turn up on the day without a reservation. Groups, of 20 or more people, make their reservations using the same system, but are required to pay a nominal deposit to guarantee the booking.

Upon arrival at Cadbury World ample parking is provided, with set-down and pick-up areas for cars and coaches directly in front of the main doors. A 'flexi-barrier' queue system is set up in front of the ticketing area. A notice at the entrance to the queue advises visitors that only one member from each group need join in order to obtain tickets. Tickets are issued with specified entry times, with each day being broken into 10-minute 'slots'. Originally 72 tickets were available for each slot, increasing to 78 when the packaging plant was closed; however, this has now been reduced to a single rate of 68 persons per 10-minute slot. Jeremy explained:

> *'We had received feedback from our market research that customers' perceived quality of the attraction was diminishing at the highest levels of demand, and in order to improve the experience we felt justified in reducing the numbers of visitors. Four people less may not sound like much, but it can mean approximately £4000 less revenue per week in the high season.'*

Average arrival times of casual visitors are also problematic; as Jeremy remarked to Peter:

'Most people who turn up without reservations tend to do so between 11.00 a.m. and 1.00 p.m. This is also when most of our pre-booked visitors wish to arrive and so the people who just turn up can have long waits: sometimes up to a few hours. We have considered limiting coach parties over this period and only allowing them to visit during the shoulder periods between 10.00 a.m.–11.00 a.m. and 1.00 p.m.–4.00 p.m., which would improve the experience of visitors who do not book. What effect this might have on our coach groups is hard to gauge.'

Apart from changes in the reservation and ticketing arrangements, much work has been done to improve the layout and flow within the exhibition. The original layout of Cadbury World, including the changes made, is outlined in Fig. 7.1.

ENTRANCE TO THE EXHIBITION

'Flexi-barrier' queues are again used in the reception area leading up to the exhibition entrance, and a permanent TV monitor displays a four-minute video previewing the main features of the exhibition. The ticket collector at the entrance to the exhibition no longer has to control the number of visitors entering at any particular time as this is determined by the timed ticketing. The ticket collector gives the first chocolate sample to the visitors (usually a popular product such as Crunchie, Curly Wurly or Wispa) and also hands out activity sheets to the younger children; they are able to answer the questions on these by referring to specific information boxes at various points in the exhibition.

CHOCOLATE AND THE SOUTH AMERICANS

The first section of the tour is unchanged, giving a brief history of the earliest discovery of chocolate by the South American Indians. Static displays, information boards and a three-minute video documentary describe how the Spanish conquered the Aztec empire and, therefore, how chocolate came to be brought to Europe. The booth, housing an attendant, issues small samples of the 'chocolate' drink, has moved to the other side of the corridor allowing the attendant to see back into the Aztec area and the jungle. This was necessary when the attendant (who is dressed in the distinctive Cadbury uniform of shirt and tie) used to control the flow of visitors into the later stages of the exhibition. This role has now been made obsolete by the recent changes to the admissions to the Cadbury Room, described later. This first section has the capacity to hold approximately 50 people and average throughput time at peak demand periods is seven minutes, two minutes of which is spent queuing for the chocolate. Next, the visitors pass into the Gallery of Europe with its static displays of King Charles II and various portraits of eminent European royals and nobles. This room can hold about 20 people, with seating for 12. A commentary describes how chocolate became adopted within the European courts, and recounts how British

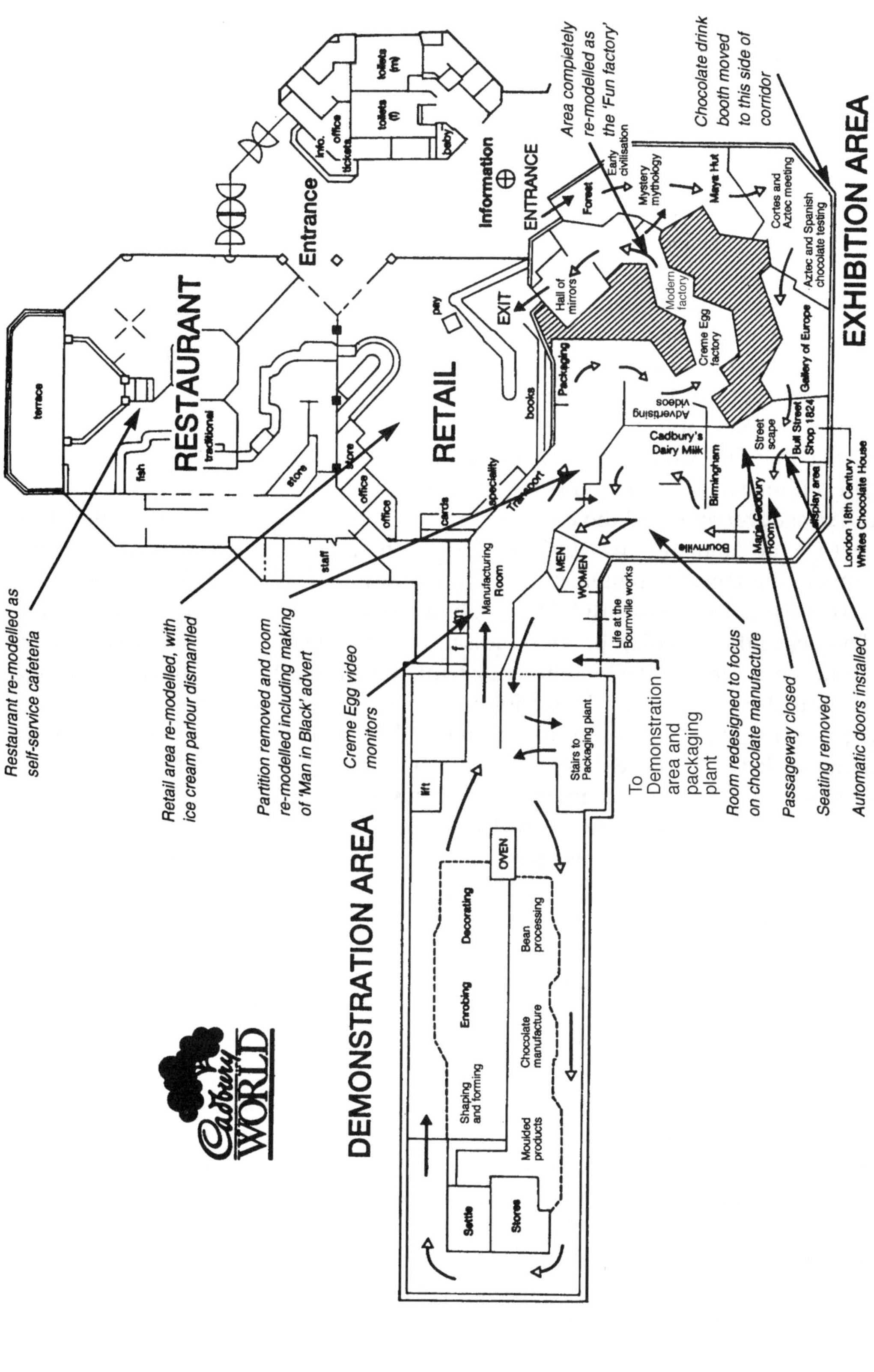

Fig. 7.1 The sketch of Cadbury World, including the changes made

pirates, raiding the early Spanish ships returning from South America, thought that the cocoa beans were sheep's droppings and so threw them overboard. The commentary lasts 2 minutes and 15 seconds, but only about one quarter of all visitors stay throughout the commentary; most others move through within one minute.

BULL STREET AND THE CADBURY ROOM

The next area is called 'Bull Street', and is a mock-up of a Georgian cobbled street in Birmingham where Cadbury first started selling and making chocolate. In the original design, an attendant would halt the flow of visitors at the end of this area, forming groups for the next stage of the exhibition; but later this person was removed and visitors were allowed to flow freely into the Cadbury Room (originally called the Marie Cadbury Room). Two weeks before Peter's arrival an automated door system had been introduced, with the intention of regrouping the visitors in Bull Street so that they would only move into the next area in time to see the beginning of the automated presentation being given in the Cadbury Room. The aim was to ensure that everyone had the chance to see one complete cycle of the 'show'. Bull Street has no animation or displays of any note, and is seen by a number of the visitors as a relatively uninteresting waiting area for the Cadbury Room. As many as 70 people can wait in the Bull Street area, although queues can sometimes develop as far back as the chocolate booth. This is most common in busy periods when flows become irregular, or if large coherent groups (such as school parties) are moving at abnormal speed through the exhibition and are either catching up with, or being caught up by, other visitors. A 30 centimetre TV monitor, located below shoulder height beside the entrance door, informs visitors exactly how long they will have to wait and when to enter. The messages it shows are reproduced in Fig. 7.2.

Seating had originally been provided in the Cadbury Room, but this has been removed and there is now only standing room in which visitors can view the three static illuminated displays located on two sides of the room. The automatically opened doors stay open for one minute, allowing an average of 45 people to enter before they close. The room has a maximum holding capacity of approximately 80 people, but since visitors' viewing pleasure was known to deteriorate above 45 persons, this number was set as the optimum capacity, and the timing of the automatic doors was adjusted accordingly. The show lasts seven and a half minutes, and the entry doors reopen 30 seconds after the end of the show, during which time most people in the Cadbury Room should have identified the exit and made their way out.

The next section has been entirely re-modelled, with most of the pictorial exhibits explaining the history of Bournville village and the social background of the firm having been removed to the Cadbury Collection. This area now focuses on the manufacture of chocolate, the processes used and the location of Cadbury's manufacturing plants worldwide. It also has a large video monitor describing the chocolate production process, from the cultivation of beans to the finished product. On one of his visits, Peter overheard a conversation between two visitors:

1 Show starts in Cadbury Room and doors close

2 Message asks guests to wait for the next show, now doors have opened

3 Messages change each minute, informing guests how long they have to wait

4 Doors open and guests are requested to enter the Cadbury Room

Fig. 7.2 TV monitor messages at entrance to the Cadbury Room

'It's a bit difficult to hear all of the video, isn't it? You can still hear the commentary from the last room, and there is something else that sounds like a helicopter and thunder!'

They were right, and Peter noticed that none of the walls between any of these sections in the exhibition extended to the ceiling, allowing noises from one area to spill over into others. This room can hold about 40 people, and visitors stay in here for an average of four minutes. Beyond this, the mock factory entrance has been retained, separating visitors through two gates marked 'Men' and 'Women' with an antique clocking-in clock and cards for the visitors to punch-in. This section can hold a further 30 people but most visitors find it only briefly amusing, passing through in an average of two minutes.

PACKAGING PLANT

From here visitors leave the main exhibition building and enter part of the main chocolate factory. If the factory is operating, visitors are escorted upstairs to the packaging plant, where they join a queue for the start of their tour. A diagram showing the layout and flow for this part of the tour is reproduced in Fig. 7.3. Here

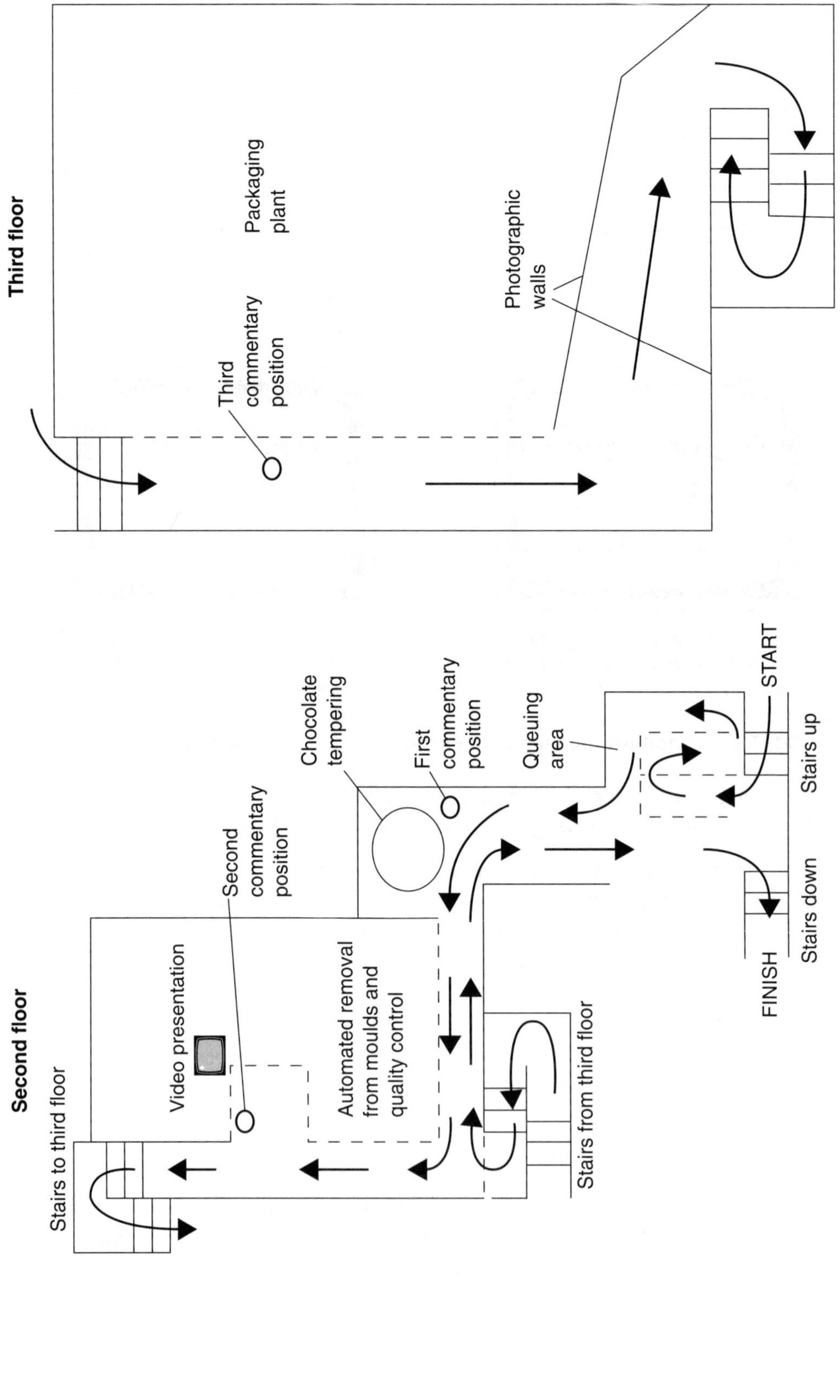

Fig. 7.3 Packaging plant layout and flow

visitors are given a second chocolate bar, and are entertained by a TV monitor slung from the ceiling that shows videos of Cadbury adverts over the ages. Visitors are grouped into batches of about 30 people, and each group is taken by a guide to three separate points in the plant on the second and third floors. At each point the group is halted, and the guide plugs a microphone into the newly installed sound system, giving an explanation of the activities occurring in front of the visitors. If excessive queues have built up in the entrance to the packaging area, size of groups is increased, and it is not uncommon for the number of people in a group to approach 50. At the second stop a pre-recorded video is shown of the unseen activity on the floor below, with a live commentary being given by the guide. Cadbury continue to experience problems with the guides' commentary. In the words of Jeremy:

'Unfortunately, the sound system is not having entirely the beneficial effects that we considered it would. There are issues of the number of people in the group, the visibility of the guide, the use of the microphones by the guides, the use of seasonal staffing, and competition with the loud radio music for the operatives in the factory; all of which impacts on the visitors' experience and reduces the overall effectiveness of the commentary. But we are making every effort to ensure that the perceived quality of Cadbury World's visitor experience is at the same level as that conveyed by its food products.'

The groups of visitors used to have to return along the same corridor, causing difficulties when one group met another, but this had been resolved by introducing a second staircase allowing the tour to take a circular path. The queuing area can hold up to 50 people, and up to three groups can be touring the packaging plant at any one time. The tour lasts approximately 15 minutes, after which the group is led directly downstairs to the Demonstration Area'. If the packaging plant is closed, either as a result of a factory holiday or because of planned scheduled maintenance, visitors move directly to the Demonstration Area. Some visitors are openly annoyed if the packaging area is closed, despite all published material clearly indicating that the packaging plant cannot be guaranteed to be open.

DEMONSTRATION AREA

The Demonstration Area can take two groups at a time, with groups consisting of no more than 30 people each. A guided batch of visitors takes about 10 minutes to move through the area. They see many of the old methods for producing and finishing the chocolates that would have been used in the factory at the turn of the century, and are able to sample fresh chocolates produced within the last few minutes. At the end of this section the visitors are told that the chocolates that have been produced in front of them cannot be bought anywhere other than in the Cadbury World shop, and would therefore make an exclusive memento of their visit. As they leave the Demonstration Area they are given a sample bar of Cadbury's Dairy Milk. If the packaging plant has been closed the size of this free bar is increased, and another chocolate bar may also be given by way of an apology.

If the queue becomes excessively long, three guides are permanently positioned at different points to give a running commentary. This allows throughput times to be reduced to eight minutes, because visitors tend not to dwell so long and can be encouraged by the stationary guides to move on. However, feedback has shown that many of the visitors dislike this system; 'It was much less personal than when we last visited,' mentioned one dissatisfied visitor. This free-flow system does not alter the total number of visitors in the area, which remains at about 60.

'MAN IN BLACK' AND THE FUN FACTORY

The remainder of the tour has been extensively re-modelled to make it 'more fun'. The Manufacturing Room has video monitors, set in life-size mock-ups of Cadbury's Cream Eggs, showing how various products are manufactured; the videos deliberately have no commentary. Other amusing novelties, like a 'Measure your height in fudge bars' and other 'Fun facts', improve the overall enjoyment particularly for the younger visitors. Most people pass through this section within 90 seconds and the room has capacity for around 25 visitors. Next, a large video screen shows a short feature on the making of the latest 'Man in Black' Milk Tray advert, shot on location in Jamaica. The film shows how both real and model helicopters were used to produce an advert lasting just 30 seconds and containing some 27 scenes. Sixteen seats are provided here but up to an additional 14 people can stand and watch the video which lasts 3 minutes and 5 seconds. There is a 15-second gap between showings. Many people find this an interesting show, and approximately one quarter of all people will watch it twice. A little further on, other displays and video screens showing Cadbury adverts from across the years add an average of 3 minutes and 40 seconds to peoples' visit, and the capacity of this area is about 30 persons.

The Fun Factory follows, giving (in the words of the Cadbury literature) 'A light-hearted look at chocolate making with help from Mr Cadbury's Parrot, the Bean Team and a touch of Cadbury magic . . .'. There are many bright colours, flashing lights, lots of noise and plenty of buttons for the children to press. This area is very popular with young and old alike, and has a capacity of approximately 35 persons, with most people spending an average of five minutes in this section before entering the final part of the exhibition, the Hall of Mirrors. By the use of mirrors, this room gives the impression of being able to see up, down and sideways into infinity. It can only hold about 10 people and most visitors do not linger, passing directly through – spending on average a mere 30 seconds before emerging in the shop.

THE SHOP

Cadbury World Shop has gone through a significant number of costly changes in response to a great deal of customer feedback. Most significant is the expenditure of over £100 000 on air conditioning, which required the whole complex to be closed for the month of January 1994. This has improved both the quality of the chocolate on display and also the visitors' comfort, causing them to linger longer than they might otherwise have done.

The floor area has been increased by 40 square metres, following the dismantling of the Ice-Cream Parlour. Five tills now operate, rather than the original three, and these are all located in a single row at the exit, similar to a checkout at a supermarket. Electronic point of sales (EPOS) systems have been installed to improve the sales information and to tie in with monitoring and control of stock.

Some customers express disappointment that chocolate prices are not lower, but they are competitive with normal retail outlets. Clearly, Cadbury World cannot deliberately undercut its retailers, but as well as selling chocolate, it offers a wide range of souvenirs and giftware. A 'Bargain corner' has been introduced, which sells mis-shapen goods (seconds), and customers can also buy the 'exclusive' handmade chocolates they saw being made in the Demonstration Area.

RESTAURANT

The original Food Court concept has been scrapped, and the restaurant redesigned as a self-service free-flow, serving a narrower range of items, including pizza, fried chicken, salads, fish fingers, a selection of sandwiches and ice-creams. This has led to a reduction in staffing costs of up to 54 per cent. There are two tills, and the number of covers has been increased from 169 to 250. An additional Outside Catering Unit, located in the children's play area, also acts as an overflow and during the summer months can generate significant revenues.

CADBURY COLLECTION

Originally called the 'Alternative exhibition', this was moved from its original location at the far end of the parking area, and is now situated on the lower ground floor of the factory, next to the children's play area. The Collection still resembles a more typical museum, with static displays explaining the history of Bournville, and the production methods employed, as well as the social history of the firm and samples of many of their products over the years. A mock-up of an old sweet shop and a 1930s film on the factory are also offered. Entrance to the Cadbury Collection is free to exhibition ticket holders.

PETER'S OBSERVATIONS

A week after his arrival Peter was meeting with Jeremy King to review his findings.

> *'In Bull Street, I got the impression that people regarded this a waiting area for the next stage. They would probably not have stopped here for more than a few minutes had they not been obliged to wait for up to eight minutes by the automatic door. Visually the street is well designed, authentically reproducing the Birmingham street as it was in 1794,*

with a London scene and Whites of St James on the other side of the room, but it lacked animation. There were sounds of horses on the cobbled streets but I can't help thinking that this audio equipment could have been better employed.

'The doors are not proving as effective as I think had been anticipated. I studied the flows of visitors through this area on four separate days, admittedly at periods of high demand, and found the problems were as follows: first, the safety sensors on the doors react so that as long as people continue to stream past the open doors, they were unable to close. The TV monitor located by the door never signalled people to stop and they continued to fill the room beyond its capacity. Children playing with the door handle caused it to open, as did someone wanting to return from where they had come. Once reopened it took over a minute for the door to close with people continuing to stream in. Groups entering just as the doors were about to close also caused the doors to stay open for far longer than should have otherwise been the case.'

The findings, showing the numbers of people entering and the delays in closing the door, which Peter had noted on the back of an envelope, are reproduced in Fig. 7.4.

Visitors entering	Delay to doors closing (seconds)
– Fri 11th August (visitor total = 1998)	
36	0
57	20
60	12
74	56
31	0
64	43
46	32
37	0
– Thur 17th August (visitors = 2369)	
64	10
49	15
32	2
56	18
70	41
61	26
32	0
51	12
– Tue 22nd August (visitors = 2420)	
69	25
47	33
76	47
69	63
64	51
94	192
– Wed 30th August (visitors = 2510)	
49	15
38	22
32	0
63	26
45	31
56	28

Fig. 7.4 Numbers entering the Cadbury Room and delays in doors closing

Visitors entering	Leaving before end
– Fri 11th August	
36	0
57	6
60	5
74	6
31	0
64	0
46	2
37	0
– Thur 17th August	
64	2
49	2
32	0
56	5
70	3
61	0
32	3
51	0
– Tue 22nd August	
69	9
47	0
76	6
69	16
64	2
94	42
– Wed 30th August	
49	1
38	4
32	0
63	6
45	4
56	2

Fig. 7.5 Numbers entering the Cadbury Room and numbers leaving before the end

'The effect of this was that peoples' enjoyment of the Cadbury Room deteriorated, and I also found that as the number of people in the room increased, the number of people leaving the show before it was completed also increased.'

These findings are reproduced in Fig. 7.5.
Peter told Jeremy:

'It was while I was in the exhibition that I noticed the continual cycle of the cleaners, which impressed me a lot. Unfortunately the visitors also notice some of the maintenance staff at Cadbury World due to the noise made by their personal stereos! Do you think we could do something about this?

'The queue lengths at the Packaging Plant entrance have apparently not reduced dramatically, but from talking to the guides, they believe that there are fewer fluctuations in the queue length. Before the doors were introduced, the queue occasionally became extremely long for a 20 to 30 minute period, whenever one group accelerated through the first part of the exhibition and joined a slower group. Now the arrival of visitors seems to be more constant, which even though it may lead to queues does not produce queues of excessive length.

'The free-flow in the demonstration area seemed to be effective at processing the visitors rapidly, reducing processing times from an average of 10 minutes to an average of 8 minutes. This clearly helps reduce queue lengths, but at what cost? The guides do not enjoy it as much, which comes over in their performance, and they suggest that the customers also prefer being given a tour by a single guide, with whom they feel more relaxed and able to question. But if the number of visitors that can be taken around by each guide and the processing time is kept at 10 minutes how else can we put more capacity into the Demonstration Area?

'Finally there do appear to be one or two "dead areas" where queuing takes place, and I am concerned that the queue lengths appear excessive to the visitors simply because they are not entertaining enough. I am keen to discover whether there are any low cost ways of improving entertainment in the queues, perhaps through the use of material that is not very effective in its current position.'

Questions

1 Calculate the hourly capacities for each of the areas in the exhibition.

2 Where may queues build up and why? What has been done so far to overcome bottlenecks? What else can be done to overcome excessive queue lengths?

3 What are the benefits and drawbacks of introducing the electronic doors?

4 What else could be done to improve the visitors satisfaction at Cadbury World?

Please note: While we gratefully acknowledge Cadbury World's help in the development of this case study, we must ask students preparing this case *not* to contact Cadbury World and its managers for any further information. However, much more detail on the operation can be obtained by undertaking the tour as a normal paying visitor, but you should not interfere with the other customers by attempting any unauthorised questioning or filming.

CASE 8

A.J. McKenzie Ltd

Nigel Slack

Case date 1992

INTRODUCTION

A.J. McKenzie was a rarity in the food retailing industry – a medium-sized supermarket chain with a very strong local market presence. Although the company operated exclusively in the East Midlands of the UK, the company had retained a healthy 22 per cent of the market in their area against increasingly aggressive competition from the national majors. Alistair Joc McKenzie, the company's founder, put their survival and success down to their size, origins and dynamism:

> *'We still have the feel of a small company even though we now have six large "town fringe" stores and three smaller stores. All the store managers were recruited by me personally, and most have been with the company for over ten years. They all have a stake, both financial and emotional, in the company. They all have a clear understanding that our success relies on keeping a fine balance between running a tight ship and being among the most innovative food retailers in the country.*
>
> *'By industry standards, we allow our managers far more autonomy than is usual, certainly more than most other supermarket groups. There is a story of an independently minded manager of one of our competitor's stores being visited by a Head Office director. When the local manager complained that he was too tightly controlled from the centre, the Head Office type took him outside to the car park, pointed up to the sign over the door and said, "It says J. Sainsbury on that sign, not your name. When it does you can do what you want." That seems to work for them but we couldn't run like that. We are too small. We need to harness the innovative drive of our staff to stay ahead.'*

COMPANY HISTORY

The history of the company showed considerable evidence of its keeping one step ahead of its competitors. Originally a stall holder in Leicester market, Joc McKenzie had foreseen the growth in larger, less central, food retail outlets in the early 1960s, and judiciously bought land, usually at the intersections of the city's ring and radial roads. During the 1960s he raised the capital for five stores around the east Midlands.

They were, by the standards of the day, large open sites with good access and plenty of parking space. Joc McKenzie explained:

'It may seem commonplace now, but it was very different then. We offered a range of products at a price unequalled by the competition, who, to be honest, were few and far between. We were one of the first smaller outfits to have our "own label" products under cutting the equivalent branded product. We piled it higher and sold it cheaper than anyone.'

By the end of the 1960s the 'pile it high, sell it cheap' approach was beginning to fail them. Tesco had expanded in the area and with far higher national volumes had the purchasing power to 'outvalue' McKenzie. The period between 1971 and 1974 were difficult years for McKenzie. Tesco, Sainsbury and Asda all opened new stores in the region; McKenzie were in danger of looking like poor local imitations of the larger, more powerful concerns.

A number of decisions were made during this period which were to shape the operational style of the stores for the next 10 years.

First, the number of McKenzie own label items was drastically reduced. The price differential between own label and branded goods was reducing anyway and the company felt that the cheaper own label products were contributing to their cheap and cheerful image. The own label products which remained were, for the most part, premium products. Second, the larger stores were given a 'face-lift'. New decor, a redesigned logo, wider aisles and a simplified layout gave the stores a more 'up-market' look. Third, the company made some small but relatively profitable moves into selling non-food products. Do-it-yourself products, small electrical appliances, kitchen equipment and, especially, gardening supplies all contributed healthy sales per square metre. Non-food products, however, never accounted for more than 10 per cent of total sales.

THE 'SPECIALIST AREA' STRATEGY

Finally, and possibly most important, the company evolved a policy of specialist areas within its stores. For example, cold cooked meats, cheeses, salads and speciality savouries were sold in a delicatessen area with decor fittings, and staff uniforms were all designed and co-ordinated to match the 'speciality' atmosphere. Promotions would be run periodically around this part of the store. For example, 'A taste of France' involved the promotion of unusual French cheeses and *charcuterie* products. Other specialist areas included the fresh fruit and vegetable area in the style of market stalls but stocking a wide range of exotic and unusual fruit and vegetables in addition to the more common types, a bakery and Patisserie area baking pre-formed chilled dough on the premises, and a 'wine merchant' area offering a 'value to vintage' selection. Joc McKenzie explained this strategy:

'We have learned how to handle this type of "specialist retailing" operation over the years. For example, you can't have too high a proportion of the store's area devoted to

this type of selling. We made the mistake at first of going over the top. Almost a third of the floor space in one store was "specialist". You quickly lose the clean open feel of the store if it goes that far.

'Similarly, the specialist areas can't be too different. It's a delicate balance, they must be distinctive without being forbidding. Customers must feel that they can "flow" from one part of the store to any other without any psychological barriers, without any threshold fear. We usually limit specialist areas to 15 per cent of floor space, and are very careful about how we design the look of each area.

'These changes have not been without their organisational consequences. It has inevitably meant more guidance from the centre, because it was the only way to make sure that we learned the lessons from our successes and occasional failures. Also, more specialised selling means that we really do need top-class central specialist buyers for each area. All of which left our store managers with less autonomy in the strategic running of their stores. Yet all the really successful changes which we have made in the last 15 years came from our store managers. It was a considerable dilemma for us.'

Dilemma or not, the strategy which emerged proved successful for McKenzie. Steady growth continued and by 1989 the group had nine stores throughout the Midlands.

THE BUSINESS PLANNING GROUP

Joc McKenzie's solution to the problem of how to harness the innovative skills of the store managers was the Business Planning Group. This body, which started in 1983, comprised all store managers together with the five senior buyers. It met regularly each month to review business and to consider all proposed changes in buying and operating policy. It also acted as the company's chief originator and evaluator of new product and operational ideas.

The Business Planning Group would also occasionally set up a working group to examine a particular issue. This allowed the more junior store managers and assistant managers to contribute to business planning. The 'fresh meat' working group was typical.

MEAT RETAILING IN MCKENZIE

Of all the food areas, the weakest for McKenzie was the fresh meat area. Unusually, the company had fallen behind current practice among their competitors. Both Sainsbury and Tesco offered a full range of value-added fresh meat products in addition to their normal range. 'Lean-cut' meats with less fat, 'matured' cuts ('for a fuller flavour'), continental cuts and fully prepared joints such as stuffed, boned (free-range) chickens, were examples of meat products offered by McKenzie's competitors. This type of 'premium' product usually commanded a higher gross margin (selling price – bought-in cost) than traditional meat products and was the fastest growing part of the fresh meat market.

McKenzie, by contrast, offered a conventional range of cut portions and joints – prewrapped, chilled and displayed in chilled cabinets. Just under 30 per cent of its meat was bought pre-packaged from meat wholesalers, a percentage which had grown from less than five per cent four years before. The remainder was cut by the company's own butchers.

Of the company's nine stores, five had their own meat preparation capability. The other four stores received their supplies in a 'cut, portioned and packed' state, partly from meat wholesalers but mainly from the other five stores. The meat supplied from McKenzie stores came cut, portioned, packed and labelled; that which came from the meat wholesalers needed weigh checking and labelling with weight, price per pound and 'this portion' price. A total of five fully skilled butchers were employed, together with seven full-time and nine part-time meat cutters. Meat cutters were semi-skilled assistants who had been trained (usually by McKenzie) but did not have the craft experience of fully qualified butchers. Table 8.1 gives details of each store's meat preparation capabilities.

Table 8.1 Meat preparation capability

Store	*Butchers*[b]	*Meat cutters*	
		Full-time[b]	*Part-time*[a]
Atherton	1	1	1(24)
Brantley	1	1	2(48)
Drakeley	NA	NA	NA
Edgeton Rd	1	3	3(72)
Hucknall	NA	NA	NA
Northampton	1	1	1(20)
Scale Hill	NA	NA	NA
Seacroft	NA	NA	NA

[a] Figures in brackets indicate staff hours available.

[b] All full-time employees work a 38-hour week.

THE 'FRESH MEAT' WORKING GROUP

On several occasions in the company's history, proposals to make fresh meat a specialist area had been raised. In two of the stores it had even been tried (at different times), but on neither occasion was it judged enough of a success for the trials to be extended to the other stores. However, the idea had not only been resurrected but was gaining momentum within the company. There were a number of reasons for this.

First, sales in the fresh meat area had fallen over the previous two-year period. This was not surprising since sales of fresh meat were declining nationally; however, McKenzie's fresh meat sales were falling away faster than most. Second, in spite of falling sales, the 'value-added' part of the market was growing steadily and was capable of sustaining high gross margins. The other two reasons for this renewed interest in fresh meat were directly related to the personalities involved in the area. After many years under the control of a technically proficient but unambitious product group manager, the fresh meat area had been taken over by Duncan Kay, an ex-butcher who until recently had been assistant store manager in the company's largest store at Edgeton Road. Possibly even more significant was the personal interest of Joc McKenzie himself.

Joc's enthusiasm stemmed partly from his belief that McKenzie needed to make a success of meat retailing if it was to maintain its innovative culture, and partly from his recent visit to a meat retailer in Leeds called the 'Real Meat Consortium' which was bucking the trend in meat sales. Seeing this successful operation had convinced him that:

'Imaginative retailing will always be more important than short-term fluctuations in the market. They are giving customers an original and attractive service; that is why they deserve their success. But it is our job to learn from them, and if we don't we not only don't deserve success, we don't deserve to survive!'

THE REAL MEAT CONSORTIUM

Originally called Morrells Meat, the Real Meat Consortium (RMC) had been trading on the same premises since 1977. Mick Morrell, whose father and grandfather had been independent butchers in Leeds, decided to move the family business across the city to larger premises at this time. Mick Morrell explained the reasons for the move:

'The main reason for the move was to get out of a declining area of the city and over to a rapidly "gentrifying" area which was already on the up. But I was also convinced that we could substantially increase our business by recognising two trends: the move towards buying meat in larger quantities and freezing it, and the demand for more personal service. There is a limit to how much personal attention supermarkets can give to customers so they are neglecting a relatively affluent part of the market.

'Originally, the design of the shop was very much a reaction to the other "bulk meat" retailers. The local co-operative was typical. In their freezer meat section the customer was faced with a large impersonal, almost clinical selling area full of freezer cabinets. Each freezer was labelled according to its contents: Pork, Beef, etc. Frozen meat is not an attractive product at the best of times. Sold like that it is even less so.'

In its first few years of operation the idea of *bulk* sales were a central part of the shop's philosophy. It was stressed in their promotional activities and it dictated their product range decisions. The shop set a minimum order weight of 3 lbs on any type of meat and set its prices to encourage customers to buy whole pieces of meat such as whole legs of pork or lamb. The types of meat were also limited to exclude low-selling types such as veal or rabbit. Also, the original shop did not prepare any of the value-added joints. What they would do though was to cut and pack the meat to order in front of the customer.

Figure 8.1 shows the layout of the shop in 1992. The selling area is L-shaped. In each wing there is a long butcher's table at which up to three butchers can work. Around the shop there are storage racks which take the meat likely to be sold that day. The decor of the shop was deliberately set in the Victorian period, with stained wood, marble shelves, brass fittings, and wooden cutting tables. All the butchers were dressed in traditional blue and white striped aprons and wore straw boaters.

Generally the shop works in the following manner. The customer enters and gives his or her order at the order desk. At busy times customers might have to queue for three or four minutes to reach the order desk, which is staffed either by a part-time assistant or, at slack times, by one of the butchers. Behind the desk is a large board

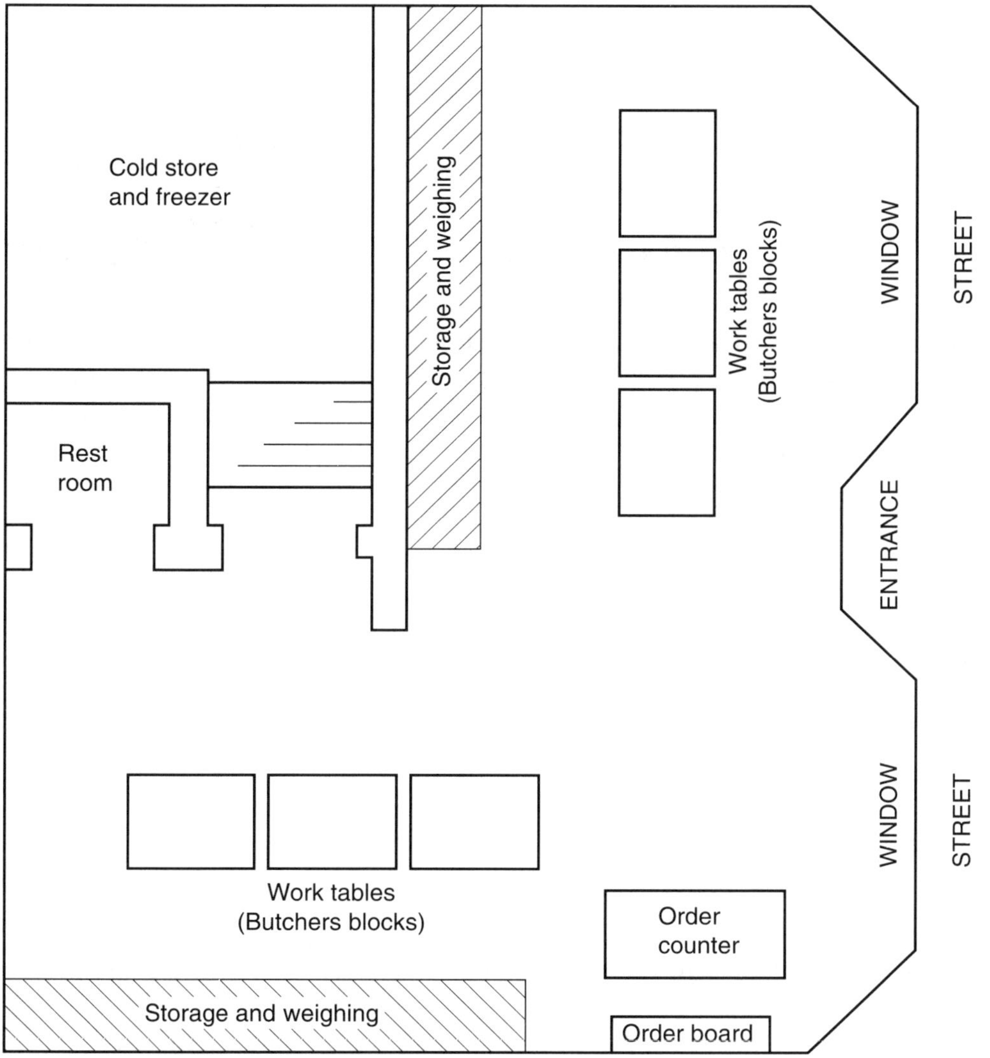

Fig. 8.1 Layout of the Real Meat Consortium

with all the types of meat on sale that day (supply varies little on a day-to-day basis). Line by line, the board displays each product, the price per piece, and the maximum price per pound. This pricing policy allows the meat to be sold 'per piece' (all legs of lamb, for example, are the same price) and discourages customers from buying less than the whole piece. Figure 8.2 shows a part of the board.

THE REAL MEAT CONSORTIUM			
ITEM	Min. weight	Price	Max. price/lb
PORK			
Whole Legs			
Loins			
Stuffed Loins			
Stewing Pork			
Fillet			

Fig. 8.2 The order board

The order taker has order forms which are almost small replicas of the order board. On these the customer's order is recorded. When the order is complete the total cost is added up and the customer is charged for the purchase (cash or card), even though the customer has not yet received the meat. At this point the customer might, at busy times, have to wait for a butcher to become free. The butcher then walks over to the customer, takes the order form and accompanies the customer back to his own work station. There he discusses the customer's requirements, and cuts, trims and bags the meat accordingly. During this process the butchers maintain a 'running banter' between themselves and sometimes with the customers. The atmosphere is good-humoured and 'jokey'. Underneath this almost theatrical facade, though, the butchers listen carefully to customers' preferences and instructions for the cutting and bagging of the meat, and also give advice and technical information for the further preparation and cooking of the meat. The bagged meat is then put into a lined box on which the shop's logo is printed. The butcher then often carries the box out to the customer's car if they are not parked too far away.

Mick Morrell explained the concept behind the operation's success:

'We have modified our original ideas a little over the years, but the original design concept has survived. We no longer think of ourselves in the "bulk meat" business although we still encourage large volume purchases and our sales of meat per head are still higher than at either supermarkets or small "corner" butchers. We came to realise that the real drawing power of our operation was the novelty of the sequence of activities,

the theatrical atmosphere of the shop itself, and the seriousness with which we took the core task of cutting meat to our customers' specification. It's the combination of fun with a highly professional service which is attractive.

'We have also changed our policy on the meat we sell. Originally we did not sell any prepared joints, such as crown roasts of lamb. Everything was done in front of the customer so we could not afford the time for speciality joints. Given changing customer tastes we now do prepare a limited range of this type of product – usually stuffed or marinaded joints. The other big change has been in the actual quality of the meat itself. When we started our meat was no better or worse than most supermarkets. Now we deal only in first-class meat which is produced in a way which appeals to our younger middle-class clientele. Most of our suppliers deal only in hormone-free, organically farmed and naturally raised "real" meat. Our product now not only satisfies your palate, it satisfies your conscience as well.'

Staffing at RMC

At its peak in 1980 RMC (then still called Morrells) employed seven butchers. Since then volume has reduced slightly (although margins and takings were well up in real terms) and five full-time butchers, including Mick Morrell, and one part-time, semi-retired butcher were employed. All were fully apprentice-trained, skilled craftsmen. Mick and two other butchers had been with the operation since the move; the other two had five and two years respectively with the business. Staff retention was an important issue for Mick.

'It takes a particular type of person to make a success of this type of job. We all have to be first-class butchers. We are, after all, demonstrating our skills in front of the customers and they can tell if a butcher is unsure or inaccurate with the knife. Any mistakes are obvious. Also, we have to be fast. At peak times slow or hesitant work would result in long queues and dissatisfied customers.

'But it's not only skill that is required. We have to enjoy serving the customers, being in front of them all the time. We need to be skilled at getting their requirements out of them and in giving advice in a tactful manner. Most of all, though, you have to be an extrovert. The banter and "theatrical routine" part of the job has to be genuine, you can't script it. You have to enjoy being a bit over the top to keep it up.'

Finding and keeping staff with all these qualities was a key problem for Mick. It had been an important factor in designing the sequence of activities in the operation. Mick had found out very early that the type of staff he needed were craftsmen who *wanted* to concentrate on performing and exhibiting their skills. They even enjoyed the 'service' implied in the bagging and carrying-out of the customer's purchases. What they liked least were taking the customer's orders and money. That was why these operations had been put together at the front end of the service so that they could be done by an assistant.

Demand and capacity at RMC

Demand at RMC varied through the week and also month by month. Both the week and the year were divided into two distinct parts. Takings were low from Monday to Wednesday, but were more than twice as high Thursday to Saturday. In the year cycle, April to September were low, with a pick-up during the autumn. This higher level continued through the winter months. Demand and capacity variation is illustrated in Fig. 8.3.

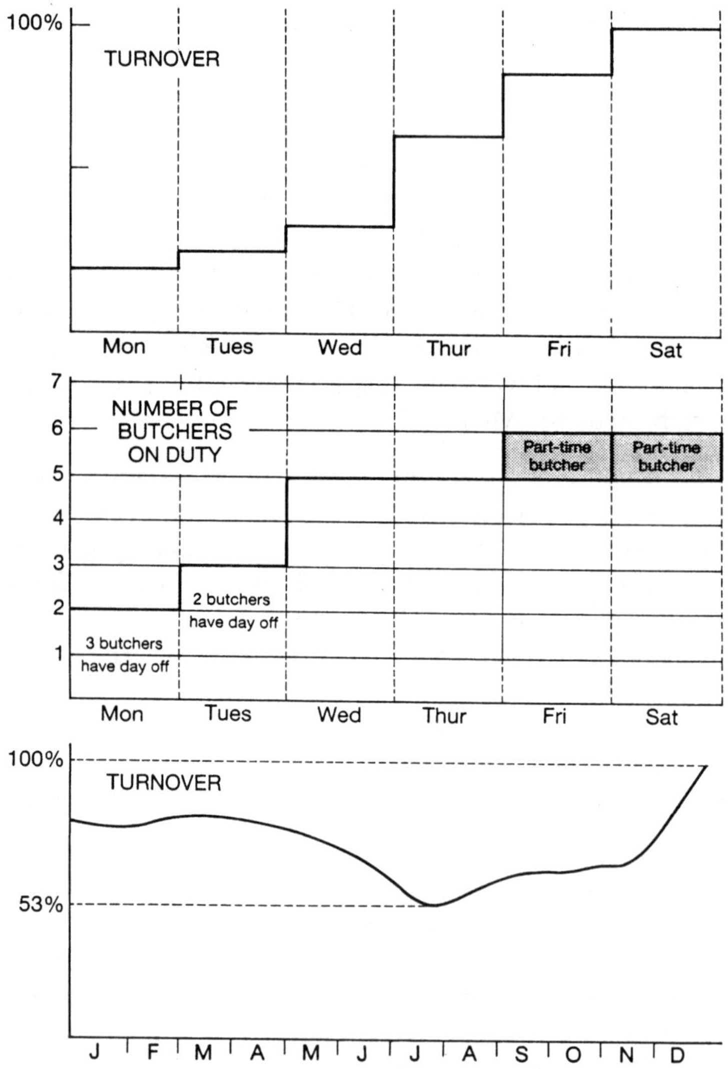

Fig. 8.3 Demand and capacity at the Real Meat Consortium

Demand variation was probably RMC's biggest problem. The staff were under-utilised for the first part of the week, but could hardly cope with demand towards the end of the week. Furthermore, on Fridays and, especially, Saturdays, customer queueing was regarded by Mick Morrell as unacceptable.

RMC AND McKENZIE

The fresh meat working group at McKenzie had all visited the RMC and spoken with Mick Morrell. They were all agreed that the RMC was an interesting and apparently successful operation, though how much of its success was due to the recent fashionability of organic and 'real' meat, and how much was due to the originality of its operation and layout, was a matter of some disagreement.

More contentious though was the issue of how much McKenzie could learn from the RMC. Those who were most enthusiastic about the RMC operation saw themselves as being able to overcome two of the RMC's biggest problems, parking and demand variation. Their idea (not worked out in detail) was to somehow use the butchers from an RMC-style operation to prepare the pre-packed value-added cuts for the supermarket in the first half of the week and move over to an adjacent 'RMC-style' customised cutting operation in the busy periods. Others in the working group had reservations about the compatibility of the two types of retailing operation.

Morrell himself tried to be non-committal on McKenzie's interest in his operation: 'They know their business best, and I wish I had their parking space, but it's taken me over 10 years to really perfect this type of retailing. I think they might be in danger of underestimating some of the difficulties involved.'

Questions

1 Compare/contrast the service concepts, types of operation and types of customer of the two retail outlets, McKenzie and the Real Meat Consortium (RMC).

2 What do you think would be the main operations problems in managing these two types of operation?

3 If McKenzie want to incorporate some of the RMC idea into their own operation, what is the range of options they have in incorporating the design of RMC into the supermarket complex?

4 What criteria would you use to judge which of these options, if any, McKenzie should adopt?

5 How would you incorporate the RMC ideas into McKenzie, if at all?

CASE 9

Aylesbury Pressings

John Bicheno, edited by Alan Harrison

*Case date 1990**

INTRODUCTION

Aylesbury Pressings (AP) is located in Buckinghamshire and has been family-owned for more than a century. The modern business is centred on the manufacture of metal pressings for UK motor manufacturers such as Ford, Austin Rover, General Motors, Land Rover, and, more recently, Nissan and Jaguar. Recent sales analysis is shown in Fig. 9.1.

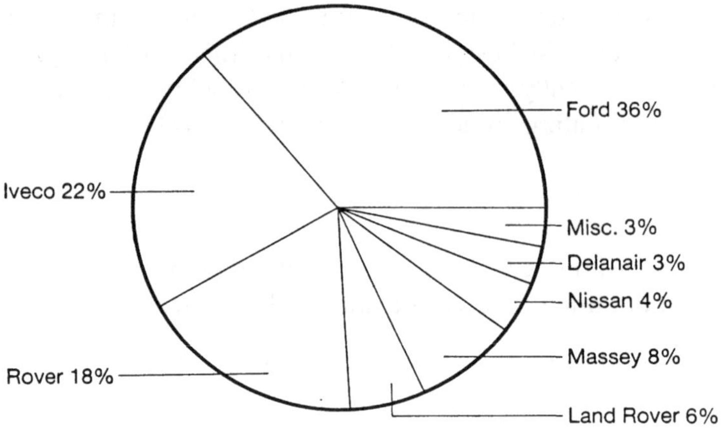

Fig. 9.1 Sales analysis mid-1988

As distinct from body pressings, which form the outer skin of a car or van, metal pressings are much smaller and are used to support such components as batteries, radiators, spare wheels, steering assemblies and dashboards. Larger parts include suspension cross-members. Within the company, pressings are classified as light (up to 2 kg), medium (up to about 5 kg), and heavy (up to about 10 kg).

*Names and data have been altered.

In harmony with much of the UK motor industry in the late 1980s, the company was in a state of higher growth. Sales were up to £10 million from £6 million only two years before, and future plans from customers indicated that sales would rise to £19 million within a further two years. Merely keeping up with demand was a challenge. The company employs 150 'directs', 70 'indirects', and some 50 other staff. The organisation chart is shown in Fig. 9.2.

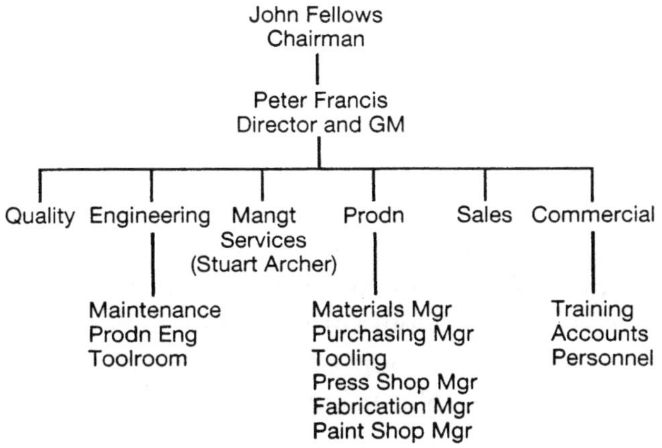

Fig. 9.2 AP organisation chart

In the manufacture of a pressing there are three main stages: press, welding/assembly and paint. A typical bill of materials is shown in Fig. 9.3. The press stage consists of several operations on various presses. Each press operation requires a die change 'set-up'. The size of a power press varies between 20 and 600 tons. In early 1988 die change times averaged about one hour. The heavy press dies have to be moved by fork-lift truck from the die store, which is located in an area adjoining the main press hall. Actual pressing times are very short. Blanking operations are typically less than two seconds per operation. A pressing is referred to as 'light' when a press

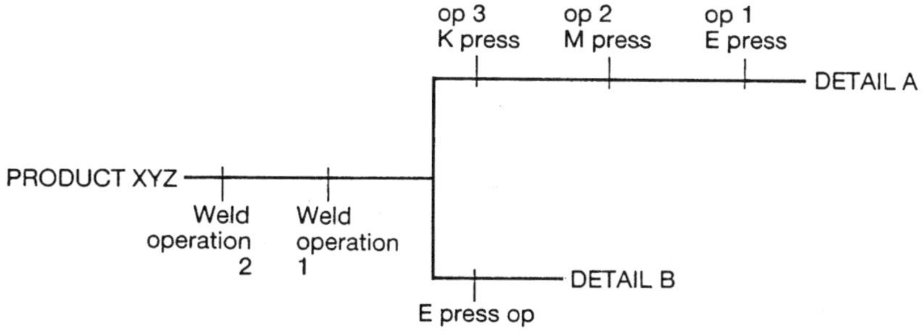

Fig. 9.3 AP typical product structure

up to 150 tons is used. While two press operators perform some of the light operations, usually only one operator is needed. Press operators are capable of operating all types of presses, but all die exchange operations are done by trained setters. One reason for using a setter is legal safety standards, and a setter has an 18-month training period. As a result of the relatively long die exchange times in relation to unit press times, the plant has long batch runs, often covering the demand for more than a month at a time.

The plant is organised in a conventional process layout, with specific areas for presses, welding and assembly and paintwork. The factory layout is shown in Fig. 9.4. Sections A and B are on two levels and transport between them is by means of fork-lift truck. Batches are not split, and one batch may fill several containers. Each container has to be moved by fork-lift truck. Occasionally, overlapping of a batch on two presses may occur. The production areas are treated as three mini factories with buffer stocks between each stage. Each stage makes a buffer stock for the next stage. The buffer stocks usually comprise several weeks' worth of work. Welding and assembly takes two or more 'details' from the press operations and joins them together. Assembly will not start until sufficient numbers of the various types of detail have been accumulated. For some products, a welding operation is required in between two press operations. Normal manufacturing lead times are six to eight weeks.

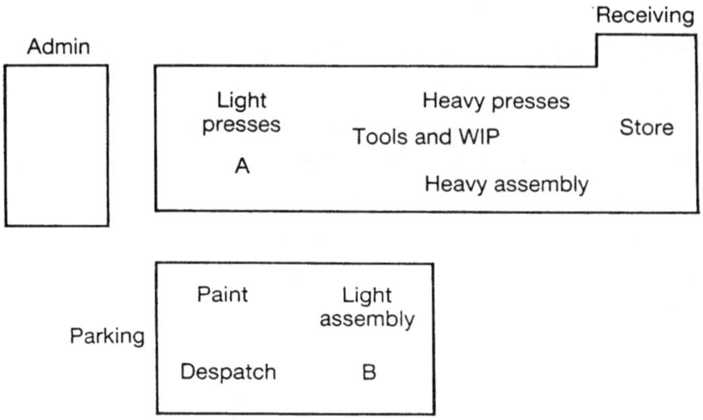

Fig. 9.4 AP factory layout prior to any JIT process

Consultants were appointed by AP in early 1988 to advise on the implementation of improved manufacturing. An AP production engineer, Stuart Archer, was appointed as Just-in-Time (JIT) project co-ordinator. He was personally enthusiastic about JIT, and enjoyed the encouragement of the General Manager. As JIT project manager, Stuart was to undertake the basic work of implementing JIT. His other duties included helping with difficulties in the Materials Requirement

Planning (MRP) system and undertaking some induction training. The consultants, working with Stuart, undertook a number of studies. A report was presented to management on the initial findings and contained recommendations for further action. The report made provision for substantial further involvement by the consultants, at a fee which was considered high by AP. Management was enthusiastic about the report since it reinforced much of what they had seen in Japan, and they decided to press ahead with implementation with some urgency, but without the consultants.

The initial study carried out by the consultants working with AP staff led to a number of initial actions.

PRODUCT LINE RATIONALISATION

A Pareto analysis showed that a large percentage of the product line was making a very small contribution to overheads. Figure 9.5 shows the situation. Clearly the 'dross', as low contribution items were termed, had to be reduced. The problem was how to do it. In some cases low contribution products were being supplied to important customers taking many highly profitable products. There was also the question of unused capacity that might appear as a result of product line rationalisation.

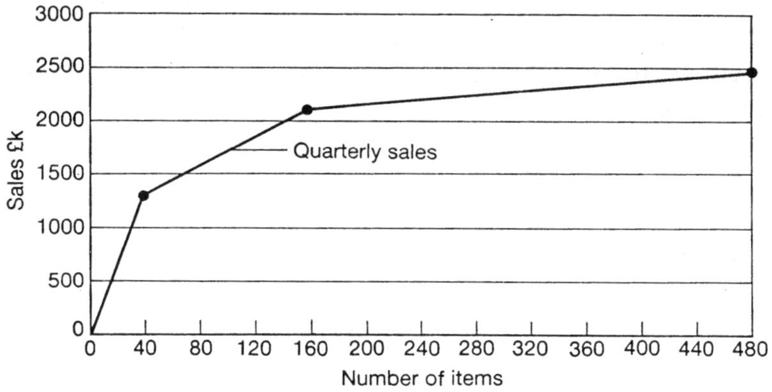

Fig. 9.5 Pareto analysis of sales

DIE EXCHANGE (SET-UP TIME) REDUCTION

Using video equipment, several press tool exchange operations were studied. Most were found to have lengthy 'external' operations, indicating the potential for considerable set-up time reductions. An example is given in Fig. 9.6. As a result, several changes were made including relocation of die stores nearer to the point of

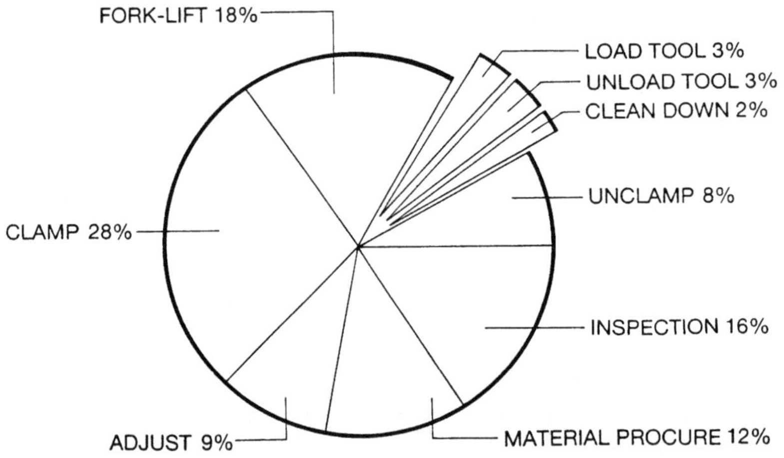

Fig. 9.6 Press change time analysis

use, training of several setter operators, redesign of some die location devices, and training operators and material handlers to prepare for die changes.

It was felt that further improvements could be made when new factory layouts were introduced. The major change was to be assistance of die movement by roller conveyor. Dies would be stored on a roller conveyor which was to be located at the same height as the press tables, and a hinged conveyor bridge would enable dies to be moved directly on to the presses. Die exchange operations were expected to fall to under 30 minutes.

Despite some initial improvements, set-up times were still substantial in mid-1988. Die exchange operations were still not being carried out with a sense of urgency. Most of the benefits had still not been realised; for instance, no changes had been made to batch sizes.

QUALITY

The practice of having roving inspectors in the press and welding shops was dropped, and operators were encouraged to undertake their own inspection. This necessitated good documentation and some training. Final inspection was retained. After some initial concern, and a brief upturn in defects, reject levels on the shop-floor soon returned to their original levels of about two per cent defective. Containers with defective parts were still to be found in some quantity. A decision rule to scrap those defective parts which had not been reworked within a given period was under consideration.

A simple cost of quality system was implemented. Each month the costs of materials, rework and lost time were recorded and displayed prominently at shop entrances. A quality performance chart, which had been started before the JIT project, was placed on display on the shop-floor.

Two members of staff attended a course on Taguchi methods and expressed some interest in trying the techniques.

PEOPLE

A selection test was developed for new operators to ensure that they had the capability to become multifunctional. A new multifunction job grading plan was developed, with only seven categories – down from some 33 previously. In future, operators would be expected to do some setting and inspection tasks; and maintenance activities may be added.

The company had been running improvement teams for some time. A special meeting room was established, and some groups met for one hour per month. There was some concern that the scheme was not working well, and with the increasing workload the groups did not meet regularly, if at all.

THE TRIAL ASSEMBLY CELL

As an initial move towards cellular production an assembly/welding cell for light products was set up. All products made in the cell were similar and went to one customer. No presses were moved, so the cell could not be considered as complete. This assembly cell used a pull system, with tote boxes as the visual signal. People in the cell were encouraged to undertake improvement activities themselves, and this led to some suggestions being made. The cell was the first experiment in taking people off the bonus incentive scheme.

THE PLAN FOR FUTURE CELLS

The consultants recommended that the whole plant be reorganised into cells, one cell at a time. The first full cell was to be for light parts and would contain both presses and welding machines. This would allow all stages of cell products to be completed, apart from painting. Later, if the first full cell proved a success, an additional cell would be added for medium and heavy parts. The first full cell would include the trial assembly cell. The cell was to include conveyors for moving and changing dies, and would have its own steel receiving bay. The cell was to incorporate a range of new concepts which management considered to be desirable in the light of their knowledge of JIT (*see* Appendix 9.1).

The range of products to be manufactured within the cell was selected on the basis of high volume, light products which were certain to be produced for some time. The concept was simply that a full range of presses and welding machines would be located together in one large area. The complete product would be made within this area, and then sent to the paint shop for painting. Initially, the cell concept was planned for single shift production, but by July 1988 the increasing volume of work forced a rethink towards two shifts. At the time of the initial design of the cell, capacity was a prime consideration. The idea was to schedule parts with a two-week cycle, that is, the same product would be manufactured every two weeks.

With half-hour exchange times, batch production was still considered appropriate within the cell. Each batch was completed on a press before it was moved on to the next press operation. The completed pressed parts would accumulate in a temporary storage area, and would be welded as soon as all sub-components were available.

The initial list of products, together with their routeings, is shown in Table 9.1. The proposed layout is shown in Fig. 9.7.

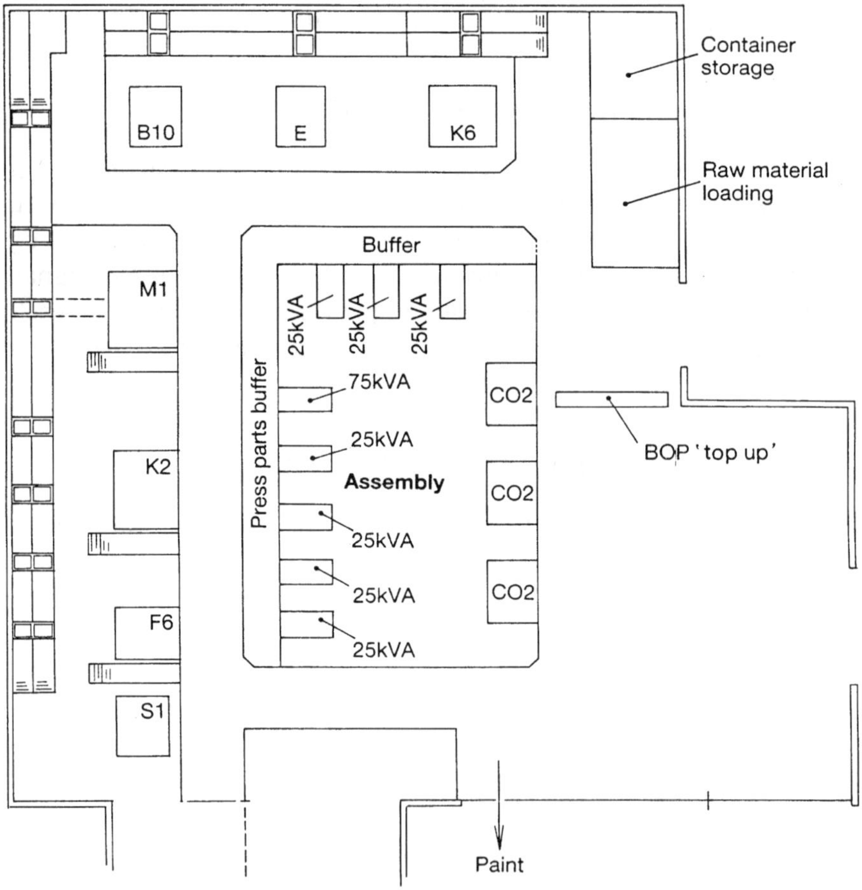

Fig. 9.7 Proposed layout

Table 9.1 Routeings of products in proposed JIT cell

Product/ detail	*m/c*	*time*	*m/c*	*time*	*m/c*	*time*	*m/c*	*time*	*m/c*	*time*	*m/c*	*time*
6123.01	K2	270	WD1	5967	K2	1767						
6123.02	E	515	F1	1111	E	1420						
6123.AA							SW2	1244				
6123									WD1	11969		
6181.01	K2	1076	E	969	E	956						
6181.02	E	690	E	1106								
6181.03	B	479	F	1426								
6181.AA					SW	93						
6181.AB							SW	6200	E	2057		
6181											SW	2097
1478.01	B	1793	S	1297	F	1122	F	1802				
1478.02	B	1215	F	1317	S	1146	B	880				
1478.03	B	1050	B	1371								
1478.04	S	323	S	950								
1478.05	S	323	S	950								
1478.AA					WD1	7350						
1478.AB									SW75	2451		
1478											WD	5312
1495.01	B	1158										
1495.02	B	45	B	1431								
1495					WD	9272						
4369.01	E	545	F	684								
4369.02	B	550	F	772								
4369					WD	9222						
4371	K2	1130	K6	1484								
4355.01	M	867	M	1369	E	1333						
4355.02	E	995	F	1145								
4355							WD	15829				
4439.01	E	1576	M	1210								
4439.05	E	653	F	828								
4439.03	E	1062	F	2031								
4439.04	F	869										
4438.AD	SW	2254										
4496.AA	WD	15218										
4496.AB	WD	15218										
4439.06	E	653	F	828								

Table 9.1 ***(continued)***

Product/ detail	*m/c*	*time*	*m/c*	*time*	*m/c*	*time*	*m/c*	*time*	*m/c*	*time*	*m/c*	*time*
4439.02	E	1576	M	1210								
4438.09	E	780	F	1099								
4496					WD	43959						
1573.01	M	2183	F	1640	M	1746						
1557.01	K6	2800	SW	1273								
1557.02	K6	2800										
1557					SW	3381						
9107.01	K2	1685	K6	1069	M	1168	E	1478	F	1456		
9107.AB	SW6	1889	SW2	1931	SW2	3234	(follows .01)					
9105.06	S	159	S	744								
9105.05	S	394										
9109.02	K2	2087	K6	2973	E	1411						
9105.03	F	1326	B	1039	F	1400						
9109.AA	SW2	5176	SW2	2745	SW2	3285	(follows .02, .03)					
9105.04	B	358	F	1021								
9105.07	S	146	S	1205								
9109	SW2	13915	(follows .AA, .AB, .04, .05, .06, .07)									
9109.02	as above											
9105.03	as above											
9105.04	as above											
9105.07	as above											
9109.AA	as above (follows .02, .03)											
9106.AB	SW6	1889	SW2	2745	SW2	3234	(follows .04, .07)					
9106.01	F	1685	K	2144	E	1478	F	1465	F	1465		
9105.06	as above											
9105.05	as above											
9110	SW2	13915	(follows .AA, .AB, .01, .06, .07)									

Notes:

- Times are given in ten-thousandths of a minute per unit. So 1695 represents 1695 minutes per unit processing time.
- Set-ups on any machine were planned to be 30 minutes maximum.
- 'Details' (shown by a numeric decimal, e.g. .01) usually have to be processed on several machines in sequence. 'Assemblies' (shown by an alphabetic decimal, e.g. .AA) are made from one or more details. The final product is shown without a decimal. The details to go into an assembly are shown by the bill of materials hierarchy. Thus in the case of 6123, details .01 and .02 are required to make sub-assembly .AA, and thereafter the final product is assembled.
- K2, K6, M, E, B, F, S are all press operations. SW is 'spot weld' and WD is 'CO_2 weld' (the assembly operations).

TIMING OF IMPLEMENTATION

The plan for implementation was to set up the cell during the August shutdown. The company was experiencing very high demand in July, and it was decided to keep part of the factory open during August. This meant that some of the people who were due to assist with establishing the cell were not available. Also, some of the presses were still in use. As a result the start date was delayed until mid-September, immediately following the September holiday. Once again, however, the pressure of work meant that most of the factory did not take a September holiday, and there were even calls from management to delay the implementation once again. Stuart Archer maintained that it was a 'now or never' situation, and the implementation went ahead. Due to the continuity of work during September, not all preparations could be made to Stuart's satisfaction. For instance, it appeared that some presses would have to be overhauled after the start of the cell, and not all inspection fixtures would be available.

In early September, it was decided to set up a new mini-cell in addition to the main cell being planned. The new cell was to produce only one part for Nissan. The volume was considered adequate to keep a number of machines busy, so at very short notice an area was cleared of inventory and the new mini-cell was set up. The mini-cell comprised only welding machines, arranged in a tight circle to facilitate flow.

Throughout this time Stuart Archer was extremely busy. He had to organise and plan for the new cell, which included:

- ordering and installing new conveyors
- selecting and ordering new containers
- procuring new distinctive overalls for the operators in the cell
- moving machines (which were still under continuous pressure to keep running, due to the increased demand)
- working out a new payment system
- introducing new supply arrangements involving more frequent deliveries to a specific receiving area for the new cell
- training supervisors and operators.

In the two months leading up to the start of the new cell he was assisted by a production engineering student who helped with part selection for the cell, the establishment of a kanban system, and in the calculation of machine loading and of the number of parts to go into a container.

Stuart was also required to assist with other duties including staff induction, running the customer system used for materials management and helping to train a new production manager who joined the company in August.

No special arrangements were made with regard to quality and maintenance in the cell. Standard procedures would apply. Likewise, measures of performance were not discussed.

THE PAYMENT SCHEME

Before the JIT project began, AP had 21 categories of hourly paid employees. All these people were paid on a straight proportional individual hours system. The incentive system was an important management philosophy. Following trips to Japan, senior management realised that an individual bonus system was not compatible with JIT, but they were nevertheless keen to retain an incentive, even if it was only group-based.

It was decided to have only six payment grades within future cells. Each grade would reflect the number of skill factors an operator had achieved. Each cell would require only seven skills, and the three grades would reflect how many of these skills an employee was capable of performing. The skill factors would not include being conversant with maintenance procedures nor with quality checks such as SPC (Statistical Process Control). These additional skills would be taught to all operators later on.

Some work categories – press operation, press setting, spot weld operation, CO_2 operations and CO_2 setting – would not be subject to incentive.

Operators for the cell were chosen on the basis of diligence, but the operators were requested rather than told to join the cell. The list of operators and their skills is shown in Table 9.2.

Table 9.2 AP Light cell: operators and skills

Shift 1 0600–1400		*Shift 2 1400–2200*	
Name		*Name*	
P. Mears	spot set, s/w	M. Bishop	power set
P. Stanton	power	P. Trower	spot set
R. Roddy	power	S. Knight	power
A. Hunter	s/w	P. Hayward	power
M. Preece	s/w	P. Bird	power
A. Sparrow	s/w	Y. Birks	s/w
B. Soulsby	s/w	G. Richards	s/w
R. Malpass	s/w	S. Ellis	CO_2
P. Whitehouse	CO_2	A. Martin	CO_2
S. Clay	power set		

Notes:
- s/w is spot welding: 25, 65, 75 kVA machines.
- Spot welders will be trained to do power press operations.
- CO_2 welders will be trained to do spot welding.
- Spot welders *cannot* do CO_2 welding (legal).

The group incentive would be based on a work plan prepared by each cell supervisor following the MPS (Master Production Schedule), and would be related to the output of quality finished parts produced. A five per cent maximum excess over weekly production figures would be imposed to discourage over-production. Production above this limit would not attract additional bonus. The actual group payment would be in the range of 75–100 per cent on a 'straight proportional' basis, dependent on the number of quality units produced. For instance, 80 per cent of target output would gain 80 per cent of the bonus payment. The bonus would be calculated on a four-weekly basis and paid monthly. Future consideration was to be given to moving direct labour over to a monthly salary. Employees were to be guaranteed no loss of earnings during the initial cell implementation period.

Questions

1 Review the status of JIT implementation at Aylesbury Pressings.

2 What would be your priorities for the future development of JIT?

APPENDIX 9.1
JIT CELLS: PROCEDURES AND DISCIPLINES

1 People must be prepared to be multi-tasking and accept constant training and change.
2 People must be prepared to work as a team to achieve a given goal rather than as individuals.
3 Productivity must be based upon number of completed (painted) good-quality units, not on individual performance/productivity of a work centre (work in progress/creating).
4 'Shop floor' accountancy is to be avoided. The old opinion that piles of work around a work centre is good has to be dispelled.
5 A mood of 'continuous flow production' must be encouraged. All work will be triggered by a 'pull' action. At any given work centre no work will be carried out unless a demand signal has been received from 'upstream'.
6 Prior to being required, any materials, press tools, assembly jigs and fixtures and working materials will be available. This includes the availability of any material handling devices. All waiting time is to be eliminated.

   Guidelines for the planning and scheduling of work within the cell shall be displayed on a centralised 'planning board' for all to see.
7 It is envisaged that the cell shall be autonomous from other cells within the factory. It shall have its own goods inwards area but will obviously share the painting, tool refurbishment and goods despatch functions.
8 People operating within the cell will be encouraged to inspect incoming product and their own work so that quality is 'built into the product' rather than being a retrospective end-of-line function. The quality and regularity of supply of product coming into and out of the cell shall be monitored.
9 People working within the cell shall be given sufficient area so that they can adequately carry out their task. Only an allotted area for necessary work in progress shall be given to eliminate the creation of pockets of inventory.
10 The overall control of the cell shall be carried out by a designated cell supervisor.

11 The assembly area of the cell shall be classed as a no-go area for fork-lift trucks. Therefore, alternative forms of material handling/transport will be investigated and utilised. Preferably these will be manually based.

12 High unit loads beyond the capability of being manually transferred are to be avoided. The movement of product singly or in low unit loads is to be encouraged rather than product multiples. (Remember that the paint line accepts products singly rather than a stillage load.) The key is small, regular movements.

13 As far as possible operations will be closely coupled and tightly linked. Labour saving ergonomics will be designed into the cell to eliminate non-added-value tasks. All effort will focus upon encouraging people to maximise the level of adding value tasks that they carry out.

14 Inventory levels (raw materials, work in progress and bought-out finished parts) will be strictly held at set levels. The raw materials and bought-out element will be restocked at regular intervals to a maximum stock holding size. This arrangement shall be self-monitoring as this will be an 'eyeball' system whereby the given levels at any point in time can be ascertained at a glance. Potential problem/bottleneck areas are detected early and solutions found.

15 Production, quality and problem data will be recorded and retained at the workplace.

16 Problem solving by the cell workforce rather than 'staff experts' will be encouraged.

17 As much as possible the cell workforce shall have greater involvement and say in their day-to-day tasks and, as a result, greater job satisfaction.

CASE 10

Warwick Castle

Robert Craven and Stuart Chambers

Case date 1991

'Warwick Castle – the finest mediaeval castle in England.'

INTRODUCTION

The Stratford-on-Avon and District Hotels and Caterers Association (SCATA) publishes a brochure which has described the Castle as follows:

> *This magnificent ancient castle, situated at the very centre of England, is a treasure house of great beauty and splendid, rare quality collections of pictures, furniture, furnishings and an outstanding collection of arms and armour which bear witness to the power and influence of the Earls of Warwick down through the centuries.*
>
> *The beautiful grounds landscaped by Capability Brown, where peacocks roam freely, are a delight in all seasons . . . Excellent catering facilities are available all year round to suit every pocket and disposition, as well as several gift shops.*

Warwick Castle is less than two hours by road from London with easy access from all major cities by motorway, road and rail. This excellent infrastructure allows the area to be part of the itinerary of any visitor to the UK. The County of Warwickshire is lyrically described in the SCATA brochure:

> *Stratford-on-Avon and Shakespeare's Country. When you think of England, and the very best of England, you are probably thinking about this fascinating region.*
>
> *Here in this most English of English landscapes, the broad rolling sweep of the Cotswolds, the classic half-timbered villages of the Vale of Evesham and leafy Warwickshire, there is an unparalleled variety of attractions.*
>
> *The birthplace of the world's greatest dramatist, William Shakespeare; the finest mediaeval castle and most-visited stately home at Warwick; England's most magnificent palace at Blenheim; and the world's most famous theatre in Stratford.*

THE CASTLE

The Castle is part of the Tussauds Group, a wholly-owned subsidiary of Pearson plc, which also owns the Financial Times Group and Royal Doulton among other varied interests. The Tussauds Group runs entertainment centres that include: Madame Tussauds, the famous waxworks in Baker Street, London; the London Planetarium and Laserium; the Royalty and Empire Exhibition at Windsor; Alton Towers, the UK's only world-rated leisure park; and Chessington World of Adventures and Zoo.

The Castle's General Manager, Martin Westwood, works in the stately home, from a majestic suite of offices overlooking the grounds. He is enthusiastic about the Castle both as a building steeped in history and as a business. In the relaxed atmosphere of his office, where he is surrounded by portraits and old paintings of the Castle, he refers to it as 'a brand leader' in stately homes for it is in the top five most visited historic sites that charge entry fees (*see* Table 10.1).

Table 10.1 Historic sites attracting more than 300 000 paid admissions in 1990

Historic site	*Paid admissions (000s)* 1989	1990
1 Tower of London	2214	2298
2 Roman Baths and Pump Room, Bath	931	950
3 State Apartments, Windsor	807	855
4 Stonehenge, Wiltshire	682	703
5 Warwick Castle	**637**	**685**
6 Shakespeare's Birthplace, Stratford	571	604
7 Leeds Castle, Kent	529	540
8 Hampton Court Palace, near London	539	525
9 Tower Bridge, London	514	528
10 Blenheim Palace, Woodstock, Oxford	524	517
11 Beaulieu, Hampshire	512	493
12 Cutty Sark, Greenwich, London	361	411
13 St George's Chapel, Windsor	412	372
14 Anne Hathaway's Cottage, Stratford	332	365
15 HMS *Victory*, Portsmouth	303	340
16 *Mary Rose*, Portsmouth	350	333
17 Royal Pavilion, Brighton	321	314
18 Chatsworth House, Derbyshire	327	306
19 Hever Castle, Kent	285	303
20 Fountains Abbey, North Yorks.	289	300

As you pass through the ticket office from the large car park you catch your first view of the Castle. The view truly takes your breath away and fully warrants the description given by Sir Walter Scott in 1828: 'the most noble sight in England'.

MARKETING

Marketing Manager, Sarah Montgomery, is another enthusiast of the outstanding beauty of the Castle. Discussing the marketing of the business she considers that the Castle's unique selling point must be that carried on all the promotional material: 'Warwick Castle – the finest mediaeval castle in England.' But she does not discount the Castle's unique state of preservation, the breadth of attractions it offers, its location on the banks of the River Avon or its thousand-year span of history.

In the year 1068 the first castle was built at Warwick and since that time it slowly developed into a mighty stronghold and later a grand mansion befitting the station of a high ranking nobleman . . . In November 1978 the present Earl sold Warwick Castle and its contents to Madame Tussauds of London.

The Castle's marketing team recognised that the Castle attracted a diverse audience, each segment of which wanted different things from a visit. So in targeting audiences the team had to decide whether it was trying to sell the castle aspect, the stately home aspect or the gardens. It was felt that all three areas attracted different audiences and conjured up different expectations.

Research had established that from the public's point of view 'castles' were not associated with grounds and formal gardens, and neither were they associated with the notion of being someone's home. On the other hand, stately homes were associated with grounds and gardens but were felt to be formal and museum-like, with ropes keeping the public away from the interesting areas. So was the 'most visited Stately Home in Britain' really a castle, or was the Castle also a stately home? This conundrum had to be solved.

The Castle management has a deliberate policy of charging one overall admission charge for all areas of the Castle and Grounds open to visitors (*see* Fig 10.1). In the past they had considered charging separate admission prices for the Castle and the Grounds but this, it was felt, would confuse the customer. The prices for 1991–92 are given in Fig. 10.1.

The Castle regularly has detailed market research questionnaires compiled by an outside company. Sarah said that market research is taken very seriously by the team:

'On average, overseas visitors represent 42 per cent of the total. Twenty-five per cent of our customers seem to come in groups of greater than 20 and these groups are predominantly from overseas. On the other hand, 58 per cent of visitors come from the UK, of which roughly half come from within a 100 km radius of the site.

'Another interesting point is that 25 per cent of all customers are repeat visitors which we feel reflects the popularity of the Castle. With UK visitors 33 per cent are repeats. Of the non-locals, that is UK residents from outside the 100 km radius, 78 per cent stay overnight in the area and the remainder have travelled over 100 km to visit the area for the day. With the recent opening of the M40 motorway into London (approximately

Warwick Castle

The finest mediaeval castle in England

What there is to see

THE CASTLE

The State Rooms and Great Hall — the magnificent and richly appointed main rooms of the Castle.

The Private Apartments — 'A Royal Weekend Party, 1898' by Madame Tussaud's — a unique award winning exhibition which by the use of 29 wax portraits in 12 room settings recreates a house party which took place in June 1898.

The Watergate (Ghost) Tower — the lodgings, by tradition of the Castle ghost, whose story is related to sound.

The Armoury — among the impressive arrays of muskets, pistols and swords rare military exhibits can be examined at close quarters.

The Dungeon — a grim reminder of the Castle's past.

The Torture Chamber — a grisley collection of instruments of torture.

The Gatehouse and Barbican — a permanent exhibition illustrating the life and times of Richard III — "To Prove a Villain — the Real Richard III" researched by the Richard III Society.

Guy's Tower, the Rampart Walk and Clarence Tower — climb the top for panoramic views of the Castle, Warwick and the surrounding countryside.

THE GROUNDS

The Victorian Rose Garden — recently recreated Rose Garden opened by H.R.H. The Princess of Wales on 8th July, 1986.

The Peacock Gardens — quiet formal gardens in front of the Conservatory.

The Conservatory — the magnificent replica of the Warwick Vase is housed in the 18th century restored Conservatory, opened by H.R.H. Princess Margaret in June 1989.

The River Island — timeless location with an impressive panorama of the massive River Front of the Castle.

Foxes Study and Cedar Walk — tranquil woodland area at the confluence of the river.

Pageant Field — open expanse of parkland skirted by many fine trees.

The Mound — the oldest surviving part of the Castle with breathtaking views across the Castle Park to the Cotswolds Hills.

Restaurant and Refreshment Facilities — available all year round.

Picnic Areas — there are several in the 60 acres of grounds open to visitors.

Special Events — Easter to September.

The Red Knight patrols the Castle precincts during the summer months and there are extra attractions on Saturday, Sunday and Bank Holiday Monday afternoons. Please telephone for details.

All inclusive ADMISSION RATES

One all inclusive admission charge covers all areas of the Castle and Grounds, which are open to visitors.

FROM 1st APRIL 1991 to 29th FEBRUARY 1992 inclusive.

INDIVIDUAL RATE

Adult	£5.75
Child (4 to 16 years)	£3.50
Senior Citizen	£4.00
Family Ticket (two adults and two children)	£16.00
Family Ticket (two adults and three children)	£18.00

PARTY RATE (minimum of 20 persons)

Adult	£4.65
Child	£3.00
Senior Citizen	£3.70

SCHOOL PARTIES

One teacher free with 20 pupils.

SPECIAL WINTER RATES (November to February inclusive)

Students (individuals)	£4.75
Students (party rate)	£4.10

REGULAR VISITOR PASS

(valid for one year)	£11.00

THE RIGHT TO ALTER ADMISSION RATES WITHOUT NOTICE IS RESERVED

Fig. 10.1 Warwick Castle information leaflet

180 km) it is felt that travel time may be a more important factor to consider than distance travelled in kilometres.'

The data are collected over a period of days, and the market research reports sent to Sarah include not only the profile of visitors but what parts of the Castle they visit. The popularity of various parts of the complex varies according to how busy the site is. For instance, on a quiet day 87 per cent might visit the Private Apartments, but on a busy day this figure drops to 68 per cent. Likewise, during one such busy period, the visitors to the Woodland Gardens increased from 17 per cent to 20 per cent, to the Mound from 46 per cent to 52 per cent, and to the River Island from 34 per cent to 40 per cent. On average, visitors stayed on the site for three hours. Coach parties tended to visit for three hours, probably because the Castle was part of a full-day, tightly scheduled excursion that included other nearby tourist attractions.

Competition for the paying tourists' disposable cash was quite fierce in the area, it was felt. Other sites competing for the 'leisure pound' were the Black Country Museum, Drayton Manor (Adventure) Park, West Midlands Safari Park, Cadbury World, Blenheim Palace, Alton Towers Theme Park, Ironbridge and Chatsworth House.

In the Undercroft Restaurant marketing researchers overheard an elderly professor in conversation with a friend he had encountered in the Castle grounds:

I came early in the morning to avoid the rush. Any major historic tourist site is going to be heaving by midday in the Summer and personally I hate all the queuing and tourists with cameras and all that.

I got here at about 10 a.m. when the place opened this morning. I was able to enjoy the pure magic of the building with relatively few other people around.

By lunch-time the queues were what I felt to be unreasonably long, but it is August and this must surely be their peak time here. I do wonder, for instance, should they not encourage more visitors out of season and what about allowing people to visit early morning or in the evening to avoid the lunch-time crush?

MANAGING DEMAND

Warwick Castle brochures show a wide variety of activities that supplement turnover outside the peak season. According to Sarah, this literature was intended 'to push up the shoulders of demand':

- Every Friday and Saturday evening the Undercroft provides the setting for splendid five-course mediaeval banquets recreating the eve of the Battle of Agincourt.
- A special events calendar has been published (*see* Fig. 10.2).
- The Warwick Arts Festival uses the Castle as a venue in the evenings for a week in July.

The Red Knight

Resplendent in the full accoutrement of a Knight of the mid 14th century Sir William de Beauchamp mounted on his splendid charger patrols the Castle precincts during the summer months.

Monday to Friday, from 13th May to 30th August. 11.15am to 12.45pm and 2.00pm to 4.00pm.

Sir William is unable to sally forth in wet weather, on Bank Holiday Mondays, and the first Monday of the Month

The 1st Regiment of French Foot Grenadiers

Evening Events Warwick Castle

WARWICK ARTS FESTIVAL
Open Air Concert and Grand Firework Display
Saturday 6th July
A programme of Russian Music including works by Shostakovich, Borodin, Moussorgsky, Khatchaturian, Prokofiev, Rimsky Korsakov and Tchaikovsky's 1812 Overture.

Played by The Britannia Building Society Band and The Jaguar Cars (City of Coventry) Band.
Conductor—Howard Snell.
Evening starts at 7pm—Concert at 9.30pm.
Advance tickets available from 15th April at Warwick Arts Festival Office.

* * * * * * * * * * * * *

Open Air Evening Performances of
WAR AND PEACE
by Leo Tolstoy
performed by **The Birmingham Crescent Theatre**

Friday 5th July, Sunday 7th July, Wednesday 10th July
Thursday 11th July, Friday 12th July, Saturday 13th July
Performances begin at 7.30pm.
Advance tickets and information from:
Warwick Arts Festival Office,
Northgate, Warwick CV34 4JL. Tel: (0926) 410747.

CHRISTMAS CAROL CONCERT
in the Courtyard
on **Saturday 21st December**
Gates open 6.45pm.—Carols from 7.30pm.
Tickets must be purchased in advance.

Open every day (except Christmas Day) 10.00am—5.30pm (November—February 10.00am—4.30pm)

Special events take place in the afternoon on Saturdays, Sundays and Bank Holiday Mondays (except where specified otherwise).

Details of timings and performance areas are displayed at the Ticket Office on the day of the event.

We reserve the right to cancel any of the attractions without prior notice due to adverse weather conditions or other factors beyond our control.

For further information:
Warwick Castle, Warwick, Warwickshire CV34 4QU.
Telephone: Warwick 0926 495421 Fax: 0926 401692

Warwick Castle Special Events

1991

Warwick Castle Special Events 1991

THERE ARE **NO EXTRA CHARGES** TO VIEW DAY-TIME EVENTS.

MARCH

Sunday 31st
The First Regiment of French Foot Grenadiers drill and mount the guard in a colourful display recalling the Napoleonic era.

APRIL

Monday 1st
The First Regiment of French Foot Grenadiers drill and mount the guard in a colourful display recalling the Napoleonic era.

Saturday 6th
Solihull Orchid Society—Orchid display in the Conservatory.
Morris Men.

Sunday 7th
Falconry Display featuring a variety of Birds of Prey.

Saturday 13th
Morris Men.

Sunday 14th
Warwick Household—mediaeval garrison.

Saturday 20th
Morris Men.

Sunday 21st
Lord Saye and Sele's Blew Regiment of Foote—a Parliamentarian Regiment of the Sealed Knot—drill and mount the guard in a display from the era of the English Civil War.

Saturday 27th
Morris Men.

Sunday 28th
Coventry Mummers.

MAY

*The Red Knight patrols the Grounds every Monday to Friday from Monday 13th May.***

Saturday 4th
Morris Men.

Sunday 5th
Warwick Castle's Red Knight patrols on his splendid charger.

Monday 6th
The Red Knight.

Saturday 11th
Morris Men.

Sunday 12th
The Golden Eagle Archery Display Troop.

Saturday 18th
Morris Men.

Sunday 19th
Earlsdon Morris Men.

Saturday 25th
Morris Men.

Sunday 26th
The First Regiment of French Foot Grenadiers.

Monday 27th
The First Regiment of French Foot Grenadiers.

Tuesday 28th
The Red Knight.

Wednesday 29th
The Red Knight.

Thursday 30th
The Royal Scottish Country Dance Society and Swiss Guests.

Friday 31st
The Red Knight.

JUNE

*The Red Knight patrols the Grounds from Monday to Friday each week.***

Saturday 1st
Morris Men.

Sunday 2nd
Falconry Display.

Saturday 8th
Morris Men.

Sunday 9th
Lord Saye and Sele's Blew Regiment of Foote.

Sunday 16th
Falconry Display.

Saturday 22nd
Morris Men.

Sunday 23rd
Morris Men.

Saturday 29th
Morris Men.

Sunday 30th
The Golden Lions of England—mediaeval foot combat display.

JULY

*The Red Knight patrols the Grounds from Monday to Friday each week.***

Friday 5th
**(Evening) Warwick Arts Festival.*

Saturday 6th
Morris Men.
**(Evening) Warwick Arts Festival.*

Sunday 7th
Falconry Display.
**(Evening) Warwick Arts Festival.*

Wednesday 10th
**(Evening) Warwick Arts Festival.*

Thursday 11th
**(Evening) Warwick Arts Festival.*

Friday 12th
**(Evening) Warwick Arts Festival.*

Saturday 13th
Morris Men.
**(Evening) Warwick Arts Festival.*

Sunday 14th
Earlsdon Morris Men.

Saturday 20th
Morris Men.

Sunday 21st
Warwick Household—mediaeval garrison.

Saturday 27th
Morris Men.

Sunday 28th
The Golden Eagle Archery Display Troop.

AUGUST

*The Red Knight patrols the Grounds from Monday to Friday each week.***

Saturday 3rd
Warwick Folk Festival.

Sunday 4th
Warwick Folk Festival.

Saturday 10th
Morris Men.

Sunday 11th
Lord Saye and Sele's Blew Regiment of Foote.

Saturday 17th
Morris Men.

Sunday 18th
Wayfarers Folk Dance Group.

Saturday 24th
Morris Men.

Sunday 25th
The First Regiment of French Foot Grenadiers.

Monday 26th
The First Regiment of French Foot Grenadiers.

Saturday 31st
Morris Men.

SEPTEMBER

Sunday 1st
Shakespeare Run passes through the Castle Courtyard between 12 noon and 2pm—300 Classic and Vintage Cars

Saturday 7th
Morris Men.

Sunday 8th
Earlsdon Morris Men.

**The Red Knight will be unable to patrol the Grounds in wet weather, on Bank Holiday Mondays and the first Monday of the Month.

*See back panel for details: separate pricing arrangements apply

Fig. 10.2 Special events calendar

- Exclusive tours of the Castle, and separately of the Gardens, are run by experts for prebooked groups. These are available during the periods October to March, and March to November respectively, except during school half-term holidays and bank holidays.

As a profit centre for the Pearson Group, the Castle is given targets that increase at a rate exceeding inflation. From these, prices are derived based on product developments, the prices that competitors are charging and known external factors that may affect demand (such as exchange rates and elections!). The Castle expected between 700 000 and 800 000 visitors in 1991 and profit projections were made based on these estimates. All catering facilities are run by the Castle, recognising that franchising to another company would result in a loss of control and reduce the potential to participate in profitable activities.

Martin Westwood commented on fluctuations in demand:

'Staffing varies relatively little with demand. It is felt that once the basic positions around the Castle are attended by staff, there is little that an additional staff member can provide. Winter weekends attract more visitors than winter weekdays, such that Saturday and Sunday combined turnover is the same as the other five days of the week put together. In summer things are more even, a Saturday or a Sunday being equivalent to two weekdays, although Sunday is usually busier than Saturday.'

BUSINESS OBJECTIVES

Martin is clear that the Castle's prime objective is 'to achieve growth in earnings per share for its shareholders'. At the same time he emphasizes the sense of responsibility the management feels 'as custodians of this precious monument' to work within it and use integrity and sensitivity at all times. Hence all signs, directions and facilities take a very low profile. Flashing neon lights are not the order of the day!

Sarah Montgomery commented on the need to underplay the commercial side of the organisation:

'Coca-Cola have offered us a sponsorship deal. They will give us money for a particular project which will increase our revenue and also the number of visitors we are getting. The problem is that Coke is the epitome of youth and fizz while the Castle's target market is adults ABC1, average age somewhere around 45! So how do we pull this deal together?'

It is the 'integrity' of the business in which the management take pride. It is not *any* business site but a very special building that is loved and cherished by the staff. Their constant concern is how to run a business from the Castle without destroying the charm and romance of the buildings, and without covering it with obtrusive signs and facilities. All staff are very polite and courteous and, though they are available to the public, tend not to interfere with the customers' visit. In fact they blend in with visitors as they wear little that suggests they are actually staff. And when the Castle is relatively empty of visitors it has a really enchanting atmosphere.

PERFORMANCE

Evaluation of the performance of the business has difficulties. On the one hand, queues are an obvious problem (*see* Table 10.2) but then the customers do not seem to mind too much! Above all, the business is going from strength to strength, and achieving healthy profit performance in the middle of 1991's severe recession. So, while the criticisms have to be noted, management has been achieving the high returns and growth that the shareholders require.

Table 10.2 Observations of queuing and flow, Tuesday 13 August 1991, afternoon

Queue to Private Apartments (number of people)	
1.00	130
1.20	147
1.40	128
2.00	153
2.20	132
2.40	119
3.00	137
Flow through doors to Private Apartments (number of people)	
1.00–1.20	104
1.20–1.40	113
1.40–2.00	107
Flow from Private Apartments and State Rooms (number of people)	
1.00–1.20	127
1.20–1.40	117
1.40–2.00	121
Queue to Rampart Walk	
0–20 people at any one time	
Number of people entering Rampart Walk	
1.40–1.50	174
Queue at top of ramparts to get down (number of people)	
6 minutes	63

Martin Westwood was defensive on the question of queues:

'What popular tourist attraction doesn't have queues, and in any case, the queues here move pretty quickly. If we get queues for one part of the Castle we simply put out a sign suggesting people move on to the next attraction, although, to be frank, that doesn't

*really work. You see, the trouble is, that once people see a queue they don't want to miss out so they still join on the end of it. Our marketing questionnaires (*see *Appendix 10.1) suggest that we've got the operation about right, but there's always room for some improvement.'*

The professor in the Undercroft Restaurant had raised several issues connected with this:

'The Castle really is in a unique condition of preservation. It's truly marvellous but I wouldn't seriously consider visiting it in the peak season. I just happen to be in the area because we're going over to Stratford tonight to see Twelfth Night *at the Royal Shakespeare Theatre. I'm really looking forward to it!*

'I wonder why they don't have off-peak rates for those not visiting around midday and maybe open earlier and close later. I would be more than happy to spend more time on the site if it weren't for all the other tourists everywhere. And another thing, couldn't they do a package deal with the theatre at Stratford? I'm sure a lot of visitors here also go there.

'In fact, I would pay a premium price to have the Castle almost to myself. For instance, I'd find it simply delightful to sip a Pimms or a gin and tonic in the grounds as the sun went down. I know that I am rambling but I am sure there's a way to re-jig the prices so that the site basically generates more income ***throughout*** *the year. And even if you say they do things out of season I've not heard about them, so what's the use of publicity if it doesn't reach the people that want to spend money?'*

Sarah Montgomery, mindful of the need to keep a close eye on customers' diverse requirements, often talked to individuals at the exit. A transcript of one such encounter is reproduced in Appendix 10.2.

Questions

1 How can you categorise/segment the visitors to Warwick Castle? Do all these visitors place the same operational demands on the management of the Castle?

2 How could the General Manager define a 'service concept' that would satisfy the diverse requirements of the customers, the staff, and the shareholders (the Pearson Group)? In what way could this concept help in the development of a Warwick Castle strategy?

3 Considering your answer to (2) above, should Warwick Castle review its policy of charging one overall admission charge?

4 In what ways could the castle modify its operations to improve the capacity/demand balance? How effective are current policies in relieving peak overloads?

5 Does the Castle provide a good quality service, and how could it be improved?

6 How could a deal with Coca-Cola be consistent with the strategy and service concept of the Castle?

APPENDIX 10.1
MARKETING QUESTIONNAIRE OF RANDOM SAMPLE OF PEOPLE LEAVING WARWICK CASTLE

Monday 12 August 1991, afternoon

Age range	
0–5	7
6–15	37
16–25	27
26–35	25
36–45	34
46–55	17
56–65	20
66+	33
	200

Area of origination	
Local (within 100 km)	34
UK (outside 100 km)	43
Europe (excl. UK)	41
USA/Canada	47
S. America	3
Australia	11
Africa	5
Asia	14
Other/unspecified	2
	200

Length of stay in area	
Day trip	96
1–3 days	50
4–7 days	13
8+ days	5
	164

Method of transport	
Coach trip	96
Own transport	74
Hire car	31
Public transport	20
Other (bicycles etc.)	12
	233

Warwick Castle: value for money?	
Yes	183
No	6
Don't know	7
No comment	4
	200

Did you find that you had to queue very much?	
Yes	186
No	12
No comment	2
	200

Did you feel that the queues were the same as other large tourist sites?	
Same	190
Better	4
Worse	6
	200

Did you visit . . .?	
State Rooms and Great Hall	191
The Private Apartments	190
The Watergate (Ghost) Tower	31
The Armory	104
The Dungeon	193
The Torture Chamber	183
The Gatehouse and Barbican	87
Guy's Tower, the Rampart Walk and Clarence Tower	186
The Victorian Rose Garden	103
The Peacock Gardens	117
The Conservatory	102
The River Island	57
Foxes Study and Cedar Walk	31
Pageant Field	101
The Mound	54
Refreshment Stall	118
Stables Restaurant and Tearoom	52
Undercroft Restaurant	71
The Bookshop	62

Did you . . .?	
Bring your own picnic	32
Did you see the Red Knight	81
Did you buy a brochure	99

How long have you spent at the Castle?	
<1 hour	5
1–2 hours	67
2–3 hours	75
3–4 hours	37
>4 hours	16
	200

Is this your first visit?	
Yes	148
No	52
	200

Would you visit again?	
Yes	144
No	31
Maybe	23
Don't know	2
	200

APPENDIX 10.2
TRANSCRIPT OF A CONVERSATION WITH A VISITOR

13 August 1991

Christabelle Tymko, Oldbury-on-Severn, Gloucester

'We got here at about midday. We came up for the day from Gloucestershire. It was quite a good trip and the kids behaved themselves in the car. We had heard a lot about the Castle from some friends who have just moved up to Stratford, which is just down the road from Warwick.

'The Castle's in superb condition! You don't know what it's going to be like until you get past the ticket office and it really is amazing. It has been kept in impeccable condition, and the gardens are beautiful as well as being far less crowded than the Castle.

'There were too many people in and around the Castle. The queues were an irritation but I parked my husband in the queue and took the kids elsewhere until he was near the front and then we joined him. I think a few people got upset because we seemed to be pushing in, but I'm not prepared to wait with three children in long queues in the sun. Mind you, it's nothing like the queues at Madame Tussauds in London, they really are crazy.

'I didn't realise quite how big the grounds were. If I had known I think we would have spent longer at Warwick Castle and made a full day of it. We should have come here at about ten and then spent the whole day here. That way the queues inside the Castle would have been shorter for us. The grounds are lovely and they've got special picnic areas which I thought was a nice idea. (I wish we'd brought a picnic.) Mind you, it does seem to be more than a bit light on entertainment for the kids.

'Nicky loved the man with the wonderful moustache dressed up in full Crusader uniform on the horse. He was very good with the kids. Nicky also liked the waxworks in the Private Apartments place. The queue wound its way up, down and around the place but apart from mild feelings of claustrophobia (that's my problem, I suppose) it went at about the right speed and I guess it lasted a bit under an hour. Oh yes, the Rampart Walk, they ought to warn you about just how many stairs you have to climb. I mean, I know there is a sign but you don't take it seriously, do you! You go up and up and then there's that great spiral staircase up the inside of that tower, I won't do that again in a rush! But it was worth it for the view.

'All in all it was a good day. More interesting than the average castle, and not full of the usual tourist-oriented rubbish associated with tourist attractions. The commercial side is very much underplayed and I like that. You don't feel obliged to buy ice creams and tee-shirts and pencils and teatowels. Maybe some of the signs were a bit too discreet – we had to ask where the toilets were – but it makes a pleasant change.

'Also I like the one price for everything. At other places, I object to paying an admission charge and then paying on top of that for particular attractions. You always feel mean if you don't pay up, and then you also feel that you might be missing something. No, I'd recommend the place and it's so much less hassle than the tourist places in London which you almost feel obliged to visit every so often.'

CASE 11

Brechten Algraphy

Nigel Slack

*Case date 1992**

INTRODUCTION

By 1992 the Brechten Algraphy group was one of the world's leading manufacturers of aluminium presensitised plates for lithographic printing. These are the plates which take the image to be printed and repeatedly transfer it onto the receiving medium. It also supplied the printing trade with a comprehensive range of lithographic equipment, chemicals and sundries, some of which were factored. Such had been the group's success over the previous 15 years that a new manufacturing plant, with increased production capacity, was completed near Cologne in 1990 for its plate-making company.

Formed when the Brechten company of Cologne had taken over Rexan-Algraphy of Bradford UK in 1985, the new company had maintained both its partners' reputations for innovation in the lithographic printing industry. Brechten, for example, had introduced the world's first fully anodised negative-working presensitised plate some years ago. The group was now the leading supplier of negative-working plates to web offset newspapers in Western Europe.

Ulrich Mayer, the group's Chief Executive, was keen to emphasize the group's continuing reliance on its technical prowess.

> *'We joined with Rexan five years ago because they were the only independent company in the industry with our dedication to maintaining technical superiority. Yet we complemented each other. Their skills were primarily in the processing technology essential for efficient production, while we had a research record which left us ahead in all of the significant new and potential product developments.'* (Financial Times, *June 1990*)

After a disappointing performance in 1990, the group experienced a very successful year in 1991, despite the printing trade worldwide being affected by a slow-down in many trading markets.

*Names and some details of the company's operations have been disguised.

THE PRESENSITISED PLATE INDUSTRY

Brechten Algraphy were the largest of the European presensitised plate-makers. The next largest European manufacturer, Hoechst, were slightly more than half the size of Brechten Algraphy. The group's share of the European presensitised plate market had been around 40 per cent in 1990 with the remainder split almost equally between other European manufacturers and imports. Even so European sales accounted for only 63 per cent of total plate sales.

In the world market, Brechten Algraphy was unusual. All their main competitors were divisions of far larger groups, for example, Fuji, 3M and Hoechst. Fuji did not manufacture in Europe but dominated the Pacific region market. Also Brechten's main competitors were far more vertically integrated. All made most of their own chemicals, for example, and two – Fuji and 3M – also manufactured offset printing equipment. Brechten Algraphy felt that this gave some advantages to their competitors, especially in terms of material costs and in the development of some new products, but considered themselves far closer to the market than the larger companies and also more innovative. Their attitude was one of, 'We have to be good at this business, it's the only one we've got.'

ORGANISATION OF THE GROUP

The Brechten Algraphy group consisted of three companies:

- Brechten Algraphy Plates, located at Cologne and Bradford, was the largest of the three and had a record turnover in 1991 of DM 902 million.
- Brechten Algraphy Vapson, located at Norwich, who manufactured the ovens and processors for the group's 'pro-techt' system. Its 1991 turnover was down slightly at DM 90 million.
- Brechten Algraphy Chemicals, located at Hamburg, manufactured some of the chemicals used in commercial offset printing and factored the rest. Turnover in 1991 was DM 17 million.

Group head office was located on the Cologne site. All shared functions were there with the exception of the research section of the technical department, which was located both at Norwich and Cologne, and the plate company's production planning department, which was located at Bradford.

The profit of the whole group for 1991, before interest, increased to DM 124 million (1990 DM 70 million) mainly due to the plate company's improved performance.

THE PRODUCT RANGE

Brechten Algraphy's breakthrough in the 1970s with its fully anodised negative-working presensitised plates had skewed the company's products towards the web offset newspaper business. But by the 1990s, the original product range of this type of plate had been supplemented with other negative-working plates, formulated for extra long print runs.

For commercial printing, Brechten Algraphy supplied positive-working plates. Some of these were for use in the demanding long-run packaging industry, and others for shorter, high-quality runs, where accuracy of reproduction, especially in four-colour work, was the major factor. The life of both types of plate could be extended by baking, using the patented Brechten Algraphy 'pro-techt' process, which hardened the image and protected the plate from solvents normally harmful to positive-working plates.

For the small commercial and in-plant printers, the company supplied small offset versions of its plates and a full range of blankets, chemicals and sundries.

The latest product being manufactured was the Electrolith 83100 electrostatic plate system. With this system no film was required as the plate was made direct from copy. The Electrolith was designed primarily for the newspaper market and was already being used successfully for several European newspapers.

Generally Brechten Algraphy's presensitised plates could be categorised by the following characteristics:

- *The type of presensitising* – that is the number and types of coating applied to the aluminium. Six types of plate were manufactured by Brechten Algraphy: three negative-working plates which are used in relatively low-quality printing such as newspapers, and three positive-working plates for high-quality work such as magazines. The three plates of each type were marketed as being suitable for short-, medium- and long-print runs.
- *The gauge of the plate* – that is the thickness of the aluminium. Seven gauges (thicknesses) were produced for each type of plate, two of them primarily for small offset work (below 0.17 mm) and five for large offset (above 0.2 mm).
- *The size of the plate* – that is the dimensions of the plate as supplied to the customer. Brechten Algraphy prided itself on accepting orders for any type of web offset machine. This meant that since there were a large number of types of machine in operation (many of them no longer manufactured) the range of plate sizes supplied by Brechten Algraphy could be almost infinite. In 1988 when an order was received for plates to fit a hitherto unheard of machine, the news was considered worthy of inclusion in the company's newsletter and later was also used in the company's promotional literature. However, the Company had customer records of over a thousand 'catalogue' sizes, of which about 800 were supplied every year.
- *The configuration of the perforations* – that is the number and shape of the fixing holes punched into the plate. Again there were an almost infinite range of possible perforation configurations, yet in practice the range demanded was not as wide as the range of plate sizes. Fifteen configurations covered 95 per cent of orders.

COMPETITIVE PRIORITIES

The variety of coatings, gauges, sizes and perforation configurations gave Brechten Algraphy a greater *product range* than any of its competitors. This had helped the company to establish themselves with smaller and medium-sized customers, especially those in the short-run, higher quality, printing business.

In this part of the market *delivery lead time* could also be important, especially in the smaller size plates which serve the small offset market. In fact, since the majority of sales in the small end of the market went through stockholding depots or distributors, speed of delivery was good provided that the plate was in stock.

Although delivery lead times were not unimportant, *delivery dependability* was particularly important for Brechten Algraphy's larger customers. It had been the major weakness in the company's performance over the previous three or four years. Several reasons were advanced by Frank Tuft, Operations Director (Bradford) to explain this:

> *'Everything has conspired against us in the last few years. The biggest problem is that our "dash for growth" policy has meant salespeople giving quick delivery promises. I admit it seems to have worked in terms of volume but it causes continual schedule changes on the lines to cope with changed priorities. Coupled with that, we seem to have been at the limits of capacity for years. Each time a new line is commissioned the backlog is such that it is immediately utilised to the full!'*

Price was becoming important in the low technology end of the market and in large newspaper plates, and hence the development of the electrostatic plate for newspaper production which was an attempt to keep ahead of the low-cost competition.

The *technical specification* of the product was probably the company's biggest advantage. By a process of continual product innovation the company had kept an edge over most of its larger rivals and had certainly kept clear of the smaller low overhead manufacturers.

Product *quality* was again a plus point for Brechten. Their quality record was at least as good as those of their major competitors.

DIRECT LIGHT SENSITIVE PLATES

The next five-year period was likely to see considerable changes in Brechten Algraphy's products and processes. The reason was the company's newly developed DLS (Direct Light Sensitive) plate which would eliminate the 'film' (middle) stage during magazine printing and allow the printing plate to be made directly from copy. The electrostatic plate had done this for newspaper printing but was unsuitable for higher quality work.

The production process for DLS plates was in some ways similar to conventional presensitised plates except that the final coatings were light-sensitive and so had to be applied in a low-intensity red-light environment. After that, all stages from final coating onwards also would have to be performed under similar conditions. This meant that the secondary operations of cutting, perforating and packing would need to be integral with the process line.

Since the market for DLS plates was relatively focused, product range in terms of gauge, plate size and perforation pattern, would be considerably less than the company's conventional production. In fact, it was initially likely that a range of less than 10 plate types would be produced. However, the number of types of coating and gauge combinations would be greater, probably by a factor of three.

Competitive priorities in the marketplace were likely to be rather different for DLS plates. *Price* was unlikely to be a major factor. Given the advantages of this technology to its target market, and given the high margin nature of their business, Brechten Algraphy were convinced that they could command a significant price premium over competitive products.

Product *quality,* however, was likely to be considerably more important. Small variations in the formulation or thickness of the coating medium, or worse still, flaws in the aluminium base sheet, could cause printing errors which could become evident only halfway through a print run. Especially in the early launch period of the DLS products, any quality problems would pose a serious threat to its acceptance by the market.

Similarly, a higher level of *technical support* would be necessary to educate customers as to which type of DLS plate was appropriate to their particular needs. The technical support service would also need to give help with the operational use of DLS plates. Bad practice in use could reduce the effectiveness of the plates considerably.

The customer service required by DLS plate customers was also likely to place more emphasis on *delivery reliability* over delivery speed.

PROCESS TECHNOLOGY FOR THE CURRENT PRODUCT RANGE

The Brechten Algraphy process for producing litho plates was somewhat different from many other manufacturers. Whereas many competitors cut aluminium sheet to size and then processed the individual sheets (either in final sizes or for further cutting), Brechten Algraphy produced coated sheet on a continuous basis, only cutting at the end of the process. The process, in Brechten Algraphy's eyes, gave them a significant cost advantage over their competitors, but did rely on relatively high total volumes, which in recent years they had been achieving. Also their larger competitors had been moving towards more continuous processing technologies over the previous five or six years.

The whole production process was divided into two stages, known within the company as primary and secondary:

1 Primary – receiving aluminium sheet in coils of different widths all with a 1550-mm outside diameter, cleaning and pretreating the material, coating with between two and five layers, straightening the sheet and shearing into 'prime sizes'.
2 Secondary – taking prime-size plate[1] material, cutting into final size, piercing side and end perforations, 'first packing' into envelope packs and final packing into boxes or crates.

Figure 11.1 shows the layout of the total production process at the Bradford plant.

PRIMARY PRODUCTION PROCESSES

Primary production was divided into four sections: feed; clean and pre-treat; coat and oven; and straighten and delivery.

Feed

The feed section collected the required gauge and width of material from the receiving stores, connected it to the pretensing rollers and inspected the material as it fed through to the next section. This last operation had become by far the most important. Sheet quality was critical. At times up to 30 per cent of the rolls had a serious rolling flaw, visible to the naked eye, and some had two or more. The effect of this on the coating process could be serious resulting in a 'flaw tail' or streak of ill-coated material for up to 15 m of sheet.

Clean and pre-treat

After feeding, the material passes through a series of six baths which chemically clean, ultrasonically clean, neutralise and surface treat the aluminium. This process is common to all types of widths and gauges of sheet. Quality problems were few, although the thinner gauges were more difficult to clean than the thicker ones.

Coat and oven

Within this section the aluminium passed through three coat and oven areas, each of which consisted of two coating heads and a drying oven. The majority of plates required three coatings so only one head in each area was used. On some plates, because of the film thicknesses involved, both heads were used. Changing

[1] Rather confusingly, the product was referred to as 'sheet' during primary production and 'plate' during secondary production.

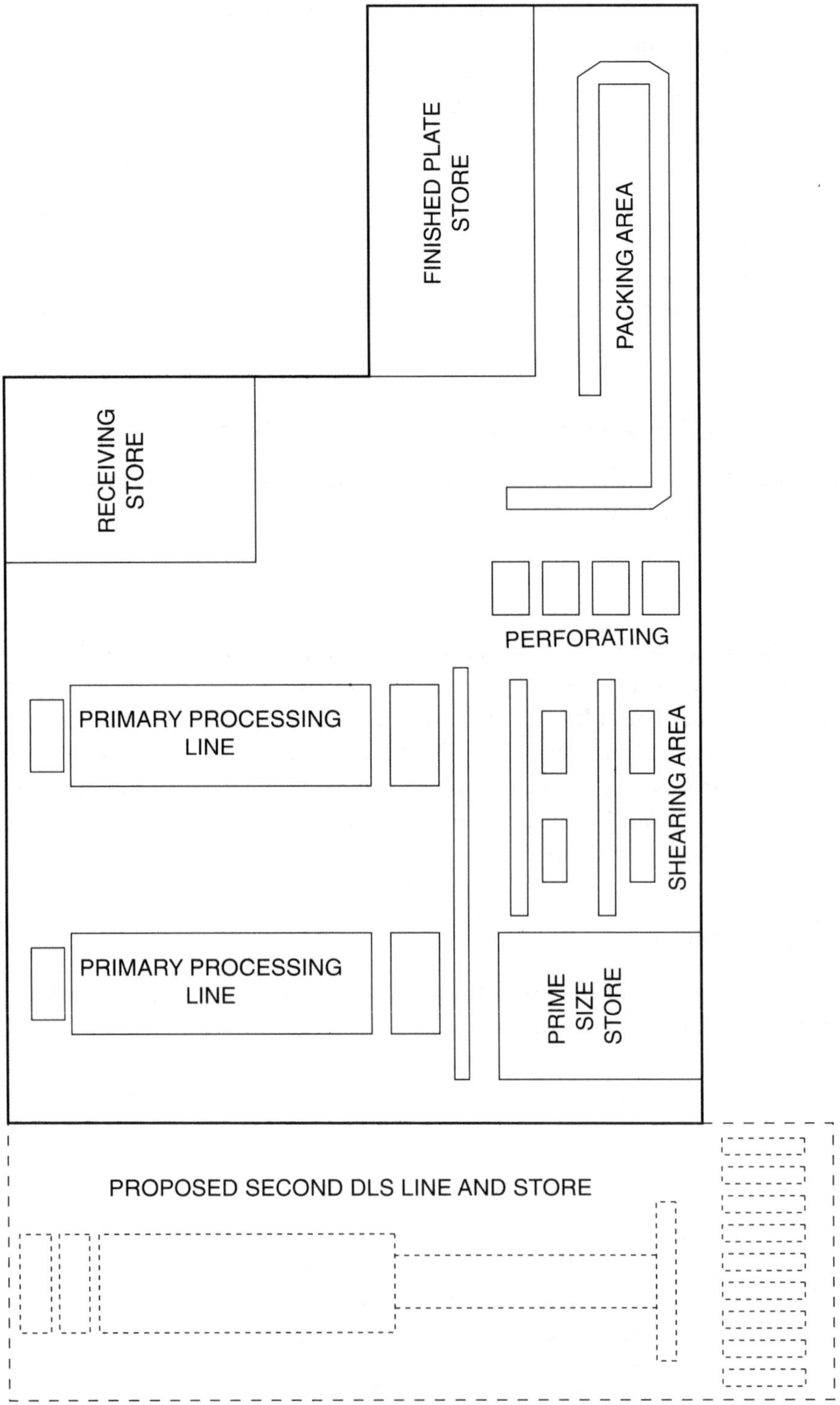

Fig. 11.1 Brechten Algraphy Bradford plant

the coating heads and the system which delivered coating material to the heads was a priority for Brechten Algraphy's plant engineers, and speeding up this part of the operation was seen as the key contributor to shortening product change-over times. It was hoped that a computer-controlled delivery system, together with 'slot-in' heads and tanks which could be pre-set off the line, would reduce change-over time substantially. However, such modifications were likely to prove expensive being estimated at approximately DM 600 000 per line. Nevertheless change-over times had reduced from 60 minutes to 40 minutes already and it was hoped that the slot-in heads could reduce the time even further, possibly down to 20 minutes. This could free some production time. The average number of change-overs per production line per 24 hours was currently 2.7.

Straighten and deliver

The straightening process simply involved passing the aluminium through a series of soft rollers and on to a flat shearing table. A semi-automatic shearing machine then cut the coated aluminium into prime-size sheets. So, once set (a 15-minute job), the shearer could cut to size automatically. The sheets were then transferred to pallets by hand with protective card placed between each sheet. Pallet loads of prime-size sheet were then transported to the secondary production department.

Figure 11.2 shows a schematic of the primary process.

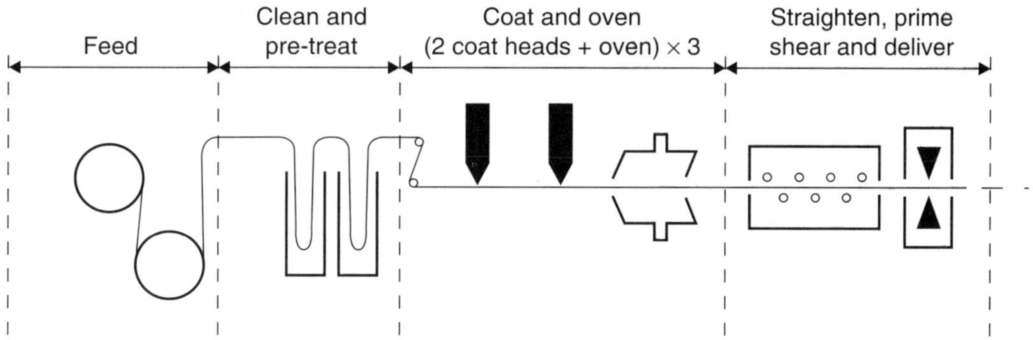

Fig. 11.2 Schematic of current process technology

SECONDARY PRODUCTION PROCESS

Secondary production was located in a combined production and warehouse area at one end of the site. When a prime-size sheet arrived in the department it was first stored in a buffer stock area, after which it passed through four operations: cutting to size, perforation, envelope pack and final pack.

Cutting to size

Four manually operated shearing machines cut the sheets to their final size. The machines could cope with up to five thicknesses of sheet but operators would only cut in fives if batch quantities of a particular size warranted it and the off-cut (that is, smaller) piece was likely to be used for a different size product in the near future. The shearing machines formed two flow lines of two machines each. The first cut to width, the second to length.

Perforate

Up until the 1970s there was little commonality between the perforations required by different printing machines in the European industry, so every machine needed its own configuration of location holes. Though some common configurations had been agreed relatively recently, the number of older machines in service still meant a wide range of styles. The current method of perforating the sheets used five relatively simple presses which could be set up to punch a line of holes through up to 10 sheets at a time. A CNC punching machine had just been ordered by the company for the Cologne plant, which, it was hoped, would replace the existing five machines.

Envelope pack

After perforation, sheets were transported by roller conveyor to packing stations where they were packed by hand into coated card envelopes in fives, tens or twenties.

Final pack

Envelopes were left as they were for 'loose transportation', or packed into card boxes in various quantities. Alternatively they were packed into crates (usually for export or for very large plates). All packing operations were manual.

PRODUCTION CAPACITY

Primary production operated on a five-day, 24-hour basis in both Cologne and Bradford. There were four process lines, two on each site, all of which were capable of handling all types and gauges of plate although the oldest line (in Cologne) was liable to some quality problems after product change-over and was therefore loaded with products needing long runs whenever possible.

Capacity was usually expressed in square metres of sheet coated and was generally reckoned to be about 76 000 square metres per week depending on the mix of products at any time. In fact, actual effective capacity would vary both with the type of sheet being processed (type of coating and coil width affected processing speeds) and production run lengths. Short process runs were unpopular with manufacturing because of the time lost in change-overs. More annoying were the quality problems associated with change-over, as these could lose a further half to three-quarters of an hour at each change-over. A new line in the Cologne plant was due to enter production service in February 1992, and would add a further 20 000 square metres per week of capacity.

The capacity of secondary production at both plants was such that one eight-hour shift and one twilight (half) shift each weekday, plus overtime at weekends, could handle primary's output. No decision had yet been taken as to how secondary production should be organised at Cologne once the third line came on-stream.

PRODUCTION SCHEDULING FOR CURRENT PRODUCTS

The Operations Director at the Bradford site, Frank Tuft, had previously been the Production Controller of an equivalent plant in the United States. His experiences there had led him to hold some very definite ideas about scheduling manufacturing operations in the presensitised plate industry.

'Given the extremely wide product range we manufacture, there are considerable benefits in making to order, or at the very least cutting, perforating and packing to order. But this is difficult when we are severely capacity-constrained at times of high demand. When we make-to-stock we are taking too high a risk as well as tieing up working capital. The new line should help us move to a largely make-to-order position.'

The balance between make-to-order production and make-to-stock production was currently about 60 per cent to 40 per cent; though some production classified by the company as make-to-order work was both predictable and regular. The UK's *Daily Telegraph* plates, for example, were a unique size but consistent orders were placed by the newspaper well in advance of delivery. Production runs at both plants were planned by manufacturing control based in Bradford about three weeks in advance, working from sales figures from each country's sales team. The production batches programmed were a mixture of regular stock requirements and specific customer orders.

Total business was seasonal to some extent but reasonably predictable, demand being heavier in the second and fourth quarters. Table 11.1 gives 1991 aggregated demand and 1992 forecasts. The closer the company found itself to capacity limits, the more it needed to rely on stocking (where possible) and backlogs to meet demand. When the new line came on stream the effect of seasonality would be more marked on production volumes.

Table 11.1 Aggregate production volume forecasts, 1992

			Average weekly volume requirements (metres^2)
Actual	1991	Jan	53 171
		Feb	63 537
		Mar	85 502
		Apr	89 010
		May	78 990
		Jun	80 211
		Jul	32 888*
		Aug	72 090
		Sep	76 132
		Oct	79 391
		Nov	80 042
		Dec	69 845
Forecast	1992	Jan	55 000
		Feb	70 500
		Mar	87 000
		Apr	90 000
		May	80 000
		Jun	85 000
		Jul	86 000
		Aug	43 000*
		Sep	86 000
		Oct	86 000
		Nov	86 000
		Dec	86 000

*Plant shut-down.

Customer orders came either directly to Cologne, in the case of larger customers, or more usually to one of the company's sales depots. All European countries and most major non-European countries had a Brechten Algraphy sales office, and usually a stockholding depot. When possible, for all but very large orders, customers were supplied directly from the depots. This allowed speedy delivery which was important, especially for smaller customers. Many depots were also investing in secondary shearing and perforating equipment. This allowed them to cut down large-size plates into smaller ones if they were out of stock of the smaller sizes. Some depots were even ordering some 'prime-size' plates directly from the factories with the deliberate policy of secondary processing them themselves to supply the less common plate types and sizes.

DLS PLATE PROCESS TECHNOLOGY

The primary end of DLS plate process technology was broadly similar to the company's current processing technology. Feed tensions needed to be very carefully controlled and some of the line's control engineering was more complex, but apart from that the only significant difference between current and DLS primary processing was that DLS coating required three coating heads in each of the three coating zones. These were required because of the more complex (and less predictable) coating characteristics of DLS products. The main difference between current and DLS processing was the integration of secondary processing (cutting, perforating and packing) with primary processing (coating). This was convenient because of the need to conduct all processing stages, from first coating operations through to envelope pack, in a low-intensity light environment. Figure 11.3 shows the schematic for the DLS line.

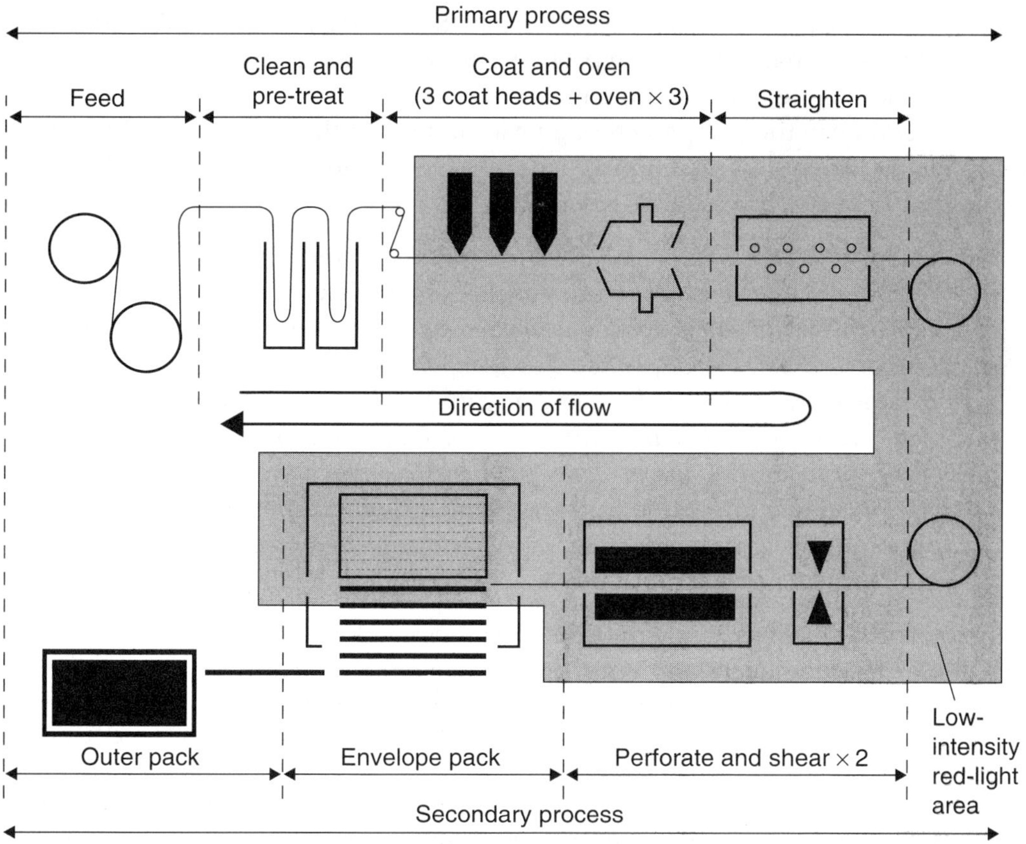

Fig. 11.3 Schematic of new DLS process technology

The technical unit in Cologne which had developed the DLS technology was delighted that initial trials on the pilot rigs were proving successful. They were convinced that their competitors would need at least three years to reach the level of expertise in this technology that Brechten had already mastered. Thorsen Lohr, Chief Engineer:

'The DLS production process is both complex and sensitive to small variations in the process parameters. At the same time it serves a market which is exceptionally quality conscious. It will be difficult for any other company to achieve the levels of consistent quality which we should be able to produce.'

While coating and gauge change-overs would be at least as much of a problem for the DLS line as they were in the current technology, changing the size and perforation configuration at the secondary end of the process had been speeded up considerably. Whereas on the current lines a size and perforation change-over could take anything from 10–20 minutes, on the DLS line it could be done in less than two minutes. The company's engineers felt that this could be a considerable advantage in keeping the primary end of the process running at a reasonably constant speed, which would help to avoid coating inconsistencies.

Not everyone in the company though was quite so enthusiastic about the way the DLS line had been designed. Frank Tuft, the Operations Director at the Bradford Plant, had already expressed his reservations:

'I am happy to admit that it looks like a fine piece of engineering, but it could be a real problem to operate. Integrating primary and secondary processes when the new primary operations are so little understood is taking too big a risk. Any problems at the primary end will halt the whole process, while any hold-ups at the secondary end will immediately slow the line down and probably cause quality problems at the primary end. I think that until we are sure that the process is well under control we should explore the possibilities of separating the primary from the secondary processes. We could prime shear the plates into their initial sizes and store them in lightproof containers until we need them for secondary processing. It would decouple the process and make us a lot more flexible and a lot less vulnerable.'

Frank Tuft's views were known and understood in Cologne. However, the consensus of the German engineers and operations managers was firmly against him. They were sure that only by keeping ahead in process technology could they maintain their lead in the market. Thorsen Lohr again:

'There is nothing exceptionally new about the basic principle of DLS plates. Most of our competitors will follow us down the same product technology path. Where we can differentiate ourselves is by developing the ability to make DLS plates of high quality in large volume, and at a lower cost than anyone else. To do this we must overcome the problems of process integration.'

The first DLS line had already been designed and planned for Cologne. Capital approval for the project had been given in November 1991 with the intention of starting work early in 1992 on a building large enough to accommodate up to two lines, together with the first line itself. The second DLS line was to be constructed at Bradford. The first line would take just under a year to reach its preproduction run state. The construction lead time for the line alone would be about six months.

The operating capacity of the DLS line was not easy to predict, but was thought to be between 17 000 square metres and 22 000 square metres per week, on a five-day24-hour basis. Similarly, demand forecasts were rather uncertain but were likely to be in the region of 20 000 square metres per week by the end of the first year of sales. Sales after that were extremely uncertain but optimistic estimates put growth at around 20 000 square metres per week each year for two or three years. Some of this growth would be substitution for existing Brechten Algraphy products and this might slow down or even reduce sales of conventional plates. The company was convinced, however, that total sales would grow rapidly after the DLS product was introduced. Further, the company's development engineers were exploring ways of converting existing lines to the DLS process should this prove necessary.

PRODUCTION SCHEDULING FOR DLS PRODUCTS

Because the first DLS manufacture would be in Cologne, it had been decided also to schedule DLS production there. Initially at least, it was uncertain how demand for the various DLS products would shape up. It was likely, however, that DLS customers would place orders in a slightly different manner to Brechten's customers for its current product range. There would almost certainly be fewer but larger customers placing fewer but larger orders. Since each customer would probably have one type of printing machine but a wide variety of types of job, they were likely to order one size of plate but in several coating types. Most important, the aggregate level of demand would be far less predictable than for the current product range.

THE FUTURE

Ulrich Mayer was clear that the company faced what he called an 'interesting' period:

> *'The challenge of DLS processing is probably the most important technical project that we have embarked on for years. If we get it right we could secure our future for the next decade by moving quickly down the learning curve. If we don't then the rest of the industry will regard us as the victims of our own technical over-ambition.'*

Questions

1. What were the main characteristics of the market for Brechten Algraphy's current range of products in 1991?
2. How is the market for DLS plates likely to differ from that for the current products?
3. What are the implications for the company's manufacturing operation of any changes in the company's competitive stance brought about by the introduction of the DLS range of products?
4. What level of flexibility should Brechten Algraphy be developing in their operation?
5. Is Frank Tuft right to argue for the separation of primary and secondary processing stages in the new DLS technology?

CASE 12

Beaver Engineering Group

Robert Johnston

Case date 1986

INTRODUCTION

Beaver Engineering Group plc, founded in 1951, is based in Norwich in a purpose-built headquarters and factory. Beaver makes a family of high-technology, high-performance machine tools, in particular CNC machining centres. (Appendix 12.1 provides a brief explanation of CNC machines.) Each machine is purpose built and made to customer's order. Beaver supplies machines throughout the EU and to many countries around the world.

In 1986 the company, faced with an expanding and yet highly competitive market, was evaluating its products, computer systems and production control systems. By 1992, as a result of the developments in its systems and the continuing design and development of its products, Beaver had emerged as one of the world leaders in the field.

BEAVER IN 1986

In 1986 Beaver had approximately 250 employees, about 80 of whom had been engaged over the previous 18 months. Figure 12.1 shows the company's organisational chart. In 1985 the company's turnover had been £7 million and was expected to be £8 million for 1986. A turnover of £11 million was forecast for 1987.

Its product range consisted of 10 basic machines. All machines, however, were made to order and so every machine was different, as each customer required special features, for example special tool changers or handling devices. Figure 12.2 depicts the basic V5 CNC milling machine.

The basic product range was under constant review. The whole range had completely changed in the previous three years. Also, modifications to components (of which there were about 2000 per machine) changed at the rate of six per day.

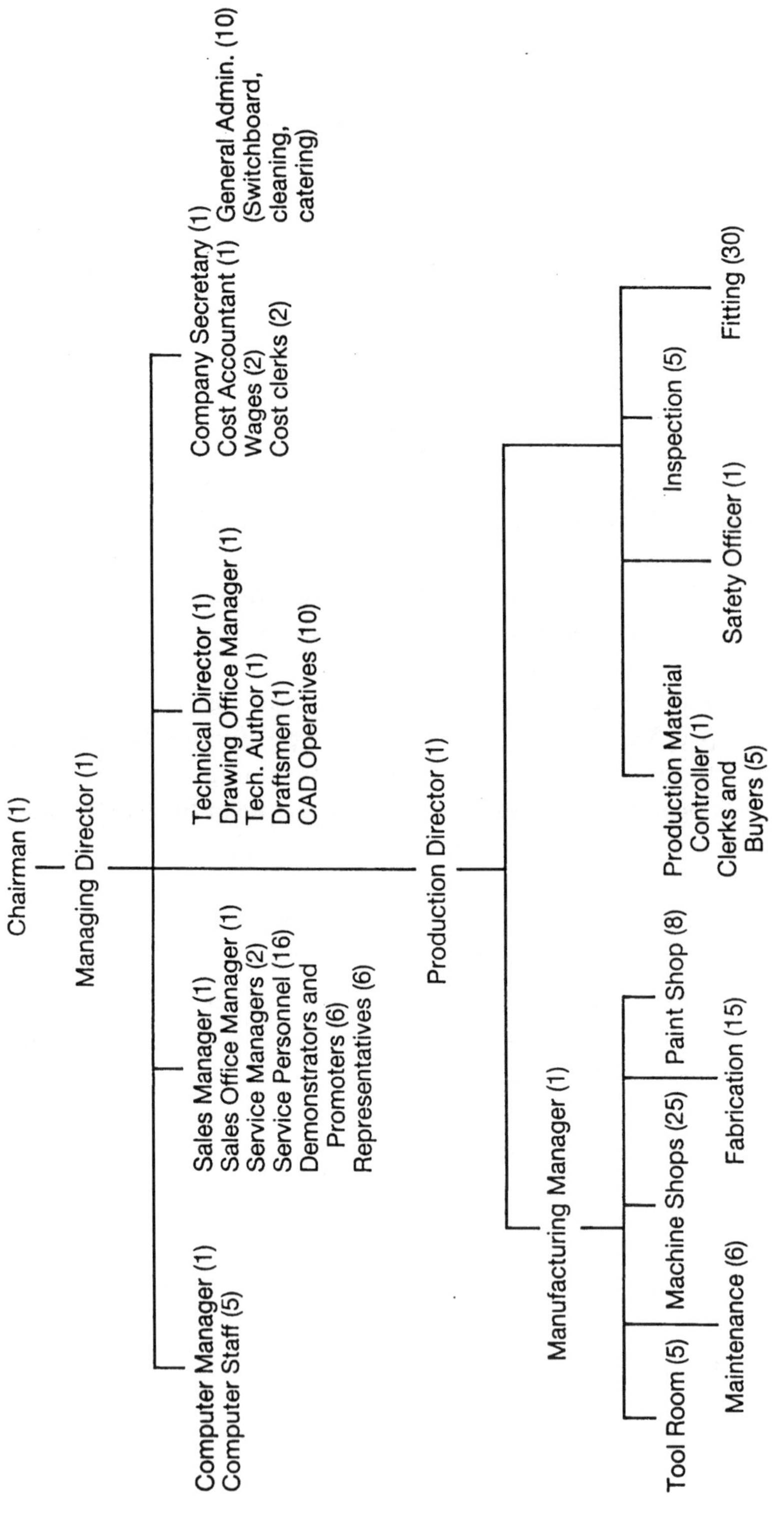

Fig. 12.1 Beaver Engineering organisation chart

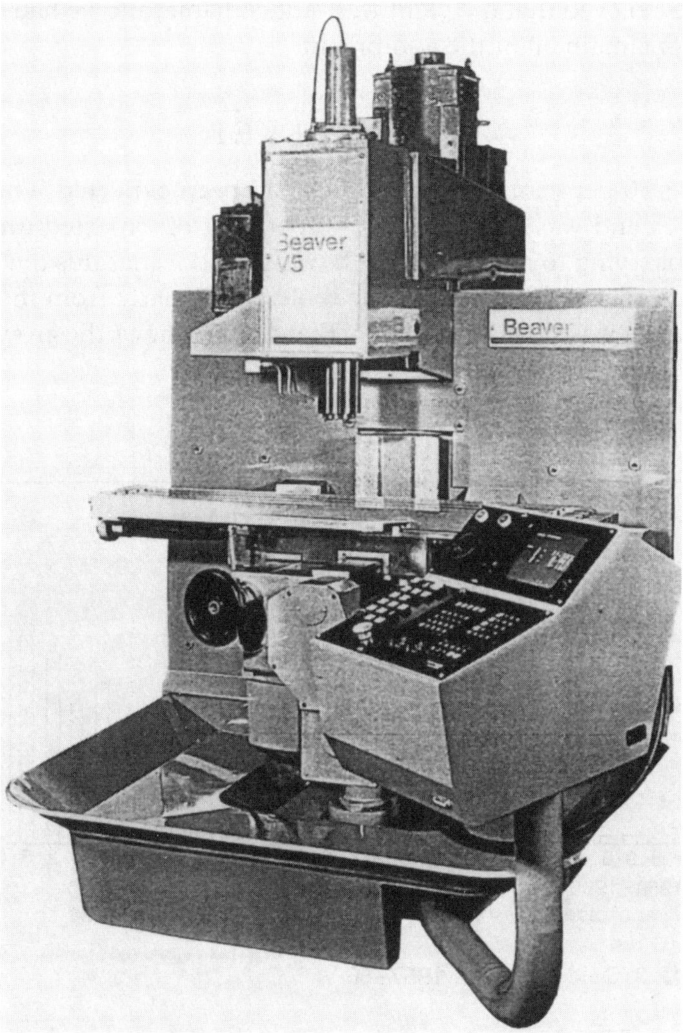

Fig. 12.2 V5 CNC milling machine

THE MANUFACTURING PROCESS

The manufacturing of each CNC machine took between 20 and 30 weeks. Final assembly of machines was a jobbing operation, though components were made in batches. The batch size was set at two months' supply to try to achieve a stock turn of 6:1 (though the actual stock turn was about 3:1). Joe Booth, the Production Director, said that his intention was to improve stock turn by reducing the batch sizes.

The Manufacturing Department used a number of NC machines (*see* Appendix 12.1) and many cheap, second-hand machines that had been dedicated to one operation. Joe believed that the plant was quite reliable, and he had the skills on site to mend and maintain all of the equipment.

THE MARKET

In 1985 about 10 per cent of the products had been exported. This was a rapidly expanding area and was being held at 40 per cent of expected turnover in 1986. The reason for trying to hold the growth was the poor margins that were the result of the intense competition for machine tools, particularly from the United States. The home market was slowly increasing. Figure 12.3 shows the growth in sales from 1957 to 1985 and the forecast sales for 1986.

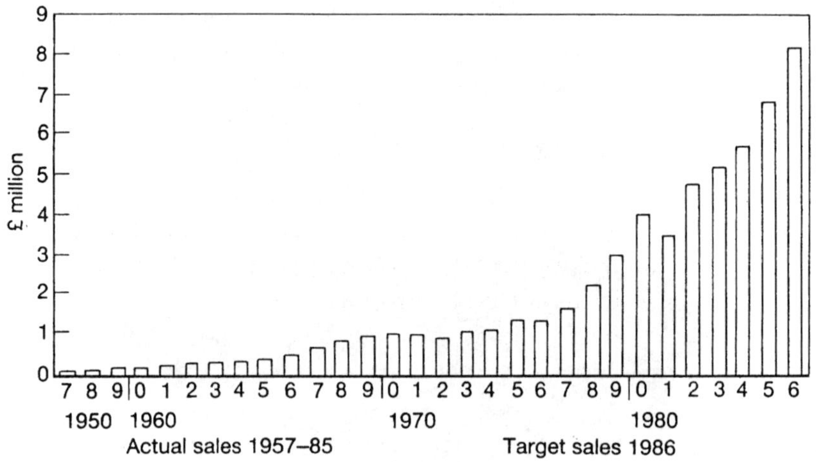

Fig. 12.3 Sales growth, 1957–86

Beaver tried to develop long-term relationships with customers as servicing and spares were required. As the company specialised in providing excellent after-sales servicing on all their products, customer loyalty was high. About a quarter of all its sales were repeat business.

Market lead times were typically 12 weeks, but salesmen often quoted as low as four to get a sale. Forecasting of average build rates of the basic types was essential, though it was difficult, if not impossible, to forecast the special options that each customer would require. The size of this problem was illustrated by the fact that they would normally expect to have about 20 machines being assembled. In fact, there were often about 50 machines part-finished, most of which were awaiting parts.

The company had about 500 'live' customers. Most were customers whose machines were being serviced. About 50 were being invoiced for new machines. Two hundred machines had been built in 1985. These had been delivered to about

150 different customers. Two hundred and thirty machines were expected to be built in 1986.

The company believed that its order-winning criteria were the ability to produce machines to customer specification and after-sales service. As the specifications were constantly being improved, customers often got a better (i.e. upgraded) machine than they contracted for because of modifications that may have been implemented between the order being taken and the completion of the machine. Beaver also claimed that its servicing was second to none. Price and delivery were qualifying criteria. Though Beaver's delivery schedule was several weeks behind, this, Joe claimed, was typical for the industry as a whole.

SUPPLIERS

Beaver had about 150 suppliers. All items were single-sourced and the company's relationships with suppliers were good. High usage-value item suppliers were chosen by price, delivery reliability, nearness to Norwich and willingness to work JIT (by which was meant suppliers should hold enough stocks to provide a two-week delivery of all items and be willing to deliver small quantities). As customers specified certain types of equipment that must be in the machine, Beaver often had to investigate where particular special items could be purchased. Lower usage-value items were sourced locally if possible. Suppliers were chosen on price and the availability of large quantities of these items. Overall, suppliers seemed to be very willing and reliable. Joe Booth stated that he did not hesitate to re-source if there were reliability or quality problems.

LABOUR

The machine operatives were relatively flexible but limited to one type of machine. NC machine operators, for example, would stay with NC machines but would operate several such machines.

There were three shop-floor grades, though there was little difference in pay between them. A group bonus scheme was in operation. There was no shortage of overtime available and there were no specific skill shortages.

OPERATING PRESSURES

Cash flow was a major problem for Beaver because of the amount of semi-finished products tied up in final assembly. The company believed that the major factor limiting profitability was the constant changes of specification, which had repercussions in production planning, stores and ordering. A second factor was the cost of poor quality. The main quality problems concerned the quality of the bought-in castings and the problems caused by the accumulation of tolerance errors in the complete and complex assembly. Joe Booth also felt that the methods employed by the company needed reviewing.

There was considerable pressure to deliver the machines on time, so machines were often put into the build programme in anticipation of customer demand in order to try to reduce the actual lead time experienced by the customer.

MANAGEMENT STYLE

The decision making in the company was totally centralised and was dominated by the two active owners, Victor Balding and his son Tony. Victor Balding was the entrepreneur who had started the company and masterminded the investment, while Tony – the modern manager with a flair for marketing, design and production – spearheaded the product growth. The directors and managers held few formal meetings. The non-owner directors, for example the Production Director, had little authority and only limited powers of influence. However, the owners had created an entrepreneurial spirit which drove the company and motivated management.

Few managers had any qualifications. Despite the fact that most managers were relatively young, the emphasis in recruitment was on experience.

COMPUTER-AIDED PRODUCTION MANAGEMENT SYSTEMS (CAPM)

Beaver set up a computer department in about 1980. The networked microcomputers which formed the basis of the CAPM system were bought then. Their link to production planning and control is summarised in Fig. 12.4. The company's investment in computing since 1980 had been predominantly in programming effort. All the CAPM systems had been developed in-house. This had provided Beaver with the flexibility that management felt was necessary. They admitted that they had made many mistakes in developing the programs but maintained that this had helped them understand their needs better and thus develop more appropriate packages.

The company had considered using packaged software but none, except the accounting software, had met their requirements. The company's computer-aided design (CAD) system and accounting systems were kept separate from the CAPM system. The company had a policy of trying to integrate computer activities for different functions, primarily to reduce duplication of input, for example cost data sent to the cost department from the CAPM was re-input to the costing programs. This integration was expected to be difficult to achieve because there were no means of co-ordinating the requirements of the different departments and flexibility was seen as essential by production control.

Inventory control had been the initiating factor in the development of CAPM and it was still the central part of the database. The base of the CAPM system was

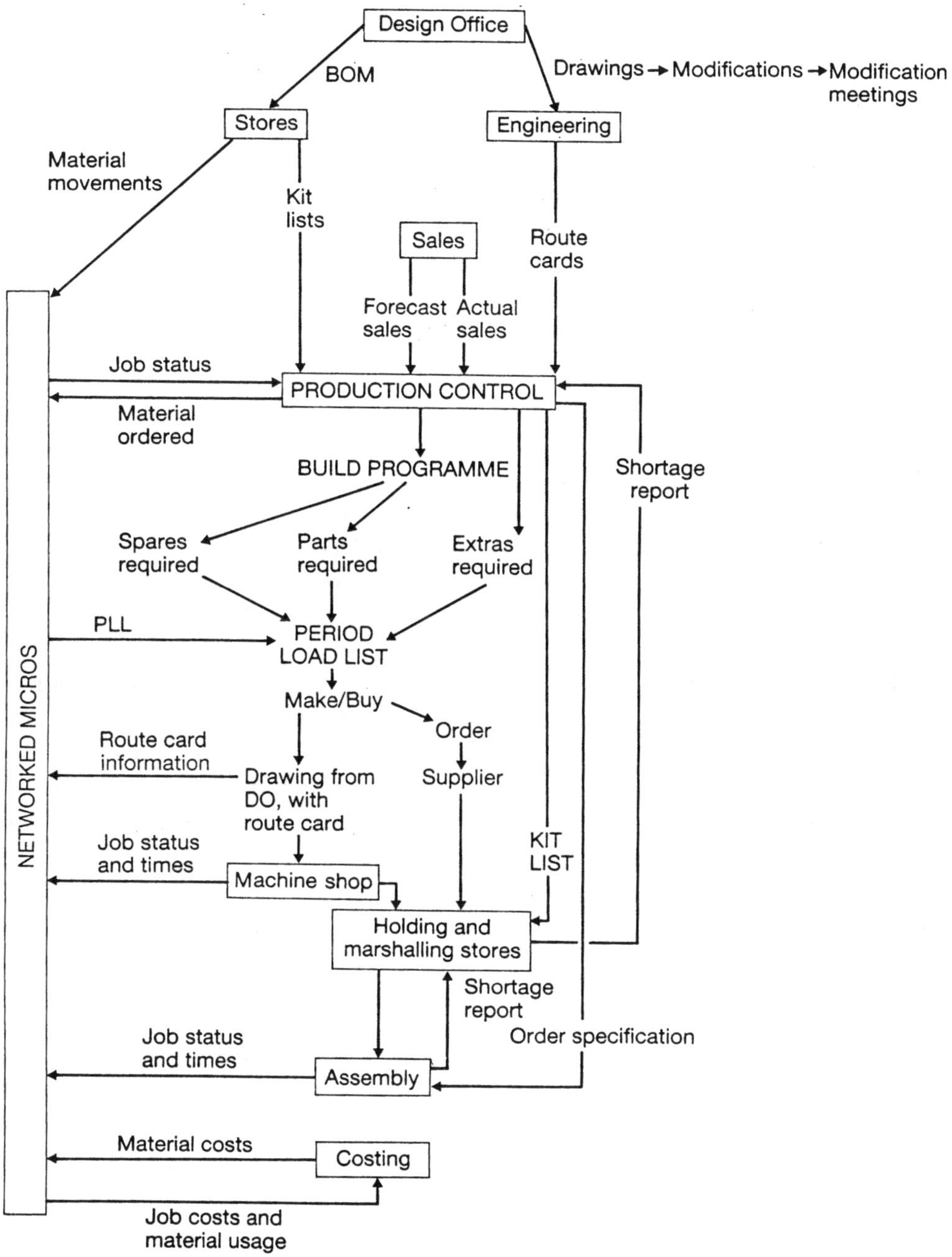

Fig. 12.4 Summary of computer-aided production management

a stock record. This had been developed into a material requirements planning-type system with shop-floor data collection. This did not work well as it was difficult to forecast the parts required in the final product until very late in the build programme. Also, although the use of micros had met with little resistance on the shop-floor, the input error rate was high – about 30 per cent – and there was a problem in motivating workers to input any data that was not linked to the payment system.

The CAPM system had real-time input and mainly overnight batch working to create the output. It was hoped to develop the system to allow real-time enquiries. In 1986 the Production Controller did not have direct access to a networked micro.

PRODUCTION CONTROL AND CAPM

The Production Controller estimated the demand for the basic product for a period of time and tried to guess what options might be required. This formed the Build Programme (*see* Fig. 12.4). This was translated into parts required, along with the extras required from knowledge of actual sales and a guess at spares consumption. This was compared to the computer-produced Period Load List (PLL). The PLL provided information on all parts: cost, current stock, orders and average build figures. All this information was inputted by Production Control. Stock figures were updated by Stores; raw material by Holding and Marshalling Stores (Marshalling Stores put together kits for assembly). By bringing together the Build Programme, the PLL and the stock figures, the Production Controller was able to identify what material was required and what was not available. Production Control decided whether to make or buy, and either sent off an order to suppliers and updated the micro or instructed the machine shop with a drawing and a route card (a card with information on the sequence and timing of activities to be performed [*see* Appendix 12.2]). The route card information was fed into the micro and the operator in the machine shop reported the completion of each stage to the computer. This gave information on job status to Production Control so that the Production Controller could load machines, allocate and reallocate priorities, and find and expedite parts – all of which was manual.

The Design Office provided the drawings for components and a bill of materials (BOM) for sub-assemblies and products. Stores would take these and amend them in conjunction with the fitters in order to create a kit list, which was the BOM rewritten in assembly sequence, noting commonalities with other machines, so that the Production Controller could amalgamate (manually) common components (in conjunction with his feeling of the probability of their being required).

The Marshalling Stores assembled the kits to the kit lists and released them to Assembly when Assembly had no more work that they were able to complete (not necessarily when the kit was complete).

Along with the kit went the actual customer order and a specification sheet – showing all the options and the due date. If an order had not been received by this time, an artificial order was created. Job status and time was recorded and fed to the microcomputer to provide cost and wage information and material usage information. The Assembly Superintendent was informed of all shortages as they occurred. He checked with Stores to see if such items were available or could be made available from kits in the pipeline. Stores then reported the shortage to the Production Controller, who checked with the PLL, decided on make/buy, expedite or the reassignment of priorities.

From the drawings from the Design Office, Engineering created the route cards, which were physically held by Production Control until that part was required.

The Production Control system was virtually isolated from the rest of the organisation. The only links were with Finance (the provision of job costing and payment information) and with the Drawing Office, who provided the Production Controller with drawings and route cards. Occasional meetings to discuss modifications were held and involved the Production Controller, the Manufacturing Manager, the design staff and engineers.

Only very recently had copies of the Build Programme been sent to Sales, so that they had some idea of the capacity of the operation and the actual lead times.

This system, although it contained many sub-systems as detailed in Fig. 12.4, was not part of a larger management information system and, indeed, provided no corporate information. If the Production Director or the owners wanted to know how well the production system was working, they would go to the Assembly Operation and count the number of part-built machines – often about 50, as compared with an operating capacity of 20 (there were about 30 near-finished machines all awaiting parts).

There were no other reports produced by the computer. All the reports that existed simply aggregated and collated production information, which Production Control used to plan their activities rather than to control events. The only real control as such was by the Costing Department, who were able (with the use of the information from the micro) to compare actual product costs with estimates, so they could better judge (90 per cent accurate) which products would provide a profit and what the margin would be.

THE FUTURE

Joe Booth explained his concerns and plans for the future:

'We are reappraising the CAPM system. To keep on top, it requires more inputting than ever before, as I try to move towards a batch size of one. Too much time is being spent just feeding the computer. We are already top heavy with indirect labour, so we must either move towards automatic input and/or removal of duplication and more integration of systems. Originally (and naively), we thought that everything would be automatic and all the files would talk to each other. There are too many manual interfaces actually having to do this.

'The largest benefit of this integration will be the benefit of a better costing system. We will be able to assess whether to take certain orders or not – or at least what the consequences will be. There will also be less production firefighting. Stocks need to decrease and we must be able to control our schedules better. However, I am concerned that the integration of the systems and better management information will not necessarily help us get our products out on time.'

Questions

1 How does Beaver compete?

2 What are the main steps in the manufacture of the company's products?

3 What do you think are the problems that are facing the Production Director?

4 What steps would you advise him to take to overcome them?

APPENDIX 12.1
ADVANCED MANUFACTURING TECHNOLOGY (AMT)

AMT is the umbrella term for the application of advanced technology (computer power) to manufacturing. Such technology has been applied in many different ways to improve, for example, machine speeds, machine control, decision making, process flexibility and design process.

Computer-aided design/computer-aided manufacture (CAD/CAM)
The use of computer graphics led to the development of computer-aided design initially for producing two-dimensional drawings and, later, three-dimensional drawings. The link between computer-aided design and computer-aided manufacture was the link between the design computer and the CNC computer. This meant it was possible to design a component on computer and use this design to program the machine directly.

Numerically controlled machinery (NC machines)
NC machines have been in existence since the end of the nineteenth century when punch cards were used to control the activities of a machine, removing some of the need for skilled operators. The punch cards, or more recently paper or magnetic tapes, carry a set of coded instructions which tell the machine the sequence of steps to be followed.

Computerised numerical control machines (CNC)
A CNC machine is linked directly to a computer where the instructions are not only stored but are also created. This direct link removes the need for tapes and cards, and makes changes to the instructions easier and quicker. As a result, change-over times are speedy and process reliability is improved.

Flexible manufacturing systems (FMS)
An FMS is a collection of computerised numerical control machines (CNCs) brought together to carry out sequential manufacturing stages controlled by a single computer. This integration allows a series of processes that are not usually carried out on the same machine to be controlled together. This increases the potential design complexity of the component or product and increases the range of products that can pass through the sub-system. The FMS comprises several general-purpose CNC machines, usually arranged in a 'cell', interfaced with automatic materials handling equipment which provides raw castings or semi-finished parts from an input buffer for machining, loads and unloads the machine tool, and transports the finished piece to an output buffer for eventual removal to its destination. The scheduling of the different parts through the system, and the operations performed on them, is controlled and sequenced by computer.

APPENDIX 12.2

Part No. BW 0180/0071-00/4	Description ROTARY ACTUATOR MOUNTINGPLATE	Batch 10	Shop No 855851	Reqd By 605	Sheet of
Used on NC15	Customer	Customer Order No.			Batch Qty. Issued
Date 18.7.84	Planning No.	Material Spec. GCQ BRIGHT (6) 160mm x 20mm x 160mm long blt.	Mod. No.		Date

Op. No.	M/C	Operation Description 9104/1160 - 20 ML	Tooling	Set up Mins	Time each Mins	Clock No.	INSPECTION Qty	INSPECTION Sign.
1	STST	Saw off to 158mm long.						
1	YANG	Load to specially M/C 3 jaw chuck to hold square section. Face.		120	7½			
		Rough & finish turn 139.968 dia.						
		139.961						
		Rough & finish bore 45.025 / 45.000. Chamfer O/D						
2	YANG	Reverse in chuck, face to 17mm width.		60	8			
3	VC15	Mitre 4 corners 5mm x 45°. Drill 4 holes 12mm dia. thro',		90	9½			
		counter bored 18 dia. x 7mm deep. Drill2 holes 11.5mm thro'.						
		Drill 4 holes 12,00mm thro(. Drill 2 holes 7.5mm thro'.						
4	SD	Drill & tap 4 holes M6 x 1.0P thro'.		45	2½			
5	HSG	Grind datum face 'X' from 1.39 face to obtain parallelism		30	15			
		tolerance if required.						
6	DB	Deburr complete.		15	1½			
7	STORES	Send out to be chemi blacked.						
8	ETCH	ELECTO MARK part number.		15	56/100 NT			

CASE 13

Royal Automobile Club

Tang Kam Hung and Stuart Chambers

*Case date 1992**

INTRODUCTION

Breaking down in the middle of nowhere or on a motorway can be inconvenient and expensive. Some 14 million motorists in the UK are prepared to pay for the reassurance that someone will come to their aid if their cars let them down. Nearly 60 per cent of motorists subscribe to breakdown services. Of those, 12 million out of 14 million are members of the Automobile Association (AA) or Royal Automobile Club (RAC). In 1990, the RAC had around 5 million subscribers, a market share of about 36 per cent.

HISTORY

The RAC is a mutual trading organisation without shareholders, any trading surpluses being ploughed back into the business to improve the quality of services for members. It was founded in 1897 and was the brain-child of a group of enthusiasts, led by Frederick R. Simms, who declared themselves to be a 'society for the protection, encouragement and development of automobilism'. In those early days, it was known as the Automobile Club of Great Britain and Ireland, which became the Royal Automobile Club in 1907 when King Edward VII extended his patronage to the organisation.

The RAC's road patrols and rescue services evolved from its origin as a countrywide network of 'specially qualified gentlemen of refinement' appointed as guides to local beauty spots in the early 1900s. A more lasting impact was made in 1912, when the touring guide service was greatly expanded to keep pace with the demands of the growing number of motorists. The new guides, mostly ex-servicemen, were in cities, large towns and major ports as well as at busy road junctions. They were on duty from 9.30 a.m. until lighting-up time. They were required to give assistance to any motorist, and to salute every private car.

During the General Strike of 1926, the guides took over traffic duties from the police in London and helped distribute the government's official newspaper. In the

*Some of the data, names and situations have been modified or disguised to suit the teaching purpose.

Second World War, patrolmen of the Club who were not called up helped guide convoys along the blacked-out roads and streets.

Services of the RAC further developed after the Second World War. In 1957, radio-equipped road service vehicles were introduced and the 'Get You Home' service was extended to cover nights. Other developments during the 1950s and 1960s included mobile offices, the Travel Service and registered motor schools.

In 1978, Sidney Lesser was appointed Chief Executive Officer to streamline and relaunch the RAC – the beginnings of the organisation as it is today. The RAC Motoring Services began to extend and grow. By 1982 there were 2.4 million associate members. The uniformed patrol staff were operating a fleet of 1000 vehicles from 17 area offices. Radio communication was provided from 80 stations. Since then, the RAC has continued to expand its services and today it is the UK's second largest motoring organisation.

THE RAC'S APPROACH AND ITS PROMISES TO CUSTOMERS

The following quotations from reports and accounts reflect the RAC's general approach to the delivery of the services.

> *As we embark on the new decade, indeed the decade in which the RAC will reach its own centenary in 1997, it is clear that the goals and values which motivated our founders in the 1890s remain of fundamental importance today.*
>
> *Our aim is to ensure that, in all aspects of our organisation, from the facilities in the clubhouse through roadside rescue . . . the service which we give to our members and to motoring in general is of the finest, not only in Britain but in Europe.*
>
> *To provide quality of service of this order requires the highest levels of care and sensitivity towards the people who are our customers.*
>
> *The service we provide will be of outstanding excellence and the RAC name on any product or service will be seen as a hallmark of quality, dependability, safety and value for money.*

'*Service beyond the call of duty*', was the rallying request from Chairman Jeffrey Rose in 1990. '*The primary aim of the RAC's service is to "get the member back on the road as quickly as possible when they have a breakdown". The motto of the RAC is "Go not tow!"*' remarked Martin Conner, the Planning and Operational Support Manager.

The story featured in the *Employee Annual Review* (1990) about Rescue Services Manager, Jim Dixon, reflected the service attitude of the staff of the RAC. Even though he was dragged out of bed at 2 a.m., Jim had pulled out all the stops in response to an SOS from stranded motorists. He took a spare part from his own car to put two holiday-makers back on the road after a quick-thinking patrol gave him an alarm call.

In 1991, the RAC accorded the following as top priorities for its rescue services:

- To reach 83 per cent of all incidents within one hour and 99 per cent within two hours.

- To recover members within two hours of initial contact on 80 per cent of occasions (to recover a member is to enable the member to continue their journey, either by repairing the car successfully or providing the tow service or 'recovery').
- To increase customer satisfaction and to move the Customer Satisfaction Index (CSI) from 85 to 88.
- To answer 80 per cent of all telephone calls within 10 seconds.
- To process enrolments, renewals, refunds, correspondence and complaints within 24 hours.

The services provided to the customer vary according to different schemes subscribed to by members. Its major service schemes include Rescue, Recovery and Reflex:

1 *Rescue service.* 'Your call to our free number will bring a patrol or RAC agent quickly to your side and get you back on the road without delay. If it's a serious problem, we'll give you a free tow to the nearest RAC-approved garage . . . If the vehicle cannot be repaired within a reasonable time, the RAC will make a contribution towards the cost of a taxi journey up to a maximum round trip of twenty miles.'
2 *Recovery service.* 'Subscribe to our recovery service and you're sure to get to your destination. We promise "one smooth journey". It provides transportation of a vehicle, the motorist and up to four passengers to a destination of the motorist's choice in the event of a breakdown or accident. The service operates throughout the United Kingdom.'
3 *Reflex service.* 'We'll keep you moving,' is the Reflex promise, 'no matter what happens, we'll organise everything you need to get you to your destination as swiftly as possible.' A Personal Incident Manager is assigned to advise members individually in the event of a breakdown.

There are other service schemes which are tailored for specific owners. These include the Sprint, which is a service specifically designed for motorcyclists. Demonstrating its concern for the special needs of vulnerable motorists, a Response scheme, tailored to the requirements of the country's 1 million disabled orange badge holders, was launched in 1990.

THE OPERATIONS STRUCTURE

The breakdown services are handled through a network which divides the country into six separate operating regions, including Bristol, Walsall, London, Stockport, Glasgow and Belfast, and in total comprises 18 areas. Each region is centred on a Control Centre which houses the region's computers, radio system and controller equipment. Each Control Centre has several Command Centres linked to it.

Each Command Centre covers services in several zones and a fixed number of patrols is assigned to each of the zones; these patrols are expected to deal with all the rescue calls in that particular zone. The zones are subdivided into cells which roughly follow the postal code areas. Each cell is allocated one or two patrols, depending on the workload of that particular cell. For example, the cells covering the city centre of Birmingham are assigned two patrols, whereas remote rural areas will have only one. Patrols move between cells if so required, but always within the assigned zone.

The Control Centres receive customers' calls, take down the relevant information and act as information relay and activity co-ordination centres. The information received in the telephone call is inputted to the computer which automatically relays it to the appropriate Command Centre, depending on the location of the breakdown. The Command Centre then allocates work for the patrols and communicates with them. Command Centres have the discretion to use subcontractors (agents) for dealing with breakdowns which happen at night or if demand is very high, overloading the RAC's resources. The Command Centres are also responsible for scheduling day-to-day operations.

THE CUSTOMERS' EXPERIENCE

Breakdowns

If members' cars fail on a motorway, members can get through to the police by using the telephones installed every mile, and the police will contact the RAC. Elsewhere, members can telephone the RAC directly using the RAC's freefone telephone number.

In 1987, a *Which?* survey (July 1987, pp. 306–9) revealed that on average a motorist needs help of some kind once every 8.5 months. This was similar for those who did and did not belong to breakdown schemes. For the RAC, there are a small number of members (less than 1 per cent in 1990) with a very high level of recorded breakdowns. Since January 1989, the RAC has introduced an excessive user policy whereby a 100 per cent surcharge is imposed on the membership subscription for members who have used the service more than eight times in the previous year.

Waiting

The 1987 *Which?* survey also revealed that the RAC did better than the AA in the sense that about 69 per cent of RAC members received service within one hour (63 per cent for AA) and only 1.6 per cent waited over three hours (2.1 per cent for AA). However, it was a much smaller rescue business (with about 150 000 members) which was found to have the best performance, with a record of 85 per cent of the breakdown callers having a waiting time within one hour and only 1.2 per cent over three hours. Over the years, the waiting time for the RAC has improved. In 1990, the RAC handled 3.25 million calls: 83 per cent of the incidents were reached within an hour and 99 per cent within two hours.

The waiting experience varies for different types of customer. Priority is given to members who are disabled, women on their own and those involved in motorway accidents. Most of those who experienced long waiting times had broken down in remote areas, in a traffic jam or in a location with an unusual and unexpectedly high demand.

The patrols

Normally, the member's explanation for the breakdown is processed through the computer and telecommunication system, together with the rescue order. On arrival at the scene, the patrol will first talk with the member about the causes of the breakdown, and then try to do the repair work by the roadside, if conditions (safety and technical) permit. In 1990, the patrols carried out 2.4 million roadside assistance interventions – 86 per cent by its uniformed service patrols – and 92 per cent of rescue despatches were successful in restoring the car to working order at the roadside.

In the cases where a vehicle cannot be repaired on the road, the car will then be towed to an RAC-approved garage. If the car cannot be towed and recovery is required, the patrol will inform the Control Centre. Unless the members are in a perilous situation, for example a single woman with a breakdown on a motorway at night, the patrol will leave. Usually, customers will have to wait up to one hour for the recovery service. In 1990, a total of 188 000 breakdowns required recovery. The recovery resource is either another suitably-equipped patrol or an appointed agent with specialist equipment.

THE TELEPHONE OPERATORS' EXPERIENCE

All telephone calls to the rescue services are directed to one of the Control Centres. There are part-time and full-time telephone operators who are required to work in shifts. For example, there are mainly three eight-hour shifts in the Walsall Control Centre, with the first shift starting at 0800 hours.

An automatic call-queuing system was installed in 1988, so that the calls are taken in turn. Members' calls are taken by telephone operators who simultaneously input the details into the Computer-Aided Rescue System (CARS) and relay them to the relevant Command Centre.

Recruitment, training and responsibility of the telephone operators

Diana Palmer, Personnel Head, said:

'We select trustworthy and committed people with proven ability in an environment similar to the RAC and good telephone manner. After recruitment, they receive a three-

week training programme which aims to provide them with the knowledge and background of the RAC, telephone manner, operation procedure and policy, and the operation of the computer-aided telephone system. This is followed by one or two weeks' hands-on experience under direct supervision before they are allowed on system. Continuous training will also be arranged, tied in with specific programmes of the RAC, for example its "People in Mind" programme, which was launched to reinforce a friendly attitude both among colleagues and to customers.'

The telephone operators record the basic information from the callers, such as the reason for and location of the breakdown, membership number, registration number and, if available, contact telephone number.

'We are the first point of contact for most enquiries and rescue calls, so we often find we have to calm down anxious or distressed members,' said Shirley Austin, a telephone operator who won the Switchboard Operator of the Year award in 1991.

THE PATROLS' EXPERIENCE

There were about 1150 patrols nationwide in 1990. On average each received 175 despatches every month. Each is allocated a patrol vehicle and basic tools and equipment. About 80 per cent of the patrol vehicles are equipped with a radio telephone and the management intends to achieve a 100 per cent installation rate when British Telecom coverage is possible in all patrol locations.

Recruitment, training and responsibility of the patrols

The RAC aims to recruit patrols who are fully-trained mechanics with the City and Guilds' Certificate or equivalent qualification. Kevin Morgan, one of the patrols, recalled:

'After recruitment, I received a 13-week training programme, which aimed to introduce me to various services provided by the RAC. The training placed emphasis on the diagnosis and repair of a wide variety of vehicle problems. The programme also concentrates on the RAC's history, our safety practice, service attitude and customer care.'

Most recruitment is done in the summer, which, allowing for the lead time for training, aims to meet the increased demand in winter. The actual demand for patrol services during the last four years, and the volume of rescue calls in a typical week in the Birmingham area, are shown in Tables 13.1 and 13.2.

The patrols are required to work shifts. For Birmingham, typically, there are three shifts per day, each of which lasts for eight to nine hours. There are also standby patrols, who are off duty or on holiday but are willing (for special payment) to provide the rescue service when requested by management.

Table 13.1 Monthly demand for rescue services in the Birmingham area

Month	*1991*	*1990*	*1989*	*1988*
January	18 698	14 377	12 187	12 887
	(8.9)	(7.9)	(7.1)	(8.5)
February	21 183	15 480	13 299	10 968
	(10.1)	(8.3)	(7.7)	(7.2)
March	20 342	15 838	17 000	14 787
	(9.7)	(8.5)	(9.8)	(9.4)
April	14 135	13 313	13 004	9 984
	(6.7)	(7.2)	(7.5)	(6.6)
May	14 230	12 603	11 477	10 263
	(6.8)	(6.7)	(6.6)	(6.8)
June	17 459	15 240	14 353	12 502
	(8.3)	(8.2)	(8.3)	(8.2)
July	14 587	13 040	12 653	10 903
	(6.9)	(7.0)	(7.3)	(7.2)
August	14 513	13 814	11 664	10 714
	(6.9)	(7.4)	(6.8)	(7.2)
September	17 600	16 113	15 259	14 117
	(8.3)	(8.7)	(8.8)	(9.3)
October	15 960	15 192	13 788	13 117
	(8.5)	(9.4)	(9.4)	(9.9)
November	17 940	17 245	16 310	14 952
	(8.5)	(9.4)	(9.4)	(9.9)
December	24 000	23 235	21 762	16 529
	(11.4)	(12.5)	(12.6)	(11.9)
Total	210 647	185 390	172 701	151 188
Increase %	13.6	7.3	14.2	13.8

Note: Figures in brackets show percentage of annual demand.

Karl Mann, one of the patrols, said:

> *'We receive rescue calls through a mobile data transfer (MDT) system linked to the Control Centre. It is a very advanced system by which we can receive the basic information of the rescue calls. The commonest causes of breakdown include flat batteries, problems in radiator and cooling systems, fuel system, clutch and gearbox.'*

After the repair work, the patrol will either stay at the scene or, upon instruction from the Command Centre, travel to locations which, historically, have been identified as breakdown black spots – the major junctions or motorway service areas. In 1990,

Table 13.2 Rescue calls in the Birmingham area, week commencing 1 March 1992

Time	*Mon*	*Tues*	*Wed*	*Thur*	*Fri*	*Sat*	*Sun*
01.00	0	0	1	0	0	4	8
02.00	1	1	0	0	0	3	8
03.00	0	1	1	1	0	4	6
04.00	0	0	0	0	1	2	4
05.00	1	1	1	0	1	2	2
06.00	2	2	2	2	20	1	2
07.00	22	19	6	16	95	13	20
08.00	51	38	12	20	98	20	41
09.00	51	39	13	28	96	30	68
10.00	45	34	10	21	86	34	66
11.00	43	33	11	16	84	33	67
12.00	42	32	10	24	85	39	75
13.00	43	35	11	22	80	37	76
14.00	44	33	9	16	98	39	79
15.00	46	32	12	23	98	36	86
16.00	46	35	14	29	106	38	76
17.00	57	44	16	41	138	33	67
18.00	53	43	20	40	132	28	57
19.00	53	39	22	41	128	22	48
20.00	45	32	13	24	116	19	33
21.00	30	23	11	19	89	11	22
22.00	16	14	8	13	49	10	21
23.00	8	6	5	9	32	8	13
24.00	6	5	2	4	26	5	9
Total	705	541	210	409	1658	471	954

on average, a patrol experienced about equal proportions of waiting, travelling and servicing time in their work.

THE DESPATCHERS' EXPERIENCE

The Command Centres are staffed by 'despatchers'. They have total authority in the allocation of the patrols, according to their experience and the priority of the rescue calls. The despatcher is also responsible for the monitoring of the waiting time of each rescue caller. Resources available to the despatchers during day-time include the patrols on duty, standby patrols and contractor agents. In 1991, the ratio of costs per rescue for each resource were 1.0:1.8:2.5 during the day-time.

FACILITIES

Martin Conner, the Planning and Operational Support Manager, said:

> *'In order to cope with the competitive market and improve the service, investment in technology becomes of paramount importance. The three new purpose-built, high-profile, modern RAC Control Centres at strategic locations by motorway interchanges, and the installation of the CARS system demonstrates the RAC's commitment to capital and technological investment.'*

These Control Centres house and link the CARS system, the Control Centres of different regions and the different functional departments of the RAC. 'The CARS system revolutionized the "Rescue Service" by the replacement of time-consuming methods of taking and passing on motorists' information', said Simon Rowland Jones, the Deputy Planning and Operational Support Manager. Now a network of computerised rescue Control Centres around the country can pinpoint a stranded motorist and, within seconds, transmit the data to a screen in the cab of a patrol vehicle. Staff in the Command and Control Centres can read from the monitor of the CARS system the individual and overall status of each rescue call, the rescue resources available, the time performance for each rescue, and comparisons of each of the 18 operational areas.

In order to achieve a high percentage of successful roadside repairs, new pieces of equipment are being added to repair kits carried by patrols: the Avo M2005 Multimeter, which facilitates the diagnosis of electrical faults; the lock-out kit to overcome the problem of lost keys; the clutch cable kit to eliminate the need for manufacturer-specific parts; and oil pressure testers.

ADMINISTRATION AND ORGANISATION

Alec Leggett, Corporate Director of Administration, said:

> *'Historically, the RAC's administrative services have lagged behind the improvements which have been achieved in our roadside services. 1992 will change all that. We have the right staff in administration and the right framework. The intention is to turn the RAC's administrative functions into centres of excellence, with everyone involved proud to be part of that success; each a major contributor to the success of the company.'*

The Rescue Services of the RAC had been reorganised since 1989 in order to achieve a streamlined and efficient administration structure. The reorganisation included a reduction in the number of levels of management, particularly at the upper end of the business.

Human resources management

'Our initial focus will be on establishing and developing a cohesive personnel function which is equipped to contribute effectively to Rescue Service's business objectives', said Alec Leggett.

In order to reinforce staff communications and commitment to service, a 'People in Mind' programme has been launched. Frank Richardson, the Managing Director, explained its success:

> *'The programme is helping us to work more effectively as a team and to better understand and meet the requirements of our customers. The way the programme is run, involving staff at all levels and in all disciplines, is important in developing our unique approach to doing business. We will continue to devolve authority to people dealing with customers. It is important that we give people control over their own work and do not stifle them with rules and regulations. We work closely with the trade union [the Transport and General Workers' Union] in order to achieve a smooth implementation of the various human resources programme.'*

To reward commitment to quality of service and the 'People in Mind' philosophy, the RAC launched the new Knights of the Road 'Awards of Excellence' during 1990. These awards single out staff who have shown initiative, gone to extraordinary lengths to assist RAC members or others at risk, helped a colleague or a charity, or involved themselves in environmental or safety issues.

Macro human resources planning

The human resources planning of the RAC starts by forecasting the number of members expected for the coming 12 months. The projection is based on historical data and market forecasts provided by marketing staff. Given the forecast number of members, the RAC then predicts the average number of breakdowns and rescue calls expected by referring to the probability of a member's vehicle breaking down each year. This gives the RAC a total national breakdown forecast for the next 12 months. Based on the historical data, the Walsall Command Centre, which covers the Birmingham area, is expected to cope with around 7.7 per cent of the national figure, thus giving the expected number of rescue calls in a particular area in that year.

Given the expected breakdowns, the RAC can work out the total number of patrols required by using the Trigger Level, which is the number of breakdowns a patrol can deal with in one year. For example, in the Birmingham area, the Trigger Level is 2800 breakdowns/patrol/year. Therefore, the number of patrols can be allocated. In 1991, the Birmingham area was allocated an establishment of 99 patrols.

These figures are reviewed monthly, since the above result is the average number for the coming year, which will have to be adjusted according to the fluctuation of demands in different seasons.

Micro human resources planning

The total number of patrols in the fleet is fixed by macro-planning. The patrols are scheduled in each area by the zone managers, who take into account the holidays, days off and training to which the patrols are entitled. After allowing for various entitlements, the number of patrols scheduled for any one day for the Birmingham area may be only 60 per cent of establishment, as illustrated in Table 13.3 for a week in March 1991.

Table 13.3 Rescue resources available in the Birmingham area, week commencing 11 March 1991

Shift structure		
Shift 1	0700–1500	(16 patrols)
Shift 2	0800–1700	(34 patrols)
Shift 3	1500–2400	(11 patrols)
Establishment		99
Strength		90
Average daily available		61

Time	*Patrol on duty*	*Standby contractors*	*Outside contractors*	*Total*
01.00	0	2	20	22
02.00	0	2	20	22
03.00	0	2	20	22
04.00	0	2	20	22
05.00	0	2	20	22
06.00	0	2	20	22
07.00	16	10	30	56
08.00	50	10	30	90
09.00	50	10	30	90
10.00	50	10	30	90
11.00	50	10	30	90
12.00	50	10	30	90
13.00	50	10	30	90
14.00	50	10	30	90
15.00	61	10	30	101
16.00	45	10	30	85
17.00	45	10	30	85
18.00	11	15	30	56
19.00	11	15	30	56
20.00	11	15	30	56
21.00	11	15	30	56
22.00	11	15	30	56
23.00	11	15	30	56
24.00	11	2	30	43

PERFORMANCE

An independent marketing survey company is employed to monitor customer expectations and satisfaction levels. The survey has been conducted twice annually since 1990 and aims to compare satisfaction with the RAC breakdown services with that of rival motoring organisations, and to assess changes over time. An extract from the 1990 survey results is given in Table 13.4.

Table 13.4 Key determinants of satisfaction of service

	% of respondents saying	
	most important factor	*very important factor*
Speed with which initial assistance arrives	43	76
Quick continuation of journey	16	64
Quick telephone contact	16	94
Car fixed at roadside	8	50
Low cost of incident	6	66
Patrol rather than mechanic	3	32
All factors equal	3	NA
Other	5	NA

Note: This survey was based on 1000 respondents nationwide.

'Comparisons with competitors are made to ensure targets are not only reached but that the RAC is without dispute "the best"', said the Director of Operations, Ron Hewitt. To achieve this, the performance of the rescue service is closely monitored. Apart from the sponsoring of market research to conduct the customer satisfaction survey, the daily performance of the response rate is monitored by the CARS system.

According to independent market research, the RAC's performance in 1991 was ahead of its major competitors when it came to delivering a fast, efficient service to stranded motorists. During the year 1991, dissatisfaction with the overall service fell from 10 per cent to 5 per cent and the satisfaction level improved from 82.7 per cent to 85.9 per cent.

'1991 was an excellent year for service performance. It is a standard we intend to maintain and improve upon', said Ron Hewitt. But Ron warned, *'We have made good progress but have not yet reached our goals of profit performance.'*

Marketing Manager, Andy Bennett, remarked:

> *'We know from our research that there is an image gap between how people perceive the RAC and where we are today. People regard us as traditional and "club-like" but not at all dynamic or high tech. But our organisation has changed over the last five years and we need to close the gap between image and reality.'*

In order to improve the image, the 'Knights of the Road' TV advertisement, which aimed to promote the high technology and customer care image, was launched in 1990 in an attempt to shake off the RAC's outdated image.

In a move designed to force better quality from garages and breakdown organisations, the RAC joined forces with the British Standards Institute to develop quality systems within BS 5750.

> *'This is the first time that specific codes of practice have been written down,'* Contractor Services Manager, Tom Atkinson, said: *'It's all about raising standards in the industry through quality assured management. The agreement set up in July 1991 should mean that poor outfits will find it difficult to stay in business. RAC contractors can save time and money by applying for BS 5750 through the RAC's quality partnership scheme.'*

RECENT DEVELOPMENTS AND ISSUES

There were a number of important membership breakthroughs during 1990, a year in which the RAC signed up nearly 1 million new members. In January 1991, the RAC strengthened its hold on the new vehicle market in a deal with Vauxhall. The motor manufacturer joined the RAC stable in an agreement which included new types of benefits, including the accident management service. In 1990, more than half of all new vehicles sold in the UK carried RAC membership. *'The provision of cover for the major motor manufacturers is a huge growth area'*, said Robert Hoare, Fleet Operations Manager of the RAC.

Ron Hewitt said:

> *'Over the last five years, the RAC has invested over £30 million in technology, people and training to provide a modern, professional, efficient and flexible service for today's motorists. In order to enhance the rescue service, better communication and information systems are being considered. The response to incidents where a recovery proves necessary still has room for improvement, as it has been identified as a source of some customer dissatisfaction.'*

While a better response and recovery rate is to be achieved, a better cost structure is required in order to maintain profitability and competitiveness. However, the unpredictable surges in volume of services pose a dilemma which needs to be addressed. For example, a wintry blast in February 1991 took its toll as patrols struggled to cope with calls from motorists stranded in the snow. Franchising or contracting out rescue services may be one possible alternative but it will raise questions about the quality and image of the service.

CASE 14

Casgo Centraal

Nigel Slack

*Case date 1992**

Jan Castel, Chief Executive Officer of Casgo Centraal, reflected on a speech he had heard some years before in 1985. It was at a computer industry conference in Fontainebleu, France, and the speaker had been the European head of one of the major computer manufacturers. He had said:

> *'The relationship between service and manufacturing in this industry is changing. Most of us think of ourselves as manufacturers of computers who also trade in additional services on the back of the boxes we sell. Even though the profit we make from the service element of the business is starting to rival the profits from our manufacturing operations, we still think like that. But in the future we will, we must, come to think of ourselves as providers of information-based services which might also pull through opportunities to sell the boxes we make.'*

The speech had had a strong effect on Jan Castel at the time, but even then he had little idea of just how prophetic those words would be for him.

CASGO CENTRAAL COMPANY BACKGROUND

In 1985 Casgo Centraal, or Casgo Research Computing (CRC) as the company was originally called, had come to the end of a period of rapid expansion. Jan, with a technical background and experience in Digital and Hewlett-Packard, had founded the company in 1979. Originally producing microcomputers for universities and research institutes, mainly in Europe but also in North America, CRC quickly gained a reputation as the 'expert's company'. Their machines were fast and technically sophisticated, they introduced updated and technically innovative models more frequently than their larger rivals, and, most important, they could relate at the technical level with the users of their machines. In the early 1980s margins were reasonably high but demand for CRC's sophisticated machinery was relatively low. Partly because of this, the company made a series of acquisitions. In 1981 they

*Names and some details of the company's operations have been disguised.

joined with their own supplier of disk drives and general memory products. Also in 1981 they bought Centraal Computers of Antwerp in Belgium and Tritan Computer Systems who, though based in Cambridge, UK, had European-wide sales. Centraal made and supplied minicomputers intended primarily to support office systems. Tritan made and supplied process control computers, mainly to the paper-making and food-processing industries. Both of these acquisitions were struggling to make money out of their manufacturing businesses, but both had growing and profitable service and software divisions. Jan Castel explained the strategy:

> *'Our idea was to exploit the obvious synergy of the merged company. The basic machines made by the three businesses were close enough to rationalise production and achieve almost a threefold increase in volume. Buying the memory company would also help us to drive manufacturing costs down. Moreover, we now could be in three markets with one set of products, our original scientific and research market, the office systems market and the process control market. Also important to us, although we didn't realise then just quite how important, was the possibility of merging the three service and software operations. Putting them together would give us a network of service centres which covered most of Northern Europe.'*

The merged company, who changed their name to Casgo Centraal in 1982, proved a success, at least in terms of revenue growth. The separate turnover of the companies in 1981 totalled DFL 54 million. By 1985 this had grown to DFL 83.7 million – an increase in real terms of more than 150 per cent. Profits, however, had not kept pace with the growth in sales, rising from DFL 6.9 million in 1982 to DFL 7.1 million in 1985. Table 14.1 shows the growth of revenue and costs for Casgo between 1982 and 1985.

Table 14.1 Financial details of the Casgo Centraal Group, 1982–5

	1982	*1983*	*1984*	*1985*
Revenue	55.3	58.7	78.1	83.7
Net profit before tax	6.9	6.8	7.1	7.0
Of which service revenue	5.0	6.5	9.8	14.3

Notes: All figures in DFL millions. All figures are in real terms (i.e. adjusted for local inflation).

By 1986 the shake-out in the computer industry was affecting Casgo seriously. During the period April 1986 to April 1987 their sales of new machines fell by 23 per cent – and that in a market which was expanding. The major manufacturers, especially Digital, and ICL in the UK, were offering product technology which was at least as good as, and often better than, Casgo's. Digital were also offering a far higher degree of product and system compatibility. But, most seriously, Casgo's prices could no longer both remain competitive and provide sufficient contribution to cover overheads.

The only optimism in the company came from the service division. Their part of the company had grown both in turnover and in profitability. Nor were they affected by the sharp downturn in the company's sale of machines in 1986/87. Two years previously they had taken the decision to offer service contracts on selected machines and systems other than their own. Although controversial within the company at the time, the move had proved very successful. By 1987 more than half the service division's contracts were to maintain and service non-Casgo machines (exclusively IBM, Digital and ICL).

In November 1987 Jan Castel acted.

'We needed to do something quickly. The losses from the manufacturing division were draining the company's vitality, and being honest with ourselves we could not see any improvement in the situation. We decided to close the Cambridge plant immediately and run down the Amsterdam plant over a 12-month period to the point where it was in effect a small support operation to the service division. It was a pivotal decision. We were getting out of our original business entirely and investing our future in what had always been regarded as a peripheral though profitable part of the company. We were transforming ourselves into a service company.'

THE POSITION IN 1991

By 1991 the wisdom of the move out of manufacturing and into service was clear to everyone in the company. Since the decision in 1987 several other small computer manufacturers had ceased trading and the industry (especially in the minicomputer markets) was dominated by relatively few major manufacturers. Casgo could never have competed as a manufacturer.

However, the scale benefits in the major manufacturers had not translated fully into their service operations. While almost all the majors also had extensive (and largely profitable) service divisions, they had come under some criticism for being less productive and less responsive to customer needs than independent service companies. Having been an independent service company for over three years, Casgo Centraal supported this view. Jan Castel:

'We have grown largely at the expense of the big manufacturers service divisions. They aren't bad as such, but they have rather relied on what they thought was a protected market. And they do have an advantage. Their sales people are there when the customer buys the hardware so they can do deals involving hardware, software and service. But after that first service deal we can move in by offering guarantees of better service, a more customised relationship, and, most important, a lower cost deal than the majors' service divisions. We are now even getting some business from customers who have chosen not to accept their hardware supplier's service deal and have come directly to us.'

This combination of low prices, a growing reputation for excellent service, and energetic sales, had proved profitable for the company. Turnover of DFL 62.1 million in 1987 had reduced to DFL 43.5 million in 1990, but this reflected the closure of the manufacturing side of the company. Profitability had risen from return on sales of 5.6 per cent in 1987 to over 10 per cent in 1990.

CASGO CENTRAAL'S PRODUCT RANGE

Casgo Centraal offered services related to the maintenance and repair of computer-based information systems. That is, they sold one-, two-, or three-year contracts to perform regular preventive maintenance on computer hardware and associated equipment such as disk drives, and repair hardware (and some software) system faults when necessary. The company offered service 'products' defined primarily by the nature of the preventive maintenance, the frequency of preventive maintenance, the maximum response time to travel to a customer's facility when a breakdown occurred and, sometimes, by the percentage of system 'up-time'. System up-time was the percentage of regular shift time for which the system would be working to specification. It was affected by the amount, nature and timing of preventive maintenance, and the number and severity of breakdowns.

Preventive maintenance regimes were specified by the 'test activity sequence'; the number and order of the various tests, checks and cleaning activities recommended by the equipment manufacturer; and the frequency with which an engineer would visit the customer's facility to run the tests. Generally Casgo offered two levels of test activity sequence – 'basic' and 'extra' – the first being the equipment manufacturer's minimum recommended standard, the second being an enhanced set of preventive maintenance activities devised by Casgo for the equipment it serviced. The frequency of preventive maintenance was also offered at two levels, one based on the manufacturer's minimum recommended frequency and one with either more frequent visits or visits for preventive maintenance which were scheduled outside the customer's normal shift times, or sometimes both.

Response times were measured from the logged time the company agreed to send an engineer out to a customer's facility to the time when the engineer phoned back to the base that he was about to start the repair. Nominally, Casgo offered three levels of response: arrival within 24 hours, arrival within four hours and arrival within two hours; recently though, the London Central district had started offering a 60-minute response to some of its financial service customers. Table 14.2 gives details of Casgo's official product structure.

In fact London Central's financial service plan was just one of many locally negotiated variations on the official product structure. All regional managers had authority to negotiate customised deals with individual customers as well as offer their own products for their specific customer needs. London's financial service plan was typical.

Table 14.2 Casgo Centraal product structure

*General Service Plans**	
Silver Basic	Covers all specified hardware and systems 1-, 2- or 3-year contracts Manufacturer's recommended preventive maintenance (PM) sequence 24-hour response (4-hour enhanced)
Silver Premium	Covers all specified hardware and systems 1- or 2-year contracts Manufacturer's recommended or enhanced PM sequence Negotiated PM schedule 4-hour response (2-hour enhanced)
Gold Basic	Covers all specified hardware and systems 1-, 2- or 3-year contracts Enhanced/negotiated PM sequence Negotiated PM schedule 2-hour response
Gold Premium	Covers all specified hardware and systems 1- or 2-year contracts Negotiated PM sequence Negotiated and flexible PM sequence 2-hour response Negotiated up-time targets
Platinum Commercial	Covers all specified hardware and systems 1-year contracts Negotiated PM sequence Flexible PM schedules 60-minute response Guaranteed up-time performance
Quick-fit Service†	Only PCs and peripherals as specified in contract 2-year contracts No PM 2-hour response guaranteed Repair or replace within 30 minutes of arrival
Resident Engineer	Covers all specified hardware and systems for repair plus general advice/help with non-specified systems 1-year contracts PM negotiated/flexible through resident engineer Engineer on site for 8 hours/day by negotiation

* Plans can be called different names in different countries. These are the names used in the UK. All plans are outlines, they provide the basic framework for negotiating individual contracts.

† No deviation from product specification.

THE QUICK-FIT AND RESIDENT ENGINEER SERVICES

The most significant of the new services was the 'Quick-fit' service, a two-hour response either to repair within half an hour or, more usually, to replace a piece of equipment. This service was usually offered only on terminals, PCs, and smaller pieces of equipment. Nevertheless it had proved popular with customers who wanted a clearly defined, 'no frills' service. The service engineers, however, were less keen. They saw the service as too basic to exploit their technical skills. The requirement to replace the inoperative equipment if it could not be repaired in half an hour meant that all but the most obvious problems were solved by replacing the piece of equipment and repairing it back at the field office. This had given rise to the feeling that they were losing their contact with customers as well as wasting their skills.

The other major development was the growth in the 'resident' or 'dedicated' engineer service. Although theoretically available for some time, the service was controversial within the organisation. The company had recently obtained new business largely on the promise of supplying a full-time service engineer resident on the customer's main site. This service had been supplied to 10 customers over the previous 12 months and was most unpopular with the district managers.

James Richards, Birmingham District Manager, said:

'It may be what some customers want, but I know that most companies taking this service don't strictly need that level of support. We have recently sold another resident contract and I am under pressure from Sales to make sure that the engineer allocated to the job is one of our better people. In effect this limits my freedom on a day-to-day basis in two ways. First, it takes an engineer out of the reckoning so I have less freedom to exploit the economies of scale of my area. Second, it takes out expertise which could be far more effectively used by being spread thinly over the area. I know that the price we get for this service doesn't seem too bad for one engineer, but the actual disruption on my area, and therefore the cost, is far greater than one would suppose.'

A recent study of three of the resident engineers put in position within the last six months had shown a large degree of difference between how they spent their time. Table 14.3 illustrates the findings.

Table 14.3 How resident engineers spend their time (%)

	Site A	*Site B*	*Site C*
Technical work (on hardware or software)	28	34	33
Site work*	53	21	39
CC administration	5	4	4
Idle	14	41	24

* 'Site work' was defined as 'general advisory and consulting work within the customer site . . . including any non-scheduled preventive maintenance and diagnostic work'.

COMPANY ORGANISATION

The company was organised on a regional (mainly country) basis. The five regions were, in descending order of size: UK, Netherlands, Belgium and France, Germany and Denmark, and Sweden and Norway. Figure 14.1 shows the regional boundaries.

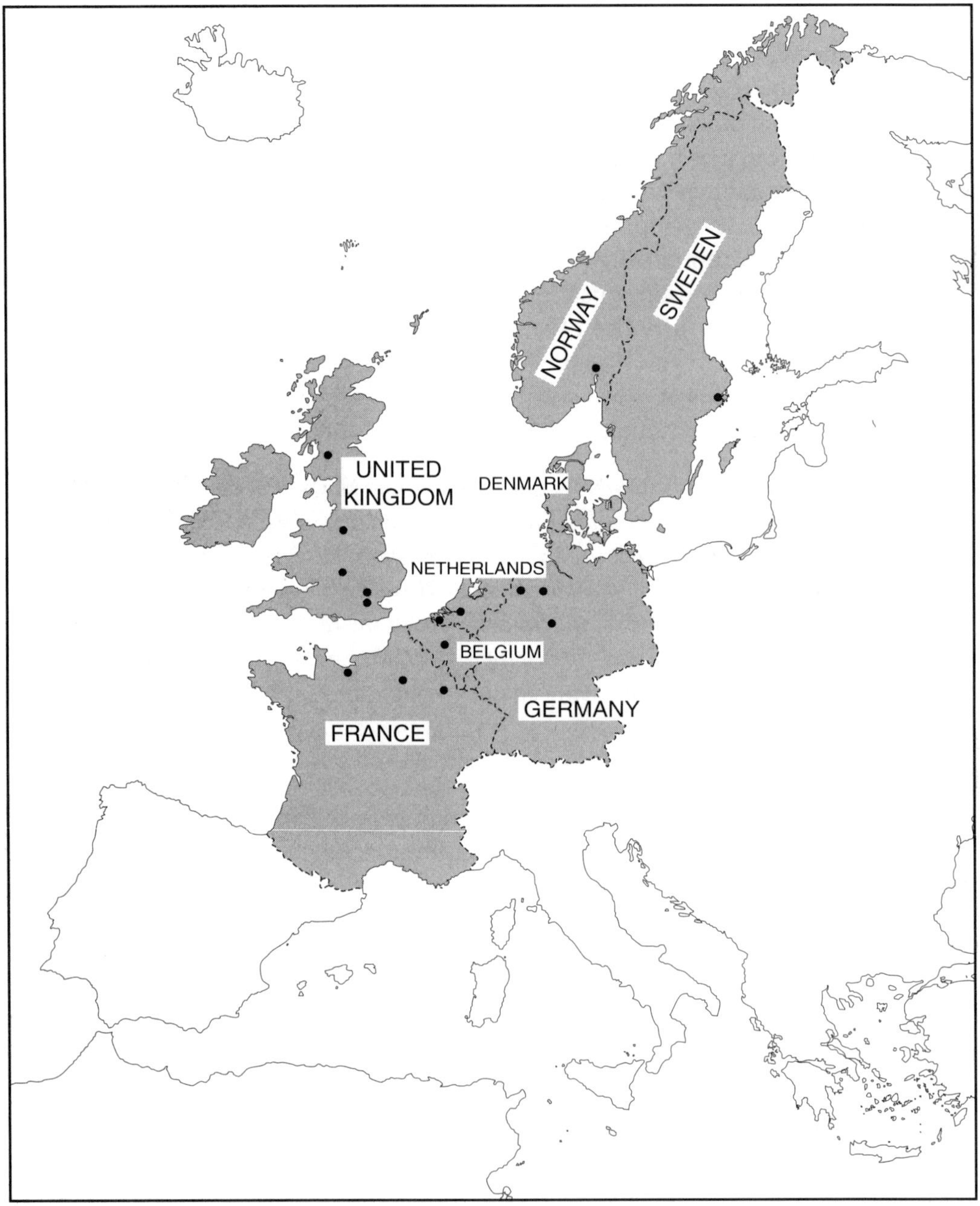

Fig. 14.1 Casgo Centraal regional boundaries

Each region was divided into a number of districts, from five districts in the UK to two districts in Sweden and Norway. Each district had a base from which the district was organised, customer calls received, support services were based and from which the engineers operated. Regional headquarters were located at one of the region's bases, usually the largest.

Each region had a Regional Operations Manager and a Regional Sales Manager. Although both were the same grade within the company's management grading system, and Casgo encouraged a 'team approach' to the management of the region, the Sales Manager was held to be ultimately responsible for the region's performance. The Regional Operations Manager had District Operations Managers in each district reporting to him. The Regional Sales Manager's staff, however, were all based at Regional Headquarters. Figure 14.2 shows the outline organisational structure for the company.

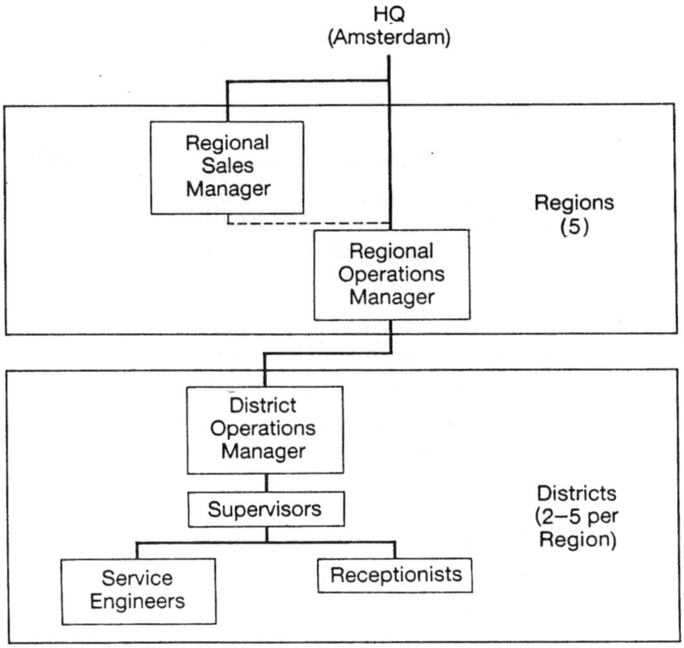

Fig. 14.2 Casgo Centraal organisational structure

Generally, Regional Headquarters were responsible for:

- all aspects of sales
- contract negotiations
- financial and operations control

- resource allocation to districts
- technical backing to districts
- spare part stock tracking and control
- most off-site repair
- customer complaints handling.

Generally the Districts were responsible for:

- engineer rostering
- telephone reception
- immediate handling of customer queries
- performance monitoring
- preventive maintenance
- all breakdown maintenance
- minor off-site repair.

THE CUSTOMER CONTACT PROCESS

Customers were provided with three telephone numbers: one for reporting hardware faults, which connected them to Casgo's district office; one for technical advice and software faults, which connected them to the technical support team at Regional Headquarters; and one for account enquiries, general enquiries and complaints, which connected them to the Commercial Department at Regional Headquarters.

Complaints or general enquiries which could be dealt with at district level were passed on to the relevant District Operations Manager to be dealt with as he or she thought fit. For complaints which were judged by Region as being particularly important, the District Manager was also required to fill in a 'complaint action' document which detailed the exact nature of the complaint and what had been done to satisfy the customer. Software faults and enquiries which could not be dealt with over the phone were either dealt with by sending one of the Regional Headquarters' software support team, or by asking the relevant district office to send an engineer. This inevitably resulted occasionally in engineers from District being sent to treat a problem which was beyond their capabilities. In such cases the Headquarters software engineer was called in immediately.

The majority of customer calls (87 per cent) were made directly to the district office and dealt with issues relating to service, mainly reports of breakdown or hardware fault or requests for a change in the timing of their preventive maintenance visits. A further 4 per cent of calls were made incorrectly to the district office when they should have been directed to the Regional Headquarters. In these cases the customer was requested to phone the Regional Headquarters.

In the case of a request for a change in preventive maintenance visits, the telephone receptionist noted the request and passed it on to the District Manager who, in most districts, was responsible for the scheduling of engineers. The manager would then try and reschedule preventive maintenance visits and call the customer back, usually the same day.

Most calls into the District, however, were reports of system failure. For these the procedure was as follows:

1 the telephone receptionist receives and logs the customer's call;
2 if the receptionist understands the nature of the query, he or she will direct the call to the relevant engineer (some engineers had a preference for particular types of work and/or equipment, some were better suited to simple servicing work such as the Quick-fit contracts);
3 if the receptionist does not fully understand the nature of the call, it is put through to the District Manager. If the District Manager does not understand the call, he or she arranges for an engineer to visit. If the manager does understand the nature of the call, then it is transferred to the relevant engineer;
4 the engineer calls up the customer's details on the screen to check on his or her service plan, i.e. what the customer has paid for and, therefore, the level of support to which he or she is entitled;
5 if the engineer cannot answer the customer's query or problem over the phone, he or she arranges to visit the customer or for another engineer to do so;
6 if the engineer can answer the query over the phone but feels that it would be safer for the customer to receive a visit, the engineer arranges for this at a convenient time for the customer;
7 if any engineer is not in the office when required, he or she is called (all engineers carry either mobile phones or pagers) and either asked to call the customer or given instructions for the visit;
8 on arriving at the customer's site, the engineer calls into the office to log arrival. Response performance measurements are based on this;
9 if the engineer cannot solve the problem, he or she calls the District Manager who decides whether to deal with it at a district level by sending another engineer, or to call on Regional Headquarters technical support. Only 7 per cent of faults need to be referred to Region, and of these 90 per cent are dealt with over the phone. Occasionally though an engineer from Regional Headquarters will need to visit the customer's site.

THE QUICK-FIT SERVICE

The simple Quick-fit service differed from this procedure somewhat. Calls were rarely diverted to the District Manager. Even if the receptionist could not fully understand the nature of the query, the call would be put straight through to the engineers. Then again, less effort would be put into trying to solve the problem over the phone and an engineer, carrying the most likely relevant replacement parts or equipment, would be sent immediately to the customer.

Usually, one of the less skilled or newer engineers would be sent on these calls because the nature of the fault was rarely complicated, and because the equipment was replaced if there looked like being any complications which would take the repair time over 30 minutes.

A further reason for dealing quickly with Quick-fit calls at district office was the very explicit nature of the service. As James Richards, Birmingham District Manager, said:

'Many large customers are not totally sure what level of service they are entitled to on our mid-range plans and anyway it is often more convenient for them that we come at a particular time rather than immediately. Often they call us when the system is faulty but still functional. They would prefer to limp along until they have got the payroll out, for example, than have us come at the end of the day. That isn't the case for Quick-fit. Because we sell it on a clear message – two-hour response then repair or replace in half an hour – and because the type of equipment it covers is prone to sudden failure, they really do expect us to be quick.'

This strict emphasis on response time meant that engineers preferred to arrive at the customer's location as quickly as possible in case they needed to return to base to collect a spare piece of equipment they had not brought with them. In fact, the Quick-fit service was popular only with the customers. James Richards again:

'There is no doubt that there is a demand for the "no frills" type of service, but it causes me a great deal of trouble. First, it is not popular with most of the engineers. They regard it as "kid's work". Second, it disrupts other work. One or two more Quick-fit calls than we expect can totally disrupt the day. Preventive maintenance schedules go to pieces because I have to divert engineers from their planned visits, who then have to call back at base to collect the relevant spares, and we then have to explain to customers why we are changing their preventive maintenance visits.'

THE RESIDENT ENGINEER SERVICE

The Resident Engineer (RE) service was also organised on different principles. Because the RE was always on-site during normal working hours (or hours agreed with the customer), customers merely used their internal phone system to contact their RE. All REs, however, were required to log all requests for service, response and repair times, as well as all preventive maintenance schedules and other work. This information was consolidated into an 'RE report' which the District Manager reviewed monthly.

The RE report gave only an outline of what the RE did. Much of their work was involved with preventing problems before they arose by informally educating users, advising the customer on how best to integrate maintenance schedules into their working schedules, and building informal contact with users within the customer's site. The better REs were also capable of giving simple business systems advice to customers.

The REs in some districts were also used to help sort out the other engineer's problems. Often informally, the practice had become established of using REs to advise on the more difficult (usually system-related) problems. If an engineer was having difficulty with a fault, before contacting the District Manager, he or she might call an RE who could possibly give advice over the telephone. The RE's customers were aware of this practice but did not seem to object, provided it did not interfere with their own company's work. They even saw some advantages in being connected to the larger network of engineers.

OPERATIONS PERFORMANCE

Regions operated as profit centres, issuing monthly reports to Group Headquarters in Amsterdam. District performance was assessed by a number of measures:

- Revenue per engineer hour, the annual value of all the district's service contracts divided by the number of engineer hours paid for by the district.
- Average to nominal response time, the average actual response time (logged customer call time to logged arrival call at the customer's site) divided by the expected average response time calculated from the district's mix of service plants.
- Number of customer complaints, graded by their seriousness.
- RE reports.

District performance was consolidated at Regional level and quarterly reports submitted to Amsterdam, where Jan Castel read them all. Yet he had expressed reservations on Casgo's reporting procedures:

> *'There are some obvious gaps. For example, we do not make any systematic attempt to assess the intangible elements of our service. What kind of an impression do our engineers make? Are they knowledgeable? Are they courteous? Do they make use of their contact with the customer to help sell further services to them?'*

THE UK SERVICE QUALITY INITIATIVE

There had been local attempts to address questions relating to 'the intangible elements' of Casgo's service, in various parts of the Casgo Centraal Group over the preceding two years. The most significant was the UK region's Service Quality Initiative (SQI).

This had arisen out of the annual Regional Management Conference in 1990.

The annual conference was a forum for the District Managers from all the Region's districts to meet with Regional management and discuss various topical issues within the company. During the evening the discussion had turned to the tough market conditions being experienced. James Richards had summed up the feeling of the group:

> *'It isn't only our customers who are getting more critical and more demanding, it is also our competitors, some of whom are sharpening their act up considerably. Even the service divisions of the major manufacturers whose business we ate into during the 1980s are now giving us a real fight. They may not yet quite match us on price but the quality of service they provide is now being compared favourably when set against ours.'*

As an initial step towards a regional service quality initiative it was decided to set up a working group of John Machine, the Regional Operations Manager for the UK, James Richards and Mark Ellis, the North London District Manager.

Questions

1 What are the different services offered by Casgo Centraal and how do they differ from each other?

2 What factors would you use to judge the performance of each of the service products?

3 How would you describe the 'customer contact' experience for each of the service products and what is important at each stage of the customer contact process to ensure high service quality?

4 What are the major skills needed by service engineers at Casgo Centraal?

5 How would you go about organising a performance improvement programme at Casgo Centraal?

CASE 15

National Westminster Bank

St James's Square Branch

David Woodgate and Nigel Slack

*Case date 1992**

Set in a graceful old square just off London's Pall Mall and just a stone's throw from Piccadilly, National Westminster Bank's St James's Square branch still retained an air of gentility from the time it was founded, 150 years ago. Yet beneath this elegant facade was the most profitable of all the Bank's West End branches, one which supplied the full range of modern business services to one of the most sophisticated clientele in the UK.

The branch had both private and business customers. The latter ranged from small sole trader businesses through to some of the largest public limited companies in the UK and multinational conglomerates. Its private customer base came from a wide variety of backgrounds although there was a predominance of professional/managerial occupations. Partly because of the proximity to the gentlemen's clubs of Pall Mall, there were also many accounts held by 'high net worth' individuals, including leading personalities in industry, commerce and government (at least one cabinet minister), well-known celebrities from the world of entertainment and members of the aristocracy. In addition, there were many overseas customers, both British expatriates and foreign nationals. All in all, the clientele were demanding and required to be treated with skill and sensitivity if their often highly individual requirements were to be met within what was still a mass service. The branch had in excess of 14 000 customer accounts in total.

BRANCH ORGANISATION

The St James's Square branch had a typical organisation chart for a large branch. (Figure 15.1 shows the organisation chart.) In brief, around 100 people worked at the branch, which was headed by a Senior Manager working closely with three 'Advances' (lending) Managers in looking after customer relationships. This involved lending money – for anything from a new car to a multimillion pound takeover bid

*Some data have been disguised.

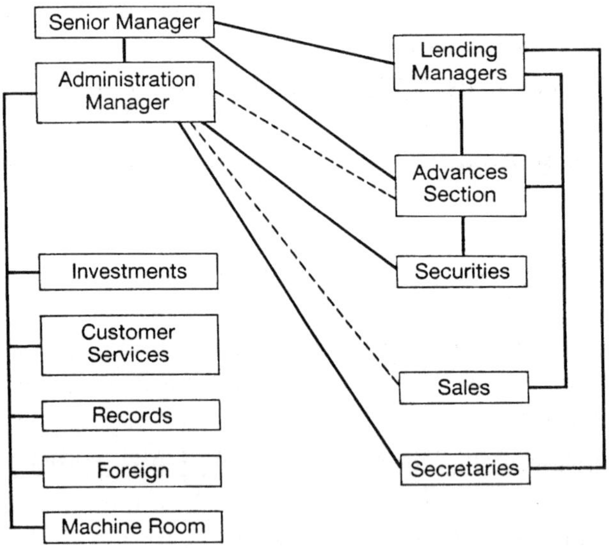

Fig. 15.1 St James's Square branch organisation chart

for another company. But also the branch was increasingly involved in the selling of ancillary financial services, such as mortgages for house purchase, insurance and pensions, savings and investment products, and the giving of general financial and business advice.

The Senior Manager was also ultimately responsible for the support functions of the branch, for example managing standing orders and managing the cashiers. From an operational point of view, however, these aspects were overseen by an Administration Manager who dealt with personnel and general organisation issues.

Below the Administration Manager were ten assistant managers who headed the nine operational sections of the branch, with the tenth providing cover for sickness, holidays, special exercises, etc. The nine sections are as follows:

1 *Advances.* This section provided direct research and technical support to the Senior Manager and the Advances Managers. It also looked after many day-to-day aspects of the relationship with customers where there was no need for a manager to be involved. For instance, the section would look after requests from small borrowers for such things as personal loans for consumer goods.

2 *Securities.* This department also worked closely with the lending managers. It was responsible for taking collateral from customers when security was required for their borrowings. For instance, a manager might lend a customer £30 000 to inject into a new business venture. As security, the Bank could take a mortgage over a property owned by the customer. The Bank would then have the right to sell if

all attempts for repayment failed. The Securities Section looked after the necessary legal formalities to ensure that the Bank could rely on its security if a customer defaulted on his or her borrowing.

3 *Investments.* This section dealt with investments and stock exchange transactions, for example the buying and selling of stocks and shares for customers. It also co-ordinated detailed portfolio advice from the Bank's specialist departments. These were used to help customers make investment decisions. In addition the section provided safe custody services boxes to enable customers to store valuables and documents at the Bank and was responsible for taking long 'money market' deposits on behalf of the bigger customers.

4 *Customer Services.* This section dealt with what were often called 'front line' services such as cashiering, as well as looking after the most basic services such as amendments to customer standing order records. Inevitably staff in this section had a very high degree of customer contact and dealt with a very large number of customer enquiries.

5 *Records.* This section maintained the basic branch records, for example customer addresses, the opening and closing of accounts, amendments to customer instructions and so on. Again, a high but erratic degree of customer contact was involved.

6 *Foreign.* The foreign department dealt with highly specialised transactions relating to the financing of foreign trade. For example, the Bank would often process the documentation relating to both imports and exports for customers. It could provide information on business opportunities abroad, and send money around the world for customers. In addition, the section also staffed a foreign till which provided currency, traveller's cheques and travel insurance.

7 *The Machine Room.* This was the paper processing part of the office. It looked after the basic accountancy procedures of the branch and was responsible for ensuring that debits and credits were transacted accurately. Although it was now a highly automated department, it nevertheless dealt with a substantial volume of paper every day.

8 *Sales.* This was the branch marketing function which provided input to all the other sections to help them sell appropriate bank services.

9 *Secretarial.* This was a seven-person section which provided general administrative support.

QUALITY OF SERVICE

Despite the highly demanding nature of its clientele, the branch generally felt that it had a first-class reputation for quality of service. This was confirmed by regular customer feedback questionnaires and unsolicited letters of praise to the Bank's West End Regional Head Office. The branch regularly outperformed its West End peer group in terms of customer satisfaction and the Bank's central Operations and Methods Department paid the branch the back-handed compliment of saying that it 'provided a Coutts style service . . . without charging Coutts style prices!'*

However, one particular area of service did attract regular negative customer comment and, indeed, letters of complaint. This was the process of opening new accounts, one of the responsibilities of the Records Section.

ACCOUNT OPENING

In general, the majority of new customers 'cold called' at the branch to open an account – that is, straight off the street without an appointment. Often they queued for service at one of the cashier's positions, instead of at the enquiries counter, where they were intended to go. This was possibly because the enquiries counter was neither well positioned nor signposted. This meant that, having waited their turn for a cashier to become free, they were often redirected to the enquiries counter. Having arrived at the correct enquiry position, the prospective customer would be served initially by an enquiries officer (usually a relatively junior member of staff) who would request a member of the Records Section to see the customer and assist with the account opening procedures.

THE RECORDS SECTION

Like the other eight sections in the branch, the Records Section was supervised by an Assistant Manager, whose role was to provide advice and guidance to the four junior clerical staff who staffed the Section. The Assistant Manager was responsible for all aspects of the smooth running of the Records Section which included overseeing the smooth running of the Bank's account opening procedures.

The Section's four clerical staff were all aged between 18 and 22 years of age with two to four years' experience of working for the Bank. All clerical staff generally passed through this Section as part of their career progression and the job was frequently the first one in which they had to undertake detailed face-to-face interviews with customers. Prior to their spell in Records, their customer contact experience would usually have been limited to telephone conversations and, possibly, relatively short transactional contact on the cashier positions.

The Records Section's responsibilities included:

- Interviewing new customers to open their accounts. The Bank required that all customers be seen by a member of staff when they opened a new account to ensure that all information was properly recorded.

*Coutts & Co. is the Bank's specialist upmarket banking subsidiary which provides a highly individual service to wealthy customers for which they pay a premium price for a level of attention which it would be impossible to provide cost effectively in a mass service outlet.

- Completing the internal formalities for opening and closing accounts.
- Maintenance of the basic customer records of the branch (for instance, recording changes of name and address).
- Responding to general queries on matters of banking procedure from the public.
- Opening accounts on behalf of other parts of the office. For instance, if the Lending Section agreed a new loan for a customer, the Records Section was responsible for all of the in-branch procedures which enabled the customer to withdraw his or her money.
- In common with all the sections of the branch, there was a general requirement for the Records Section to sell certain ancillary banking products once a customer need had been identified. Like other sections, Records had its own sales targets. The Bank's view was that a new customer interview provides an ideal opportunity to find ways in which other bank products might help the new customer.

The Section's Assistant Manager explained:

> *'It is an interesting section to manage. The mix of tasks means that the Section has a high degree of exposure to both external and internal customers with much of our work requiring an instant response. Yet at any given time at least one, and possibly two, of our staff will be new to the job and still probably receiving on-the-job training.'*

ACCOUNT OPENING PROCEDURES

One of the main reasons why customers were seen by a member of staff was to make sure that they chose the most appropriate account for their particular needs. This was regarded as being particularly important since the Bank offered such a wide range of basic current account products. It was important, for example, that the Records Officer discovered whether the customer wished to earn interest on surplus money or whether they were more likely to need to borrow from time to time. This would indicate, in part, which account was more appropriate for them. Some customers might even need a combination of both interest and borrowing facilities and there were appropriately tailored products for them. Special account products were available for differentiated groups such as students and young people. In addition, services such as credit and payment cards, cheque cards, ordinary and high interest accounts, travel services, loans and overdrafts, and personal insurance could be discussed in broad terms with the customer (although any request for credit facilities would have to be referred to the Lending Section). Depending on the customer's needs, it might be necessary to bring in somebody from one of the other sections if the customer required more specialist advice, on investments for example.

The account opening procedure also included taking and processing relevant customer information, or the *formalities* as they were known within the branch.

Appendix 15.1 shows a copy of the branch procedure checklist for opening a new 'current plus' account – an interest bearing current account with all the usual features of a normal current account. The information collected on this form was divided into three areas. First there was the checklist, which detailed the information required from the customer. The application contained personal details, name, address, employer, salary, etc., together with other useful information. This helped the Bank to market other products to the customer and also enabled credit references on the new customer to be checked so that the Bank could be protected against possible defaulters. Other formalities included completion of specimen signature cards, mandates for joint accounts to determine who could sign cheques on the account, Inland Revenue declarations to enable interest to be received without tax being deducted if the customer was so entitled, and various declarations regarding tax for persons resident overseas. A suitable piece of identification, such as a passport or employer's identity card, needed to be checked by the Records Officer at this point.

The second part of the form showed the formalities which were undertaken in the branch. The third area was the record of achievement of the branch standards for the transaction. These were seen as an important means of monitoring branch performance, and were reviewed regularly by the Administration Manager and periodically by the Senior Manager. The standards required an immediate interview and acceptable privacy, both aspects being regarded as central to ensuring customer satisfaction. The completion of internal formalities was shared by every member of the Section rather than allocated to one individual to see through from beginning to end.

Timing

The Bank felt that it was important that the customer should be seen immediately. The interview could last from 20 minutes to an hour depending on the complexity of the customer's needs, but typically would be 35 to 40 minutes. During the interview the customer was told that formalities would take up to 10 days because of the need to print cheque books, prepare plastic cards, take up references, etc. This was, to some extent, an attempt to manage customer expectations because the Bank's standards generally required the cheque book (which represented the customer's ability to use the account) to be sent out in four days. The margin was built into the time to cope with unforeseen delays. It was felt that if the cheque book could be sent out in four days it would better customer expectations and improve the customer's perception of service quality. Each of the internal formalities explained in the second part of the form generally took only a matter of minutes to complete, but the elapsed time from start to finish was considerably longer because some of the steps were out of the direct control of the branch. These steps were started first to minimise the total time the customer would have to wait.

Loading

The branch would normally open between 300 and 400 new accounts each month. For example, in November 1989, 351 accounts were opened, with the following profile:

current accounts	147
deposit accounts	86
loan accounts	37
personal loan accounts	32
high interest accounts	40
internal accounts	9

Nearly all of the 147 new current account holders would have been seen by one of the four Records Officers, but the formalities for most of the remaining accounts would be originated elsewhere in the branch. In these cases, the Records Section transacted only the internal formalities and had no direct customer contact.

Customers called into the branch to open accounts in an uneven flow which was impossible to predict accurately. However, peak demand generally occurred over the lunch-time period from about 11.45 a.m. to 2.15 p.m. This coincided with the period when Records Section staff were expected to cover for the cashier positions, in order to help with the lunch-time rush for cashier services.

COMPETITION IN THE RETAIL BANKING INDUSTRY

By the late 1980s competition in the UK banking industry was generally considered to be tough, with a growing number of players offering a broadly similar range of products. This meant that a customer could easily shop around if dissatisfied with any of the Bank's services. Competition was particularly intense in London's West End. Within a few minutes' walk of the St James's Square branch, disgruntled customers could take their business to any one of the English or Scottish clearing banks, a branch of most of the major building societies, National Girobank/the Post Office and even branches of French, Irish and other overseas banks. Quality of service, it was felt, could deliver a strong differential advantage for the branch.

The account opening process was one of the activities which was particularly important in creating an impression on the customer of a high quality of service. One manager at the branch observed:

> *'If we can't get it right at the start of our relationship, it is very difficult to fight your way back up in the customer's esteem. Account opening is crucial in setting the tone of the relationship. It gives us the opportunity to advise customers on which type of accounts are right for them and it makes sure that we haven't missed any sales opportunities. It also gives us our best chance of educating customers to what they can expect. In overall terms the intention is to create a feeling in the customer's mind that he is not going*

through a bureaucratic form filling process but rather that the Bank is trying to make things as easy as possible for him or her and that this is the start of an excellent new relationship.'

The general feeling among the staff at the branch was that customers probably expected a certain amount of bureaucracy, not least because they were conditioned by the traditional image of UK retail banking. But their requirements were probably quite simple. They were:

- To be able to complete the basic formalities as quickly as possible at their own convenience (which meant seeing a member of staff 'on demand').
- To have any formalities clearly explained and to receive general guidance.
- To be in a position to operate the new account as soon as possible. While customers accepted that taking up references, printing cheque books and preparing 'plastic' all took a little time, they expected it to take no more than a few days.
- Perhaps most importantly, they expected the highest degree of accuracy. Nothing infuriated a customer more than a basic spelling mistake in their name and Ms Smith had a right not to be inconvenienced by receiving a cheque card embossed with the name of Mr Smith.

THE CUSTOMER SURVEY

In late 1989 the branch decided to investigate customers' views of their account opening procedures. The survey confirmed their anxieties. The results did not make comforting reading:

- 36 per cent of respondents, all of whom had opened a new account over the period of the survey, felt that the opening forms/formalities were not properly explained to them.
- 76 per cent had not received the Bank's standard account pack which provided useful advice and information directed at new customers.
- 31 per cent received their cheque book and card within nine days, and could thus make full use of their account, but 44 per cent waited 10 to 14 days, and 25 per cent 15 days or more (an unacceptable delay in all but the most exceptional circumstances).
- 19 per cent had personal details wrongly recorded on statements, cheque books, etc.
- 71 per cent of new customers were broadly happy but 13 per cent found the staff inefficient and 6 per cent found them uninterested in the customer's needs.
- Finally, 24 per cent would not recommend the branch to others and the same percentage found the whole account opening procedure unsatisfactory.

This final point was felt to be quite crucial, word of mouth recommendation being an important factor in a customer's choice of branch.

RECORD SECTION STAFF VIEWS

The Assistant Manager of the Records Section was well aware of the problem. 'One of my staff put it in a nutshell,' he explained somewhat ruefully, 'when they said it would be a great job if it wasn't for the customers!' There was a general feeling that smooth work flow was continually being interrupted by customers calling without an appointment and needing to be seen immediately, a factor which impacted far less markedly on other sections of the branch. This had led to a feeling that the Records Section was burdened with an unfair share of the branch workload, a sentiment made worse by the fact that they consistently worked overtime (which added to branch overheads) whereas other sections often finished their work early and were able to leave earlier than the official time. Because of this the Section's morale and motivation had begun to suffer, which in turn impacted on the level of service.

The Assistant Manager summarised how he saw the problem by describing four 'typical' staff attitudes and the effect these could have on customers:

- 'I know that the customers deserve more of our time and attention, but we are just too overloaded.' Result: the customer gets a poor impression of the Bank just when they are at their most impressionable.
- 'At least the standard form is helpful. If you strictly follow it you can get through the interview without wasting too much time.' Result: the customers feel that they are 'on a production line'.
- 'It's all right for the other sections, they either have a queue of customers in front of them all the time or they keep to the back office. We have to do both types of work. You no sooner sit down to get on with a job than you are dragged away to the enquiry desk to see to a customer.' Result: the customer gets the feeling that they are an irritant to the staff.
- 'The pressure of work is not only high, it is also erratic, so it's not surprising that we occasionally make mistakes.' Result: customer and other parts of the branch suffer from any errors which are introduced right at the beginning of the process.

THE IMPROVEMENT TASK

Not surprisingly the Senior Manager was concerned at the level of customer dissatisfaction. The survey results contrasted sharply with the image the Bank wished to portray. In the Bank's own account opening literature it stated, 'Opening a bank account is an important step and should ideally lead to a lasting and helpful relationship between you and the bank.' He charged the Administration Manager with finding a solution.

The Administration Manager knew the constraints under which he was working:

'We can't throw money at the problem. Branch establishment cost constraints mean that it is not possible either to switch staff permanently from other sections or to increase the

overall level of staff in the branch. In any event, according to the Bank's sophisticated work measurement analysis the branch is properly staffed to meet the usual business requirements and to provide adequate cover for sickness, holidays, peaks in demand, etc. It will have to be a case of working more effectively with the staff we have.'

TWELVE MONTHS LATER

'It has been a total success story. Far better than we could have hoped for. It just shows you that, if you tackle these types of problem in the right manner, you can always find a better way to do things.' The Administration Manager was clearly delighted.

Questions

1 Analyse the customer contact process during the account opening procedure. What aspects of the branch's operation impact on each stage?

2 How would you improve the process?

A form dealing with the 'formalities' of account opening is shown in Appendix 15.1.

APPENDIX 15.1
'FORMALITIES' OF ACCOUNT OPENING

New Current Plus Account – Opening Procedure Checklist

Account Number

Customer Name ______

Date Opened ______

Customer Interview

Panel member to complete for all Accounts

	Required	Seen/Completed
Account opening application completed as appropriate		
Specimen Signature Card		
Identity confirmed by comparing documents with account opening form		
Mandate		
Statement Dispensation Form completed by Customer		
If Access/Visa Cardholder transferring from another Bank complete appropriate application form		
Composite Rate Tax–advise customer of implications Determine status by reference to ***Within scheme/exempt**		
Is non–resident TMA/CRT declaration 1 required?		
Is a Fiduciary Account Statement required?		

*delete as appropriate

Service Standards

Initial request made to open account	Date	
Immediate interview by member of panel?	Date	* Yes/No
Acceptable privacy of interview?		* Yes/No
Plastic Cards – customer advised issue dependent on satisfactory reference		* Yes/No
New Account Pack issued with tariff leaflet and Current Plus Terms and Conditions		* Yes/No

see over for Conversion of Accounts

Branch Records

Cautionary Notices checked		
Account Number allocated/Master Index completed		
Entered in Record of Accounts Opened		
Cheque Book ordered (Credit Book if required)	Date	
CRT status determined – write if necessary		
TMA/CRT Exemption–Declaration		
CRT exemption marker applied (if necessary)		
Fiduciary Account Statement		
Non–Resident marker and Geographical Code applied (if necessary)		
VAT Zero Rate marker (if necessary)		
Copy application sent for credit scoring (includes credit reference search)	Date	
Reply received and action taken	Date	Appt Officer's Initials
Decline letter sent if appropriate	Date	
Status enquiry written for (if applicable)	Date	
Satisfactory reply received	Date	Appt Officer's Initials
Servicecard ordered		
Cashcard ordered		
Cheque Card ordered (in exceptional circumstances)		

*Group Services Record Card raised/marked as appropriate		
*Control and Information Card raised/marked as appropriate		
Mandate checked		
*Kardex Card raised		
*Kardex Cross Reference Card raised (if necessary)		
Specimen Signature Card completed		
'No Central Marketing' marker applied (if required)		
Insurance Application to NWIS (if required)	Date	
SIC Code 00077 checked	Appt Officer's Initials	
Commission Code G checked	Appt Officer's Initials	
Application of CRZ or PNL checked	Appt Officer's Initials	

Service Standards

Cheque Book (Credit Book if required) issued	Within 4 days/ immediately formalities completed?	Date	
Letter of welcome sent			Yes/No
Delays advised/further information sought		Date	
Diary raised to contact customer		Date	

Service Standards reviewed. Branch Standards Achievement Register to be completed if standards not achieved — Appt Officer's Initials

Formalities completed and discharged from Record of Accounts opened — Appt Officer's Initials

Date

***Not appropriate for Branch Processor Branches**

APPENDIX 15.1
'FORMALITIES' OF ACCOUNT OPENING

New Current Plus Account – Opening Procedure Checklist

Account Number [ ]

Customer Name ______________________

Date Opened ______________________

Customer Interview

Panel member to complete for all Accounts

	Required	Seen/Completed
Account opening application completed as appropriate	[ ]	[ ]
Specimen Signature Card	[ ]	[ ]
Identity confirmed by comparing documents with account opening form	[ ]	[ ]
Mandate	[ ]	[ ]
Statement Dispensation Form completed by Customer	[ ]	[ ]
If Access/Visa Cardholder transferring from another Bank complete appropriate application form	[ ]	[ ]
Composite Rate Tax–advise customer of implications Determine status by reference to	[ ]	[ ]
*Within scheme/exempt		
Is non–resident TMA/CRT declaration 1 required?	[ ]	[ ]
Is a Fiduciary Account Statement required?	[ ]	[ ]

*delete as appropriate

Service Standards

Initial request made to open account	Date [ ]	
Immediate interview by member of panel?	Date [ ]	*Yes/No
Acceptable privacy of interview?		*Yes/No
Plastic Cards – customer advised issue dependent on satisfactory reference		*Yes/No
New Account Pack issued with tariff leaflet and Current Plus Terms and Conditions		*Yes/No

see over for Conversion of Accounts

Branch Records

Cautionary Notices checked		[ ]
Account Number allocated/Master Index completed		[ ]
Entered in Record of Accounts Opened		[ ]
Cheque Book ordered (Credit Book if required)	Date	[ ]
CRT status determined – write if necessary		[ ]
TMA/CRT Exemption–Declaration		[ ]
CRT exemption marker applied (if necessary)		[ ]
Fiduciary Account Statement		[ ]
Non–Resident marker and Geographical Code applied (if necessary)		[ ]
VAT Zero Rate marker (if necessary)		[ ]
Copy application sent for credit scoring (includes credit reference search)	Date	[ ]
Reply received and action taken	Date [ ]	Appt Officer's Initials [ ]
Decline letter sent if appropriate	Date	[ ]
Status enquiry written for (if applicable)	Date	[ ]
Satisfactory reply received	Date [ ]	Appt Officer's Initials [ ]
Servicecard ordered		[ ]
Cashcard ordered		[ ]
Cheque Card ordered (in exceptional circumstances)		[ ]

*Group Services Record Card raised/marked as appropriate		[ ]
*Control and Information Card raised/marked as appropriate		[ ]
Mandate checked		[ ]
*Kardex Card raised		[ ]
*Kardex Cross Reference Card raised (if necessary)		[ ]
Specimen Signature Card completed		[ ]
'No Central Marketing' marker applied (if required)		[ ]
Insurance Application to NWIS (if required)	Date	[ ]
SIC Code 00077 checked	Appt Officer's Initials	[ ]
Commission Code G checked	Appt Officer's Initials	[ ]
Application of CRZ or PNL checked	Appt Officer's Initials	[ ]

Service Standards

Cheque Book (Credit Book if required) issued / Letter of welcome sent	} Within 4 days/immediately formalities completed?	Date [ ]	Yes/No
Delays advised/further information sought		Date	[ ]
Diary raised to contact customer		Date	[ ]

Service Standards reviewed. Branch Standards Achievement Register to be completed if standards not achieved	Appt Officer's Initials	[ ]
Formalities completed and discharged from Record of Accounts opened	Appt Officer's Initials	[ ]
	Date	[ ]

*Not appropriate for Branch Processor Branches

Part 3

PLANNING AND CONTROL

Introduction

One of the most important tasks of an operations manager is to ensure that the organisation has sufficient input resources to be able to meet demand. This is the task of operations planning and control, the objective of which is to ensure that the operation runs effectively and produces products and services as it should do. It is concerned with the timing, quantity, quality and choice of transformed and transforming resources to ensure that the supply of products and services meets customer demand (*see* Fig. P3.1). Planning and control involves both managing demand for its products or service from actual or potential customers and matching them against its capability to supply them, today and in the future.

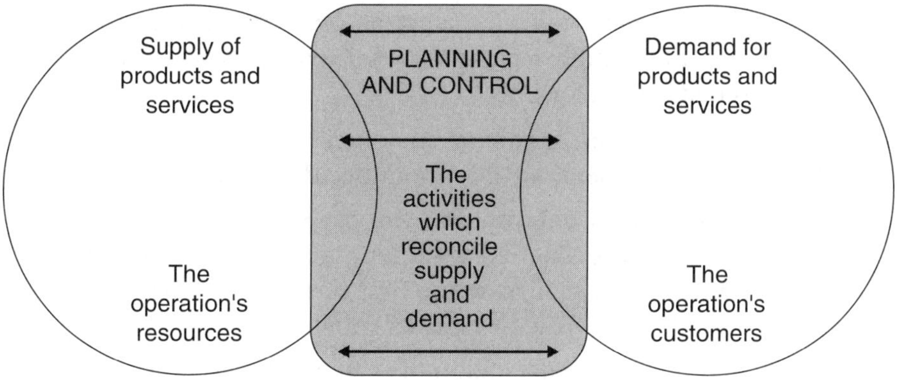

Fig. P3.1 Reconciling demand with supply

Planning versus control

A plan is a statement of intention based on expectations about the future. Planning the future allows an organisation to commit itself to longer-term expenditure which will be required to ensure that it can cope with the future. The plan may need to be reworked, or re-planned, to deal with known or anticipated changes as the date of implementation nears.

When the plan is implemented many things may go wrong and thus control is required to try to cope with whatever changes have occurred. Control is about making the necessary measurements and changes to allow the operation to meet its objectives – the objectives set by the plan. The closer to implementation, the more the task concerns control; the further away, the more it concerns planning.

Long-, medium- and short-term planning and control

In the long term, the planning and control task is primarily concerned with long-range planning. It is concerned with taking long-range forecasts and making appropriate long-term investments, or dis-investments, to try to meet the level of expected demand. This is done at a broad or aggregate level and may effect the number and size of operations locations, the approximate number of employees needed and the broad skills required, for example.

By the medium term some of the resources will be fixed and the forecast a little more certain. Planning is still usually at an aggregate level. Most operations use some form of master plan, schedule or timetable. This should be a realistic, achievable statement of what the organisation is planning to do; and it is checked against the operation's expected ability to supply, to see if meeting the forecast demand is feasible. If it is not, the plan must be altered. Any imbalances are usually dealt with using one, or a combination, of the following approaches: level capacity, chase demand, demand management (*see* below).

In the short term, the master plan provides the base for detailed planning of the day-to-day provision of goods or services, such as the operating theatres at Hillingdon Hospital (Case 18). The detailed planning of the operation will include loading, sequencing and scheduling decisions.

- *Loading* This task involves assigning customers/products to work centres, i.e. staff and/or machines. Essentially it is about deciding who, or what, will do what.
- *Sequencing* This concerns determining the order of jobs at each stage of the process. It is usually approached by allocating priorities to the jobs using predetermined rules, such as 'first come first served', or is based on a sequence of sizes, such as wide to narrow or large to small.
- *Scheduling* Scheduling is the allocation of start and finish times to each task and involves statements of the detailed timing of activities.

Furthermore, as the actual demand and mix will vary from day to day and hour by hour, control is needed in the short term to deal with the impact of queues, staff shortages, material shortages, equipment failures, etc. by re-loading, re-sequencing and rescheduling the work.

Dependent and independent demand

Planning is easier for some organisations than for others. If demand is relatively predictable and dependent upon some known factor then planning will be relatively logical and easy, certainly in comparison with an organisation which can only base plans or forecasts on what its management *believes* the market will require – based on, for example, historical demand for their products or services.

The first type of demand is referred to as dependent demand and is illustrated in the cases of Sheepbreeder (Case 25) and Farnray Tools (Case 27). Other cases document the problems of dealing with independent demand, without any firm future orders; see, for example, Holly Farm (Case 16) or Hillingdon Hospital (Case 18) where some 'demand' derives from unpredictable accidents.

There are many important activities involved in planning and controlling an operation. The remainder of this Part deals with each in turn:

- *Capacity planning and control* – planning and control at an aggregate level
- *Inventory planning and control* – managing physical inventory to meet intermediate or end demand
- *Supply chain planning and control* – ensuring the best flow of goods and services through the supply network
- *Materials Requirements Planning (MRP)* – planning and control of independent demand with the aid of a computer-based information system
- *Just-in-time planning and control* – producing goods and services exactly when needed
- *Project planning and control* – the planning and control of large and complex sets of interrelated activities
- *Quality planning and control* – ensuring the quality of the goods and services produced.

CAPACITY PLANNING AND CONTROL

Capacity planning and control is also sometimes referred to as *aggregate planning and control*. This is because demand and capacity (or resource) calculations are usually performed on an aggregated basis which does not discriminate between the different products and services which an operation might produce. Holly Farm (Case 16) uses customers and litres of ice-cream, Crocodile Ice House (Case 17) uses the number of orders and Peas (Case 24) uses tonnes of peas harvested. The essence of the task is, at a general and aggregated level, to reconcile the supply of capacity with the level of demand which it must satisfy.

Capacity planning and control, as dealt with here, is concerned with setting capacity levels over the medium and short terms *in aggregated terms*. That is, it is making overall, broad capacity decisions while not concerned with all of the details of the individual products and services offered. Thus aggregate plans assume that the mix of different products and services will remain relatively constant during the planning period.

What is capacity?

The capacity of an operation is the maximum throughput of an operation over a period of time. Capacity may be measured in terms of inputs, process or output capacity, and there will usually be some constraints upon the organisation's capacity. For Holly Farm (Case 16), for example, there is a limit to the number of cars and coaches that it can accommodate (input capacity) although maximum depends on the mix of cars and coaches and how long they stay. The organisation's ice-cream processing has a maximum daily capacity, limited by its ability to fast freeze its output. Its ice-cream storage is also limited by its freezer capacity.

Capacity plans

There are three main ways of managing capacity, that is trying to reconcile supply and demand at an aggregate level:

- *Level capacity plan* Ignore demand fluctuations and keep activity levels constant
- *Chase demand plan* Adjust capacity to reflect the fluctuations in demand
- *Demand management* Attempt to change demand to fit capacity availability.

In practice, most organisations will use a mixture of all of these 'pure' plans, although often one plan might dominate.

Level capacity plan

In a level capacity plan, the processing capacity is set at a uniform level throughout the planning period, regardless of the fluctuations in forecast demand. This means that the same number of staff operate the same processes and should, therefore, be capable of producing the same aggregate output in each period. Level capacity plans of this type can achieve the advantages of stable employment patterns, high process utilisation, and usually also high productivity with low unit costs. Unfortunately, they can also create considerable inventory which has to be financed and stored. Perhaps the biggest problem, however, is that decisions have to be taken as to what to produce for inventory rather than for immediate sale. Some organisations have little alternative but to adopt a level capacity plan because they are physically constrained. Hillingdon Hospital (Case 18), for example, is constrained by the number of operating theatres it can use. Yet because some elements of demand (emergencies) must be treated quickly, other elements of demand (non-urgent operations) are disrupted.

Chase demand plan

An alternative capacity plan is one which attempts to match capacity closely to the varying levels of forecast demand. This is much more difficult to achieve than a level capacity plan, as different numbers of staff, different working hours – and even different amounts of equipment – may be necessary in each period. Also, for particularly capital-intensive operations, the chase demand policy would require a higher level of physical capacity, some of which would only be used occasionally.

Crocodile Ice House (Case 17), for example, is a mail-order operation serving the Christmas gifts market, so most of its order processing is conducted on a chase demand basis in October to December.

Manage demand

A third approach is to try to 'manage' demand to match more closely the organisation's productive capacity. There are several ways of doing this, for example: changing the level of demand through the price mechanism or using promotions; creating alternative products or services to use spare capacity; or attracting customers away from heavily used capacity. Careful target marketing is crucial to get the best demand profile:capacity match.

The Holly Farm case (Case 16) provides opportunities to investigate these capacity plans. Sometimes the capacity plan is influenced by the supply of transformed resources (inputs) and this is illustrated in the Peas case (Case 24). Murray Rock Drilling Ltd (Case 19) has run into trouble on its delivery dates. All products essentially go through the same sequence of operations; however, an order seems to spend a large amount of time with little happening to it. Understanding capacity problems is at the bottom of Murray's problems.

INVENTORY PLANNING AND CONTROL

Inventory is the stored accumulation of physical material resources in the operation. These could be stocks of blood (Case 22) or stocks of ice-cream (Case 16), for example. In some organisations the value of the inventory might be quite small, in others it is large. The Blood Supply case (Case 22) case is an interesting example as the value of the inventory is very high but has no intrinsic 'price'.

Types of inventory

Inventory is often classified into raw material, work-in-progress and finished goods. However, it is often more useful to categorise it in terms of its role in the operation's system.

- *Buffer inventory.* Buffer inventory is also called safety inventory; its purpose is to compensate for the uncertainties inherent in supply and demand. By holding buffer inventories organisations can help ensure that they can meet demand even if it is greater than anticipated or in case the delivery of goods, either from the operation or a supplier, does not arrive on time (*see* Vector Valves Ltd, for example, Case 23).
- *Cycle inventory.* Cycle inventory occurs because an organisation chooses to produce or purchase in batches or lots in quantities greater than are immediately required by subsequent operations or customers (*see*, for example, Farnray Tools, Case 27).

- *Anticipation inventory.* Anticipation inventory is made in anticipation of changes in demand or supply. It is most commonly used when seasonal demand fluctuations are significant but relatively predictable. It might also be used when supply variations are significant, such as in the freezing of seasonal foods (*see* Peas, Case 24, for example).
- *Pipeline inventory.* Pipeline inventory exists because materials cannot be transported instantaneously between the points of supply and the points of demand. Material 'in transit' is referred to as pipeline inventory. Cadbury Ltd (Case 20) includes an example of *internal* pipeline inventory.

Inventory decisions

There are three key decisions associated with inventories:

- How much to order – every time a replenishment order is placed, externally or internally, how big should it be?
- When to order – at what point in time, or at what level of stock, should the replenishment order be placed?
- Which items are the most important – should different priorities be allocated to different stock items?

How much to order?

This decision usually requires the balancing of two sets of costs: the costs associated with purchasing the items and the costs associated with holding inventory. One option would be to hold very small stock and to purchase when needed. Although this approach has the benefit of only spending money when materials are needed, there may be a high cost in terms of time and inconvenience in having to make frequent purchases. Alternatively, purchasing very large amounts infrequently would have the effect of minimising the cost and inconvenience of making the purchases but would result in very large stock holding. This is an important issue raised in the Crocodile Ice House (Case 17). Organisations, therefore, have to make a balance of judgement between all the costs involved in stock holding and replenishment, including:

- the costs of placing orders (or setting-up processes)
- price discounts for bulk purchases
- working capital costs
- storage costs
- obsolescence costs.

When to order?

If stock arrived immediately after it was ordered this would be a simple decision. However, in reality there may be a variable lag in the system between order and arrival and also variability in the use of the item, so both supply and demand is uncertain. Operations managers can try to make their decisions on the best time to order, based on their understanding and experience of order lead times (and their variability) and demand variability. However, again, it is a case of balancing judgements about the most appropriate levels of safety stock and optimum ordering times, and is often problematical. This is a particularly difficult problem for the National Blood Transfusion Service (Case 22).

Which items are the most important?

In any inventory which contains more than one stocked item, some will be more important to the organisation than others. Some items, for example, may have a very high usage rate, so if they ran out many customers would be disappointed. Other items may be of particularly high value, so excessively high inventory levels would be particularly expensive. One common way of discriminating between different stock items is to rank them by their usage value (their usage rate multiplied by their individual value) and categorise them into class A, B and C items:

- Class A items – those 20 per cent or so of high value items which account for around 80 per cent of the total usage value;
- Class B items – those of medium value, usually the next 30 per cent, which account for around 10 per cent of the total usage value;
- Class C items – those low value items which, although comprising around 50 per cent of the total types of items stocked, probably only account for around 10 per cent of the total usage value of stocked items.

Vector Valves Ltd (Case 23) has a number of inventory related problems. This case brings together the issues of managing inventory with the problem of dealing with distant suppliers with long lead times.

SUPPLY CHAIN PLANNING AND CONTROL

Supply chain planning and control is concerned with the flow of goods and services through the supply network, from suppliers through to customers. In large organisations there can be many hundreds of strands of linked operations through which goods and services flow into and out of the operation. These strands are usually referred to as supply chains. A supply chain as a whole can be likened to the flow of water in a river: organisations located closer to the original source of supply are described as being 'upstream', those located closer to the end customer are 'downstream'.

There are three main areas in understanding supply chain planning and control:

- *purchasing and supplier development* – the role of the purchasing function in forming contacts with suppliers to supply the organisation (upstream activities);

- *physical distribution management* – the movement of products or services to the customer (downstream activities);
- *supply chain management* – co-ordinating the whole of the supply chain.

Purchasing and supplier development

At the supply end of the business, the purchasing function forms contracts with suppliers to buy-in materials and services. Some of these materials and services are used in the production of the goods and services sold on to customers. Other materials and services are used to help run the business: for example, staff catering services or oil for machinery. These do not make up part of the finished goods or service but are still essential purchases for operations.

There are four key objectives for the purchasing function and these are discussed below.

Purchasing at the right price

This is an important way of providing the organisation with a cost advantage as the cost of materials may have a significant effect on an organisation's overall costs. This is a transitional activity of purchasing – to secure the best possible deal.

Purchasing for delivery at the right time and in the right quantity

Purchasing at the right time and in the right quantity can also have an important impact on the operation's overall performance. Success in this area requires the purchasing function to understand the operations processes and forecast activity, and the intricacies of lead times, volumes and seasonalities, for example. Successful management of timing and quantities has a big influence on inventory levels (working capital).

Purchasing at the right quality

The quality of incoming goods and services will have an important impact on the quality of the processed goods and services, and also on their reliability and dependability. While in the past many organisations would carefully inspect all incoming items, purchasing functions are now working closely with suppliers to ensure that incoming goods and services will conform to the agreed quality specifications, through supplier quality programmes, for example.

Purchasing from the right source

One key function of a purchasing department is to make choices between various suppliers. Decisions may not only rest on price and quality but also on future potential, and willingness to develop what they do, and to work with the downstream organisations. A second issue here is the decision of whether to have just one organisation to provide the goods or services (single source) or to reduce the risk in problems of supply through multi-sourcing.

Physical distribution management

On the demand side of the organisation, products (and sometimes services) need to be moved to the customer, involving the physical transportation of materials through the supply chain. The main issues which confront the manager concerned with distribution are:

- The mode of transport to be used – for example, road, rail, water, air or pipeline.
- The use of warehousing, or hubs, to simplify routes and communication, whereby many products can be distributed to regional warehouses so that end customers only need to deal with one warehouse instead of many.
- Deciding contract terms, in particular agreeing who takes the risks involved in transporting the products and deciding when the products will be paid for.

Supply chain management

In the past, some organisations have seen purchasing, distribution and even inventory management as almost independent and distinct functions. This approach tends to underrate the importance of management of the whole flow of materials from upstream suppliers to downstream users through many distribution channels. Supply chain management is concerned with the management of the *whole* supply chain, from raw material supply right through to distribution to the end customer.

The three main objectives of supply chain management are discussed below.

To focus on satisfying end customers

Because supply chain management includes all stages in the total flow of materials and information, it must be based on consideration of the needs of the final customer. It is only the final customer who has the only 'real' currency in the supply chain. When a customer decides to make a purchase he or she triggers action along the whole chain. All the businesses in the supply chain pass on portions of that end customer's money to each other, each retaining their margin for the value they have added. If each link in that chain does not understand their role in the supply chain, the final customer's needs may not be met.

To formulate and implement strategies based on capturing and retaining end customer business

The key operation in a chain is the strongest business which is in a position to influence and direct the others, so that they work together in the common cause of capturing and retaining the end customer's business. This organisation may then take responsibility for setting the standards and determining the design of the infrastructure, such as the information systems used, to which the downstream dealer network needs to comply.

To manage the chain effectively and efficiently

Taking an holistic approach to managing an entire supply chain opens up many opportunities for analysis and improvement, especially in shortening time-to-market, dealing with 'bottleneck' organisations, and performing cost and value analysis of the whole supply chain to try to generate cost savings across the whole supply chain.

MRP

The purpose of MRP is to help organisations plan and control their resource requirements with the aid of computer-based information systems. Over the last 20 years, the concept of MRP has developed from an operations tool which helped in planning and controlling materials requirements (MRPI), to become, in recent years, a broader business system which helps plan all business resource requirements (MRPII).

MRPI – materials requirement planning

Materials requirement planning, usually referred to as MRPI, is a computerised control and information system that provides a formal plan for every part, raw material, component and sub-assembly. It co-ordinates all manufacturing decisions – based on forecast demand and actual orders – from ordering, through the control of stock levels and work-in-progress, to the supply of the finished products. Its aim is to help organisations calculate how many materials of particular types are needed and when they are needed in order to manufacture their products to meet the actual and anticipated needs of their customers.

Because of the often complex nature of this activity, due to the numbers of different components involved in products and the varieties of products produced, this activity is usually undertaken by computer.

MRP generates purchase orders and work orders for items, based on forecasts and actual orders, and so is a dependent demand system. It involves a number of stages:

1 *Demand management* – this involves generating customer order and sales forecasts for the products and also the physical distribution of the finished items. This information is fed into the master production schedule.
2 *Master production schedule* – this provides the main input into the MRP system and is a statement of time-phase records of each end product, current and expected demand and available stocks.
3 *MRP* – the MRP system takes the master production schedule together with the bills of materials (BOM) for the products and the inventory records of all existing component parts and effectively explodes the top level demand through bills of materials, taking into account inventory and lead times at each level in order to generate:

- purchase orders
- works orders and
- material plans.

The Farnray Tools case study (Case 27) provides an opportunity to understand in detail how MRPI works and to discuss some of the problems involved in using MRP systems.

MRPII – manufacturing resource planning

During the last 20 years the concept of MRPI has expanded and been integrated with other parts of the business, each of which may have held their own computerised databases. A product structure or bill of materials, for example, may be held in the engineering department and also in materials management. If engineering changes are made to the design of products, both databases have to be updated. It is difficult to keep both databases entirely identical and discrepancies between them cause problems, which often are not apparent until a member of staff is supplied with the wrong parts to manufacture the product or stocks of the required items are unavailable. Similarly, cost information from finance and accounting, which is used to perform management accounting tasks such as variance analysis against standard costs, needs to be reconciled with changes made elsewhere in the operation, such as changes in inventory holding or process methods.

Manufacturing resource planning, or MRPII, is based on one integrated system containing a database which is accessed and used by the whole company according to their functional requirements. This ensures the updating of bills of materials as design modifications are made, allowing for updates of stock costs and product costings to take place, for example. However, despite its dependence on the information technologies which allow such integration, MRPII still relies on people providing the right information at the right time and doing the right things with that information!

JUST-IN-TIME PLANNING AND CONTROL

The aim of a JIT approach is to produce goods and services exactly when they are needed, with perfect quality and no waste, and is a philosophy of manufacturing embodying a collection of tools and techniques.

The JIT philosophy

JIT is a philosophy founded on doing the simple things well, or gradually doing them better, and on squeezing out waste every step of the way. It involves three core principles:

- *The elimination of waste* – the removal of any activity which does not add value.
- *The involvement of everyone* – JIT is a 'total system' approach which aims to pull together everyone in a system.
- *Continuous improvement* – the JIT objective, which, being an ideal, aims to promote continuous improvement through an organisation.

JIT tools

JIT comprises a collection of tools for reducing waste and these include:

- *Basic working practices*, such as the use of standards, fair personnel policies and working practices, flexibility of responsibilities, autonomy, 'line stop' authority (allowing people to stop the process if problems are occurring) and an improvement in problem solving, data gathering and personal development.
- *Design for manufacture* – fostering a close relationship between design and operations to ensure that what is designed can be made well.
- *Operations focus* – focusing on simplicity, repetition and experience.
- *Small simple machines* – using several small machines instead of one large general-purpose machine as smaller machines may perform more reliably, are easy to maintain, and produce better quality over time. Small machines are also easier to move and to modify.
- *Layout and flow* – layout techniques can be used to promote the smooth flow of materials, of data, and of people in the operation. Long complex process routes may cause large quantities of inventory and slow the process, both of which are contrary to JIT principles.
- *Total productive maintenance (TPM)* – TPM aims to eliminate the variability in operations processes which results from unplanned breakdowns.
- *Set-up reduction (SUR)* – set-up times can be reduced by a variety of methods such as cutting out time taken to search for tools and equipment, the pre-preparation of tasks which delay change-overs, and the constant practice of set-up routines, all of which contribute to the elimination of waste.
- *Total people involvement* – total people involvement is concerned with providing people with the training and support to take full responsibility for all aspects of their work, including dealing directly with suppliers, measurement and reporting, process improvements, budgets and plans, and dealing directly with customers and their problems.
- *Visibility* – problems, quality projects and operations checklists are made visible by displaying them locally so that they can easily be seen and understood by all staff.

JIT planning and control techniques

There are three techniques which deal specifically with the planning and control of operations using JIT:

- *Kanban control* – Kanban is the Japanese for card or signal. It is sometimes called the 'invisible conveyor' which controls the transfer of materials between the stages of an operation. In its simplest form, it is a card used by a customer stage to instruct its supplier stage to send more materials. This is a key signal to produce and ensures that production only takes place when items are required, in the quantity in which they are required.
- *Levelled scheduling* – this activity attempts to equalise the mix of products or services made each day to create a simple and repetitive cycle. This makes control easier and more visible.
- *Synchronisation* – Many companies make a wide variety of parts and products, not all of them with sufficient regularity to warrant levelled scheduling. Synchronisation dictates that parts need to be classified according to the frequency with which they are demanded, and tries to make production as regular and predictable as possible.

Some of these issues are addressed in the Massey Ferguson JIT purchasing and supply case (Case 26). The case centres on the difficulties of providing a 'seamless' relationship between the operations planning and control systems of supplier and customer.

PROJECT PLANNING AND CONTROL

A project is a set of activities, often large scale and complex, which has a defined start point and a defined end state, pursues a defined goal and uses a defined set of resources. Projects have several elements in common:

- they have a defined objective or end result;
- they are complex, consisting of many related events;
- they are unique, that is they produce 'specials' – non-repeated outputs;
- they are also uncertain and contain an element of risk;
- they require a temporary allocation of resources until completion;
- they follow a predictable life cycle which affects the nature of planning and control activities.

The project planning and control process

Project management planning and control can be categorised into four stages relevant to project planning and control.

Stage 1 Understanding the project environment – the internal and external factors which may influence the project

The project environment comprises all the factors which may affect the project during its life, such as political, geographic, economic, other projects being carried out, or even the history of previous projects carried out for the customer. Each of these may influence how the project is carried out and will affect the degree of risk inherent in the project.

Stage 2 Defining the project – setting the objectives, scope and strategy for the project

Before starting the complex task of planning and executing a project, it is necessary to be as clear as possible about what is going to be done: the objectives, the scope of the project and the strategy for meeting the objectives. Some projects are simpler to define than others. Projects where all the major tasks have been done before, where methods and equipment have already been proven, can be defined reasonably well in advance (*see* The Glastonbury Festival, Case 3). Completely new projects may be much more difficult to define.

Stage 3 Project planning – deciding how the project will be executed

Project planning involves the detailed step-by-step planning of all the activities involved in the project. It involves breaking the overall complex task down into separate activities, estimating the time and resources required for each activity, and the relationships and dependencies between them. This information is used to create a schedule of activities and to identify the time critical or resource critical activities in the project.

The planning process fulfils four distinct purposes:

- It determines the cost and duration of the project. This enables major decisions to be made – such as the decision whether to go ahead with the project at the start.
- It determines the level of resources which will be needed.
- It helps to allocate work and to monitor progress. Planning must include the identification of who is responsible for what.
- It helps to assess the impact of any changes to the project.

Stage 4 Project control – ensuring that the project is carried out according to plan

This stage deals with the management activities which take place during the execution of the project. The process of project control involves three sets of activities:

- Monitoring the project in order to check on its progress using a variety of measures such as cost, overtime and delays.
- Assessing the time performance of the project by comparing monitored observations of the project with the project plan.

- Intervening in the project in order to make the changes which will bring it back to plan. This can be a complex decision due to the interrelatedness of the activities in a project; so making changes in one area will have knock-on effects elsewhere.

Vixen Instruments: the 'Scantel' project (Case 21) illustrates all these essential characteristics of project planning and control. You may also want to consider some of the issues discussed in product/service design studying this case. The Tesco Composites case (Case 28) tracks the planning and control of a major project for the implementation of a new system of warehousing, from the early contractual phase through to operationalisation. The four-stage model above can be used to follow the progress of this project.

QUALITY PLANNING AND CONTROL

Quality is often defined as 'consistent conformance to customers' expectations'. This definition does not take account of the fact that the quality of a product or service may be perceived differently by different customers. A definition that integrates the operations' view of quality, concerned with trying to meet customers' expectations, and the customer's perceived view of quality is: 'quality is the degree of fit between customers' expectations and their perception of the product or service'. If the product or service experience was better than expected then the customer is satisfied and quality is perceived to be high. If the product or service was less than his or her expectations, then quality is seen as low and the customer may be dissatisfied. If the product or service matches expectations then the perceived quality of the product or service is seen to be acceptable.

Diagnosing quality problems

The gap between expectations and perceptions may be caused by four related gaps:

1. *The customer specification – operations specification gap* Perceived quality could be poor because there may be a mismatch between the organisation's own internal quality specification and the specification that is expected by the customer.
2. *The concept – specification gap* Perceived quality could be poor because there is a mismatch between the product or service concept and the way the organisation has internally specified the quality of the product or service.
3. *The quality specification – actual quality gap* Perceived quality could be poor because there is a mismatch between the actual quality of the service or product provided by the operation and its internal quality specification.
4. *The actual quality – communicated image gap* Perceived quality could also be poor because there is a gap between the organisation's external communications or market image and the actual quality of the service or product delivered to the customer.

The quality planning and control activity

Of the four gaps described above, the one for which operations managers bear the most responsibility is to ensure that the product or service conforms to its required specification (gap 3). Quality planning and control tries to ensure that gap 3 does not exist. This involves six sequential steps (the first four are dealt with here and the remaining two in Part 4):

Step 1 Define the quality characteristics of the product or service

The detailed design specification of the product or service should provide operations managers with a clear understanding of the characteristics of that product or service and how it is expected to perform. The characteristics will include functionality, appearance, reliability, durability, recovery (ease of repair) and contact (the nature of person-to-person contact involved in the delivery of the product or service).

Step 2 Decide how to measure each quality characteristic

For every product or service these characteristics must be defined in such a way so that they can be measured and then controlled. This involves taking a very general quality characteristic, such as functionality or appearance, and breaking it down into its constituent elements. Measures for each element need then to be established, either objectively in the case of size or shape for example, or subjectively in the case of customer perceptions of courtesy or empathy.

The measures used by operations to describe quality characteristics are of two types – variables and attributes. Variable measures are those that can be measured on a continuously variable scale, for example length, diameter, weight or time. Attributes are those which are assessed by judgement and are dichotomous (that is, have two states), for example right or wrong, works or does not work, looks OK or not OK.

Step 3 Set quality standards for each quality characteristic

When operations managers have identified how any quality characteristic can be measured they need a quality standard against which it can be checked, otherwise they will not know whether it indicates good or bad performance. The critical task for operations managers is setting reasonable and achievable targets which will be appropriate to the level of customers' expectations. In the case of variables these are usually called 'tolerances' within which the variable is required to conform (for example plus or minus one millimetre).

Step 4 Control quality against those standards

After setting up appropriate standards that are capable of being met by the operation and that will meet customers' expectations, the operation will then need to check that the products or services conform to those standards. This involves three key decisions:

- Where in the operation should they check that it is conforming to standards? The key task for operations managers is to identify the critical control points at which the service, products or processes need to be checked to ensure that the product or services will conform to specification.
- Should they check every product or service or take a sample? Having decided the points at which the goods or services will be checked the next decision is how many of the products or services to check. While it might seem ideal to check every single product being produced or every service being delivered, operations usually work on samples since 100 per cent inspection may be too costly, time-consuming or even dangerous.
- How should the checks be performed? There are two main methods which can be employed to help operations check samples and make reasonable predictions about all the products or services created. Statistical process control (SPC) aims to achieve good quality through prevention rather than detection. Once a process is under statistical control, predications can be made about how it should behave. Regular sampling of the process enables managers to make rational decisions about what action to take, if any, in order to maintain control. Acceptance sampling is concerned with whether to regard a complete incoming or outgoing batch of materials or customers as acceptable or not, on the basis of inspection of a representative sample.

Step 5 – Find and correct causes of poor quality *and* Step 6 – Continue to make improvements are dealt with in Part 4

Valley District Council Cleansing Services (Case 29) illustrates the application of SPC in a service setting. The case also brings up the issue of the 'total quality' nature of the business environment in which SPC is used. Sun Products (Case 30) provides an exercise in control charting and data are supplied to enable the calculation of process capability indices and to compile run charts.

SUMMARY

Planning and control is a central and critical responsibility of operations. It involves ensuring that the operation has sufficient resources to be able to meet demand. It involves decisions in the short term to ensure current demand for products and services can be met and also long- and medium-term decisions to prepare for future anticipated demand. Key planning and control activities include:

- planning and controlling the use of resources (capacity planning)
- managing physical stocks to meet end demand (inventory planning and control)

- ensuring the optimal flow of goods and services through the supply network (supply chain planning and control)
- planning and control of independent demand with the aid of a computer-based information system (MRP)
- producing goods and services exactly when needed (just-in-time planning and control)
- the planning and control of large and complex activities (project planning and control)
- ensuring the quality of the goods and services produced (quality planning and control).

Key points

- The purpose of planning and control is to ensure that the operation runs effectively and produces products and services as it should do.
- Planning is the act of setting down expectations of what should happen. Control is the process of monitoring events against the plan and making any necessary adjustments.
- The balance between planning and control changes over time. In long-term planning and control the emphasis is on the aggregated planning and budgeting of activities. At the other extreme, short-term planning and control usually operates within the resource constraints of the operation but makes interventions into the operation in order to cope with short-term changes in circumstances.
- In planning and controlling three distinct activities are necessary: loading, sequencing and scheduling.
- The capacity of an operation is the maximum level of value-added activity which it can achieve under normal operating conditions over a period of time.
- There are three basic plans for capacity planning and control: the level capacity plan, the chase demand plan and demand management.
- There are three major types of decision which operations managers need to make regarding the planning and control of their inventory. These are:
  - How much to order
  - When to order
  - Which items are the most important.
- The purchasing function attempts to obtain goods or services at the right price, for delivery at the right time, in the right quality, in the right quantity, from the right source.
- Supply chain management is concerned with the management of the entire supply chain from raw materials supply, manufacture, assembly and distribution to the

end customer. It includes the strategic and long-term consideration of supply chain management issues as well as the shorter-term control of flow throughout the supply chain.

- Materials requirements planning (MRPI) is a system for calculating materials requirements and creating production plans to satisfy known and forecast sales orders.
- Manufacturing resource planning (MRPII) incorporates engineering, financial and marketing information in an integrated business system for manufacturing businesses.
- The aim of just-in-time (JIT) operations is to meet demand instantaneously with perfect quality and no waste.
- JIT can be seen both as an overall philosophy of operations but also as a collection of tools and methods which support its aims.
- A project is a set of activities which have a defined start point and a defined end state, that pursue a defined goal and that use a defined set of resources.
- Project management has four stages relevant to project planning and control: understanding the project environment; defining the project; project planning; and project control.
- Quality is the degree of fit between customers' expectations and their perception of the product or service.
- There are six steps involved in quality planning and control: define quality characteristics; decide how to measure each of the quality characteristics; set quality standards for each characteristic; control quality against these standards; find the correct cause of the poor quality and continue to make improvements.

Recommended reading

Slack, N., Chambers, S., Harland, C., Harrison, A. and Johnston, R. (1998), *Operations Management* (2nd edn), Pitman Publishing. Chapters 10, 11, 12, 13, 14, 15, 16 and 17.

Selected further readings

Bailey, P. and Farmer, D. (1990), *Purchasing Principles and Management* (6th edn), Pitman Publishing.

Bicheno, J. (1991), *Implementing JIT*, IFS Publications.

Bounds, G., Yorks, L., Adams, M. and Ranney, G. (1994), *Beyond Quality Management: Towards the emerging paradigm*, McGraw-Hill.

Burns, O. M., Turnipseed, D. and Riggs, W. E. (1991), 'Critical success factors in manufacturing resource planning implementation', *International Journal of Operations and Production Management*, Vol 11, No 4 pp. 5–19.

Dale, D. G. (ed.), (1994), *Managing Quality* (2nd edn), Prentice Hall.

Evans, J. R. and Lindsay, W. M. (1993), *The Management and Control of Quality* (2nd edn), West Publishing Company.

Fiedler, K., Galletly, J. E. and Bicheno, J. (1993), 'Expert Advice for JIT Implementation', *International Journal of Operations and Production Management*, Vol 13, No 6 pp. 23–30.
Gilbreath, R. D. (1986), *Winning at Project Management*, Wiley.
Harrison, A. S. (1992), *Just-in-Time Manufacturing in Perspective*, Prentice Hall.
Jessop, D. and Morrison, A. (1991), *Storage and Control of Stock*, Pitman Publishing.
Lockyer, K. and Gordon, J. (1991), *Project Management and Project Network Techniques*, Pitman Publishing.
Meredith, J. R. and Mantel, S., (1989), *Project Management: A Managerial Approach* (2nd edn), Wiley.
Oakland, J. (1995), *Total Quality Management: Text with Cases*, Butterworth-Heinemann.
Orlicky, J. (1975), *Material Requirements Planning*, McGraw-Hill.
Owen, M. (1993), *SPC and Business Improvement*, IFS.
Primrose, P.L. (1990), 'Selecting and evaluating cost effective MRP and MRPII', *International Journal of Operations and Production Management,* Vol 10, No 1.
Primrose, P .L. (1992), 'The Value of Inventory Savings', *International Journal of Operations and Production Management*, Vol 12, No 5.
Tersine, R. J. (1987), *Principles of Inventory and Materials Management* (2nd edn), North Holland.
Vollmann, T. E., Berry, W. L. and Whybark, D. C. (1992), *Manufacturing Planning and Control Systems* (3rd edn), Irwin.

CASE 16

Holly Farm

Stuart Chambers

Case date 1989

INTRODUCTION

In 1983, Fred and Gillian Giles decided to open up their mixed (dairy and arable) farm to the paying public, in response to diminishing profits from their milk and cereals activities. They invested all their savings into building a 40-space car park and six-space park for 40-seater coaches, a safe viewing area for the milking parlour, special trailers for passengers to be transported around the farm on guided tours, a permanent exhibition of equipment, a 'rare breeds' paddock, a children's adventure playground, a picnic area and a farm shop. Behind the farm shop they built a small 'factory' making real dairy ice-cream, which also provided for public viewing. Ingredients for the ice-cream – pasteurised cream and eggs, sugar, flavourings, etc. – were bought out, although this was not obvious to the viewing public.

Gillian took responsibility for all these new activities while Fred continued to run the commercial farming business. Through advertising, giving lectures to local schools and organisations such as Women's Institutes, and through personal contact with coach firms, the number of visitors to the farm increased steadily. By 1988 Gillian became so involved in running her business that she was unable to give so much time to these promotional activities, and the number of paying visitors levelled out to around 15 000 per year. Although the farm opened to the public at 11 a.m. and closed at 7 p.m. after milking was finished, up to 90 per cent of visitors in cars or coaches would arrive later than 12.30 p.m., picnic until around 2 p.m., and tour the farm until about 4 p.m. By that time, around 20 per cent would have visited the farm shop and left, but the remainder would wait to view the milking, then visit the shop to purchase ice-cream and other produce, and then depart. The entry fee was £2.

VISITORS TO THE FARM

Gillian opened the farm to the public each year from April to October inclusive. Demand would be too low outside this period, the conditions were often unsuitable for regular tractor rides and most of the animals had to be kept inside. Early experience had confirmed that mid-week demand was too low to justify opening, but Friday through Monday was commercially viable, with almost exactly twice as many visitors on Saturdays and Sundays than on Fridays or Mondays. Gillian summed up the situation thus:

'I have decided to attempt to increase the number of farm visitors in 1989 by 50 per cent. This would not only improve our return on the "farm tours" assets, but also would help the farm shop to achieve its targets, and the extra sales of ice-cream would help to keep the "factory" at full output. The real problem is whether to promote sales to coach firms or to intensify local advertising to attract more families in cars. We could also consider tie-ups with schools for educational visits, but I would not want to use my farm guides staff on any extra weekdays, as Fred needs them three days per week for "real" farming work.

'However, most of the farm workers, and their wives, are glad of this amount of work as it fits in well with their family life, and helps them to save up for the luxuries most farm workers cannot afford.'

THE MILKING PARLOUR

With 150 cows to milk, Fred invested in a 'carousel' parlour where cows are milked on a slow-moving turntable. Milking usually lasts from 4.30 p.m. to 7 p.m., during which time visitors can view from a purpose-built gallery which has space and explanatory tape recordings, via headphones, for 12 people. Gillian has found that on average spectators like to watch for ten minutes, including five minutes for the explanatory tape.

'We're sometimes a bit busy on Saturdays and Sundays and a queue often develops before 4 p.m. as some people want to see the milking and then go home. Unfortunately, neither Fred nor the cows are prepared to start earlier. However, most people are patient and everybody gets their turn to see this bit of high technology. In a busy period, up to 80 people per hour pass through the gallery.'

THE ICE-CREAM FACTORY

The factory is operated 48 weeks per year, four days per week, eight hours per day, throughout the year. The three employees, farm workers' wives, are expected to work in line with farm opening from April to October, but hours and days are by negotiation in other months. All output is in one litre plastic boxes, of which 350 are made every day, which is the maximum mixing and fast-freezing capacity. Although extra mixing hours would create more unfrozen ice-cream, the present equipment cannot safely and fully fast freeze more than 350 litres over a 24-hour period. Ice-cream that is not fully frozen cannot be transferred to the finished goods freezer, as slower freezing spoils the texture of the product. As it takes about one hour to clean out between flavours, only one of the four flavours is made on any day. The finished goods freezer holds a maximum of 10 000 litres, but to allow stock rotation it cannot in practice be loaded to above 7000 litres. Ideally no ice-cream should be held more than six weeks at the factory, as the total recommended storage time is only 12 weeks prior to retail sale (there is no preservative used). Finished goods inventory at the end of December 1988 was 3600 litres.

Gillian's most recent figures indicated that all flavours cost about £1 per litre to produce (variable cost of materials, packaging and labour). The factory layout is by process with material preparation and weighing sections, mixing area, packing equipment, and separate freezing equipment. It is operated as a batch process.

ICE-CREAM SALES

The finished product is sold to three categories of buyers. See Appendix 16.1 for sales history and forecast.

Retail shops

The majority of output is sold through regional speciality shops, such as delicatessens, and food sections of department stores. These outlets are given a standard discount of 25 per cent to allow a 33 per cent mark-up to the normal retail price of £2 per litre. The minimum order quantity is 100 litres and deliveries are made by Gillian in the van on Tuesdays.

Paying visitors to the farm

Having been shown around the farm and 'factory', a large proportion of visitors buy ice-cream at the farm shop and take it away in well-insulated containers that keep it from melting for up to two hours in the summer. Gillian commented:

> *'These are virtually captive customers. We have analysed this demand and found that on average one out of two coach customers buys a 1-litre box. On average, a car comes with four occupants, and two 1-litre boxes are purchased. The farm shop retail price is £2 per box, which gives us a much better margin than for our sales to shops.'*

'Farm shop only' visitors

A separate, fenced road entrance allows local customers to purchase goods at a separate counter of the farm shop without payment for, or access to, the other farm facilities.

> *'This is a surprisingly regular source of sales. We believe this is because householders make very infrequent visits to stock up their freezers almost regardless of the time of year or the weather. We also know that local hotels buy a lot this way, and their use of ice-cream is year-round, with a peak only at Christmas when there are a larger number of banquets.'*

All sales in this category are at the full retail price (£2).

Appendix 16.2 gives details of visitors to the farm and ice-cream sales in 1988. Gillian's concluding comments were:

> *'We have a long way to go to make this enterprise meet our expectations. We will probably make only a small return on capital employed in 1988, so must do all we can to increase our profitability. Neither of us want to put more capital into the business, as we would have to borrow at interest rates of up to 15 per cent. We must make our investment work better. As a first step, I have decided to increase the number of natural flavours of our ice-cream to ten in 1989 (currently only four) to try and defend the delicatessen trade against a competitor's aggressive marketing campaign. I don't expect that to halt fully the decline in our sales to these outlets, and this is reflected in our sales forecast.'*

Questions

1 Evaluate Gillian's proposal to increase the number of farm visitors in 1989 by 50 per cent. You may wish to consider:
- What are the main capacity constraints within these businesses?
- Should she promote coach company visits, even if this involves offering a discount on the admission charges?
- Should she pursue increasing visitors by car, or school parties?
- In what other ways is Gillian able to manage capacity?
- What other information would help Gillian to take these decisions?

2 What factors should Gillian consider when deciding to increase the number of flavours from four to ten?

Note: For any calculations, assume that each month consists of four weeks. The effects of Bank Holidays (statutory holidays) should be ignored for the purpose of this initial analysis.

APPENDIX 16.1
ANALYSIS OF ANNUAL SALES OF ICE-CREAM (£000), 1984–8, AND FORECAST SALES FOR 1989

	1984	*1985*	*1986*	*1987*	*1988*	*1989 forecast*
Retail shops	8	26	39	62	75	65
Farm shop total[a]	10	16	20	25	27	40
Total	18	42	59	87	102	105

Note:
[a] No separate records are kept of those sales to the paying farm visitors and those to the 'farm shop only'.

APPENDIX 16.2
RECORDS OF FARM VISITORS AND ICE-CREAM SALES IN 1988

	Jan	*Feb*	*Mar*	*Apr*	*May*	*June*	*July*	*Aug*	*Sept*	*Oct*	*Nov*	*Dec*	*Total*
Total number of paying Farm visitors[a]	0	0	0	1200	1800	2800	3200	3400	1800	600	0	0	14 800
Monthly ice-cream sales (£s):													
to retail shops	3900	3050	7950	5100	6600	8550	8250	7500	7350	4800	3450	7500	75 000
farm shop total	600	1000	800	1600	2400	4000	4400	4800	2400	1600	1000	2600	27 200

Note:
[a] Farm visitors are those that pay the £2 entrance fee. This figure does *not* include local visitors to the farm shop only that are able to use a separate entrance and sales counter.

CASE 17

Crocodile Ice House

Graham Wittington and Stuart Chambers

Case date 1990

INTRODUCTION

It is February 1990, and Robin Baker, the Managing Director of the Crocodile group of toyshops, suspects that he has a problem. His company, formed in 1962, consists of five profitable shops and a mail-order operation, which, though profitable, has never been able to capitalise fully on the quality of its product and the loyalty of its customers.

The mail-order operation, established in 1973, is run from a renovated eighteenth-century ice house in Bristol (south-west England), which the company acquired in 1981 when property was easy to find. But the current state of the property market makes relocation unrealistic, and suitable warehouse space in the Bristol area is either inconveniently situated or too expensive, or both.

The building consists of three floors, all of which have been divided into two working areas of 600 square metres each. At present, one of the ground floor areas is used to store stock for the company's shops, but it has been decided to reallocate this space to the mail-order operation from the beginning of September 1990. The other ground floor area is used as the packing room for the mail-order operation. Of the remaining four work areas in the building, three – two on the first floor and one on the second – are mail-order stockrooms, while the fourth contains the office. As is normal in an ice house, ceiling height is restricted: stock is stacked to use all the available height.

SALES

Crocodile brings out three mail-order catalogues every year, each of which contains approximately 280 different toys and games, all of which are standard products manufactured in the UK, Europe and the Far East. The major catalogue is the Christmas one, despatched in the first week of October to 160 000 customers. In 1989, this had resulted in a total of 22 600 orders with an average order value of £42. The Winter Sale Catalogue and the Spring Catalogue were each sent to 45 000 regular customers, and in 1989 achieved a combined total of 6900 orders with an average order value of £23.

The stock for the Christmas Catalogue is ordered by the end of July, and is delivered in two phases: the first, representing approximately 75 per cent of total requirements, arrives in the first week of October, filling the stock areas to capacity. The remainder is ordered when the first 2500 customer orders have been processed and the results analysed, and is delivered during the fourth week of November. The possibility of receiving deliveries of smaller quantities of stock has been considered on several occasions in the recent past; but, taking loss of discount and advantageous terms of payment into account, the resulting 7.5 per cent reduction in profit margins has been considered to be unacceptable. See Appendix 17.1 for a detailed breakdown of costs.

In 1989, stock with a total resale value of £1.1 million was ordered. This was based on a projection of 21 000 orders with an average value of £45, plus a 15 per cent margin for error which Robin traditionally added to guard against unexpected demand for a particular item, or the failure of some suppliers to deliver an order in full. Any surplus at the end of the Christmas Catalogue period could be disposed of through the Winter Sale Catalogue, or through the Crocodile shops.

Table 17.1 Orders received in 1989

Month	*Week*	*Orders*
October	1	0
	2	300
	3	800
	4	1800
November	1	2900
	2	3300
	3	3700
	4	3500
December	1	2800
	2	2200
	3	1300

In 1989 the orders arrived as shown in Table 17.1, in a pattern which varied very little from year to year.

Given the 24 December delivery deadline for Christmas, all orders have to be despatched by the end of the third week in December. Any customers who send orders received in the fourth week of December (only 75 in 1989) are contacted by telephone, and generally agree to their order being despatched when the warehouse reopens in the first week in January.

OPERATIONS

Any order arriving at the warehouse passes through three stages, in the following sequence: recording, assembly and packing, despatch. A detailed analysis of each of these stages follows.

Recording

All orders are entered into the computer on the day on which they arrive, so that the earliest possible notice is given of any stock shortages. There are currently facilities in the office for up to seven VDU operators, who are hired from a local agency and paid by the hour. They each work a seven-hour day. Each operator is able to process an average of 22 orders per hour, which involves entering either the customer number or name and address for new customers into the computer, followed by the customer's order and payment details. A packing note and address label are then printed out two floors below in the parcels room, where both the assembly/packing and despatch operations are situated.

Assembly and packing

The assembly operation is divided into two stages, both of which, according to both internal and external work studies, are performed efficiently. For every batch of 20 orders the computer produces an aggregate picking list, which enables each of the three stock collectors to go round the stockrooms and, in an average of 45 minutes, select the stock required for the 20 orders. This stock is then given to two packers who work together to divide the stock up among the individual orders, check that each order is correct and then carefully pack each order in a suitably-sized box. The completed orders are then passed on, with packing note attached, to the despatch stage of the operation. Each packer can complete an average of 4.3 parcels per hour, which enables a single stock collector to provide sufficient stock for six packers.

The total space allocated to the packing operation is 330 square metres, which is sufficient for a maximum of 16 packers at any one time. This department, like the despatch department, is staffed entirely by part-timers who work either four-hour (morning) or five-hour (afternoon) shifts. The warehouse is operated Monday to Friday from 9 a.m. to 6 p.m.

Despatch

The workers in the despatch department are, like their colleagues in assembly and packing, employed as and when they are required. Their job is to take each parcel, attach to it an address label which has been printed by the computer and to enter the order number into the computer to confirm that the order has been fully processed. The parcels are then stored in a secure area on the loading bay, and are collected by a parcels carrier at regular intervals six times each day. Each person in the despatch team can complete 9.5 orders per hour, and requires at least 30 square metres in order to be able to operate effectively.

FUTURE PLANS

Robin is determined to expand catalogue sales considerably in 1990:

'The 1989 figure of 22 600 orders from 160 000 catalogues sent out was close to the average total of the previous ten seasons. For 1990, however, we intend to exchange addresses with another mail operation, which will add some 30 000 to our current list. We would expect an order from one in twelve of these addresses. In addition we have decided to spend a further £18 000 on advertising. In the past, each £1000 spent has led to 190 extra orders.

'The only thing that worries me is that this expansion will lead either to the warehouse walls falling down due to the sheer volume of stock, or to us being forced to accept unprofitable business due to having to pay overtime to open the warehouse at evenings or weekends.'

Questions

1 Evaluate Robin's targets for the 1990 Christmas Catalogue. You may wish to consider the following:
- What are the main capacity constraints within the mail-order operation?
- To what extent can they be resolved by the planned 1990 increase in the amount of warehouse space allocated to the mail-order operation?
- In what other ways could Robin attempt to influence demand so as to overcome capacity constraints?

Assumption: Selecting smaller toys for the Catalogue is not a solution.

2 Is it possible to construct an argument which could justify the company accepting a 7.5 per cent reduction in gross profit margin through the adoption of a purchasing policy which would significantly reduce stock levels?
Assumptions:
- Zero inflation.
- Increase of 15 per cent in orders each year for five years, resulting in 57 000 orders in 1995.
- It is company policy to despatch all orders within three days of receiving them.
- Crocodile likes to keep sufficient stock to cover ten working days, so as to allow a buffer for late delivery from a supplier, or sudden unexpected demand for a particular item.

3 Is it reasonable for Robin to be horrified at the idea of overtime payments?

APPENDIX 17.1
CHRISTMAS CATALOGUE

Breakdown of costs for one parcel (1989 figures)

	£
Sales	42.00
Cost of stock	(23.00)
Gross profit	19.00
Share of fixed costs[a]	(10.08)
Catalogue production[b]	(3.25)
VDU	(0.35)
Stock collector	(0.12)
Packer	(0.77)
Despatcher	(0.35)
Net profit	4.08

Notes:

[a] Total fixed costs £228 000 per annum, absorbed over 22 600 orders.

[b] 160 000 catalogues are printed and mailed at a cost of £0.46 each, resulting in 22 600 orders.

CASE 18

Hillingdon Hospital

Karen Turner and Nigel Slack

Case date 1992

INTRODUCTION

In January 1992, Philip Brown, Chief Executive of the Hillingdon Hospital, was sitting in his office thinking back over the hospital's performance as the financial year drew to a close. The number of treated patients had risen considerably, waiting lists were falling and overall costs had been contained. 'Not a bad year at all,' he thought to himself, 'but I must keep the pressure up. Our position in the marketplace is still by no means secure, and we must do more to ensure patients don't wait too long for surgery.'

BACKGROUND

The UK's National Health Service (NHS) was organised on a national basis, with all parts of the service eventually reporting through to the Department of Health's Management Executive. Primarily, though, it operated at three levels. At the first level were the Regional Health Authorities (RHAs), of which there were fourteen in England. At the second level were the District Health Authorities (DHAs). Normally there were about 10–15 DHAs in each region. The third level comprised the individual units, the hospitals and community service units which operated within the district boundaries and provided their services directly to the public. Appendix 18.1 provides an organisation chart of the NHS in England.

The Hillingdon Hospital was located to the south of Hillingdon Health Authority, a DHA with around a 250 000 resident population. The DHA was situated within the boundaries of North West Thames RHA and was accountable to it for the provision of health services to the district's residents. Hillingdon DHA purchased health services from a variety of hospitals in the area and also from teaching hospitals in central London. It was free to purchase from any hospital which, in the DHA's opinion, offered the best value services (judged by such criteria as their quality, timeliness and cost) within reasonable proximity.

The Hillingdon Hospital had one major contract with Hillingdon DHA for the provision of the full range of services which the hospital provided. This contract was negotiated annually and included conditions covering the following:

- A defined level of work for in-patients, day patients and out-patients by speciality.[1]
- Accident and emergency services for 60 000 patient attendances (within a 5 per cent range).
- A defined maximum waiting time for surgery where the exact length of time depends on speciality, for example six months for gynaecology, 16 months for orthopaedics. See Appendix 18.2 for further information on numbers of patients and waiting times.

Also stipulated in the contract were many performance standards which described service quality, including such things as waiting times for out-patients and their standard of care.

This contract was of major importance to the hospital and represented 85 per cent of its total workload. Appendix 18.3 details the size of the hospital's contracts as a proportion of its total workload. The hospital's other contracts were important, but it was overwhelmingly dependent on Hillingdon DHA – its key customer – for its future. Philip Brown was keenly aware that to prevent the DHA looking elsewhere for its services, he must be able to give them quality services, with competitive waiting times for surgery, at competitive prices. At the moment they were struggling with waiting times.

A major influence on the hospital's workload was its high proportion of accident and emergency (A&E) patients, those who arrived at the hospital for treatment without an appointment. Attendance at A&E was high at Hillingdon because of the large number of people who came to work every day in the hospital's catchment area. These are the figures for a typical year:

- There were 60 000 attendances to the A&E Department.
- An average of 24 patients were admitted every 24 hours.
- An average of 7 patients required emergency surgery every 24 hours.

This made the hospital one of the largest emergency receiving centres within the region, and it was likely to remain so because of its close proximity to the M4, M40, M25, Heathrow Airport and some major business parks. Yet, in spite of this large daily influx, the hospital had earned a reputation for never closing its A&E Department. Its policy was that a bed, if needed, would always be found. Other local hospitals did not always follow this practice. If, for example, there was a sudden influx of A&E patients combined with an unusually large number of patients who could not be discharged, then a hospital might close its A&E Department for a short period. Most hospitals, however, do try and avoid this type of action. Hillingdon

[1] In-patients are patients whose treatment involves at least one overnight stay. Day patients are those who are admitted, treated and discharged on the same day. Out-patients are not formally admitted to the hospital although they may receive treatment.

Hospital was proud of its reputation for never closing its A&E Department but recognised the impact such a policy had on planned surgery.

OPERATING THEATRES

Kate Emmerson, the hospital's Theatre Manager (*see* Appendix 18.4 for the operating theatres' organisation chart), was the person who bore the brunt of unplanned emergency patients coming through A&E and requiring emergency surgery. She had to provide reasonable A&E surgery cover while not letting it disrupt the planned operations too drastically. The hospital's current drive to reduce waiting times for surgery made the issue even more significant. Whereas the operating theatres were not the only bottleneck in the hospital, it was generally felt that any improvement in patient throughput in the theatres could very effectively speed up the flow of patients through the whole surgery process.

In January 1992 Kate was reviewing the operating theatres' performance:

> *'It is now two months since I agreed with all the surgeons and anaesthetists that operations would start half an hour earlier, at 8.30 a.m. instead of 9 a.m. Yet in spite of this we don't appear to be doing many more cases, and we are still cancelling too many, usually because of emergency operations. The earlier start has led to one important improvement, though, more operations are finishing on time. This means that we don't have to pay as much overtime to theatre staff, which is a significant cost saving.'*

There were six operating theatres in the hospital, five for surgery and one for endoscopy (that is non-invasive work). Kate had to staff all of these to support the theatre sessions. These sessions are shown in Appendix 18.5 as they were organised for the various surgeons. The staff worked shifts (*see* Appendix 18.6) to cover the two theatre sessions each day, from 8.30 a.m. to noon and 1.30 p.m. to 5 p.m., from Monday to Friday. The one and a half hour lunch break was used for cleaning and restocking the theatres and to enable the staff to have lunch.

The problem certainly was not the surgeons' enthusiasm. Most of them wanted to reduce their waiting lists and all were keen to be in the theatre and operating. One enthusiastic surgeon has asked Kate if he could work on into the evening to clear more patients from his waiting list. 'Who is going to pay all the staff overtime?' she wondered. Her budget was stretched already, largely by the agency payments she had to make for the operating department assistants (ODAs).[2] Three surgeons, at their own request, had moved to all-day operating lists. This enabled them to operate on a larger number of major cases. They were reluctant to stop for lunch

2 ODAs are considered to be key members of the theatre staff because of their flexibility. They act as technical assistants, porters and do some basic nursing duties. Their salaries in the NHS are notoriously low. There are relatively few of them, and they can usually earn a much higher rate working through an agency. The hospital then has to pay the higher rate plus the agency fee. Several hospitals had recently negotiated their own salary packages with the ODAs to get around this problem.

but Kate had asked them to finish before 5 p.m. to give the staff chance to catch their breath. Another surgeon had asked if he could do a routine list on Saturdays and if he could have more space allocated to him in the Day Care Unit. Again this was to enable him to tackle more of his waiting list.

The Day Care Unit was a unit with 12 'day bed' trolleys (Fig. 18.1 depicts a patient being wheeled to the operating theatre in a 'day bed') and two reclining armchairs. It was open from 8 a.m. to 8 p.m. (Appendix 18.7 provides the numbers of beds in other wards and the costs associated with each ward.) Patients were booked into the unit from 7.30 a.m. onwards, were undressed and laid on the trolley which was then wheeled directly to the operating theatre suite. The trolleys are similar to the usual theatre trolleys but have a double-thick mattress for extra comfort. Alternatively, they would walk under 'their own steam' or be wheeled in a wheelchair to the theatre. After the operation the patient could be wheeled back to the unit on the trolley or in a wheelchair to rest in a reclining armchair.

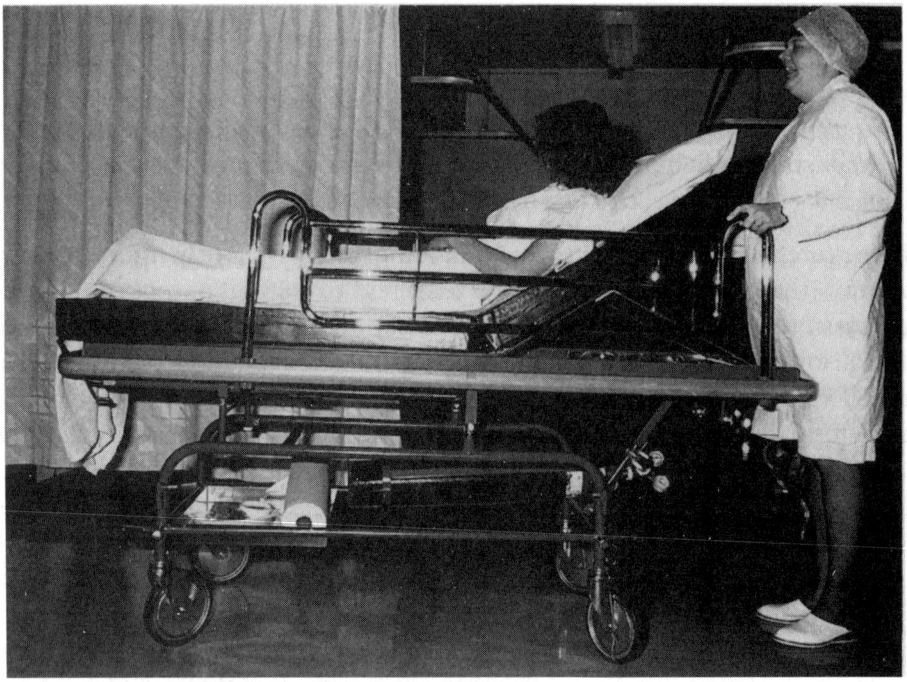

Fig. 18.1 A 'day bed'

The following are considered to be the advantages of the Day Care Unit:

- Guaranteed admission for planned operations because it did not take patients requiring emergency treatment. (It had neither the facilities nor the staffing resources to do so.) Therefore operations could not be disrupted by A&E admissions.

- Experienced staff who gave a high standard of care with high quality patient information.
- A competent contact point if patients needed advice following treatment.

THE THEATRE SCHEDULES

Kate knew she had to find a solution that would enable more planned operations to be undertaken. She looked at her current staff rotas and theatre timetable for inspiration. There was very little flexibility in the consultant surgeons sessions because the majority had a fixed schedule all week in out-patients or other hospitals. Yet apart from the endoscopy theatre, which was not equipped for invasive surgery, any theatre could be used for any type of operation, although many surgeons had their favourite.

The theatres were staffed 24 hours a day to undertake any emergency work, but the majority of staff were on duty between 8 a.m. and 5 p.m. to cover routine operations. (Appendix 18.8 shows how patients arrive at the operating theatre for routine surgery.) Yet the requirement for 24-hour emergency staffing did lead to under-utilisation of these staff. Additional routine sessions with her existing staff and existing rotas would be impossible.

One solution to the problem might lie with the new Clinical Assistant in General Surgery – an experienced, non-career grade surgeon, below Consultant status in the hierarchy. This new Clinical Assistant had recently been appointed to work two and half days a week and hadn't yet finalised his timetable. He would be able to operate on patients from whoever's list was the longest. In other words, rather than be a fixed member of a particular consultant's firm (team) he could be used in a flexible way wherever he could best contribute to shortening the lists or dealing with emergencies.

The disruption caused by the emergency work was the key issue – on average there were seven emergency operations out of a total of about thirty-nine each day. Most of these were done after hours, but many interrupted the routine lists if the surgeon on call had his operating list on the same day. If the emergency operation was major, it could 'block' the theatre all day. Not only did the surgeon have to delay or cancel his planned operations to do an emergency, but he was frequently called away to see patients in the A&E Department in between operations, which would also cause delays. Kate would have liked to have scheduled a dedicated A&E theatre during normal working hours to give some protection for the planned operations.

THE TOTAL CARE PROCESS

With the continuous emphasis on cost reduction and improved efficiency, the hospital had steadily reduced the number of its 'seven-day' beds (beds which were fully staffed and supported at all times) in favour of more planned 'five-day' beds (available Monday to Friday) and 'day care' beds. It was much cheaper employing staff for the day, or part of the day only, than paying the enhanced costs incurred at weekends. However, the result of this reduction in the number of beds available for 24 hours, seven days a week, had placed constant pressure on those seven-day beds which remained to take both emergency patients and patients from their own speciality. So, for example, some surgical wards quickly had any empty beds filled up with emergency admissions. If the patient who had been admitted as an emergency needed a prolonged stay, they not only occupied the bed for the current period, but also prevented the next round of planned surgical admissions.

The hospital had two wards dedicated to planned admissions only, that is protected against emergency admissions. Because these wards were not distracted by frequent urgent admissions they were better able to make sure that patients arrived at the operating theatres on time. It was regarded as particularly important for the operating theatres to receive patients on time. When patients arrived late it led to all manner of problems. For example:

- The surgical team had to hang about, unable to do much else (their next patient would not necessarily be ready until just before their scheduled slot).
- The operations ran late causing subsequent cancellations and extra overtime payments to staff.
- If day patients were operated on late, it could prevent them recovering adequately to be discharged home that day. They would then need to be accommodated overnight which would disrupt the wards.

From the wards' point of view, when patients were admitted for a planned operation, they were anxious to ensure they had their operation on schedule. Only then could their discharge be planned with confidence and subsequent admissions be assured. Operations cancelled today meant admissions cancelled tomorrow. Kate was well aware of this.

> *'Patients complain bitterly when their admission is cancelled. It is not surprising really, they are anxious anyway and many have had to make elaborate arrangements to come into hospital, getting help for elderly relatives or children, or putting the dog into kennels, for example.'*

Kate also knew that a high proportion of patients were discharged between 24 and 48 hours after their operation. She wondered if there might be scope for opening a 'post-operative' ward attached to the operating theatres to relieve ward staff of patient care immediately after the operation. This might also result in specialised (and therefore possibly better) post-operative care, although she recognised that this would be difficult to measure.

CONSIDERING THE ISSUES: THE THEATRE USERS GROUP

The Theatre Users Group comprised the Clinical Director responsible for the operating theatres, the Theatre Manager (Kate Emmerson), two representative Consultant Surgeons and Anaesthetists, the Director of Operational Services (also the Senior Nurse) and Philip Brown, the hospital's Chief Executive. It met monthly to review the processes in the operating theatres and plan improvements. The group met early in February 1992 and included in their agenda were the two items, achievements during the previous twelve months and current major issues.

Achievements during the previous twelve months

Philip Brown was quick to draw members' attention to and congratulate them on the substantial achievements that had taken place. These included the following:

- The successful introduction of 'day case' operations for cataracts and varicose veins. These were running smoothly and had reduced the waiting lists for these two operations dramatically.
- The reorganisation of theatre sessions which had enabled three consultants to move to all-day operating. The consequence of this was that they could do more major cases, that is three in one day rather than one in half a day.
- The earlier shift had resulted in fewer operations being cancelled.
- A significant new technology in the form of 'keyhole' surgery[3] for gynaecology and general surgery had been introduced. This had required retraining for the surgeons, but the results were already significant. Theatre time was reduced by up to 50 per cent and post-operative length of stay reduced from ten days to two or three. Usually patients were back at work within two weeks rather than six as previously, and so far feedback from patients was very positive.

Philip was keen to consider with the group what could be learnt from these achievements. Certainly one lesson was the importance of involving everyone in the planning process who was concerned with or affected by any changes.

The current major issues

There was general agreement in the Theatre Users Group that there were four major issues to be considered:

[3] Keyhole surgery involved the surgeon making a few very small incisions in the patient rather than one large one as in previous techniques. This reduced the trauma to the patient. The operation was undertaken through one tube, with a camera inserted through another. The surgeon viewed a screen to guide him.

1 The length of time for which patients were waiting for surgery. The lists differed significantly between surgeons and specialities, both because of the different demands for the various types of surgery and because of the reputations of particular surgeons.
2 The recruitment of key staff and the costs of paying overtime, enhanced hours and agency payments. The ODAs were a good example of this.
3 The number and type of emergency admissions causing disruption to both the wards and the theatres.
4 Theatre layout (Appendix 18.9) which was clumsy, inflexible and made poor use of available space.

The potential solutions were far-reaching and caused much debate. One suggestion was to 'pool' waiting lists by type, for example, orthopaedics or ophthalmology, or even between type, for example general surgeons could do some urology. The rationale for pooling was that it would spread the load, especially the routine operations, evenly between the surgeons and ensure better surgeon utilisation. This had been done once before, to a limited extent and for a short time. The surgeons were unanimously against it however on the grounds that 'experience led to better results' and if a surgeon hadn't undertaken a type of operation for ten years, it was better that he didn't start now. In effect some surgeons had specialised almost by default.

Philip Brown wasn't sure that the issue was as clear-cut as this but brought the discussion back to pooled lists within the same specialty. One of the surgeons spoke for many by saying, 'I can see how attractive it looks to you, Philip, there could be some efficiency gains, but if a GP refers a patient to me, it is because he wants me to do the operation.' Philip replied, 'But how many such patients do you then delegate to your Registrar?'[4]

Kate Emmerson was keen to start preparing a 'special package' (that is more money) for the ODAs to avoid agency costs. Others felt the pay review should go further and should be included in a general review of the shift organisation for staff. Philip asked members to consider the introduction of a third shift and Saturday operating, but stressed that such a move should be funded from existing resources, perhaps by a move to more short-stay beds.

The emergency admissions issue also caused much discussion. Suggestions included the designation of an existing ward to an A&E receiving only ward. Many emergency admissions stayed less than twenty-four hours and could therefore be discharged the following morning without a regular in-patient bed having to be found. This would reduce disruption on the wards. It would also mean that only one ward would take emergencies, and at night patients in other

[4] The 'Registrar' is the second in command (or third, when a Senior Registrar is in post) in the Consultant Surgeon's team.

wards would not be disturbed. Another suggestion was that one theatre should be dedicated to emergencies. There was general support for the idea of a post-operative ward. But it would require structural changes to the theatre suite, if it was to be part of theatre. Philip had already told the group that no capital funds would be available for such a scheme in the foreseeable future.

'If we see this as a priority, it will have to be found within our existing ward space and bed complement,' he said.

Questions

1 How should the organisation of the operating theatres contribute to the effectiveness of the hospital?

2 What are the main operational issues which need to be addressed if the theatres are to improve their performance?

APPENDIX 18.1
ORGANISATION CHART FOR THE NATIONAL HEALTH SERVICE IN ENGLAND, 1992

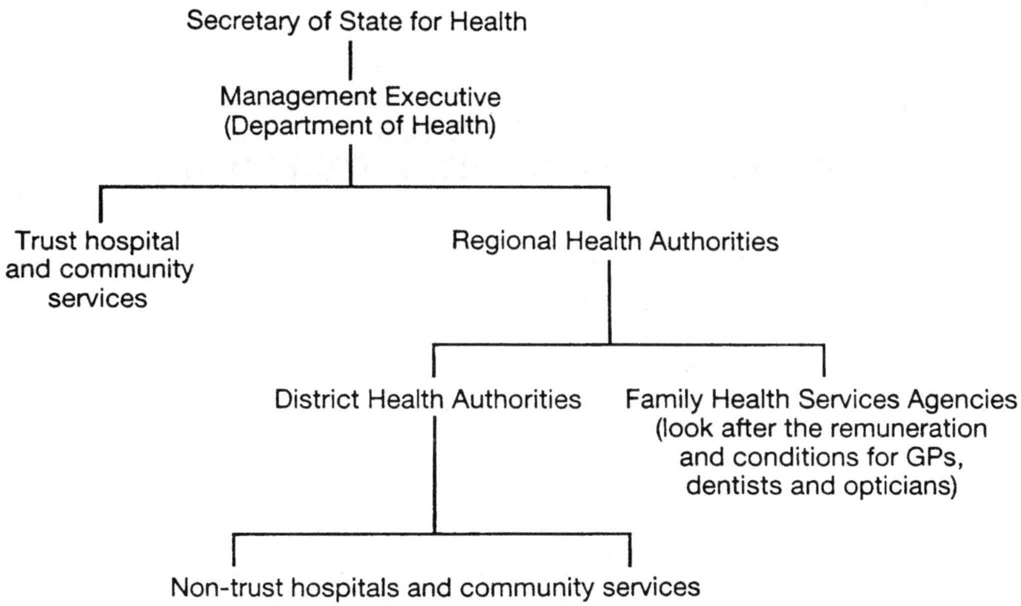

APPENDIX 18.2
PATIENT NUMBERS AND WAITING TIMES

Numbers of patients

	1990/1	*1991/2*
In-patient stays[a]	18 565	18 252
Day cases[b]	3 215	4 561
Out-patients[c]	94 968	100 462

Waiting times

	31.3.90	*31.3.91*	*30.11.91*
Under 12 months	828	722	573
12–23 months	504	561	442
Total number (i/p and d/c)	2271	2692	2379

Notes:

[a] 'In-patients' are patients who are in the hospital for at least one overnight stay.

[b] 'Day cases' are patients who receive treatment (often surgical treatment such as hernia operations) but do not need to stay in the hospital overnight; that is they are discharged on the same day as they arrive.

[c] 'Out-patients' are patients who are not 'admitted' to the hospital as such but are treated at the various out-patient clinics.

APPENDIX 18.3
THE HILLINGDON HOSPITAL WORKLOAD (%)

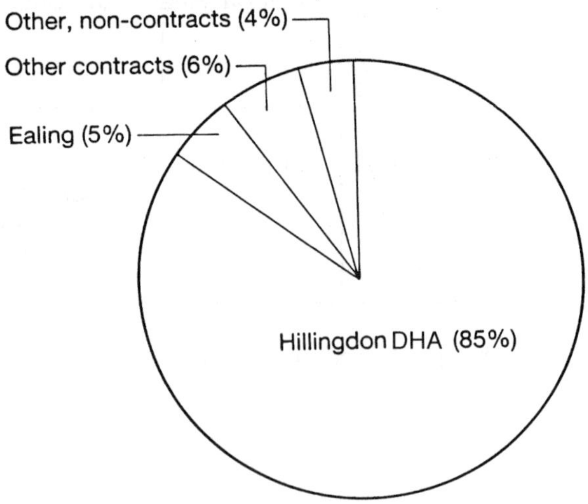

APPENDIX 18.4
OPERATING THEATRES ORGANISATION CHART

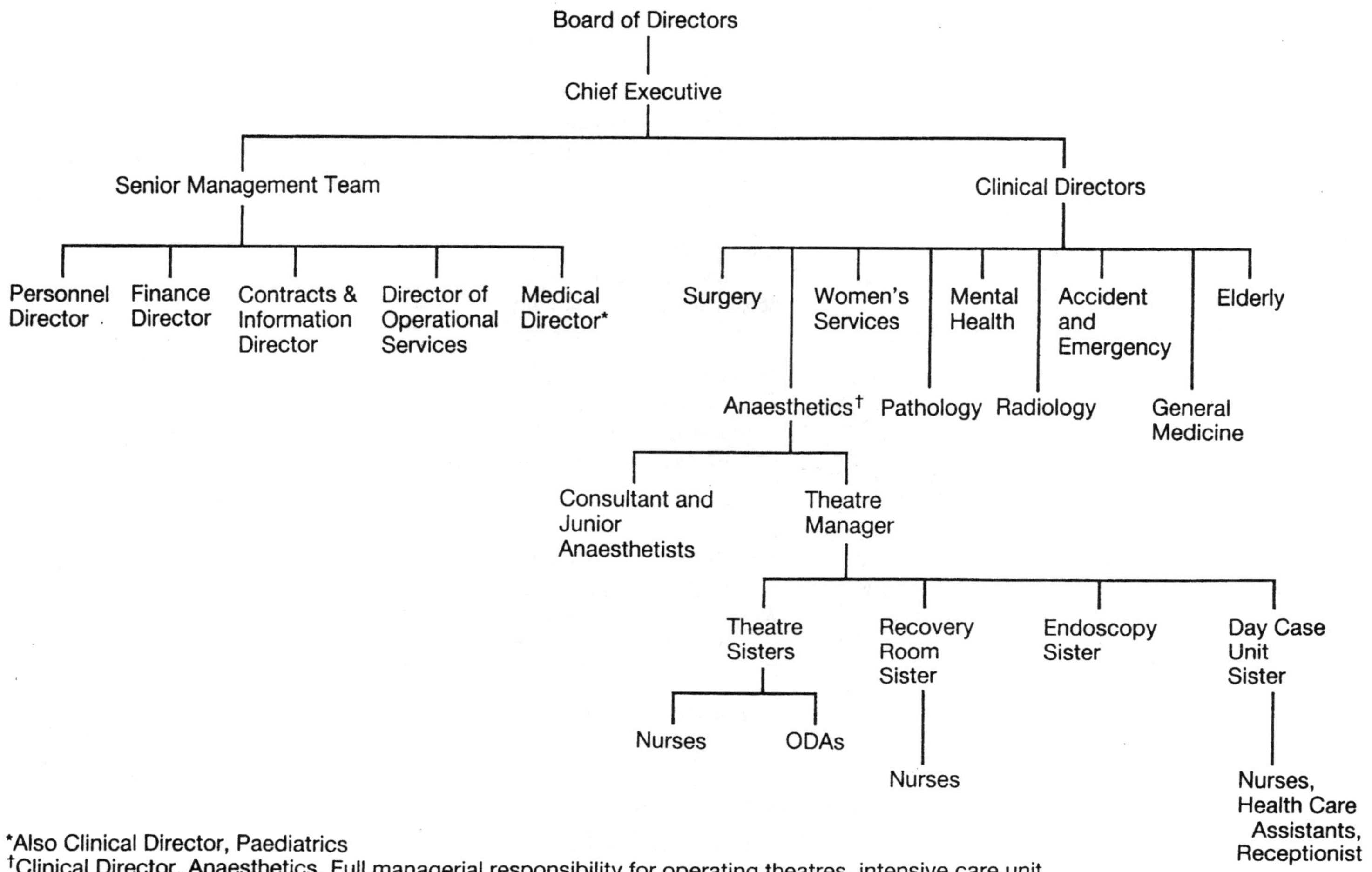

*Also Clinical Director, Paediatrics
†Clinical Director, Anaesthetics. Full managerial responsibility for operating theatres, intensive care unit

APPENDIX 18.5
WEEKLY OPERATIVE SCHEDULE

Day		*Theatre 1*	*Theatre 2 (endoscopy)*	*Theatre 3*	*Theatre 4*	*Theatre 5*	*Theatre 6*	*Other*
Monday	a.m.		*Mr Smith* Endoscopies	*Mr Fox* Urology	*Mr Smith* Gen. surgery	Ophthalmics	*Mr Smith* Gen. surgery	
	p.m.	*Mr Vincent* Orthopaedics	*Dr Lapin* Endoscopies *Mr Snood* LAs	*Mr Fox* Urology	*Mr Brown* Gynaecology	*Mr Brown* Gynaecology		LSCs in maternity
Tuesday	a.m.	*Mr Patel* Orthopaedics	*Mr Wilson* Endoscopies	*Mr Wilson* Gen. surgery	*Mr First* Gynaecology	*Mr Dean* Dental	*Mr Peters* Gen. vascular	ECTs in Psych. Day Hosp.
	p.m.	*Mr Patel* Orthopaedics	Flexible Cystoscopies	*Orthopaedic* *Registrar*	*Mr First* Gynaecology		*Mr Peters* Gen. vascular	
Wednesday	a.m.	Pain list	*Med. Registrar* Endoscopies	*Mrs Prentice* Urology	*Mr Down* Gynaecology	Ophthalmics	*Mr Rees* Gen. surgery	
	p.m.	*Mr Vincent* Orthopaedics	*Mr Peters* LAs	*Mrs Prentice* Urology	*Mr Down* Gynaecology	*Sen. Registrar* Gen. surgery	*Mr Rees* Gen. surgery	
Thursday	a.m.	*Mr Burton* Orthopaedics	*Dr Straw* Bronchoscopies		*Mr Hay* Gynaecology	*Mr Dean* Dental	*Mr Clayton* Ophthalmics	Epidural LSCs in maternity
	p.m.	*Mr Burton* Orthopaedics		*Clin. Asst.** Gen. surgery	*Mr Hay* Gynaecology		*Mr Smith* Gen. surgery	*Dr Page* ERCPs in X-ray
Friday	a.m.	*Mr Corkery* Orthopaedics	*Dr Page* Endoscopies		*Gynae. Sen. Reg.* Gynaecology		*Mr Smith* Gen. surgery	ECTs in Psych. Day Hosp. Dental opd.
	p.m.		*Dr Page* Endoscopies			Dental	*Mr Wilson* Gen. surgery	

* Relatively new non-career grade, at sub-consultant level.

APPENDIX 18.6
THEATRE STAFF ROTAS

Shifts
8.00 a.m.–5.30 p.m.
1.00 p.m.–9.00 p.m.
8.00 p.m.–8.00 a.m.

Allocation of staff

All operating theatres	3 trained nurses 1 ODA 1 student
Endoscopy suite	1 trained nurse
Recovery room (for ward patients only, not DCU who return there directly after their operation)	1.5 nurses for 2 patients
Night shift and weekends	3 trained nurses 1 ODA 1 ODO (Operating Department Orderly who who undertakes portering and cleaning duties)

Approximate costs (1992)
Without overtime, but including employer costs.

Sister/Charge Nurse	£20 000
Registered General Nurse	£15 500

APPENDIX 18.7
NUMBER OF BEDS AND APPROXIMATE COSTS* PER WARD BY SPECIALITY, 1992

Speciality	*No. of beds*	*£000*
General medicine (2 wards)	24	300
General medicine	30	320
Trauma and orthopaedics	30	380
General surgery	30	380
Gynaecology	30	380
Surgery (mixed)	30	380
Day Care Unit	12 trolleys	200
Elderly	30	400

* Costs comprise staff costs, cleaning and all other costs directly attributable to the ward. They are, therefore, approximate.
Notes: All 30-bed wards are laid out as 6 × 4-bed bays, 6 × single rooms. All 30-bed wards take both male and female patients and the 24-bed take either male or female.

APPENDIX 18.8
HOW PATIENTS ARRIVE AT THE OPERATING THEATRE FOR ROUTINE SURGERY

Patient at home in anguish

↓

Goes to see GP

↓

Refers patient to consultant for advice/treatment

↓

Patient goes to see consultant in out-patients

↓

Consultant assesses urgency of condition – routine or urgent, and sends patient to admissions office.

↓

Patient put on waiting list
or
Patient given a date to come in

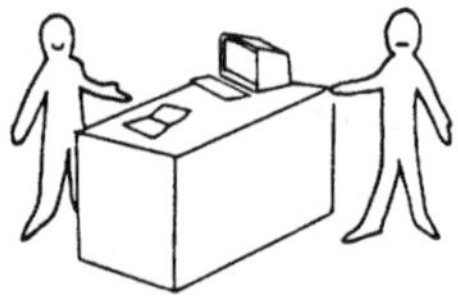

→ Patient sent date/telephoned for admission. Asked to telephone on morning to confirm bed available. If so, patient arrives at the hospital at stated time, goes directly to Day Care (if previously instructed) or to admissions office to be allocated a bed. Goes to ward, details are taken, information given. Patient is now ready for operation.

APPENDIX 18.9
THEATRE LAYOUT

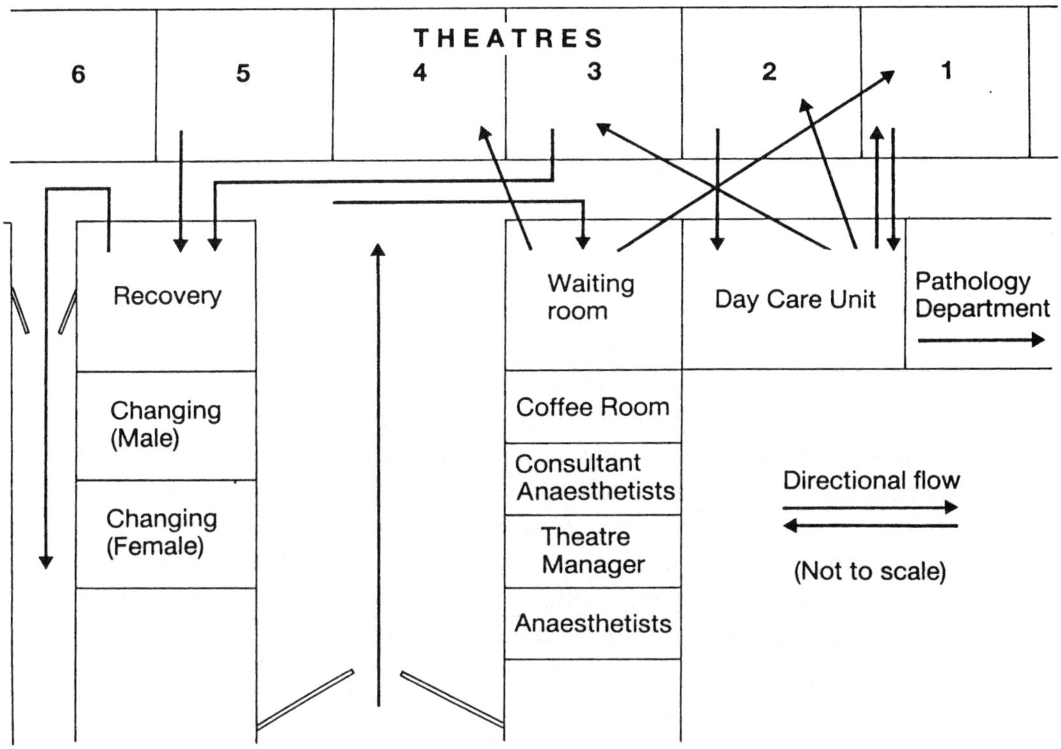

CASE 19

Murray Rock Drilling Ltd

Iain Young and Alan Harrison

*Case date 1992**

INTRODUCTION

Murray Rock Drilling Ltd ('Murray') is a subdivision of the Murray Engineering Group, part of the large conglomerate PH Holdings plc. Murray Rock Drilling Ltd manufactures a range of machined steel products, designed to drill rock for mining semi-precious ores and general quarrying. Murray shares certain functions with other parts of the group but it has its own production engineering, purchasing and production control functions. Murray's Production Manager accepts sales orders from Quick Tools Ltd, the direct sales arm of Murray's, and from two main customers, Kerhandt (a German company, also a member of PH Holdings) and Barstrom (a large international manufacturing and distribution group). Barstrom is Murray's principal customer and comprises 80 per cent of sales by volume.

The Murray manufacturing group has two production units located adjacent to one another. The main unit produces around 90 per cent of output, concentrating on catalogue items with batch sizes of ten units or more. The smaller unit concentrates on 'specials', bespoke tools and volumes of nine units or less.

The current lead time from order receipt to dispatch is in excess of twelve weeks. Management believe this to be unacceptably high; a figure of six weeks should be achievable. One of the main areas of concern is the amount of time spent setting up the various machines between batches. Management believe that this is primarily due to the wide range of products manufactured and the consequent small average batch size. The Managing Director, Sid Beckett, feels that the introduction of group technology methods may help.

THE PRODUCT

The product range is basically a drill bit, usually called a tool, plus a range of drill rods, couplings, adaptors, etc. The drill bits, shown generally in Appendix

*Names and data have been altered.

19.1, have two main features, a head and a shank. Without exception the tools are produced from steel bars and then turned/milled and heat-treated after which carbide inserts are added to give the finished product. The carbide inserts may be of rectangular section, which are brazed into position, or they may be small and cylindrical, which are inserted into circular holes and retained by the interference fit between hole and carbide. Where rectangular type inserts are used only two or four per tool are fitted, but where the cylindrical type are used the number may vary from 10 on a 50-mm diameter tool to 120 on a 200-mm diameter tool. This latter type of bit is called a button bit and accounts for 70 per cent of production. The other type is called a cross bit and is a more traditional design.

The product range, while limited in its geometric variations, is very large with some 1000 catalogue items to which must be added a wide variety of specials to suit particular needs. The grade of carbide, number and pattern of buttons, design of flushing hole, etc. are all varied to enable the tool to perform better in varying geological conditions. Thus in reality the product range consists of 2000 to 3000 items. The variations are:

- Shank types:
  - Splined: 4 types
Head diameter range 115–200 mm
  - Threaded: 6 types
Head diameter range 45–100 mm
  - Tapered: 2 types
Head diameter range 38–50 mm
- Head diameters:
  - Range 38–200 mm
  - Number of diameters 42
- Carbide grades: 4
- Steel types: 1

THE MANUFACTURING PROCESS

The process is predominantly a flow batch process. The vast majority of the product range, tools, follow virtually identical routes (*see* Appendix 19.2).

Set-up time accounts for approximately 26 per cent of capacity of the machines. Keeping set-ups to a minimum is currently achieved by both grouping identical product orders together to form larger batch sizes and using the current set-up on any machine as a sequencing guide, that is do all the jobs that require the same setting first and then change the setting.

MANUFACTURING FACILITIES

Murray recently purchased most of the machines from Barstrom's old plant in Bristol. The transfer of the machines began in January 1991 and took three months. Some machines are still not in their final positions and a number are still giving problems – one grinding machine has never run properly.

This resulted in a substantial increase in the number of employees, the number of machines to be operated, the volume of material to be processed and the complexity of the whole operation.

The layout of the machines is consistent with the stages of the manufacturing process. Infrastructure, such as industrial engineers, maintenance, plant engineers, accounts, etc. is shared with other parts of the group.

MANUFACTURING STRATEGY

Murray believe that their competitive advantage in tool-bit manufacturing lies in the price at which they can provide a wide range of tool-bit products. Their strategy is to use economies of scale to achieve lower costs. To this end, they have created a small plant within plant to produce low volume items (less than 10 off), allowing the main plant to concentrate on the higher volume orders. Hard state operations, however, were all grouped together.

BARSTROM AGREEMENT

Barstrom used to have their own production facility in Bristol but closed it in favour of a sole supplier agreement with Murray for a substantial discount on list price.

The agreement on order quantities is that the minimum order quantity should be 30 units, unless annual demand is less than 30, in which case the minimum quantity is 12 units. Approximately 40 per cent of orders are for the minimum quantity of 12.

However, there are many instances where a series of orders for 12 off have been placed in consecutive months for the same product. Therefore there is room for improvement at Barstrom. Orders are processed on a make-to-order basis and usually go into stock at Barstrom.

QUICK TOOLS LTD

Although part of Murray Group, Quick Tools Ltd is run as a separate company. Order intake at Quick Tools is handled separately and delivery dates are quoted by Quick Tools salesmen without reference to Murray where the parts are manufactured.

The standard lead time for Quick Tools orders is only eight weeks, because work pack drawings and route cards are put together by Quick Tools and are ready for loading at Murray.

INVESTIGATION OF LEAD TIME

The Managing Director

Sid Beckett, the new MD of Murray has complained:

'Our biggest problem here is the amount of time spent setting up. Our average batch size is only 30 bodies. If only we could reduce the set-up times and introduce cellular manufacturing, the released capacity could be used to shift all this inventory faster and bring our lead times down.'

Commenting on the high level of WIP, Beckett stated that the latest report suggested around 10 000 bodies and added:

'We've not been reaching our output targets recently. We were aiming for 1500 bodies per week but only seem to be managing 1200. You should have seen the WIP inventory earlier in the year, we were up to our waists in the stuff!'

Asked if sales had been hit by the recession yet, Beckett commented that Murray sales this month were down on the previous months but it was difficult to say whether or not this was due to the recession.

Commenting on the twelve weeks quoted lead time, Beckett informed:

'Some jobs are still here after four or five months but, usually, they are non-urgent jobs. We can push a job through in just over a week when we have to. But, in general, most jobs are going through in 12 weeks, two to three weeks in the office and nine to ten weeks on the shop floor.

'We use a standard costing system, so we do not really know what each item costs because we do not have a standard set-up time. Standards are only calculated for run times. We are having our costing system looked at by our accountants. They are due to report in a couple of months.

'Lost time can be determined from the operators' time sheets. Scrap and rework are recorded each day in the Inspection Logbook. Inspection also log the work going to and from subcontractors and into stores.'

The Production and Materials Controller

The WIP report produced on the computer system was out of date and not regarded as reliable by any of the staff, including Fred Pearse, the Production and Materials Controller (PMC):

'Many of the entries for batches of one and two units are items which have been scrapped but not yet taken off the system. Also, some of the items on the list have been dispatched but the records have not worked their way through the system yet.'

Overall, the computer report overestimates WIP by about 10 per cent.

The report was produced weekly and comprised a list of part numbers with quantities sorted by due date and then by location. For example:

Due date	*Location*	*Part no.*	*Description*	*Quantity*
Week 17 off	Soft State	972364222	150 DTH Spline	2

It was normally only printed out for due dates which had already passed. It was, therefore, being produced to monitor arrears rather than to monitor material flow through the plant.

Monitoring delivery performance proved to be a difficult task, which required a special exercise to be carried out. The results are shown in Appendix 19.3.

When asked about a record of lost time, Pearse replied that the Senior Foreman kept the operator time sheets and that they would contain that sort of data but that he did not monitor lost time:

'The Industrial Engineers occasionally monitor it. As for scrap and rework, that is monitored. Speak to Phil Johnson, the Production Manager, he has the figures.'

The Production Manager

On receipt of order enquiries from Barstrom, Kernhandt or Quick Tools, a 'due date' would be issued in line with capacity and the order entered into a register by due date. Over a period of three to four weeks, the register would be checked for orders of identical part numbers and, where found, a single larger batch created. This would then be issued to the shop-floor. Phil Johnson, the Production Manager commented:

'It would probably take about 48 hours to machine an average tool, if you include set-ups, but that would be for an average batch, which is around 30 bodies.'

Asked about capacity calculations, Johnson said:

'From our dispatch figures, it would appear that our capacity is around 1200 bodies per week at present. Prior to the Barstrom deal, we were making around 800 per week. We should be capable of reaching 1500 per week but some of the foremen aren't pulling their weight and some of the new machines aren't capable of producing what Barstrom said they would.

'We've had a lot of trouble with the machines we bought from Barstrom. They have been breaking down a lot and we have been unable to reach the output levels we expected. Also, we are short of setter operators, so some of the younger lads have to wait for a setter operator before they can proceed with their set-up. A few months ago, we also had a

problem with a shortage of inspectors, but we have solved this by reducing the amount of inspection required. During the early months of the year, when we were installing the new machines, we had higher than usual scrap and rework levels but this is now under control.'

Capacity calculation

It was possible to analyse the output history of both of the main sections of the plant (Soft State and Hard State). The Inspection Logbook logged jobs out of Soft State to heat treatment and shotblast, and they were also logged out of Hard State to Inspection and then to Stores. The throughput figures, together with the average batch size, are shown in Appendices 19.4 and 19.5. The average throughput for Hard State, that is logged to Stores, was 1050 bodies per week – less than the figure of 1200 quoted by Phil Johnson. At no point had output reached 1500 bodies per week.

Appendix 19.6 was prepared to show the machine hours needed for an average batch size of 26 in soft machining and an average batch size of 23 in hard machining. These were based on an analysis of the route cards of the most common products, covering 80 per cent of the previous eight months' output and some supporting data.

The average batch size in Hard State is lower, due to the inclusion of the small batches from the low volume plant.

Shop-floor scheduling

Shop-floor scheduling was carried out by looking first at the set-up of a particular machine and then at the requirements of the various jobs in the queue. If there was a job with similar set-up requirements close to the front of the queue, it would be pulled forward. If not, the next job in sequence was loaded and the machine re-set. The due dates on the route card were often no help to the foremen, since they had often expired. In the foremen's office was a large board with 'T'-cards slotted into it for each batch going through the plant. These cards were inserted under the particular machine heading at the top of the board and had the dispatch date for the batch marked on the card.

The foremen had no information on what works orders were going to be released next and only the 'T'-card board information on which jobs were waiting upstream of Hard State. The sequence of work the foremen had given to the machine operators was frequently changed by instructions given by the MD and Production Manager. These instructions were usually issued in response to calls from customers trying to expedite overdue orders.

Asked about the lack of information, the foremen agreed the system was chaotic, but what could they do? The Hard State Foreman mentioned that previously they used a report which listed the complete WIP inventory by plant section, subcontracted activities, etc. but had stopped using it because it was so unreliable, and anyway priorities were always being altered. So now they just planned from day-to-day using due dates as a basis and tried to reduce the number of set-ups where they could.

Sales discipline

Sales were received in two ways. First, Barstrom would send an order to the Production Manager each week. He would allocate a date by which the work could be completed. In theory, this was based on a 12-week lead time plus or minus a few weeks, depending on the quantity of tool-holders due for delivery at that time. The same approach was used for Kerhandt orders. Second, Quick Tools would top up the Barstrom orders if they could or raise an additional order for those products not ordered by Barstrom. Quick Tools were supposed to be supplying their customers from stock but this was often not possible because of shortages. Thus, many of the Quick Tools orders were required by customers as soon as possible. If a competitive delivery time could not be given, the customer would often phone around for a faster delivery quote.

This prompted the salesmen to quote unrealistic delivery dates in the hope that Production would rush them through:

> *'Oh, but we can't turn down £6000s' worth of business because they wanted delivery in four weeks. I know that is less than the normal lead time, but if we push it through we can make the due date. Anyway, we can't afford to refuse important customers. If we don't have the stock, we have to rush it through.'*

Phil Johnson often accepted this situation and this resulted in orders going through with due dates that were impossible to achieve or had even passed.

An analysis of orders received against bodies logged to stores (the nearest measurement available to orders despatched) showed that there was virtually no correlation between the two, even allowing for a twelve-week or longer lead time (*see* Appendix 19.7). By physically counting the WIP on the shop-floor and extrapolating the order input/output data back to the beginning of the year, historical WIP inventory and order backlog could be plotted (*see* Appendix 19.8). Due to the lack of any records of works order releases to the shop-floor, Soft State WIP inventory cannot be separated from the order backlog.

Lead time

With a measure of capacity and WIP inventory, it was now possible to make an estimate of manufacturing lead time. By making a rough assumption that the throughput of 1200 bodies per week was the same for each machining stage in Soft State and 1050 per week for each Hard State stage, the lead time broke down to roughly four weeks' administrative lead time (office processing and batching up) plus nine weeks' manufacturing lead time (*see* Appendices 19.9 and 19.10). Eighty per cent of the manufacturing lead time was due to queueing and 75 per cent of the administrative lead time due to the practice of delaying works order releases in the hope of creating larger batches.

Final assembly

Another area where lead time was increased was in final assembly. Finished bodies were often delayed due to the lack of carbide inserts and packaging materials. The system employed was for the PMC to order the bought-in parts when ordering the raw material for the bodies and to place works orders for any in-house components at the same time as placing the works order for the bodies themselves. Often the quantities were small and therefore the placement of the orders would be delayed to increase the order size – and occasionally forgotten or lost. The same often applied to in-house works orders.

The information system

Information was gathered and passed on by several individuals: the Managing Director, the Production Manager, the PMC and the Senior Foreman. All did so separately, on handwritten sheets of paper which they used at progress meetings. The PMC used computer system reports but system data were not kept up-to-date. No one had definitive information and even when the Managing Director passed photocopies of his sheets round, no sooner were they issued than they were changed.

In effect, Murray had no single systematic method of processing the information necessary to run the factory effectively.

Questions

1 What are the issues facing Murray Rock Drilling Ltd?

2 What action would you propose to improve delivery performance and reduce lead time?

APPENDIX 19.1
ROCK DRILLS WITH TUNGSTEN CARBIDE INSERTS

Alternative shank styles for rock drills

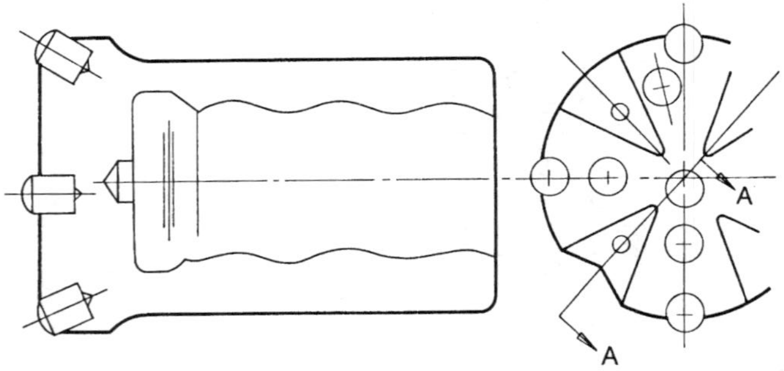

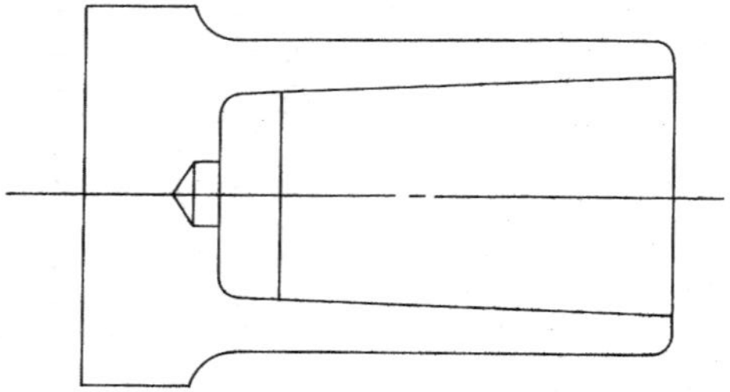

Taper socket bit

Section AA
showing side and
face flutes and
flushing hole

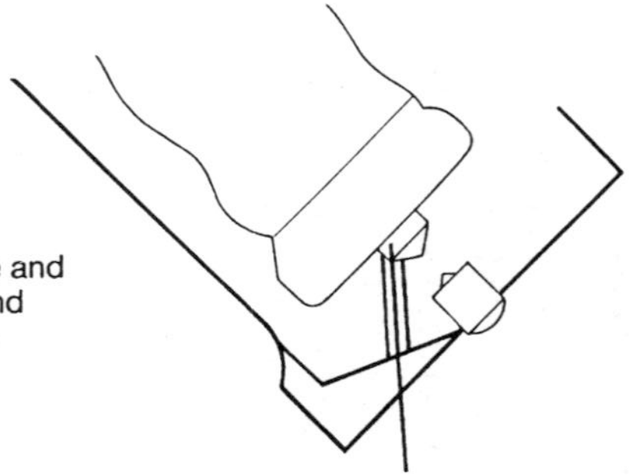

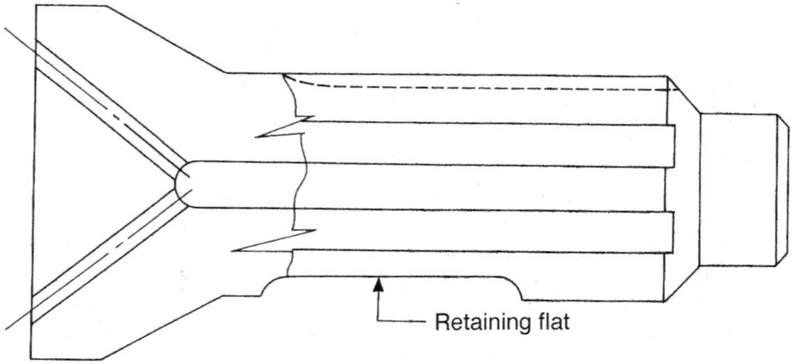

Diagram of 70-mm dia. button bit
with centre flushing and $1\frac{1}{2}$-inch rope thread

Splined depth bit

APPENDIX 19.2
BUTTON AND TAPER SOCKET-TYPE ROCK DRILLS: BASIC MANUFACTURING ROUTE

Button socket type Sheet 1

Splined type

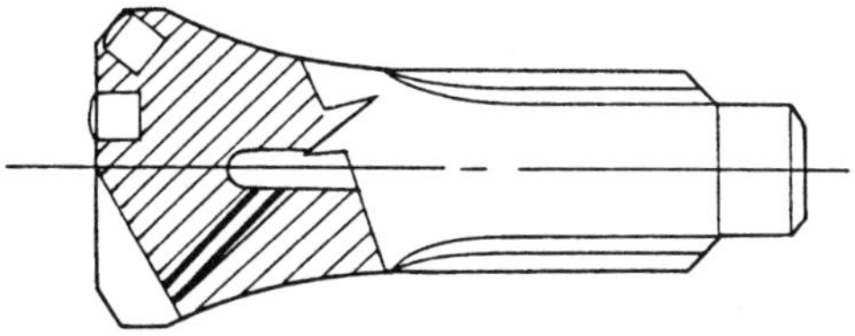

Threaded type

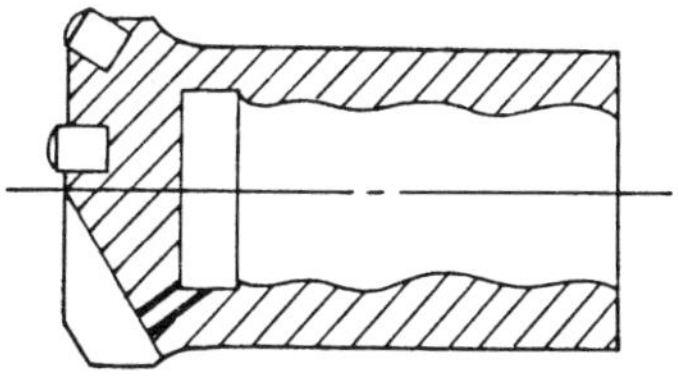

Operation	Splined type	Threaded type
1. Turn	✓	✓
2. Turn	✓	✓
3. Mill face flutes and side flutes	✓	✓
4. Drill axial hole (flushing)	✓	
5. Drill flushing holes (angled)	✓	✓
6. Mill spline	✓	
7. Stop – off button faces	✓	✓
8. Inspect and mark	✓	✓
9. Heat treat	✓	✓
10. Shotblast	✓	✓
11. Inspect	✓	✓
12. Grind spigot	✓	
13. Drill and ream button holes	✓	✓
14. Assemble buttons	✓	✓
15. Hand grind and deburr	✓	✓
16. Inspect and etch	✓	✓
17. Box and label	✓	✓
18. Store	✓	✓

APPENDIX 19.2 *(continued)*

Taper socket type Sheet 2

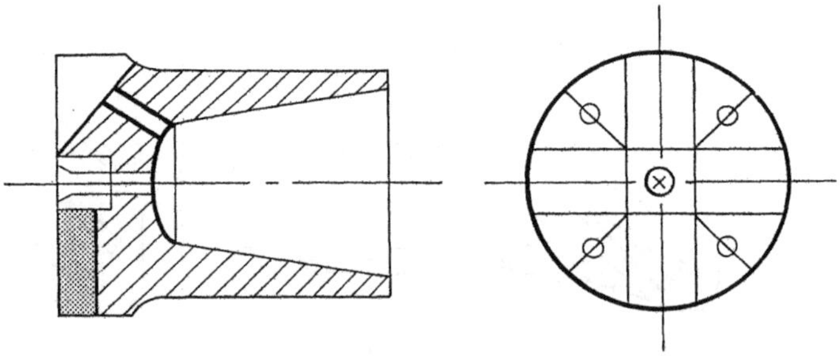

Operation

1. Saw and drill centre pellet
2. Deburr
3. Store

Operation

1. Turn body
2. Turn
3. (a) Mill face flutes
   (b) Mill side flutes
4. Drill flushing holes
5. Stop-off insert faces
6. Inspect and mark
7. Heat treat
8. Shotblast
9. Inspect

9A. Mill slots

10. Assemble centre pellet, carbide inserts, flux and braze pellets
11. Braze
12. (a) Machine grind outside diameter
    (b) Hand grind and deburr
13. Inspect and etch
14. Box and label
15. Store

APPENDIX 19.2 *(continued)*

Combined process route – all types

Sheet 3

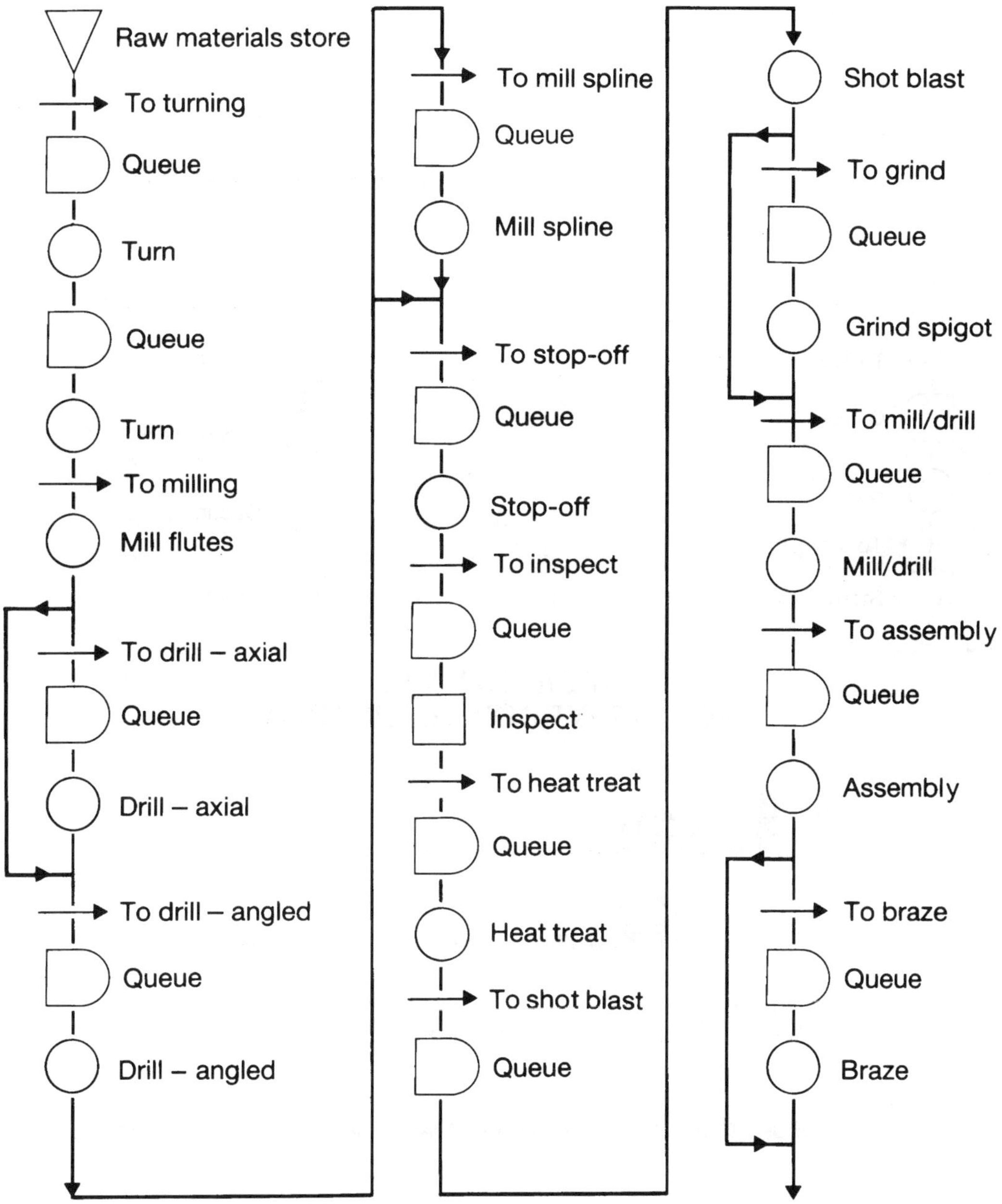

APPENDIX 19.2 *(continued)*

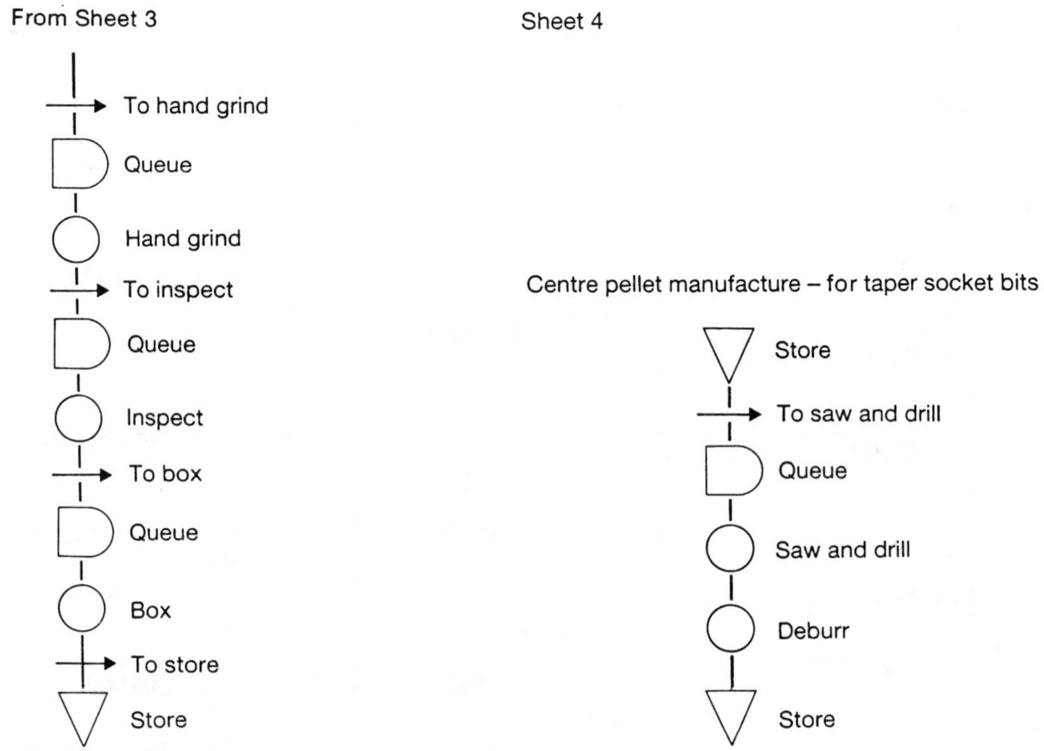

APPENDIX 19.3
LATE DELIVERIES (BARSTROM)

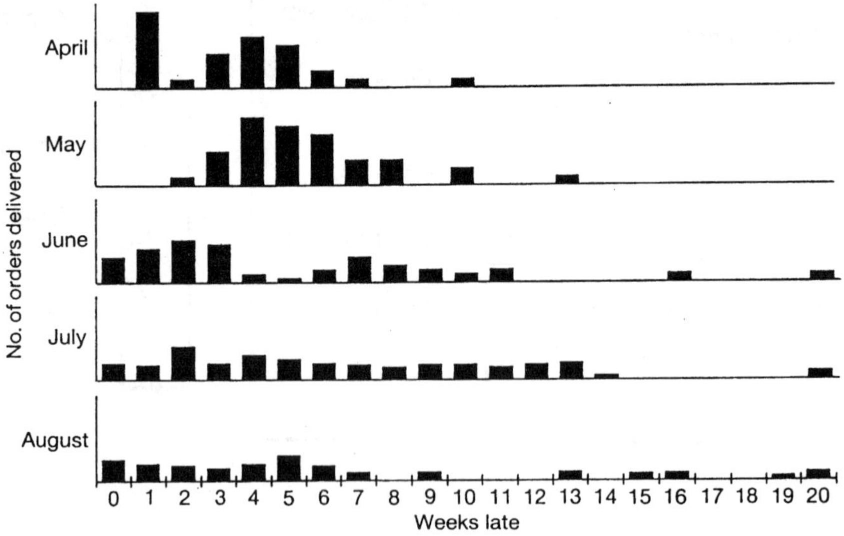

APPENDIX 19.4
SOFT STATE THROUGH-PUT

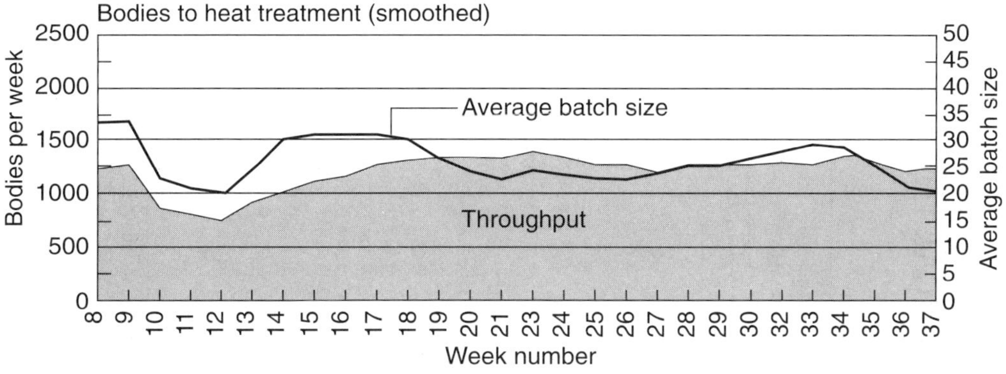

Average throughput approximately 1200 bodies/week
Average batch size 26

Note: Although much of this data was initially collated in weeks 27 and 28, it was monitored over the whole period of the study. Thus the data is given through to week 37.

APPENDIX 19.5
HARD STATE THROUGH-PUT

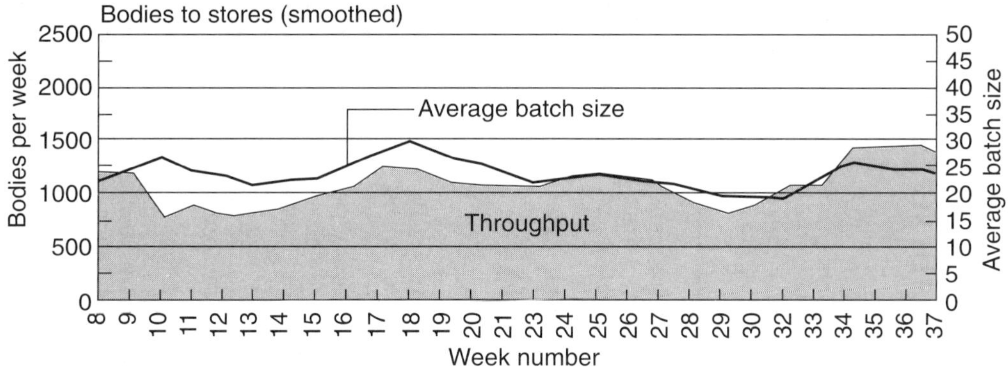

Average throughput approximately 1050 bodies/week
Average batch size 23

Note: Although much of this data was initially collated in weeks 27 and 28, it was monitored over the whole period of the study. Thus the data is given through to week 37.

APPENDIX 19.6
MACHINE LOADING FACTORS FROM EIGHT MONTHS HISTORICAL THROUGHPUT DATA

Lot size	Operation	Av. set-up (hrs)	Av. set-up (hrs/unit)	Wt. Av. run time (mins/unit)	Wt. Av. (run time) (hrs/unit)	Operator perform level	Total (hrs/unit)	Reqd m/c hours for 1200 body/wk	No. of m/cs	No. of men		No. of manned m/cs available				Manned m/c hours available	Spare manned m/c hours	Loading factor (%)
										D	N	D	O/T	N	O/T			
	Soft State																	
26	Turning	0.50	0.0192	7.2	0.1200	0.87	0.1572	189	4.0	3.0	2.0	4.0	2.0	2.0	2.0	250	61	75
	Turning	1.75	0.0673	5.4	0.0900	0.87	0.1708	205	4.0	3.0	2.0	4.0		3.0		273	68	75
	Drill – axial	0.10	0.0038	1.1	0.0183	0.87	0.0249	30	1.0	1.0		1.0				39	9	77
	Drill coolant holes	0.25	0.0096	0.6	0.0100	0.87	0.0211	25	0.8	0.8		0.8				31	6	81
	Mill spline	0.25	0.0096	4.8	0.0800	0.87	0.1016	122	2.2	2.2	1.0	2.2	1.0	1.0	1.0	133	11	92
	Mill face flutes	0.50	0.0192	3.1	0.0517	0.87	0.0786	94	4.0	3.0		3.0	2.0			125	31	75
			0.13		0.37		0.55	665	16.0	13.0	5.0					851	186	78
	Hard State																	
23	Shotblast	0.10	0.0038	0.43	0.0072	0.87	0.0121	15	2.0	0.2	0.2	0.15		0.20		14	–1	106
	Grind spigot	0.45	0.0196	0.43	0.0072	0.87	0.0278	33	0.5	0.4	0.5	0.40		0.45		33	0	101
	Drill and ream	0.20	0.0077	0.59	0.0098	0.87	0.0190	23	0.5	0.5	0.4	0.45		0.35		31	8	73
	Mill	0.45	0.0196	4.01	0.0668	0.87	0.0964	116	2.0	1.5	1.0	1.5	1.0	1.0	1.0	106	–10	110
	Assemble – button	0.60	0.0261	1.21	0.0202	0.87	0.0493	59	1.5	1.5		1.5	1.0			63	3	95
	Assemble – brazed	0.60	0.0261	3.01	0.0502	0.87	0.0837	100	2.0	1.0	1.0	1.0	1.0	1.0	1.0	86	–14	117
	Grind O/D	0.50	0.0217	5.79	0.0965	0.87	0.1327	159	3.5	2.0	2.0	2.0	1.0	2.0	1.0	164	5	97
	Hand grind/deburr	0.10	0.0043	1.87	0.0312	0.87	0.0402	48	2.0	1.0		1.0	1.0			43	–5	112
	Inspect/etch	0.50	0.0217	0.89	0.0148	0.87	0.0388	47	2.0	1.0		1.0	1.0			43	–4	108
			0.15		0.30		0.50	529	16.0	9.0	5.0					504	–25	105

Notes: This table uses the available data for set-up times, run times, manning levels and machine hours available to calculate the machine loading factors at each stage of the process. Appendices 19.4 and 19.5 plot the historical throughput data. The average through-put of Hard State is 1050 bodies/week, significantly lower than the 1200 bodies/week in Soft State. This is reflected in the loading factors in Hard State.

Weighted average run times were averaged from product route cards weighted in accordance with the volumes produced of each product over the previous eight months. A day or night shift is 39 hours per week. Overtime amounted to four hours per week.

APPENDIX 19.7
ORDERS *v* OUTPUT

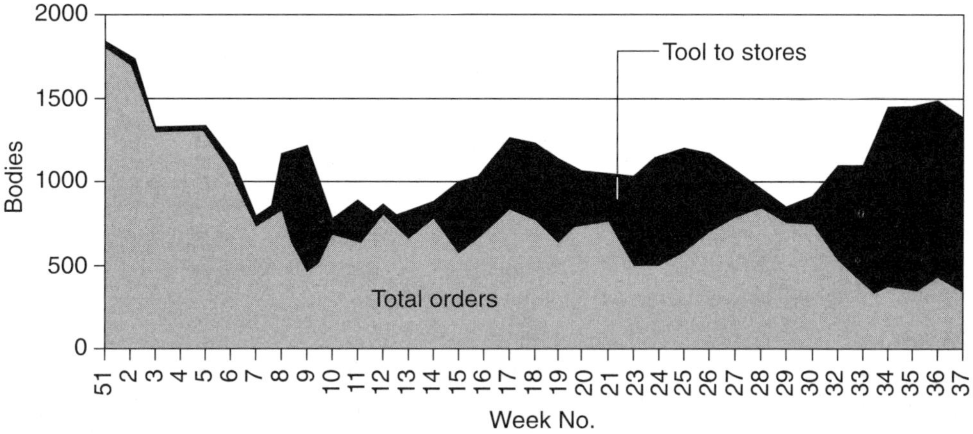

Note: Tool to stores data begins at week 8.

APPENDIX 19.8
ORDER BACKLOG AND WIP INVENTORY

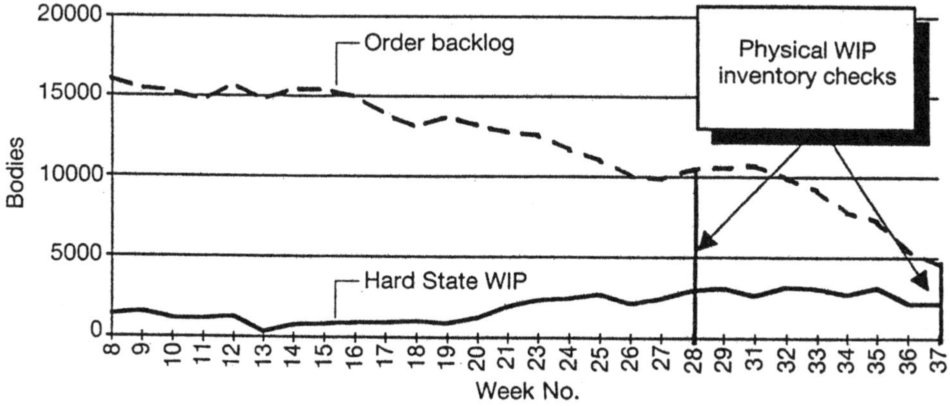

Note: The data was extrapolated from order receipt, transfer to stores and dispatch records. There is no means of distinguishing Soft State WIP from the order backlog.

APPENDIX 19.9
MANUFACTURING LEAD TIME FROM WEEK 28 WIP

Operation	*Bodies per week*	*Week 28 WIP*	*Lead time weeks*		
Turning	1200	2407	2.0		
Turning	1200	1110	0.9		
Drill-axial	1200	485	0.4		
Drill coolant holes	1200	95	0.1		
Mill spline	1200	796	0.7		
Mill flutes	1200	438	0.3		
				4.4	
Shotblast	1050		0.0		
Grind spigot	1050	91	0.1		
Drill and ream	1050	435	0.4		
Mill	1050	619	0.6		
Assemble – button	1050	386	0.4		
Assemble – brazed	1050	633	0.6		
Grind O/D	1050	14	0.0		
Hand grind and deburr	1050		0.0		
Inspect/etch	1050	137	0.1		
				2.2	
					6.6
Office processing			1		
Batching			3		
Heat treatment and shot blast			1		
Inspection, etch, box and dispatch			1		
				6	
Total lead time					12.6

APPENDIX 19.10
BREAKDOWN OF ORDER LEAD TIME

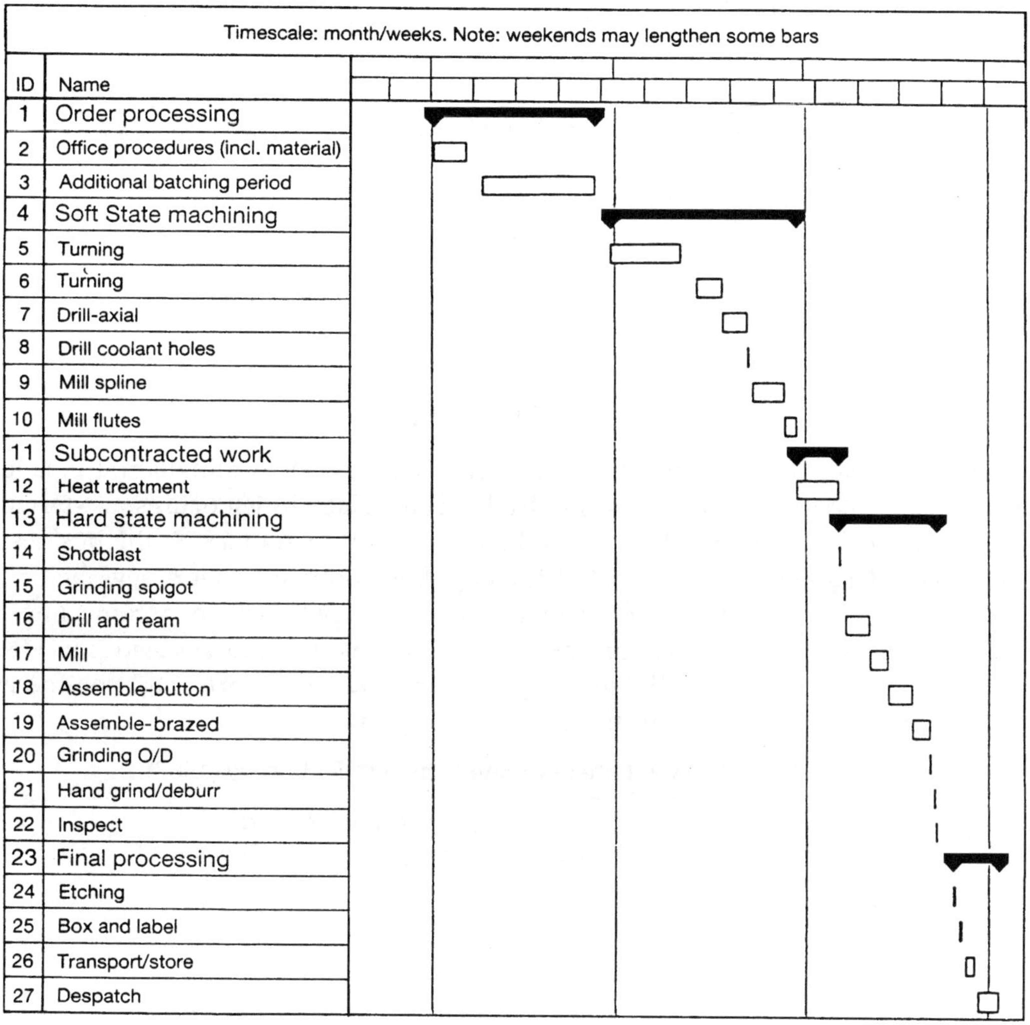

CASE 20

Cadbury Ltd: A Routine Investment Decision?

Stuart Chambers

*Case date 1992 (additional text added 1995)**

INTRODUCTION

Cadbury Ltd was founded by a Quaker, John Cadbury, in Birmingham, England in 1794 and sold tea, coffee, cocoa and drinking chocolate. In 1866, his sons started producing chocolate bars, which proved so successful that, in 1879, the business moved to a larger site on the edge of the city. The company built a new factory, along with housing and recreation facilities at Bournville which became internationally famous as a model community. Cadbury is now market leader in UK chocolate confectionery (*see* Table 20.1), with worldwide exports, and volume is continuing to increase by about five per cent per year.

Table 20.1 UK market share of chocolate confectionery (1988)

	% Market Share	
Company	*By volume (kg)*	*By value (£)*
Mars	30	24
Cadbury	26	29
Rowntree-Nestlé	26	27
Others	18	20

Chocolate-making starts with a series of primary processes, which convert full cream milk, sugar and cocoa into a wide range of recipes of thick (viscous) liquid chocolate. This chocolate is used at secondary processes to mould bars such as Cadbury Dairy Milk (CDM), to coat biscuits and assortments, and to make speciality products such as Easter eggs. Often, UK and export markets require different recipes to cater for legislative and climatic differences.

The conching process is a later stage of the primary processes. These enormous machines take fatty powders from earlier primary stages and, through a shearing action between large contra-rotating rollers, release fats and disperse the solids, to produce

*Based on research originally conducted by Helen Valentine. Names and data have been disguised.

liquid chocolate with various controllable physical properties, such as temperature and viscosity. The main steps in the primary processes are outlined in Fig. 20.1. Late in 1991, at a regular meeting of the Management Committee, a routine discussion centred on the purchase of additional equipment for the Chocolate Department. David Manuel, Manufacturing Director of the Bourneville site, was supporting his recent £1.5m. capital application for a fifth conventional 'conch' machine, to provide an additional 25 per cent capacity for the department.

'We really should not delay this decision again! If we can't approve the purchase of another conch machine, we will not be able to meet the forecast growth in demand for 1992/3, and we will be forced to cut back on all our expansion plans. We are already experiencing frequent capacity problems in the chocolate plant ... it is certainly our worst bottleneck! It is now sometimes nearly impossible to plan an efficient sequence of production of different grades of chocolate to satisfy the various needs of all the secondary user departments. My proposal is that we should purchase another conventional conch machine which could be installed and working in under six months. Because it would be identical to the existing four machines, we would have considerable flexibility ... for example, to move staff around the different conches, to plan for any type of chocolate on any conch, and to hold standard spare parts. There would also be greater opportunity to dedicate one conch to one grade of chocolate, so cutting out many costly change-overs. I really cannot support Chris' proposal to buy the "new technology conch". Because it could take 12–15 months to make and install, it's certainly not going to solve next year's capacity problems. It would require completely different skills, both in production and maintenance, and would even require different planning rules. All this would be far too disruptive at a time when we need to concentrate on output and new product development. I'm sorry, Chris, I do think that you've done a good job on the development of the new small-scale conch, but I would rather invest the extra capital at Bourneville in more in-line viscositising and much more chocolate storage, to decouple primary and secondary processes.

'However, I am certain that the new technology conch would be well-suited to a greenfield development such as at one of our new joint-venture operations in Eastern Europe where we could standardise on this new equipment. This would also eliminate the risks of potential subtle changes in taste being noticed by our customers. With the greatest respect to Chris and his team, I cannot understand how we've ended up with a new technology without first establishing a clear market need for it!'

Mark Mitchell, Marketing Director commented:

'I really must agree with David. I too support the idea of purchasing another conventional conch, as otherwise we can get into production by mid-1992; the new technology conch would not be into production until at least six months later. But, even more importantly, while we know that the small trial machine has made chocolate which the tasting panel cannot distinguish from our standard product, there is no guarantee that would be the case for a machine ten times larger. We know that conching is critical in creating our

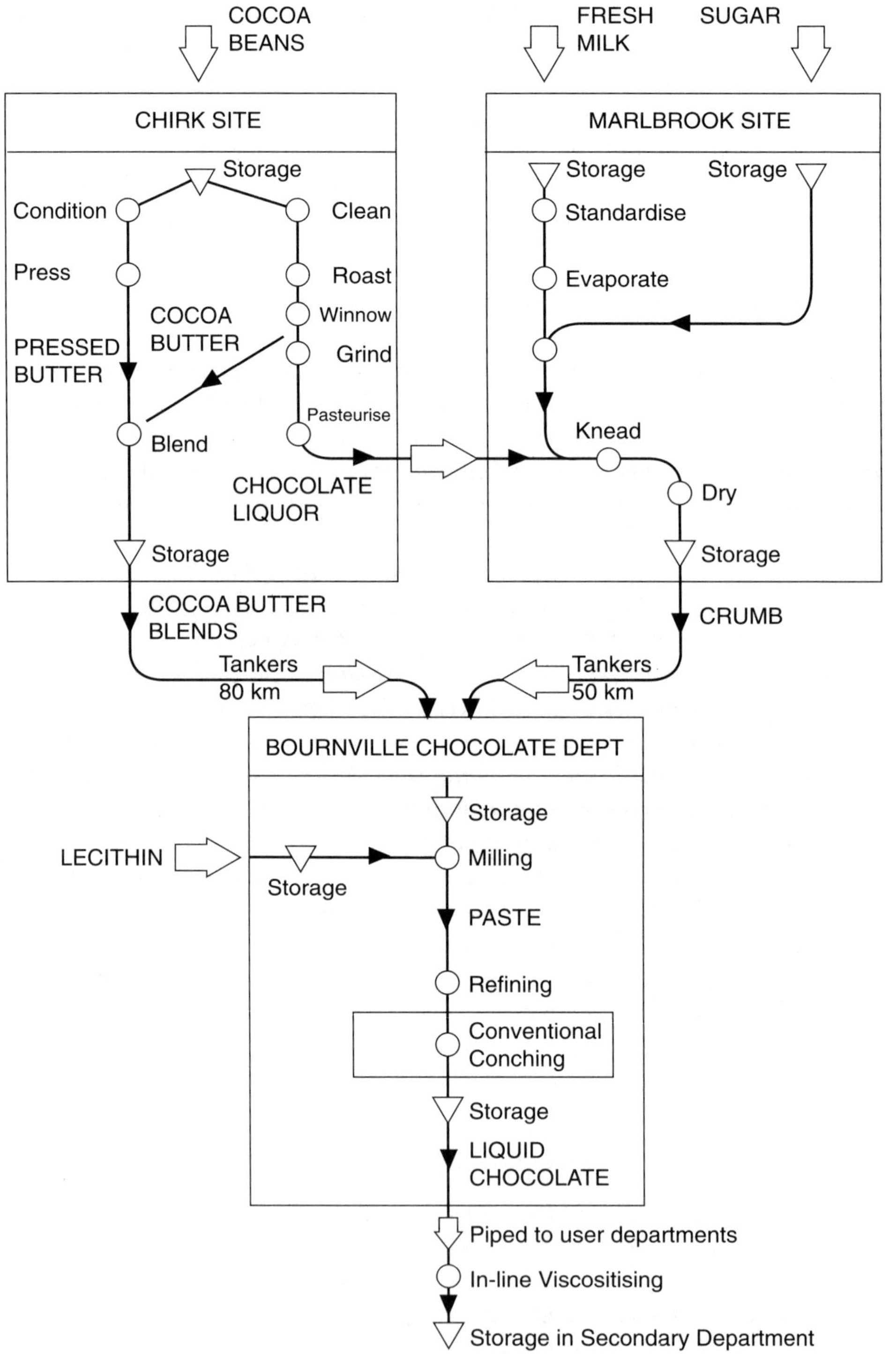

Fig. 20.1 Primary chocolate processes

unique "Cadbury Dairy Milk" (CDM) flavour and texture, so we should take no risks and stick with the type of process we have been using for at least eighty years. At least 70 per cent of our customers, particularly in the UK, can distinguish the taste of CDM from competitors' products such as "Galaxy" (Mars) and "Yorkie" (Rowntree-Nestlé). The early commissioning of the extra capacity will allow us to go ahead with our schedule of planned trials and new product launches, which are already being disrupted by capacity and planning constraints. How could we possibly justify the delays and risks associated with the new technology, Chris?'

Chris English, the Director of Engineering Development, had been expecting resistance to his proposal from Marketing, but had already made some attempts to convince David of the advantages of the new conch technology in manufacturing. It seemed that all his colleagues were against his proposal, even the Finance Director objected on the grounds that the new process would cost about £2m. as opposed to £1.5m. for conventional conching of similar capacity. It appeared that two years of research and trials had been for nothing but he sprang to the defence of his proposal:

*'I am convinced that the new technology offers too many advantages to be dismissed so lightly. I accept that it could delay the availability of capacity by around six months and would cost more – but there are at least six advantages which I have listed separately (*see *Appendix 20.1), some of which could be quantified in money terms, to justify the extra capital cost. You will understand that I am not in any position to calculate all these cost savings throughout the company, but I think that they could be obtained if we required them, but that would create months more delay. Our conventional capital expenditure (Capex) applications have always had to demonstrate clear departmental cost savings such as reductions in direct labour and associated overheads which result from automation technologies. The opportunities for further automation of high volume production processes are diminishing as the variety of our products is expanding. Payback periods for this type of investment are extending . . . perhaps we are experiencing the law of diminishing returns. The days are long gone when we can design dedicated production lines for single products.*

'The relative annual cost saving of the new technology conch (compared to a conventional conch) in the primary processes would be around £140 000. The labour saving is only small, perhaps half a person or around £10 000. Space savings are estimated by Finance to be worth around £20 000 in opportunity cost. Improved control of cocoa fat content will save the department around £30 000 based on our trials on the prototype machine. The biggest saving is reduced material wastage at change-overs: we could expect a £80 000 reduction here, since there will be dramatic reductions in the quantity of mixed grade outputs which are used up on the lower specification products. But the big benefits will be seen in the secondary departments, where there will be much more control of coating thickness and less quality and productivity problems. Unfortunately, these savings are much more difficult to predict. I believe that we cannot survive and grow without this type of development. In my view, the old technology is

often barely able to achieve the demands placed on it by the complex new products being dreamed up by our Development Department. These modern and efficient process technologies will be critical in our future developments. Mars and Rowntree-Nestlé are certainly investing heavily in their factories.'

The Chairman was alarmed to find that there was no agreed strategy for the purchase of conching capacity but recognised that the decision had to be made quickly and appropriately:

'Before we decide what to do next, let's just have another look at our marketing strategy; that might give us some insights on the best solution. Mark, what do you think are the key aspects of our strategy in this context?'

Mark was well prepared to brief the Board, having just completed his first draft of the marketing strategy.

Table 20.2 Consumption of chocolate confectionery per capita in selected countries

Country	*Per capita consumption kg/year*
Switzerland	8.8
United Kingdom	8.0
Germany	6.7
France	4.2
Italy	1.1
Spain	1.1

'As you all know, chocolate eating is an obsession in the UK (see *Table 20.2), which gives us a solid base of loyal consumers. However, the environment is changing quickly! While Cadbury holds the top position in the UK consumer's mind (70 per cent refer to Cadbury when questioned about chocolate), we know this is based on volume brands like CDM and Roses. There is ample evidence that they are demanding more varieties and experimenting with new tastes. The European manufacturers are already making major attacks on our market and some of our comfortable dominance of retail chains could be lost in the 1990s. Competition for retail shelf space will be intense. Our strategy is clear. First, we will have to defend existing volume brands by maintaining price competitiveness and quality. The factories must be able to continue to support this by corresponding cost reductions. Second, we must be able to launch new, high quality, high margin products (based on the trusted Cadbury name) at a faster rate than ever before, to satisfy the niche opportunities provided by changing consumer and retailer demand. If we can't do this*

successfully, I know there are plenty of eager competitors out there ready to erode our shelf space in the corner shops and supermarkets. Realistically, not all of these new products will be a success and few will ever even reach 10 per cent of the weight of sales of CDM. But, together, they will be very profitable and will provide most of our projected growth.

'We will also continue to export existing and selected new brands, particularly into Europe. The marketing strategy recognises that this decade will bring unprecedented competition but, also, unbelievable opportunities for our chocolate business. With the right support from the factories, I am confident we will become the leading European manufacturer. I think you can see why I favour the conventional conch technology. It minimises the fixed-cost burden of extra capacity and ensures low-cost production without any risks associated with new processes.

'I have heard it said that one of the strengths of Japanese companies is that they would almost never make new products on new, uncertain processes. They first try out any new technology on well-established products in order to minimise any impact on the market of unforseen problems. Thus they always have the back-up of the old processes in case of problems. In my view, the new conch would be an expensive distraction at a time when we should be concentrating on the new product launches. The last thing we want is any unnecessary delays or risks!'

The Chairman leaned back thoughtfully in his chair and sighed:

'Well, we have a problem but I'm not prepared to put this issue to the vote today. I propose that we wait just two weeks, while you give one last thought to Chris' proposal, and re-examine the Capex. We must see an analysis of the likely savings from receiving more consistent chocolate at the Secondary Processes; perhaps that would put a better perspective on the incremental cost. I always feel that new technology is only of use if it helps us competitively. *What we must decide is how the new conch process would help, if at all. Clearly, this is* not *one of our routine investment decisions!'*

A report was received from the secondary processes manager ten days later. A summary of her findings is shown in Appendix 20.2.

Questions

1 What are the main concerns of the managers involved, when choosing between the 'conventional' conch and the new technology conch process?

2 How did Cadbury compete for sales of its various chocolate products, and how is that expected to change in the 1990s?

3 The Manufacturing Director refers to flexibility when considering the purchase of the new asset. What is meant by 'flexibility', and what will be the main differences in flexibility between the two types of conch machine?

4 What do you think the management should decide to do?

APPENDIX 20.1
MEMORANDUM ON THE ADVANTAGES OF THE NEW PROCESS

To: Members of the Board 30th September, 1991
From: Chris English,
Director of Engineering Development

NEW CONCHING PROCESS

Trials have now been completed on the one-tenth scale new technology conch. All output has been used successfully on our full product range. The tasting panel reports no detectable changes in taste, texture or aroma.

There are at least six advantages of this technology, which I list below; not all can be evaluated in money terms:

1 Fat Content
Trials have indicated that, for about half of our recipes, fat content can be reduced by up to 1% without significant changes to flavour or texture. As cocoa butter is expensive, this could give significant savings for some products.

2 Viscosity*
The new process gives much greater control over viscosity, allowing more precise coating of biscuits and fondants. This should reduce the level of rejects on all coated products, but the greatest saving would be that the chocolate can be used immediately without further adjustment, eliminating the need for 'in-line viscositising'.

3 Change-over Time and Cost
Conventional conches take eight hours to completely clear of material during a recipe change, during which time the output is a mixture of two recipes, which can, therefore, only be used on the 'lower quality specification' product (usually a product that sells at a lower price). The new conch, in comparison, fully clears all material in less than half an hour, reducing the cost of materials.

4 Variety Capability
The new conching process will allow a much wider range of chocolates to be produced, as it can produce to a higher viscosity and to tighter tolerances.

5 Scalability
We believe that the technology will work at any size from one-tenth to double the size of conventional conches. They can be custom-built for our specific needs.

6 Reduced Size
The new conch occupies 150 m^2 on one level, whereas a similar sized, conventional machine occupies 200 m^2 on three levels (total 600 m^2). The saved space would provide opportunities for further expansion.

* Viscosity is the 'thickness' of a liquid; it is a measure of how quickly it flows.

APPENDIX 20.2
EDITED MEMORANDUM ON THE ADVANTAGES OF THE NEW PROCESS IN THE SECONDARY PROCESSES

To: Members of the Board
From: Christine Thompson,
Secondary Processes Manager

NEW CONCHING PROCESS

Now that we have had experience of using the chocolate from the small scale conch, we have been able to estimate the potential costs benefits to the secondary processes. These are entirely due to the improved viscosity consistency which gives us more control over the thickness of the chocolate in the case of coated products and shells (e.g. Easter eggs).

1 Material Savings
We estimate that the tighter performance to our viscosity requirements will yield savings on these products of approximately £100 000 per year based on current output levels. This saving has been calculated from our statistical records of standard deviation of coating/shell thicknesses.

2 Reduced Scrap/Rework
Where viscosities have been too low, some coatings or shells have suffered from defects such as holes, and are therefore rejected as are underweight eggs. The improved viscosity control should eliminate at least 75 per cent of this problem, saving £140 000 per year.

We should like to point out that this improved control means that we should not need any more in-line viscositising between primary and secondary processes. The improved consistency of the chocolate will eliminate many of the uncertainties in our department, which should, in turn, allow us to give a more reliable service to our customers.

CASE 21

Vixen Instruments: the 'Scantel' project

Nigel Slack

Case date 1992

INTRODUCTION

Peter Middleton, Chief Executive Officer of Vixen Instruments Ltd (VIL), was conscious that the project in front of him was one of the most important VIL had handled for many years. The number and variety of the development projects under way within the company had risen sharply in the last few years, and although they had all seemed important at the time, this one – the 'Scantel' project – clearly justified the description given it by the President of Vixen Instruments Ltd's American parent company, Photonics Corporation: '*. . . the make or break opportunity to ensure Vixen's long-term position in the European instrumentation industry*'.

THE COMPANY

Vixen Instruments, originally the 'Leicester Engineering Instrument Company', had been founded in the 1920s as a general instrument and gauge manufacturer for the engineering industry. By expanding its range into optical instruments in the early 1930s, it eventually moved also into the manufacture of high precision and speciality lenses, mainly for the photographic industry. Its reputation as a specialist lens manufacturer led to such a growth in sales that by 1939 the optical side of the company accounted for about 60 per cent of total business and Vixen Instruments (as it was now known) ranked one of the top two or three optics companies of its type in the world. Although its reputation for skilled lens making had not diminished since the 1940s, the instrument side of the company had come to dominate sales once again in the 1970s and 1980s.

In 1957 the company had been acquired by a large UK engineering group but had been largely left to its own devices. In 1980 it was sold to the Photonics Corporation, a US-based industrial group with interests in electronics, optical products and defence products. VIL, together with the US instrument company Allman Taylor, formed the Instruments Division of Photonics. The two companies' products complemented each other well and each marketed the other's products in Europe and the USA respectively. Appendix 21.1 shows the divisional structure of the Photonics corporation.

One organisation oddity remained. VIL's optical side was kept within VIL in the Instruments Division even though Photonics Optical Division would have been a more natural home. The reasons for this were that both instrument and optical manufacturing at VIL occupied the same site in Leicester, and, of more long-term significance, Photonics aspired to develop products incorporating both optical and electronic instrument expertise. The optical side of VIL did have a 'dotted line' relationship with the Optical Division, but since the division was otherwise based entirely in the USA, this had not proved a strong relationship as of 1985, when the Scantel project formally reached the board of VIL for a decision.

VIL'S PRODUCT RANGE

VIL's product range on the optical side included lenses for inspection systems which were used mainly in the manufacture of microchips. These lenses were sold both to the inspection system manufacturers and to the chip manufacturers themselves. They were medium-precision lenses mounted in relatively simple housings. However, most of the company's optical products were specialist photographic and cinema lenses. In addition about 15 per cent of the company's optical work was concerned with the development and manufacture of 'one or two off' very high precision lenses for specialist scientific instrument-makers and other optical companies.

The instrument product range consisted largely of standard metrology products such as probes for co-ordinate measuring machines, flatness and surface finish measurement equipment and concentricity measurement equipment. These products were essentially precision electro-mechanical assemblies with an increasing emphasis on software-based recording, display and diagnostic abilities. This move towards more software-based products had led the instrument side of the business towards accepting some customised orders. The growth of this part of the instrumentation had resulted in a special development unit being set up – the Customer Services Unit (CSU). The CSU was a small group of four engineers and six technicians who modified, customised or adapted products for those customers who required an unusual application which the base manufacturing factory could not satisfy. CSU would work on and adapt the whole range of Photonics products, but mainly it dealt with products originating from Leicester. Often CSU's work involved incorporating Photonics products into larger systems for a customer, either at Bracknell or at the customer's site. Although nominally in the Development function, CSU worked closely with Sales and Marketing.

In 1985 VIL's turnover was approximately $120 million, of which optical products accounted for around 22 per cent, electronic instruments 55 per cent and Allman Taylor products 23 per cent. Neither profitability nor ROCE figures were published for product groups but margins were generally higher on the instrument than on the optical side of the business. Even the instrument business however was starting to feel the effects of competition, mainly from Japanese manufacturers.

COMPANY ORGANISATION

VIL occupied three sites, two at Bracknell in southern England and one a hundred miles north at Leicester. One of the Bracknell sites housed the company head office, Sales and Marketing, Personnel, Finance, Management Accounting functions and part of the Development function. Half a mile away the other Bracknell site housed the rest of the Development engineers with their development laboratories and the CSU. Practically all the development activity at Bracknell was instrument development. Optics development was based at Leicester.

The Leicester site was VIL's main manufacturing site. As well as Manufacturing Operations it also housed Purchasing, Plant Engineering, Manufacturing Engineering, and Development. All Optics development engineers were based at Leicester as well as the 'Build Shop', a general workshop for larger development projects.

Appendix 21.2 shows VIL's organisational structure and locations.

THE SCANTEL PROJECT

The idea for Scantel had come out of a project which the CSU had been involved with in 1984. At that time the CSU had successfully installed a high-precision VIL lens into a character recognition system for a large clearing bank. The enhanced capability given by the lens and software modifications had enabled the bank to scan documents even when they were not correctly aligned. This had led to CSU proposing the development of a 'vision metrology' device which could optically scan a product at some point in the manufacturing process, and check the accuracy of up to twenty individual dimensions. The geometry of the product to be scanned, the dimensions to be gauged, and the tolerances to be allowed, could all be programmed into the control logic of the device. It was envisaged that it could also be connected to conventional materials handling equipment which could then take the defective products out of the production process.

The CSU team were convinced that the product, if successfully developed, could have considerable potential. The introduction by several large companies of computer-controlled flexible manufacturing systems (FMS) and automated assembly was thought to be an especially promising source of demand. Such a vision metrology system could easily be integrated into this type of manufacturing system. The proposal, which the CSU team had called the Scantel project, was put forward to Bob Brierly, the Development Director, in August 1984. Brierly both saw the potential value of the idea and was impressed by the CSU team's enthusiasm:

'To be frank it was their evident enthusiasm which influenced me as much as anything. Remember that the CSU had only been in existence for two years at this time – they were a group of keen but relatively young engineers. Yet their proposal was well thought out and, on reflection, seemed to have considerable potential.'

Mainly due to Brierly's championing of the project, in November 1984 CSU were allocated funds outside the normal budget cycle to investigate the feasibility of the Scantel idea. The investigation was led by Brian Callister, the 29-year-old engineer and acting manager of the CSU, who had been the prime mover behind the idea thus far and had been instrumental in putting the idea up for special funding. Callister was given one further engineer and a technician, and a three-month deadline to report to the VIL board. In this time he was expected to overcome any fundamental technical problems, assess the feasibility of successfully developing the concept into a working prototype, and plan the development tasks which would lead to the prototype stage.

THE CALLISTER INVESTIGATION

Brian Callister, even at the start of his investigation, had some firm views as to the appropriate 'architecture' for the Scantel Project. By 'architecture' he meant the major elements of the system, their functions, and how they related to each other. The Scantel system architecture would consist of five major sub-systems:

1 Lens and lens mounting: an exceptionally high-precision lens mounted in a high-precision adjustable mounting.
2 Vision support system: the support and control and recording electronics which were associated with the lens.
3 Display system: the visual display and associated graphics software and control.
4 Control logic system: the overall control software which integrated the whole Scantel system.
5 Chassis and body: the physical support chassis and outer casing.

Callister's first task, once the system's overall architecture was set, was to decide whether the various components in the major sub-systems would be developed in-house, developed by outside specialist companies from VIL's specifications, or bought in as standard units and if necessary modified in-house. Callister and his colleagues made these decisions themselves, while recognising that a more consultative process might have been preferable:

'I am fully aware that ideally we should have made more use of the expertise within the company to decide how units were to be developed. But we just did not have the time to explain the product concept, explain the choices and then wait for already busy people to come up with a recommendation. Also there was the security aspect to think of. I'm sure our employees are to be trusted but the more people who know about the

project the greater chance there is for leaks. Anyway we did not see our decisions as final. For example, if we decided that a component was to be bought in and modified for the prototype building stage it does not mean that we can't change our minds and develop a better component in-house at a later stage.'

Security was of concern to Callister, and had influenced some of his design decisions. He had already realised that VIL had an opportunity to get into the market well in advance of any competitor provided they were first in completing the design and development phase. He wanted no word of the Scantel project to get out of the company.

'Perhaps we have been influenced towards modifying standard components rather than exploring whether we could commission original engineering work because of the security aspect. We have put some of the work out for design of course (we could not have done all the investigative work ourselves in time) but we have not been totally open with our suppliers as to the shape or purpose of the total project.'

By February 1985 Callister's small team had satisfied themselves that the system could be built to achieve their original technical performance targets. Their final task before reporting to the board would be to devise a feasible development plan to move the project through to the prototype stage.

PLANNING THE SCANTEL DEVELOPMENT

As a planning aid Callister's team drew up a network diagram for all the major activities within the project from its start through to completion when the project would be handed over to Manufacturing Operations. This rather detailed diagram is shown in Appendix 21.4 and the complete list of all events in the diagram is shown in Appendix 21.3. The duration of all the activities in the project were estimated either by Callister himself or, more often, by Callister consulting a more experienced engineer within the company. While he was reasonably confident in the estimates, he was keen to stress that they were just that – estimates.

Two draughting conventions on these networks need explanation. The three figures in brackets by each activity arrow represent the 'optimistic', 'most likely' and 'pessimistic' times (in weeks) respectively. The left-side figure in the event circles indicates the earliest time the event could take place and the figure in the right side of the circles indicates the latest time the event could take place without delaying the whole project. Dotted lines represent 'dummy' activities. These are nominal activities which have no time associated with them and are there either to maintain the logic of the network or for drafting convenience.

Callister, having compiled the network diagram himself, understood it perfectly well, but he did realise that it might look rather daunting to the board. So, for the presentation he had reduced the full network to one which illustrated the major *composite* activities (Appendix 21.5).

The development of each of the five major sub-systems required different types of technical effort and each type of effort was described in the network by a separate activity. As an example, for any one item the initial engineering, testing and re-engineering modifications after testing (rework) were shown as separate activities. The five sub-systems are described below.

1 **The lens.** The lens (events 5–38–43–44) was particularly critical since the shape was complex and a degree of curvature of no more than 0.0005 on the projected image would be permissible if the system was to perform up to its intended design specification. Callister was relying heavily upon the skill of the expert optics group at Leicester to produce the lens to the required high tolerance. Since what in effect was a trial and error approach was involved in their manufacture, the exact time to manufacture would be uncertain. Callister realised this:

> *'The lens is going to be a real problem. We just don't know how easy it will be to make the particular geometry and precision we need. The optics people won't commit themselves even though they are regarded as some of the best optics technicians in Europe. It is a relief that lens manufacture is not amongst the "critical path" activities.'*

2 **Vision support system.** The vision support system included many components which were commercially available. However, considerable engineering effort would be required to modify them for the Scantel system. In addition, some parts would need to be developed in-house and integrated into the system. To expedite development, it was planned that separate groups would perform the modification and re-engineering of these units. They would, however, be assembled as one unit. Although the development design and testing of the vision support system was complicated, there was no great uncertainty in the individual activities, or therefore the schedule of completion. If more funds were allocated to their development some of the tasks might even be completed ahead of time.

3 **The control logic.** The control logic system represented the most complex electronics design and software engineering task, and proved to be the most difficult to plan and estimate. It was the only area of the Scantel project where the investigating team felt they had no alternative than to consult at length with their colleagues in Instrument Development. In fact the Instrument Development section had very little experience of this type of work but (partly in anticipation of this type of development) had recently recruited a young software engineer with some experience of the type of work which would be needed for the Scantel control logic. He was confident that any technical problems could be solved even though the system needs were novel, but completion times would be difficult to predict with confidence.

4 **Chassis and body.** The task of designing the chassis and casing (events 37–42) was largely that of mechanical layout and planning the internal wiring (integration) within the body of the equipment so that all other units would be properly connected. The major uncertainty involved in the design of this unit was the timely receipt of data concerning the other units in the system.

5 **Display system.** The simplest of the sub-systems to plan, the display system (events 5–32–33) would need to be manufactured entirely out of the company and tested and calibrated on receipt. The only uncertainty was likely to be the delivery time.

Brian Callister was anxious not to give the impression that the network diagram in Appendix 21.4 was a complete picture of the project. The reality would usually be more complex than the network suggested. For example, in the network, the main tasks associated with each sub-system were separated into their engineering, testing and rework phases. This gave the impression that each package was relatively independent. In fact the rework or engineering (to be done after compatibility testing) would be strongly dependent upon the amount and quality of prior engineering. Because of this what might appear, during the project, to be a cost or time overrun in an early work package might actually be a superior design effort which would reduce the time and money required for the entire effort. This was often true, but would apply especially in the Scantel project. If early work packages seemed expensive, it was possible that they could bring costs into line later in the project. Also the network did not fully convey the way information needed to flow between parallel activities. For example, the progress of some of the later activities in the control logic sub-system would depend partly on the way the vision support development was shaping up.

MARKET PROSPECTS

In parallel with Brian Callister's technical investigation, Sales and Marketing had been asked to estimate the market potential of Scantel. In a very short time the Scantel project had aroused considerable enthusiasm within the function, to the extent that Desmond Plant, the European Marketing Vice President, had taken personal charge of the market study. The major conclusions from this investigation were:

- The European market for Scantel-type systems was unlikely to be less than 50 systems per year in 1988, climbing to more than 100 per year by 1992. The American market would be only slightly smaller.
- The volume of the market in financial terms was more difficult to predict, but each system sold was likely to represent around $200 000 of turnover.
- It was likely that only a small number of Scantel 'basic model types' would be needed but some customisation of the system would be needed for most customers. This would mean greater emphasis on commissioning and post-installation service than was necessary for VIL's existing products.
- Timing the launch of Scantel would be important. Two 'windows of opportunity' were critical. The first and most important was the major World Trade Show in Geneva in April 1986. This show, held every two years, was the most prominent show-case for new products such as Scantel. The second set of opportunities was related to the development cycles of the original equipment manufacturers who

would be the major customers for Scantel. Although these were not in phase for all OEMs, critical decisions would be taken in the autumn of 1986 for many of the larger manufacturers. If Scantel was to be incorporated into these company's products it would have to be available from October 1986.

THE SCANTEL GO-AHEAD

At the end of February 1985 VIL's board considered both the Callister and the plant reports. In addition estimates of Scantel's manufacturing cost had been sought from George Hudson, the head of Instrument Development. His estimates indicated that Scantel's operating contribution would be far higher than the company's existing products. The board approved the immediate commencement of the Scantel development through to prototype stage, with an initial development budget of $4.5 million. The objective of the project was to 'build three prototype Scantel systems to be "up and running" for April 1986'.

The decision to go ahead was unanimous. Exactly how the project was to be managed provoked far more discussion. The Scantel project posed several problems. First, it would involve the instrument and the optics sides of the company working together on the project. There had in the past been some ill-feeling between engineers in the two parts of the organisation. The optical engineers regarded the newer, but now larger, part of the company as rather arrogant.

Instrument engineers were also much younger on average. The instrument engineers thought the optics people 'craft-centred' rather than 'science-centred'. Second, neither of the two groups of engineers had much experience of working on such a major project. Their normal work was in making comparatively minor modifications to existing products. Third, the crucial deadline for the first batch of prototypes meant that some activities might have been accelerated, an expensive process which would need careful judgement. A very brief investigation into which activities could be accelerated had identified those where acceleration definitely would be possible and the likely cost of acceleration (Appendix 21.6). Finally, no one could agree either whether there should be a single project leader, which function he or she should come from, or how senior the project leader should be. Pete Middleton knew that these decisions could affect the success of the project, and possibly the company, for years to come.

Questions

1 Who do you think should manage the Scantel Development Project, and why?

2 What are the major dangers and difficulties which will be faced by the development team as they manage the project towards its completion?

3 What can they do about these dangers and difficulties?

APPENDIX 21.1
THE DIVISIONAL STRUCTURE OF THE PHOTONICS CORPORATION, OCTOBER 1984

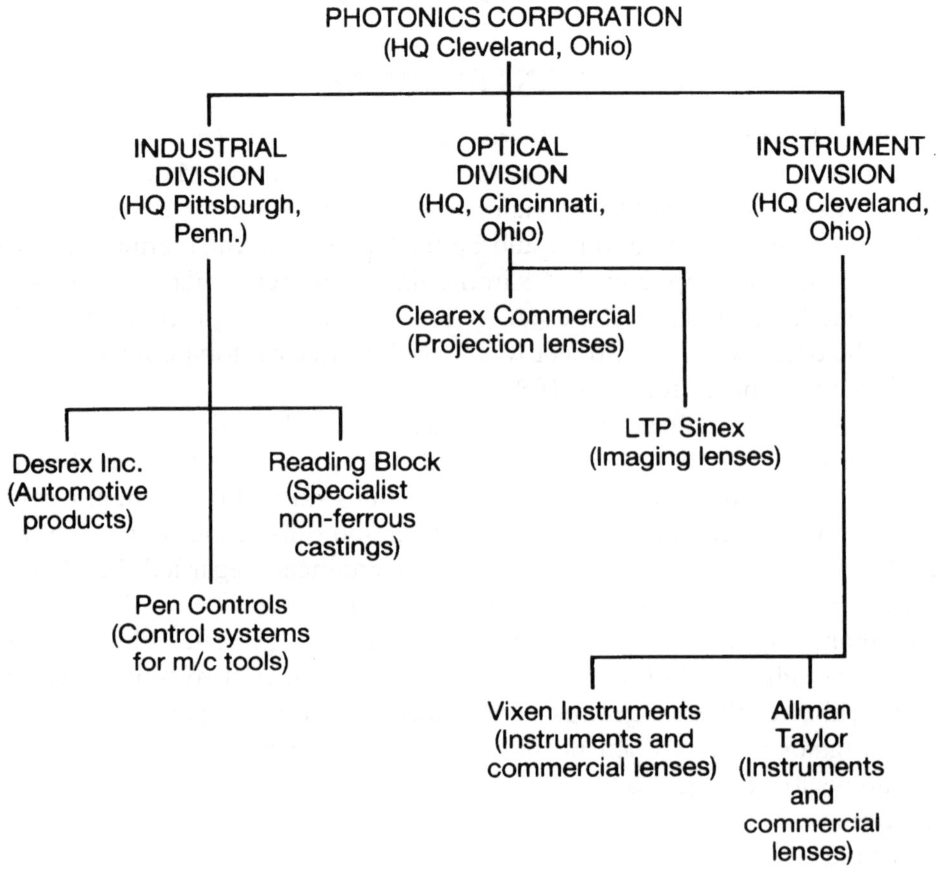

APPENDIX 21.2
PHOTONICS CORPORATION ORGANISATION

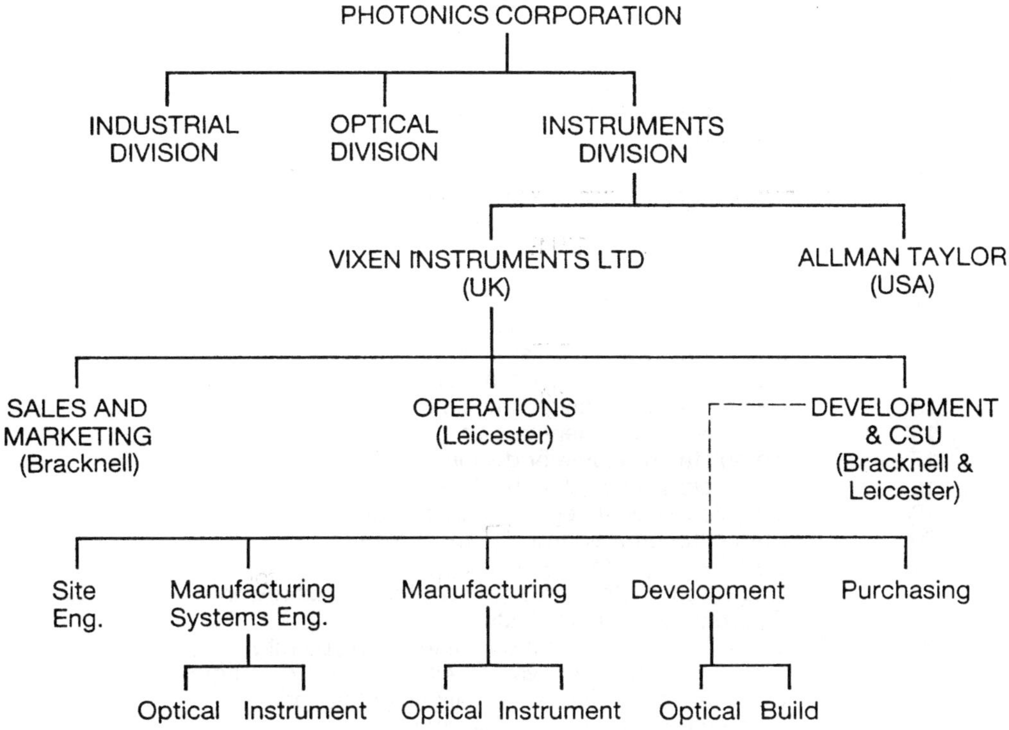

APPENDIX 21.3
EVENT LISTING – SCANTEL I(a)

Event no.	*Event description*
1	Start systems engineering
2	Complete interface transient tests
3	Complete compatibility testing
4	Complete overall architecture block styling and simulation
5	Complete costing and purchasing tender planning
6	End alignment system design
7	Receive S/T/G, start synch mods
8	Receive Triscan/G, start synch mods
9	Complete B/A mods
10	Complete S/T/G mods
11	Complete Triscan/G mods
12	Start camcorder sub-system compatibility tests
13	End camcorder sub-system compatibility tests, start rework
14	End camcorder sub-system rework, start S/A design
15	Camcorder S/A design complete
16	End Triaxis alignment design
17	Complete chronometer design
18	Complete comparator chip integration
19	Complete wave integrator chip design
20	Start chronometer and alignment testing
21	Start interface (tmsic) tests
22	End chronometer and alignment tests, start rework
23	End interface (trinsic) tests
24	End interface development, start prototype mfg
25	Complete alignment system rework, start S/A integration
26	Complete chronometer and alignment rework
27	End interface (tmnsic) programming
28	Complete manufacturing of alignment system
29	Start manufacture of tmnsic comparator
30	Complete (interface) prototype manufacture
31	Complete manufacture of trinsic comparator
32	VDU sub-system received, start VDU cycle tests
33	VDU cycle tests complete
34	Begin all logic system tests
35	Complete all logic system tests, start reintegration tests
36	Complete reintegration tests
37	Start physical outline product geometry design
38	Complete optics design and specification, start lens manufacture
39	Complete POG design
40	Start final casing design and integration
41	Complete final casing design, start manufacture
42	Complete manufacture of final casing
43	Complete lens manufacture, start lens housing S/A
44	Lens S/A complete, start tests
45	Lens S/A tests complete
46	Complete camcorder integration system interface
47	C/C integration system interface complete
48	Start assembly of total system
49	Complete total system assembly
50	Complete final tests and dispatch

APPENDIX 21.4
SCANTEL NETWORK DIAGRAM

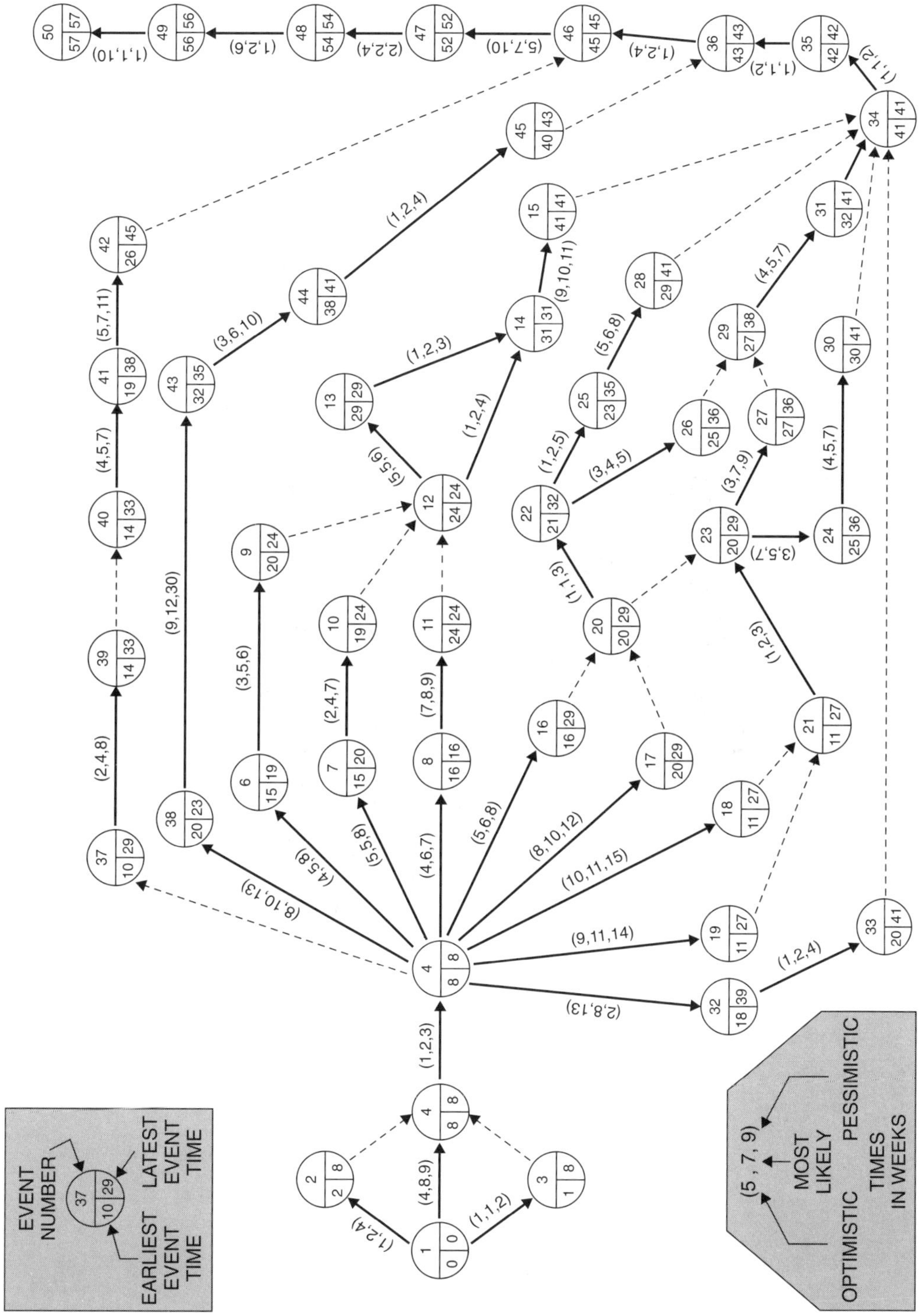

APPENDIX 21.5
SIMPLIFIED NETWORK DIAGRAM

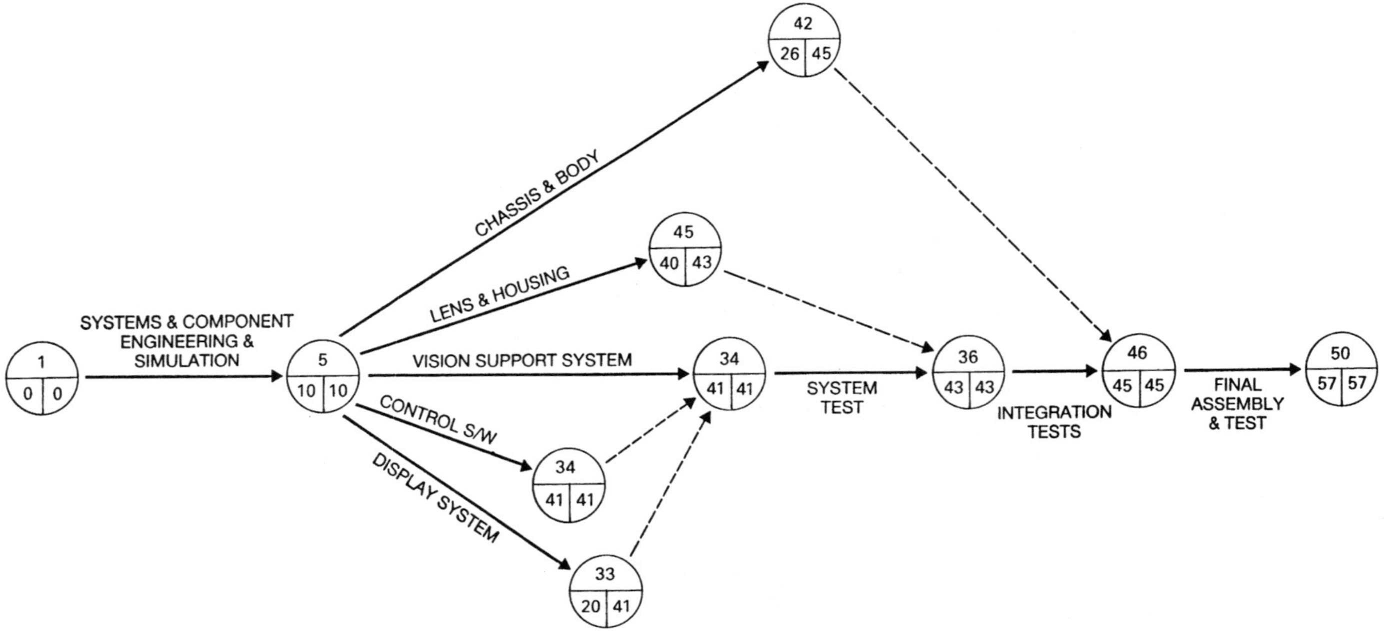

APPENDIX 21.6
POSSIBLE ACTIVITIES FOR ACCELERATION

Activity	*Acceleration cost in £/week*	*Likely minimum activity time with acceleration (weeks)*	*Normal expected activity time (weeks)*
5–6	11 700	3	5
5–7	15 200	4	5
5–19	17 900	8	11
32–33	7 800	1	2
8–11	19 400	5	8
40–41	19 000	3	5
22–26	9 100	2	4
25–28	10 700	4	6
14–15	18 300	7	10
46–47	15 150	6	7

Note: The table identifies the activities that can definitely be accelerated and the cost per week of accomplishing the acceleration, along with the minimum time the project can take. For example, activity 5–6, the alignment system design can be accelerated at a cost of £11 700 for each week gained. Since the maximum acceleration that may be accomplished is from 5 weeks to 3 weeks, the cost of the greatest acceleration possible (2 weeks) is £23 400.

CASE 22

Blood Supply and the National Blood Transfusion Service

Christine Harland

Case date 1995

NATIONAL LEVEL

Founded in 1946, the National Blood Transfusion Service was established to manage the collection of blood from donors and its provision to hospitals. The service was incorporated into the National Health Service in 1948. In the UK the Scottish Blood Transfusion Service has always been managed separately to the service in England and Wales.

The service was organised regionally with each regional centre being responsible for the collection from donors and the provision of blood to hospitals in the region. Each regional centre collected, tested, stored and issued blood. In addition to the regional blood transfusion services, a laboratory in Elstree processed and tested blood.

Until April 1991, the Regional Health Authorities (RHAs) used to supply funds to the regional Blood Transfusion Services (BTSs); these regional BTSs used to serve their own areas, with some helping out across regions. The National Directorate at Manchester co-ordinated the transfer of any surpluses of blood products to regions of shortage.

After April 1991, funding devolved to District Health Authorities (DHAs), and was allocated on the basis of previous usage of the Blood Transfusion Service. Instead of giving the BTS what was then £9m per year, the service charged hospitals this amount for blood provided. The hospitals then added this cost to their own range of health care provision for subsequent purchase by the DHAs under the new contracting arrangements of the NHS internal market.

In April 1994 the English Blood Transfusion Centres were incorporated under a single executive body called the National Blood Authority (NBA) and the service was renamed the National Blood Service. This service collected a total of 2.1 million donations of blood each year.

The assistance of the West Midlands Regional Blood Transfusion Service is gratefully acknowledged.
It should be noted that substantial reorganisation of the National Blood Service occurred in 1996.

REGIONAL LEVEL

The West Midlands Blood Transfusion Service (WMBTS) served a population of 5.2 million people. Within the region 20 District Health Authorities and approximately 50 major hospitals with local blood bank facilities supporting a network of over 200 NHS and private hospitals were served by the WMBTS. The service comprised of fixed site blood donor centres in Birmingham and Coventry city centres, a laboratory and a distribution centre in Edgbaston, Birmingham and a team of mobile collecting units that covered the region.

In 1994/95 the WMBTS was the second largest regional blood transfusion service in the country with a forecast income for 1994/95 of £14m. It had a staff of about 390 whole time equivalents, 150 of which were involved in taking donations. There were eight teams of 15 collectors, each team being equipped with a lorry and a coach to travel out in the region to collect blood. Other staff were involved in medical, clinical, scientific, administrative, technical testing and clerical functions.

Blood can be collected in two ways, first as whole blood and second as plasma only donations through an *apheresis* procedure. Plasma only donations are performed by taking whole blood from the donor, immediately spinning it in a centrifuge releasing the plasma, then returning the red blood cells to the donor. The apheresis procedure takes longer than whole blood donation but the donor can donate more frequently as the red cell level is not depleted and the plasma is regenerated relatively quickly. In 1994/95 240 000 whole blood and 800 apheresis donations were processed by the WMBTS.

In addition to collecting, storing and distributing blood and blood products, this regional service also performs other functions including ante-natal screening and tissue typing for solid organ and bone marrow transplant programmes. In 1994/95 about 130 000 ante-natal screenings were performed. WMBTS also acts as the national frozen blood bank and has recently established a bone bank. In addition it performs some other special tests and maintains an active research and development programme. Table 22.1 shows the approximate proportionate income of WMBTS products and services.

Table 22.1 Approximate proportionate percentage income of WMBTS products and services

Products and Services	*Approx. % of total income*
Blood and blood products	71
Plasma	16
Ante-natal	4
Tissue typing	3
Special tests	1
Exported blood to other BTSs	1
Bone marrow	1
Other	3

BLOOD COMPONENTS

Blood is essentially made up of cells and plasma, a protein solution. Cellular component products are whole blood, red cell concentrates, platelet concentrates, white cells and frozen cells. Plasma component products are frozen fresh plasma, cryoprecipitate, albumin, Factor VIII concentrate and specific immunoglobulins. Different blood components are administered to treat different medical conditions.

Plasma Components

Factor VIII

Factor VIII concentrate is the plasma component required by haemophiliacs. The Bio Products Laboratory (BPL) at Elstree forecasts demand for Factor VIII with the assistance of the regions. The amount of Factor VIII required is so significant it is this which drives the recruitment of plasma only donors. To satisfy the national requirement for plasma, each region is targeted to collect so many tonnes. In 1994/95 WMBTS was targeted to collect 53.6 tonnes of plasma per year.

Because of the large demand in the UK for Factor VIII, the USA and other countries have been used as a supply source. However, the much publicised problem of HIV contamination of haemophiliacs from imported blood was attributed largely to the fact that American plasma providers were paid. The payment system attracted drug abusers who had AIDS. The World Health Organisation recommended that all countries moved towards a volunteer donor system to help prevent this. It is possible that a Factor VIII artificial substitute could be available in the future though it is likely that this will be significantly more expensive than the human donation.

Albumin

Albumin is a plasma component which, at different levels of concentration, can be used to treat different conditions. A solution of 4.5 per cent albumin is used to treat burns victims who lose body protein and body fluid (i.e. blood volume) but don't actually bleed. The albumin dosage required is directly related to the severity of the burn. Twenty per cent albumin solution is used to raise the protein level of kidney dialysis patients and patients with malabsorption syndromes.

Cellular Components

The cellular components of blood are also used by different groups but are mainly required for surgical procedures and for the treatment of anaemia. Freshness of blood can be important; children's hospitals use blood less than two weeks old. This is because young children's circulations cannot cope with the potassium leakage and haemoglobin release that occurs as blood ages. Children's hospitals ship blood to other hospitals when blood is too old for their use but not too old for use by adults. This causes some logistical and transfer pricing problems.

Red cell concentrate

Red blood cell stock is fairly low in the region. Recent research indicates a possibility that an engineered substitute may be available in the future. Until this is proven, donations represent the only medium-term source.

Platelets

Platelets, which help blood to clot, are used mainly by leukaemia victims and in bone marrow transplantation. The demand for platelets is extremely variable, however, with a range of 200–500 units per day being demanded from the West Midlands regional centre. The variability in demand for platelets arises because leukaemia patients may suddenly require platelets when they go into relapse. Each leukaemia sufferer can use six donors' platelets per day when in relapse. As with whole blood, platelets need to be of a particular blood group. A significant additional problem with platelets is that they only have a safe, usable shelf life of five days and there is, therefore, a much higher risk of outdate and product wastage than with blood or plasma.

White cells

White cells are necessary to fight bacterial infection in the body. For example, child cancer patients need help to fight off something like measles, so large doses of white cells are given. The demand for white cells is intermittent; there are very few white cells in each donation so when they are demanded, 20 donations may be required for one therapeutic dosage.

Whole blood

Whole blood is used for accidents and emergencies; if there is no time to take a blood test of the recipient, group O is given as this is less likely to cause the patient a fatal reaction. Also, unborn babies are given O Rhesus negative if their blood group has not been determined. Fresh whole blood, i.e. which has not been treated, processed or frozen, may be used for some operations such as open heart surgery but its usage is relatively small.

Planned operations always have the correct blood group available; this is performed by cross-matching patients' blood. For example, it is recommended that there must be two units of blood on standby for each Caesarian section, though statistically it is unlikely that this will be used. These recommendations are made to doctors to reduce the risk of litigation that could result from having inadequate supplies of blood available.

There are about 600 blood groups identified, but the main groupings are ABO and Rhesus groupings; blood is either Rhesus positive (85 per cent of the population) or Rhesus negative (15 per cent). The percentage of the UK population in each of the ABO groups is shown opposite:

Table 22.2 Percentage of the UK in each of the ABO groups

Blood type	*UK population (%)*
A	42
B	8
AB	3
O	47

The incidence of blood groups varies by race; for example, it is exceptionally rare that Chinese are Rhesus negative and group B is more common in Asian communities. The most significant problem, however, is with West Indian and African negroes who may have very rare blood groups. If they are transfused with Caucasian blood, they can produce an antibody and have a potentially fatal haemolytic reaction. As the majority of the donor population is Caucasian, there can be imbalances between demand mix and supply mix. The WMBTS is increasing its efforts to collect from ethnic minorities to help alleviate this mix problem. As blood group is inherited, it is necessary sometimes to look to family members for donations as there is a one in four chance that a brother or sister will have the same blood group.

TOTAL DEMAND FOR BLOOD

In total, demand for blood is rising at about 2.6 per cent per year, largely because technology and knowledge improvements are enabling more operations to occur. The demand for blood is not even around the country; the large teaching hospitals and organ transplant hospitals used to be centred around the south of England, generating a larger demand in that area. However, increasingly these hospitals are moving into the regions. For example, a major liver transplant programme has started at the Queen Elizabeth Hospital in Birmingham. Liver transplants are some of the most bloody operations, using 30–130 donations per operation. A heart and heart and lung transplant programme started in the region in 1992 which increased regional demand.

Because blood is donated, it cannot be sold on. However, when donations collected elsewhere in the country are transferred to other regions, the value added (which represents the collection and production handling charges) is charged at £34.45 per whole unit. In practice whole units are rarely sold; it is more usual to sell the components. Appendix 22.1 shows the pricing for blood and blood component products.

COLLECTING

Attracting Donors

The United Kingdom policy is that donors are not paid for the blood or plasma they donate. In the West Midlands, all blood collection is organised by the Regional Blood Transfusion Service; fully equipped teams travel out to different sites each day to make it easier and less disruptive for people to give blood. About 1760 collection sessions were held at venues throughout the region in 1994/95. In interviews with staff of WMBTS, some changes in collection were indicated:

'We're having to reduce collection in areas where supply is falling. Take Longbridge, for example, we used to be in there for four solid weeks – now we only do a week there. I

think in this region we've been affected by the fall in employment in the major manufacturers. We also detect a hardening of attitude of management to their people having time off during the day to give blood. Because of this, we've had to put more effort into public sessions in church halls, youth clubs etc.'

The fixed site Blood Donor Centres in Birmingham and Coventry city centres enable donors to visit without an appointment. However, fixed location centres are falling out of favour with an increasing emphasis on more flexible, lower cost mobile units. The West Midlands region has a database of 600 000 donors, though many are relatively inactive. Most donors are requested to attend sessions two or three times a year to give blood at a specific session. About half the donors requested actually turn up.

As each donor is given at least 10 days notice of the session, it is difficult for the service to react to short-term demand. In the case of an urgent need for blood, such as a large scale accident, the centre is inundated with donors ringing up offering to help. The Gulf War increased the public's donation rate and allowed the service to build up depleted stocks. At the time of the Birmingham pub bombings, the switchboard to the service was jammed with donors offering to be bled. This caused such a problem that a hot line radio link with the hospitals and field staff had to be set up separate to the phone system.

Certain donors with rare blood groups are called in more frequently, possibly at short notice, to donate. These donors are asked to be on a national blood panel for rare blood groups. Plasma only donors give monthly or even every fortnight. A plasma donor can give 600ml of plasma per session compared to 200–250ml from a normal whole blood donation. Instead of the normal 10 minutes per donation, plasma collection takes around an hour. It is also preferable to use plasma only donors as a source of plasma because if a normal donation is separated for plasma, this must be done by the laboratory staff within a day of the donation being made.

A further constraint on the collection of blood is with regard to platelets; platelets must be made within six hours of the collection, therefore some collection must be done close to the regional centre to take blood back hourly for platelet production. Within the service, those involved with issuing and processing blood determine which blood products are needed; when collecting, the platelets demand is considered first because they have a short shelf life, as will be described later.

If any fresh blood has been demanded, this is usually collected the morning of the operation. This is only done in exceptional circumstances, such as for neonatal heart operations. In cases of emergency, it is usually possible to bleed a donor at very short notice or to obtain blood from another region.

The Collection Process

For each collection session a sheet is sent to the session with the details of all donors requested to attend. At the time of collection, all donations are given a unique bar code showing when and where the donation was given. This is stuck onto the bag at the collection point. If the donor is one of those anticipated to attend, their details are added to the donation. New donors are bled even though their details are not available. When their donation arrives at the WMBTS Edgbaston site, a new set of registration details is added to the donation. For each donor a record is kept of what was donated and when it was donated. For every donation made, the blood transfusion service records all the components into which it was divided and to which hospitals they went.

Blood used to be collected in a standard glass bottle. However, blood can now be collected in different types of bags, depending on what products the donation is allocated to provide.

Not all donors who turn up are allowed to donate. At the time of donation, all donors are asked to read a wide range of questions and say if they have been ill or taken medication. The donor is relied on to tell the truth as there is no practical means of validating this information. The transfusion to a sick person of mild food poisoning, for example, which is relatively insignificant to a healthy person, could cause serious consequences. Usually if the donor is on medication, has a cold, high blood pressure or received an anaesthetic at a dentist that day, his donation is deferred. About 20 000 people per year (i.e. approximately 10 per cent) have their donations deferred for this reason. Some viruses can be carried and passed on through blood without the donor being aware that they are infected. The testing process is therefore a vital part of the blood transfusion service's operation.

TESTING

Two samples, bar coded with donation details, are separated from the donation at the collection session to go for testing. Blood grouping and virology testing usually occur the day after bleeding. All blood is tested for ABO and Rhesus blood grouping. In addition some virology tests are performed on all donations – these are tests for Hepatitis B, Hepatitis C, Anti HIV (the antibody to HIV1 and HIV2) and syphilis. Any blood where the donor has visited or lived in a malaria area is tested for antibodies to the malaria parasite. Depending on the demand for blood free of cytomegalovirus (CMV), a flu like virus, selected blood donations of the appropriate groups in demand are screened for this. Sixty per cent of the population have had CMV. Blood from donors with CMV can be used but it has to be ensured that it is not given to very vulnerable groups such as premature babies or transplant patients. The immuno-suppressants given to transplant patients effectively make CMV a death sentence for them. Treating CMV infection can only be done by reducing the suppressants, increasing the risk that their transplant organ is rejected. HIV, Hepatitis B and Hepatitis C tests that are positive are sent to a reference laboratory for confirmatory testing.

BLOOD PROCESSING AND STORING

Each region sends the plasma collected for Factor VIII to the Blood Products Laboratory (BPL) at Elstree; this is transferred at nationally agreed transfer prices. Factor VIII concentrate is made at BPL in Elstree. The concentrate is then returned to the regions, again at national transfer prices. Factor VIII is stored at four degrees Celsius and has a shelf life of three years.

Red cells are reconstituted with a solution – saline, adenine, glucose and mannitol (SAG-M) – to make them flow better and to provide nutrients. Red cells can be stored at four degrees Celsius and have a shelf life of 35 days. They can be stored for much longer periods in liquid nitrogen but this is an extremely expensive process. For example, frozen/thawed red cells are charged to hospitals at £149.35 per unit compared to £34.45 for fresh. Because of this large cost, few red cells are frozen in the UK (in the USA freezing red cells is more common). Freezing may be appropriate for very rare blood groups. The WMBTS is the UK Blood Transfusion Service's national red cell freezing facility. Outside the service only the army operates its own independent facility.

Most blood is broken down into its components; between 90 and 95 per cent goes through processing and separation. To take platelets off, blood is spun in a centrifuge at a different speed to plasma separation. Platelets only have a shelf life of five days and need to be constantly agitated during that time. They need to be stored at 20–24 degrees Celsius. It is not currently feasible to freeze platelets. White cells need to be stored at 18 degrees Celsius (room temperature) and have a shelf life of only six–eight hours. Cryoprecipitate can be frozen for six months at –30 degrees Celsius or below. Albumin has a shelf life of three years.

ISSUING AND DISTRIBUTING BLOOD AND BLOOD PRODUCTS

The hospitals keep a certain amount of blood in blood banks from which they issue to the wards and theatres, based mainly on requests from anaesthetists. The banks will also cross-match (checking that the patient can receive the blood without a haemolytic reaction) and reserve blood for a particular patient. Not all operative procedures require cross-matching; a simpler group and screen test is sufficient in some cases which can be done at shorter notice – less blood is allocated than if it were all cross-matched and put aside in advance. It is quite possible that blood, if cross-matched, could be done so two or three times without being used, by which time it may become too old to be used. The hospitals are becoming increasingly aware that their predicted demand for blood for various operations needs to be aggregated into a blood schedule which can be checked against their bank and any shortfall ordered from the service.

In addition to becoming out of date, there are several points in the supply chain at which blood may be lost (*see* Fig.22.1).

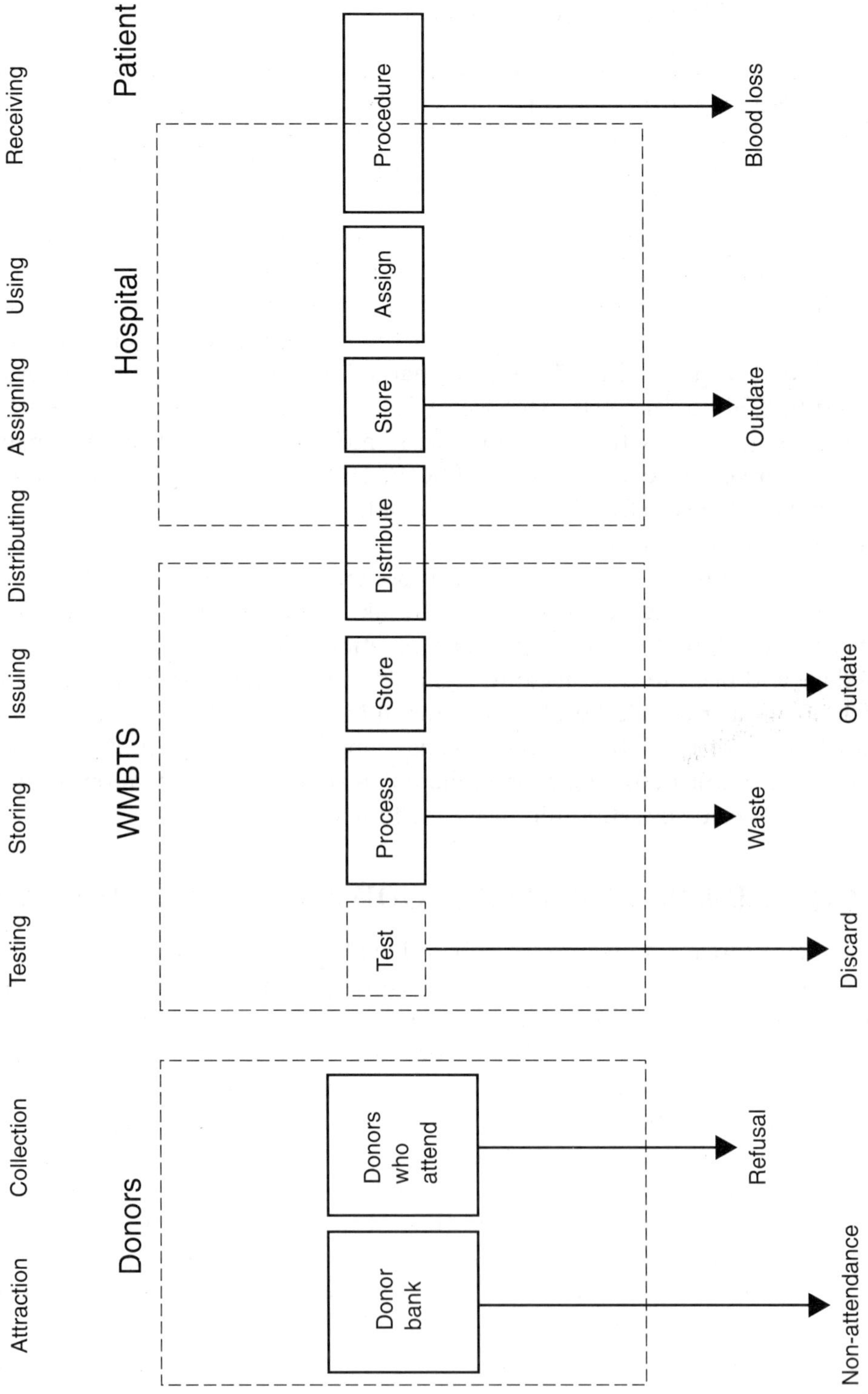

Fig. 22.1 Blood loss in the supply chain

Hospitals record ratios of cross-match to usage in order to monitor their blood consumption and their use of the cross-matching technique. Maternity hospitals have very low cross-match to usage ratios because quite large amounts of blood may be required at very short notice. The hospitals are supposed to record to which patient a particular donation was given. However, it is reported that not all hospitals can always identify which patient had which unit or blood product.

The hospitals order on a regular basis from the blood transfusion service. The West Midlands takes orders on a daily basis from the local Birmingham hospitals. In addition it delivers three times a week to other towns including Stoke, Hereford and Coventry. If hospitals do not accurately predict demand and subsequently require an additional delivery, an extra charge is made.

Emergency deliveries are made to hospitals or to the site of an accident. To make short demand deliveries, the centre uses its own drivers; sometimes it may use taxis or rail. Usually the centre prefers not to lose control of the delivery wherever possible.

Questions

1 Draw the total supply network for the supply of blood and blood components from donors right the way to end-customers.

2 What are the main demand factors that would impact on the total network?

3 What are the main supply factors that would impact on the network?

4 How has the network adapted to serve end-customer segment needs?

5 What inventory management problems do you think would be encountered by
   (a) the hospitals; and
   (b) the WMBTS?

APPENDIX 22.1

Blood Product Prices 1994/95 (at 1993/94 prices including capital charges)

Red cell products		£
00163	Whole blood CPD A1	34.45
00150	Whole blood (CPD)	34.45
04060	Red cell concentrate	34.45
04233	Red cell concentrate (supplemented with SAG-M)	34.45
04750	Red cell concentrate – buffy coat depleted – (supplemented with SAG-M)	34.45
04160	Red cell plasma reduced (limited availability)	34.45
00166	Whole blood (small volume)	19.00
Plasma Products		£
10160	Cryoprecipitate	20.25
18460	Plasma – cryoprecipitate depleted	10.75
18260	Fresh frozen plasma	24.00
18266	Fresh frozen plasma – small volume	14.00
Other Cellular Products		£
12060	Platelet concentrate – recovered	28.80
12552	Platelet concentrate – leucocyte poor	28.80
12559	Platelet concentrate – leucocyte poor therapeutic dose	144.00
12055	Platelet concentrate – cytapheresis therapeutic dose	144.00
16460	Leucocyte concentrate (CPD-A1) – price per unit (20 units per treatment)	32.95
Red Cell Products – Modified		£
04464	Red cell concentrate – leucocyte depleted – filtered	58.90
06460	Red cell concentrate – thawed and washed	149.35
04463	Red cell concentrate – washed (saline)	61.00
04066	Red cell concentrate – small volume	19.00
Other Cellular Products – Modified		£
12769	Platelets – filtered	32.00
12068	Platelets – volume reduced	20.00
12069	Platelets – filtered washed resuspended in ringers/CPD-50	102.00
16461	Leucocyte – concentrates – pooled and red cell depleted	37.30

APPENDIX 22.1 *(continued)*

Other Products	£
Autologous transfusions – per unit bled	60.00
Bone (femoral head – quarantined for 6 months)	150.00
Fibrin glue	FREE
Reagents	
ABO cells	3.00
Screening cells	7.50
Coombs control cells	2.50
WMRTC cell panel	12.00
Weak anti-Rh	2.50
AB serum	3.00
Anti-A1 lectin	2.50
Anti-D 2.50	
Papain 0.25%	1.00
Antibody identification panel in LISS	15.00
Antibody identification panel, pre-enzyme treated cells	15.00
Services	
Red cell cross-matching (per unit cross-matched)	10.00
Group and save	20.00
Investigation of incompatibility	25.00
Supply of antigen typed red cells (per antigen)	5.00
Irradiated units	10.00
CMV negative units	5.00
Antibidy investigation/confirmation	25.00
Full antigen typing	60.00
ABO/Rh anomaly	20.00
AIHA investigations	30.00
Plt IFT by FC	25.00
Plt IFT by FC (acid stripped)	35.00

APPENDIX 22.1 *(continued)*

PLA1 phenotyping	15.00
Identification of platelet specific antibodies (MAIPA)	35.00
Platelets cross-match	40.00
Assessment of foetal maternal haemorrhage by flow cytometry	5.00
P.N.H screening (CD 59)	10.00
Specialist Services	
Autologous bone marrow: cryopreserved for up to 2 months	450.00
cryopreserved for 2–12 months	600.00
each subsequent year or part	104.00
Individual PBSC harvest	450.00
Allogeneic bone marrow: T lymphocyte depletion	600.00
Red cell depletion	600.00

CASE 23

Vector Valves Ltd

Alan Harrison

Case date 1996

INTRODUCTION

Vector Valves Ltd is another division of Murray Engineering. It was formed following the acquisition of a US company by Murray's parent group, the large conglomerate PH Holdings plc. Initially, Vector acted as the UK sales arm, and marketed a range of valves for specialised petrochemical fluid control applications. Valves were manufactured in the USA, and sold via the UK company to markets in Europe. However, customers increasingly demanded specific designs to meet their own applications. It was found that, while the US affiliated company could meet such specific demands, Vector's sales were suffering because of the costs, and the relatively lengthy delivery times involved.

It was therefore decided some six years ago to establish manufacturing facilities in the UK. A factory was built on an industrial estate at Ebbw Vale in Gwent, South Wales, and the machines and equipment purchased to enable Vector to manufacture many of the components themselves. This helped considerably to reduce costs and improve capability of meeting specific customer orders, and sales surged ahead. By 1995, Vector was buying only 30 per cent of the parts it used from the USA.

THE COMPANY

Although Vector had grown rapidly after it had established UK manufacturing facilities, sales turnover had flattened out in recent years. Table 23.1 shows the profit/loss statement, and Table 23.2 the balance sheet for this period. Vector is

Table 23.1 Consolidated profit and loss account (£'000)

	1990	*1991*	*1992*	*1993*	*1994*	*1995*
Turnover	2784	4192	6462	8961	8349	9073
Cost of Sales	1953	2934	4394	5735	5594	6069
Gross Profit	831	1258	2068	3225	2755	3004
Admin Expenses	1011	1360	1807	2320	2210	2720
Trading Profit	(180)	(102)	261	905	545	284

Table 23.2 Consolidated Balance Sheet (£'000)

	1990	*1991*	*1992*	*1993*	*1994*	*1995*
Fixed Assets						
Tangible Assets	270	1021	1507	2294	2095	1943
Current Assets						
Stocks	1189	1487	1589	1907	2288	2794
Debtors	565	979	1152	1356	1648	2010
Cash in Hand	(200)	(103)	(53)	752	505	230
Creditors	432–	621–	1207–	1564–	1156–	1023–
Net Current Assets	1122	1742	1481	2451	3285	4011

currently regarded as a poor performer within Murray, and is now finding it difficult to attract investment for further growth in sales the company believes is possible.

The organisation chart for Vector is shown in Fig. 23.1, and the main functions can be briefly explained as follows:

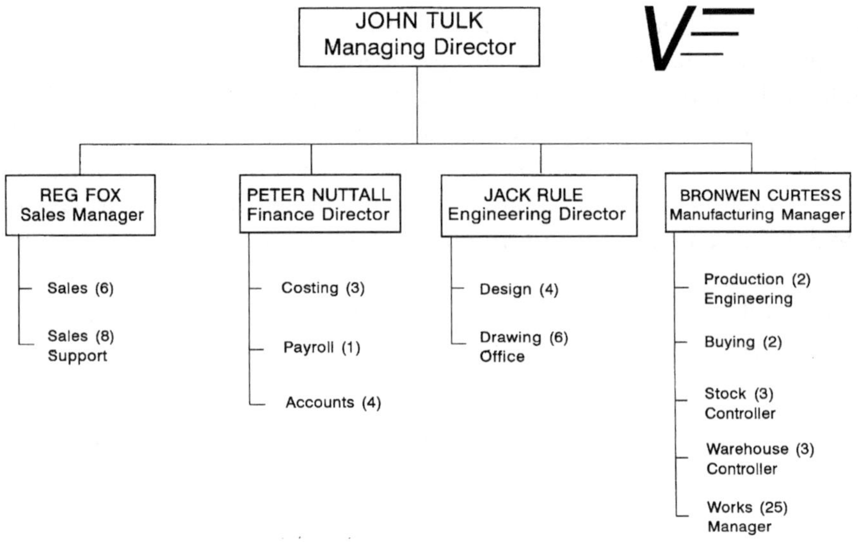

Fig. 23.1 Vector Valves: Organisation chart

Managing Director

John Tulk has been with Vector from the start. He has been successful in establishing the company as a force in the marketplace, and has led the sales initiatives 'from the front'. In common with Murray Group policy, he is required to prepare and have approved an annual budget and to submit monthly reports of current and forecast financial performance. He is under increasing pressure to improve ROCE to the group target of 15 per cent.

'After our initial sales successes in the European market, competition has become much more intense in recent years. Further progress depends on improvements in the level of service we provide to our customers while at the same time making substantial inroads into our cost base. It is apparent that our manufacturing operations have a major role to play in achieving these twin objectives.'

Sales

Reg Fox joined Vector four years ago, and his responsibilities now range from the sales force to sales support. The latter department handles telephone orders and enquiries, processes contracts and orders from the sales force. Sales have led the development of Vector, and take full ownership of processing customer orders from pricing to quoting delivery dates through manufacturing to delivery. In the last year, Reg has become increasingly concerned about Vector performance.

'We are getting a lot of complaints about late deliveries. My salespeople are wasting a lot of their time chasing orders through manufacturing, and are increasingly delivering urgent orders themselves. I know that opportunities are being missed: we are simply finding it difficult to keep our promises.'

Vector holds about 12 per cent of the market for their range of products. The major player holds about 30 per cent and a number of smaller players each hold less than 10 per cent.

Finance

Peter Nuttall is responsible overall for Vector's budgets and period financial reports. Sales produce a forecast in November for the 12 months commencing January. The forecast is in financial terms covering each main product range. Peter Nuttall operates a standard costing system with direct labour performance reporting. Prices are negotiated individually by the sales team, but Peter or John Tulk sign off contracts above £10k in value. The overall product cost breakdown is as follows:

- direct material 67 per cent
- direct labour 8 per cent
- works overhead 12 per cent
- commercial and administrative overhead 13 per cent

Peter echoes John Tulk's concern about ROCE:

'It is not surprising that we are under pressure from the group about our financial performance. In spite of our commitment to improve returns last year, our performance this year has actually deteriorated. I estimate that the cost of holding and servicing these inventories alone is 20 per cent per year. Murray's patience is not inexhaustible!'

Engineering

Jack Rule started with Vector at the same time as John Tulk in order to develop a sound technical base for the UK operation. Initially presiding over a sales and service operation, his responsibilities now cover design and drawing office. The main activities of these areas of the business are maintenance of designs for standard products, and the ongoing design of make-to-order contracts.

> *'We have made considerable progress in transferring American designs to European practice in recent years. My aim is to be importing less than 15 per cent of our parts from our US affiliate within the next two years.'*

Manufacturing

Bronwen Curtess was hired six years ago to develop Vector's product support expertise. She soon found herself making the major decisions on factory layout and equipment. She comments:

> *'The job has grown like Topsy. I am now responsible for product support, production engineering, buying and the factory. In the factory, we have 12 hourly-rated machine operators and eight assemblers together with some support staff. We intended to install sufficient equipment to meet peak sales demand easily. However, sales forecasts in this business are notoriously unreliable, and the sales force do tend to drop big orders with short delivery dates onto us with no warning! I must admit that our production planning leaves much to be desired, and I'm starting to look much more closely at this.'*

THE PRODUCT

Vector's sales catalogue describes some 500 types of standard valves. These are produced in 10 different sizes and three different materials. The basic types are further subdivided into products with different outlets, mountings, automatic controls, etc. All of the standard valves are quoted for delivery within two weeks of placing an order. Customers may also specify their own individual requirements, which are made to order with delivery dates quoted individually. Sales by type of valve range from about £500k for the most popular to about £10k for lower volume types. Sales of new valves for 1995 were 70 per cent standard designs and 30 per cent made-to-order. The made to order sales have been increasing by 10 to 15 per cent each year.

There are some 2500 active components listed in the stores system, of which about 500 are raw materials (bar, tube, sheet and castings), 1250 are made in-house and 750 are bought-out – mostly from the US affiliate. The part numbering system became somewhat disjointed after Vector set up its UK factory. Parts from the US affiliate are numbered on a different system which starts with a prefix 'A', and the designers tend to use suppliers' catalogues when selecting a part. This has resulted among other things in a very limited number of common components used in the different types of valve.

The manufacturing lead times for a batch of standard products vary from three weeks for smaller types to 12 weeks for the larger ones. Urgent jobs can be rushed through in three days for smaller jobs to 12 days for larger ones. Lead times cover purchase of bought-out materials – which takes up about half of the lead time – through to delivery of the valves into the finished goods warehouse. Component machining takes from one to four weeks, and the rest is allowed for assembly and test. Because of the manufacturing and shipping times involved, the US affiliate requires four months advance notification of UK requirements. Minor substitutions only are allowed up to one month prior to production at Vector, and no changes at all after this time.

Parts are controlled by means of a stock control system, which is similar for both components and finished products. The key points of this system and the accompanying manufacturing operations are described briefly below.

Component Stock Control

Stock cards are maintained for every component used in a standard type of valve. An example is shown in Fig. 23.2 for raw material from the tube store. The card contains the following information:

- size and spec (the tube size and specification)
- parts made (the part number of the Vector component(s) which are made from this)
- bar code (the Vector part number for the tube)
- conversion factor (allows the stores to convert from delivered measure (weight) into used measure (length))
- safety stock (the stock balance which triggers a requisition to be raised for more parts to be ordered)
- re-order quantity (the weight of steel ordered each time a requisition is raised)
- receipts (records date received into store, the supplier, order number, weight and length)
- movements (records issues (iss) and receipts (rec) into and out of stores, together with the quantity moved and the balance).

If the stock has been physically checked, the letters 'S/C' are entered in the movements record, together with the physical quantity. The stock cards are the responsibility of a stock controller. Records are maintained manually, and some 300 entries are made each day. Errors once made are carried forward on the card, and are not spotted until the stock becomes zero or the discrepancy is shown up at the stock check. Requisitions for fresh deliveries of parts are raised by stock clerks when the stock level falls below the re-order level. Re-order quantities are based on the last three months usage, but this usage figure is rarely adjusted and so is typically out of date. The requisition is passed to the stock controller who checks the order details against the stock record card. It is then routed to buying (for raw materials and bought-out parts such as the steel tube) or to production control (for made-in parts). The cost of raising a purchase order is reckoned to be £30.

Requisitions rarely state the date that the delivery is needed. Re-order levels on the stock cards are based on estimated lead times. If the stock has already fallen to zero, or a large demand arises which cannot be covered by existing stock, the stock clerk will enter 'ASAP' in the delivery date box on the requisition. Otherwise, buying or production control assume that the usual lead times will apply.

Most of the deliveries to stores of made-in parts were executed in not one but several part-batches. This was usually traceable to production exigencies, whereby

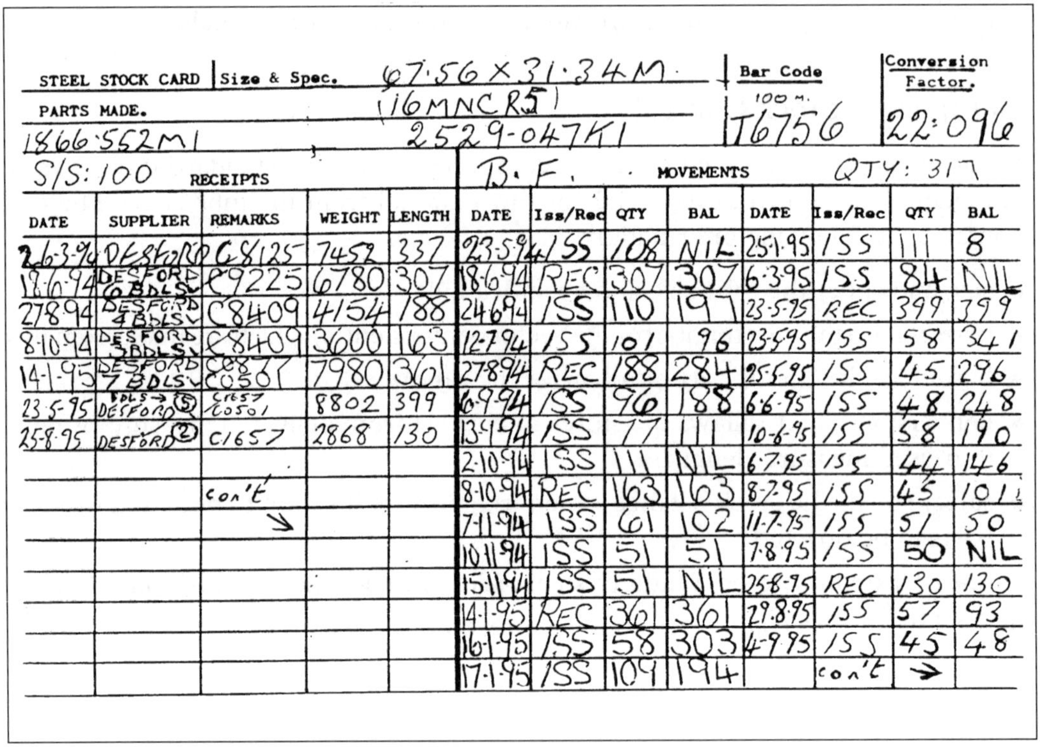

STEEL STOCK CARD | Size & Spec. 67·56 X 31·34 M. (16MNCR5) | Bar Code 100 M. T6756 | Conversion Factor. 22·096

PARTS MADE. 1866·552M1 2529-047K1

S/S: 100 RECEIPTS | B.F. MOVEMENTS QTY: 317

DATE	SUPPLIER	REMARKS	WEIGHT	LENGTH	DATE	Iss/Rec	QTY	BAL	DATE	Iss/Rec	QTY	BAL
26-3-94	DESFORD	C8125	7452	337	23-5-94	ISS	108	NIL	25-1-95	ISS	111	8
18-6-94	DESFORD 6 BDLS ✓	C9225	6780	307	18-6-94	REC	307	307	6-3-95	ISS	84	NIL
27-8-94	DESFORD 4 BDLS ✓	C8409	4154	188	24-6-94	ISS	110	197	23-5-95	REC	399	399
8-10-94	DESFORD 3 BDLS ✓	C8409	3600	163	12-7-94	ISS	101	96	23-5-95	ISS	58	341
14-1-95	DESFORD 7 BDLS ✓	C8877 C0501	7980	361	27-8-94	REC	188	284	25-5-95	ISS	45	296
23-5-95	BDLS → ⑤ DESFORD	C1657 C0501	8802	399	6-9-94	ISS	96	188	6-6-95	ISS	48	248
25-8-95	DESFORD ②	C1657	2868	130	13-9-94	ISS	77	111	10-6-95	ISS	58	190
					2-10-94	ISS	111	NIL	6-7-95	ISS	44	146
		con't			8-10-94	REC	163	163	8-7-95	ISS	45	101
		→			7-11-94	ISS	61	102	11-7-95	ISS	51	50
					10-11-94	ISS	51	51	7-8-95	ISS	50	NIL
					15-11-94	ISS	51	NIL	25-8-95	REC	130	130
					14-1-95	REC	361	361	29-8-95	ISS	57	93
					16-1-95	ISS	58	303	4-9-95	ISS	45	48
					17-1-95	ISS	109	194		con't	→	

Fig. 23.2 Example stock card from the tube store

Notes:

Steel is ordered and delivered by weight. The conversion factor (22.096 in this case) converts from weight (kg) into metres. All of the stock movements are recorded in metres.

'Parts made' gives the Vector parts which are produced from this raw material. The numbers in the 'Remarks' column refers to the steel mill cast code for traceability purposes. Under 'supplier', the storemen often note the number of bundles received in a delivery.

Under 'size and spec', the dimensions 67.56 × 31.34 refer to the external and internal bores of the tube, and 16MNCR5 to the specification of the steel. 'Bar Code' refers to the Vector part number for the material. 'S/S' refers to the safety stock for the part, and 'QTY' the re-order quantity. 'S/C' indicates that a physical stock check has been carried out.

According to records in the buying dept, the purchase price is £717/tonne.

only part of a batch would be made in order that a machine could be set up for the next part which was also urgently wanted. The rest of the batch would be completed when it too became urgent.

It is hoped that a 100 per cent service level to production would be provided on this system, but in practice, stocks of many parts are excessive while stocks of others are nil. Figure 23.3 shows a representative sample of 35 bought-out parts from the range held at Vector, which serves to illustrate this and other points. Further, stock

Part number	*Unit cost (£)*	*Annual usage*	*Annual expenditure*	*Physical stock*	*Physical value*	*Order quantity*
B-010	2.34	106	248	126	295	40
C-011	63.45	111	7043	28	1777	30
D-012	31.68	5	158	15	475	5
E-013	34.38	42	1444	24	172	50
F-014	3.00	1133	3399	363	1089	300
G-015	38.04	244	9282	121	4603	100
H-016	9.91	13	129	6	59	10
J-017	0.89	180	160	Nil	Nil	200
A-018	29.90	10	299	59	1764	10
A-019	4.06	51	207	Nil	Nil	50
B-020	37.20	4	149	43	1600	20
A-021	0.90	5353	4818	3167	2850	2000
B-022	25.32	23	582	2	51	10
C-023	14.65	13	190	108	1582	10
A-024	440.86	30	13226	1	441	20
B-025	0.45	618	278	1701	765	2000
C-026	92.44	9	832	3	277	20
A-027	0.42	360	152	90	38	300
B-028	2.00	811	1622	1630	2656	20
C-029	1.78	66	117	7	12	50
D-030	0.36	246	89	3	1	300
A-031	125.55	20	2511	13	1632	10
B-032	8.10	40	324	27	8	30
C-033	15.00	73	1095	3	360	50
D-034	37.20	4	149	43	1600	20
E-035	243.90	16	3902	24	5854	10
F-036	0.27	396	107	136	37	300
A-037	1.34	102	137	Nil	Nil	100
A-038	10.95	68	745	Nil	Nil	100
A-039	42.80	4	171	1	43	10
A-040	94.00	1	94	5	470	1
A-041	0.45	822	368	280	126	200
B-042	13.98	145	2027	190	2656	20
C-043	27.30	6	164	7	191	10
D-044	3.13	214	671	600	1878	50
Totals			56,823		35,362	

Fig. 23.3 A representative sample of component parts from the Vector range

Notes:
Part Numbers have been simplified and shortened for the purpose of this analysis. Those beginning with 'A' are purchased from the American affiliate. The sample of 35 parts has been chosen to be representative of the 2500 total in the range held by Vector.

record accuracy, determined by comparing stock check quantities with the stock cards, averages only about 40 per cent. This is a matter of grave concern for Peter Nuttall.

Finished Goods Control

Stock records are also kept in the warehouse for each standard type of valve. The card carries similar information to the component stock control cards described above:

- description (the description of the type of valve which is being stocked)
- part number (the Vector part number for this type of valve)
- safety stock (the stock level at which the clerk raises a new factory order for a fresh batch of valves to be made)
- re-order quantity (the batch size for the factory order)
- receipts (the number of valves received from the factory)
- order quantities (the outstanding number of valves on factory orders)
- issues (the number of valves issued to meet a given customer order).

When the balance on a finished goods stock card falls below the re-order level, the clerk raises a factory order which is signed by the warehouse controller and passed to the Production Controller. The re-order quantity is intended to represent six weeks' usage of the more popular types to 10 weeks' usage of the less popular. These quantities were last set two years ago after discussion with Sales.

The warehouse processes customer orders in the sequence in which they are received, unless Sales instruct otherwise – which they frequently do. If there is insufficient stock to meet a customer order, a note is made of the customer order and it is clipped to the back of the card so that it can be cleared as soon as a fresh batch of valves arrives from the factory. No regular report is made of the outstanding orders and their age, but the usual procedure is for Sales to circulate lists of unfulfilled orders which are currently being expedited by customers to members of the senior management team, production control and the warehouse controller.

Stores Procedure

A stock check of stores and work-in-progress is held twice each year. Volunteers from the shop-floor and from offices come in over a weekend, and enter the stock check figure onto the stock cards. If there is a major discrepancy between the physical figure and that on the stock card, the stock controller is expected to identify the reason. 'Major' is not specifically defined, and the controllers do not have time to investigate more than a few items.

Keeping track of component stock is particularly difficult. When batches are split for the reasons outlined above, the operator is expected to identify the part batch with a slip of paper. Urgently needed batches of made-in components often bypass the stores, and the foreman is supposed to notify the stock controller of his actions. Issues from raw material and component stores are made on requisitions which can be authorised by many different members of staff from production controller, stock controllers, foremen and service engineers. A frequent problem in the finished goods warehouse is that salespersons enter the stores in search of valves which are missing or reported as out of stock.

Assembly orders are raised by production control one week in advance of the assembly of a batch of valves. The stores assembles kits of parts and report any shortages to production control. It is up to the assembly foreman to accept a kit which has shortages: if he rejects it, then it will have to wait until the shortages have been made good. Meanwhile, he will bring forward a batch from another week to maintain satisfactory labour productivity figures.

Questions

1 What problems are being created for manufacturing by:
   (a) sales;
   (b) engineering;
   (c) current procedures for stock control and production control.

2 Vector's customers are complaining that deliveries are unreliable, and that promises are often broken. But stocks are high and stock turns are sluggish. How should Vector plan to overcome these problems?

CASE 24

Peas

Stuart Chambers and Tammy Helander

Case date 1995

INTRODUCTION

John Lincoln nodded goodbye to the guard and drove out of the gates of his large factory, situated in a fertile coastal region of eastern England. He drove home through a soft rolling landscape, surrounded by shimmering green fields towards a darkening early September sky, but the sight of this beautiful summer scene gave him little peace of mind. It just made him worry more about peas and pea fields. Peas that had to be harvested, transported to the factory, cleaned, processed, frozen, and packaged. And soon plans had to be completed for *next year's* pea crop, because as Factory Manager, he had to look ahead to ensure that all the production processes would be prepared to cope with the requirements of the increasingly demanding customers.

This year had been difficult. The weather had been exceptionally good, which meant that the harvesting period had been much shorter than usual, putting pressure on the factory, which only had a limited daily processing capacity. The factory was designed to produce a range of frozen vegetables including carrots, cauliflowers, beans, peas, petit pois, broccoli, and sprouts. It belonged to a large specialist food group, and had an enviable reputation for its high quality standards.

Despite John's many years of production management experience, the pea processing operation had always been his greatest headache during the summer season. The previous year had turned out to be an exceptionally long harvesting period of 65 days, which was relatively easy to cope with. However, this year's season, because of the fine weather, had shrunk to a more normal 44 days, which had meant an immense pressure in getting about the same tonnage of peas through the factory, in the much shorter period. Peas always caused the worst problems, as they were by far the largest crop handled by the factory, and had to be processed in a very short time after being picked.

John had discussed many times with the Crop Planning Manager, Dave Ronson, the possibility of extending the pea growing season to lessen the pressure on the factory but it was difficult to make any further changes. As Dave explained:

'Well, unfortunately you can't plan the weather! Certainly, we do influence when the peas should be ready for vining (picking) by using the best possible planning to ensure that the harvest is spread out over as long time as possible. You know as well as I do, that the distribution of harvest times can be manipulated; for example, by using selected south and north facing fields, different varieties of seed, and planting at different altitudes above sea level. We have continuously worked to make this planning better, and to have better co-operation with the growers. We have managed to get them to agree on a target growing plan period of 44 days instead of 36, which is the normal contract period for growers supplying other factories. But there is a limit in how much we can extend the season – the peas will simply not grow over a longer period, and I believe we have reached the limit. The yields are also different, depending on the harvesting period. For the first and last quarter of the period the yield is only around 3.5 tonnes per hectare, whereas in the middle the yield is as much as six tonnes per hectare. The growers are naturally more interested in having their main harvest in the middle, for obvious economic reasons.'

It was only two weeks after the last of this year's harvest had gone through the factory, and the group's operations director had scheduled the following Wednesday to meet with John and the management team. They would go through this year's output figures compared to targets. Each year's targets were set on how many tonnes of frozen peas they would have to produce to satisfy anticipated customer demand.

THE COMPANY

Although the frozen vegetable business had achieved only slow organic growth, it had continued to invest in improved processing facilities, and to develop better product quality through agricultural technology and practices, as well as by using leading freezing technology. In this way, the company ensured that the products were fresh and of high quality, and this was controlled by taking appropriate measurements on samples at every stage of processing from the field to the final packing in the factory. Most of the immediate customers were large and powerful retailers with very specific requirements for taste, colour, size, tenderness, etc.

The number of factory employees varied between 400 and 200, depending whether it was the peak harvest season or not. Most of the important functions were all on-site, including production and marketing, but some additional cold storage, and transportation resources were provided by contractors.

THE MARKET FOR PEAS

The total market for vining peas (the pea type that is best suited to quick freezing) in the UK is about 200 000 tonnes per annum and the growing area is around 40 000 hectares. The human consumption markets (there are some sorts of peas used for

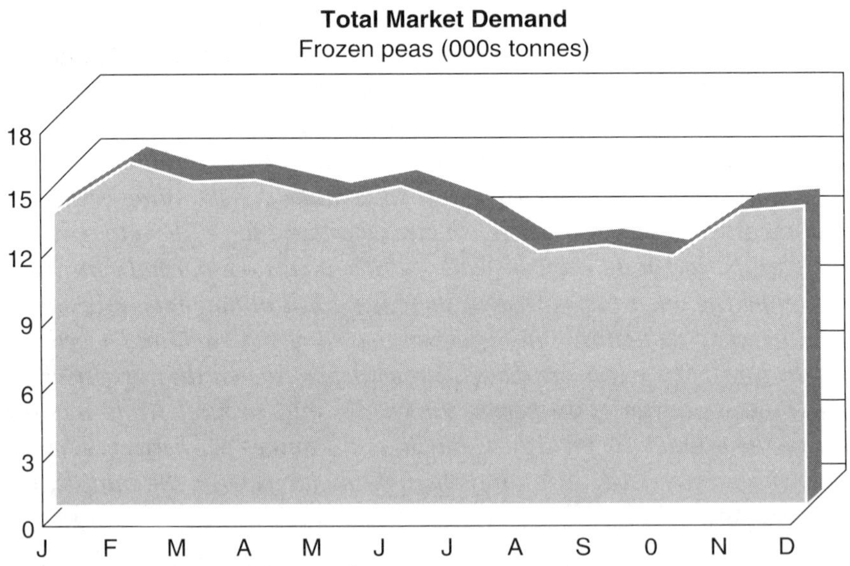

Fig. 24.1 Market for peas in the UK (previous year)

Table 24.1 Current year pea output in frozen tonnes

Date	*Tonnes*	*Date*	*Tonnes*	*Date*	*Tonnes*
28/6	29	13/7	467	28/7	489
29/6	–	14/7	449	29/7	370
30/6	134	15/7	411	30/7	404
1/7	241	16/7	463	31/7	350
2/7	320	17/7	524	1/8	450
3/7	349	18/7	492	2/8	488
4/7	454	19/7	452	3/8	514
5/7	543	20/7	358	4/8	435
6/7	500	21/7	337	5/8	351
7/7	476	22/7	336	6/8	226
8/7	462	23/7	335	7/8	120
9/7	461	24/7	179	8/8	102
10/7	376	25/7	305	9/8	36
11/7	379	26/7	363	10/8	13
12/7	401	27/7	452	TOTAL	15396

animal feed) are quite static, but remain important for vining pea growers, who have invested in expensive, specialised equipment for harvesting the crop.

The typical annual pattern of demand in the UK for frozen peas is just the opposite of that of supply. Peas from growers all come in during three summer months with the harvesting lasting between 40 and 60 days, and with the main peak in July. In contrast, sales are at a minimum in the summer, because of the good availability of fresh vegetables, but peak during the winter from October to May, as shown in Fig. 24.1. The company's sales target throughput of frozen peas for this year had been 15 115 tonnes, measured in the frozen state. Actual output had been slightly higher at 15 396 tonnes as shown in Table 24.1, much to the satisfaction of the management team.

RETAIL CUSTOMERS

Most of the total market is held by the bigger retailers, including Asda, Safeway, KwikSave, Iceland, Somerfield, Tesco, and Sainsbury. For a producer to be approved by a large retailer, it is critical to offer the right price and the right quality. John's factory focused mainly on the needs of these very demanding UK retailers.

Sales can be either in bulk form (which are subsequently prepared for retail sale by contract packers), or in branded or own-label retail packs within cardboard cases, according to requirements. Exports are only in this packed form and only account for a small proportion of sales. Prices depend on which quality the customers ask for, as the peas are graded in qualities ranging from AA to D, where AA is the top grade. The goal is to make as many AA graded peas as possible. The factory had built up an enviable reputation with the retailers for the quality of the product and services provided.

Despite this, everyone was continually seeking ways of further increasing quality. For instance, it was known that the recently installed steam blancher should improve final pea quality. A blancher is basically the equipment where the peas get a rapid pre-cook, either in water, or in steam, to stop enzymes action which breaks down natural sugars in the peas. This would give tangible benefits in terms of texture and taste, which could then be marketed at premium prices. By improving the overall quality of output, the resulting improved profitability would make it possible to reinvest in order to further improve the equipment, thereby achieving even higher levels of quality in the future.

MARKETING AND COMPETITORS

There were about six direct competitors that operated on a sufficiently large scale to supply the major retailers. One in particular was privately owned, and sometimes used aggressive pricing, apparently to gain market share. In contrast, John tried to maintain high utilisation of capacity in order not to increase unit fixed costs, but some competitors were known to hold considerable spare plant capacity which was only in full use during the peak harvest season.

According to the Marketing Manager, Chris Johnson, the most important factor in the success of the business was its ability to enhance the customers' frozen vegetable business, and to initiate quality projects, in line with detailed knowledge of the retailers' requirements. They had the market understanding, and good development resources and skills to achieve this success. Unlike many competitors which offered a wider range of frozen foods including pizzas, pies, and gateaux, the account managers here were able to focus only on selling vegetables, which keep their knowledge and interest high.

Chris was very conscious of the necessity of close co-operation between the factory and Marketing, in order to sustain and improve success in terms of customers. He liked the fact that the marketing function was now located at the factory, creating an understanding and ambition for the site from the customers account managers. Chris was quite proud both of their external and internal relations:

> *'I think our customers like dealing with us, because we are usually able to provide them with exactly what they want. We specialise in vegetables and we always try to help them with all their special requirements, for example special pack sizes and graphics to assist in their promotions. We have good co-operation with the factory as well. We simply would not ask the factory to do something that it could not do. We talk every day to the planning people at the factory.'*

FACTORY PROCESSES AND CUSTOMER SERVICE

Another important factor was the short line of communication along the supply chain, and the ability to adapt. The company had extremely good trade relations and supply partnerships, and the factory tried to always be very responsive. The target service level of 98.5 per cent delivery dependability was usually met or exceeded. Marketing was constantly updating its demand forecasts, and checked these against the factory capabilities. They also gained from having big company back-up, as they at any time could call upon the technical or commercial help of the group.

An important characteristic of the operation was that it had good control of the whole process, from the farms to the cold storage rooms. Some of the competitors had great difficulties in controlling their supply chains, and tended to depend more on the open market for the vegetables as it unfolded each season. In contrast, the close and detailed co-operation here between the marketing and factory operations, and between the suppliers and factory, impressed most customers.

However, there were some unique difficulties in the planning of the pea business. The sowing/growing plan had to be set nearly one year ahead of the demand for peas in the following year. Therefore, the forecast from the marketing/sales department had to be made long before getting firm orders from any of the customers. The customers committed themselves firstly around May, by which time all the peas were planted and some of them were in flower.

CONDITIONS FOR PEA GROWING

Commercial pea crops are mainly grown in the east of England because of the particular weather pattern needed for a good quality crop. High summer rainfall would make it messy and expensive to harvest and to clean, so reasonably dry weather is an advantage. In the eastern areas these conditions are met, as there is usually less than 75mm of rain in the whole of July and August.

The economics of pea growing is affected by things like crop rotation, soil condition, feed, weed control, machinery, as well as post-harvest handling. The crop has to be rotated, using a field only every fifth year or sometimes even only each seventh year before it is possible to grow peas or related crops again. The peas provide a valuable soil-improving crop, since they 'fix' nitrogen from the air into the soil. There are many types of peas, but vining peas are harvested mechanically for processing and quick freezing.

SUPPLIERS: THE PEA GROWERS

The farmers that supply the factory are members of trading groups, which mutually own equipment and hire personnel for the vining pea season. The factory closely co-operates with five of these farmer groups. In co-operation with the growers, a sowing plan and a harvesting plan are prepared each year, which details the number of hectares and tonnes to be harvested every day during the season. The sowing of peas usually starts in the last week of February.

Some of the farmer groups have exclusive contracts with the business, but there are also some who have contracts with other processors. The crops are normally situated within a 60 kilometre radius of the factory, because the growers have to be able to deliver within a short elapsed time from beginning each harvest run. This is to ensure that the time from picking to blanching does not excede 140 minutes, a demanding internal specification designed to produce the highest quality peas.

THE VINING IN THE FIELDS

Before vining can begin, the 'sample man' visits the fields and measures the tenderness of the peas, and when this reaches exactly the right level, it is time to begin harvesting the following day.

At each farm, a foreman is responsible for the detailed control of the vining process, and maintains constant radio contact with the control room at the factory. He is in charge of the planning and ordering of lorries, and for the timing of the emptying of the peas from the vining machines, which is done during harvesting, without having to stop. The tractor and trailer simply drives alongside the vining machine, and the crop is discharged in one or two tonne batches into the trailer. These are then driven to lorries, and the peas are discharged into them up to the maximum required weight.

The work shifts are different for each of the farmer groups, but in most cases the vining machines are used for around 19 hours a day, with five hours for cleaning and preventative maintenance. There is an average of three harvesting machines per farming group. Usually, two machines work all the time and the third is held in reserve, to be used if one suffered a breakdown or if the pea factory asks for more peas. The workers are employed on two shifts; a night shift from 6 p.m. to 6 a.m., and a day shift from 6 a.m. to 6 p.m., continuing seven days a week, every week until the pea season is over. This is demanding work, and sometimes stressful when vining on sloping fields. The huge machines, known affectionately as 'big drums' by the drivers, eat their way up and down the fields, irrespective of the weather. The only break in the humming driver's cab is the contact with the staff in the other viners and the tractor using the walkie-talkie radio. There is one full-time maintenance man, as it is important to keep these £250 000 machines going, not least because of the potential costs of delays in terms of lost revenue and scrap peas, but also because of the importance of keeping a reliable supply for the factory.

When the peas are being vined, the whole plants are cut and rolled over drums to separate the peas from the pods and stems. They then pass into a drum, where the peas roll down to the transporter belt, which take them up to the hopper, where they can be seen from the driver seat. The normal harvesting speed is around six tonnes/hour, but in ideal conditions can achieve around eight tonnes/hour.

TRANSPORTATION TO AND ARRIVAL AT THE FACTORY CONTROL ROOM

The time from the beginning of harvesting to arriving at the factory should be below 90 minutes. This is vital in order to ensure a consistent high quality of the frozen peas, and so the farmers are careful to keep within the time, particularly as they are being paid on the quality of the peas they are delivering. The lorries are owned both by large haulage firms, and by individual lorry owners who come back and operate during the pea season year after year. The capacity of the lorries ranges from four to 18 tonnes, but they do not normally load more than about five tonnes per journey, as the lorries need to get quickly to the factory. They average around 45 km per hour on the journey along country roads and lanes.

When the lorries arrive at the factory, they first stop at the control room for the quality check, to see if the load will be accepted. A collection tube is put into the load, and sample peas are extracted and taken directly into the quality room. Three samples are taken, from which the tenderness of the pea, percentage of unwanted material, and dirtiness is measured. Should any of the values not be within control standards, the load will not be accepted. The whole checking procedure takes between five and ten minutes. Once accepted, the lorries are weighed with the full load of peas and after having tipped the load into the receiving hoppers, the lorries are weighed again empty. The drivers are given receipts detailing the tonnes delivered and quality. The whole weighing-tip-weighing procedure takes ten minutes on average, provided that there is a receiving hopper immediately available.

Records are kept of the total daily deliveries from farmers, and of the expected tonnage (the 'daily plan'), based on the previous day's field inspections by the Sample

Man, as shown in Table 24.2. The expression 'dirty tonnes' simply means that the peas are delivered as they are without being cleaned. They are cleaned when they come to the factory, and go into processing. The target for the supply from growers this year in dirty tonnes had been 18 660 tonnes, but the actual deliveries were slightly higher at 18 813 tonnes.

Table 24.2 Actual and planned intake of peas in dirty tonnes

Date	*Actual*	*Daily plan*	*Date*	*Actual*	*Daily plan*	*Date*	*Actual*	*Daily plan*
28/6	36	40	13/7	568	564	28/7	609	562
29/6	–	–	14/7	543	496	29/7	460	505
30/6	169	196	15/7	496	521	30/7	496	547
1/7	295	374	16/7	524	488	31/7	438	491
2/7	394	437	17/7	633	622	1/8	558	573
3/7	427	392	18/7	596	608	2/8	600	615
4/7	562	557	19/7	548	621	3/8	626	711
5/7	661	616	20/7	433	496	4/8	527	625
6/7	613	624	21/7	408	474	5/8	428	435
7/7	590	624	22/7	401	416	6/8	273	376
8/7	565	566	23/7	418	420	7/8	148	220
9/7	559	580	24/7	220	366	8/8	122	110
10/7	466	513	25/7	379	382	9/8	46	88
11/7	464	480	26/7	451	455	10/8	17	48
12/7	486	488	27/7	560	469	*Total*	18813	19791

IN THE CONTROL ROOM

John Lincoln often talked to the staff in the control room, the hub of the linkage between the harvest, transport and production processes. He was thinking back to some of the comments he had heard during the day. When John had come in to the control room, Tim Wallace, the shift manager, had been explaining their role to a visitor:

> *'You can see, from this position, how the whole factory is planned and run. Whatever is done here, affects the whole process. From the tipping of the lorries of peas, to the feeding of the lines, blanchers and freezers.'*

Behind him was the babble of voices of the other people working in the room. One had just received a call from a farmer, apologising that they could not deliver as many peas as planned at their sceduled five minute 'slot' one hour later. One of the new summer planners had immediately changed the figure on the board, the main planning instrument, according to the new information. Tim had crossed out and changed the figure just written down, and had quietly explained to the visitor:

'You have to keep an eye on them all the time! We have so many new employees during the summer. Our workforce increases from 200 in the winter to almost 400. You have to teach them everything, from the start.'

On his way back to his office, John had walked past the cleaning lines, one of which was standing idle, so he asked an operator what the problem was.

'Oh, it has just clogged again, but it will soon be back running! It was much worse yesterday . . . a load of peas was accidently tipped outside the hoppers, which prevented us from tipping there for a time while we cleared up. They had to stop one of the viners for an hour or so, I heard.'

There are three shifts in the control room: one night shift from 23.00–7.00; and two day shifts, from 7.00–15.00, and from 15.00–23.00. There is a CB (citizens band) radio to communicate with the viners and lorries, and everything that has affected the schedule of deliveries is recorded in detail.

THE FACTORY

Once the lorries have been emptied into the hoppers, the peas are conveyed in segregated batches into one of three production lines in the factory. According to the control room manager, the maximum planned input is 12 tonnes/hour of dirty feed for Lines 1 and 3, and 10 tonnes/hour for Line 2. The peas go into bulk feeders and up on to the weighing belt, and then to the 'pod and stick machine' to take out stones, pods, small lumps of earth, and other unwanted materials. When processing peas, approximately 10 per cent of tonnage is removed in transforming dirty peas to clean, and around a further 10 per cent is lost when transforming clean to frozen. The segregation of batches is critical, to maintain traceability and to ensure that different grades are not inadvertently mixed.

The peas then go into small hoppers known as 'scacos' which hold a small buffer of inventory to smooth out the flow, and then to collecting points, from there they are transported in water, pumped along pipes. These lead directly to the water or steam blanchers, where the peas are heated in approximately 90 seconds to 98 degrees Celsius. After the blanching, there is a cooling down process and quality check, where the content of starch can be sampled.

The peas are then pumped in water to the freezer house, where there are three freezers, with capacities which are detailed in Table 24.3. The peas flow continuously into the freezers and are collected at the end into bulk pallet containers, each of about one tonne capacity. The output of frozen peas is weighed and labelled, allowing traceability of each harvested batch, before being transported into the cold store by fork-lift truck. Peas must exit the freezers at, or below, minus 18 degrees Celsius. Figure 24.2 illustrates the main process stages.

Each freezer is made up of five separate sections, each with refrigeration coils (cold surfaces behind which refrigerant is passed). The outside of these tend to 'ice-

Table 24.3 Nominal capacity of the three freezers

Freezer number	*Tonnes/hour*
1	10
2	7.5*
3	10
Total	27.5

* No 2 revised from 10 to 7.5 because of age (19 years)

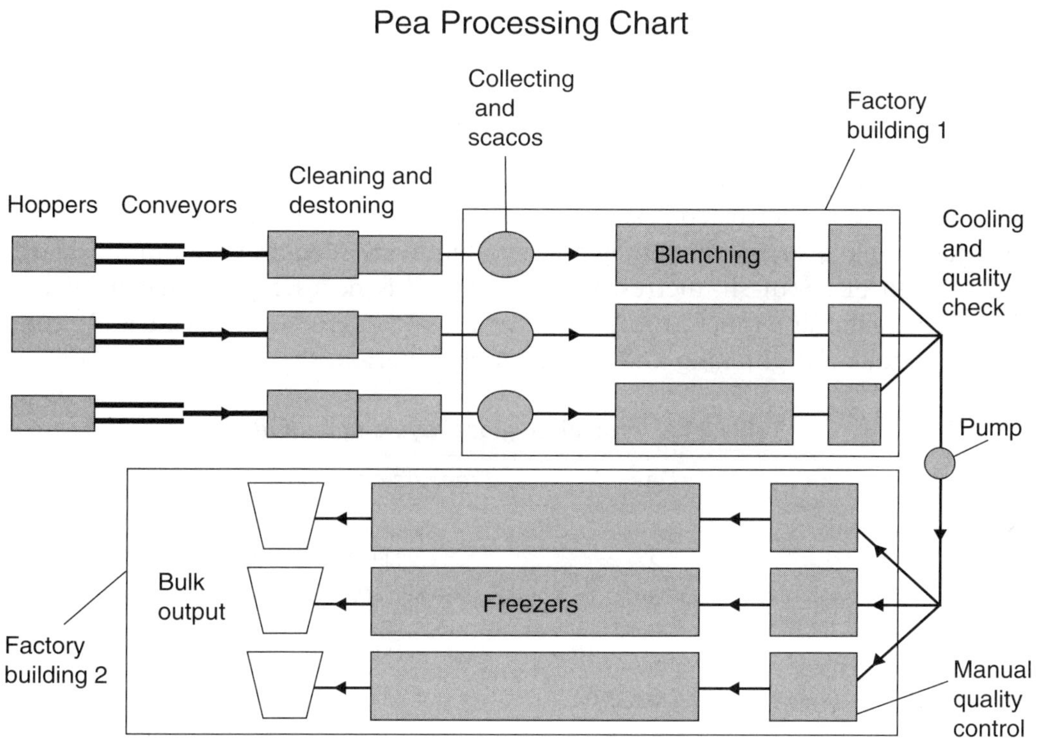

Fig. 24.2 Factory processes and layout

up' fairly quickly, reducing their cooling efficiency, so each section is automatically defrosted while the peas continue to be frozen in the remaining sections. Depending on certain factors, such as temperature, the moisture of the inputs, and the weather, the rate of icing-up increases, and overall effectiveness of the process declines, being detected by an upward trend in the output temperature of the peas. At this point, the input feed rate must be reduced, affecting the actual output capacity of the freezer, and slowing down the feed rate for the cleaning and blanching process, because there is almost no in-process storage between blanching and freezing. For the same reason, any problems with the cleaning and blanching processes quickly deprive a freezer of its input, wasting valuable freezer capacity.

QUALITY AND HYGIENE REQUIREMENTS

Through the whole process there are stringent quality checks, and if batches of peas are not immediately accepted, they are quarantined and labelled accordingly. There are three standard places for quality checks: one in-process quality check; one check at the freezer output, and one when the peas are repackaged later for retail sale. Whenever capacity is a constraint, the bulk pallet containers of quarantined peas are taken into cold storage and dealt with later. Up to 30 per cent of the peas may be quarantined, but this does not seem to be a problem, as they can be dealt with later. The frozen peas can be fed through the automated 'Sortex' colour sorter, where any that are discoloured (and may therefore have a sour taste) or are otherwise bad are extracted.

In order to operate under hygienic conditions and to operate the freezers at as near to maximum capacity as possible, they are scheduled (*see* Table 24.4) to be regularly defrosted, completely cleaned out and sterilised. It takes eight hours for each freezer to be defrosted. Visiting the inside of a working freezer, one can see why defrosting is so essential: they are very big, with a length of about 15 metres and a width of about six metres. Before entry, it is necessary to wear insulating clothes, since the air temperature is around minus 35 degrees, and a wind is blowing, making it quite a frightening and breathtaking experience!

Table 24.4 Typical 'hygiene' cycle schedule

Day	*Freezers defrosted*
1	3 and 2
2	Nil
3	1 and 2
4	3
5	2
6	1

A series of conveyor belts go through the whole freezer, and cold air is blown up from underneath making the peas jump and circulate some centimetres above the conveyor while they freeze. Snow can build up on the floor to more than ten centimetres deep, and icicles hang from everywhere in the roof. The walls are covered with snow and ice.

BREAKDOWNS AND MECHANICAL DOWNTIME

Problems in form of breakdowns are dealt with by the process manager, who has a team of full-time skilled employees, plus contractors if required. Unplanned engineering downtime can arise because of mechanical, electrical, refrigeration, or other technical problems. Time is planned for preventative maintenance, in order to keep the equipment in optimal condition to cope with the pressures of the harvest. This planned downtime reduces operating utilisation on each of the cleaning/blanching lines to 95 per cent of operating time. Planned maintenance of the freezers is carried out during the hygiene downtime described above.

Because of the complexity of the equipment, and variability of the condition of the peas, small unplanned breakdowns are frequent, and records are kept of the time, time lost, the line involved, and the type of breakdown. One of the most common reasons is 'WFP' (waiting for product; that is input of peas); another is clogging (the produce getting stuck and making the lines stop), which is recorded as production downtime. In the control room any changes to the plan are recorded on the wall charts, using a blue pen for changes originating from factory problems, and using a red pen for changes created by the growers. The actual downtime for the year turned out as shown in Table 24.5:

Table 24.5 Actual recorded downtime, this season. Total for cleaning and blanching lines.

Downtime	*Hours lost*
Engineering	83.59
W.F.P. (Waiting for Product)	125.97
Production problems	39.97
Total (unplanned downtime)	249.53
Planned hygiene	82.30
Total (Recorded Downtime)	331.83

PACKAGING

There is a review of the sales plan every fourth week. It is prepared by the sales department covering 13 weeks ahead, and is given by specified product in cases per week. This plan is downloaded on the systems for all departments to use. A weekly plan is delivered, first and foremost, to the packaging department for repackaging from bulk into retail packs and outer cases.

Sometimes the department has to deal with lingering quality problems, which can slow down the process. These can normally be completely sorted out by running the bulk peas through the Sortex colour sorter, if necessary several times. The packaging shift manager, Andy Burton, was not always happy with having to do this rework:

> *'There have always been some arguments between production and packaging about quality. There are quality checks, both in the beginning of the line, at the flow-end, and in the packaging area, but in spite of these checks it is this department that has to deal*

with any remaining problems, which can take quite some time to sort out! When we get in bulk packs of peas, which are clogged, iced, or contain sours, it means that we have to run them through the Sortex several times. This sometimes results in time delays in delivering to customers, since most of the packing is planned on a just-in-time basis.'

From time to time, especially in the spring season, the factory can run out of peas, which then have to be bought in. Usually there are the right amount of peas in store, but not the right mix of quality and grade of peas required. Other quality problems can involve the supply of cases, labels, or polythene bags.

COLD STORE

In addition to the factory cold store, the company uses six contractors' stores, all at temperatures around –30 degrees Celcius. Only 2700 tonnes can be stored on site, comprising 1500 tonnes in bulk containers on pallets, with the remainder kept for cases of packaged peas awaiting dispatch to customers. Over the whole year there is a need for a maximum of 22 000 tonnes of cold storage, not only for peas but for all other vegetables produced at the site. The cold store manager, Martin Stover, commented:

'We have a much better system in the cold store after the recent reorganisation. Now we can access the piles of containers from all sides. However, the piles of peas bought in from other companies cause a bit of a problem as they often don't fit in well with our own bulk containers. It is quite expensive to buy in from others, of course. But even though we have lots of peas, we do not always have the right quality grade according to the retailers wishes, and we have to do everything we can for these customers. They pay our salaries, you know.'

Questions

1 What are the capacities at each main stage of the pea processing?

2 Which is the bottleneck process, and how is this managed to maximise throughput?

3 (a) What is the design capacity of the overall operation?
(b) What is the effective capacity?
(c) Calculate the efficiency and utilisation for the operation over the current year's pea season. Would this give a good indication of the factory performance, for example in benchmarking against other factories in the group, such as frozen pizza manufacturing?

4 Prepare graphs showing:
(a) the daily output compared to design and effective capacity
(b) cumulative output compared to cumulative design and effective capacity
What do these tell us about the operation?

5 Summarise the reasons why capacity is lost on some days in mid-season.
What could be done to reduce this problem?

6 Do you think that John Lincoln's desire to extend the pea harvest period is the best strategy for the overall operation?

CASE 25

Sheepbreeder

Adam Bates and Stuart Chambers

Case date July 1995

INTRODUCTION

Jane Bishop, senior clerk at 'Sheepbreeder' was chatting to a colleague during her lunch break:

> *'There has to be a better way of organising things around here. Right now, we are rushed off our feet and we have a huge backlog of data to be processed, but I know that in a month we will be quiet again. Still, I'm off on holiday this weekend, and don't have time to think about it right now, but when things are quieter we are going to have to re-organise the way we operate once and for all.'*

BACKGROUND

'Sheepbreeder' is a relatively new service provided by the Meat and Livestock Commission (MLC), that helps independent sheepbreeders improve the quality of their animals through analysis of key physical attributes, allowing them to decide which animals to dispose of, and which to mate.

The MLC was established by the British Government in 1968 to encourage improved production techniques, and to promote increased consumption of all meats. It is funded by a statutory levy on the slaughter of all calves, cattle, sheep and pigs, as well as fees which are charged for services and consultancy work undertaken, such as that offered by Sheepbreeder. Recent changes in the corporate objectives of the MLC have determined that all funds received from the 'slaughter levy' should be allocated in greater proportions to the promotion and marketing of meat; and that all other technical services, such as Sheepbreeder, should achieve break-even within 12 months. Consequently, all the technical services have had to become more commercially aware, by providing their existing clients with value for money in order to encourage further growth in demand for the services, and by improving operating efficiency wherever possible.

It is recognised that Sheepbreeder is currently operating at a cost recovery of only about 75 per cent. The foreword in the brochure issued by Sheepbreeder to its customers summarises the role of the service, and is reproduced in Fig. 25.1.

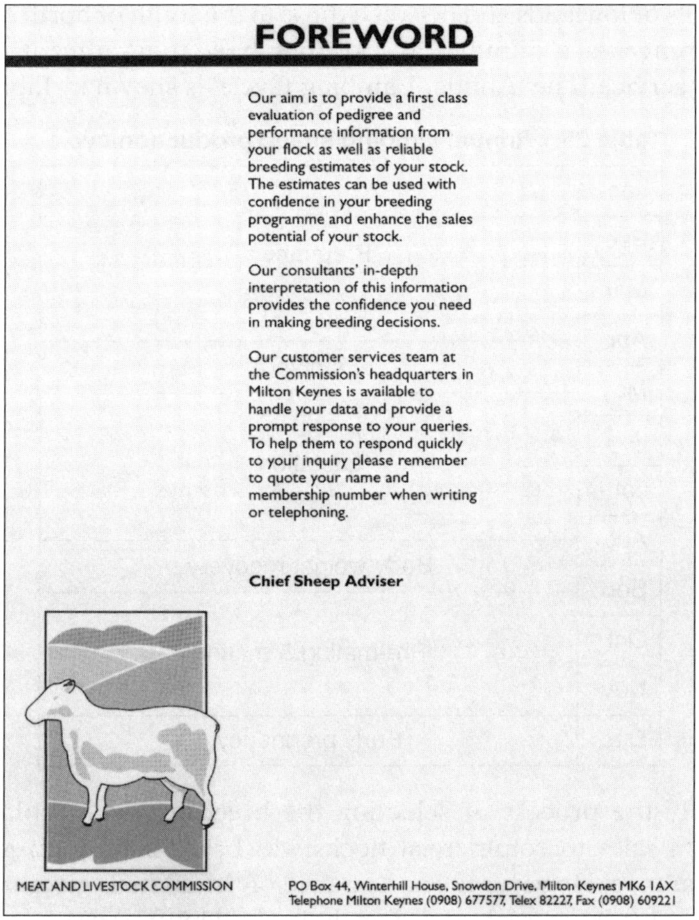

FOREWORD

Our aim is to provide a first class evaluation of pedigree and performance information from your flock as well as reliable breeding estimates of your stock. The estimates can be used with confidence in your breeding programme and enhance the sales potential of your stock.

Our consultants' in-depth interpretation of this information provides the confidence you need in making breeding decisions.

Our customer services team at the Commission's headquarters in Milton Keynes is available to handle your data and provide a prompt response to your queries. To help them to respond quickly to your inquiry please remember to quote your name and membership number when writing or telephoning.

Chief Sheep Adviser

MEAT AND LIVESTOCK COMMISSION

PO Box 44, Winterhill House, Snowdon Drive, Milton Keynes MK6 1AX
Telephone Milton Keynes (0908) 677577, Telex 82227, Fax (0908) 609221

Fig. 25.1 Sheepbreeder instructions to breeders – foreword

THE SHEEP INDUSTRY

The sheep farming industry can be roughly divided into two types of farmer; *pedigree sheep breeders* and *commercial farmers*. In the UK there are approximately 1800 pedigree sheep breeders, most of whom have flocks of more than 30 ewes, or female sheep. A single male sheep, or ram, would normally be mated with between 40–50 ewes each year, and both rams and ewes would normally have a useful breeding life of approximately seven years, with each ewe producing on average 1.5 lambs per annum.

The annual cycle of sheep production begins in the autumn (Oct–Nov) when mating takes place; pregnancy occurs during the winter months, and then 'lambing' takes place in the spring. The lambs suckle their mothers until weaning, and then the best ram lambs are sold to commercial flocks that autumn or a full 12 months later when they are 18 months of age. Some ewe lambs are kept as flock replacements while the remainder are sold along with the rams to commercial flocks as 'finished lamb', and then the cycle repeats itself. Differences in timing do occur between breeders on hills or lowlands and between those in the south or north of the country, but the differences are minimal and do not have a significant effect on the Sheepbreeder service. The 'Annual Lambing Cycle' is shown in Table 25.1.

Table 25.1 Annual lambing/sheep production cycle

Jan	Pregnancy
Feb	
Mar	
Apr	Lambing
May	
Jun	Lactation
Jul	
Aug	Body weight recovery
Sep	
Oct	Pre-mating & mating
Nov	
Dec	Early pregnancy

Traditionally the process of selecting the breeding flock replacements and promoting ram sales to commercial flocks was based simply on judgements of physical appearance. However the appearance of the animals gives no quantitative information about the animal, and does little to identify those lean, high quality sheep likely to produce better lambs in the future.

SHEEPBREEDER SERVICE

In order to be able to supply this quantitative information to overcome this problem, Sheepbreeder monitors the performance of lambs in the pedigree flocks under standard conditions and periodically takes objective measurements which can then be used as an aid to the differentiation between good and bad lambs. The best ones can either be sold to commercial flocks or retained for breeding purposes, while the poorer ones can be fattened for immediate slaughter, either by the breeder or a commercial farmer.

The records held by Sheepbreeder fall into two main categories: adults (rams & ewes) and lambs. Regular updating of the Sheepbreeder records by the breeders ensures that 'active' animals on the Sheepbreeder computer file match the current stock in the breeders flock, allowing Sheepbreeder to provide the breeder with accurate results in its final report. However the ongoing flow of data is heavily reliant upon the breeder returning forms promptly, as each data input generates the next data output.

Similar services exist for breeders of pigs (*Pig Plan*) and cattle (*Beef Breeder*) although seasonality of production is less obvious, and therefore these services do not experience such serious fluctuations in demand as those experienced by Sheepbreeder.

Communication

The cycle of communications between Sheepbreeder and the breeders follows the annual breeding programme, and typically starts in the autumn when Sheepbreeder sends the breeders a list of six-month-old ewe and ram lambs assumed to be in the flock. This list is derived from lambing details provided earlier and takes account of previous years' sale and disposal records. The breeder then updates the list by deleting animals disposed of and circling animals retained (*see* Fig. 25.2) and returns it to Sheepbreeder for processing. Sheepbreeder then issues the breeder with a 'Ram Mating Inventory' (*see* Fig. 25.3) and a 'Ewe Mating Inventory' (*see* Fig. 25.4). The breeder gives each ram a code number and identifies on the Ewe Mating Inventory which ram was used for mating. He then sends these forms back to Sheepbreeder at the end of the mating period. A separate form is used if newly purchased ewes are added to these inventories, giving full details on the animals' background and parentage. Other standard forms are detailed in Fig. 25.5.

At the same time as the mating inventories are issued, Sheepbreeder issues a 'lambing details' form (*see* Fig. 25.5) which allows the breeder to identify the lambing date for the ewe, the number of lambs born, and their sex, weight and individual identification number. Once the lambing details have been received, 'weigh sheets' (*see* Fig. 25.6) are then issued to the breeders, who are required to weigh the lambs at about 8 and 21 weeks (weigh dates are stated on the forms) and then return these to Sheepbreeder. A Sheepbreeder consultant will attend one of the weighings to verify the results.

All lamb weights are then analysed to enable comparisons to be made with other lambs in the Sheepbreeder program. In addition, at the second weighing, some breeders have their rams ultrasonically scanned*, by the Sheepbreeder consultant, to measure back fat and muscle depth, which helps quantify differences in conformation and fatness.

All of the performance information is then collated to produce indexes on all animals in the flock, which the breeder then uses to guide decisions about which animals to breed, to sell or to fatten and slaughter. These selection decisions usually take place soon after the second weighing, and therefore the breeders expect to receive the final report from Sheepbreeder as soon after the second weighing as possible. This is always the busiest period for Sheepbreeder, and the office receives numerous telephone calls from breeders enquiring after their animals' results.

If we examine Fig. 25.7 we can see that over this three-year period the breeders had received an average of £3.00 for each increasing millimetre of muscle over fat on their lambs, and so it is possible to see how they had benefited financially from enrolling in the Sheepbreeder service.

*Similar to the ultrasonic scanning of unborn human babies.

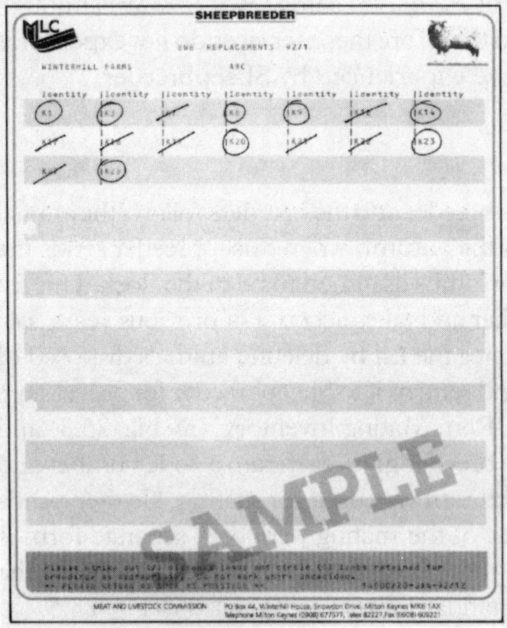

SHEEPBREEDER

EWE REPLACEMENTS 92/1

WINTERHILL FARMS ABC

Identity	Identity	Identity	Identity	Identity	Identity	Identity
K1	K2	[illegible]	K5	K9	[illegible]	K14
[illegible]	K16	[illegible]	K20	[illegible]	[illegible]	K23
[illegible]	[illegible]					

MEAT AND LIVESTOCK COMMISSION PO Box 44, Winterhill House, Snowdon Drive, Milton Keynes MK6 1AX Telephone Milton Keynes (0908) 677577, Telex 82227, Fax (0908) 609221

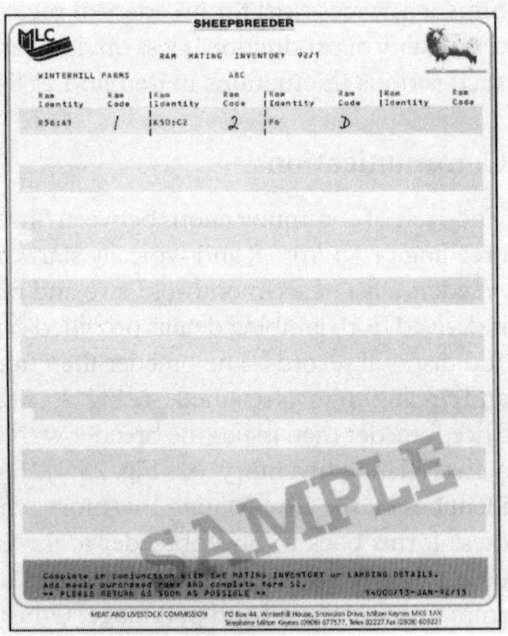

SHEEPBREEDER

RAM MATING INVENTORY 92/1

WINTERHILL FARMS ABC

Ram Identity	Ram Code	Ram Identity	Ram Code	Ram Identity	Ram Code	Ram Identity	Ram Code
R56:A1	1	K50:C2	2	F6	D		

Complete in conjunction with EWE MATING INVENTORY or LAMBING DETAILS.
Add newly purchased rams AND complete form S2.
** PLEASE RETURN AS SOON AS POSSIBLE **

MEAT AND LIVESTOCK COMMISSION PO Box 44, Winterhill House, Snowdon Drive, Milton Keynes MK6 1AX Telephone Milton Keynes (0908) 677577, Telex 82227, Fax (0908) 609221

Figs. 25.2 and 25.3 Samples of Sheepbreeder 'pre-lists'

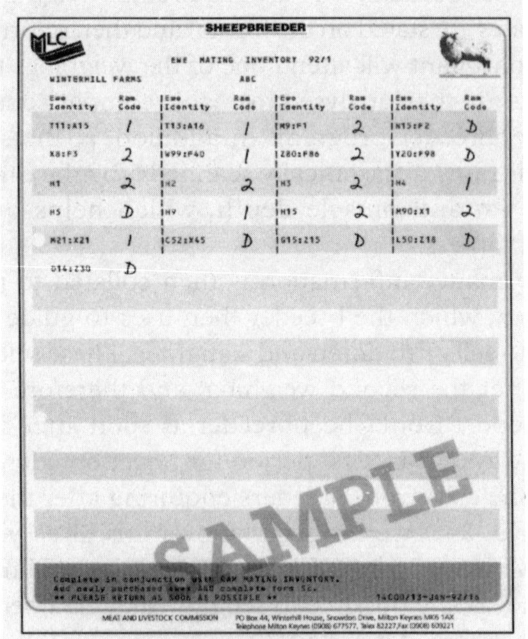

SHEEPBREEDER

EWE MATING INVENTORY 92/1

WINTERHILL FARMS ABC

Ewe Identity	Ram Code	Ewe Identity	Ram Code	Ewe Identity	Ram Code	Ewe Identity	Ram Code
T11:A15	1	T13:A16	1	M9:F1	2	N13:P2	D
X8:F3	2	W99:F40	1	Z80:F86	2	Y20:F98	D
H1	2	H2	2	H3	2	H4	1
H5	D	H9	1	H15	2	M90:X1	2
M21:X21	1	C52:X45	D	G15:Z15	D	L50:Z18	D
D14:Z30	D						

Complete in conjunction with RAM MATING INVENTORY.
Add newly purchased ewes AND complete form S2.
** PLEASE RETURN AS SOON AS POSSIBLE **

MEAT AND LIVESTOCK COMMISSION PO Box 44, Winterhill House, Snowdon Drive, Milton Keynes MK6 1AX Telephone Milton Keynes (0908) 677577, Telex 82227, Fax (0908) 609221

Fig. 25.4 Sample of Sheepbreeder 'pre-lists'

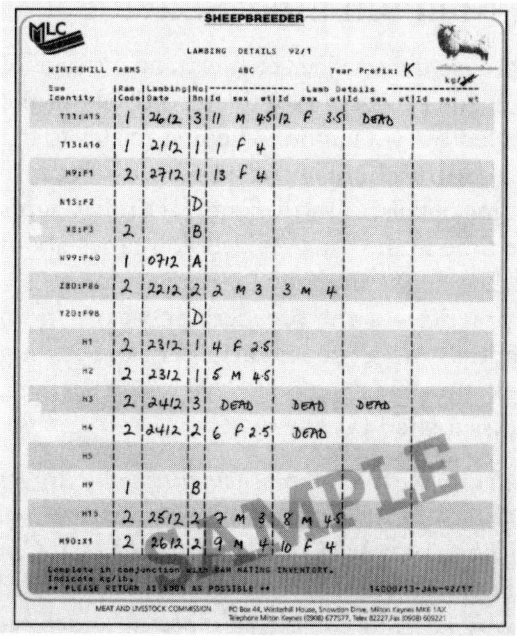

SHEEPBREEDER

LAMBING DETAILS 92/1

WINTERHILL FARMS ABC Year Prefix: K kg/~~lb~~

Ewe Identity	Ram Code	Lambing Date	No Bn	Id	sex	wt	Id	sex	wt	Id	sex	wt	Id	sex	wt
T11:A15	1	2612	3	11	M	4.5	12	F	3.5	DEAD					
T13:A16	1	2112	1	1	F	4									
N9:F1	2	2712	1	13	F	4									
N15:F2			D												
X8:F3	2		B												
W99:F40	1	0712	A												
Z80:F86	2	2212	2	2	M	3	3	M	4						
Y20:F98			D												
H1	2	2312	1	4	F	2.5									
H2	2	2312	1	5	M	4.5									
H3	2	2412	3	DEAD			DEAD			DEAD					
H4	2	2412	2	6	F	2.5	DEAD								
H5															
H9	1		B												
H15	2	2512	2	7	M	3	8	M	4.5						
M90:X1	2	2612	2	9	M	4	10	F	4						

Complete in conjunction with RAM MATING INVENTORY.
Indicate kg/lb.
** PLEASE RETURN AS SOON AS POSSIBLE ** 14000/13-JAN-92/17

SAMPLE

MEAT AND LIVESTOCK COMMISSION PO Box 44, Winterhill House, Snowdon Drive, Milton Keynes MK6 1AX
Telephone Milton Keynes (0908) 677577, Telex 82227, Fax (0908) 609221

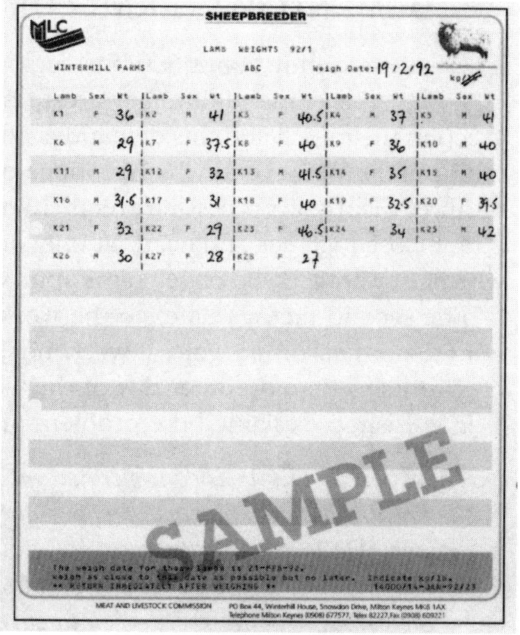

SHEEPBREEDER

LAMB WEIGHTS 92/1

WINTERHILL FARMS ABC Weigh Date: 19/2/92 kg/~~lb~~

Lamb	Sex	Wt	Lamb	Sex	Wt	Lamb	Sex	Wt	Lamb	Sex	Wt	Lamb	Sex	Wt
K1	F	36	K2	M	41	K3	F	40.5	K4	M	37	K5	M	41
K6	M	29	K7	F	37.5	K8	F	40	K9	F	36	K10	M	40
K11	M	29	K12	F	32	K13	M	41.5	K14	F	35	K15	M	40
K16	M	31.6	K17	F	31	K18	F	40	K19	F	32.5	K20	F	39.5
K21	F	32	K22	F	29	K23	F	46.5	K24	M	34	K25	M	42
K26	M	30	K27	F	28	K28	F	27						

The weigh date for these lambs is 21-FEB-92.
Weigh as close to this date as possible but no later. Indicate kg/lb.
** RETURN IMMEDIATELY AFTER WEIGHING ** 14000/14-JAN-92/23

SAMPLE

MEAT AND LIVESTOCK COMMISSION PO Box 44, Winterhill House, Snowdon Drive, Milton Keynes MK6 1AX
Telephone Milton Keynes (0908) 677577, Telex 82227, Fax (0908) 609221

Figs. 25.5 and 25.6 Sheepbreeder 'lambing details form' & 'weight sheets'

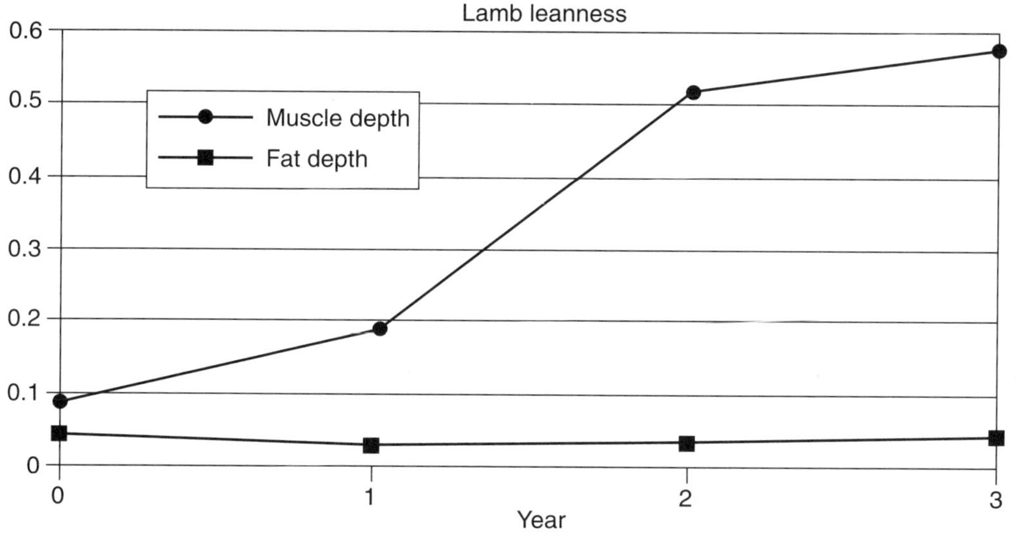

Source: Species Development Strategy. MLC Corporate Plan.

Fig. 25.7 Improvements in leanness resulting from Sheepbreeder

DEMAND PATTERNS FOR SHEEPBREEDER SERVICE

There are currently about 600 breeders who use the service, each with an average of 100 ewes. The demand that they create is for the processing of the records about the sheep in their flock and this demand is affected by two factors. The first relates to the timing of the main events which produce an *annual cycle of demand.* This occurs because the three main data processing events (Lambing details, Lamb weights 1, Lamb weights 2) are close together and occur at only one time in the year. As decision times about whether or not to keep or sell rams approaches, so the urgency for results increases.

The second factor relates to the work practices of the breeders, most of whom tend to do their office work at weekends, and so more records arrive for processing on Mondays than on other day of the week, thus creating a *weekly cycle of demand.*

Jane Bishop explained the problem of dissatisfied breeders:

'Most of the activity is concentrated into the spring and summer months, not only for the breeder, but also for the Sheepbreeder service. This seasonal peak means we are not always able to process the records as quickly as we or the breeders would like. Our problem is made worse by the fact that the most important aspect of quality as perceived by the breeders is the speed of data turnaround. How can we be expected to achieve break-even within Sheepbreeder, if we already have difficulty satisfying those breeders who are using the service?'

This issue is further complicated by data processing queries, which appear to occur more frequently when Sheepbreeder is busier. A list of complaints that Jane had noted from a recent staff meeting with the clerks showed the types of problems that were occurring:

- Breeders do not always send in lambing details, and therefore are not issued with lamb weighing forms. This results in numerous unnecessary telephone calls.
- Breeders often lose forms and therefore send lamb weights on plain paper, usually in a format different from that required by Sheepbreeder.
- The timing of data received at Sheepbreeder may cause breakdowns in the forms and reports which must then be issued to the breeders.
- Lambing details are occasionally sent in together with weight details, therefore increasing processing times at already high demand periods.
- The forms which the breeders receive from Sheepbreeder are not consistent with their current farm documentation and so are not used, again resulting in information being issued on blank sheets.
- Breeders are unfamiliar with the service as it is still relatively new, and so make mistakes when completing the forms.

These all serve to further complicate the processing of records, and frequently require the clerks to telephone the breeder to verify or correct information.

In the four years since Sheepbreeder had been operating, the resulting improvements in sheep fertility and the quality of meat produced was apparent. Figure 25.8 summarises the improvements in leanness resulting from the use of the service.

Annual cycle of demand

There are five different types of data received by Sheepbreeder which must be processed for the animals in the flock and these are:

1 replacement lists (also 'Breeding stock inventory/Purchased breeding stock);

2 mating inventories (rams and ewes);

3 lambing inventories;

4 lamb weights 1; and

5 lamb weights 2.

After the second weighing the Final Report, consisting of up to 20 pages is produced for the breeders and the information contained in it is copied to disk, so that it can be referred to in future years. If ultrasonic scanning has also been used, the additional data can be combined with the information already obtained, to provide even more detailed final reports. This additional work does not place much demand on the resources of the Sheepbreeder office, and its timings are already included in those provided in Table 25.2.

Processing of data

The processing of data on arrival at Sheepbreeder follows the path illustrated in Fig.25.8.

Jane explained:

'Every day the clerical team batches up work for each operation; first ensuring that all mail to be expedited is issued, then that all mail received is opened, checked and stacked in chronological order by data type. After that one person takes the stacks of forms in batches of 20–30 and records their details in the postbook, which registers the receipt of the data against the members' details. Once the data type, date received, and number of records provided has been entered into the postbook, two other people start processing the data, dealing with any queries as they arise. Towards the end of the day the computer processing is started and allowed to continue throughout the night. No priority is given to any particular data type or any particular breeder, so you can see the system is very equitable. However, we do have periods where we appear to be building up a never ending backlog of forms for which the next set of "Pre-Lists" is not being issued.'

The opening of envelopes, entering membership details in the postbook and the despatch of results takes a fixed amount of time per member, whereas entering data is a function of the number of records. The processing of these records is monitored

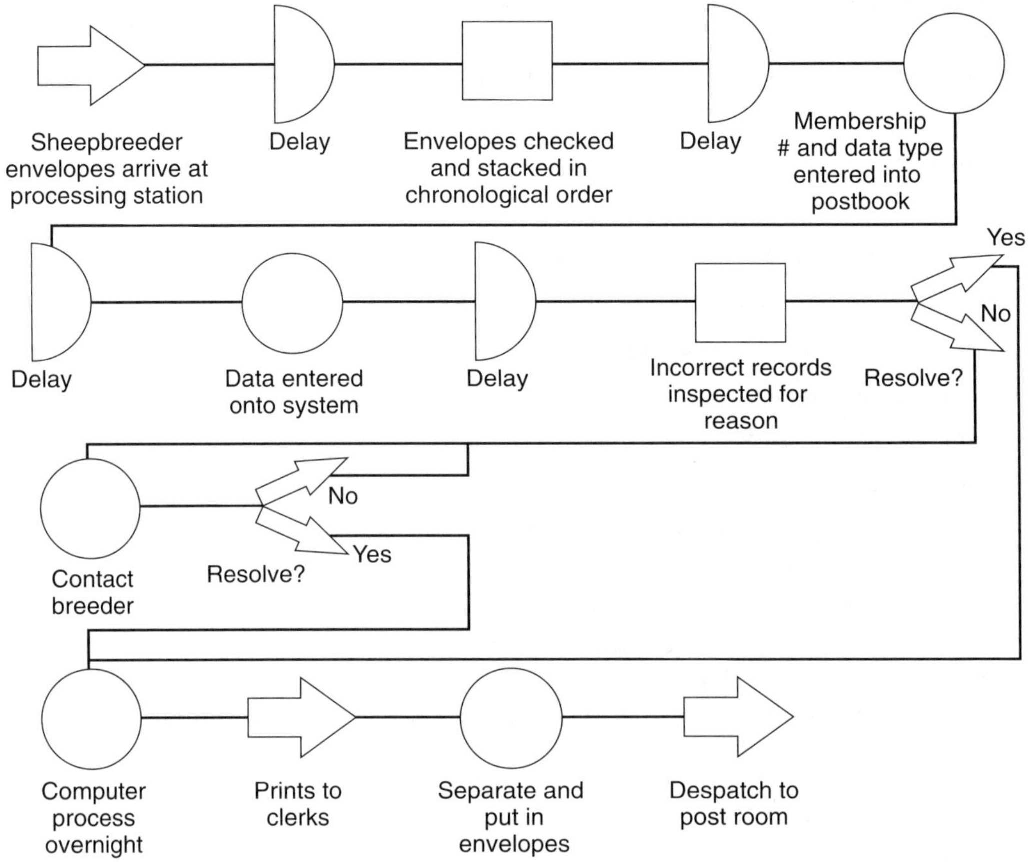

Fig. 25.8 Data processing flow chart

as 'Ewe Events Processed' (EEPs). The time taken to process the EEPs depends on the type of data (replacement list, mating inventory, lambing inventory etc . . .) and the format of the data entry document ('Pre-List' or 'Random'). Pre-List documents are those issued by Sheepbreeder with many of the details already printed on them and require the breeder to only update them with the required additional information. Random documents on the other hand are blank input documents which require the breeder to enter all of the animals details by hand. The processing of data on the Pre-Lists is faster than on Random documents as the Sheepbreeder computer program has been designed to mirror the Pre-List. If documents have been completed by hand, all the data must be re-entered and the computer system then checks the existence of the record. The Random documents also tend to generate far more queries than the Pre-Lists.

Based on many random observations over a three-month period, the time taken to process the different documents in the different formats has been determined and is presented in Table 25.2.

Table 25.2 Time taken to complete each operation

Operation times	*Replacement list*	*Mating inventory*	*Lambing inventory*	*Lamb weights 1*	*Lamb weights 2*	*Final report*
Time to handle post on arrival per member (minutes)	5	5	5	5	5	–
Time per EEP as 'Pre-List' (seconds)	9	6	24	6	3	–
Time per EEP as 'Random' (seconds)	45	30	135	30	15	–
Time per EEP per Query (seconds)	60	60	60	60	60	–
Despatch/member (minutes)	2	2	2	2	2	10
Disk copy/member (minutes)	–	–	–	–	–	10
% of forms on 'Pre-List'	50	50	50	15	50	–
% of forms on 'Random'	50	50	50	85	50	–
% EEP Queries	5	5	10	5	2	–

The volume of data received in the current year, presented in EEPs and number of reports issued to the breeders, is displayed in Table 25.3. This demonstrates the marked seasonal nature of demand. The peak demand requirements tend to be accentuated still further because the type of data being processed takes longer and tends to have a higher percentage of queries.

Table 25.3 Annual cycle of demand in current year

	Replacement list (EEPs)	*Mating inventory (EEPs)*	*Lambing inventory (EEPs)*	*Lamb weights 1 (EEPs)*	*Lamb weights 2 (EEPs)*	*Final report (# breeders)*
January	7900	8200	–	–	–	–
February	6900	7400	2800	–	–	
March	6600	2800	19500	8800	1500	
April	3100	600	22100	14300	11800	
May	4000	–	14900	24100	11100	
June	900	–	14100	26600	22400	
July	–	–	13300	13600	21500	90
August	–	–	5500	5600	14100	105
September	16400	3300	2800	–	7600	135
October	12400	12200	–	–	–	135
November	14900	13400	–	–	–	105
December	8700	11100	–	–	–	30

Weekly cycle of demand

The demand also fluctuates within any week, with approximately 26 per cent of the data arriving on Mondays. A full analysis of weekly demand is shown in Table 25.4.

Table 25.4 Typical weekly cycle of demand (EEPs)

	Number	*% in total*
Monday	1950	26
Tuesday	1350	18
Wednesday	1425	19
Thursday	1425	19
Friday	1350	18

Capacity determinants

The ability to process this data is in the form of one senior clerk and two junior clerks who each work 42 hours per week and have an entitlement of 27 days leave as well as public holidays. All the clerks are fully cross-trained and can do any role within the Sheepbreeder bureau.

Monitoring of the time spent actually working, however, reveals that on average each person spends only 7 hours and 20 minutes working on Sheepbreeder data processing every day. The remainder is taken up attending meetings, collecting drinks from vending machines, collecting stationery, taking breaks, etc. Overtime is used as a last resort to increase capacity temporarily, but is avoided wherever possible. An analysis of the clerical capacity available in the current year (before the use of overtime) is presented in Table 25.5.

Table 25.5 Office capacity

Month	*Working days*	*Gross staff days: 3 people*	*Annual leave & sick leave (days)*	*Nett working days available*	*Total hours available*	*% of maximum*
January	22	66	7.5	58.5	430	89
February	20	60	3	57	419	95
March	22	66	6	60	441	91
April	20	60	5	55	404	92
May	18	54	11	43	316	80
June	22	66	7	59	434	89
July	21	63	23	40	294	63
August	21	63	17	46	338	73
September	22	66	7.5	58.5	430	89
October	22	66	17.5	48.5	356	73
November	21	63	3	60	441	95
December	20	60	5	58	426	97

Whenever demand exceeds capacity the turnaround times on data processing become extended. Jane summed up their predicament:

> *'Clearly having turnaround times of over two weeks does not provide the quality of service on which fees can be increased or additional membership encouraged, to meet the corporate objective of increased cost recovery.'*

Ultrasonic scanning service

This additional service which is offered by Sheepbreeder, allows the breeders to obtain even greater detail on the performance of their flock. It provides them with more accurate statistics, which they can use as a sales tool when taking the animals to market.

The service is generally offered at the same time as the second weighing, and is carried out by one of the MLC's on-site consultants who offer expert advice and consultancy to breeders on all areas of breeding, mating and animal performance. Access to the consultants is included in the fee charged by Sheepbreeder, although there is an extra charge for the scanning. The work of these consultants generally covers all animals, and they cross-charge the relevant MLC department proportionally to the amount of time spent working for each particular service.

Scanning does not create additional paperwork for the clerks at the Sheepbreeder bureau, as the information is processed and printed at the time it is obtained on the breeder's farm. The only work carried out at the Sheepbreeder bureau is the copying of the data from the on-site consultants disk onto the Sheepbreeder master-copy retained for the breeder. This function takes a negligible amount of time and has been included in the 'Disk Copy' times given in Table 25.2.

Sheepbreeder revenues and costs

Sheepbreeder derives revenue by charging an annual fee of £260.00 per breeder which covers the first 50 ewes in every flock and charges an additional £1.45 for every ewe thereafter.

Data about lambs born of any ewe registered at Sheepbreeder is processed without the breeder incurring any additional cost. Effectively the fee is charged on the lamb's parents regardless of the number of lambs they produce. The lambs only become charged by Sheepbreeder if they are retained within the flock for breeding purposes in future years.

The sheep scanning service charges a minimum fee of £83.00 for every flock, with the cost per lamb being £1.55.

Overtime for the three clerks costs approximately £12 per hour including employment costs such as insurance. Average annual Sheepbreeder costs are shown in Table 25.6.

Table 25.6 Average annual sheepbreeder costs

Item	*Annual Cost £000*
Rent	35
Utility charges & other operating costs	25
1 manager	25
1 senior clerk	15
2 junior clerks	20
12 national on-site consultants (Sheepbreeder share)	110
Vehicle leasing costs (Sheepbreeder share)	20
Annual rental of scanning equipment	10
Total	260

Questions

1 Calculate the monthly demand for the service and compare this to the capacity at Sheepbreeder. What causes the differences, and what is the effect on Sheepbreeder and the breeders?

2 What effect does the weekly demand pattern (Table 25.4) have on the operation?

3 What action should be taken to improve the management of capacity and demand?

4 How might the cost recovery at Sheepbreeder be improved, and what changes might this require? You should consider both the operations design and also the quality of service provided to the breeder.

5 Are there any other issues which may affect the operation in the next five years? You may consider issues such as the ongoing potential for improvements in leanness, costs to the breeder versus value, barriers to exit, knowledge transfer, uniqueness of service, etc.

CASE 26

Massey Ferguson JIT purchasing and supply

Alan Harrison and Christopher Voss

*Case date 1992**

INTRODUCTION

The Massey Ferguson (MF) plant at Banner Lane in Coventry has been described as the 'largest tractor plant in the Western World'. In the mid-1980s, like other automotive assemblers, MF were keen to implement Just-in-Time (JIT) delivery. An off-site wheel and tyre assembly operation combined with deliveries to track schedules had worked extremely well, and had greatly reduced stock holding. MF was now keen for other suppliers of class 'A' materials and components to deliver only as needed. This was not as simple a task as was originally envisaged.

A case in point was provided by Car Products (CP), a supplier of starters and alternators. CP's plant was 20 miles away from Banner Lane, and supplied MF with eight different part numbers. Like MF, CP was operating in very competitive international markets, was under heavy financial strain and had strong policies to minimise investment. For example, CP aimed to keep five days' worth of finished goods stock, while MF aimed to keep five days of incoming parts. Although CP had been supplying MF for many years, relationships had recently become somewhat strained.

Three years previously, CP had raised prices unilaterally to 'market levels'. MF had responded by second sourcing from a Japanese supplier (Nisachi) in order to 'keep CP on their toes'. It was felt that this move had greatly improved CP's attitude to price negotiation. The Nisachi deal, negotiated by one of the MF's lead buyers, had been competitive on price, and protected from exchange fluctuation by a currency 'banding' agreement. In addition, Nisachi had agreed to a lengthy credit period (120 days), and to keep a ten-day buffer stock at their expense in the UK. The business is now split between CP and Nisachi on a roughly 70/30 basis. A summary of the main points of the two supply contracts is shown in Appendix 26.1.

Negotiations to set the 1986 price level had been bogged down for six months, and MF currently gave CP a 'D' rating (the worst) on its vendor rating system (*see* Appendix 26.2). The principal causes of this low rating are:

*Some of the names and figures have been disguised.

- CP insisted on shorter payment terms than the 60 days MF was seeking to establish with other suppliers.
- CP was unwilling to maintain more than a five-day buffer stock of finished product in their warehouse. Five days was their 'standard' stock level for all customers.

There was also resistance to MF's demand to take over the shipment of parts of CP's factory (an aspect of MF's 'ex-works' programme). The 'D' rating meant that MF buyers were required to seek further alternative sources of supply.

On the other hand, CP found great difficulty in dealing with the frequent MF schedule changes. Appendix 26.3 analyses these changes over a representative period for four different part numbers supplied by CP. Among other problems, this resulted in CP holding 1177 starter motors and 2852 alternators which had been made against MF schedules which were subsequently cancelled under short notice. CP regarded MF as their worst customer for schedule changes.

Many of the problems related to scheduling and stocking at both MF and CP. A report prepared at the time by the Operations Management Group at the University of Warwick analysed the systems in both companies, and the problems caused by their interaction.

MF SCHEDULING AND STOCKING

Scheduling is performed at two levels as shown in Fig. 26.1. The two levels can be summarised as follows:

- Strategic forecast (six months), exploded through MRP to give the material delivery schedules to suppliers. It is intended that the detailed schedule for the next eight weeks is 'firm', but this is rarely so. Because it must be processed through several stages, the demand information on which the supply schedules are based is up to six weeks out of date. CP suffers from further delays in receiving their schedules because the system cannot cope with the 'fixed' demand for Nisachi. This has to be sorted out manually, and typically causes a further one-week delay.
- Tactical forecast (20-day) used for internal material control purposed and based on the same information used to schedule both CKD (Completely Knocked Down, i.e. the customer is given a kit – a box of components which they assemble themselves) and track requirements. The 20-day delivery planning report is used by the expeditors to chase parts. Therefore, suppliers can be confronted with further

Fig. 26.1 Two levels of demand scheduling at MF

demands for which they do not get a hard copy. In practice, even the 20-day demand is changed on a week-by-week basis, as is shown in Appendix 26.4.

- MF are looking for five-day stocks on the supplied parts. This is the lead time to organise a delivery and process it through goods inwards and on to the track. However, an analysis of a recent 20-day planning report (*see* Table 26.1) indicated that stocks of these parts were either too high or too low.

Table 26.1 20–day report dated 2 August 1986

MF part no.	*Stock level*	*Days covered*
1676689 M92	1108	20
1676690 M92	978	20
1680065 M1	1015	20+
1680065 M2	–8	nil
1691745 M91	217	20
1695613 M91	565	15
1695614 M91	122	20
1868283 M5	459	15
1868285 M3	1551	20

CP SCHEDULING AND STOCKING

The main steps in processing order/supply schedules at CP are as shown in Fig. 26.2.

Sales Order/Schedule
↓
Customer liaison
↓
*Customer and Delivery Schedule (CDS)
↓
*Sales Amendment Request (SAR)
(specifies new order, or change)
↓
Planning Department – Inform customer
(decide whether delivery possible)
↓
Master Production Schedule – factory targets
↓
MRP* (weekly)
↓
CP Supplier Schedules

*Denotes computer system

Fig. 26.2 Steps in processing orders and supplies at CP

CP establish factory targets on a rolling, five-month basis as illustrated in Table 26.2. Therefore a request by MF at the end of August for the 1680065 M3 from 257 to 685 per week was rejected by CP because the September programme had already been set, and could not be changed at such notice. CP will only officially accept demand which has been generated by the MF material

Table 26.2 Scheduling routine at CP

Meeting date: 1st week in September			
		Schedule	
Sept	*Oct*	*Nov*	*Dec/Jan*
Already set	Confirm	Set now	Set tentative schedules

delivery schedules. Short-term changes (that is changes to the master schedule for the next four weeks) are generally resisted because of the knock-on effects to labour and material scheduling.

Note that schedules for two and three months out are based on the demand forecasts from the MF material delivery schedules. These schedules are processed through MRP, and in turn determine delivery schedules on CP suppliers. The scheduling of long lead parts at CP is therefore crucially dependent on the accuracy of MF delivery schedules. While improvements can often be made to pull forward scheduled demand for ongoing products, it is much more difficult to inject demand for new long lead parts within the 12/15 weeks delivery cycles involved.

CP aims to maintain a five-day buffer stock of MF units at their finished product warehouse. However, an analysis of free stock at the end of period three, detailed in Table 26.3, shows that this is rarely the case.

Table 26.3 CP free stock as at August 1986

MF part no.	*Free stock*	*Current MF 5-day demand*
1695614 M91	–	–
1695613 M91	–	189[a]
1691745 M91	–	–
1676690 M92	–	–
1676689 M92	1177	–[b]
1868283 M5	575	136
1868285 M3	2852	453[b]
1680065 M1	–	257[a]
1680065 M3	–	685[c]

Notes:

a MF had recently called in all free stock on these units.

b MF had cancelled previous schedules on these units, leaving CP with excessive stock.

c MF introduced a new demand on these products at short notice (*see* below).

While the situation obviously changes from one week to the next, it is apparent that free stocks at CP also are either too high or too low.

Changes to the 1680065 part illustrate further communication problems in the supply system. MF have experienced various launch problems on the CX tractor, and introduced two new modifications (M2 and M3) to this part. The new schedule for M3 was first given to Customer Liaison at CP on 18 July 1986 by Material Supply at MF. CP pointed out that a new part was involved, that the M1 version could be modified at extra cost, and that the order should be processed through Sales with a drawing so that a formal quote could be made. After threatening to withdraw the business, MF gave CP new schedules of the M3 version on 18 August and asked for delivery to start in September. CP have stated that this is impossible, and have offered October delivery. Meanwhile much valuable time has been lost.

EFFECTS OF DUAL SOURCING

The effects of dual sourcing with fixed quantities on Nisachi, and with CP taking total schedule variability, can be illustrated as shown in Table 26.4.

Table 26.4 The variability at CP is exaggerated by the Nisachi contract

Month No.	1	2	3	4
Total MF call	1400	1800	1200	1600
variability %		+29	–33	+25
Nisachi	400	400	400	400
variability %		nil	nil	nil
CP	1,000	400	800	1200
variability %		+40	–42	+50

This is obviously creating much greater raw material and free stock problems at CP. If the total demand illustrated were to be broken down to individual part numbers, then the demand variability seen by CP would be greater still. CP have pointed out – with some justification in our view – that the highly variable schedules they have to deal with merit a price differential in comparison with a monthly, fixed quantity schedule. Alternatively, Nisachi should be exposed to the same schedule variability for the same price structure as CP.

One consequence of this is that CP is less willing to make short-term changes in their factory targets. Their programming section thinks that they would gain nothing by so doing, and would risk giving away their capacity to a competitor. Schedule changes over the next eight weeks therefore get added up and netted off the programme three months ahead. Schedule changes within the next eight weeks are resisted.

INTERACTION OF CP AND MF SYSTEMS

The consequence of the interaction of the inventory control systems at CP and MF is as follows:

1 In reality, there is little attempt to control free stocks to MF delivery schedules. These are only used by CP to create demand for raw materials on MRP, and to control free stocks in the absence of any better information.

2 CP schedules are actually determined by telephone contact between MF Material Supply and CP Customer Liaison.

3 CP attempt to maintain programmes based on MF delivery schedules. CP do accept changes to these programmes, but only grudgingly. MF are actually expediting to their twenty-day schedules, of which CP do not get a copy. (Under current arrangements, CP would challenge the validity of schedules other than the official monthly delivery schedules anyway.)

4 Finished product inventories are considerably at variance to five-day stockholding objectives at both CP and MF. MF are particularly worried about inadequate security stock in the system.

5 CP are currently carrying about £140 000 excess MF inventory, while MF want CX starters now, not in October.

As a result, there is a mutual feeling of dissatisfaction between supplier and user. Commercial negotiations about the supply contract have been bogged down since February 1986. Yet both parties to the supply contract feel that, although relationships are currently at their lowest, progress towards JIT supply can surely be made.

Question

1 What actions would you recommend to:

(a) the customer (Massey Ferguson)
(b) the supplier (car products)

in order to facilitate the movement towards JIT supply?

APPENDIX 26.1
MF SUPPLY CONTRACTS – MAIN POINTS

Starters and alternators are dual sourced by MF between CP and Nisachi on a roughly 70/30 basis.

The CP supply contract

- There is no letter of understanding about security of business. The contract could therefore be terminated by MF with little more than one month's notice.
- Payment terms are 30 days nett.
- CP aim to maintain a five-day stock of MF parts in their finished product warehouse.
- Detailed quantities by part number are called off by MF using a material delivery schedule. This is supposed to arrive at CP at the beginning of each month and covers the next eight weeks in weekly quantities (firm) and the following four months in total quantities.

- In practice, schedules can arrive at CP piecemeal, and up to the second half of the month in which they were supposed to arrive. Scheduled quantities can also change considerably from month to month (*see* Appendix 26.4).
- CP do not currently supply the MF-branded goods as 'Perkins Powerparts'. MF-compatible spares of CP manufacture are sold through the CP service organisation, and are currently only made available to MF at a discount on retail prices (two-tier structure).

The Nisachi supply contract

- Payment terms are 180 days nett. A 'banding' system buffers exchange rate fluctuations.
- Nisachi aim to keep a two-week buffer stock of MF parts in the UK at their expense.
- The supply contract is for fixed quantities (360/month starters and 432/month alternators) which are not subject to change.
- Parts are delivered under the 'Perkins Powerpart' label, and can therefore be used by the MF service organisation at the same price to MF as OEM (Original Equipment Manufacturer) parts (single-tier structure).

APPENDIX 26.2
COMMERCIAL ASSURANCE PROGRAMME

The Commercial Assurance Programme is a method to evaluate and rate the total performance of a supplier. It assesses the delivery, quality and commercial performance. The method of arriving at the rating for each of these factors is by the following:

Delivery performance measurement

The Material Control Section evaluate:

- *Supply* (50 points):
  - Stock-out, missing, line stopped.
  - Response to shortages.
  - Maintaining supply to high value criteria.
  - Rejects (replacement/rework/sorting/removal).
- *Security stocking* (20 points):
  - Do stocks exist?
  - Supplier effort to replace stock?
  - If no stock, is it supplier or MF fault?

  Note: Cases exist where we have accepted security stocking is not necessary; therefore supplier gets maximum points.
- *Communication* (30 points):
  - Access to immediate contacts and others.
  - Returning calls as promised.
  - Attitude to MF.
  - General response to problem solving.

The points total is converted to overall rating by comparing thus:

Delivery performance	*Points to CAP rating*
95	40
80–94	35
70–79	30
60–69	20
50–59	10
Less than 49	0

Quality standards

The total number of rejected parts are expressed as a percentage of the total number of parts delivered. The rejected number does not include any MF liability rejects. For example:

Total number of parts delivered (all part numbers) = 2500
Total number of parts rejected (all part numbers) = 100
Reject rate = 100/2500 = 4%.

This reject percentage is converted to a rating accordingly:

	%	*Points*
	0.50 equals	40
0.51 to	0.75	35
0.76	1.00	30
1.10	1.00	25
1.26	1.50	20
1.51	1.75	15
1.76	2.00	10
2.01	2.50	5
Greater than 2.50 =		0 points

Commercial performance

The Chief Buyer and Buyer assess the commercial aspects against the following:

Responsiveness	15
Payment terms	15
Competitiveness	15
Security stocking	15
Open factory approach	10
Investment	10
Post supply quality service performance	10
Financial soundness	10

The total score is expressed as a percentage of the maximum rating of 20 to give the commercial performance.

Final rating

The final rating is found by totalling:

- Delivery rating
- Quality rating
- Commercial rating

The total is compared:

- A rating 100–95
- B rating 90–94
- C rating 89–80
- D rating below 80

The rating is carried out monthly and will be notified to the supplier by the buyer.

APPENDIX 26.3
MF: CHANGES IN MATERIAL DELIVERY SCHEDULES

Owing to the pressures of the market in which they operate, MF are constantly revising sales forecasts and build commitments to take advantage of opportunities as they arise. This is reflected in considerable variability of demand scheduling. After processing through MRP, the material delivery schedules, which are used to schedule parts delivered from MF suppliers, are therefore also highly variable. The graphical analysis in the following figures was prepared from an analysis of MF delivery schedules:

- For each month in turn (e.g. Feb. 1986), the scheduled demand three months prior to the month (Nov. 1985) is compared with revised demand two months (Dec. 1985) and one month (Jan. 1986) prior to production. The actual demand for the month (Feb. 1986) is also shown.
- Although MF provides scheduled demand for six months ahead, only the three months immediately prior to demand were selected. Demand for months 6 to 4 prior to demand show even greater changes, but are outside the CP lead time for long-lead components.

Note that CP pick up the total schedule variability under current sourcing arrangements. This can be further amplified by certain territories (e.g. Turkey) insisting on 100 per cent CP supply.

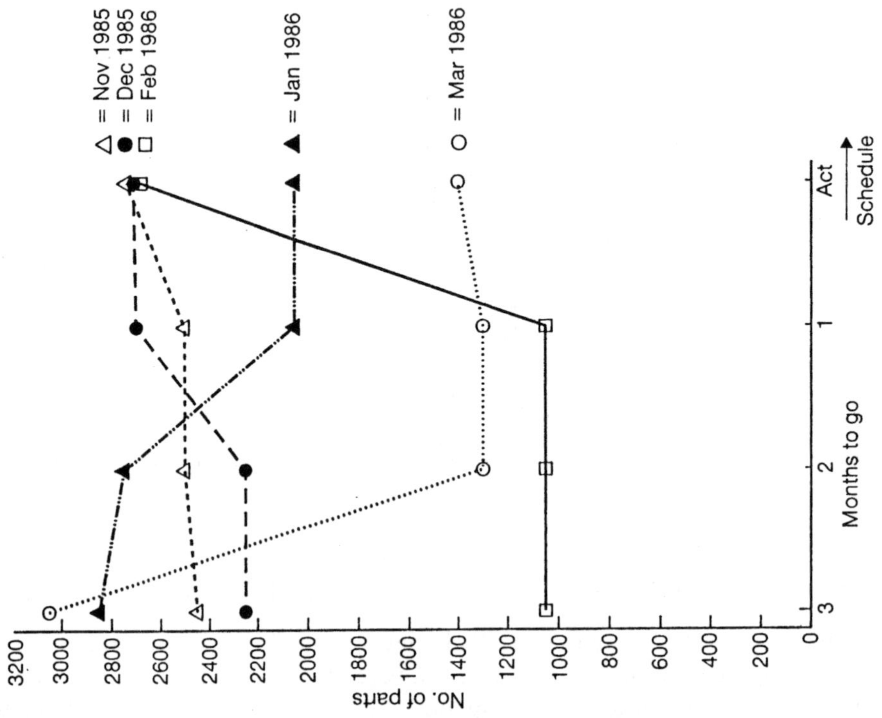

No. of parts
3200
3000
2800
2600
2400
2200
2000
1800
1600
1400
1200
1000
800
600
400
200
0
3
2
1
Act
Months to go
Schedule
△ = Nov 1985
● = Dec 1985
□ = Feb 1986
▲ = Jan 1986
○ = Mar 1986

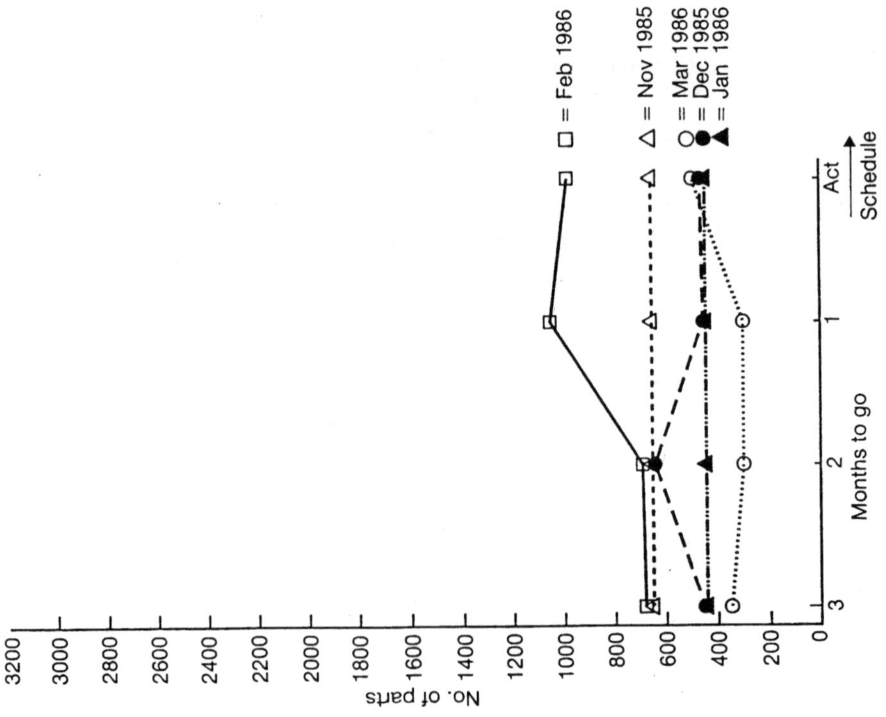

No. of parts
3200
3000
2800
2600
2400
2200
2000
1800
1600
1400
1200
1000
800
600
400
200
0
3
2
1
Act
Months to go
Schedule
□ = Feb 1986
△ = Nov 1985
○ = Mar 1986
● = Dec 1985
▲ = Jan 1986

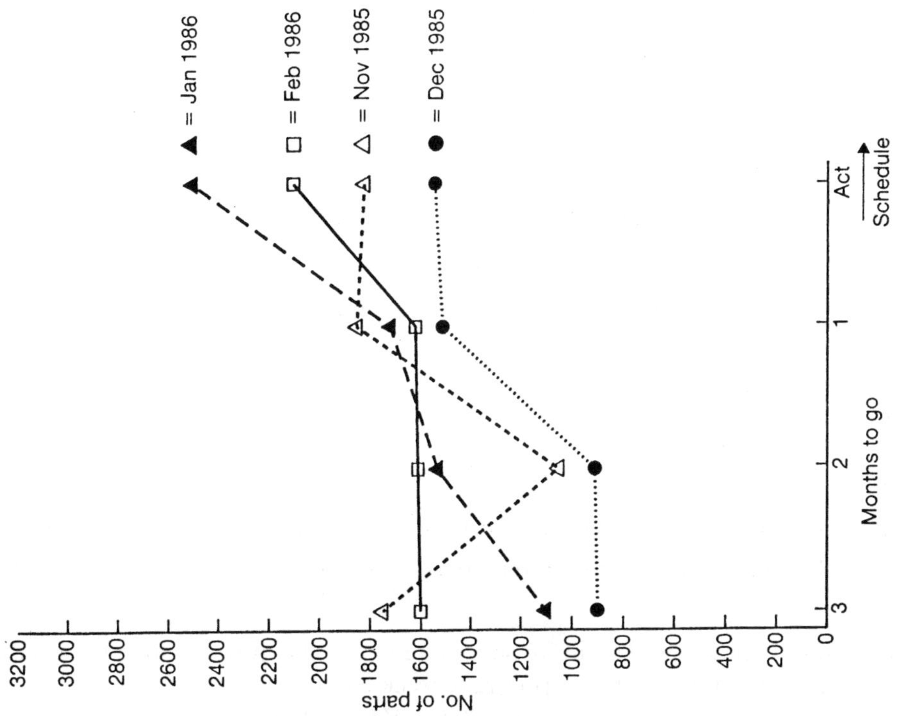
▲ = Jan 1986
□ = Feb 1986
△ = Nov 1985
● = Dec 1985
No. of parts
3200
3000
2800
2600
2400
2200
2000
1800
1600
1400
1200
1000
800
600
400
200
0
3
2
1
Act
Months to go
Schedule

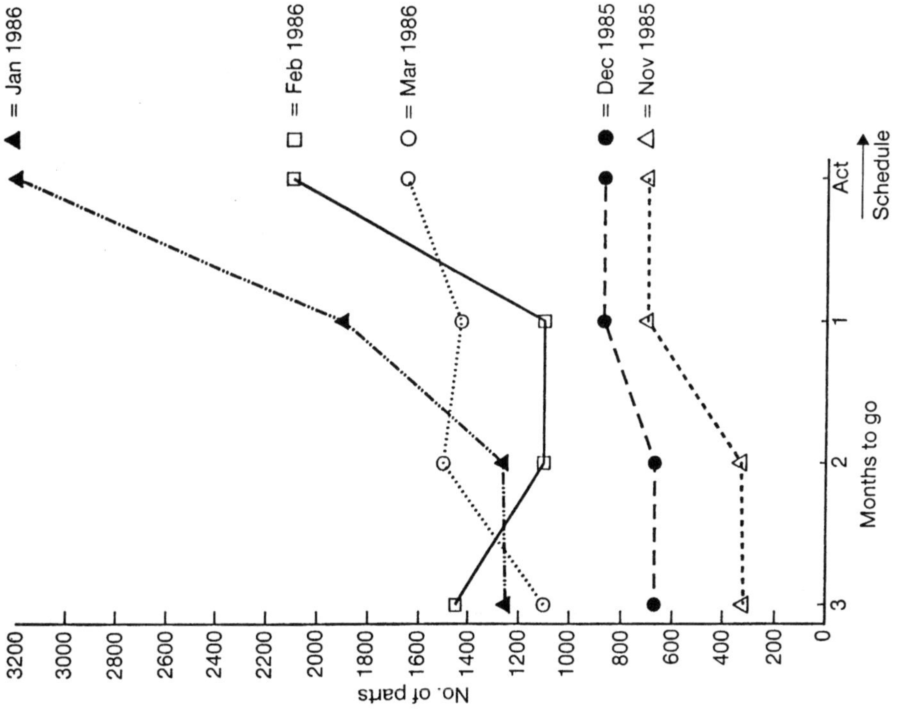
▲ = Jan 1986
□ = Feb 1986
O = Mar 1986
● = Dec 1985
△ = Nov 1985
No. of parts
3200
3000
2800
2600
2400
2200
2000
1800
1600
1400
1200
1000
800
600
400
200
0
3
2
1
Act
Months to go
Schedule

APPENDIX 26.4
MF: CHANGES IN 20-DAY DELIVERY PLANNING REPORTS

The 20-day delivery planning reports are based on firm orders with a minimum of forecast information, and are based on more recent information than the material delivery schedules. Demand is exploded into 15 buckets covering the next four weeks as follows:

- Weeks 1 and 2: track and CKD in detail.
- Weeks 3 and 4: track and CKD in total.

The reports are run weekly, and it is intended that schedules for weeks 1 and 2 should be firm. In fact, some rescheduling takes place even in these weeks to cater for such problems as material shortages.

The analysis below in Table 26.5 follows changes in seven consecutive 20-day reports. Information is arranged in such a way that it is possible to see the successive schedules for each week:

- Report date is given down the left-hand side (e.g. week commencing 26.7.86).
- The week ending date for the requirements shown is given along the top (e.g. week ending 8.8.86).

The changes in scheduled demand from one report to the next can then be seen from the figures in the column under the appropriate week ending date.

Note that week 1 changes can be caused by CKD packs which have not been closed and the demand cancelled (e.g. part no. 1676690 M92). Twenty-day reports do not require interpretation in the light of known stock movements.

Table 26.5 Changes in 20-day delivery planning reports

Part no.	*Week commencing*	*Week ending*							
		8.8	*15.8*	*22.8*	*29.8*	*5.9*	*12.9*	*19.9*	*26.9*
1676690 M92	26.7	190	217	134	104				
	4.8	262	145	158	77				
	11.8		275	110	128	128			
	18.8			264	183	149	32		
	25.8				261	84	150	86	
	1.9					202	144	111	152
	8.9						146	120	153
1691745 M91	26.7	16	80	80	31				
(DX phase out)	4.8	16	80	80	31				
	11.8		19	80	80	41			
	18.8			65	65	71	10		
	25.8				61	80	38	3	
	1.9					72	62	–	–
	8.9						62	22	–
1868283 M5	26.7	54	97	157	215				
	4.8	55	97	157	215				
	11.8		133	155	239	111			
	18.8			173	168	158	215		
	25.8				162	128	123	181	
	1.9					112	140	164	205
	8.9						129	167	193
1868285 M3	26.7	266	223	294	306				
	4.8	291	319	270	179				
	11.8		357	367	218	307			
	18.8			379	160	315	310		
	25.8				404	283	266	184	
	1.9					509	275	128	238
	8.9						514	187	249

CASE 27

Farnray Tools

Christine Harland

Case date 1992

THE BEGINNINGS OF THE COMPANY

Mike Ray and Tony Farnham had formed a small engineering company in 1977, Farnray Tools, that made small wooden-handled garden tools such as trowels and hand forks.

Mike and Tony had started in a small unit on what was grandly called an industrial estate in Woburn Sands, just outside Milton Keynes. In reality it was a few outbuildings attached to an old farm at the end of a lane. When the business started and was making two main products, trowels and forks, it was reasonably easy to calculate how many of which products should be made and when they should be made. Mike used to go out on the road selling to the smaller garden centres, using samples. When he gained an order he and Tony would work out what materials they needed then make the required quantity for that particular order. When they had several orders at the same time, Tony would tend to concentrate on manufacturing while Mike handled the liaison with the customers, bought the parts and raw materials they needed, and ensured they were delivered on time.

Mike Ray bought the timber for the handles from a local timber merchant who gave him a good deal if he bought reasonable quantities, so he tended to place an order with him about every three months and stored the timber at the back of the workshop. He bought the fixings when he noticed the bin was getting low; again this tended to be every few months. The blades of the garden tools were forgings which they bought in from a forge in Brierley Hill in the West Midlands. It was prohibitively expensive to buy these as required from the forge so Mike did a calculation of how many he thought they would use over the next couple of months and had them forged in one go. This was always a bit speculative because the garden centres and distributors he sold to were reluctant to commit themselves ahead; he accepted their best guesses of future business then hoped the orders would come in. Occasionally they had a problem when their stock of an item was wiped out unexpectedly by a large order; on the whole, though, they managed to keep a reasonably safe amount of stock around them.

Since the company was formed it had grown in size and expanded its product range to include building and DIY tools and also larger garden tools like spades and hoes. By 1992, Farnray had a turnover of nearly £2 million and employed 28 people in total, 18 of them direct shop-floor operatives. The roles of the other ten are shown in the organisation chart in Fig. 27.1.

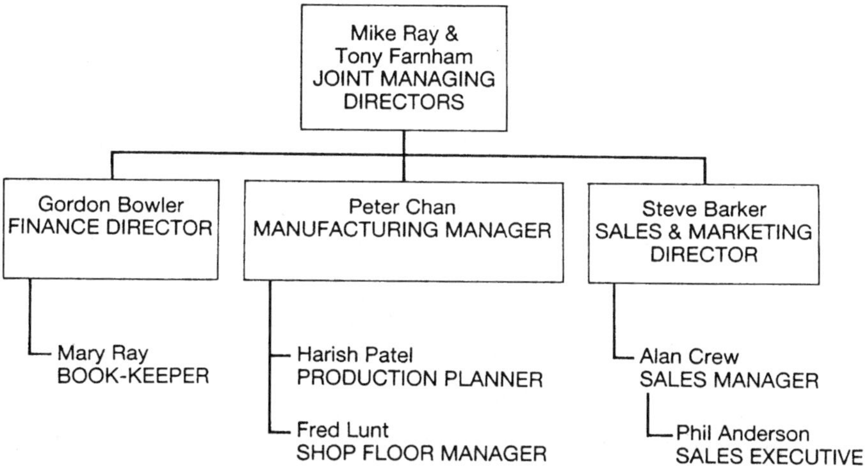

Fig. 27.1 Farnray Tools organisation chart

Farnray had moved to a newly built industrial estate on the edge of Milton Keynes which had more shop-floor space into which to expand. As the company had grown, Mike's and Tony's roles were similar to before; Tony looked after product design, manufacturing and the operations of the business while Mike concentrated on ensuring the customers were satisfied and keeping the company afloat financially. They had found it necessary to bring in a finance director and a sales and marketing director. Mike had brought in his wife, Mary, to help with the book-keeping, payroll and some typing.

While everyone in the company respected Mike's selling abilities, he had never managed to sell to the buyers in the centralised purchasing units for the 'sheds' (the large warehouse DIY chains). Steve Barker was recruited as Sales and Marketing Director specifically because of his experience of dealing with these buyers; he had previously been a sales manager for a large power tools manufacturer. Within six months of joining, Steve had managed to get a small order from Sellecks, one of the largest UK DIY superstores, for part of Farnray's range of builder's tools and all of their range of garden tools. It was recognised that this was a trial order and that if they performed well and kept to the delivery schedule there were possibilities of significant orders from them in the future.

Sellecks was over twenty times the size of any of Farnray's existing customers. They were a professional organisation who were used to dealing with organised sales departments with good information systems. The systems at Farnray were likely to be somewhat of a shock to them.

THE SYSTEMS

Farnray's systems were still largely manual and time-consuming to operate. They were also prone to such inaccuracies as misfiled invoices, purchase orders that were placed by telephone and never confirmed in writing and many other irritating occurrences. Mistakes had been made in the past because of this overloaded manual system.

Gordon Bowler, the Finance Director, used to be a finance manager at a powder coatings company where he had been responsible for computerising the ledgers, invoicing and payroll of the accounts department. He proposed that they buy a reasonable size PC-based integrated financial system with sales order processing as part of it. Mary Ray had been pushing her husband for some time to computerise the ledgers as the volume of ledger transactions was becoming more than she could handle.

After reviewing the available systems with their local dealers, a quick decision was made to buy the following modules from the OWL suite, a business management system:

- purchase, sales and nominal ledgers
- invoicing
- sales order processing
- inventory management
- job costing
- payroll.

Gordon passed the details of the inventory management module to Peter Chan, the Manufacturing Manager, for implementation.

When Peter dropped the details of the inventory management module on the desk of his Production Planner, Harish Patel, it brightened up Harish's day. Up until then, Harish had been manually calculating the purchase requirements for the next three months on all of the 850 parts used in the business. Each week of the month he looked at the records for one-quarter of the parts. For each one he had to check the bin card to see the balance of inventory, look at the usage over the last few months, then place orders to cover them for the next few months, trying to keep a few weeks safety stock as protection. One of the bin cards is shown in Fig. 27.2.

Harish's job was quite routine really. On Mondays he issued the production plan for the week and raised all the works orders for the shop-floor. On Tuesdays and Wednesdays he checked inventory and raised purchase orders. On Thursdays he went to college and on Fridays he worked out the following week's production plan, taking into account the arrears from the current week. He drew up a plan for production of the numbers of each finished product, an extract of which is shown in Table 27.1.

STOCK RECORD CARD PART NUMBER DESCRIPTION SUPPLIER			
ISSUE/RECEIPT	BALANCE	ISSUE/RECEIPT	BALANCE

Fig. 27.2 Bin card

Table 27.1 Production plan, end items

	Arrears	*24*	*25*	*26*	*27*	*28*	*29*	*30*
00265	290	400	450	400	400			
00310	680	0	1000					
00311	3500	1200	1400	1200	1200			
00326	890	60						

Harish asked if he could go for a day's training to the systems dealer from whom they had bought the inventory management module. One day's training on each module was included in the package so Peter thought it was a good idea. Harish had been going to night school and doing one-day-a-week day release at a local technical college to study for a diploma in production and inventory control. Quite a large part of the course had been on manufacturing planning and control systems, and in particular materials requirements planning (MRP I). When he returned to work after the one-day training course, Harish was full of what the new system could do in the way of production planning and control. He thought they should buy the following additional modules to improve their control of production:

- bill of materials
- materials requirements planning
- purchase order management
- works order management.

At the time, Peter was working on a large problem. Harish left brochures with him for these additional modules, for him to look at when he had time. The problem Peter was working on was calculating the implications for manufacturing of a very large order just in from Sellecks. Steve Barker was full of it and was making demands left right and centre to ensure that this big important customer was 100 per cent satisfied.

Later that evening, still trying to work out how they would cope with the big Sellecks order, Peter picked up the brochures for the OWL modules in production planning and control. He had been thinking for some time that Harish would be better used managing exceptional problems than spending his time doing routine calculations. He saw the light on in Tony Farnham's office and went along to talk to him about it.

Stopping outside, he heard Steve Barker's voice. The Sales and Marketing Director was on the phone in Tony's office. Knocking first, Peter put his head round the door. Tony and Mike were both in there. Tony gestured for him to come in and sit down. Steve was obviously talking to Sellecks and his part of the telephone conversation went like this:

> *'There's no problem in delivering to a schedule or into a delivery window. You must understand though that this sudden increase at the front of the schedule may cause us a bit of a problem.* [Pause] *Yes, I'm well aware of that and we're very grateful for the opportunity. We won't let you down.* [Pause] *No, you won't need to do that, you can rely on us.'*

Mike explained to Peter that it was imperative that they got this right. He felt they had adequate space in the current workshop for the additional work and he was taking on extra staff to help them through the initial peak. Their main materials supplier, Brierley Forgings, was able to handle the extra business and he had personally negotiated a good deal with a new timber supplier, a national firm with better prices. This order could really be the breakthrough for them into the national chains. When Steve had finished on the phone, he and Mike went off to the pub to continue the chat, leaving Peter with Tony.

Peter Chan explained what it would mean to Farnray in terms of improved speeds of getting information and the reduction in time of doing manual materials and works order calculations if they computerised their production planning and control. But, most important of all, there would be the benefits of operating a planned production facility instead of the erratic operation they had at the moment. Peter expressed some concern that with their current manual system, which used historical usage to calculate materials requirements, he couldn't confirm with confidence that they could meet Selleck's order 100 per cent. The MRP systems on which Harish had brought back the details would let them project ahead the materials required and tell them when they were needed. Tony agreed to discuss it with Mike and support the suggestion to computerise the production planning and control system.

THE CONFLICT

It was obvious that something was wrong when Tony walked into Peter's office. He placed the OWL system brochures on his desk and sat down. He explained to Peter that he had joined Mike at the pub later the previous evening and mentioned Peter's concerns about their ability to cope with the Sellecks order. Mike's response was immediate and hostile. Steve had joined in the conversation to emphasize that they had to cope: there was no choice in this one. Besides, there was no capacity reason why they shouldn't manage.

Tony had suggested they at least should buy the additional production planning and control modules to help Peter and Harish with the workload. This seemed to add fuel to the fire. Mike seemed to think they would waste time playing about with computers while they should be making sure the Sellecks order was made on time. His wife Mary had also chipped in at this point and said the computer wasn't for production planning anyway, it had been bought for her to do the ledgers. That had killed the debate.

Meanwhile, Harish had been given the first sales order and schedule information on Sellecks and had been doing some calculations on what materials would be required to meet it. The first part, a new design of spade, part number 00289, had the following requirements:

Period 24 300
Period 25 200
Period 27 400
Period 29 500

As it was a new design of spade, he got the BOM from Tony Farnham. Tony had already calculated the batch sizes that would enable them to recover the set-up costs on the machines. He had also worked out how long should be allowed for the batches to be made or bought. This information is shown below in Tables 27.2 and 27.3.

Table 27.2 Bill of materials for new spade

Level	*Part No.*	*Description*	*Quantity*
0	00289	Spade	1
.1	10089	Handle Assy	1
..2	10278	Handle	1
..2	10062	Nail	2
.1	10077	Shaft	1
.1	10023	Connector	1
.1	10062	Nail	4
.1	10045	Rivet	4
.1	10316	Blade Assy	1
..2	10992	Blade	1
..2	10045	Rivet	2

Table 27.3 Manufacturing data for new spade

Part No.	*Order quantity*	*Lead time*
00289	500	1
10089	1500	1
10278	500	2
10062	2000	1
10077	400	1
10023	700	1
10045	2000	1
10316	200	1
10992	200	4

As most of the parts were already used in existing designs, Harish did a quick check of the stock situation for each one by looking at the bin cards. This is shown in Table 27.4.

Table 27.4 Stock position

Part No.	*On hand*
00289	300
10089	350
10278	800
10062	0
10077	50
10023	350
10045	400
10316	0
10992	30

Harish set to work to calculate manually how many of each part were required and when. To help him he drew up a form similar to that used in an MRP system (copy attached in Appendix 27.1). From his calculations, he immediately saw a problem in satisfying the Sellecks order.

Questions

1 What problem became evident to Harish? Fill in the blank materials requirements records headed 'MRP exercise' to find this out.

2 What are the likely difficulties that Farnray will face if they continue to use their existing system of calculating materials requirements?

3 What practical problems do you think Peter Chan faces?

APPENDIX 27.1
MRP EXERCISE

Part number	00289	21	22	23	24	25	26	27	28	29	30
Requirements (gross)											
Scheduled receipts											
On hand inventory											
Planned order release											

Part number	10089	21	22	23	24	25	26	27	28	29	30
Requirements (gross)											
Scheduled receipts											
On hand inventory											
Planned order release											

Part number	10278	21	22	23	24	25	26	27	28	29	30
Requirements (gross)											
Scheduled receipts											
On hand inventory											
Planned order release											

Part number	10062	21	22	23	24	25	26	27	28	29	30
Requirements (gross)											
Scheduled receipts											
On hand inventory											
Planned order release											

Part number	10077	21	22	23	24	25	26	27	28	29	30
Requirements (gross)											
Scheduled receipts											
On hand inventory											
Planned order release											

Part number 10023	21	22	23	24	25	26	27	28	29	30
Requirements (gross)										
Scheduled receipts										
On hand inventory										
Planned order release										

Part number 10045	21	22	23	24	25	26	27	28	29	30
Requirements (gross)										
Scheduled receipts										
On hand inventory										
Planned order release										

Part number 10316	21	22	23	24	25	26	27	28	29	30
Requirements (gross)										
Scheduled receipts										
On hand inventory										
Planned order release										

Part number 10992	21	22	23	24	25	26	27	28	29	30
Requirements (gross)										
Scheduled receipts										
On hand inventory										
Planned order release										

Part number	21	22	23	24	25	26	27	28	29	30
Requirements (gross)										
Scheduled receipts										
On hand inventory										
Planned order release										

CASE 28

Tesco Composites

Alan Harrison

Case date 1992

INTRODUCTION

Tesco is one of Europe's largest retailers with annual sales of over £6 billion and with over 9 million square feet of sales area. The company is committed to growth and is currently involved in a £1 billion investment programme with over 20 new stores being opened each year. A Tesco Superstore has over 25 000 square feet of selling area and carries some 16 000 different products.

During the 1980s, distribution to retail stores was handled by 26 depots. These operated on a single temperature, single product basis and were small and relatively inefficient. The delivery volume to each store was also relatively low, and it was not economic to deliver to all stores each day. Goods which required temperature controlled environments had to be carried on separate vehicles. Five of these were needed to deliver the full range of products to each Tesco store. Each product group had different ordering systems, some of which were owned by the distribution contractor and were not specifically designed for Tesco needs. This network of depots simply could not cope with the growth in volume and the increasingly high standards of temperature control. A new distribution strategy was needed.

COMPOSITE DISTRIBUTION

Such a new approach to distribution had been pioneered in the UK by Sainsbury. Many small depots with limited temperature control facilities were replaced by a smaller number of 'composite' depots which can handle many products at several temperature ranges and so provide a cost effective daily delivery service to all stores. Typically, a composite depot can handle over 30 million cases per year on a 15 acre site which includes vehicle maintenance and repair facilities. The warehouse building comprises 250 000 square feet broken down into temperature zones such as ambient, –25°C (frozen), 0°C (chilled), +5°C (chill) and +10°C (semi-ambient).

Each depot serves a region which contains about 50 retail stores. Delivery vehicles for composite depots use insulated trailers which can be divided into chambers by means of movable bulkheads so they can operate three different temperatures simultaneously. Short life products are received by each composite during the afternoon and evening and delivered to the stores before trading commences the next day. This is called the 'first wave'. Longer life and ambient products which are stock lines are delivered to stores on the 'second wave' between 8.00 a.m. and 8.00 p.m. Deliveries to stores are made at agreed, scheduled times. The composite operates 24 hours a day, 364 days per year.

TESCO'S DECISION

Tesco undertook a detailed appraisal of their distribution policy, and used NFC consultancy group to analyse their requirements and to produce a tender specification. NFC is the UK's largest logistics and moving company, and comprises a number of divisions of which the consultancy group is one. The tender specification could be used as a blueprint for quotations from third-party distribution specialists such as NFC Contract Distribution. By early 1987 Tesco Distribution took the decision to completely modernise their distribution system by opening eight composite depots in one year, a very ambitious and high-risk strategy. To minimise this risk, they chose third-party operators with a proven track record in the design, building, implementation and operation of such composite depots. Tesco Retail were sceptical that such a departure from current methods could be made to work without a major disruption to the smooth and accurate flow of goods. It rarely happened, but Tesco Retail were over-ruled on this occasion.

THE CONTRACTS FOR CHEPSTOW AND DIDCOT

NFC Contract Distribution were invited to tender for two sites, one for the south-west region (Chepstow) and one for the central south region (Didcot). Both were scheduled to open in March 1989, as shown in Table 28.1:

Table 28.1 Schedule of depot start dates (goods out)

Depot	*Goods out*
CHEPSTOW	6th March, 1989
Harlow	13th March
DIDCOT	20th March
Doncaster	3rd April
Middleton	10th April
Livingstone	17th April
Hinckley	17th April
Snodland	6th June

These two large contracts represented high growth potential to what was at the time a relatively small company in the distribution business. Acceptance of the NFC tender was indicated by Tesco in June 1987 and heads of agreement were signed in August of that year. The main operational aspects of the contract were as follows:

1 *Warehouse* Each warehouse was to operate on a three shift basis from midday Sunday to midday Saturday. One hundred and forty warehouse staff and 39 clerical and administrative support staff would be employed at each site. Over 4000 product lines would be handled at four temperature regimes. The latest high level racking and material handling techniques would be used. NFC were to be responsible for stock management using Tesco's DALLAS computer system.

2 *Transport* Using a fleet of 40 units and 60 composite trailers on each site, the transport function was also to operate on a multishift basis, providing two delivery waves to the retail stores. Absence of a suitable composite trailer on the UK market determined the need for NFC Engineering to design a trailer with three adjustable compartments capable of operating at different temperatures.

3 *Management* The two composites would operate under the control of a general manager, supported by a commercial manager. A distribution centre manager would report to the general manager at each site. The management structure under the Distribution Centre Manager is shown in Appendix 28.1, representing a total of 54 management staff.

4 *Industrial Relations* The depots were to operate as independent locations with their own unions agreements and their own terms and conditions of employment. It was expected that USDAW would be appointed at Didcot, and that T&GWU would be given Chepstow. Single status terms and conditions would apply to all levels, with a minimum number of grades to promote flexibility. All staff were on salaried status and to assist motivation, quarterly merit bonus payments would be based on individual performance.

5 *Contractual Agreement* Formal five-year contracts effective from the commencement of operations at each depot were due to be concluded in mid-1988. The main principles were:

   (a) 12 months notice;
   (b) annually agreed revenue and capital budgets;
   (c) provision of management accounts and formal review meetings to approve NFC costs;
   (d) payment of budgeted amounts in week two of each period;
   (e) provision for half yearly audits by Tesco, and access to accounts at other times;
   (f) agreement of stock lost tolerance;
   (g) redundancy to be borne by Tesco unless termination of the contract due to NFC default.

6 *Financial* A total annual revenue of £1.6m was targeted with management fees of £1.7m linked to 33m cases. The management fee would be adjusted to take

account of changes in throughput volumes by reference to an 'S' curve with a fallback limit. The management fee would be adjusted by inflation. An incentive/penalty scheme was planned whereby up to 10 per cent of the management fee could be gained or lost during the development and start-up phase. All project management and start-up costs were to be reimbursed by Tesco. No management fee was expected at this stage. Instead a modest recovery of overhead would be made. A government grant (the Welsh Office) of up to £600k was to be obtained, the full benefit of which would be passed back to Tesco.

Full site capacity was established at 52m cases. Tesco had chosen 'open book' contract terms, whereby all information about operating methods within the depots, productivity ratios and detailed costs are made available by the contractor. The information is jointly reviewed every four weeks together with plans for future months. Performance at different depots can thereby be compared and best practice learned and incorporated at each as the business develops. In this way, Tesco retain maximum control over the distribution network, and gain full benefit from productivity savings. From the contractor's point of view, 'open book' terms virtually guarantee that all reasonable operating costs will be recovered. A bar chart for the project is shown in Appendix 28.2.

START-UP

This phase of the project is documented a year later. By this time, although Chepstow had started operating on schedule, Didcot was delayed by 13 weeks. This meant that NFC Contract Distribution could not achieve the budgeted contribution. In addition the payment of the management fee was fixed from the goods-in date to the goods-out date (a loss of two weeks contribution). The initial budgeted volume was not achieved, which resulted in the fallback management fee being charged in the first year.

Tesco increased the specification of the depots so that they were required to be open on Saturday afternoon and on Sunday from 6.00 a.m. This meant that more shifts were needed, and resulted in an increase in warehouse staffing from 140 full-time equivalent heads to 163. The number of temperature regimes was increased from four to five to include a +1°C chamber in addition to ambient, –25°C, 0°C and +5°C. A change in Tesco strategy to deliver produce (e.g. fresh fruit and vegetables) and fresh meat and poultry in trays initiated the requirement for an on-site traywash facility which increased the operational areas from 250 000 square feet to 283 000 square feet at Chepstow and from 260 000 square feet to 280 000 square feet at Didcot.

The original plans to equip the sites with new fleets of composite trailers was changed so that Tesco's ex-produce fleet could be integrated into composite by modifications to two temperature compartment trailers. This had three knock-on effects:

1 an increase in the number of journeys which was compounded by environmental delivery restrictions in the London area;

2 an increase in the number of drivers from 65 to 80 at Chepstow and from 55 to 76 at Didcot;

3 an increase in resource levels to cope with the restrictions on temperature flexibility in transit.

The following table summarises the changes in equipment which were needed.

Table 28.2 Summary of necessary equipment changes

Depot	*Units*		*Trailers*		*Rigids*	
	Proposed	Actual	Proposed	Actual	Proposed	Actual
Chepstow	42	60	67	64	None	10
Didcot	36	51	54	77	None	4

During the course of 1988 Tesco, using the basic NFC specification, built two prototype three-compartment composite temperature trailers. Exhaustive experiments led to the adoption of the NFC-designed frontmounted Marshal-Thermoking refrigeration units, for the NFC sites and a small number of 8m trailers, with underslung refrigeration units.

Due to the need to cover additional shifts and the increased complexity of the warehouse operation, not least in relation to the extra temperature regime and the traywash, the management resource was increased from 27 to 47 at Chepstow and from 27 to 48 at Didcot.

One third of the way through the building programme Tesco decided to incorporate traywash operations on-site with the result that the handover to NFC was piecemeal, chamber by chamber. This caused considerable problems for the operational management and staff, particularly with regard to the maintenance of the required standards of hygiene, in the control of the ingress and egress of vehicles to the yard area. However the 16-week take-on programme for both depots agreed with Tesco distribution was adhered to throughout with no disruption to their retail organisation.

Formal contracts for each site were eventually signed. The main difference from the original concept was that six months notice of termination was agreed instead of 12 months.

Difficulty was experienced in agreeing the first year operational budget. Tesco insisted on a productivity of 65 cases per warehouse hour overall. This would have equated to a productivity level of 84 BSI, which was impossible in a non-incentivised environment. Subsequently, Tesco had to revise their productivity figures in line with the original NFC budget proposals. In addition, Tesco imposed a ceiling on warehouse salaries at Didcot against NFC management advice which was based on an independent survey of local wage rates. The extreme difficulty experienced in recruiting staff as a consequence forced Tesco to reappraise the situation and resulted in salaries being offered in line with the original NFC budget proposals. The delay in coming to this decision caused considerable disruption to the recruitment programme. Formal period reviews were initiated and held throughout the start-up phase. All pre-operational start-up costs were reimbursed.

When the project was prepared, it was envisaged that capital expenditure would be incurred as is shown in the table below:

Table 28.3 Envisaged capital expenditure

	1989	*1990*
	£'000	*£'000*
NFC Leasing: Vehicles, equipment, trailers	10695	289
NFC Finance – sundry equipment	160	10
Own Account	40	None
Total (£'000)	10895	299

In the event, Tesco decided in principle to acquire substantially all of the assets for their composites, mainly to make for an easier divorce if the contract should fail, but also having regard to the competitive terms available to them.

NFC put forward proposals for a Lincoln scrubber and CCTV system; both of which were rejected by Tesco. However, NFC management were convinced that both items represented a good investment and entered into five-year agreements with the suppliers at an annual cost of £24k per site.

EARLY OPERATIONAL PHASE

A year has since elapsed. After 14 weeks at Chepstow and 18 weeks at Didcot from the first day of goods-out, both depots were delivering in excess of 500 000 cases per week. In the case of Chepstow these actual volumes were 23.8 per cent above budget, due to the fact that the summer peak in demand in the south west brought about by the holiday trade was not anticipated when the budget was originally set. Despite these high volumes, the very demanding take-on programme was adhered to while at the same time Tesco resisted NFC management's requests for increased resource in line with these volumes. Staff turnover was significantly higher than expected and the learning curve was unnecessarily elongated for this reason.

Tesco eventually recognised that higher staffing levels were needed and advised NFC to recruit. This requirement to recruit a considerable number of staff in a very short timescale put additional pressure on the local management team, already stretched due to the start-up. The shortfall was addressed through the use of agency staff who were not of the right quality resulting in a drop in standards, particularly hygiene, and thereby straining the relationship between Tesco and NFC management.

Tesco believed that they had the corporate muscle to ensure an even flow throughout the day of goods-in from suppliers. NFC management did not share this view and were proved, unfortunately, correct in the light of experience. The immediate impact was the rescheduling of employees' hours to meet this demand which, together with the higher volumes, created a potentially difficult industrial relations situation.

This compression of workload was detrimental to the quality of assembly and severely stretched the administrative support system. As a result of the level of picking accuracy (the accuracy with which orders were selected from composite depot stock for delivery to the stores) being below that which was anticipated Tesco retail lost confidence in the system and applied pressure on their Distribution division to abandon the 'no claims' drop and drive policy. As a result Retail was able to charge Distribution for delivery shortfalls. NFC was given the go-ahead to recruit clerical staff, and their numbers were increased from 39 to 66, but not in time to deal with the number of claims that followed. Tesco distribution insisted on maintaining the fast 'drop and drive' turn around times with the result that product checking at the store back doors could not take place. As a result, NFC could not prove the accuracy of their service which they believed, from independent checks in their warehouses, was much higher than retail claims would suggest.

NFC's senior management were criticised for their inadequate support of Administration from Head Office. This situation was further exacerbated by the long lead time for implementation of a new computer system. Recognising this shortfall, NFC management took the decision to split the on-site administration function and appoint an accounts/statistics manager for each site. This cost was borne by NFC and as a consequence, contribution was reduced. The resulting benefits were recognised by Tesco. However, for the last five accounting periods of the 1989/90 year they imposed expenditure limits.

Questions

1 Evaluate the list of changes to the original project plan:
   (a) what is the likely effect of the changes on NFC's sales and profitability during the first two years of operation?
   (b) which of the changes is likely to have a harmful effect on the original project objectives?

2 Evaluate the description of the contract terms set out in the case. What are the major risks to NFC and to Tesco?

3 What are the advantages and disadvantages of 'open book' contract terms in this situation?

APPENDIX 28.1
DEPOT ORGANISATION STRUCTURE

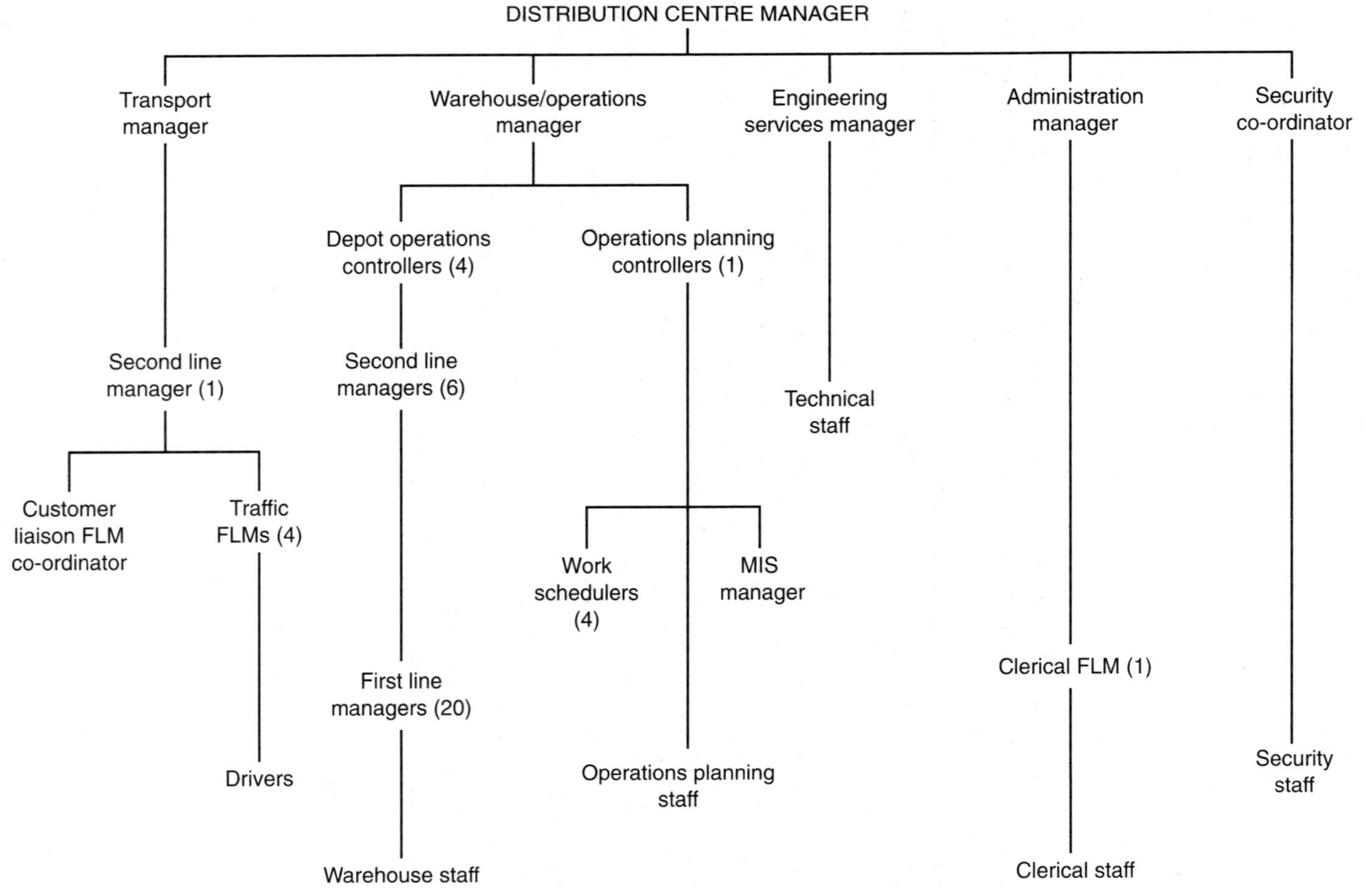

APPENDIX 28.2
PROJECT BAR CHART

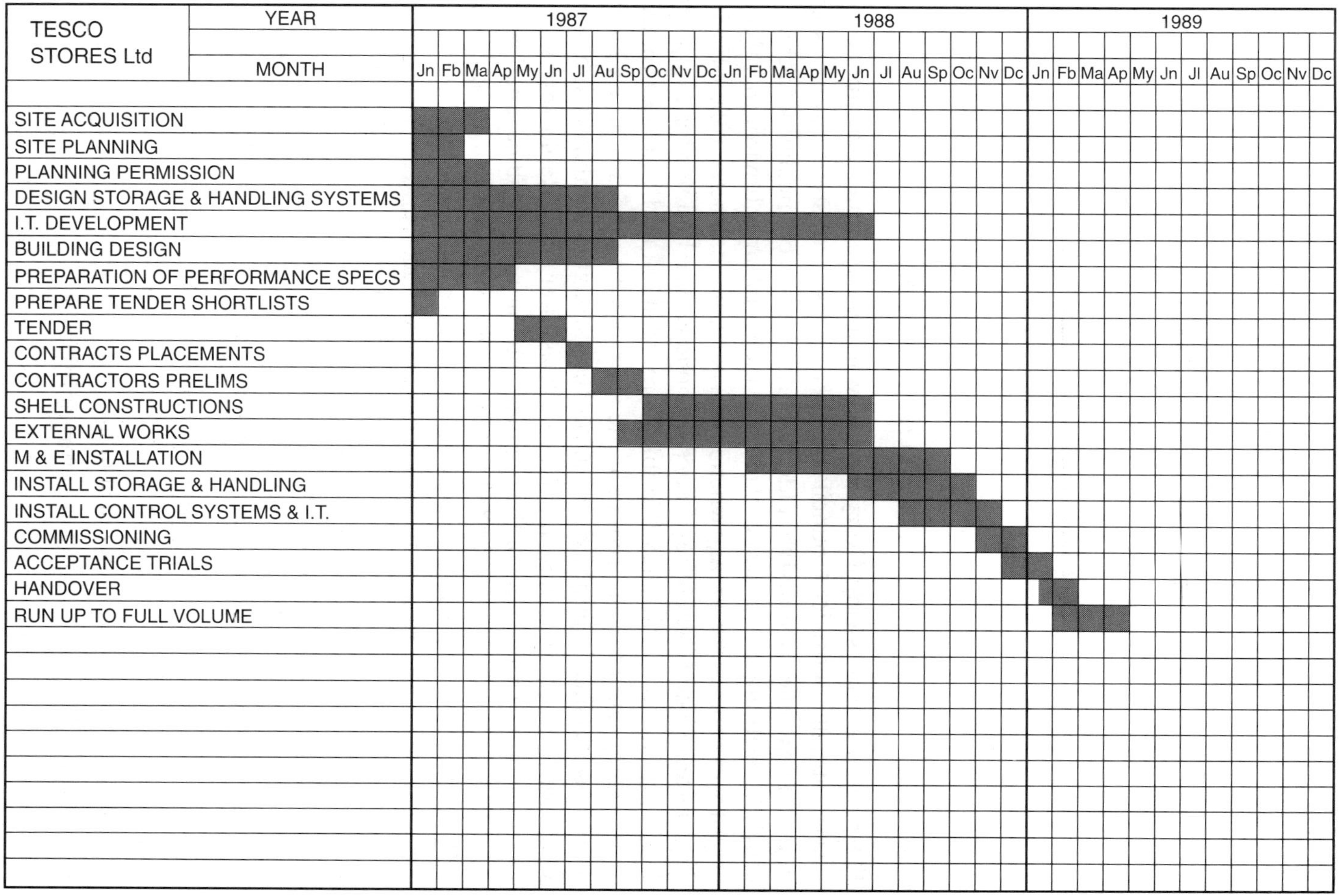

CASE 29

Valley District Council Cleansing Services

John Bicheno and Alan Harrison

Case date March 1996

INTRODUCTION

The party was in full swing. Everyone who was anyone connected with the Cleansing Service at Valley District Council was there. Dustmen, street sweepers and civic amenity site workers rubbed shoulders with the mayor, councillors and chief officers. Why? To celebrate the success of Valley Council's 'Cleaner Environment' campaign.

It all began some 10 years ago when Teresa New, the chairperson of the Environment Committee, visited the United States on holiday. She had used the opportunity to call in on the 'Keep America Beautiful' organisation, and had been impressed by their systems approach to reducing the sources and causes of litter. Each source should be specifically targeted and improved through a combination of awareness, education, enforcement and facilities such as litter bins. Rapid response to litter accumulation was also part of the organisation's approach, since it had been shown that a cleaner environment tended to remain clean, while litter promoted yet more littering. One particular point that stuck in Teresa's mind was 'if you don't measure the incidence of littering, you will never know if you are wasting your ratepayer's money, and you won't know how to focus your campaign'. As a hard-nosed accountant, this had particular appeal to Teresa.

On returning home, Teresa made a bee line for the Tidy Britain Group (TBG). This is an independent charity, part-funded by the Department of the Environment, with a specific brief as the national litter abatement agency. TBG works through six initiatives:

- *Awards.* Recognising excellence through campaigns such as *Britain in Bloom*
- *Consultancy.* Through the group's Environmental Research and Consultancy Unit
- *Research.* Such as developing standard ways to measure litter
- *People and Places.* Working at community level
- *Campaigning.* To raise awareness and the need for action
- *Education.* Targeting schools in particular.

TBG offered invaluable assistance, and recommended use of the international 'Tidyman' symbol shown in Fig. 29.1.

Several years and seemingly innumerable meetings later, Valley Council had adopted a complete package of measures proposed by the Environment Committee. Today's party was being held to celebrate the achievements these measures had made, that is a 40 per cent reduction in the litter count from an average 27 pieces to the current 16.

Fig. 29.1 International 'Tidyman' symbol

Valley District Council is one of three local authorities in a county in South Wales. The Council's area includes one town of moderate size, four smaller towns and over 40 villages. The population and most of the industry is concentrated in the south. The Council undertakes the normal range of services required of a non-metropolitan district council. Services include recreation and tourism, environmental health, housing, planning and economic development, and cleansing services.

The Cleansing Service basically undertakes refuse collection and disposal and street cleansing. It runs civic amenity sites where garden waste and bulky objects can be left, and container services comprising both compacted waste from office buildings and other waste removed in open skips. The Cleansing Service has been subjected to compulsory competitive tendering and the compactor vehicles used for refuse collection are now run by contractors, with crews supplied by the District Council. For operating purposes, the Cleansing Service is divided into three depot areas, known simply as North, Mid and South, each controlled by a superintendent.

Street sweepers at Valley have a routine which requires them to cover all high street areas on their 'beat' once per day. Other areas are covered in a specified frequency which ranges from twice per week to once per month. Actual sweeping may not be needed, so the sweepers spend much of their time picking up litter with a scoop which looks like a domestic dustpan with a long handle. Their other equipment comprises a trolley with bins and brushes. A proportion of each day is left to the sweepers' own initiative. During these periods, sweepers can clean whatever area they think has highest priority. Since all of the sweepers live close to or on their beat, this has proved quite successful.

Apart from competitive tendering, several innovations have been undertaken in the last few years. These include new crew sizes, different plastic bags, trials with wheeled containers for business uses, mechanised sweeping in the Mid region, more litter bins of various types, and most recently 'doggy' bins. The doggy bin scheme had enjoyed priority since a private members' bill had gone through Parliament. A dog owner who did not clear up after their pet could now be fined up to £1000. Councillors and officers were now considering how the law could now be enforced, and in the light of the success with the litter campaign, how it might be measured.

Over the last two years, Valley had embarked on a Total Quality programme. Senior and middle-ranking officers had attended courses and were encouraged to adopt a 'TQ' philosophy by becoming more 'customer focused'. Several of the courses, however, made use of manufacturing examples and it was not always clear how the tools and techniques discussed in the courses could be adopted for use within the District Council.

MEASURING PERFORMANCE

The principal performance measures used at Valley are based on quality and productivity. Productivity is measured by sacks per man per year, and by cost per sack and per tonne removed. Were possible, these figures are compared with corresponding national data, but there is always controversy over such comparisons. Areas with relatively poor performance go to considerable lengths to explain why they are 'different'. 'Quality' of the Cleansing Service has traditionally been measured by complaints received. A recent analysis is shown in Table 29.1 for the Mid depot area:

Table 29.1 Analysis of complaints received during 20 days last month

Complaint	*Number received*	*Maximum in 1 day*
Late collection	158	31
Missed collection	29	4
Spillage	89	16
Broken bags	22	3
Bags not delivered	67	6
Litter	10	4
Dog fouling	14	2
Dangerous driving	5	2
All other	18	2

Since her visit to the United States, Teresa had been convinced that measurement was fundamental to the success of the litter campaign, and insisted that additional measures to these must be devised. Eventually, the Cleansing Service decided on a modified version of methods recommended by TBG and 'Keep America Beautiful'. This required that 12 sites should be selected, each comprising 200 metres of typical high street pavement. Each day, four of the sites would be selected at random, and all pieces of litter would be counted whatever their size between the building line and the roadside edge of the gutter. Thus sweetpapers, cigarette ends, matches, soft drink cans and newspaper pages each count as one item. The sites themselves were kept secret, known only to four people within the Cleansing Service. Even the method used was kept confidential to a selection of council officers and councillors on the Environment Committee. In particular, neither the method nor the sites were disclosed to street sweepers or to shopowners adjoining the sites. Table 29.2 gives a sample of recent measures.

Table 29.2 Items of litter by sample area

		Area	*Items*	*Area*	*Items*	*Area*	*Items*	*Area*	*Items*
Week 1	Mon	S	111	N	10	M	109	S	90
	Tue	M	3	N	12	N	8	N	16
	Wed	S	29	M	15	N	20	M	14
	Thurs	N	11	S	36	M	69	N	13
	Fri	S	27	N	6	S	3	N	5
Week 2	Mon	M	90	N	13	N	14	N	15
	Tue	S	24	M	24	M	14	S	18
	Wed	N	19	N	11	S	27	N	11
	Thurs	S	11	S	22	S	12	N	6
	Fri	M	4	S	15	N	1	S	28
Week 3	Mon	N	15	M	144	S	44	N	8
	Tue	M	15	N	13	M	10	S	28
	Wed	M	14	S	25	M	5	S	34
	Thurs	M	16	M	18	N	19	S	31
	Fri	N	21	S	37	N	10	M	12
Week 4	Mon	S	49	M	88	S	83	M	120
	Tue	M	9	M	16	N	15	M	17
	Wed	S	22	N	9	S	35	N	17
	Thurs	M	15	N	13	S	24	M	6
	Fri	M	19	M	5	N	4	M	18
Week 5	Mon	S	73	S	44	M	60	M	127
	Tue	N	3	M	17	M	18	N	10
	Wed	M	54	N	9	S	25	M	38
	Thurs	S	15	S	20	N	10	N	19
	Fri	S	27	S	29	S	34	M	7

AT THE PARTY

During the party the Chairman of Valley District Council, Kevin Anderson, was introduced to staff by the Chief Cleansing officer, Stan Verrier. In talking to one of the street sweepers, A.J. Williams, Councillor Anderson asked A.J. what he thought about the state of the streets. A.J. replied that he thought that while some areas had improved, 'there are still some very bad streets where people just don't seem to care. No matter how many times I clean them, they're always a mess the next day'. Councillor Anderson took Stan to one side, and said 'People like A.J. are just trying to protect their jobs. We have to translate the success of our litter campaign into cost reductions that we can pass on to the ratepayers.'

In another part of the room, Councillor Teresa New was speaking to two of the street sweepers. 'But how do you know that there has been a 40 per cent reduction in litter?' asked Dai Jones. This put Teresa on the spot. 'We have a measurement system', she said, 'but you'll have to ask Mr Verrier how it works.' This rather spoiled the evening for the two sweepers. Were they being spied on, they wondered?

Later at the party, Stan Verrier was speaking to Councillor Gareth Edwards, a management consultant and member of the Environment Committee. Gareth suggested to Stan that the litter data could be plotted on an SPC chart. Stan said that he had heard about SPC at the Total Quality courses, but was reluctant to try SPC because 'no one in Cleansing Services is a statistician'. Gareth then said to Stan that SPC really stands for making a process 'Stable, Predictable and in Control'. 'I had never thought of it that way', said Stan.

Questions

1 Should the measurement system for the litter campaign be more widely understood?

2 What do you think about Councillor Anderson's remarks about 'protecting jobs'?

3 How could SPC be used at Valley to analyse the number of litter items by sample area? (*Clue*: use a Number of Defects (c) control chart, and analyse the data by depot area ignoring Mondays.)

$$\bar{c} = \Sigma c/n, \text{ and } UCL = \bar{c} + 3\sqrt{\bar{c}},\ LCL = \bar{c} - 3\sqrt{\bar{c}}$$

What do the control charts suggest about the litter process at Valley?

4 Which of the other '7 Tools of SPC' could be used to analyse the litter problems at Valley, and how?

CASE 30

Sun Products Company:
An exercise in variables control charting

Alan Harrison

Case date March 1996

SUN PRODUCTS COMPANY

Sun Products Company (SPC) makes a range of components for various customers in the automotive industry at home and abroad. One of these customers made an approach a year or so ago with a quality concern about the sunroof which was supplied by SPC. The customer delegation told the Sun QA Manager, Fred Jarvis:

'This is on our top 40 list of quality concerns at present. The height of the glass on the roof is often noticeably uneven, or sits too proud of the car body. We'd like to take a look around your processes to see if there are any immediate improvements we can make.'

After looking round the sunroof line at SPC, the customer delegation suggested to Fred that some improvements should be made to materials handling within the Sun works, and in the way that parts were transported from Sun suppliers. A detailed inspection of the production process with Fred and his colleagues had been made, and a process flow chart drawn up. But attention had eventually focused on the profile setting operation where the glass was fitted into the sunroof mechanism. A sketch of this is shown in Fig. 30.1. A 100 per cent inspection of the profile was made by probes at the end of the production process. The probes measured the height of the glass at four points on the sunroof near to the corners, represented by P1, P2, P3 and P4:

The customer specification called for a profile measure with a tolerance of ±1.00mm for each point P1 to P4. If the probes detected a condition which was out of specification for one of these points, the inspector called for the profile setting to be altered.

A month later, the customer delegation returned to Fred, and told him that they had made further investigations of their own assembly process.

'We have made a number of immediate improvements on our assembly line, such as giving the operator a step block to make the fitting process more exact and less visual.

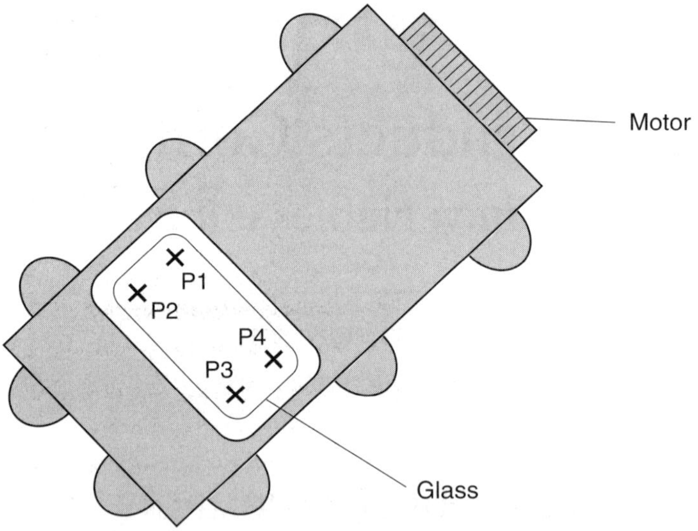

Fig. 30.1 The sunroof at Sun Products Co
(NB: Sketch only: not to Scale!)

Now we want you to introduce variable control charts on your profile setting operation. You are generating a lot of data at the inspection stage, but you're not doing enough with it! Further, you're reacting to events rather than controlling them'

These comments had come as rather a shock to Fred, who thought that Sun had installed the best kit, and that it was virtually impossible (given 100 per cent inspection of the profile) for defective products to be shipped. Nevertheless, Fred got to work, first tackling a process capability study. This came as an even greater shock! The process was clearly out of control. It seemed very difficult to maintain specification on all four points at the same time. Thus C_{pk} values of less than 1 were initially quite common. Fred concentrated first on getting rid of special causes of variability. For example, he found that when the glass supplier changed batches, the curvature of the glass could change significantly and cause problems at Sun. But once these problems had been recognised and dealt with, Fred was satisfied that control charting could start.

Although the inspection process would be left at 100 per cent for the timebeing, Fred decided on taking two samples each hour and recording the difference to specification for all four points P1 to P4. Samples would be taken for the two readings made closest to the hour. Tables 30.1 and 30.2 shows the data which were used for calculating the grand average, and the upper and lower control limits for the averages chart (X Bar Chart) for point P3. It also provides the data used to calculate the upper control limit for the range chart (R Chart) for P3.

Table 30.1 P3 data used to calculate the process capability indices

		Reading 1	*Reading 2*
Saturday 2/12	06.00hrs	+0.6mm	+0.2mm
	07.00	+0.3	+0.2
	08.00	+0.4	+0.1
	09.00	+0.1	–0.3
	10.00	–0.2	+0.0
	11.00	+0.0	+0.0
Monday 4/12	06.00	+0.2	+0.2
	07.00	–0.3	+0.1
	08.00	–0.3	+0.0
	09.00	+0.1	+0.3
	10.00	+0.6	+0.4
	11.00	+0.0	–0.2
	12.00	+0.5	+0.0
	13.00	+0.1	+0.2
	14.00	+0.1	+0.0
	15.00	+0.2	+0.3
	16.00	+0.4	+0.3
	17.00	+0.1	–0.1
Tuesday 5/12	06.00	+0.0	+0.6
	07.00	+0.2	+0.0
	08.00	–0.3	–0.1
	09.00	+0.0	–0.2
	10.00	+0.5	+0.2
	11.00	+0.1	–0.2
	12.00	–0.2	–0.1
	13.00	+0.0	+0.1
	14.00	+0.1	+0.1
	15.00	+0.0	+0.4
	16.00	–0.3	–0.1

Table 30.2 P3 data from a subsequent day's production

		Reading 1	*Reading 2*
Thursday 18/1	06.00	–0.3	–0.1
	07.00	–0.4	–0.1
	08.00	–0.2	–0.3
	09.00	–0.2	–0.2
	10.00	–0.5	–0.2
	11.00	–0.4	–0.8
	12.00	–0.7	–0.3
	13.00	+0.1	–0.1
	14.00	–0.1	–0.3
	15.00	–0.3	–0.1
	16.00	+0.1	+0.2
	17.00	+0.1	–0.1
	18.00	–0.2	–0.1
	19.00	–0.1	+0.2
Friday 19/1	06.00	–0.6	–0.4
	07.00	+0.0	–0.4
	08.00	–0.3	–0.8
	09.00	–0.5	–0.2
	10.00	–0.5	–0.2
	11.00	–0.5	–0.2
	12.00	+0.0	+0.0
	13.00	+0.1	–0.2
	14.00	+0.2	–0.1
	15.00	+0.0	+0.6
	16.00	+0.2	–0.1
	17.00	+0.2	–0.1
	18.00	+0.0	+0.0

Questions

1 Why was Sun's process before SPC implementation prone to giving problems to customer in spite of 100 per cent inspection?

2 From Table 30.1, calculate the grand average and the upper and lower control limits for the P3 profile height setting process at Sun. Use the formulae and constants given on the control chart. Plot the hourly data on the chart. Given that action on special causes is called for if there is any point outside the control limits, or if there is a run of seven points all above or all below the central line, is the process under statistical control? Does this mean that Sun no longer ships defective product?

3 Given the ±1.00mm engineering tolerance for all four profile points, calculate the C_p and the C_{pk} of the process.

For a sample size of 2, assume that $6\sigma = 5.319\ \bar{R}$.

[C_p = tolerance $\div 6\sigma$ of the process,
C_{pk} = the smaller of (the upper specification limit – the grand average) $\div 3\sigma$
and (the grand average – the lower specification limit) $\div 3\sigma$]

4 Table 30.2 shows data for P3 that was collected on a subsequent day. Again, plot the data on the $\bar{X}$ and R chart. Comment on the degree of process control this indicates.

5 The customer is now pressing for the engineering tolerances to be reduced to ±0.5mm. What effect would this have on process capability at Sun?

6 Comment on the sequence of events leading up to the introduction of control charting for the sunroof at Sun Products.

Part 4

IMPROVEMENT

Introduction

Even when an operation is designed and its activities planned and controlled, the operations manager's task is not finished. All operations, no matter how well managed, are capable of improvement. In recent years the emphasis has shifted markedly towards making improvement as one of the main responsibilities of operations managers. This section deals with four main areas:

1 *Performance measurement.* If organisations are concerned to improve what they are doing they need to know how good or bad they are at the moment and also know by how much they are improving. Performance measurement is therefore a prerequisite and essential tool for improvement.
2 *Types of improvement.* There are two different, and to some extent, opposing philosophies to improvement, breakthrough and continuous improvement.
3 *Improvement techniques.* There are many techniques that can help improve an organisation's operational performance.
4 *Total quality management (TQM).* Probably the best known philosophy of improvement.

PERFORMANCE MEASUREMENT

Performance measurement is the quantification of the performance of an operation. This may be carried out at a broad level in terms of the operations performance objectives, quality, speed, dependability, flexibility and cost, although this does not help operations managers make decisions about exactly what to change. These performance objectives will usually be measured using a variety of more detailed second order measures, some of which may impact on one or more performance objectives. Some examples of performance measures are:

- *Quality.* Number of defects, scrap level, customer complaints, or a customer satisfaction rating.
- *Speed.* Order lead times, customer processing times, frequency of delivery.
- *Dependability.* Percentage of late orders, adherence to schedule, availability of products or services.
- *Flexibility.* Time to market of new products or services, range of products and services, ability to make changes to schedules (volume and timing).
- *Cost.* Variance against budget, utilisation of resources, added value.

Measuring performance in itself is often sufficient to bring about improvement in an organisation as it shows that management is concerned about the activity being measured. However, by adding performance targets, managers can provide a better means to display the amount of change required and check progress against it. Several types of targets can be used:

1. *Historical standards.* Historical standards allow organisations to assess improvement against previous performance as historical standards are based on what has been achieved in the past.
2. *Competitor performance standards.* Competitor performance standards compare the achieved performance of the operation with that which is being achieved by one or more of the organisation's competitors.
3. *Benchmarking.* This is used to compare an organisation's performance with other organisations, often using organisations from quite different environments. The purpose is to help the organisation search out new ideas which might be copied or adapted. Deciding which organisations to benchmark against is not an easy decision and is explored in the Bristol & West case study (Case 33).
4. *Absolute performance standards.* An absolute performance standard is where perfection is required. Although this might be very difficult, if not impossible or extremely expensive for organisations to achieve, some organisations have to work hard to try to achieve it, such as safety levels at nuclear waste processing plants or railways.

The problems of setting appropriate performance standards is addressed in the GlobalAir Cargo case (Case 31).

TYPES OF IMPROVEMENT

Breakthrough improvement

Breakthrough improvement or step-change improvement looks for dramatic changes to the operation. This might involve the creation of a new factory, the total re-design of a computer-based reservation system or a total re-design in the methods of working. Such changes are usually costly and do not necessarily realise the required improvements quickly. Business Process Re-engineering (BPR) is one such approach. Underlying the BPR approach is the belief that operations should be organised around the total process which adds value for customers, rather than around the functions or activities which perform the various stages of the value adding activity. BPR is about undertaking a radical re-think and re-design of all business processes, not just operations processes.

Continuous improvement

Continuous improvement involves a more incremental approach to improvement, concentrating on encouraging many small step improvements. Continuous improvement is also known by the Japanese word *kaizen*. Continuous improvement is less concerned with the size of the steps taken more with the nature of ongoing improvement activities. The repeated and cyclical nature of continuous improvement is best summarised by what is called the PDCA (Plan, Do, Check, Act) cycle:

- *Plan.* The examination of the current method or the problem area being studied and the formulation of a plan of action.
- *Do.* The implementation of the plan.
- *Check.* The evaluation of the plan against expected performance improvement.
- *Act.* The consolidation or standardisation of successful change and the re-planning, doing, checking, acting of unsuccessful change.

IMPROVEMENT TECHNIQUES

There are many techniques that can be used by organisations to help gain improvements in performance:

- *Flow charts.* Flow charts provide a detailed picture of the flow of materials, information or customers. This technique can quickly show poorly organised flows, highlight areas where procedures do not exist, identify non-value-added delays and movements and allow managers to assess where control and measurement should take place. The Executive Holloware case (Case 35) uses a simple flow chart to understand the points where quality problems might occur.
- *Scatter diagrams.* Scatter diagrams are a quick and simple method of identifying whether there seems to be a connection between two sets of data. It will highlight the strength of their relationship though is not necessarily evidence of a cause–effect relationship.
- *Cause–effect diagrams.* Cause–effect diagrams are used to search for the root causes of problems. This is done by asking what, when, where, how and why questions. Cause–effect diagrams (which are also known as 'fish bone' or *Ishikawa* diagrams) have become extensively used in improvement programmes.
- *Pareto diagrams.* Pareto analysis attempts to identify what is most important and what is less so. It is a relatively straightforward technique which involves arranging information on the types of problem or causes of problem into their order of importance and/or frequency. This can then be used to highlight areas where further analysis will be useful.
- *Why–why analysis.* This technique starts by stating the problem and asking *why* that problem has occurred. Once the major reasons for the problem occurring have been identified, each of the major reasons is taken in turn and again the question is asked *why* those reasons have occurred, and so on.

- *Failure detection.* There are several ways of trying to detect whether a failure has occurred so that not only can it be put right but also the organisation can learn from the mistake and improve its operation, such as process control (statistical process control – *see* Section 3), diagnostics checks by machines, customer interviews or phone surveys and complaint cards. Case 34, Talleres Auto, provides an example of an organisation where one customer experienced a series of failures, but the organisation failed to learn and improve as a result.

TOTAL QUALITY MANAGEMENT

Total Quality Management (TQM) is arguably the most significant of the new ideas which have swept across the operations management scene over the last few years. TQM is concerned with the improvement of *all* aspects of operations performance, not just quality.

TQM is a philosophy, a way of thinking and working, that is concerned with meeting the needs and expectations of customers. It attempts to move the focus of quality away from being a purely operations activity into a major concern for the whole ('Total') organisation. Through TQM, quality becomes the responsibility of all levels, departments and sections in the organisation. TQM also embodies the process of continuous improvement.

Meeting the needs and expectations of customers

TQM approach is about more than just meeting the expectations of customers, it is about seeing things from a customer's point of view. This involves the whole organisation in understanding the central importance of customers to its success and even to its survival. It requires that the implications for the customer are considered at all stages in corporate decision making and that decisions are made and systems created that will not detract from the customers experience. The Courage case (Case 36) and London Zoo (Case 32) are examples of the processes involved in gaining understanding of customer expectations and/or perceptions.

Covering all parts of the organisation

One of the most powerful aspects to emerge from TQM is the concept of the 'internal customer' and supplier. This is a recognition that everyone is a customer within the organisation and consumes goods or services provided by other internal suppliers (or micro-operations), and too is an internal supplier of goods and services for other internal customers (or micro-operations). The implication of this is that errors in the service provided within an organisation will eventually pass through the internal supply chain and affect the product or service which reaches the external customer.

Including every person in the organisation

TQM is sometimes referred to as 'quality at source'. This notion stresses the impact that each individual staff member has on quality as well as the idea that it is each person's own responsibility to get quality right. Everyone in an organisation, not just those with direct contact with customers, has the potential to impair seriously the quality of the products or services received by customers. They also, therefore, have the ability to improve quality. The Eurocamp Travel case (Case 39) is an illustration of how one organisation involved all its workforce.

Examining all costs which are related to quality

TQM is concerned with examining all the costs associated with quality. These costs of quality are usually categorised as prevention costs, appraisal costs, internal failure costs and external failure costs. In traditional quality management it was assumed that there was a trade-off between improved quality and increased costs, and hence reduced profits. Furthermore it was assumed that there is an optimum amount of quality effort to be applied in any situation which minimises the total costs of quality. TQM rejects the 'optimum' quality level concept and strives to reduce all known and unknown failure costs by preventing errors and failures taking place.

Getting things right first time

The emphasis on TQM, as indicated by its approach to quality costs, is on prevention. TQM therefore tries to shift the emphasis from reactive (waiting for something to happen) to proactive (doing something before anything happens). This change in the view of quality costs has come about with a movement from an inspect-in (appraisal driven) approach to a design-in ('getting it right first time') approach. 'Design', of course, involves the original design of the product or service and of the macro and micro processes.

Developing the systems and procedures which support quality and improvement

Improving quality is not something that happens simply by getting everyone in an organisation to 'think quality'. Very often people are prevented from making improvements by the organisation's systems and procedures. Indeed there is a belief that direct operators can only correct a small percentage of quality problems, the majority are management's responsibility because they are due to 'the system', or the lack of one.

Developing a continuous process of improvement

TQM is not a one-off activity but an ongoing process of development and improvement. As such it is a mistake to consider it as an 'initiative' or 'programme'. TQM is a way of thinking, and, simply put, just good management practice.

Many of these elements of TQM are not easy to mobilise in an organisation which has become accustomed to managing quality only in the traditional ways as described in Section 3 as 'quality control'. Changes in management style and culture are required, as well as the use of new quality tools and techniques. These difficulties are illustrated in Executive Holloware (Case 35) and EuroCab SA (Case 37).

Implementing TQM

Many organisations have launched a TQM initiative with high expectations as to the likelihood of fast pay-offs. This is contrary to the nature of TQM as described above and not surprisingly has resulted in many failures. A number of factors appear to influence the eventual success of performance improvement programmes such as TQM:

- *A quality strategy.* This means having clearly thought-out long-term goals for TQM, including setting out the role and responsibilities of various parts of an organisation in its implementation and planning the resources to pursue it.
- *Top management support.* The full understanding, support and leadership of an organisation's top management emerges as a crucial factor in almost all the studies of TQM implementation.
- *A steering group.* Successful implementation requires a steering group to plan the implementation of the improvement programme.
- *Group-based improvement.* TQM programmes are usually implemented by teams as improvement usually involves people from several departments in an organisation, each of whom will have direct experience and understanding of the processes involved.
- *Success is recognised.* Formally recognising success stresses the importance of the quality improvement process as well as rewarding effort and initiative. Celebration of individual, team or company success may be crucial.
- *Training is the heart of quality improvement.* Improvement techniques should be provided to help people work towards the basic objective – the elimination of errors.

The evolution of TQM implementation is illustrated in two cases: Problems in TQ Implementation at Company A (Case 38) and Eurocamp Travel (Case 39).

SUMMARY

The task of improving operational and organisational performance is emerging as a key task of operations managers. It involves measuring performance in order to help managers make decisions about what to change and understand the impact of their decisions, not just on quality but the other operations performance objectives, speed, dependability, flexibility and cost. There are many techniques that can be used to help gain improvements in performance, including flow charts, scatter diagrams, cause–effect diagrams and pareto diagrams. Total Quality Management (TQM) is one of the best known improvement philosophies and involves:

- meeting the needs and expectations of customers
- covering all parts of the organisation
- including every person in the organisation
- examining all costs which are related to quality
- getting things 'right first time', i.e. designing-in quality rather than inspecting it in
- developing the systems and procedures which support quality and improvement
- developing a continuous process of improvement.

Key points

- Performance measurement and appropriate choice of targets underpins performance improvement.
- Improvement activities are usually either breakthrough activities or continuous improvement programmes.
- There are many techniques which can be used to help organisations improve their performance, such as pareto analysis and cause–effect analysis.
- TQM is a philosophy which applies to all parts of the organisation. If everybody in the organisation can detract from the company's effectiveness, then everyone also has the potential to make a positive contribution. A central concept of TQM is its use of internal customer/suppliers to enable each part of the organisation to identify its contribution to overall quality.
- TQM puts customers at the forefront of quality decision making and places considerable emphasis on the role and responsibilities of every member of staff within an organisation to influence quality.

Recommended reading

Slack, N., Chambers, S., Harland, C., Harrison, A. and Johnston, R. (1998), *Operations Management* (2nd edn), Pitman Publishing. Chapters 18, 19 and 20.

Selected further readings

Armistead, C. G. (ed.) (1994), *The Future of Services Management,* Kogan Page.
Berry, L. L. and Parasuraman, A. (1991), *Marketing Services: Competing Through Quality*, Free Press.
Bounds, G., Yorks, L., Adams, M. and Ranney, G. (1994), *Beyond Total Quality Management: towards the emerging paradigm*, McGraw-Hill.
Collier, D.A. (1994), *The Service/Quality Solution: Using Service Management to Gain Competitive Advantage*, Irwin and ASQC Quality Press.
Crosby, P. B. (1979), *Quality is Free*, McGraw-Hill.
Dale, B. G., (ed.) (1994), *Managing Quality* (2nd edn), Prentice Hall.

Deming, W. E. (1986), *Out of the Crisis*, Massachusetts Institute of Technology Press.

Feigenbaum, A. V. (1986), *Total Quality Control*, McGraw-Hill.

Fitzgerald, L., Johnston, R., Brignall, S., Silvestro, R. and Voss, C. (1991), *Performance Measurement in Service Businesses*, The Chartered Institute of Management Accountants.

Garvin, D. A. (1988), *Managing Quality: The strategic and competitive edge*, Free Press.

Heskett, J. L., Sasser, W.E. and Hart, C.W.L. (1990), *Service Breakthroughs: changing the rules of the game*, Free Press.

Imai, M. (1986), *Kaizen*, McGraw-Hill Publishing.

Ishikawa, K. (1985), *What is Total Quality Control? – The Japanese Way*, Prentice Hall.

McNair, C. J. and Leibfried, K.H. J. (1992), *Benchmarking: a tool for continuous improvement.*

Oakland, J. S. (1989), *Total Quality Management*, Butterworth-Heinemann.

Oakland, J. S. (1993), *Total Quality Management* (2nd edn), Butterworth-Heinemann.

Taguchi, G. and Clausing, D. (1990), 'Robust Quality', *Harvard Business Review*, January–February, pp. 65–75.

CASE 31

GlobalAir Cargo – Import Operations

Adam Bates and Stuart Chambers

*Case date 1995**

INTRODUCTION

Richard Thompson, General Manager at GlobalAir Cargo's (GAC) London Heathrow Operations explained to a visiting group of potential customers:

> *'Musical instruments, exotic fruits, deceased persons, fish, reptiles, beer, autoparts, chemicals, jewellery, newspapers and textiles are just some of the goods which we transport for our customers. We have the flexibility to offer you the highest levels of service, speed and security, as well as being able to meet any other specialised handling needs you may have. We are fully aware that our success depends upon your success and we are prepared to gear all of our efforts to serving you right first time, every time.'*

A little later that afternoon Richard was reviewing the latest 'Weekly Performance Appraisal' (*see* Table 31.1) for 'Import Operations' and was disappointed to see that they still did not appear to be meeting the target service specifications, although they were definitely an improvement on previous years. Richard was pleased with the improvements which had been made, but he remained concerned that he was not receiving the necessary information to help him determine how effectively he was meeting his business objectives and whether his operations were really running smoothly and efficiently.

BACKGROUND

GlobalAir Cargo is the world's seventh largest airline freight carrier, transporting over 600 000 tonnes in the last financial year, and contributing £460m to group revenues. The scale of its cargo operations is immense, with over 100 destinations and a GAC aircraft taking off somewhere every three minutes. GAC is often better placed to meet the needs of its customers than other smaller competitors.

*Based on the original ideas and materials kindly supplied by Alistair Nicholson of London Business School.

Table 31.1 Weekly performance appraisal – GlobalAir Cargo Import, London, Heathrow

CARGOCENTRE IMPORT WEEKLY PERFORMANCE week ending 24/10		
1. THROUGHPUTS	*Actual*	*%Variance*
a) Commercial Arrivals		
–Tonnes	1481	6.4
–Consignments	3834	28.3
b) Transshipments		
–Tonnes	1374	33.0
–Consignments	6998	37.3
c) Services Arrivals		
–Tonnes	18	–25.0
–Consignments	310	2.6
d) Express Services		
–ESU Tonnes	57	
–ESU Consignments	1120	
–Courier Tonnes	123	
–# Bags	6001	
e) Other Airline Received		
–Tonnes	56	
–Consignments	156	
TOTAL THROUGHPUT		
TONNES	2996	
CONSIGNMENTS	11142	

2. STANDARDS	*Target%*	*Actual%*
a) Documents available within aircraft arrival + 90 mins (Terminal 4)	90	85
b) Documents available within aircraft arrival + 2 hours (Terminal 1)	90	81
c) Status X within aircraft arrival + 6 hours	85	58
d) Caller collections. Cargo available in 40 minutes of release note issue	95	87
e) Slotted collections. Cargo available at slot time	95	95
f) Telephone answering: Total # calls		
–% calls answered in 20 seconds	80	45
–% calls lost	10	25
g) Transshipments flown as booked:		
–Europe	90	67
–America's	90	83
–Far East	90	85
–Trucks	90	58
h) Terminal deliveries 100% in 1 hour: Total units	100	54
i) Express Handled Units Status X performance:		
– + 45 minutes		33
– + 1 hour		12
– + 2 hours		39

3. COMMENTS FOR WEEK
a) High percentage of incoming goods for transshipment
b) Storage problems with two fewer operational aisles
c) Manpower resource levels dropped over weekend leading to decline in Status X standards
d) ETV breakdown on Tues. caused severe problems, leading also to decline in Status X

In the same way that containers revolutionised the handling of cargo in the shipping industry, so modularisation of cargo has been adopted in air freight, and most items are now transported in large aluminium containers especially adapted for the shape of the large long-haul aircraft.

While most airlines use a mixture of 'all-freight' aircraft and 'passenger' aircraft to meet the needs of their cargo customers, GAC has decided to solely utilise the under-floor capacity of their passenger aircraft. They have avoided investing the capital in all-freight aircraft, believing it to be an unnecessary risk, and an unprofitable decision by most airlines, only adding to the excess capacity within the industry. However at periods of extremely high demand GAC has been known to charter all-freight aircraft for limited periods.

Richard's role covers both import and export operations at Heathrow. Within the import business he felt his responsibility was divided between two major tasks: first, ensuring profitability, in accordance with plans and budgets, and second, making certain that the operations are working smoothly and efficiently. Richard explained his current predicament:

> *'I am getting some information about how well our operations are running, with regards conformance to standards; I have access to feedback from our customers about how well we compare with our competitors, and I have information about how much business we are achieving in terms of consignments and tonnes shipped, which gives a good indication of our profitability. However I am not certain from this information whether I should be happy or disappointed with the results we are achieving. On one hand we are making many operational improvements and productivity gains, but on the other we still seem to be often outperformed by our competitors, which suggests that perhaps we are trading off one against the other. Also I am not certain whether the information is the most relevant for me to perform my dual responsibility of ensuring profitability and making certain that the operations run smoothly. None of the information I am receiving either gives me a 'real time' window into my operation, nor a clear picture about our likely levels of success or failure in the future.'*

Richard's primary business target was to increase the freight productivity (measured in tonnes/person) by 5 per cent per annum. Essentially this measure correlated strongly with the profitability of the operation since the tonnage determined revenue and the manpower costs represented the largest operating expense. The actual growth figure which Richard had maintained for each of the last three years had dramatically exceeded the arbitrary 5 per cent and stood at 11 per cent for the current year.

CARGO CUSTOMERS

GAC customers are as varied as the items they carry. However, the majority of goods which they transport are in fact consolidated and shipped by organisations known as 'Freight Forwarders'; agents who consolidate freight items and deliver in bulk direct to GAC. They book their freight on the basis of route/airline capacity availability, and make commercial judgements in the trade-off between price and delivery time. The freight forwarders arrange delivery to and collection from the airlines and either handle the paperwork themselves or nominate a 'Clearing Agent' at the destination to do the paperwork on their behalf.

Air freight industry market research had been published showing some of the criteria upon which the freight forwarders judged the airlines, giving the perceived performance of GAC relative to its competitors at Heathrow. This is reproduced in Table 31.2.

Table 31.2 Importance of customer service features and GlobalAir cargo performance

Features of the freight service	*Relative importance (1=low; 10=high)*	*Relative performance of GlobalAir (rank within top 7 airlines)*
General service features		
Rates (cost of delivery)	10	4th
Capacity availability	9	7th
Speed of answering telephones – reservations	7	7th
Attitude of phone staff – reservations	5	4th
Speed of answering telephones – post flight enquiries	5	4th
Attitude of phone staff – post flight enquiries	3	3rd
Import service features		
Speed of making documents available	9	7th
Speed of achieving 'Status X'	9	7th
Speed of handling vehicles at import despatch	5	6th
Attitude of phone staff at service centre	2	3rd

GAC has attempted to build longer-term relationships with these customers by achieving agreed delivery and quality performance objectives (*see* Fig. 31.2 for the Charter), and had introduced Total Quality Management (TQM) into its cargo operations. Prior to the introduction of TQM, the import operations had been experiencing capacity and quality problems. The successful introduction of TQM had improved the utilisation of capacity of the storage area, for example through better labelling of stored items, more accurate recording of cargo storage and movements, more rapid locating of items during collection, and fewer 'lost items'.

THE PHYSICAL PROCESS

At 'Un-bundling' the cargo items are removed from the container, placed onto pallets and put into racks in the main storage area. Their location is noted on a storage card

This Charter defines the principles and ideals which GlobalAir Cargo believe are central to successful air cargo management. By striving towards these goals we can all share in the many benefits that flow from a successful business commitment.

A COMMITMENT TO THE HIGHEST LEVELS OF SERVICE

The success of our business is dependent on the success of our customers. For all of us to grow and develop, we aim to provide consistently high levels of service in every area of air cargo.

A COMMITMENT TO QUALITY

We care about our customers' freight as much as they do. It is in our interest to ensure their goods are transported efficiently and arrive in perfect condition. We shall provide expert advice where required. We shall offer a flexible and reliable cargo handling and transport service, utilising service, utilising trained staff and sophisticated handling equipment.

A COMMITMENT TO SECURITY

We will take all necessary precautions to protect the security of our customers' goods, from the moment they are entrusted to our trained staff until their collection at the point of destination.

A COMMITMENT TO CARE AND ATTENTION

We care equally for our customers' goods and their business requirements. From reservation to collection at the destination airport we will work actively to solve any customer problems. At all times we encourage customers to tell us how or where we may be of assistance. Our Customer Service Centre will work pro-actively to avoid problems rather than simply dealing with them as they happen.

Where problems occur we will provide answers, not excuses.

A COMMITMENT TO VALUE

We pledge ourselves to offering true value for money with competitive prices on all products and services. We shall offer Business Partnership customers exclusive packages and added value wherever possible.

A COMMITMENT TO CONTINUED INNOVATION

We are committed to innovation wherever it may produce benefits for the customer. We will continue to lead the air cargo industry in the development of information and handling technology. And we will endeavour to keep our customers abreast of any industry developments that may enhance their own efficiency and profitability.

A COMMITMENT TO THE FUTURE

We shall continue to invest millions of pounds towards our service infrastructure. An investment in manpower, resources and ideas for the future of the world cargo industry. We recognise the opportunities and we invite you to share in our success.

Fig. 31.2 GlobalAir Cargo Charter

(*see* Fig. 31.3) and items then wait here until they are cleared by Customs and may be collected. *'It's a very simple system, so we don't experience many problems, but if we lose the storage card or simply enter the wrong information on it, well, it's like looking for a needle in a haystack! One parcel out of 15 000 every week can take a very long time to recover,'* reflected the storeman. When the cargo reaches this stage it is known to have reached 'Status X', which means that the clearing agent can start clearing the items with Customs. Richard Thompson explains, *'GAC aims to have 85 per cent of its freight reach Status X within six hours of arrival'.*

Once the clearing agent has had Customs clear the items, and all necessary paperwork has been completed, the items are ready for collection. On arrival at the collection area, a driver would go to the reception area, where the paperwork is verified, release documents are supplied, and the reception then contacts the warehouse with the relevant 'Air Waybill' numbers. The warehouse then locates the items and brings them to a loading bay for collection by the driver. Major customers have predetermined pickup timeslots, to speed up their collections. A diagram showing the layout of the physical process is shown in Fig. 31.4.

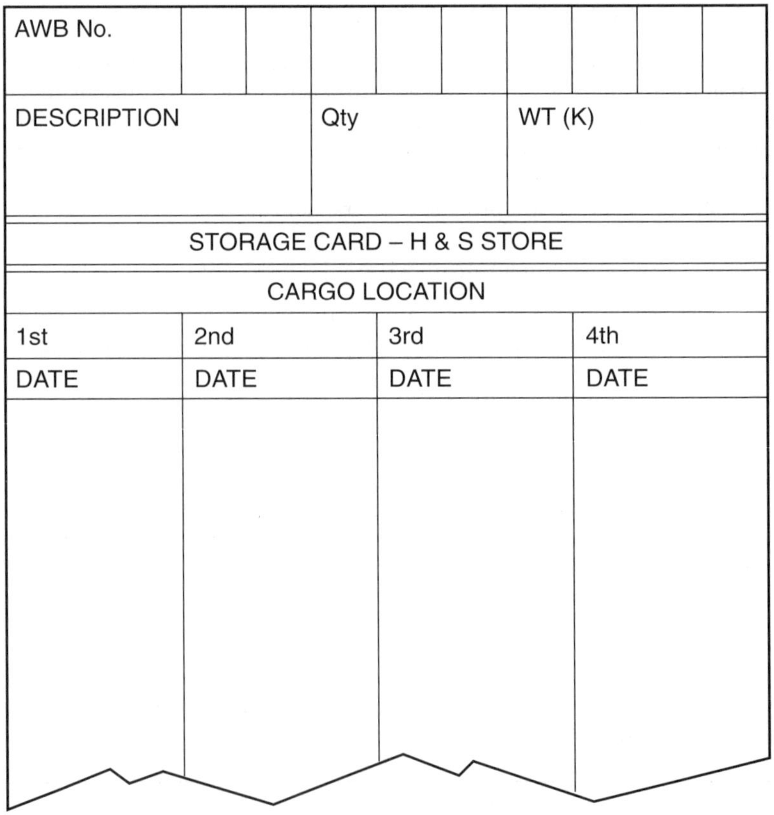

Fig. 31.3 Warehouse storage card

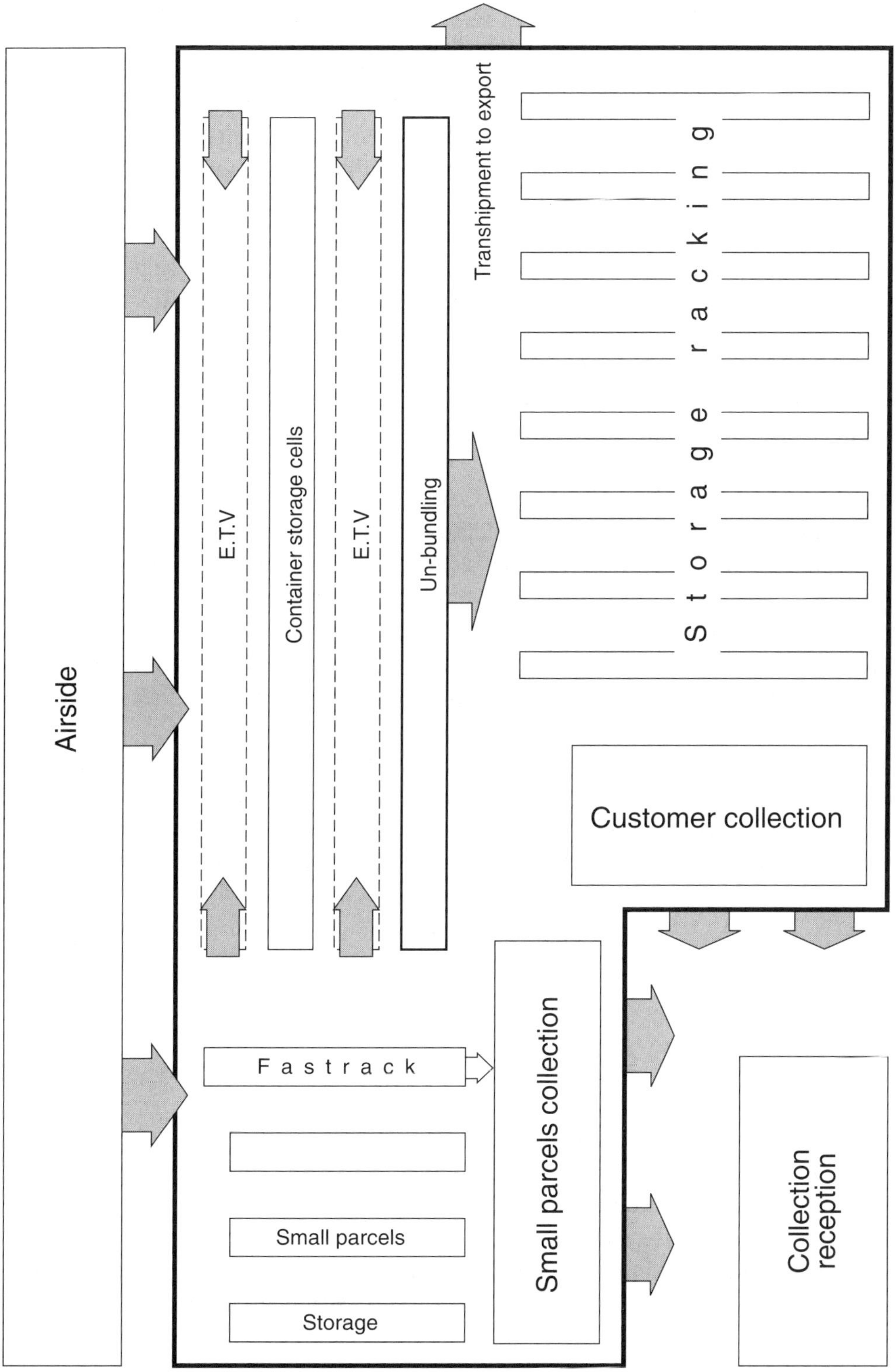

Fig. 31.4 Diagram of the GlobalAir Cargo import operation at Heathrow

THE ADMINISTRATIVE PROCESS

The administrative process runs simultaneously to the physical process. As the containers reach 'Airside', the manifest is checked by the warehouse, and the 'Air Waybills' are extracted and taken to 'Document Control'. 'Air Waybills' (*see* Fig. 31.5) detail the goods in transit showing the expediter, nominated clearing agent, number and type of items and amount charged. At document control the information from the AWB is keyed into 'GAC-Trac', the Global Air Cargo operations computer system. This gives a full record of each item in transit from the moment it is delivered by the freight forwarder, to the time it is collected, tracking its movement anywhere in the world. The details of the AWB should already exist on GAC-Trac, as they were first entered when the item was exported and now only require updating, however a number of GAC's stations, affecting approximately 4 per cent of packages, are not networked onto the system and therefore all of the details must be entered and a new record created.

After this information is entered onto GAC-Trac, copies of the AWB are passed to the accounting department, so that billing can be arranged, to the reception area for their records, and also to the regular clearing agents, many of whom have their own pigeon holes within the GAC offices. This 'document availability', as it is known, allows the clearing agents to start processing the formal paperwork, and once the items themselves reach Status X, the customs clearance can take place. The document availability is fairly rapid with GAC aiming to release 90 per cent of all documents within two hours of the aircraft arriving.

After customs have cleared an item, they inform both the clearing agent and GAC. Their direct interface into GAC-Trac system updates the items file and produces an automatic print-out highlighting which items are free to be collected.

From the time that an item arrives on an aircraft until the time that it is collected by the freight forwarder takes an average of three days, most of which is spent waiting for paperwork and customs clearance. Obviously perishable goods and express items proceed much faster, while other less urgent items may sometimes take weeks.

COMPETITORS

GAC's competitors at Heathrow include all those airlines who have inbound flights arriving at Heathrow. Companies such as British Airways, Virgin, Lufthansa, KLM, Air France, American, United are Global Air's largest competitors. Global Air Cargo's performance against these airlines was shown in Table 31.2.

Overall improvements in these measures can be seen in Table 31.3, which shows the previous two years' statistics at GAC for the month of October.

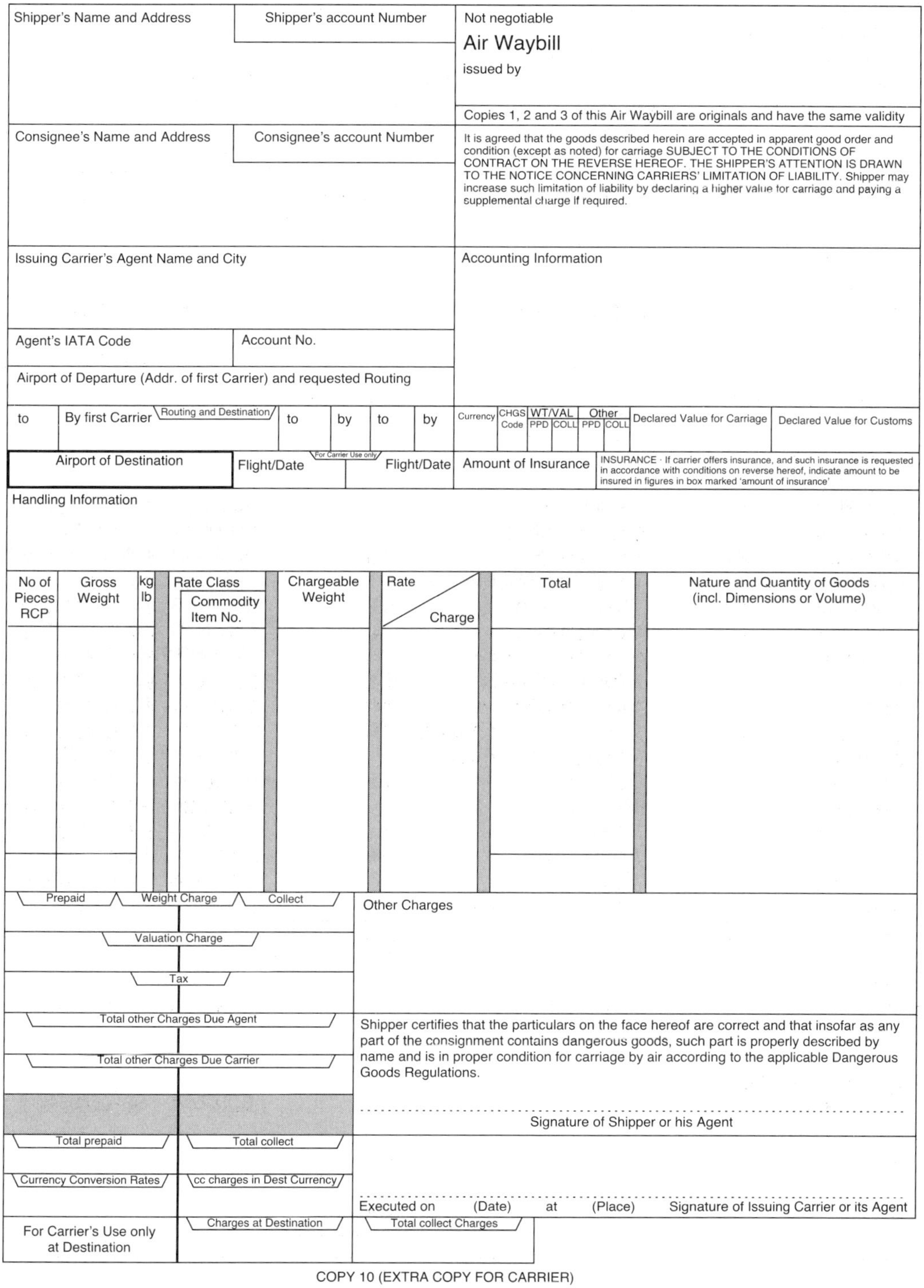

Shipper's Name and Address | Shipper's account Number

Not negotiable
Air Waybill
issued by

Copies 1, 2 and 3 of this Air Waybill are originals and have the same validity

Consignee's Name and Address | Consignee's account Number

It is agreed that the goods described herein are accepted in apparent good order and condition (except as noted) for carriage SUBJECT TO THE CONDITIONS OF CONTRACT ON THE REVERSE HEREOF. THE SHIPPER'S ATTENTION IS DRAWN TO THE NOTICE CONCERNING CARRIERS' LIMITATION OF LIABILITY. Shipper may increase such limitation of liability by declaring a higher value for carriage and paying a supplemental charge if required.

Issuing Carrier's Agent Name and City

Accounting Information

Agent's IATA Code | Account No.

Airport of Departure (Addr. of first Carrier) and requested Routing

to | By first Carrier (Routing and Destination) | to | by | to | by | Currency | CHGS Code | WT/VAL (PPD, COLL) | Other (PPD, COLL) | Declared Value for Carriage | Declared Value for Customs

Airport of Destination | Flight/Date (For Carrier Use only) | Flight/Date | Amount of Insurance | INSURANCE - If carrier offers insurance, and such insurance is requested in accordance with conditions on reverse hereof, indicate amount to be insured in figures in box marked 'amount of insurance'

Handling Information

No of Pieces RCP	Gross Weight	kg lb	Rate Class / Commodity Item No.	Chargeable Weight	Rate / Charge	Total	Nature and Quantity of Goods (incl. Dimensions or Volume)

Prepaid | Weight Charge | Collect

Other Charges

Valuation Charge

Tax

Total other Charges Due Agent

Shipper certifies that the particulars on the face hereof are correct and that insofar as any part of the consignment contains dangerous goods, such part is properly described by name and is in proper condition for carriage by air according to the applicable Dangerous Goods Regulations.

Total other Charges Due Carrier

Signature of Shipper or his Agent

Total prepaid | Total collect

Currency Conversion Rates | cc charges in Dest Currency

Executed on (Date) at (Place) Signature of Issuing Carrier or its Agent

For Carrier's Use only at Destination | Charges at Destination | Total collect Charges

COPY 10 (EXTRA COPY FOR CARRIER)

Fig. 31.5 GlobalAir Cargo Air Waybill

CARGO MANIFEST

Name of Operator	**GLOBALAIR**		
Marks of Nationality & Registration	**GBDX**	Date	**27-Nov.**
		Flight No.	**GA/79**
Point of Lading	**BOMBAY**	Point of Unlading	**LONDON**

Air Way Bill No.	Number of Packages	Nature of Goods	For Use by owner or operator only Gross Weight	Remarks	For Official Use Only
AIR CARGO					
AC5BA					
5301 4296	1	DYE INTERMEDIATES	1	BOM/LON	SB205404/25.11
5301 4297	1	DYESTUFF	1	BOM/LON	SB205404/25.11
2	2	FRT ATTACHED WITH DOCS	2		
CC202BA					
5027 3015	4	GARMENTS	50	BOM/LHR	DB69736/23.11
5302 5336	1	CASSETTES	12	BOM/MRU	DB69896/23.11
5025 8541	20	GARMENTS	210	BOM/LHR	DB69864/23.11
5302 1921	1	DYES INTERMEDIATES	1	BOM/CHI	SB200542/8.11
5412 0774	1	SILK FABRICS	14	CCU/DUS	EX IC273/25.11
5412 1171	1	GARMENTS	20	CCU/NYC	EX IC272/25.11
5189 0695	3	PRINTED MATTER	129	TRV/LHR	EX IC168/20.11
5412 4321	4	HANDKERCHIEFS	82	CCU/BIO	EX IC176/22.11
5412 4354	1	SILK FABRICS	37	CCU/LBA	EX IC274/24.11
5190 2892	1	COMPUTER SOFTWARE	17	HYD/PIT	EX IC118/24.11
5190 2971	18	COMPUTER SOFTWARE	11	HYD/LHR	EX IC119/23.11
5412 4365	1	TOOLS	5	CCU/DUS	EX IC273/24.11
5760 2780	1	MACHINERY	4	HYD/DAR	EX IC118/25.11
5060 2775	3	GRANITE	1	HYD/DBW	EX IC118/25.11
5412 4343	4	ENVELOPES	53	CCU/PHL	EX IC273/24.11
5028 2375	1	NECKLACES	37	AMD/LHR	EX IC616/25.11
5412 0123	2	AIR COMPRESSORS	179	BOM/NYC	DB69786/23.11
17	50		862		
HOLD FIVE					
5028 2933	1	DIPLOMATIC MAIL	7	BOM/WAS	APICO1/24.11
1	1		7		
SEALED LOCKER					
5602 3144	1	SILVER ARTICLES	5.5	BOM/DTT	SB205798/23.11
1	1		5.5		
21	**54**		**876.5**		

Fig. 31.6 Typical Cargo Manifest

Table 31.3 Performance comparison for previous two years

	Two years ago	*Last year*
Tonnes	11082	12447
Number of consignments	41609	48690
Status X	66%	78%
Caller collections. Cargo available in 40 minutes	81%	96%
Slotted collections. Cargo available at slotted time	94%	96%
Overtime. Manpower equivalent	338	344
Tonnes per man	8.19	9.05
Phones: answered in 20 seconds	63%	71%
Phones: lost calls	20%	15%
Phones: total calls	15081	12545

SUMMARY

Richard is left wondering:

> *'I need to re-think the information I receive regarding performance here at the Import Operations. I must have both a real time window on the state of the operations, as well as an indication of how likely I am to achieve my business targets both in the current year and in the longer term; say* up to five years. *But what sort of information should I ask for? We handle 15 000 items a week and, with seven documents on each item, I can't review every piece of information, I must be selective!'*

Questions

1 Prepare a flow chart showing both the physical and administrative processes. What can you conclude from this?

2 What problems might occur in getting a parcel through GlobalAir Cargo's Heathrow import operations? What will ensure that the throughput rate can be maintained?

3 Which measures should Richard ask for? Suggest both a model for evaluating the business both in the short and long run, and a model for evaluating the operation. You should show which measures should be used, why they should be used, where the information will come from, and at what frequency.

4 Are full storage shelves good or bad? Discuss.

CASE 32

London Zoo

Adrian Watt and Stuart Chambers

Case date 1995

INTRODUCTION

Dr Jo Gipps, the Director of London Zoo turned away from his window:

'I have quite a good view of Regents Park and the zoo from here. I can also see the visitors arriving and walking to the main entrance from the car park or the tube station on the other side of the park. You get quite a good feel for the attendance numbers just from watching the stream of people walking along the pavement. By late morning on really busy days we have quite a queue building up at the ticket kiosks. Of course, that doesn't happen as often as it did some years ago, but we would like to see if we could bring the crowds back. We have a huge fluctuation in daily numbers. Our busiest times are obviously weekends and the summer holidays when we regularly get attendance levels of between 4000 and 6000. On the Easter and August Bank Holidays we can easily reach 10 000. The busiest day we have had in the last few years was on a special "Save Our Zoo" day when visitor numbers topped 18 000; the zoo was packed, you could hardly move, the whole operation was bursting at the seams, there were queues everywhere, we were running out of food, it was chaos! Yet our lowest budgeted attendance figure is for Christmas Eve with just 48 people. The place is like a ghost town, it lacks any atmosphere and there are hardly any staff around as they are all getting on with their work behind the scenes.

'We certainly need to increase our visitor numbers, but it is vital that we still provide a high quality of service; and there lies our problem. We have had all the usual market research done for us: we know the age range, group size, average length of visit, where the visitors come from, and even which newspapers they read. We also know which animals they like best: the monkeys, big cats, elephants and penguins are always popular, but we do not really know what the public thinks of the quality of the service we provide throughout their visit. Apart from providing the animals, what are we doing right and when? If we do not know that, how can we improve and build on our successes? Marketing is all very well at getting people here, but once they are here we have to keep them and organise our operations to give them a good day out.

'The second problem is largely concerned with society's attitude to animals, and this is really one of the reasons for the zoo being in the difficulty it is today. The public's views

have changed a great deal over the past few years: they have become far more aware of issues such as animals rights and welfare, and conservation, they are far more sceptical of the need to keep animals in captivity, and they are questioning the role of zoos in today's society. London Zoo (and the Zoological Society as a whole including the Institute of Zoology) has long been primarily dedicated to animal welfare and conservation, but in the past there has been no real need to emphasize this because people did not really seem to care. All they wanted to do was to come to the zoo to see some exotic large animals and did not think about the welfare of the animals in the zoo or the wild. Now things have changed completely! Many people now still want to see the animals, but are worried about their happiness, their well-being and their conservation in their natural habitats. Some people think that zoos are one of the problems rather than part of the solution.

'I suppose this encapsulates our problem; having got the visitors to come, are we treating them well by giving them a good quality service, and indeed are we giving them what they want?'

BACKGROUND INFORMATION ON LONDON ZOO

Ever since it opened in 1828, London Zoo has played a major part in the country's interest in natural history both as a scientific and recreational activity, and has frequently been in the news headlines. London Zoo is the UK's premier zoological collection and has one of the most prestigious animal collections in the world. It was designed to house and display the 'grand collection of live animals', for the Zoological Society of London. Although initially only occupying a small corner of Regents Park, it expanded rapidly to reach its present size of 36 acres. From the start the zoo had a wide range of exotic species including Indian elephants, llamas, leopards, kangaroos, bears and numerous birds. The collection grew rapidly with the addition of an orangutan, an Indian rhinoceros, giraffes, and chimpanzees all arriving over the next 10 years. The first of a series of gorillas arrived in 1887.

As the collection expanded so building work continued, with major periods of construction and refurbishment occurring in the 1830s, 1850s, 1880s and 1920/30s. For the first 65 years all the animals were permanently housed inside in the mistaken belief that they would not survive the cold outside. The world's first aquarium was built in 1853. The original lion house was replaced in 1876, and the first reptile house which opened in 1849 was replaced in 1883. The existing aquarium was built in 1924, the present reptile house in 1927, the penguin pool in 1934, and the Cotton and Mappin Terraces were also built during the 1930s. The latter are closed awaiting refurbishment, and have been for a number of years. These, and many of the other buildings are listed, and can not simply be demolished, but must be renovated within strict guidelines.

There was a severe lack of capital investment in the zoo's infrastructure in the 1960s and 1970s. However a spate of building did occur in the 1970s with the Sobell ape and monkey pavilions opening in 1972, followed by the big cat enclosures, and the Snowdon Aviary. In the late 1980s and 1990s there was the re-development of the Clore Small Mammal House into the Moonlight Centre and the rebuilding of the Children's and Petting Zoo (which has been present in some form since 1924), the construction of the Lifewatch Centre, Macaw Aviary, and Barclay Court and the fountain area. Recently the zoo has been awarded £2 million from the National Lottery Heritage Millennium Fund to go towards building an education centre.

Visitor attendance levels have always fluctuated as fashion and public interest have increased and waned with the introduction of new exhibits and developments, or as investment declined. In the 1830s annual attendance levels exceeded 250 000, but fluctuated considerably during the latter half of the century. The zoo's popularity increased after the turn of the century with a sustained period of expansion, attendance figures reaching 2 million per annum before the Second World War. After the war, attendance figures leapt to 3 million due to the desire for post-austerity recreation, but by the mid-50s the visitor numbers had settled back down towards their pre-war 2 million level and remained stable for some time. In the late 1960s and early 1970s a new decline began and by 1975 attendance levels started to fall rapidly. By the early 1980s visitor levels were just over 1 million, and the budgeted 1995/96 attendance level was just 900 000.

This decline in attendance levels was due to a number of socio-economic changes including changing social habits, growth in car ownership, leisure preferences and inflation. In the 1950s there was very little competition from other animal or general leisure attractions. Coupled with this there was a general lack of transport, usually only public transport being available and there being very little private means of transport with only a few cars. This restricted the ability of people who lived in and around London to travel widely beyond the city, or for other people to go anywhere far except to the capital. With the expansion of the road network and increased car ownership, as well as the growth of foreign travel, people found it easier and were more willing to go further for their leisure activities. Competition also grew rapidly with respect to animal based organisations, there were nine zoos in Great Britain in the 1950s but there are now over 250 attractions which include animals. The fastest growing visitor segments were leisure, amusement and country parks. Historical buildings, and the museums and galleries sector remained constant, and wildlife attractions showed the lowest consistent absolute growth, and as a consequence a fall in percentage terms. Thus London Zoo was in a market sector which had a rapidly increasing number of new entrants and competitors, but at the same time its segment was showing a relatively decreasing market size while other visitor attractions expanded rapidly.

The proportional decrease in the attendance of animal attractions was coupled with the change in the public's perception of the rights of animals, the care of animals in captivity and the effect of caging animals on their health, behaviour, and psychology. The morality, function and need of zoos was also questioned with an emphasis being placed on the requirement for conservation to occur in the wild.

Over the last 25 years, there has been a general lack of investment in the zoo's infrastructure, new attractions, facilities, educational and conservation development or its image. This occurred just at the time when alternative leisure attractions, both animal based and otherwise, were starting to present substantial competition. The performance of the zoo in the early 1960s to mid-1970s had generated considerable profit which could have been used for the reinvestment in the zoo's infrastructure, but the Zoological Society decided to use the money to support and expand its scientific work at the Institute. In the mid-1970s attendance levels fell sharply and the zoo went into a major financial deficit. At the same time many private donations dried up, and the government was no longer willing to provide money for capital development. A severe money shortage resulted at the very time when capital investment was desperately needed. The zoo reached a desperate position by 1981/82. It was realised that it was imperative to increase gate revenues, by developing new exhibits and improving the facilities and the service offered to the public. Between 1985 and 1988 government grants totalled £7.5m, without which the operating deficit would have been £6.5m. In 1988 the zoo applied for £13 million for immediate work and £40 million for long-term development. The government gave a one-off £10 million grant, and informed the zoo that it had to be self-supporting.

Following a number of strategy reports in 1990 the society announced it plans for major changes in the collection. There was a large reduction in the number of species kept, and many animals were moved to its sister collection at Whipsnade in order to reduce costs. Throughout 1991 the zoo produced 80 per cent of its revenue from gate receipts but remained open due to private donations received. Further development plans and fundraising activities took place throughout 1991 and 1992. The incumbent Director of the zoo resigned and was replaced by Dr Jo Gipps, the present Director. Following disappointing attendance levels to early summer 1992 it was announced that the zoo would close by Christmas. However at a special council meeting this decision was reversed by the Fellows, and this was confirmed at the Annual General Meeting in September 1992. A new Council was elected by April 1993.

THE 1992 DEVELOPMENT PLAN

With the support of the zoo's staff, Dr Gipps' development plan was published and adopted, in June 1992. This would cost an estimated £21 million over ten years. The plan focused on the conservation of animals with breeding programmes for endangered species including Asiatic lions, Sumatran tigers, and Lowland gorillas. The aim was summarised in the statement that *'there will be less emphasis on the zoo as a good day out. We are going to appeal to people's intelligence. Zoos have no right to exist in the late 20th century unless they can show they are good for animals'.* The plan also detailed the proposed infrastructural changes and reorganisation required as well as the finance required, and the consequences of the changes. Developments were to include a children's zoo, an education centre, the long-term restoration of the dilapidated Mappin Terraces and the re-introduction of the bears. The reorganisation and rationalisation involved the shedding of 90 staff and a reduction in the size of the animal collection, although the remaining animals had enlarged enclosures. An emphasis was placed on cost-cutting and the evaluation of the species in the collection; with particular consideration to those for which the captive breeding programmes were an integral part of their conservation, and in line with the zoo's mission statement.

The 1993/4 period was largely one of financial structural and organisational consolidation after years of upheaval so stabilising and equating income and expenditure and thereby ensuring a secure future that did not exceed income. A new charter and mission statement was ratified in 1994/5. The Zoological Society's mission statement is summarised in Appendix 32.1. There was an organisational restructuring into a series of departments with defined roles and responsibilities. These included the departments for animal management, education, marketing, events, projects, visitor operations, general services and the retail departments, with outside franchises awarded for catering and peripheral visitor activities e.g. face painting. Attendance figures still continued to fall.

CONSERVATION IN ACTION

In 1993 in association with the launch of its marketing campaign, summarised by its slogan 'Conservation in Action', London Zoo commissioned its first ever market research poll to establish a visitor profile and to measure the public's awareness of its advertising campaign. This indicated the family and children orientated nature of the visitor profile, that 41 per cent came from London, and 14 per cent from overseas. Overall views were positive, with 76 per cent saying that they were likely to return within two years. The decision to visit was largely at the request of the children, was only made a few days prior to the visit, and was strongly influenced by the weather on the day. There was also a high awareness of the zoo and its advertising campaign.

Throughout 1994/5 a small rise was seen in visitor numbers although there was an underlying deficit in revenue of £600 000, offset by a £900 000 private donation. Further market research revealed that the average visit was of four hours, and that the apes and monkeys, big cats, elephants and penguins were the most popular exhibits.

THE MANAGEMENT OF LONDON ZOO

London Zoo consists of eight departments, the heads of which report to Dr Jo Gipps, the Director of London Zoo. The departments consist of the animal management division, marketing, development, general services, projects, retail and visitor operations. In total the zoo directly employs 161 staff. In addition there are catering and other franchise staff employed by outside contractors. The permanent staff are supplemented by temporary staff employed during peak periods such as school and bank holidays. These are largely used at the catering and retail facilities.

THE SERVICE QUALITY RESEARCH PROJECT

In June 1995, Jo Gipps was addressing a meeting of the monthly management committee:

'For us to manage the budget and to breakeven we must maintain an attendance level of at least one million visitors a year . . . but even then there will be very little money available to carry out the much needed modification of the infrastructure, and the addition of new exhibits. A secure financial future would enable us to carry out our development and expansion plans, and to adapt further as views and perceptions of the public and of society as a whole change. It is therefore essential that we accurately define our target market segments, identify what our customers expect when they come to the zoo, and then provide them with their needs and requirements at a consistently high quality of service. Of course, we must target and attract these customers using accurate and effective marketing, promotions and PR, but to build and maintain a reputation we must be able to deliver what the customers want, or they will not come back. If we fail to do that, the customer will be disgruntled and dissatisfied, and when they return home they will spread their dissatisfaction or disappointment by 'word-of-mouth'. The consequence will be that visitors will not return, and new visitors will not be attracted. If, however, the service is as wanted and expected, or even exceeds expectations, the visitors will leave satisfied and delighted. They will spread the zoo's positive reputation, returning themselves and helping to increase the level of new visitors.'

'In order to ensure that we achieve our aim of providing the visitors with an excellent day out and so attract them back again in even greater numbers, it is essential that we find out how they rate their visit. This involves two basic issues: the first is to discover how the zoo performs with respect to the service it provides, and the second is to ensure that it is delivering the services that the customers want. It is only after we have some measure of these things that we can hope to fine tune our operating procedures, and develop a plan of action to tackle problem areas in some order of priority. I have decided to seize an opportunity to use an MBA student, Adrian Watt, to undertake a major customer research programme over this summer, so I hope you will all find the time to assist him when necessary. His work should give us a much better understanding of what we must do, but first it is important to ensure that an accurately defined segment of visitors is targeted. We have three general categories of visitors: school and education groups; large parties and coach trips; and individuals, couples or family groups. Each category requires different services from the zoo during their visit. The latter group

represents our largest category of visitors, particularly during the summer months, so Adrian should only target these this year. Overseas visitors can be included as long as they are fluent in English, because they account for about 15 per cent of the total visitors, and could provide us with a valuable means of international competitive benchmarking. Perhaps Adrian could explain to you all how he intends to go about his project?'

Designing a questionnaire

Adrian explained that he would first need their help in designing the questionnaire:

'What I would like to do is to use a list of the "18 determinants of service quality" (see *Appendix 32.2) as a guideline for the design of the questionnaire. I would like you all to help me translate these into a comprehensive list of appropriate questions that we could ask about the zoo and the visitors' day here. We should word them so that people can make a judgement of their perceptions of the quality of the service they have experienced, on a 1 to 5 scale, where 1 is very bad and 5 is very good, and hence 3 is average. The scores will then be analysed using statistical software.*

'It is essential that our questions also reflect the areas that are relevant and of importance to the zoo, and that are within the control of the zoo, so that you can act to alter or influence the provision of the quality of those aspects of the service. It is equally important that the questions are not ambiguous, too complex, or leading. Consequently the wording must be kept simple and the phraseology might use terms such as "how did you rate" to avoid leading statements such as "how good" or "how bad", which may influence the respondents' rating score.

'Having ascertained how the visitors perceive the quality of the service the zoo provides, the second part of the questionnaire will be designed to discover what customers expected from the zoo during their visit. This can be achieved by providing a list of short statements derived from each of the questions asked in the first section of the questionnaire. Each statement will be a non-committal sentence which does not indicate that this is the standard actually provided by London Zoo, but rather it is a desired standard that should be provided. The respondent will be asked to consider their expectations of the zoo, and to select and rank the top ten statements. This would enable us to obtain an indication of exactly what visitors wanted from their visit to the zoo.'

After several attempts at designing the questionnaire, including a reduction in the number of questions to manageable levels, a final version was agreed (*see* Appendix 32.3). It was necessary for visitors to have experienced a large proportion of the zoo's facilities and service process, as a result all respondents had to have been at the zoo for at least two hours prior to the interview (half the average visit duration) in order to be allowed to complete a questionnaire, assisted by Adrian. As a result, interviewing only started after 12.30 p.m. on any given day so that visitors could have been at the zoo for the requisite time, and interviewing continued until 5.30 p.m. when the zoo closed. Because each interview took approximately 15 minutes, it was considered necessary to approach potential interviewees who were already resting, as would often be the case for visitors who had already been at the zoo for two hours.

As a result the areas used to select potential respondents were predominately those in which people were likely to be resting and eating, namely seating areas, and near to the restaurant and cafe facilities.

The interviews were conducted on a group basis with all members of the group taking part. It was stressed that the questions should be answered with respect to the group as a whole. For example, the visibility of the animals would include a child's ability to see as well as an adult. Access would include the ability to gain access for those with pushchairs and small children or elderly people as well as adults. Other questions involving perceptions were usually answered following a discussion which gave rise to a consensus, if a strong divergence of views occurred, which was rare within a group, either those with the strongest (not necessarily the most extreme views) or a majority vote usually prevailed. A consensus group view was also obtained for the second part of the questionnaire to obtain a top ten priority ranking of those aspects of the visit that they felt the zoo should provide.

The expected subjective variability of the responses that would be obtained, required a large sample size over a broad range of attendance levels. The survey was carried out over the summer months of July, August and September 1995. This included the school summer holidays, a bank holiday and a pre and post-holiday period. This would sample a wide range of attendances, which were predicted to be between 1000 to 9500 visitors per day. The sample days selected reflected this range. The size of the overall sample was therefore determined by the fact that each individual day had to have a potentially statistical credible size group, the size only being limited by the number of people that could be questioned on any given day. The target number of completed questionnaires per day was 20.

Having agreed the design of the questionnaire, and selected the appropriate segment of visitors for interviewees, the range of sample days, the sample times and other criteria, Dr Gipps concluded:

> *'All our previous market research has been on a very different track. We know a great deal about our visitors' demographics, where they come from, and the newspapers they read. However, I can now appreciate that we didn't find out anything about what they thought about their visit, or how we performed in giving them a good day out, nor what they actually wanted or expected from us or their visit in the first place. The one commonality with Adrian's work is that we also carried out the survey on a wide range of days from the slowest to almost the busiest, so that when we averaged the results we got a really representative view of the average visitor on an average day. The only days we didn't survey were the really busy ones, because we felt that it might only add to any problems. If people were tired due to queues and the general bustle, the last thing they would want to do was answer a list of questions!'*

RESULTS

Over the three-month period of the survey (July, August and September 1995), a total of 755 questionnaires were completed on 38 separate days. The first was carried out on 20 July before the school summer holidays had begun, and the last on 18 September after the schools had gone back. The attendance levels varied between 1046 on 18 September and 9554 on the August Bank Holiday Monday. The total number of people to visit the zoo on these days was 183 395, with an average daily attendance level of 4826 visitors. The mean group size was 3.6 with a modal group size of 4. This represented mainly family parties, and of these a mean of 1.9 or 43 per cent of all visitors were children under 16. Most people arrived between 11.00 a.m. and 12.29 p.m., and the mean visit time was four hours 50 minutes. The weather was consistently excellent during the entire research period, as the UK experienced one of its hottest and driest summers on record.

The results for the performance and priority sections of the survey were digitised and fed into a spreadsheet in order to analyse the huge quantity of data, using a combination of standard and specially written software. The results were analysed and the scores scaled onto a 1 to 5 scale, with 1 representing the poorest performance or of very low priority, and 5 representing an excellent performance or the highest priority to be provided by the zoo. This scaling was simple for the performance ratings as the visitor had already awarded a score of 1 to 5, and so the final rating was simply an average of the scores achieved for each day or appropriate attendance band. The scaling of the priorities assigned to each aspect of a visit was more complex. The priorities were given as rankings and were therefore relative. Each priority ranking was assigned a score with the highest priority (1) receiving the highest score, the lowest priority (10) receiving the lowest score, and all those not included in the top ten list were given a score of zero. All the scores assigned to any given aspect were added together for any given day or attendance band, and these were then ranked in order of scores, with the highest overall score representing the highest overall priority. To scale these scores onto a 1–5 scale, the highest score achieved by any aspect in any attendance band was awarded a score of 5, and then all the other scores were scaled by the same factor to achieve a score between 0–5. As only the highest score achieved in any set of attendance bands was awarded a 5 it enabled a true comparison to be made between attendance bands, to see how priorities changed under different conditions.

The results were collected and presented in four categories:

1 The overall results averaged for all the data sets obtained

2 The data divided into three groups of daily visitor attendance levels:
   (a) (b1) 0 to 2999 visitors per day;
   (b) (b2) 3000 to 5999 visitors per day;
   (c) (b3) over 6000 visitors per day.

The performance and priority results are tabulated in Appendix 32.4 and 32.5 respectively.

At first sight the data appeared to show that the zoo was performing well overall, although there was significant variation between different attributes of quality. Also, as could be expected, there was a wide variation in the priority rankings with some factors scoring almost a maximum score of 5, and others only a quarter of that.

Adrian's task was the interpretation and use of the data to help the zoo's management derive some idea of how it was performing in providing their visitors with a good day out and where it was failing to provide a reasonable quality of service, and under what conditions this occurred. He would have to summarise the visitors' rankings of the zoo's performance and of what they expected from the zoo. And finally he would have to help the zoo determine a prioritised plan of action to improve its service delivery system.

Questions

1 (a) Using the 18 determinants of service quality, devise your own questionnaire for the zoo. Compare your questionnaire to the one actually used.
  (b) Which determinants of service quality are investigated by which question?

2 What do the various sets of figures tell you about the zoo's performance from the visitors' perspective? In which are the zoo performing best of all, and where are the areas of poor performance? Which areas and type of the operational processes do they reflect? How and why do they vary?

3 Do the visitors' priorities vary in a similar manner and why?

4 Derive a plan of action and priority list which will help the zoo decide which aspects of its service provision to tackle first. What factors may need to be taken into account while formulating this order of action?

5 Evaluate the strengths and weaknesses of the questionnaire in its objective of providing a priority agenda for improvement to operations.

APPENDIX 32.1
THE MISSION STATEMENT OF THE ZOOLOGICAL SOCIETY OF LONDON

To promote the worldwide conservation of animals and their habitats by presenting outstanding living collections, breeding threatened species, increasing public awareness through information and education, conducting relevant research, and undertaking action in the field.

The Society pursues this mission by:

1 keeping and presenting animals in accordance with best practice;
2 giving priority to species that are threatened in the wild;
3 increasing public understanding of animals and their welfare and of the issues involved in their conservation;
4 maintaining an outstanding education and information programme, particularly for school children and families;
5 undertaking field conservation programmes, both in the UK and abroad;
6 developing its role as a leading centre for research on conservation biology and animal welfare;
7 fulfilling its role as a learned society and force for zoology and animal conservation through publications, scientific meetings, lectures, the award of prizes for outstanding achievement and the promotion of conservation policy.

(Source: The Annual Report 1994–95 of The Zoological Society of London).

APPENDIX 32.2
DEFINITIONS OF THE 18 DETERMINANTS OF SERVICE QUALITY

Determinant	*Definition*
Access	The physical approachability of service location, including the ease of finding one's way around the service environment and clarity of route.
Aesthetics	Extent to which the components of the service package are agreeable or pleasing to the customer, including both the appearance and the ambience of the service environment, the appearance and presentation of service facilities, goods and staff.
Attentiveness and helpfulness	The extent to which the service, particularly contact staff, either provide help to the customer or give the impression of being interested in the customer and show a willingness to serve.
Availability	The availability of service facilities, staff and goods to the customer. In the case of contact staff this means both the staff/customer ratio and the amount of time each staff member has available to spend with each customer. In the case of service goods availability, includes both the quantity and range of products made available to the customer.

Determinant	*Definition*
Care	The concern, consideration, sympathy and patience shown to the customer. This includes the extent to which the customer is put at ease by the service and made to feel emotionally (rather than physically) comfortable.
Cleanliness and tidiness	The cleanliness, neat and tidy appearance of the tangible components of the service package, including the service environment, facilities, goods and contact staff.
Comfort	The physical comfort of the service environment and facilities.
Commitment	Staff's apparent commitment to their work, including the pride and satisfaction they apparently take in their job, their diligence and thoroughness.
Communica-tion	Ability of the service to communicate in an understandable way with the customer. The clarity, completeness and accuracy of both verbal and written information, and the ability to listen to and understand the customer.
Competence	The skill, expertise and professionalism with which the service is executed. This includes the carrying out of correct procedures, correct execution of customer instructions, degree of product or service knowledge exhibited by contact staff, the rendering of good advice, and the general ability to do a good job.
Courtesy	The politeness, respect and propriety shown by the service, usually contact staff, in dealing with the customer and his or her property. This includes the ability of staff to be unobtrusive and uninterfering when appropriate
Flexibility	A willingness and ability on the part of the service worker to amend or alter the nature of the service or product to meet the needs of the customer.
Friendliness	The warmth and personal approachability (rather than physical approachability) of the service, particularly of contact staff, including cheerful attitude, the ability to make the customer feel welcome.
Functionality	The serviceability and fitness for purpose or 'product quality' of service facilities and goods.
Integrity	The honesty, justice, fairness and trustworthiness with which customers are treated by the service organisation.
Reliability	The reliability and consistency of performance of service facilities, goods and staff. This includes punctual service delivery and ability to keep to agreements made with the customer.
Responsiveness	Speed and timeliness of service delivery. This includes the speed of throughput and the ability of the service to respond promptly to customer service requests, with minimal waiting and queuing time.
Security	Personal safety of the customer and his or her possessions while participating in or benefiting from the service process. This includes the maintenance of confidentiality.

Source: Johnston, R. 'The determinants of service quality, satisfiers and dissatisfiers', *International Journal of Service Industry Management*, Vol 6, No 5, 1995, pp. 53–71.

APPENDIX 32.3
LONDON ZOO CUSTOMER QUESTIONNAIRE

The first page of the questionnaire recorded details of the respondents' group size, ages, times of arrival and of anticipated departure, the time and date of the interview, and the weather conditions

These questions are intended to be answered relatively quickly to reflect your general perceptions of your visit. If you are completing the questionnaire as part of a group, please feel free to discuss your answers briefly within your group.

Questions 1–29 are scored on a 1–5 scale, where 1 reflects the lowest degree of satisfaction and 5 the highest, or you can leave it blank *(a separate card as below was provided for reference).*

1 = Very bad / very disappointing / unacceptably poor / never or rarely.
2 = Bad /disappointing / poor / not frequently enough.
3 = Average /usually / could be improved.
4 = Good /above average / most of the time.
5 = Very good indeed /very satisfactory / delighted / always

Or leave blank

Please answer questions 1–28 on the separate answer sheet (*not included in this case*) by ringing the appropriate number (1 ... 2 ... 3 ... 4 ... 5)

1 How do you rate the parking facilities (being able to find a parking space)?

2 How do you rate being able to find your way around the zoo?

3 How do you rate the access and being able to move freely around the zoo?

4 How do you rate the visibility of the animals?

5 How do you rate the happiness of the animals with their environment?

6 How do you rate your overall impression of the appearance of the zoo?

7 How do you rate the attentiveness and helpfulness of:
(a) The staff?
(b) The volunteers (Information *etc.*)?

8 How did you rate the level and usefulness of the contact with staff?

9 For your needs:
(a) How do you rate the number of animals available to see?
(b) How do you rate the number of events and presentations?

10 How would you rate how London Zoo looks after its animals?

11 How do you rate London Zoo as a conservation organisation?

12 How would you rate how London Zoo looks after you, its visitors?

13 How would you rate your visit to London Zoo as an educational experience?

14 How do you rate the cleanliness and tidiness of London Zoo?

15 How do you rate the smartness and tidiness of the staff at London Zoo?

16 How do you rate the comfort of the animals at London Zoo?

17 How do you rate the quality and provision of toilet facilities throughout the zoo?

18 How do you rate the quality and provision of catering facilities throughout the zoo?

19 How do you rate the commitment of London Zoo to:
(a) The animals?
(b) You, its visitors?
(c) Conservation and Education?

20 How do you rate the degree to which the information available arond the zoo answered any questions or interests you had?

21 How do you rate the professionalism of London Zoo at:
(a) Caring for their animals?
(b) Customer care?

22 How do you rate London Zoo as a friendly place to be?

23 Overall how do you rate your day out at London Zoo?

24 Having been to London Zoo, how do you rate the honesty of London Zoo in its aim of *Conservation in Action*?

25 How do you rate the quality of the events and presentations?

26 How do you rate the time you spent queuing at London Zoo?

27 How do you rate your safety and that of your group, during your day at London Zoo?

28 How do you rate London Zoo for value for money?

29 When thinking about today's visit to London Zoo, **which 10 of the factors** listed below would you consider that a zoo should provide generally or during your visit when you are deciding whether to come again and/or recommending London Zoo to friends or family? **Please number these in order of priority (1 = highest priority)**.

For example; If you think being able to see the animals is the factor of highest priority when you consider visiting London Zoo again, or recommending it to friends and family, put a '1' in the priority box in row 4. Then put a '2' in the priority box of the next most important factor, and so on until '10'.

No.	*Factor*	*Priority*
1	It is easy to find a parking space.	
2	It is easy to find your way around the zoo.	
3	There is good access and it is easy to move freely around the zoo.	
4	It is easy to see the animals.	
5	The animals are happy with their environment.	
6	The zoo is in a good condition.	
7a	The staff are attentive and helpful.	
7b	The volunteers are attentive and helpful.	

No.	*Factor*	*Priority*
8	There is plentiful contact with the staff.	
9a	There are enough animals to see.	
9b	There are enough events and presentations to see.	
10	The animals are looked after well.	
11	The zoo is an important conservation organisation.	
12	The visitors are looked after well.	
13	A visit to the zoo is a good educational experience.	
14	The zoo is clean and tidy.	
15	The staff are clean and tidy.	
16	The animals are comfortable.	
17	There are enough high quality toilet facilities.	
18	There are enough high quality catering facilities.	
19a	The zoo is committed to its animals.	
19b	The zoo is committed to its visitors.	
19c	The zoo is committed to conservation and education.	
20	There is sufficient information available to answer your questions and interests.	
21a	The zoo is a professional organisation with respect to the care of its animals.	
21b	The zoo is a professional organisation with respect to the care of its visitors.	
22	It is a friendly place to be.	
23	Overall a visit to the zoo is an enjoyable day out.	
24	The zoo is honest in its aim of *Conservation in Action*.	
25	The events and presentations are of high quality.	
26	There is minimal queuing.	
27	It is a safe place to spend the day.	
28	It is good value for money.	

Any Other Comments:

APPENDIX 32.4
PERFORMANCE SCORES

This table shows the mean performance scores achieved by each attribute investigated. The mean scores are calculated overall, and for three bands of attendance levels.

		Adjusted mean performance score (1–5 scale)			
Question number	*Aspect of visit*	*Overall*	*0–2999 visitors*	*3000–6000 visitors*	*over 6000 visitors*
1	Parking	3.36	4.31	3.53	1.82
2	Find way around zoo	2.41	2.38	2.66	1.99
3	Access, free movement	3.49	4.46	3.57	2.45
4	Visibility of animals	2.18	2.18	2.17	1.96
5	Happiness of animals	1.96	2.23	2.13	1.78
6	Appearance of zoo	2.08	2.28	2.65	1.32
7(a)	Attentative & helpfulness: staff	2.45	2.70	3.03	1.76
7(b)	Attentative & helpfulness: volunteers	3.69	3.58	4.27	3.80
8	Contact with staff	1.10	0.60	1.62	1.07
9(a)	Number of animals to see	2.88	2.79	3.08	2.64
9(b)	Number of events and presentations	2.01	1.77	2.53	2.19
10	Care of animals	3.77	4.07	3.88	3.46
11	Conservation organisation	4.01	4.90	3.91	3.44
12	Care of visitors	2.31	2.08	2.69	1.86
13	Educational experience	3.58	4.12	3.57	3.01
14	Cleanliness and tidiness	2.76	4.46	2.99	1.73
15	Smartness and tidiness of staff	2.54	3.13	2.79	2.03
16	Comfort of animals	1.73	2.43	1.87	1.51
17	Quality and provision of toilets	2.46	2.79	2.56	1.49
18	Quality and provision of catering	1.72	1.67	2.29	1.18
19(a)	Commitment to animals	4.37	4.47	4.47	3.99
19(b)	Commitment to visitors	2.86	2.11	3.24	1.97
19(c)	Commitment to conservation/educn.	3.37	3.93	3.56	3.13
20	Availability of information	2.66	2.38	2.89	2.31
21(a)	Professionalism: care for animals	4.37	3.77	4.58	4.01
21(b)	Professionalism: customer care	2.29	1.87	2.64	1.72
22	Friendliness	3.36	2.29	4.02	2.33
23	Overall as day out	4.39	3.10	4.35	3.32
24	Honesty of aims of London Zoo	3.09	3.34	3.22	2.66
25	Quality of events and presentations	3.42	3.02	3.99	2.67
26	Time queueing	3.22	4.36	3.46	2.64
27	Safety of you/group	3.46	3.33	3.43	3.43
28	Value for money	2.68	2.27	2.99	2.45

APPENDIX 32.5
PRIORITY SCORES

This table shows the mean priority scores achieved by each attribute investigated. The mean scores are calculated overall, and for three bands of attendance levels.

		Adjusted mean performance score (1–5 scale)			
Question number	*Aspect of visit*	*Overall*	*0–2999 visitors*	*3000–6000 visitors*	*over 6000 visitors*
1	Parking	2.48	1.29	2.66	3.28
2	Find way around zoo	3.29	3.17	3.39	3.47
3	Access, free movement	3.27	3.21	3.05	3.40
4	Visibility of animals	4.78	4.72	4.94	4.69
5	Happiness of animals	4.79	4.89	4.52	5.00
6	Appearance of zoo	2.60	2.86	3.04	2.03
7(a)	Attentative & helpfulness: staff	3.01	2.63	2.89	3.46
7(b)	Attentative & helpfulness: volunteers	2.83	1.92	2.86	3.50
8	Contact with staff	3.07	2.88	3.09	3.36
9(a)	Number of animals to see	3.78	3.57	3.83	4.01
9(b)	Number of events and presentations	3.30	3.08	3.17	3.74
10	Care of animals	4.65	4.78	4.31	4.76
11	Conservation organisation	3.07	3.30	3.22	2.88
12	Care of visitors	2.38	2.37	2.12	2.87
13	Educational experience	3.67	3.51	3.29	3.75
14	Cleanliness and tidiness	3.54	3.44	3.19	3.79
15	Smartness and tidiness of staff	2.19	1.88	2.43	2.05
16	Comfort of animals	3.43	3.47	3.70	3.44
17	Quality and provision of toilets	2.73	2.87	2.60	2.73
18	Quality and provision of catering	2.37	2.52	2.14	2.54
19(a)	Commitment to animals	3.82	3.84	3.58	3.87
19(b)	Commitment to visitors	3.39	3.52	3.22	3.77
19(c)	Commitment to conservation/educn.	3.71	3.62	3.41	3.48
20	Availability of information	2.99	2.99	2.68	3.27
21(a)	Professionalism: care for animals	3.08	3.52	2.86	2.87
21(b)	Professionalism: customer care	2.68	2.54	2.32	3.08
22	Friendliness	3.00	2.73	2.92	3.01
23	Overall, as day out	4.10	3.96	4.16	4.42
24	Honesty of aims of London Zoo	2.89	2.85	2.51	3.17
25	Quality of events and presentations	2.31	2.88	1.87	2.73
26	Time queueing	3.23	3.17	2.88	3.06
27	Safety of you/group	2.81	3.08	2.33	3.16
28	Value for money	3.18	3.26	2.66	3.66

CASE 33

Bristol & West Building Society

Robert Johnston

Case date 1996

BENCHMARKING

Peter Woodrow, the Information Management Manager with Bristol & West Building Society:

> *'We are doing well but we cannot afford to be complacent. To keep us on our toes and help us keep improving what we do I think we need to benchmark ourselves against other organisations. Though the problems are which measures do we use and which organisations should we benchmark ourselves against?'*

With a head office in Bristol and 158 branches mostly focused in the south and south-west of England, Bristol & West is one of the top ten building societies in the UK.

> *'We are currently using the EFQM framework to help us develop our measures and improvement activities and we have found, maybe not surprisingly, that we have quite a few measures of results but that we are less good at measuring the enablers.*
>
> *'We obviously have a lot of information in terms of volumes about all of our products; mortgages and savings, for example, and details of all money flows on a daily basis – all the "day to day measures" needed for running such a business. We use these performance measures to compare the activities of our various branches. We also have lots of measures of "competitiveness" and we send monthly returns to the Building Society Association (BSA) and Building Society Commission (BSC). The material they produce allows us to compare ourselves with the rest of the building society industry (though not on a one-to-one basis). We do measure customer satisfaction and employee satisfaction but maybe not in a particularly sophisticated way, though we are working on this at the moment.*
>
> *'We want to do some benchmarking to see how we can improve what we are doing and also to try to ensure that what we do is adding value to our customers and other stakeholders. Should we look, for example, at the Cheltenham & Gloucester? They are very focused in terms of their products and services or should we look at the Halifax because it is the biggest, or Midshires because they have a good reputation for customer service . . . or British Airways?*

'I don't want us to waste our time creating measures for the sake of measuring things. I want us to choose things that will help us improve and know how far in front or behind we are.'

Questions

1 Which organisations do you think Bristol & West should choose to benchmark itself against? Explain the reasons for your choice.

2 What is the purpose of benchmarking?

CASE 34

Talleres Auto

Christine Harland

Case date 1996

INTRODUCTION

Many businesses were identifying in the early 1990s that Spain was a market ripe for development. Business consultancy practices were focusing more attention on this market and were posting consultants to Spain to take advantage of opportunities arising there. One such opportunity arose for Taylor Associates, an international consultancy company, in the form of a brief from a Spanish businessman.

THE BRIEF

Antonio Playan was a dapper, amiable man, short in stature but with his silk bow ties he had a certain presence. He was a selfmade businessman who had started life buying automotive components working for Seat but had quickly formed his own local parts distribution business – Distribucione Barcelona – which had grown rapidly. He prided himself with a caring, attentive attitude to business, customers, employees and suppliers. Antonio's style of conducting business was to build close relationships with customers over years; many of his customers were friends of the family. The majority of customers had been doing business with him for over 10 years. His sales representatives were trusted to top up their customers' stores with regular stock items periodically. The garage owners used the representatives as a source of expertise for technical advice; each rep. had his own forte so they all helped out with technical support for each other's accounts. Playan's people would always source a part for customers that they did not have in stock.

Many people in the industry that knew him believed that it was this attention to detail which had brought him success over the years.

By 1991, in addition to the central Barcelona parts distribution branch, Playan also owned a warehouse that fed this and six other wholly owned branches in a radius of 25 kilometres. Playan also owned half the equity in a further six branches, five in Barcelona and the sixth in Cerida, all fed from the central warehouse. In addition, this warehouse supplied 135 independent parts shops and garages spread over Cataluna. The split in sales between these is shown in Fig. 34.1.

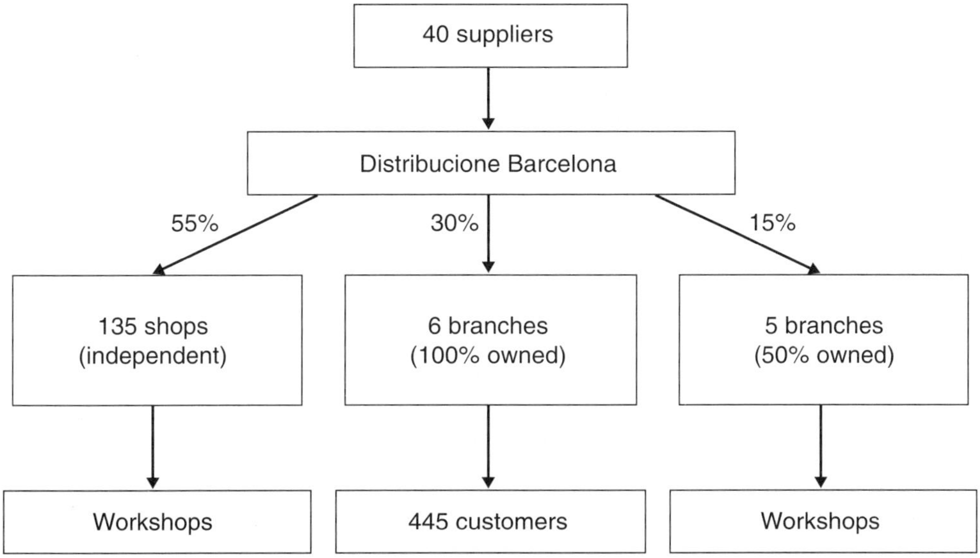

Fig. 34.1 Distribucione Barcelona Supply Network

Antonio Playan had been watching the aftermarket (the service, repair and parts supply market) in Spain very carefully. It was apparent to him that the less developed countries in the EU, such as Spain, Portugal and Greece, exhibited more of a DIY repair culture, rather than using garages to replace complete parts. However, Spain was changing and he thought that while owners in suburbs and villages would still do many of their own repairs, city centre dwellers would tend to replace parts. This, he felt, was partly because most people in the cities lived in apartments without garages. As 76 per cent of Spaniards now lived in urban areas this represented a substantial replacement market. Another factor of change in Spain was the mix in the car parc (the profile of makes and models in existence in a country at any one time). In what was traditionally a market dominated by small Seats, there was a significant increase in variety of cars in Spain.

Playan wanted his business to grow to be the major automotive aftermarket distributor in Cataluna but, having seen several differences between the aftermarkets in cach country he had been to, he was unclear how they, the Spanish aftermarket, may develop. Taylor Associates had been given the brief to assess the best development route for his automotive parts business in this market.

THE SPANISH AND UK AUTOMOTIVE AFTERMARKETS

In Spain, there was a lower percentage of car ownership than in the UK. The models bought still tended to be 'cheap and cheerful' small family cars in comparison to the UK where there was a reasonable spread of types of vehicles including larger, more expensive models such as BMWs and Mercedes.

The total car parc and the content of the parc affects the automotive aftermarket. New cars tended to need little attention, and therefore fewer parts, other than regular servicing. Most new car owners take their cars back to the franchised Vehicle Manufacturer's agent for two main reasons. First, many new cars are owned by company fleets who have them serviced regularly by main agents and second, many new cars are supported by warranties tied to servicing by approved agents. As cars get a little older, they need more repairs, therefore visits to the garage become more frequent. Third, many cars are sold after three years, passing to a different set of owners. Secondhand car buyers are often less willing to use VM agents because they perceive their charges to be substantially higher than independent garages. Therefore, cars from 0–3 years old are usually serviced and repaired by VM agents but most cars from 3–7 years old are taken to independent garages. Once cars are seven years old or more, many owners do their own repairs, buying parts from parts shops and scrap yards.

Figure 34.2 shows the structure of the Spanish aftermarket, taking the example of a wheel cylinder, and the various routes that parts passed through until they are installed on owners' cars.

In well developed markets such as the UK and the US, specialists had evolved. These specialists were of three major types – the fast-fit operator, the menu service and the technical specialists. Fast-fit operators focused on one or two products, such as tyres or exhausts, and kept large ranges of model types. Their name came from the speed of service, for which vehicles need not be pre-booked. Menu service operators dealt with a slightly larger range of tasks such as brake and clutch repair and routine service. Rather than stock a large range of parts they stocked the volume movers then ordered parts for delivery within an hour. Their name came from the fixed price menu offered to customers so no five o'clock surprise bill was given when the car was picked up. Generally no pre-booking was required for these. The technical specialist concentrated on repairs usually requiring a high level of expertise and diagnostic equipment, for example autoelectro injection centres.

Taylor Associates identified that the Spanish market was ripe for menu service outlets which weren't then a feature of the industry. They proposed that Playan set up a chain of menu service operations. A year later Playan had opened eight menu service outlets under the name of Talleres Auto. Taking his consultants' advice, Playan had recruited a manager from the UK who had managed both menu service and fast-fit operations.

THE CUSTOMER EXPERIENCE

The Need

Wendy Harrison was nipping along the side streets off the Ramblas in Barcelona at 11.15 p.m. on a November night when suddenly it seemed to go very dark. Braking hard, she squinted out of her windscreen into the darkness and noticed the headlights

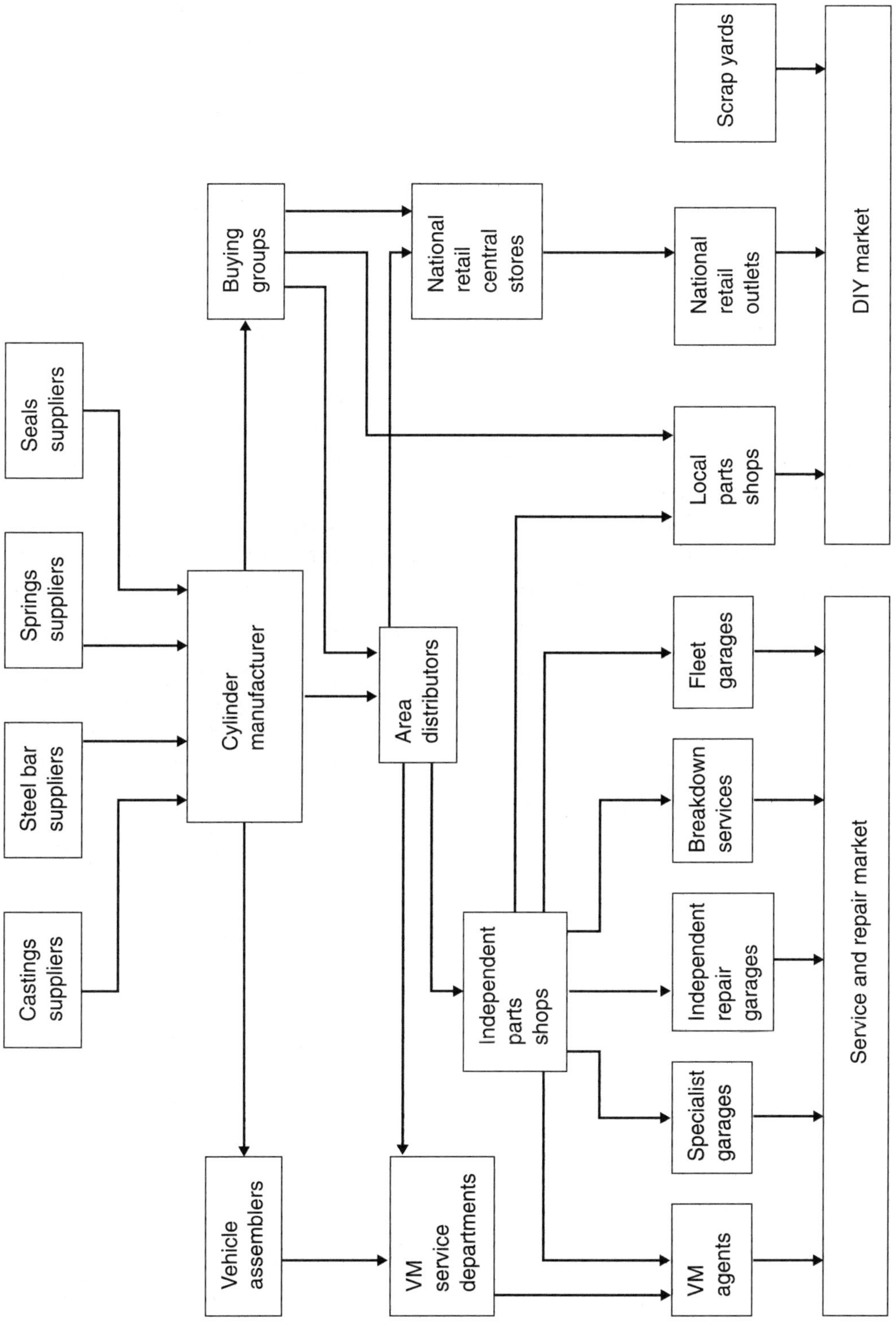

Figure 34.2 Spanish aftermarket structure

of her VW Scirocco flickering. She turned them off and on again and found that when she pressed hard on the headlight switch they stayed on but when she released her finger, they faltered and went out. Her first reaction was to lock the car doors centrally as she was aware that women driving cars slowly in that area had fallen prey to opportunist attackers who usually mugged to steal handbags. Wendy then drove, as carefully as she could, with one finger pressed on the lightswitch, except when she needed to change gear.

When she got home she was greeted by her boyfriend, Tom, who listened sympathetically. Wendy complained that she did not have time to leave the car at the local garage Tom had used last for servicing his Audi Coupe; it seemed to take them ages to get the parts and then the car was in for a few days. As she had recently started her own company with a friend, she was very busy driving round large organisations such as Seat to sell their services which were business English courses. The VW franchised agents were so expensive, she was reluctant to take the car there as it was now coming up to five years old and they intended to sell it in a few months, hopefully buying a company car if the business took off.

Tom was over in Spain working for a large consultancy house, Taylor Associates, focusing on distribution; he specialised in the automotive sector. He explained the following to her:

'Back in the UK there are a lot of service centres cropping up who are stealing business from the local garages and the larger, more expensive franchised agents. These service centres offer a "menu" for a range of standard repairs, such as clutch replacement, and regular services. They target working women in particular who represent an increasing percentage of car owners and who want a friendly, unintimidating place to take their cars and not feel as though they are being gawped at or ripped off by dirty mechanics.

'We were doing some work a few months ago for a great bloke called Antonio Playan who has just opened a chain of these in Barcelona, Bilbao and Sans Sebastian. It's called Talleres Auto. He's even employed an English guy who's managed service centres in the UK to run the biggest branch in Barcelona. It's five minutes from here; why don't you try them? While you're at it, your car is due for a service so get that done at the same time.'

This was his normal forthright style of talk but it did strike a chord with Wendy who had always felt a bit awkward going to garages. She decided that she might as well try them out because she really needed the car and she couldn't continue driving with one hand on the headlight switch. She would book it in the next day.

The Experience

Wendy rang Talleres Auto the next morning and explained that she urgently needed the car to be repaired and serviced. She spoke to a polite man who took all the details of the make, model and year of the vehicle and the work to be done. Wendy emphasized that she needed the lights to be done as a priority; he assured her that a faulty switch would be easy to replace and not to worry. She also mentioned that it seemed to have a cold start problem and could they check the brakes for her – they felt a little spongy. She was told that if she brought the car in first thing the next morning she could pick it up by 7 p.m. the following evening. Wendy felt she ought to find out roughly how much to expect to pay so she asked him; he said it would probably be about 16 000 ptas (about £90) for the service and repair but that if it was going to be much more they would ring her first to authorise it.

Next morning, Wendy was in a hurry, as usual. She had to do a presentation to a large insurance company at 8.30 a.m. She just had time to drop the car off and get a taxi to her appointment. On arriving at Talleres Auto, she was greeted by a different man to the one she had spoken to on the phone. Wendy gave her name, took the car keys off her key ring and handed them over and was just about to leave when the man behind the counter asked her what was to be done to the car. Wendy paused, slightly confused, then said she'd given all the details already. However, she was shown the form with her name and vehicle on it but there were no details of the service and repair to be carried out. Feeling rushed now, Wendy quickly described the problem with the headlights, said the brakes were spongy and could they do a full service – the cold start problem slipped her mind in the rush. A little irritated as she was now running late, she turned and briskly walked out to hail a taxi.

Later in the morning, the man who had been on reception at the service centre in the morning rang her on her mobile phone. He explained to her that they had found a few problems when they examined the car; the wheel cylinders were cracked and she needed new brake pads. Wendy's heart sank and she asked how much this would cost; she was told it would be about 30 000 ptas (about £170) altogether. There seemed little choice other than to authorise it, so she did. Once again she asked if the car would be ready that evening, conscious that she was going out to dinner with some girlfriends that night. She also had a 5 a.m. start the next morning with a long drive ahead of her to Zaragoza. She was assured that there was plenty of time before 7 p.m. to finish it.

Wendy struggled through the afternoon to get taxis to her appointments which, though local, were just too far to walk to. She was relieved when, arriving at 6.45 p.m. at Talleres Auto, she saw her Scirocco on the forecourt, ready for collection. A lorry delivering parts was completely blocking the door into the reception; an English man talking to the driver in Spanish offered to take her through the workshop to get into reception the backway. Wendy said she was English and followed him, remembering the conversation with Tom and deducing that this must be the English manager.

Once inside the workshop, Wendy lowered her head, embarrassed, as several mechanics shouted out comments to her as she walked through. The chap leading her smiled and said in a loud voice, 'Ignore these animals – they're not used to a pretty face in here'. Feeling her face slightly flushed, Wendy arrived in reception and was shown to the customer's side of the counter by the Englishman who then proceeded to serve her. He explained that the wheel cylinders had been repaired, new pads fitted, a full service had been done and once the light switch came in in a couple of days she could drop the car off and they'd fit it immediately. The conversation then went something like this:

WENDY: *'What do you mean, when the light switch comes in? Do you mean to say that you haven't repaired the lights?'*

MANAGER: *'No, we couldn't because the part was out of stock but it's promised for two days time; as soon as it comes in we'll give you a ring and fit it for you straightaway.'*

WENDY: *'But I need the car now, tonight, and I've got a long drive tomorrow which will start and finish in the dark. I can't drive part the way to Zaragoza with my finger on the headlight switch, can I?'*

MANAGER: *'I'm sorry but there is very little we can do if we can't get the part. We've ordered it and requested it as urgent.'*

WENDY: *'Why didn't anyone tell me this before?'*

MANAGER: *'Well, somebody should have but it wouldn't have made any difference would it?'*

Wendy flinched at his tone. It was at this point that she became aware of people behind her. Red in the face with anger, Wendy turned round to see three men, presumably customers, waiting to be served. She paid her bill, said she'd bring it back in two days time and left.

Wendy climbed into her car. Looking at her watch, she tried to think through her options and decided to drive slowly home with her finger pressed on the headlight switch, and ask her boyfriend if she could borrow his car. Tom was going out as well that night but she knew it was close enough to use a taxi. As far as she could remember, he was planning to work from home the next day to finish off a report, so she might be able to borrow the Audi for her trip to Zaragoza. Feeling a bit more positive, the feeling only lasted for a minute as she turned the ignition. Failing to start, she turned the key again with no joy. After trying four times, Wendy got out, slammed the door and marched back into the reception. The Spaniards and the Englishman were all having a laugh and a joke. The manager shouted across the others to her, saying, 'What's the trouble, love?' Wendy's eyes closed to slits; she replied through clenched teeth, 'My car has cut out four times on your forecourt.' The manager suggested to Wendy, grinning widely, that she should try the choke. Slightly baffled, Wendy replied that it was fuel injected. He said, 'Oh, so it's got automatic choke.' She said, 'No, that it was fuel injected – it didn't have a choke at all.' The manager suggested Wendy took a seat and he would have someone come and see to her. He then turned to the Spanish men and said, in Spanish, 'I find the same difficulty explaining these things to my wife.' At this Wendy became incensed and replied in Spanish that maybe if he could find a mechanic who understood something about fuel injected cars to come and speak to her, they might get somewhere. Sheepishly, the manager disappeared into the workshop, leaving Wendy puffed up and angry, being stared at amusedly by the other customers.

After a few minutes, an inoffensive looking mechanic, who had probably just been given an earbending, came out and asked her for the keys. He went out to the car, tried it a few times then, when he managed to get it to spring to life, revved it hard for a minute or so and then drove it back into the workshop.

Wendy returned to her seat. Looking at her immediate surroundings, she started to notice that the table and the chairs opposite her were quite grimy. Moving her leg, she sighed in dismay at the state of the chair she was sitting on in her best suit. Nevertheless, she chose to sit quietly and calm down, feeling that she had already drawn enough attention to herself. After a long ten minutes, Wendy saw her car being driven back out from the workshop. The manager came over to her with the carkeys and apologised for keeping her waiting, but said that the car was ready now. He said that the mechanic had been a little over-zealous in tuning the engine for economy. As Wendy enjoyed the acceleration on her car, she said, 'Why would you tune a performance car for economy?' The answer to beat all others was, 'It means you use less petrol that way.'

Wendy mentally gave in at this point and just wanted to go home and have a bath. As she took the keys from the manager and was leaving the reception, his parting remark to her was that next time it would be better if she told them in advance of the problems; they hadn't been told before it had a cold-start problem. Wendy left.

Tired and fed up, Wendy poured out her saga to Tom as he made her a cup of tea in the kitchen. At the point about borrowing his car, he stopped her and explained that tomorrow he had to go to Gerona to visit a client. It wasn't possible for him to lend her it that evening either as he had volunteered to pick two others up. By now, Wendy didn't really feel like going out to dinner, so she rang her friends and cancelled. She also rang her business partner and managed to persuade her to do her next day's appointment, but she knew this was a big favour. With a headache, Wendy took two Panadol and went to bed.

Two days later, just before leaving home to go and have her light switch fitted (she still had to work out how to return the hire car she'd been using, with a busy day ahead) she rang Talleres Auto just to make sure they were ready to fit it immediately. The manager answered and told her that they were still waiting for the light switch to come in, but it was sure to arrive during the day; they'd ring her up as soon as it did. Wendy had such a hectic day, she didn't notice until after the service centre had closed that they hadn't rung. Cross that another day had gone by, paying for a hire car, she went home to have dinner with Tom.

Tom enjoyed the opportunity to impart his knowledge of the business by asking Wendy if it had been ordered VOR. Apparently, there were different levels of urgency ascribed to orders and if a vehicle was off the road (VOR) parts could be couriered at an express speed to the garage within hours. He said it was probably coming from the VW franchise garage they used to use. Wendy mentally cursed Tom for suggesting she tried the service centre and wished she'd paid the extra to use the VW garage. Tom insisted she rang up and found out when it was coming in and if it had been ordered VOR. He also said they should be providing loan cars if they genuinely wanted to compete with the VM agents who would automatically lend a car in this situation (at this point Wendy could have cheerfully crowned her beloved).

Wendy decided to sort things out for herself; the next day she rang the VW agent who said that they were out of stock but would locate a switch for her; in the meantime they could fit a substitute switch which was in plentiful supply. He explained to Wendy that on the Scirocco there used to be a switch which didn't automatically dim the lights when you turned the ignition off. This was improved to one that did, to protect the battery; however, fitting the old switch would at least mean she could use her car safely. Wendy took her car in straightaway and the switch was fitted in two minutes at an additional cost of 3800 ptas. It was worth every peseta.

Wendy didn't ring the service centre and they didn't ring her. As far as she knows, her light switch is still on order. Next time the service was due, Wendy had no hesitation in booking it in with the VM franchised garage.

Questions

1 In what ways did the operation fail?

2 What strategic, structural and infrastructural improvements could be made to ensure the operation did not fail in the future?

CASE 35

Executive Holloware Ltd

Kevan Scholes

*Case date 1990**

INTRODUCTION

'We must get to the bottom of this quality problem,' said Hugh Preston, Managing Director of Executive Holloware Ltd, at one of his regular monthly meetings with senior managers in June 1990.

> *'I've just seen some figures from Jean Lipson's accountants and it appears that it may be costing us more than £3000 each month – and that's only reworking costs and customer returns, heaven only knows what the total cost might be. I've asked Paul Stone from Quality Assurance to look at this problem and report back to me by the end of July. I hope you'll all give him every assistance in sorting this one out.'*

Quality had always been of importance at Executive since many of their products were aimed at the top end of the market and commanded high prices. Their most important product line was silver-plated Georgian tea-sets retailing at anything from £200 upwards. Other products included silver-plated candelabra, small items of giftware (silver-plated), and tea-sets made from pewter and stainless steel.

Executive had been founded in 1948 in Birmingham and began by manufacturing a wide range of cutlery and tableware items. The company had gradually narrowed its range and by 1990 had become one of the leading UK suppliers of top quality holloware as well as continuing to produce items for the less expensive end of the holloware market. Turnover in 1989 exceeded £6 million although the pre-tax profits of only £80 000 had been very disappointing compared with the company's profit performance over the previous ten years. The Chairman's report for the year had sought to explain this poor profit situation:

*This case is based on a real organisation and was prepared by Professor Kevan Scholes, Sheffield Business School, and adapted by Robert Johnston, Warwick Business School. The case is not designed to illustrate either the effective or ineffective handling of an administrative situation, but as a basis for class discussion.

The author gratefully acknowledges the financial assistance of the Nuffield Foundation who supported the writing of this case study.

The results are, of course, a disappointment but are largely a result of production inefficiencies during this period of transferring our traditional craft methods to a batch production, light engineering, type system. We are confident that the new methods will give us the necessary competitive edge and help us return to, and exceed, our previous levels of profitability.

Paul Stone, the Quality Assurance Manager, decided to approach his brief in two ways. First, his department would undertake a quality survey on a sampling basis to assess the scale of the problem and, second, he would talk to people in the company who were either directly or indirectly concerned with quality. He decided to concentrate his efforts, in the first instance, on silver-plated teapots since they were by far the most important item made at Executive.

QUALITY CONTROL AT EXECUTIVE

The Quality Assurance Department's task was to ensure that goods leaving the factory were of the required quality. In addition, the department dealt with customer complaints. Internal quality assurance was performed on a batch sampling basis (10 per cent for most items) of goods leaving the final polishing process (*see* Fig. 35.1

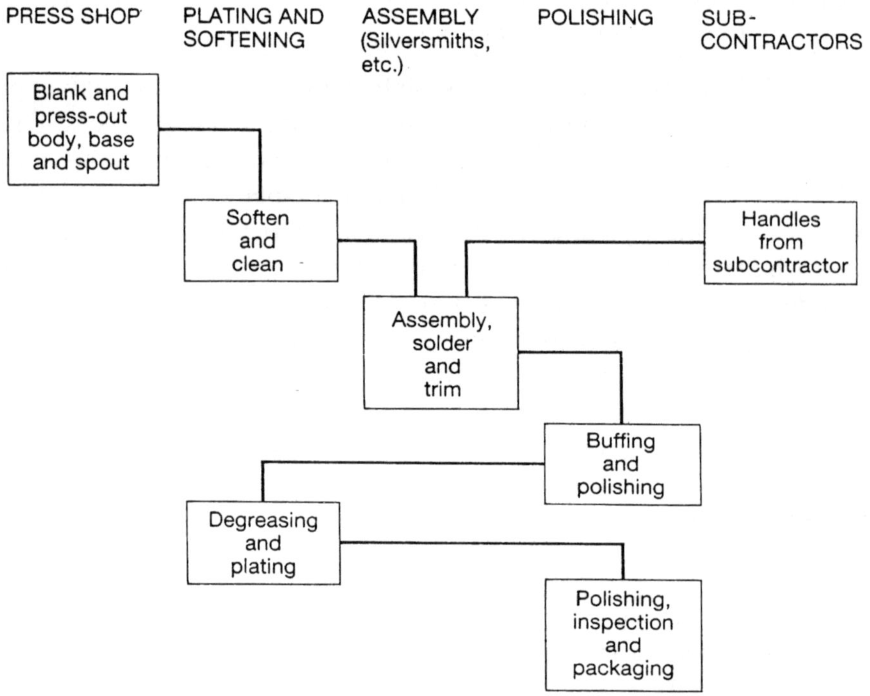

Fig. 35.1 Production route and responsibilities

for the production route and responsibilities). In the case of teapots, they were inspected for both dimensional accuracy and surface finish (scratches and bruises). Batches rejected on a sampling basis were subjected to 100 per cent inspection and rejects either renovated or scrapped (depending on the nature of the defect). Certain items, for example candelabra and top quality tea-sets, were subjected to 100 per cent inspection as a matter of course.

The Quality Assurance Department was, from time to time, involved in investigating quality problems arising during production, or with bought-in components, teapot handles for example. The majority of these investigations arose as a result of complaints from the Buffing and Polishing Department about the number of scratched or bruised items they were having to deal with.

PAUL STONE'S QUALITY SURVEY

In addition to the records that were already available from final inspection (*see* Table 35.1) and customer complaints (Table 35.2), Paul Stone decided to take a random sample of 100 teapots at various stages in the production system and assess their 'quality' in terms of dimensional accuracy and surface condition. The results of his survey are shown in Table 35.3.

Table 35.1 Summary of rejects at final inspection

	Reason for rejection			
	Dimensional accuracy	*Scratches*	*Bruises*	*Total*[a]
Percentage rejected on inspection	0	5	1	5

Note:
[a] Some teapots were rejected for more than one reason.

Table 35.2 Summary of customer complaints

	Nature of complaint			
	Dimensional accuracy	*Scratches*	*Bruises*	*Total*[a]
No complaints per 100 despatches[b]	1	3	2	5

Notes:
[a] One teapot was both scratched and bruised.
[b] Sample size 10 000.

Table 35.3 Quality survey, silver-plated teapots

Stage of production process	*Percentage sub-standard*[a]			
	Dimensional accuracy	*Scratches*	*Bruises*	*Total*[b]
Leaving press shop (bodies only)	2	24	6	28
Prior to assembly (all items)	2	32	6	32
Leaving assembly	0	30	8	32
Leaving buffing and polishing	0	20	1	20

Source: Paul Stone's survey July 1990.
Notes:
[a] Sample size = 100.
[b] Some teapots were rejected on more than one count.

Having completed the survey Paul decided to discuss his findings with Andrew Keegan, the new Production Director at Executive. Andrew Keegan's reaction to the figures was as follows:

'Well, Paul, on the face of it, it looks as though I should have asked you to do a survey like this when I first arrived. There certainly does seem to be a serious problem, particularly on scratching. I know that nickel-silver's not the easiest material to deal with but I'm surprised at the scale of the problem. What I find difficult to swallow is the fact that most of these scratches and bruises are being removed by reworking, so why did they get through the system in the first place? I think we'd both better have a word with Jim Dyer, the Senior Shop Foreman.'

Knowing Jim's reluctance to speak too frankly when Andrew Keegan was around, Paul decided that he had better chat with Jim by himself if he was to get any useful information on the quality angle. He met Jim later that day in his office. Paul explained the results of his survey and asked for Jim's opinion:

'I don't doubt that your people have done a good job, Paul,' said Jim, 'but you know the problems as well as I do. First of all, how do you decide what is and what is not a scratch? Even after twenty years I'm not sure how consistent I am on that one. Then of course there's Keegan breathing down my neck all the time about output – I mean he can't have it both ways, can he? What's more, the lads in the shop can't spend all day worrying about every little scratch – what would their pay packet look like at the end of the week if they did? I think it'd be quite a good idea if you had a chat with Alan Jones in the buffing shop. He had a go at me only last week about this one!'

Paul decided to take up Jim Dyer's suggestion and managed to speak to Alan Jones a couple of days later. He told Alan he was particularly interested in his views on the scratching and bruising problems. Alan was only too willing to tell him!

'You probably know that I had a bit of a barny with Jim Dyer over this last week. It was about one batch of teapots we got from assembly which were in a dreadful state. Apart from some deep scratches, half of them were bruised and should never have been let out of the shop. Jim seemed to feel I was being too fussy but quite honestly if we've got to sort out rubbish like that we'll never earn a living wage. I don't think the assembly workers care any more. When I worked up there we used to do our own buffing and polishing and problems like this never arose but with the new set-up "the sooner they get them out and on the worksheet the better" seems to be the attitude. They don't seem to care if we send half of them back – it gives them more work to do.'

Paul decided that before he could put his report together he needed to see John Wells, the Sales Director, and Jean Lipson in Finance. He managed to see John Wells the following week and asked him about the customer complaints situation:

'Frankly you probably know as much about this as I do since it's your people who investigate the complaints. As you know, most complaints come from the shops and very few from the public, although this may not be a fair picture as the shops may not be passing on customer complaints. In the case of Georgian tea-sets, I'm sure that we're very often accepting responsibility for scratching that isn't our fault, but it's difficult to prove that, of course. The trouble is that the tea-sets usually need to go back to buffing and then replating, which must cost us a penny or two. One thing I find funny is that we've had very few complaints about the new range, probably because they're fighting each other to get hold of them as they're selling like hot cakes apparently. The thing that worries me most at the moment is the backlog of work in the factory is lengthening my delivery times.'

Paul met with Jean Lipson, the Finance Director, that afternoon and asked for her opinion on the whole quality problem:

'I raised this with the MD because it's something that worried me for a long time,' said Jean. 'The trouble, as I see it, is that we really don't know what's going on. For example, it's almost impossible to sort out reworking from normal work and even if you manage that its only guesswork as to the costs of reworking. I know that Andrew Keegan seems to think that a lot of the overtime in the buffing shop must be due to reworking and he'd like to cut it down.'

Following this chat Paul decided it was about time he sat down and started work on his report if he was to meet the MD's deadline. The situation certainly didn't seem so straightforward as he had assumed it might be!

Questions

1 Why is quality important to Executive Holloware?

2 What do you understand by the term 'quality'?

3 How would you specify 'quality' for Executive Holloware?

4 What are the underlying causes of the problems for Executive Holloware?

5 How should Executive Holloware measure quality at each stage in the process?

6 What steps would you advise Paul Stone to take to improve quality performance at Executive Holloware?

CASE 36

Courage Ltd

Robert Johnston

Case date 1988

CRISIS IN THE BREWING INDUSTRY

In 1987 the public house trade was facing a crisis. People were spending less and less in public houses in the UK, not only because of the current economic recession but also as a result of increasing pressures to reduce the nation's consumption of alcohol. Each company in the industry was having to work hard just to maintain its share of a slowly declining market. There were many attempts being made by the breweries to deal with the situation: divestment, changing public houses into eating houses, increasing the range of products, improving the appeal of pubs to certain market segments, and so on. The situation was expected to become even more difficult, this time for demographic reasons, as the population of 18–30 year olds, the majority of drinkers, was starting to decline.

THE COURAGE SOLUTION

Courage Ltd was a part of Imperial Brewing and Leisure Group and had bases in Bristol, Reading and Tadcaster. The company sold its beer through its 1356 managed public houses, which were situated mainly in the north of England.

Kevin Flanagan was the senior manager responsible for staff training and development at Courage. He had some firm ideas as to how Courage could face this crisis:

> *'There is a need for any brewery that is to survive in the beer, wine and spirit retail trade to be able to differentiate itself from the competition. This is not an easy task as all our competitors have similar locations, similar products and similar prices. Even when a competitor brings out a new product, it is relatively easy for us or anyone else to reproduce it at similar prices. The problem is that Courage does not have a unique selling point. There is nothing that differentiates us from the competition.*
>
> *'One factor that I believe is the underlying key to success is based on the observation that the volume of trade in a pub does not seem to be too closely related to products or promotions or to market strengths or weaknesses, but is very much dependent upon the*

licensed house manager (LHM), his or her attributes, abilities and the way he or she runs the pub. I believe that seeking a competitive edge through service *as opposed to* products *could have a substantial impact on volume. I really believe that we should differentiate ourselves by concentrating our time and efforts on the way the service is provided; how the customer is dealt with.*

'You may argue that good customer service is equally as reproducible as products. However, I believe that to achieve real and lasting service improvement is relatively difficult and requires changes not only in the pub itself but to overall company culture and central control systems. This I believe could be difficult for a less forward looking and flexible company to follow.'

There was some evidence to substantiate Kevin's claim. A recent survey commissioned by Courage suggested that good customer service was important to customers. During a survey of 80 managed houses it was shown that staff attitudes were felt to be crucial in creating the right atmosphere and that customers expected them to be friendly, happy, smiling, polite and efficient. Every single person in the survey agreed that pubs should provide a warm, friendly and happy atmosphere. Furthermore, customers believed that the high turnover of staff was an indication of poor management.

Kevin Flanagan continued:

'If we can achieve a high standard of service, I believe our turnover and profits will increase. In all fairness many people believe that we are not doing badly at the moment. The company only receives about ten written complaints a month. This, you must realise is out of over one million transactions per day. However, what this really shows is that we are giving "not bad" service, but it does not show that we are giving "good" service. I believe that if we could make an improvement in this area, and move from providing not bad service to providing good or even outstanding service, we will be far ahead of the competition.

'The problem is, how do we know what constitutes "good" service as each and every customer's idea of what is good service might be different. Courage have tried to identify different types of pubs that attract different market segments, to help them understand the different types of service that may exist. Nine pub types have been identified: the Local, Young Entertainment, Young Traditional, Traditional, Estate Pub, Office Pub, Lad's Bar, Restaurant and Family Destination Pub.

'However,' Kevin added, 'in reality we have 1356 different pub types, as each and every one of our pubs is different and attracts different people. You see, we are not branded, and I don't think we want to be. Our customers don't have a McDonalds-type expectation of what they will get.'

THE STAFFING PROBLEM

Courage employed about 13 500 staff in their managed public houses, 96 per cent of whom were part-time. Part-time can be anything from one evening a week to every lunch-time and evening. The LHM and spouse are accommodated on the premises and the bar staff usually live nearby. The typical bar person is a married housewife who is trying either to supplement the family income or save up for a particular need, like a holiday. Most pub managers experience difficulty in recruiting good staff. They require someone who is neat, numerate, reliable and honest but who will work for quite low pay. Kevin continued:

> *'The crux of the problem is that our staff change more often than our customers. Our staff turnover is not unusual for the industry and is running at about 200 per cent per annum. We employ about 26 000 new people every year and they stay with us an average of six months. This is not quite as bad as it seems for we have a core of good people, about 38 per cent of the total workforce, who have been with us for some time. There is only a small turnover in this core.*
>
> *'You will realise that training staff is a bit of a headache! Our small central training staff cannot deal with that many new staff each year, and quite rightly we leave it to managers to train their own staff. However, we give them a lot of help and support in this area. We provide videos and written guidelines and we also provide a training programme, TS1 (Training Skills 1), for the LHM. This involves one-to-one instruction and involves training the LHMs on how to train their staff. This is a relatively new idea in the business. Already one hundred pub managers and their spouses have been through this programme. We are hoping to put all of them through it by the end of this year.'*

CENTRAL CONTROL

There is strict control of the performance of each pub and pub manager. Each pub manager reports directly to a District Manager (DM). Each year the District Manager negotiates with the LHM and discusses the budget for the future year and the possible promotional campaigns. The pub's budget is based on the previous year's contribution plus a bit more, to account for proposed changes in prices, volumes, costs and promotional efforts. The LHM receives bonuses on a sliding scale depending on his/her performance over the agreed target. There is careful and frequent monitoring of his/her performance in terms of turnover, profits, stocks, food sales, staff turnover, general effectiveness and competence by the DM who is seen to be there to help and advise, and, if necessary, remove.

IMPROVING THE SERVICE AT COURAGE

'We need to start understanding what the regular customers see as good service, and we must also try to understand what attracts passing trade as today's passing trade could be tomorrow's regular,' said Kevin.

A second survey of 100 managed houses found that 84 per cent of the customers described the pub as their 'local' – the pub that they usually frequented, and that passing trade only accounted for 16 per cent of the business. The most common reason for visiting the pub, according to the survey, was that of convenience. Friends, friendly staff, good service and food were secondary. The type of beer also appears to have little significance on pub selection. Forty per cent of those surveyed came into the pub unaccompanied suggesting that the pub is a place of social gathering and companionship for the lonely. Kevin continued:

*'We are currently working to improve our service. We are presently trying to test about 20 per cent of our houses in order to develop an understanding of the link between good management, profit and customer service. And we are auditing most of our pubs on specified service criteria [*see *Appendix 36.1] using senior central staff, who visit pubs incognito and send the audit sheet to the DM as additional feedback on his or her public houses. We are concentrating on three areas at the moment. First, the "welcome": we believe that every customer wants a good welcome which includes acknowledging their presence when they arrive at the bar. Second, the service: everyone wants good and efficient service and we have instituted a few rules like if a customer wants beer or lager then they are offered a choice of a glass with a handle or a straight glass or if a customer wants a short, then they are always offered ice and the appropriate fruit. Third, we are trying to persuade the staff always to provide a "good-bye".'*

Kevin readily admitted that it is not easy trying to improve customer service:

'The problem is that our performance measurement of the LHM is very much financially oriented. A lot of LHMs even have their own microcomputers and get regular print-outs of their own profit and loss accounts and spend hours analysing them. While this shows real financial keenness and control it significantly reduces the time they spend with their staff and customers.

'The company, understandably, is financially oriented and our control systems mirror this. It would be a bit of an overstatement to say that all DMs assume that all LHMs are thieves, but in reality the control systems that we use seem to imply it. It would also be a bit of an overstatement to say that all LHMs assume that their staff are incompetent, but, again, some of their house rules imply it. For instance, managers did not use to allow staff to accept a cheque for over £5 without the manager checking it first, despite the fact that most bar staff have bank accounts and handle the family budget. They are just as able and competent as the manager to check the cheque. This has now changed and the limit is £50, which is much more sensible. It's just like the unthinking beer delivery system that delivers on a Friday lunch-time at the busy office pub. There are a lot of other crazy things that happen but we are now thinking about them and stopping them.

'The biggest difficulty is the bar staff. How do I interest an eight-hour-a-week part-timer who is only with us for six months to get some spending money for the summer holiday in providing good service. Most staff don't even see it as a "real" job and they feel that it has low status not only because of its low pay but because they think that anyone can do it. Despite the fact that all staff in a recent survey said that coping with the customer is the most difficult aspect of the job, none of them had received guidelines

on it and even felt that the only formal training they did require was on how to use the electronic cash register. My worry is that if we try a "put people first" type campaign they may feel that either they know it already or they will see it as a "two-day wonder" package.'

THE WAY FORWARD

'Somehow we need a training or communications exercise to increase people's awareness of the problem. I don't believe we can change, especially people's attitudes to the customer, just by saying that it is a problem. Somehow we need to create awareness and appreciation. We need an output called "customer service". But it is almost against current culture, not only at HQ level but also in the pub where, unless you are in the right circle of locals, you may not get good friendly service.

'Somehow we have to be able to define good customer service and we have to measure it and somehow reward it. We have to change the bar staff from being beerpushers and moneytakers to being service providers.'

The signs are hopeful that Courage can achieve this. Recently one DM organised a staff training session in an evening. Attendance was entirely voluntary but there was a buffet at the end of the evening. The DM's colleagues said that no one would turn up as people would not be paid. The DM hoped that about 20 people would attend. On the day 70 turned up and it was a great occasion. At the end of the evening that DM concluded that not only were staff desperate to learn more, they were also desperate to contribute more.

Kevin concluded:

'Most of our bar staff are housewives and mothers with families. We need to understand what makes them give only adequate service at work when they give good service to their families at home. Also we need to get managers to demonstrate good service and to set high physical and interpersonal standards. Somehow he or she has to become a coach not a cop.'

Questions

1 Why is Courage considering improving its service quality?

2 How good or bad is its service?

3 What do you think will be the barriers to improving its quality of service?

4 Evaluate the Customer Service Report Form as a means of measuring service quality.

5 If you were asked to advise Kevin Flanagan as to how to improve the quality of service provided by the pubs what would you recommend he do?

APPENDIX 36.1
CUSTOMER SERVICE REPORT

PUB: ____________________ TIME: ____________________

DM: ____________________ DATE: ____________________

	A	B	C	D	E	NOTE
THE WELCOME						
1. Greeting						
2. Acknowledgement						
3. Invitation						
SERVICE (as appropriate)						
4. Passing off*						
5. Selling up**						
6. Choice of glass						
7. Ice						
8. Fruit						
9. Cleanliness of glass						
10. Correct glass						
11. Correct drink						
12. Correct price						
13. Correct change						
14. Bar counter clear						
15. Speed of service						
16. Staff appearance						
17. Staff friendliness						
18. Clean tables						
19. Clean ashtrays						
20. Clean toilet						
21. Food – selling up						
22. Clean plates						
23. Convenient condiments/ serviettes						
THE GOODBYE						
25. Goodbye						
OVERALL STANDARD						

Notes:

*Passing off is the offering of an alternative product to the one that is requested because it is not stocked.

**Selling up is the offering of a more expensive alternative than that requested.

CASE 37

EuroCab SA

Stuart Chambers

Case date 1995

INTRODUCTION

'I was brought in to sort out manufacturing, and that is what I'm going to do – and fast! Honestly, I was shocked by what I saw in my first week here; but I am sure that you will both want to help get to the bottom of the problems, and sort them out. Materials management must be our top priority if we are to get back on course and bring manufacturing here at least up to the high service standards shown by other departments, such as design and sales. At the moment all I can see is scrapped materials, shortages, wasted effort, and a large overhead which seems to be there only to make absolutely sure that good products reach our customers. We've certainly got a big task ahead, but I need your input. First, however, I am bringing in an experienced materials manager to take overall responsibility for planning, materials handling, inventory management and performance measurement within manufacturing. I would like you both to work directly with me and the new manager, over the next year, to develop our improvement strategies and to get them into action.'

Pierre Dumas, the new VP of Operations at EuroCab's Lille factory in northern France, was talking at his first meeting with Sara Montenay and Jean Brasfort, two young graduate production engineers who had joined the company about nine months earlier as trainees in the operations department. The previous VP of Operations had recognised the importance of giving them an important, but not high-risk project based on their recent training in the latest thinking in manufacturing. He had decided to ask them to prepare outline plans for introducing 'best practice' manufacturing to the company, with a particular emphasis on at least halving the ten-week lead time needed to produce the products. They had then drawn up an outline project plan which involved them in a series of activities such as capacity planning, 'de-bottlenecking', the introduction of *kanban* control, inventory planning, facilities layout, and improvements to a basic MRP system which had been allowed to fall into disuse because of outdated data, failed working practices, and inaccurate data entry.

EuroCab is one of the leading European manufacturer of customised metal cabinets (known by the employees as 'cabs'), of various sizes and designs. These are sold to a wide range of high-technology industries to contain, support and securely protect electrical and electronic control systems from dirt ingress, the weather, and accidental or deliberate interference or damage. The main applications include cabinets for large traffic signalling systems, industrial controls, and cable television equipment. EuroCab had experienced rapid growth in sales and profits (*see* Appendix 37.1) during the last five years, for three main reasons.

First, the market had grown fast during this period, with substantial new opportunities in the rapid development of Eastern Europe's infrastructures, modernisation of railway signalling in several European countries, huge growth in cable/satellite television systems, and a similar growth starting in South America and SE Asia. Suppliers who could cope with rapid growth in volume were valued by the electronic system manufacturers, who often wanted to concentrate on their core competencies of electronic design and system development.

Second, EuroCab provided excellent technical support, designing increasingly sophisticated products which exactly met the customers' technical and aesthetic requirements, and rapidly making prototype cabinets.

Finally, EuroCab had been particularly willing and eager to do more of the value-added work on these products, initially fitting and testing many of the electrical and electronic systems, and more recently, purchasing these components directly from vendors. The company was also accredited to quality systems standard ISO 9002 and had passed all external quality audits with rarely more than trivial errors found in records, and high levels of adherence to documented procedures. However, the management team had always recognised that there must come a time when these factors would no longer play such a big part in EuroCab's growth; maturing markets would probably not require constant technical revisions, and there was even an increasing risk that customers might take back the value-added assembly work, and do it in-house.

CEO, Philippe Legrand, spoke at the last board meeting of his expectations:

> *'At the very least, we should expect the market prices to become tighter over time, and customers will start to pay more detailed attention to schedule adherence and the quality of what they are getting, so there will be no room for complacency. We must start raising productivity throughout the business if we are to survive and prosper.'*

Most of Sara and Jean's time had been spent acting as the improvement team for the 'Signal Cell' which had been established just before they joined the company, to assemble cabinets for one of the largest customers, accounting for over 4000 cabinets per year. In line with their work plan, they had spent the last two months beginning to look at quality issues in this area. They had decided to share the analysis by dividing it into two categories: Jean would concentrate on the physical aspects of the processes; looking at work specifications, the causes of damage in material handling, and assembly faults. Sara would look at the human side of quality; starting with an attitude survey to determine employees' views on quality in the company and on this cell. She would also recruit and train 'Improvement Teams' on the cell, to demonstrate the benefits of *kaizen* principles in gradually eliminating the causes of faults on the cabinets. This approach would then be extended to the whole factory with teams for each area.

Jean's experience

'Some of the most critical components used in these particular products are the corner posts and cross-members, since if they have been processed incorrectly, the cab built can be completely disrupted. These components are made from long lengths of bought-out purpose-made aluminium extrusions which are first cut to length; fixing holes are then made using dedicated punching and drilling jigs, they are then sent out to subcontractors who provide a special chemical EMC finish (Alocrom), and they are finally returned to the company for painting, if required, and then to mechanical assembly to be built into cabinets.'

(Appendix 37.2 gives an indication of the process route involved)

'When I started looking for quality problems, I didn't have to look far! A brief inspection of the scrap bins revealed hundred of posts and cross-members in amongst the normal offcuts and scraps of metal associated with the cutting and drilling processes. Many of these had obviously been through most of the operations. I decided to start by evaluating the cost of the scrapped posts and cross-members, and then to try to identify the causes of the scrap. Some of these components were obviously bent or scratched, but what or who had caused this was not at all obvious. I then collected samples of all types of defect that had been found, and showed them to the supervisors of the component supply areas concerned. I have written down some of their comments to highlight the nature of the problems we face [Appendix 37.3]. Lack of product standards was seen to be a big problem: people seemed to have little understanding of what level of quality was actually required or acceptable . . . for example, the position, depth, length of any scratches. Surprisingly, many of the technical drawings issued to the shop-floor included dimensions without clear tolerances, or with ambiguous ones. Most people in the assembly areas admitted that they had absolutely no idea of what they were looking for in terms of the visual appearance of the components, and when in doubt, they tended to use rather than reject them, to save money and to keep to the build schedule.

'The first shock to both of us had been the enormous variety and cost of all this scrap. A typical finished post costs around ff200 (French francs) and a typical cross-member ff80! I prepared a Quality Standards Board for the Mechanical Assembly area, which used physical components and photographs to show the assemblers (for the first time) what were the acceptable standards of finish: posts and cross-members below this standard were to be put aside for the reasons to be identified and recorded. Data for two months was analysed, and the true cost of scrap was highlighted. [This is summarised in Appendix 37.4] Unfortunately, this only emphasized that scratching was the biggest problem, but did not tell us precisely where it was coming from.

*'To highlight where we should focus our efforts, I then looked at cross-members in more detail. I introduced random sampling at the four check points. [*See *Appendix 37.5] A sample of four components was taken at each point every hour, and was thoroughly inspected against the standards. The percentage failure due to scratching was recorded in this way for a period of five weeks, and the results were recorded [Appendix 37.6]. This exercise focused our initial improvement efforts on the saw and pierce activities, where the scratching problem was greatest. Analysis of these processes highlighted three areas where scratching occurred: on the saw table; at the pierce operation where the cut length of aluminium is pushed into the punching jigs; and in-transit between the saw, deburring, and piercing operations.*

'Jigs were designed to prevent the extrusion coming into contact with the metal table of the saw. Swarf (sharp metal cuttings) from the saw and punching operations was removed by the addition of a constant controlled supply of compressed air, preventing build-up of swarf that could cause scratching. Special tubular plastic carriers, similar to large crates for beverage bottles, were designed to protect the components between operations. Further monitoring at the check points [Appendix 37.7] indicated that our efforts were paying off, with noticeable improvements downstream. Unfortunately, at this point in the project I was asked by M. Dumas to work with Jules Lecabec, the new materials manager, on the scheduling system for the press shop, so I was no longer able to pursue this work.'

Sara's experience

'My first task was to determine the attitudes of the workforce to quality in general, in order to discover whether the quality problems we had seen around the factory were due to carelessness, or inability of the people to do their jobs well . . . perhaps due to problems with the design of products or processes, lack of training, inadequate tools and equipment, and so on. I started by talking informally to the Signal Cell management and supervisors, and finally to a small cross-section of the shop-floor employees. Extracts from some of their replies is included in my report.' [Appendix 37.8]

'Clearly, while the managers and supervisors were emphasizing the importance of good quality, their generally held view was that the shop-floor workers didn't care about quality, and were the source of most of the mistakes and damage. I therefore decided to find out the views of those on the shop-floor, so conducted a more structured employee survey, initially in the electrical assembly section. Most of the questions required the employee to rate their opinions on a 1–6 scale, but the last few questions were more open, asking for descriptions of good and bad quality practice. [A copy of the questionnaire is included as Appendix 37.9] What I want to do next is to repeat this in other parts of the cell, and then to present the results of these surveys to the managers and supervisors for comment. The results might also be a valuable introduction to the second improvement team which I hope to get under way in the next few weeks; but I don't know if its a good idea to start with that or not. I know

that Pierre is very keen to get teams established in every area within the next few months.

'I believed that membership of improvement teams should be voluntary, and so arranged for Pierre to authorise overtime to allow meetings be conducted after work, to avoid conflict with production output requirements. In practice, however, Anne preferred to nominate some brighter and more company-minded people in her section, and to conduct the meeting in working time. On balance, I felt it was best to agree to this because if I were to go against this I might loose her co-operation and interest. Unfortunately, in practice, two of the team members are not as keen as the others, but even so, have started to make a useful contribution to the work. Another problem I had to face is how a team should be run. I had assumed that we should allow them to identify problems and solve them, supported by my training sessions in 'tools and techniques'. Anne and Pierre, however, both felt that we must direct the agenda – setting a limited number of important problems to be solved. I don't know how we will get their full support and enthusiasm that way, but only time will tell!

'I devised and ran a training programme with the team to teach the basic ideas of quality and some problem-solving techniques such as brainstorming, cause-and-effect analysis, SPC charting, and preparation of simple graphs. The team now meets on an ad hoc basis, often with only two members involved, to solve problems which have shown up recently on the inspection of finished cabs. I am now aiming to have the team meeting held twice a week to work on problems, and once every two weeks to review progress and for further training. They are already producing some good solutions, and are establishing the root causes of some of the more obscure problems. However, they are still very dependent on me. Over the next three months, I would like to gradually hand over more responsibility until they are telling me about their meetings and the problems they have solved. One obstacle that I have encountered is the way in which the company is geared up to productivity. Everyone is working flat out to meet production targets, so I am finding it almost impossible to pull people off production to solve quality problems . . . so I tend to resort to doing the implementation work myself! That is not what I had intended, but at the moment, if I don't do it, nobody else will!'

Questions

1 How important is quality to the company, given its current growth situation?

2 What are the underlying causes of the quality problems in this company?

3 What action is being taken by management to overcome these problems, and is this sufficient to create lasting improvements?

4 Should more inspectors be recruited and/or trained to cope with the growth in output?

5 What other actions could be taken to improve quality in the company?

APPENDIX 37.1
EUROCAB SA:
FINANCIAL PERFORMANCE 1992–1995

	Year ended 31 Mar (ff million)			
	1992	*1993*	*1994*	*1995*
Turnover (continuing activities)	115	252	310	750
Cost of Sales	(72)	(167)	(215)	(575)
Gross Profit	43	85	95	175
Other Operating income and charges	29	67	70	104
Operating Profit (continuing activities)	14	18	25	71
Retained Profit	2	2	11	41
Fully diluted earnings per share (ff)	31	32	47	124

APPENDIX 37.2
PROCESS ROUTES FOR MAIN COMPONENTS OF SIGNAL CABINETS
(white areas are used for other products)

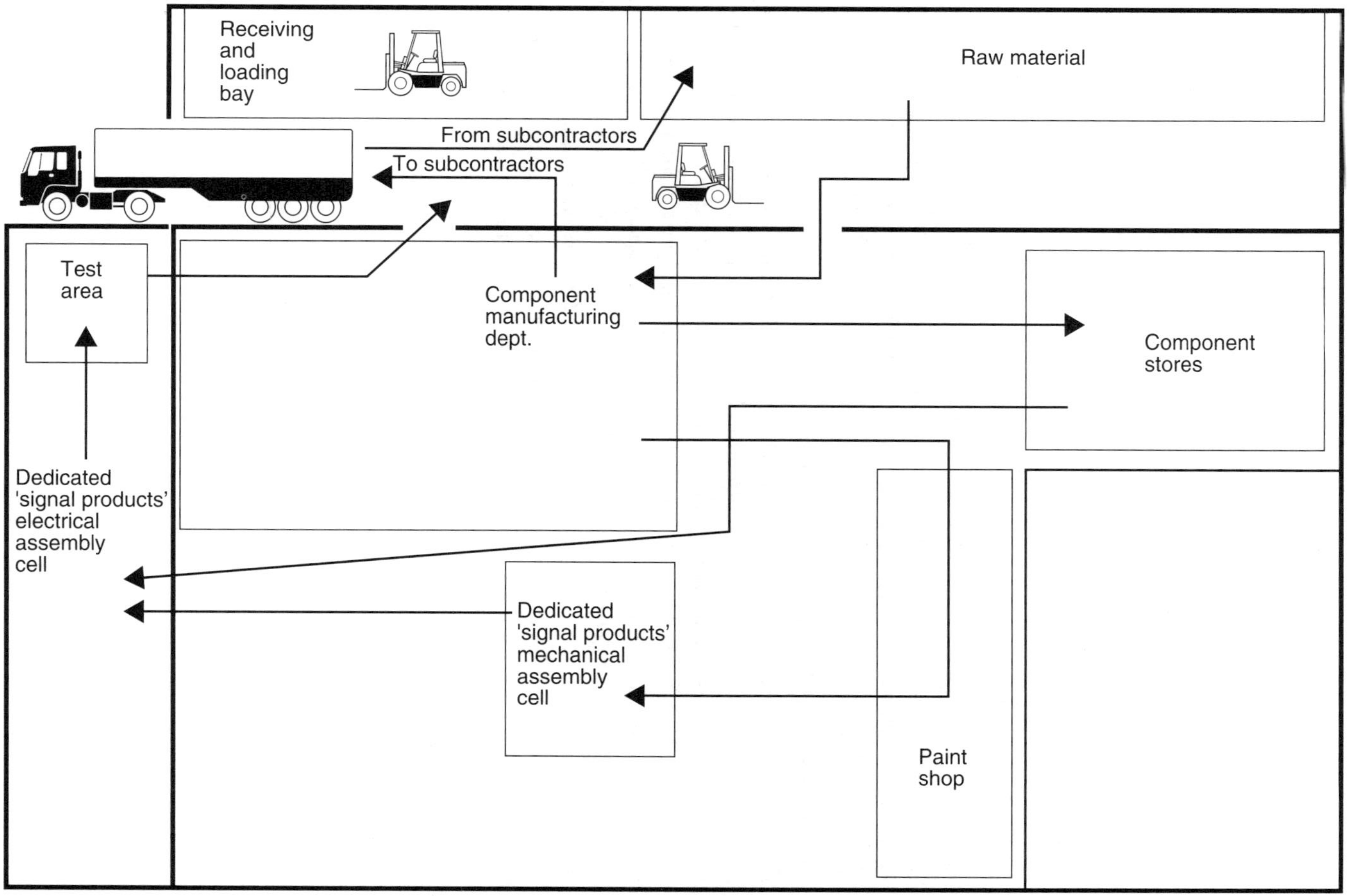

APPENDIX 37.3
EXTRACTS FROM JEAN BRASFORT'S NOTES

Some of the causes of non-conformance on signal posts and cross-members, as reported by supervisors

Charlotte Lorcy, Final Inspection

'We have to reject a completed cab if we find any visual defects on the posts, either inside or on the outside. If there are obvious dents or bent edges, this needs assemblers to remove the electrical parts (about three person hours' work), change the offending posts, and rebuild the cab. Scratches and damaged paint are more of a problem, because they show up a lot in our section's strong lighting, but are not always so obvious in the factory. I have to admit, however, that we've had very few returned because of this type of fault, but it certainly doesn't convey a good impression of the company if these are seen by the customer's engineers. M. Cahor, the Quality Manager, has often told us that we (in the Quality Department) are here just to make absolutely sure that only good cabs get to the customers, so we are usually quite careful in our final checks, and record every blemish we can find. It's then up to management to decide what to do.'

Anne Cardignac, Electrical Assembly

'Being in the same area of the factory, we work closely with Charlotte, so we try to pick up any faults for her before we start our work, but that's not always easy because we aren't qualified to say whether a small scratch or dent is acceptable or not. Very often we find holes missing which we need for fixing parts to. This is really frustrating, particularly if we have already done most of the assembly and have to take everything out again. I have to admit that sometimes we do a little damage getting some of the larger and heavier electrical assemblies into position into the cabs; they are a tight fit at the best of times, but sometimes they have to be pushed in hard. A small variation in the size of the inside of the cabinet creates an interference fit which I don't think is what the designers intended, and this can cause paint damage.

'I must say that most of the problems seem to be caused by Mechanical Assembly. I've seen them walking over posts and cross-members rather than picking them up! There's a lot of bad work like that – lack of care, poor discipline. What really annoys me is that they manage to assemble the cabs wrongly – all the posts and cross-members upside down and back-to-front, not once, but over and over again! However, for many of the cabs there aren't any clear Build Instructions to show the new employees in Mechanical Assembly, so it's really no surprise that mistakes are made. Taking cabs apart again not only takes time, but also almost always causes some damage. We used to run out of cabs when this happened, so now I keep a reserve of cabs to work on, in case there are any problems in Mechanical. They are a bit in the way, in the corridor near the office, but it's nice to have the back-up stock. As you know, at the end of every week all the managers are accountable for their output achieved. It's really the only performance measurement taken seriously here, so it tends to make me angry when these problems make me miss my target.'

Quentin Latour, Mechanical Assembly

'Many of the people on my section are temporary staff and they're new to the job, so that's a problem for a start. Trying to achieve high targets for efficiency is bad enough without having to train

temporary contract people to do it. Management thinks that our job is as straightforward as assembling Lego, but our components are not always that consistent, and we have to constantly watch out for missing holes and damaged components, while suffering from constant shortages from our suppliers. We often get batches of components which are well outside the tolerances, which I am told is because of a backlog of repairs on worn tooling or machines. If we were to do our job properly, we would stop production every time we see a problem, but of course, we wouldn't be allowed to do that! I think the manager should stop criticising us and look at where the posts and cross-members are coming from before they get to us. We get bad quality from the Alocrom subcontractors for a start – bits of the post are sometimes untreated so the paint falls off, and I know for certain that they damage good posts. The Sawing and Piercing Section is very bad as well. There's a complete lack of care in there. We sometimes get cross-members which are sawn off a few millimetres too long or short, or with holes punched out of place – we only find this out when we can't get the cab doors to fit properly! The manager of the Components Department has been complaining that the dimensional tolerances on new designs of cab are often tighter than he can achieve with the existing machines and tooling, but since we don't use any SPC, he'll have a job convincing management that this is the cause of all of his problems! The first thing they taught me on my quality course at the local Technical College was how to use SPC, and it amazes me that we haven't got that going here! How they expect us to do a good job with all this rubbish I don't really know. One thing's certain; it's always us that gets the blame if a bad one gets out, and they don't want to listen to our explanations.'

Hubert Montielle, Components Manufacturing Dept.

'I know that everyone feels it is always our fault when bad components are found, but I really don't agree! You specifically highlighted posts and cross-members, but these are only a few of the thousands of different things we make. Because these components are large and are easily seen on the final cabs, we take every precaution to protect them in our department. We have made containers with tubular plastic inserts which we drop the posts into, for protection when they are ready to go to the Alocrom subcontractors; so they certainly aren't getting damaged by us. I admit that there have been problems with the occasional missing holes or wrong lengths, but now that the employees are more experienced at making these parts, these mistakes don't happen anymore. We all get better at a product the longer we have been doing it! We try to get well ahead with production of the posts so that if any get damaged or incorrectly Alocromed it doesn't stop Mechanical Assembly.

'I'm not always happy with the long lengths of aluminium extrusions which come from our suppliers. Because they are banded in bundles with a cardboard outer protection, the outside ones are sometimes crushed by the banding, or have obviously been damaged by other things on the truck. We only find this when we come to open up the bundle, and we take care to avoid using the damaged pieces. This is the price we pay for going to the cheapest supplier of extrusions! I think that our buyers should stop being proud of the savings they screw out of the suppliers, and spend a little time down here looking at the problems we have to cope with.

'For example, I'm not really happy with the attitude of the Alocrom subcontractors. We try to keep the posts and cross rails clean, but it's inevitable in our environment that some oil and grease gets on the parts, which we wipe off as best as we can. When they get a bad batch of Alocrom finish, their excuse is that our material is contaminating their liquids, but they are supposed to degrease everything first anyway. It seems like a feeble excuse for their bad work, if you ask me! Our buyer should look for a better supplier; and quickly too, before they damage our reputation for quality cabinets.'

Gaston Cahor, Quality Manager

'This site has expanded very quickly over the past two years with all the new business. What this has meant is that the products have been introduced very quickly so that we can fulfil our orders. Often, there have been a lot of design and assembly problems which had not been forseen, and it usually takes some time to iron them out. I know that the design office has a huge backlog of changes to do, largely because most of their time is taken on new products. Quality isn't really considered enough – a problem will be solved but not at its root cause, so it'll show up again and again.

'We need to build quality into the design and process before manufacturing starts but this isn't easy – our design and prototyping facility is on the other site 200km away, so generally communication is poor. We can go back and try to improve everything on a piecemeal basis, but inherently it's our way of doing things as a company which should be addressed by senior management. To be honest, I just haven't got the resources or authority to do that! All I can do is to solve problems as they're found now, and allow the general build standard to improve that way.

'It's very difficult to get people involved in quality when they're so preoccupied with output. Also, and let's be honest here, most of them think that quality should be the responsibility of somebody else, usually me! I can't really accept their excuse that they haven't got time for quality. They've got time to rebuild it, that is to build it twice, but they haven't got time to build it once, properly!'

APPENDIX 37.4
IDENTIFICATION OF SCRAP CAUSES ON MECHANICAL ASSEMBLY
two-month period: 23/03/95 to 23/05/95

Part no.	*Description*	*Scratches*	*Operation omissions*
SP-1361501	X Member	40	0
SP-1361502	X Member	91	10
SP-1361701	X Member	60	0
SP-1361702	X Member	172	0
SP-1361800	Rear Post	100	23
SP-1361900	Hinge Post	44	0
SP-1361902	Lock Post	43	20
SP-1404200	X Member	27	0
SP-1404300	X Member	122	15
SP-1405000	X Member	99	0
SP-1643301	R/Post	20	6
SP-1643302	R/Post	15	10
SP-1643401	Hinge Post	10	0
SP-1643501	X Member	15	30
SP-1643502	X Member	10	10
SP-2103801	X Member	51	0
SP-2103802	X Member	110	50
SP-2116101	X Member	79	30
SP-2116501	Hinge Post	40	21
SP-2116502	Lock Post	150	15

Costing

Average Cost for posts	ff200
Average Cost for X Members	ff80

Cost of scrap over the two-month period

Posts	ff10 3400
X Members	ff81 680

APPENDIX 37.5
THE DETAILED PROCESS ROUTE FOR POSTS AND CROSS-MEMBERS

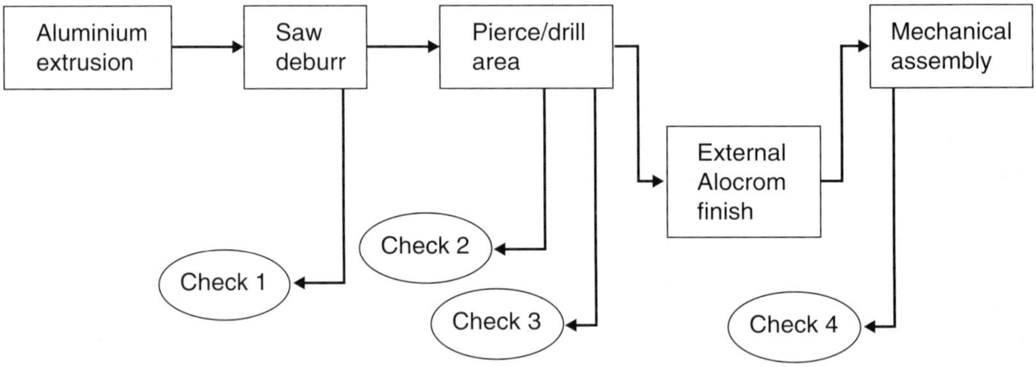

APPENDIX 37.6
INITIAL ANALYSIS OF CROSS-MEMBER FAULTS

Four components selected at each check point every hour. Inspected against 'scratch standard' on Quality Board

Check point		*Weekly failure rate %*					
Number	Description	week 1	week 2	week 3	week 4	week 5	Average
1	Saw	45	37	50	43	38	43
2	Pierce	31	28	36	30	31	31
3	Drill	22	28	19	25	21	23
4	Mech. Assy.	24	19	20	28	16	21

APPENDIX 37.7
CONTINUED ANALYSIS OF CROSS-MEMBER FAULTS

Four components selected at each check point every hour. Inspected against 'scratch standard' on Quality Board

Check point		*Weekly failure rate %*					
Number	Description	week 6	week 7	week 8	week 9	week 10	Average
1	Saw	35	32	28	26	25	29
2	Pierce	21	21	19	23	20	21
3	Drill	18	19	19	20	17	19
4	Mech. Assy.	13	14	13	14	13	13

APPENDIX 37.8

Some representative extracts from Sara Mountenay's interviews with employees in the mechanical and electrical assembly department

Anne Cardignac, Electrical Assembly Manager

'I have a lot of quality problems in here – I don't really know where to start!

'One of the main causes of problems is just lack of care. Nobody accepts responsibility for their work around here! For example, in one cabinet we found this morning, there are holes missing which we need for fixing parts to. Now we're going to have to take everything out and start again. It's very frustrating, I can tell you – and we'll probably find a few more like it before the end of the day!

'Suppliers are a problem as well. For example, with one type of connection cable we had to go over to just one supplier to get the lowest price, but they're often causing a problem – they're not made properly and we have to adjust them when fitting them. Their delivery is also bad. I've complained but it takes ages to get anything put right here and when it is, we don't hear about it until weeks afterwards.

'I do think that improvements are beginning to happen, though. We'll be moving to our new layout soon and that should tidy things up – all the stock at one end, and lines for assembly. They're also going to start using the MRP system properly which means that my shortages should be a thing of the past!'

Fabrice Tripont (Electrical Assembly Team Leader: 5 years' service)

'I agree that in theory we need better quality, but it's not so easy in practice. We've just been told that we have to produce 25 per cent more cabinets each week. To meet that target, we're just going to have to use everything in sight or we'll end up with shortages!

'The problem with the Improvement Team is that we just haven't got the time to do it. If I lose people from the line it'll affect productivity and I can't afford to do that! Anyway, why should we do it? We're here to build cabs, and it's management's responsibility to sort out the quality of the suppliers and the Components Department! I think that we really need more quality engineers to solve all the problems we get. The Quality Department is too small here – it definitely needs to be bigger and more effective. It has never kept up with the expansion that we have been through!'

Sophie Lambert (Assembly: 3 years' service)

'The problems we face are really unnecessary. We get cabs from Mechanical Assembly that look okay, but right at the end of our work we find something wrong. Last week it was a few which had no hole for the earth strap. We had to strip about ten cabs right down, so that the faulty post could be removed and replaced. All this wasted time could have been avoided if they employed inspectors in the Mechanical Assembly to make sure everything's right before we get it. We haven't got time to do all this extra work – Pierre Dumas keeps telling us that we have to make more cabinets every week or we'll let the customer down badly, and the company will lose money too.'

Bernard Dupond (agency worker in Assembly: 2 months' service)

'I fit doors to the finished cabs, which is the same for every type of cab, and so was quite an easy job to pick up. I reckon that I do it just as well as the old-timers now! Training? Well, somebody showed me what to do and that was it, but I wouldn't really say that was training, would you?

'My basic wage is fairly low but we end up with a good bonus if we reach the output targets, which we do almost every week, unless there have been problems with cabinets coming late from Mechanical Assembly. Some of the tools here are a bit worn but we have to make do with what we've got. I had trouble with the torque wrench slipping, but if you set it a little on the high side, it seems to do the job okay. I had to ask Quentin to get me a new one, but he told me that the manager had said that the old one could be repaired, but it never was. Management here seem to pass all the problems back to the shop-floor . . . that's what they called 'empowerment' at my last factory, but it really didn't seem to work! I mean, I think that at the end of the day, nothing really improves unless Management get down onto the shop-floor and start putting a few basic things right. The only time we see them here is when there's a problem to sort out!'

Amandine Fouquet (Union Representative in Electrical Assembly: 2 years' service)
'We're under far too much pressure here – it's getting ridiculous! I know that Anne has been threatened with the sack if we don't get out the scheduled cabs, which is hardly the way to get morale up in the Cell. Because she's the supervisor, she isn't in our union, but she does seem to take it out on us. There is a very aggressive style of management right from the top, and all this pressure ends up on our shoulders. Of course, we'd have no trouble meeting the targets if supplies were good and came in on time, but there are problems with shortages both from here and outside.

'I don't think that the Management respects or appreciates the workforce at all. We pull out all the stops for them, time and time again to meet deadlines and we don't get anything back at all. It's hardly surprising that nobody cares around here.'

Emile Verpeau (Electrical Tests Inspector: 5 years' service)
'Having worked here so long, I know from experience what the customers will accept and what they won't. Although our main job is to check out the circuits with the computerised testing equipment, we also look for visual and mechanical faults; parts missing, scratches, poor paint finish and so on. This is the last chance before the cabs are packaged up and sent to the customer. If we find one of these faults, it is usually on several cabs which quickly build up on our section and get in our way. What we need is quick decisions from management, but because of meetings, it may be hours before they get down here to sort things out. And nine times out of ten, they decide to let cabs go out of the door that shouldn't . . . then a week later they shout at us for having missed a quality problem and the cabinets come back!

'Sometimes we find damage caused by lack of clearance between the components; for example, doors that won't shut tightly because of a build up of tolerances on the hinges and posts. I think these could be sorted out by the designers, but we get the same problems over and over again. They don't solve these problems at the design stage and leave us to sort it out the best way we can, even if someone has to use a hammer!'

Charlotte Lorcy (Final Inspection: 5 years' service)
'Scratched and damaged components shouldn't be there, they should be rectified or replaced, but we have regularly been completely overruled by the Cell Manager or even by M. Dumas, and these cabs are immediately sent out to the customer.

'As the number of cabs has gone up we're having to short-cut inspection and we're sure to miss faults occasionally because of the rush to get products out of the gate. We could really do with at least two more inspectors to add to our current four, to ensure that everything is checked, and so

that we don't hold up dispatch. My biggest fear now is that we will find a batch of bad cabs and the customer won't get the scheduled delivery.'

Francoise Alon (Electrical sub-assemblies, 2 years' service)

'I've been doing assembly work like this for 15 years now so I've worked in quite a few places. But I've never come across anywhere as chaotic as this! I mean, there doesn't seem to be any proper understanding of what needs to be done and how! Some of the girls don't even know which spanners and screwdrivers to use!

'We're under a lot of pressure here. If management wants better quality they should give us the right tools and training and take the pressure off output! But really I think that the main problem is with Inspection. There just aren't enough qualified inspectors.'

APPENDIX 37.9 EXTRACTS FROM THE EUROCAB SA QUALITY SYSTEMS MANUAL

Dated Nov 1994, and signed by Philippe Legrand

Mission Statement

To completely satisfy our customers' needs by . . .

How Will We Achieve This?

delivery of a quality product on time every time.

We will undertake to monitor and improve our processes on a continuous basis. Our aim is to constantly improve in all areas of our operation to:

1 reduce the manufacturing cycle time;

2 bring product to the market quicker;

3 reduce costs;

4 strive for zero defects;

5 keep to our promises and plans.

Our People

To achieve the goals we have set, we must aim to develop an environment with:

1 a bias for action and improvement;

2 emphasis on teamwork;

3 integrity and respect for others;

4 training and development of our people;

5 recognition for achievement.

CASE 38

Problems in Total Quality implementation at Company A

Alan Harrison

Case date 1992

INTRODUCTION

Many companies in recent years have enthusiastically set about implementing Total Quality. Sometimes there are fatal flaws in how the implementation is planned, or in how it is carried out. This was the case in a traditional manufacturing company in the UK. Two years after the start of Total Quality implementation, an investigative group from Company A's parent (the holding group which owned Company A) concluded:

- A major effort was needed to improve the fundamentals of the business. The first priority was to establish effective disciplines and controls within each function.
- TQ consumes a great deal of management time and resource. Additional time and effort in further development should be deferred until the priority issues have been addressed.

This marked the end of TQ development at Company A. But the background to the investigative group's conclusions are highly instructive.

SOME OF THE MAJOR ISSUES

Early initiatives directed at improving product quality at Company A had been very successful, but the board realised that progress had plateaued, and that new ideas were needed to propel the company into the 'world class' league. It was decided that a study team of senior managers would be set up to examine the company's approach to 'putting quality first', and to report in three months' time. The study group concluded that there was no magic solution to improving quality. Although previous one-off initiatives had yielded some benefits, several examples were quoted where an inconsistent and uncertain management approach still prevailed:

- While management preached quality, production quotas were always the real priority.
- New product introduction always led to many late modifications and high costs of returns.
- While management preached 'right the first time', mass inspection and large areas for rectification were still features of the business.
- New tools and techniques like SPC (Statistical Process Control) had been introduced in a disjointed way. Some areas used SPC but didn't know why.

The study group identified over 30 specific, quality-related issues which needed to be addressed as a matter of urgency. These included the need to:

- review the role of the supervisor and shop-floor control;
- improve discipline and control on working practices;
- reduce the number of suppliers, some of whom had a poor quality record;
- improve the control of design changes;
- introduce process failure mode and effect analysis (FMEA);
- considerably improve preventive maintenance disciplines.

A list of some of these items, together with the action which was proposed to deal with them by the study group, is shown in Appendix 38.1.

The study group went on to stress the need to commit everyone in the company by means of a single management quality philosophy which encompassed the elimination of waste and an integrated human resource plan. In order to bring about progress on this point, it was recommended that the board should seek the advice of Dr Deming, the American quality 'guru', and a series of seminars took place. This phase of development culminated in the appointment of consultants to help facilitate the initial stages of TQ implementation.

The time from presentation of the internal study group report (which the board had accepted in its entirety) to the decision to go ahead with TQ implementation had been less than five months. It is important to take stock here of some of the issues:

- The managing director was totally convinced that acceptance of TQ was the only way forward. He became very enthusiastic. When it was stressed that adoption of some TQ ideas and perceived benefits could take five years to bear fruit, he replied: 'We are Company A, we do things quicker here. We'll do it in two.'
- While some board members shared the chairman's enthusiasm, others were totally unconvinced about TQ and very lukewarm to some of the key issues.
- The need to address the list of over 30 quality-related issues referred to above as a matter or urgency was quickly forgotten in the rush to progress with TQ implementation.

Some of the seeds of failure had already been sown.

THE NEW QUALITY MANAGEMENT SYSTEM

Changes were to be implemented by means of a structure of committees and teams with clearly defined roles. These are illustrated in Fig. 38.1. The new system mirrored existing organisational structures, so that the transition from process improvement being a 'special' activity to becoming a normal way of life was managed by the same group of people. The following is a brief summary of the structure:

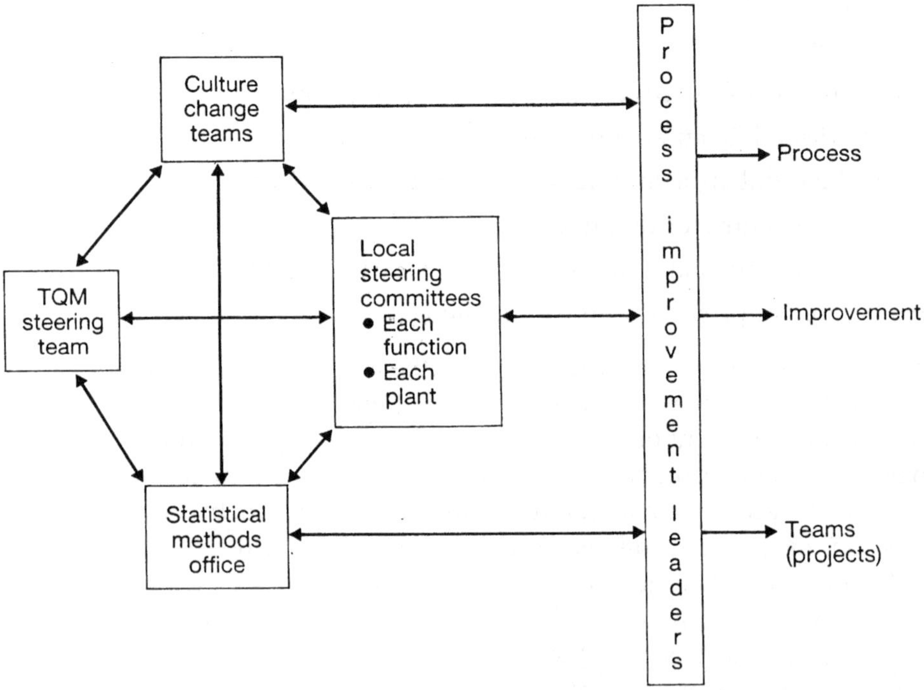

Fig. 38.1 Structure of committees and teams for new quality management system

- The steering team was the board, and its task was to lead the transition by supporting the work of other groups.
- Local steering committees were set up to manage the improvement activities in each function and each plant. They were chaired by a member of the steering team.
- The statistical methods office provided technical support in the areas of training, behavioural science and statistics and worked on the structure and systems of the change process.
- Process improvement leaders were statistical facilitators who helped members of project teams and local steering committees.

- Culture change teams examined Deming's 14 principles and identified areas where there was conflict with existing management culture. The teams' recommendations were championed by a board member for implementation.

While this was the theory of the new Quality Management System, the reality was somewhat different. The lukewarm commitment of some board members meant that some of the steering committees floundered and that some of the culture change teams never got off the ground.

THE CHANGE PROCESS

Figure 38.2 shows how actions were planned and implemented under four distinct but related fronts. These were education and training, quality planning and focus, management culture and style and communication and recognition.

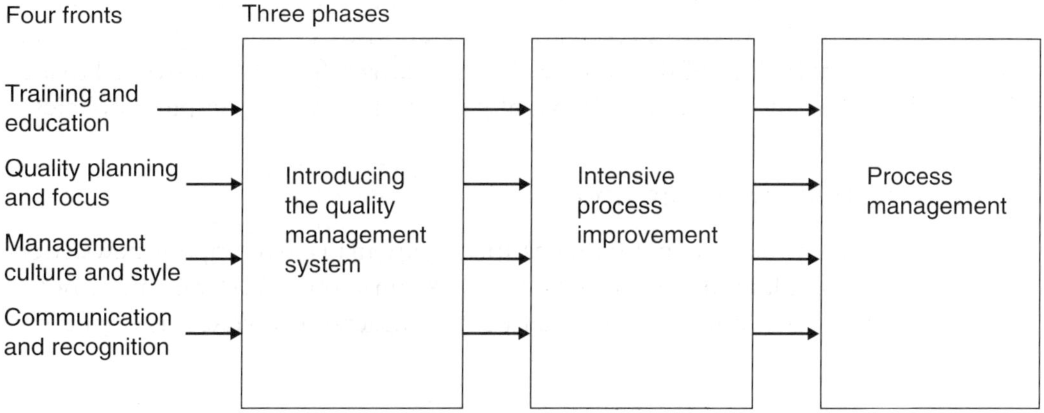

Fig. 38.2 Planned evolution of change process

Training and education

This was carried out as a 'cascade' exercise, with consultants and the statistical methods office training the board who in turn trained their direct reports and so on down the hierarchy. The method was a huge success. But training in philosophy was not followed up with training in tools and techniques for some months. Philosophy training emphasized attitude changes, like driving out fear and treating everyone as if they want to do a good job. But no new systems were in place to support the new philosophy. Also, without tools and techniques, nothing could be done with philosophy training alone.

Quality planning and focus

This was intended to cover priorities and measures of quality improvement, integration of quality initiatives like SPC and improvement of management processes like reward systems and appraisal. This whole area proved to be a particular problem. Because existing processes were in many cases not under adequate control, there was little that could be done to improve them. Major changes in systems were required. Appraisal systems were addressed by replacing management by objectives and target numbers by a less specific 'process improvement plan' which managers never properly understood. Issues of work measurement were also never sorted out. (Appraisal systems and management by numbers are strongly criticised by Dr Deming.)

Management culture and style

This covered corporate and functional missions, values and goals, the interpretation of Deming's principles, and work on the recommendations of the culture change teams. While the corporate missions, values and goals were well handled, functional efforts depended very much on the attitude of the board members concerned. Those keen on TQ were the first to present. Interpretation of Deming's principles was never undertaken. Failure of the culture change teams referred to above led to lack of progress in defining operating philosophy and in reviewing company policies.

Communication and recognition

This was handled by means of conferences, management briefs, company newsletters and handouts to explain the new philosophies. A conscious effort was made not to overplay the publicity, but to ensure that people understood what was happening and why.

It was intended that these four actions would evolve through the three phases shown on Fig. 38.2 and would not therefore have defined start or finish dates.

Questions

1 List the good and bad aspects of the way in which Company A introduced TQ into its operations.

2 What lessons can be learnt?

APPENDIX 38.1
SOME OF THE ISSUES DESCRIBED BY THE STUDY GROUP

The company has made many quality-related improvements over recent years. The directors view quality as the primary objective, but progress has levelled off, and existing quality levels are only being maintained by means of major, piecemeal projects.

The study group identified a number of quality-related issues that require immediate attention. A selection of these is listed below. They serve to highlight that a fundamental change is needed in the company's approach to quality and productivity.

Issue	*Action*
Quality training is not linked to a quality philosophy.	An integral plan is needed for all employees.
Quality circle application is patchy.	Every supervisor must be responsible for a QC by the end of the year.
Role of the supervisor is currently inappropriate.	A working party has been set up.
Working practices a problem in many areas.	A new personnel strategy is needed.
Suggestion scheme is little used by employees.	New scheme designed to be in operation by the end of the year.
Existing bonus scheme has little emphasis on quality.	A working party has been set up.
Product plans are not well defined from the outset, and they are not supported by plans from functional areas.	A strategy committee has been set up to develop a formal planning system.
Design and manufacture are not well integrated.	A new system is needed to integrate design and manufacturing engineering.

CASE 39

Eurocamp Travel

Stuart Chambers and Jim Crew

Case date 1996

BACKGROUND

Eurocamp Travel was founded in 1974, specialising in the provision of family camping holidays in France, based on car travel. The service package initially comprised ferry crossings from the UK, fully-equipped tent or mobile home accommodation on high specification campsites, the services of on-site couriers, and insurance. The company soon gained a reputation for the high quality of its equipment and services, and became market leader in this rapidly-growing sector, with high levels of re-purchase and recommendations. Growth averaged around 15 per cent per year in the period 1985–90, and at the same time, the business became much more complex: sales offices were opened in The Netherlands and Germany, and the geographic coverage was extended to include sites throughout Europe, totalling 160 by 1990. The service package also offered more choice, including en-route hotels, short stays on sites, and a range of company-provided site services including sports equipment, children's entertainment's, baby-packs, etc. As the business became larger and more complex, the demands placed on the office systems also became greater, reinforcing the need for functional specialisation of staff, yet requiring more interdepartmental understanding and co-operation. At this time, batches of customers' files were moved physically between departments for each stage of processing, and this resulted in delays and excess costs when amendments or corrections were requested by customers. Feedback from customers has always been valued, primarily through analysis of questionnaires issued to every customer. Levels of satisfaction with many aspects of the services, including the initial reservation, were closely monitored throughout each season and from year to year.

THE QUALITY CHALLENGE

By 1990 it was clear that almost every element of Eurocamp's service package could be, or was being, copied by competitors eager to attract away some of the premium customers. The best defence would be to reinforce quality at every stage in the process, since this was believed to be the main criterion that already differentiated

Eurocamp, and this was also potentially the most difficult for lower priced competitors to follow. Under a UK Government Department of Trade and Industry (DTI) initiative, a consultant was brought in to initiate and facilitate a major quality improvement programme. This was conceived as a 'top-down' approach, whereby important projects would be identified and tackled by trained teams. It was intended that the entire workforce would eventually be affected and involved by this 'cascade learning' approach, but it soon became apparent that these early projects were not achieving the anticipated sustainable improvements. It became clear that the failure of the early work was largely the result of only involving senior managers, who couldn't devote the time required to projects, and did not fully understand the processes concerned. Conversely, those employees who did have a very detailed understanding of the processes and the problems had been excluded from the problem definition, evaluation of potential solutions, and implementation of changes (although few projects actually reached the implementation stage). It was decided to learn from these failures, and to continue in the quest for sustainable, tangible improvements in quality. A complete rethink of the company's approach would be required.

INTRODUCTION OF TOTAL QUALITY MANAGEMENT

Now free from the constraints of the prescriptive approach of the consultant, the quality manager reviewed the latest thinking on TQM, and found inspiration in the clear approaches described in the book *Total Quality Management* by Oakland (1989) which then became compulsory reading for the members of the board of directors. In 1991, the company launched the Quality Management System (QMS) initiative, but also decided *not* to pursue ISO 9000 registration. A clearly structured organisation for quality was set up, headed by the directors Quality Council. Each department established a Quality Steering Committee which comprised at least one director, a trained facilitator, and volunteers from every grade of employee. The emphasis at this stage was on the identification and improvement of internal processes, with emphasis on satisfying the internal customer. Each departmental committee initially chose three such processes to analyse and improve, not necessarily including the biggest known problems. Early successes demonstrated the validity of this approach, and generated a high level of enthusiasm throughout the company.

One example of a project involved analysis of the process of entering telephone bookings data onto the computer system. The objective was to reduce the number of key strokes, so that the length of telephone calls could be minimised without affecting the quality of the customer–staff interaction. Unnecessary steps were identified and improvements were made to the booking screens. The number of key strokes was reduced from 123 to 85, a saving of 32 per cent.

In 1992, a new approach was developed to tackle specific problems concerning processes that affected operations in several departments. These problems were initially identified and selected by individual departmental managers, but their selection was then controlled more rigorously with structured feasibility studies, before release to the ad hoc 'Improvement Teams' of around five to seven people. These were established and given substantial training, both in the tools and techniques of quality improvement, and more significantly in a compulsory 'seven-stage project methodology', which is outlined in Appendix 39.1. In the early projects the team leaders were usually junior managers, but now almost any grade of employee, including part-timers, may act as leader. An example of a successful project of this type was the redesign of the brochure requests system, which brought together formally disparate parts into a single operations centre, which included the brochure requests telephone lines, label printing facility, assembly and enveloping operations and despatch.

Although many of these projects were unquestionably successful, and had brought great credibility to the programme, it was increasingly apparent that further stimulation of the process would be required if results were to be sustained. It was decided to introduce occasional elements of fun or humour, and 'Dragon Days' were conceived and implemented. Briefly, this involved the search for hidden green dragon eggs (dyed hard-boiled hens' eggs) throughout the offices, prizes were awarded for their discovery, and a mechanism was introduced for employees to report problems called 'hatched dragons' which still had to be identified and slayed! Employees were issued with a number of blank 'Dragon Cards', on which they could detail any problems, however minor, that were affecting them or their work, (an example is shown in Fig. 39.1), for example:

- a process that they did not fully understand
- a slow process
- a process that they found difficult to do
- discomfort, such as distracting noises, poor seating position, draughts, etc.

Usually these cards were then passed to the person that owned the process, for action or further analysis as appropriate. Some of this 'slaying of dragons', or problem resolution, could be done individually, with a reward of appropriate T-shirts, but more complex problems were handled by improvement teams. Prizes were also awarded for the best dragon problems, as judged by the Quality Steering Committees and Quality Council. Some examples of prize-winners were:

1 suggested changes to the late-amendments system, including a new form of reminder to reservations staff;
2 amendments to brochure information concerning opening and closing dates in Scandinavian sites in relation to complex ferry schedules, to reduce customer confusion.

No attempt was made to quantify the number of problems identified, or solved. The success of the system relied simply on the interest and enthusiasm of the staff,

Name *Linda Lowry*

Department *Reservations*

Dragon *Amendments 10 wks. Prior to departure, need to be put through to liaison*

A notice board with the week commencing date could be on display in reservations as a reminder.

PRIZE
T-SHIRT-
WALLET

Fig. 39.1 Example of typical 'Dragon card' completed by an employee in Reservations

and on the culture of continuous improvement, rather than on numerical targets or quality cost reductions.

Having concentrated efforts on satisfying the internal customers and improving the processes that linked them, it was then decided to refocus the programme on satisfying the end-customers; the paying holiday-makers. In 1994 the company launched a Customer Focus Programme, beginning with two half-day consultant-facilitated workshops in a local theatre, for all employees. This programme emphasized the value of a customer, both in terms of retaining existing and gaining new ones. One outcome of this programme was a recognition of the need to re-examine the handling of complaints, which led to a more generous, professional, and respectful, service recovery policy. This considerably enhanced the empowerment of all contact staff to resolve customer complaints or disappointments without having to get permission from managers. Sometimes this involved issuing free days, discounts, or upgrading, but often was simply a more personal way of responding quickly, sensitively and constructively to genuine problems as they arose. The customer-orientation approach of the organisation is reflected in recent independent customer research, which reported one of the highest scores was for Eurocamp's telesales which came near the high scores of Hewlett-Packard. For the 1995 season, the telesales and booking administration departments received an average score of 9.3 out of 10, with 57 per cent of respondents giving a rating of 10 out of 10! This excellent performance was also recorded by Eurocamp's own highly developed market research; nearly 50 per cent of customers go to the trouble of completing and returning a post-holiday questionnaire, which gives feedback on a wide range of quality attributes. An annual bonus based on a customer satisfaction score is paid equally to all employees. Managers feel that the early resolution of customers' problems through greater staff empowerment has saved the time and costs involved in handling ongoing disputes, and has therefore had a significant role in improving the productivity of the overall system.

The latest initiative to create an even greater customer orientation is the 'Listen and Learn' programme. As with most large organisations, there is considerable specialisation of work, whereby individuals develop knowledge and skills in their own role, but lack experience in, and understanding of others. The company devised an initial menu of ten 'modules' in which employees could experience other customer-oriented jobs within the company, either actively or passively, as observers. These experiences focused on getting people into customer contact roles, either directly or alongside customer-facing staff. Participation in the programme was voluntary, and each module of experience was clearly defined in a booklet and advertised internally. Table 39.1 lists the available modules and points awarded for each experience, and Table 39.2 describes a typical module. As can be seen, each completed module earned a number of points which an employee could record and collect towards an award on the scale: Green Standard (250 points), Red Standard (500 points), and Gold Standard (750 points). The directors showed their commitment by each promising to achieve Green Standard by a certain target date, and they were soon seen taking telesales bookings, analysing customer feedback questionnaires, and working in the Customer Services Department. A 'Heros and Heroines' awards ceremony is now held annually, when attractive rewards are presented. All award winners receive a customer focus memento such as an inscribed mug and passport holder, plus gift vouchers for purchases in a popular store. It had been hoped that this scheme would be of interest to backroom staff, such as the accountants and IT people, but to date their involvement has been considerably below average, as indicated in Table 39.2.

Table 39.1 'Listen and Learn Programme' contact modules and points earned

Contact module		*Points*		*Maximum points*	
No.	Description	Number	Per	Number	Equivalent
1	Reservations / Reception	25	2 hour session	125	5 sessions
2	Reservations / Liaison: Listen-in facility	15	2 hour session	75	5 sessions
3	Customer call-back: Post travel-pack, pre-hol	2	call	80	40 calls
4	Customer call-back Post-holiday	3	call	150	50 calls
5	Adopt-a-customer 5 calls per customer	10	customer	100	10 customers
6	Site visits	5	customer	250	50 contacts
7	Work as a courier	250	5 days	250	1 visit only
8	Work as a cleaner	85	3 days	85	1 visit only
9	Read questionnaire comments	6	Batch of 50	60	500 questionnaires
10	Questionnaire call-back	2	call	100	50 calls

Table 39.2 Analysis of 'Listen and Learn programme' involvement

Category	*Number (Percentage) of category achieving*		
	Green Standard 250 points (%)	*Red Standard 500 points (%)*	*Gold Standard 750 points (%)*
Directors	3 (75)		
Senior managers	2 (33)		
Supervisors	4 (40)	1 (10)	
Customer sales/support	20 (25)	7 (9)	2 (2)
On-site service	5 (14)		
Accounts	2 (33)		
Computer department	2 (16)	2 (16)	1 (8)

Table 39.3 Eurocamp's Seven-stage Methodology for Improvement Projects

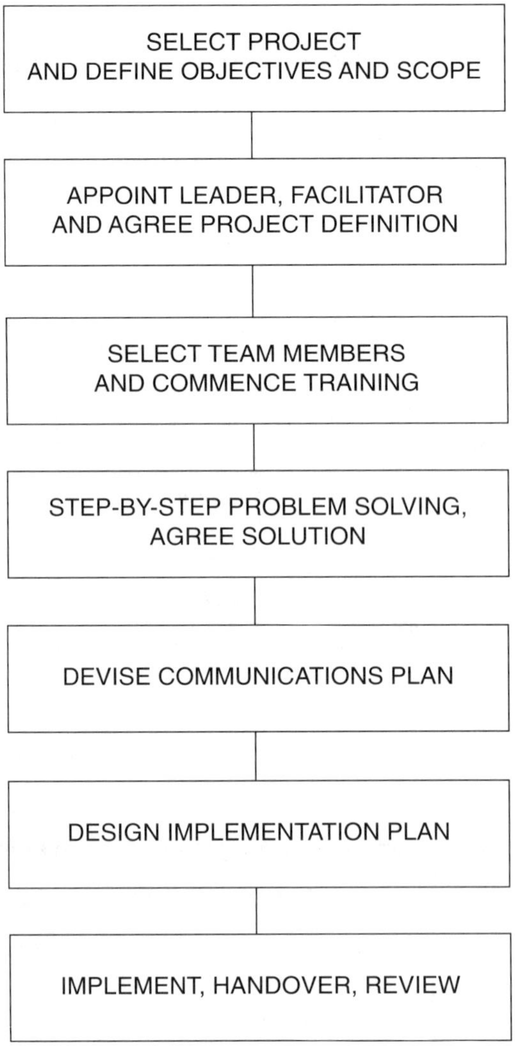

While the programme is considered to have been a success, the directors now feel that there is a need for it to be revised and updated to maintain interest, and to bring in those whose participation has not yet been significant. The menu of contact options certainly needs regular review and updating, and the points allocation will have to be adjusted. Currently, the programme encourages the 'easier' passive activities, such as observing and reading, so greater rewards will be needed for more proactive tasks involving direct customer contact. New objectives for 'Look and Learn' might include greater staff flexibility, continuous improvement, and personal development.

TOWARDS THE PAPERLESS SYSTEM

Since the early beginnings of the company, an envelope-style file had been used for every booking, to hold all the associated information and correspondence including copies of invoices, acknowledgements, letters, amendments, and handwritten 'Contact Sheets' which recorded details of every telephone conversation with the customer. The file was also used as a trigger for each specialised stage of the processes involved in completing the associated administrative requirements of the order.

The file, in a colour representing the start-of-holiday month, was prepared in 'Bookings Reception', and this triggered an acknowledgement of order being sent to the customer. This department then passed on the file to the required next stage in the process, such as the 'Travel Department' which booked ferries and/or Motorail if required by the customer. It would then be passed to 'Hotel Reservations' if appropriate, or to the Sales Ledger Department for invoicing, and then to the Records Department to await receipt of deposits, and so on.

At each stage of this essentially 'batch' process, staff used computers and had access to the basic details of each order, but the file remained the core of the system. No work could be done by any department without the file. Where amendments were required, either at the request of the customer, or as a result of problems in providing exactly what the customer wanted, this was dealt with by specialists in the 'Liaison Department', who also needed the file to be fully informed about all previous discussions and negotiations with the customer. Under these circumstances the file had to be found from within the normal system, and temporarily diverted to Liaison, until the problem was resolved. When not in immediate use and when completed, the file would be returned to 'Filing'. In 1994, a total of fifty large filing cabinets were in use, holding 40 000 files, and occupying a large area of office space. At the end of the season, all this paperwork was carefully sorted, and archived in a warehouse for five years.

This file-based system had been the stable core of the bookings administrative system, and had been constantly improved and adapted while the departments developed and used more computer systems and electronic links to the suppliers and external operations. Most ferry bookings, for example, are now made on-line with direct links into the operators' systems, and communications with hotels and campsites are usually by fax. The use of conventional files was, by contrast, slow and labour-intensive. Sometimes it was also far from ideal in terms of flexibility, for example when amendments were required; and a few files could be mislaid, affecting dependability.

The biggest problem was when files entered the Liaison Department, since they would have to be held there until the amendment was confirmed by the supplier, such as a ferry company, French Motorail, or a hotel. This could delay the file by many weeks, delaying later critical stages such as invoicing.

The difficulties of locating files resulted in delays in responding to customer queries, often leading to anxiety and a general impression of sub-standard service.

Equally serious was the cost of unproductive searching for files by liaison staff, the most skilled and highest paid administrative grade, and the time and cost of extra telephone calls back to customers. Customer files had to be found quickly in the event of cancellations, and everyone involved with that booking alerted, so that associated external reservations could be reversed. All of this took large amounts of staff time and effort, which could have been used more productively and proactively in direct contact with customers.

In 1994 it was decided to change the system, with the objective of 'reducing or eliminating the dependency on customer files, such that costs are reduced and service is improved'. A six person improvement team including members of each department involved in the process and a computer systems expert, was established. It carried out its work in accordance with Eurocamp's well-tried 'Seven-stage Methodology' (Table 39.3) described earlier. The objective was to develop new systems and procedures that would reduce the need for customer files, and that these would be working before July 1994, the start of the 1995 booking season. Targets were set for the proportion of customer files still in use: 50 per cent for 1995, and 20 per cent for 1996. There was significant resistance to this project, since physical files had been a normal part of everyone's job, and there were implicit threats to employment levels.

The improvement team brainstormed the issue with all the departmental managers, and collected data on all the existing uses of files. Many further meetings refined the specification of the proposed system changes. Involvement with users in this way helped to reduce resistance to change, and facilitated the later implemented work. The recommendations were that the new system should be installed in three phases. Phase one transferred all existing routine correspondence including acknowledgements and invoicing onto an internal paperless system, the customer receiving the only hard copies. Phase two involved 'electronic contact sheets' to replace the handwritten ones. All discussions with customers were now keyed directly into the system, which recorded the date and time and member of staff involved. This record could not be amended, and also provided immediate communication of required actions to other departments for action, along with a 'to do' list for every user. Phase three, not yet implemented, will involve scanning all incoming correspondence, which is the only remaining reason to open a conventional customer file.

The targets set for the project have been exceeded, with only 9.5 per cent of conventional files in 1995, and only 1 per cent in 1996. The system has clearly worked extremely well, and has had significant effects on productivity. Table 39.4 indicates the changes in permanent staff levels and bookings made over the last three years. It is believed that most of the improvement in productivity has been as a result of the new system. The reduction in staffing during this period has been through natural wastage and voluntary redundancy.

Table 39.4 Productivity of bookings system 1993 to 1995

	Number of permanent staff (excludes seasonal staff)				*Bookings processed*		*Productivity Bookings / Staff*	
Year	*Administration*	*Liaison*	*Reservation*	*Total*	*Gross*	*Net**	*Gross*	*Net**
1993	62‡		30	92	34937	31231	380	339
1994	48.6‡		24	72.6	39880	36091	549	497
1995	25.6	14	19	58.6	41525	37997	709	648
Productivity Improvement 1993 to 1995							87%	91%

*Net refers to the final number of bookings after deduction of cancellations
‡Refers to combined number of staff for Administration and Liaison before they were separated organisationally (no separated figures available).

THE FUTURE

Jim Crew, Eurocamp's Managing Director, believed that the past five years demonstrated the value of TQM for the business:

> *'One of the most striking effects has been our ability to analyse and improve our processes. This has resulted both in improved quality as experienced by the external customers, and in increasing productivity. With the current adverse economic conditions for our market in Europe, our growth has slowed somewhat, so the savings that we have achieved have been essential for the ongoing development of the business. Now is certainly not a time for complacency. We will need to consider how we can continue to motivate everyone to continue to look for the thousands of little improvements which are so essential in sustaining the vitality of the business. We have to ensure that the individual initiatives, such as the "Listen and Learn Programme" are developed or replaced. We must also give more thought to quality improvements in the back office. How important is it for our computer experts and accounts staff to learn to interface with our external customers? And what about our campsite couriers? Every year we take on over one thousand employees, mostly students, to look after our customers on sites spread all over Europe. They are all very well trained and supervised, but perhaps there is much more we could do to get them involved in improvement, in addition to their basic "maintenance" tasks of cleaning equipment and being helpful to customers.'*

Questions

1 Why has Eurocamp's 'Seven-stage Methodology' been so important in managing the company's quality improvement projects? How does this compare with 'best practices' for project management in general?

2 What are the main features of Eurocamp's approaches to quality improvement, and why have these been so successful? How has the company avoided 'Quality Droop'?

3 Should the 'Listen and Learn Programme' be reviewed or scrapped, now that the level of participation is declining? Could it be modified to encourage more proactive participation and to identify more opportunities for process improvement?

4 Why was there a lower than average participation in the 'Listen and Learn Programme' by back-room staff? How could this resistance be overcome, and what benefits, if any, would accrue from their involvement?

5 Would it be possible to get the active involvement of temporary staff, and particularly of the couriers, in continuous improvement activities?

6 Now that many of the larger process improvements have been achieved and customer satisfaction ratings are so high, further changes will inevitably be less spectacular. How can the momentum of improvement be maintained? Should improvements be recorded and counted? Should Eurocamp undertake self-assessment under the European Foundation for Quality Management (EFQM) Quality Award model?

APPENDIX 39.1
EXAMPLE OF 'LISTEN AND LEARN' MODULE

6 Site Visits

Manager: Ruth Stubbs

WHAT'S INVOLVED: Meeting and talking to customers on the campsite. This would include:

- Making an initial contact.
- Asking a short series of questions and recording the responses.
- Asking a specific series of questions if required for any special market research.
- Following these up with general discussion as appropriate.
- Feed-back of information including record of additional anecdotal information.
- Post-holiday response to customer if appropriate.

TRAINING AND PREPARATION: Staff wishing to undertake this module will be provided with a pack including a preparation sheet for their guidance and a set of question sheets for completion. Further support will be available from Ruth Stubbs, Marketing. Points will be accrued for each set of responses returned.

TIMING: For many employees, site visits will have to be carried out during holidays, staff educationals etc. However, staff taking up module 8 (Cleaner) would finish work at 3.00 p.m. and would have the opportunity to use 'time off' to speak to customers.

Part 5

THE OPERATIONS CHALLENGE

Introduction

This part returns to the strategic view of operations management. It is suggested that the key challenge for operations managers is the creation and implementation of an operation strategy. This section:

- examines the difficulties in formulating operations strategies
- identifies four generic operations strategies
- identifies the key steps in formulating an operations strategy.

It also assesses four key challenges related to the creation of an operations strategy:

- ethical – the moral imperative to develop ethical operations strategies
- international – the necessity of considering the international dimension of operation strategies
- creative – the need for creativity in devising operations strategies
- implementation – the ultimate challenge of implementing the chosen strategies.

THE STRATEGY CHALLENGE

By now it should be clear that managing most operations is a complex task involving the design, planning and control and improvement of not only the products and services themselves but also the processes by which they are created. The complexity arises not just from the range of tasks, but also their interrelatedness. The real challenge for operations managers though, is not just their understanding and command of the detailed complexity of all the operations decisions, rather it is whether they can make enough sense of the operation to fit it into a strategic context, reshape and improve it, and then make sure that its contribution to competitiveness is both clear and ongoing.

Creating an operations strategy involves putting together a set of policies, plans and improvement projects which, when they are taken together, define the direction of the operation so that it becomes the source of competitive advantage.

Difficulties in formulating operations strategy

Trying to make strategic sense of a business and the operations role within it is not easy for a number of reasons:

- Operations management is highly complex involving many decisions about the effective use of most of an organisations resources.
- Operations managers may be geographically dispersed, located in all the operations parts of the organisation rather than grouped together at its headquarters.
- Operations managers operate in 'real time' with pressure to deliver goods and services, and may not be able to allow their attention to move beyond the running of the operation for more than relatively short periods.
- The cost of the resources under the operations managers control is usually high and there is often a degree of difficulty in getting the business to accept innovative and imaginative changes.
- Operations managers often are just not used to thinking, acting or influencing the organisation in any strategic manner; they tend to be more used to concerning themselves with the day-to-day detailed running of the operation.

Generic operations strategies

There are four generic operations strategies:

1 *The caretaker strategy.* This strategy is often employed when an organisation believes that there is little competitive advantage to be gained by differentiating itself from its competitors. Operations managers are expected to make sure things do not go wrong, rather than provide much in the way of innovation or creativity.

2 *The marketeer strategy.* Marketeer strategies are often used by organisations which experience increased competition and respond by enhancing or extending the level of customer service which they offer. This might include such things as broadening the range of their products or services, increasing quality levels or giving delivery guarantees. The operation function tries to do this by developing its infrastructural resources such as planning and control systems, working practices, or quality management methods.

3 *The reorganiser strategy.* This strategy implies a change in the way an organisation designs and manages its processes. This could mean investment in new technology and (more significantly) a different way of organising its methods of producing goods and services.

4 *The innovator strategy.* The innovator strategy is a combination of the marketeer and the reorganiser strategies. Not only has the organisation adopted an enhanced approach to designing its operations, it also expects enhanced customer service from its operations function. In other words, it has enhanced not only its structure but also its infrastructure.

Formulating an operations strategy

There are several procedures available that can help organisations formulate their operations strategy. Typically many of the formulation processes include the following elements:

- A process which formally links the total organisation strategic objectives (usually a business strategy) to resource level objectives.
- The use of competitive factors (called various things such as order winners, critical success factors, etc.) as the translation device between business strategy and operations strategy.
- A step which involves judging the relative importance of the various competitive factors in terms of customers preference.
- A step which includes assessing current achieved performance, usually as compared against competitor performance levels (often referred to as 'benchmarking').
- An emphasis on operations strategy formulation as an iterative process.
- The concept of an 'ideal' or 'green field' operation against which to compare current operations. Very often the question asked is 'If you were starting from scratch on a green field site how, ideally, would you design your operation to meet the needs of the market?'. This can then be used to identify the differences between current operations and this ideal state.
- A 'gap based' approach. This is a well tried approach in all strategy formulations which involves comparing what is required of the operation by the marketplace against the levels of performance which the operation is currently achieving.

Some of these steps are considered in the Jeyes Wet Wipes case (Case 40).

Judging the effectiveness of operations strategy

An effective operations strategy should clarify the links between overall competitive strategy and the development of the company's operations resources. More specifically, an operations strategy should be:

- *Appropriate*. It should support the company's competitive strategy.
- *Comprehensive*. It should indicate how all parts of the operations function are expected to perform.
- *Coherent*. The policies recommended for each micro-operation must all lead roughly in the same direction, and interrelate positively with other functional strategies.
- *Consistent over time*. The lead time of operations improvement means that consistency must be maintained over a reasonable time period.

- *Credible.* The strategies and associated improvement targets should be seen as feasible and realistic.

At a broader level operations strategies must also be ethical, international, creative and implemented.

Strategies must be ethical

The concept of ethical decision making permeates operations management. There are ethical implications in almost every operations management decision area. Product or service design, for example, may affect customer safety or energy consumption, the layout of facilities may affect worker safety, process technology may affect waste product disposal.

In operations management, as in other areas of management, ethical judgements are often not straightforward. What might be unremarkable in one country or company's ethical framework could be regarded as highly dubious in others. Nevertheless there is an emerging agenda of ethical issues which at the very least all operations managers should be sensitive to. The first step in this sensitisation process is to identify the groups to whom an ethical duty is due. These groups can be categorised as, the organisation's customers, its staff, the suppliers who provide it with materials and services, the community in which the environment operates and the shareholders and owners who invest their capital in the business. Some of these issues are addressed in the Indian Metals Corporation case (Case 41).

Strategies must be international

Few organisations can afford to limit their operations strategies to within their national boundaries. Only the smallest organisations do not buy any of their supplies from abroad, or do not sell any of their products and services abroad, or should not be, considering doing so. For operations managers the 'environment' within which they make their decisions is, increasingly, a global one.

Large multinational organisations may also have the additional problem of different operating practices in different parts of the world because of their differing cultures, economic conditions, history, market needs and demography, for example. The question, therefore, which multinationals have to face is should it allow its facilities in different parts of the world to develop their own operations strategies to suit their own conditions, or should it encourage a uniformity of practice which reflects its corporate values?

Strategies must be creative

Faced with a given set of circumstances different sets of operations managers will probably come out with very different strategic solutions. Some might follow fairly conventional and orthodox routes while others might be more imaginative and creative in coming up with their own original strategic solutions. Many successful operations are successful because they thought of an original way of creating their products and services and are therefore able to offer new forms of differentiation and associated competitive advantage (*see* Singapore Airlines, Case 42).

There are several blockages to being creative:

- *Trade-offs.* Believing that prioritising operations performance objectives and improvements in one area will lead to a natural and consequential deterioration in another, for example, an increase in quality will have a consequent increase in costs.
- *Focus on efficiency.* Developing operations planning and control systems which emphasize efficiency over creativity.
- *Specialising creativity.* Dividing staff's jobs into those who are expected to be creative and those who are not, or expecting certain functions in the organisation (such as research and development or marketing) to be creative while other functions (such as operations and finance) are not expected to be creative.
- *Not rewarding creativity.* Not recognising or rewarding those staff who do generate creative solutions to operations strategy.

Strategies must be implemented

Too often operations strategies fail at the implementations stage. A strategy may set the direction of the operation but implementation defines how it gets there, which is a more difficult task. Operations managers need to start the task by addressing their implementation agenda – the list of general questions, whose answers set the basic plan for implementation. The questions are:

- *When to start.* Implementation should not be begun until there is a clear idea as to how the strategy is to be implemented. Also some start times may be better than others, such as during a relatively settled period rather than during the launch of a new product.
- *Where to start.* Either start where the operation is likely to get most benefit or where there is the best chance of success.
- *How fast to go.* Managing the speed of improvement means understanding (and often combining) the two modes of improvement – breakthrough improvement and continuous improvement.
- *How to co-ordinate the programme.* An operations strategy implementation needs managing like any other project. It requires planning, resource allocation and controlling to achieve the plan.

There are several important success factors to implementing an operations strategy:

- *Top management support.* Top management is needed not only to offer support to the activity but also to allocate and co-ordinate resources.

- *Business driven.* The organisation's overall competitive imperatives must be linked to the operations strategy programme.
- *Strategy drives technology.* Competitiveness should drive operations strategy which in turn determines the way technology is developed, not the other way round.
- *Change strategies are integrated.* Successful operations strategy programmes involve change over several fronts; technological, organisational, cultural.
- *Invest in people as well as technology.* Changes in methods, organisation or technology must be supported by changes in knowledge and attitude by all employees.
- *Manage technology as well as people.* Technology needs integrating into the operation and 'managing' after its implementation to achieve the most out of it.
- *Everybody on board.* Any effective operations strategy must be understood and supported throughout the organisation, at all levels.
- *Clear explicit objectives.* If staff know what is expected of them and believe in the objectives, it is easier to succeed.
- *Time framed project management.* Objective setting, schedules, resource plans, and milestones are as important here as for any other project.

The Rover case (Case 43) describes the rapid progress of the company in its improvement strategies which are strongly founded on a carefully devised programme incorporating most of these 'success factors'. It also begs the question – how can the momentum of improvement be maintained?

SUMMARY

It has been suggested that a key challenge for operations managers is to be able to make sense of the operation and all its complexity and fit it within a strategic context in order to ensure that it contributes to the competitiveness of the organisation as a whole. This task is complicated by a frequently held belief that improvement in one area will lead to deterioration in another. Operations managers need to work out how to do all things well and important things excellently. Furthermore, they have a responsibility to ensure that their decisions and actions are ethical, to take into account the global economy of which they are a part, and also to be creative in their development and implementation of operations strategies.

Key points

- A key challenge for operations managers is fitting the operation into a strategic context and creating a set of policies, plans and improvement projects to provide the organisation with a competitive advantage.
- Operations strategies can be classified into four generic strategies; caretaker strategies, marketeer strategies, reorganiser strategies, and innovator strategies.

- Formulating an operations strategy involves linking the total organisation strategic objectives (usually a business strategy) to resource level objectives.
- Nearly all decisions made by operations managers have some kind of ethical dimension.
- Managers need to understand the international implications of managing their operations.
- Creativity is needed to overcome trade-offs between performance criteria. This also involves overcoming some of the blocks to creativity present in most organisations.
- Successful implementation involves deciding when to start, where to start, how fast to proceed and how to co-ordinate the implementation programme.

Recommended reading

Slack, N., Chambers, S., Harland, C., Harrison, A. and Johnston, R. (1998), *Operations Management* (2nd edn), Pitman Publishing. Chapter 21.

Selected further readings

Fine, C. H. and Hax, A. C. (1985), 'Manufacturing strategy: a methodology and an illustration', *Interfaces*, Vol 15, No 6.

Harrison, M. (1993), *Operations Management Strategy*, Pitman Publishing.

Hayes, R. H. and Wheelwright, S. C. (1984), *Restoring Our Competitive Edge*, Wiley.

Hayes, R. H., Wheelwright, S. C. and Clark, K. B. (1988), *Dynamic Manufacturing*, Free Press.

Hill, T. (1993), *Manufacturing Strategy* (2nd edn), Macmillan.

Platts, K. W. and Gregory, M. J. (1990), 'Manufacturing audit in the process of strategy formulation', *International Journal of Operations and Production Management*, Vol 10, No 9.

Skinner, W. (1985), *Manufacturing: the formidable competitive weapon*, Wiley.

Slack, N. (1991), *The Manufacturing Advantage*, Mercury Books.

Slack, N., Chambers, S., Harland, C., Harrison, A. and Johnston, R. (1998), *Operations Management* (2nd edn), Pitman Publishing.

Stonebreaker, P. W. and Leong, G. K. (1994), *Operations strategy: focussing competitive excellence*, Allyn and Bacon, Boston.

Voss, C. A. (1992), *Manufacturing Strategy*, Chapman and Hall.

CASE 40

Jeyes Wipes

Stuart Chambers, Tammy Helander and Stephen Mottram

Case date 1994

INTRODUCTION

Jeyes Group Ltd of today can trace its origins back to late-Victorian Britain. During the last two decades of the nineteenth century, Jeyes established itself in the newly born disinfectants industry, making products used to destroy undesirable microorganisms. This industry was created at a time when large numbers of people were living in cities under unhygienic and primitive sanitary and housing conditions, and so disinfection almost became an obsessive fashion.

COMPANY HISTORY

John Jeyes

John Jeyes was born in 1817, into a wealthy country family of land owners that also had some commercial interests including a retail pharmacy business. John's brother, Philadelphus, had the main responsibility for this shop after their father's death. As a result, John went into business, including the manufacture of mattresses, boots, shoes and wool, before coming up with his famous disinfectant fluid. It was patented 1877, and was to become the start of the company Jeyes Group Ltd of today.

It seems that John Jeyes' strengths were not as a businessman, and so he did not earn much with his business, but he was an amiable, genial and charitable character. He was a very big man, and every morning he had to be pushed up the stairs to his office! He also seems to have been a philanthropist, and he and his wife mixed fluids in the kitchen that they sold cheaply in order to try to stop epidemics of childhood diseases like smallpox. However, his real talents and strengths were in his outstanding abilities as an inventor and in making technical innovations. Between 1854 and 1891 he patented 21 different products. However, he made very little impression on the company's finances or ability to grow. Commercial success came later as a result of a hard-headed businessman exploiting his inventions.

The company was first registered in 1879 as Jeyes' Sanitary Compounds Company Ltd, and went through many changes before it acquired its present name, Jeyes Group Ltd. The role of the investors at the time was purely financial in seeking a lucrative investment opportunity. John Jeyes discovered 'the fluid' through working with solutions of timber preservation. It was a disinfectant based on creosol, derived from coal tar distillation. Most disinfectant products at the time were based on carbolic acid (phenol), and they were both more harmful to humans, and had less disinfecting power than the fluid that John Jeyes discovered.

The Handover to Shareholders

The company made an impressive start both home and abroad, and by 1882 a good profit was being made. However, bad credit control, unsuitable accounting systems and ineffective management, led to the collapse of the business in 1884. Control of the Jeyes patents was then acquired by seven well-established businessmen, who saw Jeyes as a good investment, with a product that fitted exactly the buoyant market for disinfectants. Jeyes evolved and established itself as a leading manufacturer of disinfectants and related products. By 1906, as many as 38 products were available, and Jeyes operated in more than 30 different countries.

A Buoyant Market

Demand for Jeyes' products was stimulated by big epidemics throughout the world: cholera in Hamburg and Egypt, plague in South Africa, smallpox in Japan, for example. Jeyes extensively exploited these crises in their marketing materials. They immediately capitalised on an order for 15 000 kg of fluid to wash the streets of Alexandria in order to prevent further outbreak of cholera. In a circular issued to medical officers, Jeyes strongly recommended use of the company's products, referring to Alexandria. Another area from which Jeyes benefited, was the growth in passenger ships, where disinfection was considered very important.

Jeyes also regularly received many government orders, and won prizes for its products, which undoubtedly gave a very prestigious image; all of this happening within the first thirty years of the founding of the company. Besides the excellent use of advertising, further success was enhanced by a combination of factors such as the extended product line, new patents registrations, technical expertise, its enthusiastic and competent salesforce, and a continuous attack on new markets.

Jeyes success continued throughout this century, with many large government contracts from around the world, and general growth in retail sales. Jeyes brand became well known and trusted in many countries. In 1970, UK production was brought together in a new factory at Thetford.

THE CADBURY-SCHWEPPES YEARS

From 1972 to 1986 the company was part of the Cadbury-Schweppes Group. The group's main objective in the purchase of Jeyes was to diversify from confectionery and beverages into other food and health businesses. From its health food product range came the introduction to hygiene products, and so to Jeyes. The Cadbury-Schweppes bid was welcomed, as the move to Thetford had put considerable pressure on the Jeyes company finances.

Jeyes worked fairly independently during the Cadbury-Schweppes years, and continued to trade under the name of Jeyes. During this time the company acquired complementary businesses, sold off non-core activities, and adopted a strong customer focus. In 1986, after more than a year of negotiations with the group, a management buy-out (MBO) was agreed and implemented.

AFTER THE MBO

Jeyes continued to build and secure its strong customer base, both in the UK and internationally, and strengthened its portfolio of bleaches and disinfectants. There was a group culture of a customer- and marketing-led approach, and the developments of the product lines and promotional activities were extensive. However, the power of private label products was growing.

In 1988, discussions were started with Sterling Drug, with the objective of buying their 'moist wipes' business. Jeyes was already involved with wipes, having obtained the selling and distribution rights for moist toilet tissue made by the German firm Hakle. In early 1990 Jeyes diversified by making some further acquisitions in related businesses, and had moved successfully into several new areas including wipes, and slow-release insecticides.

There were also some divestments. The washing-up liquid business was sold off. In 1992, the blowmoulding operations (the manufacture of plastic bottles used for most of the products) were sold to the LMG group, which continued to operate on site, supplying the needs of the packing lines on a 'hole-in-the-wall' supply basis. The vehicles fleet was contracted out, and the manufacturing sites were rationalised.

THE ARGENTI PLAN

A new corporate strategy was formulated in 1989 with help from the strong corporate strategist Argenti, ending up with what was known as the 'Argenti Plan'. From the plan it was recognised that there was a need to increase the number of core categories in which the group was operating, as at the time it was involved mainly in mature markets. Wipes were to become one of these essential new categories.

When Jeyes unexpectedly got the offer to buy Stirling Drug's wipes business, it seemed to suit all of its identified strategic needs. The overall outlook for wipes seemed very promising. The US moist wipes market was growing at a rate of 18 per cent per year, and the UK, at an earlier stage in the life cycle, appeared to offer even faster initial growth.

In the spring of 1989, Jeyes completed its £1.1million acquisition of the moist wipes business from Sterling Drug, which comprised the brands *Wet Ones* and *Baby Wet Ones*. As well as already having UK selling and distribution rights for Hakle's moist toilet tissue, Jeyes also produced flat pack toilet tissue, so Jeyes was already fairly familiar with the wipes market.

At the time of the acquisition, a financial plan was made for wipes, summarised in Table 40.1. Everything indicated large margins and fast growth. The payback period for the investment was estimated to be under three years. At that time the wipes category consisted primarily of canisters which are wide-mouthed plastic bottles in which the moist wipes are packed. Gross margins as high as 50 per cent were expected, although private-label products accounted for around 20 per cent of turnover, and normally had significantly lower margins than branded wipes. Own-label, if adequately controlled, was felt to be an important segment of the retail market, but if it was ignored, could allow entry into a growing market by lean 'followers'.

Table 40.1 Wipes business financial forecast at acquisition

	Forecast for year (£000)					
	1988	*1989*	*1990*	*1991*	*1992*	*1993*
Sales revenue	5800	6400	6500	7200	8600	11000
Gross margin*	1738	2095	2504	2826	3486	4552
Gross margin (%)	30.0	32.7	38.5	39.3	40.5	41.4
Direct marketing costs	(1170)	(1250)	(1300)	(1400)	(1800)	(2400)
Gross margin less mktg.	568	845	1204	1426	1686	2152
Overhead	(200)	(300)	(500)	(650)	(750)	(800)
Trading profit	368	545	704	776	936	1352
Sales margin (%)	6.3	8.5	10.8	10.8	10.9	12.3

*Gross margin defined as revenue less materials and direct labour

THE ACQUISITION OF RUFUS

The Swedish firm Rufus Förpacknings AB was acquired 1991 to further expand Jeyes' wipes business. The products consisted of smaller wipe travel packs in flexible packaging, which complimented Jeyes' existing wipes range. Its turnover was £1.3m, and the company was acquired for just under £1m. A further acquisition of the *Quickies* and *Allfresh* sachets brands from SmithKline Beecham was made in 1992, for approximately £1.7m.

It was anticipated that these moves would improve the overall margin of the wipes business, since the travel packs commanded higher margins, and Rufus was thought to have been bought for a very good price. Rufus came with a fully operational Swedish factory, and its own management, and brought with it a totally different culture from that of the UK operation.

MATERIAL AND PRODUCT TYPES

Moist wipes are normally made from a wide range of non-woven materials or fabrics. There are numerous ways in which these are produced by the suppliers; for example wet-laid, dry-laid, hydroentangled, and spunbonded. In the UK, the type of fabric selected for a wipe is often determined by the type of outer packaging that will be used in the production of the wipe.

When wipes first appeared they were manufactured using wet-laid fabrics which have a tissue-type appearance; but the fabric retains its strength even when wetted, because chemical binders are used to hold the cellulose, viscose, and rayon fibres together. Rolls of fabric are first slit and perforated, and then rerolled to create small rolls or 'logs' which are packed into cylindrical plastic cannisters. The consumer draws sheets from the inner part of the log, through the top closure of the canister which also serves to break the sheets at the perforations. Canisters have two disadvantages compared to the later flatpack wipes. First, the use of a canister is a two-handed operation, and second, the wipes are rather thin.

More expensive flatpack wipes arrived in the late 1980s, led by the brand Scott, and the user benefits were immediately apparent. Flatpacks generally use air-laid fabric which is thick, soft, and feels much more like cloth. The cut sheets are z-folded, packed in a flat stack, and presented in rigid plastic boxes which allows one-handed use; important when using them on active babies. Shortly after the introduction of the box, flow-wrapped refills were introduced. These comprised standard packets of wipes in flexible, impervious printed wrapping similar to the type used on many food products.

Cosmetic wipes are made from circular, die-cut pads of more expensive non-woven materials. These pads are dosed with non-aqueous formulations using specialised, custom-built fillers.

PRODUCTION PROCESSES

When Jeyes bought the wipes business it acquired all the manufacturing plant for producing canisters. Within two years further equipment had been purchased to make thick wipes using air-laid fabric. Recent developments using stronger and softer alternatives to air-laid fabric are beginning to stretch the capability of these high capital cost converting machines. Jeyes has the equipment to manufacture all these types of wipes, and can handle a wide variety of fabric types. However there is little flexibility across the production lines, because of the necessary specialisation of the equipment associated with each type. Thus the seasonal sales patterns for the different products has to be planned for in terms of capacity on an individual line basis, although there is sufficient labour flexibility to permit movement of staff between the lines as necessary.

The production of canisters begins at the winder which converts the large parent reels of fabric (up to one metre in diameter) into perforated logs which can then be held as WIP until required on the assembly line. The winders are very flexible in that they can be quickly changed in terms of sheet length and width, the sheet count per log, and the type and weight of fabric. The logs are manually placed into canisters on the line, and the fluid is then dosed in automatically. Closure caps are then pressed onto the canisters, and then labels and any secondary packaging are applied. Apart from the winder, the other equipment is simple and poses few barriers to entry for low-overhead competitors. Some fabric suppliers are able to supply converted logs to these companies.

Thick wipes use much more expensive equipment, and thus high volume demand is required to justify the initial investment. Parent reels of fabric, up to two metres wide and 1.5 metres in diameter are hoisted into the unwinding section of the converter. Fabric is drawn into the machine through slitters which cuts it longitudinally, and then it passes over a dosing section where fluid is forced into the fabric. The wet strips pass through a series of folding plates to produce the z-fold and finally into a cutting/packing section producing the assembled wet stacks of between 40 and 90 sheets. These are then passed by conveyor into the box-loading or flow-wrapping equipment. The thick wipes converting machines have low flexibility, since they are designed for a specific sheet size and fold. Those change-overs that are possible, such as variations in fabric specification and sheet count are time-consuming, so batch sizes and inventory levels tend to be much larger than for canisters.

Because canisters use the lower priced and thinner wet-laid fabric, the production lines run at output rates two to three times faster than those of a thick wipes line. Set-ups on the simple filling lines can be completed quickly and with very low material losses. This allows smaller batches to be produced economically, resulting in lower finished goods inventory levels and greater flexibility in response to sales fluctuations. The machinery for travel pack production is complicated and slow to set-up, and costly in terms of material wastage as the type of fabric or fold is changed.

The cosmetic wipes are quite distinct from other wipes in that they use non-aqueous fluid formulations. To successfully produce these wipes the manufacturing plant has to inject the correct amount of fluid into the pads of material which are naturally more resistant to oil-based than water-based formulations. Because of this, change-overs are relatively time-consuming, and flexibility is limited.

THE PLANT

The rented Wigan factory was new to Jeyes but had previously been used as a warehouse, and was chosen as it was considered a low-cost, low-risk location to introduce the wipes business. Labour availability was good, and there was felt to be a good industrial work ethic in the area. The site was cheap to rent, and communications and transport were good. Most fabrics were supplied from Scandinavia, and the blowmoulded canisters and labels from several different UK sources. Because of the relatively high value/weight ratios involved, there was no need to either locate near suppliers, nor customers.

When Stephen Mottram, the new factory manager, started January 1993, he had been impressed by what Gary Swanton, the quality control and hygiene manager, had been telling him during the round tour.

> *'When we started, all we had was this empty storage building of 4000 square metres, not at all suited to hygiene conditions. Ideally, it would have been best to set up a new building, where we could have adopted strict standards without difficulties. However, we have succeeded in developing a very well functioning site, and today we have rigorous hygiene controls, and we fill all requirements according to the standards required by the cosmetics industry.'*

In September 1994 all the Rufus production of travel packs was moved to Wigan when the Bjuv site was closed. At one extreme these could be packs containing 25 sheets of air-laid fabric; simpler and smaller versions of the more usual 40 or 80/84 sheet thick box refills. At the other, they could be a 10-sheet pack of crepe fabric, in a very small sheet size for spectacle cleaning wipes. The products generally had high gross margins, but production throughput rates proved to be much slower than for other wipes products. Some of the differences mentioned earlier became more apparent. Jonas, the Swedish Planning and Logistics Manager explained:

> *'It is a very different culture here from that of Bjuv. The qualifications of the people in Bjuv were much higher, and I worked side by side with engineers. Everyone was so aware of how important it was to keep the lines running to remain profitable. I did not have to tell them every minute what to do. I mean, I really like people here, but they have to be trained. Things are much better now, but it has taken time to reach the same efficiency levels as we had in Sweden.'*

THE WIPES MARKET

In 1993 the total UK wipes market was valued at £70m, as detailed in Table 40.2. Market experts judged market penetration to be around 87 per cent. Jeyes' part of the market was around £10.5m or 15 per cent. In addition, approximately one fifth of Wigan's wipes, by value, were exported. Since the entrance of Jeyes into the wipes market competition had increased, with fights both for market share and for increased differentiation, through developments such as 'hypoallergenic', 'alcohol free', and 'natural' to name a few.

Table 40.2 The UK wipes market (£ million)

Market segment	*Year*									
	1988	*1989*	*1990*	*1991*	*1992*	*1993*	*1994*	*1995f*	*1996f*	*1997f*
Baby	20.9	26.9	35.5	44.4	51.5	56.4	60.9	64.6	67.8	70.5
Adult	4.6	4.6	4.6	4.6	4.2	4.2	4.2	4.2	4.2	4.2
Cosmetic	2.6	2.6	2.6	2.6	2.5	2.4	2.4	2.4	2.4	2.4
Moist toilet tissue	2.0	2.2	2.8	3.4	4.6	6.6	8.6	10.6	12.6	14.6
Others*	0.3	0.3	0.4	0.4	0.5	0.5	0.6	0.7	0.8	0.9
TOTAL	30.4	36.3	45.9	55.4	63.3	70.1	76.7	82.4	87.8	92.6

*Others category includes shoe-care, insect repellent household wipes, etc.
f = forecast for market

The customers mainly consisted of big retailers, and since they had a lot of market power, they were demanding in terms of low prices. The market seemed to contain many product offerings, many competitors, and have a wide range of distribution channels. There were now many different base fabrics, packaging formats, and ranges in terms of branded, private-label and commodity 'generic' offerings. From a marketing point of view the easiest way to segment the market was according to product type (canisters, box, flow-wrap, thick/thin, etc.) and distribution channels (major retailers, minor retailers, pharmacies, etc.). However, commercial market research data is obtained in the categories shown in Table 40.2, which focuses on the ultimate use of the wipes.

It seemed to Stephen, that Jeyes was being asked to make more and more private 'own label' for big retailers, and that it was becoming increasingly difficult to promote their own brands in the supermarkets, particularly for mature products such as canisters of wipes. The market trend for other retail outlets had also changed, with more customers buying cheap generics, rather than the highly promoted, quality branded products. Newer innovative products (such as thick wipes in plastic boxes used in the baby market) tended to begin as branded only, but because of intensive competition in the wipes market, were soon copied for own-label sales. Then, within a relatively short time, if sufficient volume of sales were available, these could become generic and much more price sensitive. Any future growth was expected to be driven both by greater competition between strong brands and own label, and continuously improved products and packaging. In the US market, a forerunner to that in the UK and Europe, there were constant innovations in materials, fluids, and packaging, and new applications for wipes.

PERFORMANCE SINCE THE ACQUISITIONS

When Stephen looked at the financial situation in early 1994, as outlined in Table 40.3, the wipes business accounted for around 20 per cent of the group's turnover, but compared to some of the other, and more mature group businesses of bleach, disinfectants and toilet cleaners, the poor profitability of wipes had been a continuing headache. He was concerned about the way these losses had been derived, since the apportioned head office overhead seemed to have increased dramatically since the earlier financial planning. Knowing that overhead of the Wigan site had been relatively static and tightly controlled, he felt that the underlying wipes business probably was much more profitable than the figures were indicating. Since the wipes category was growing, it was suffering from the way the head office overhead was being absorbed; apparently this was proportional to Wigan's percentage of group turnover.

Table 40.3 Actual financial performance

	Results for year (£000)					
	1988	*1989*	*1990*	*1991**	*1992*	*1993*
Sales revenue	7828	9294	9663	10246	11879	13182
Gross margin	2897	3139	3390	3611	4153	4572
Direct marketing costs	(1391)	(1414)	(1511)	(1664)	(1942)	(2152)
Overhead	(1300)	(1900)	(2300)	(2500)	(2800)	(3100)
Trading profit (loss)	206	(175)	(421)	(553)	(589)	(680)

*Rufus included from 1991.

Margins were under much more pressure than had been anticipated, and the *'Baby Wet Ones'* brand failed to get adequate distribution. Other factors affecting profitability were the unexpectedly rapid changes in the marketplace. When the wipes category was bought it mainly consisted of canisters of thin wipes, but shortly after the acquisition, sales of canisters started to decrease, and sales of plastic boxes of thick wipes increased rapidly. Even though these were a lower margin product, Wigan had invested in the necessary production machinery, as this product was in general demand by most customers, and because the considerable investment in special process technology required for thick wipes raised the barriers to entry. The accompanying flow-wrapped refill packs were higher margin products. However, the generally broadened range and complexity brought new demands on the processes, and on the factory infrastructure.

Fortunately, the Wigan site was quick to adapt to the changing circumstances, and it was felt that these problems could quickly be overcome. The management team felt that the broader range would never pose any problems they could not solve, so they worked towards creating solutions that would be beneficial to both customers and the company. They had passed the learning stage, and successfully produced a whole line of different wipes for a wide range of totally different customer requirements.

THE SURVEY

Shortly after Stephen had started as Factory Manager at Wigan, he decided to conduct a survey of the account managers' views of order-winners and qualifiers, in order to get a better knowledge of the business, and hopefully to add something to the wipes business in terms of manufacturing. He found that the segmentation used by marketing, described earlier, was not very useful from a manufacturing perspective. He first divided the one hundred or so different products into eight main operations-based categories. These segmented the business on the basis of the type of product and process technology used (e.g., canisters, boxes, refills) and the market positioning of the products (e.g., branded, private label, commodity).

The operations director, based at the head office in Thetford, some 300 km from the plant, fully supported Stephen's investigation. His view of the wipes market was pretty clear:

> *'I don't believe that there are any unique competitive advantages that can come just from manufacturing in the wipes category. The retailers are very strong, and the specifications of the products are now very much dictated by them. The products have to fulfil certain requirements, for instance quality and cost levels, but nothing else seems to be needed above that level. We have been able to serve these requirements very well, and our customers are coming back again and again for more business.*
>
> *'Possibly something more progressive could be done with product innovations, but that concerns our R&D department more than manufacturing. We have to be careful with our choice of process investments. It would not be very sensible to invest in expensive automated equipment in a market where it seems that the customers, even just after a couple of years, demand completely different products. We have to be flexible enough to adapt quickly, and that requires that we have not locked ourselves in with old solutions.'*

The twenty account managers had been asked to rank Stephen's operations-based segments on price, volume flexibility, range flexibility, lead time from order, product innovation and design, delivery reliability, and quality, or any other criteria of their choice. The survey was based on the Hill Methodology for manufacturing strategy development, but was adapted by using Slack's Importance/Performance Matrix. The scales ran from 1 to 9, with 1 as the top ranking, as described in *Operations Management* by Nigel Slack *et al.* The research findings are summarised in Tables 40.4(a) and 40.4(b), which show the average scores assigned to each criterion by the survey respondents.

Table 40.4(a) Survey result – Importance to customers

	Importance to customers						
Product / Market	*Price*	*Lead time*	*Delivery reliability*	*Volume flexibility*	*Range flexibility*	*Quality*	*Product innovation and design*
Commodity canisters	1.3	4.7	2.4	4.5	5.8	4.1	6.5
Branded canisters	2.4	4.9	3.0	4.8	4.6	2.9	4.2
Branded box	2.3	4.6	3.1	5.0	4.7	2.6	3.4
Private label box	1.7	4.8	2.5	3.8	3.9	2.8	3.6
Branded box refills	2.1	4.5	3.2	4.8	4.8	2.9	3.5
PL box refills	1.3	5.1	2.4	3.9	3.9	2.7	3.6
Canister refills	1.9	4.6	3.2	4.7	4.5	2.7	3.8
Cosmetic wipes	2.6	4.3	3.1	4.9	4.3	2.7	3.1

Table 40.4(b) Survey result – Performance rankings versus competitors

	Performance relative to competitors						
Product / Market	*Price*	*Lead time*	*Delivery reliability*	*Volume flexibility*	*Range flexibility*	*Quality*	*Product innovation and design*
Commodity canisters	4.3	5.4	5.4	4.3	4.8	4.1	4.8
Branded canisters	4.1	5.2	5.7	4.0	4.1	4.2	4.7
Branded box	5.3	5.3	5.4	4.7	3.6	3.9	4.4
Private label box	4.7	5.6	5.9	4.1	4.1	4.4	5.0
Branded box refills	5.4	2.5	5.4	4.7	3.7	4.0	4.7
PL box refills	5.1	4.7	4.6	4.0	3.7	4.3	4.7
Canister refills	4.5	5.8	5.5	4.5	3.9	3.8	4.4
Cosmetic wipes	3.6	4.9	5.8	4.2	4.5	3.7	4.8

1994 CHANGE OF DIRECTION

In 1994 a new chief executive was appointed to the Jeyes Group. He immediately set about reorganising financial controls, strengthening operational management, and building a strong executive team. Three profit centres were established to achieve improved profit accountability, as shown in Fig. 40.1.

Rationalisations were carried out to make the groupís operations more cost efficient. For instance, marketing and promotional costs were cut in 1994 compared to 1993 levels. There were continuing difficulties in terms of not being able to pass on the rising raw material prices and cost increases for packaging and chemicals, which put pressure on margins. Sales grew in Germany, as well as internationally. In the UK there had been an increasing demand for low price and lower specification generic products, but this trend appeared to be slowing.

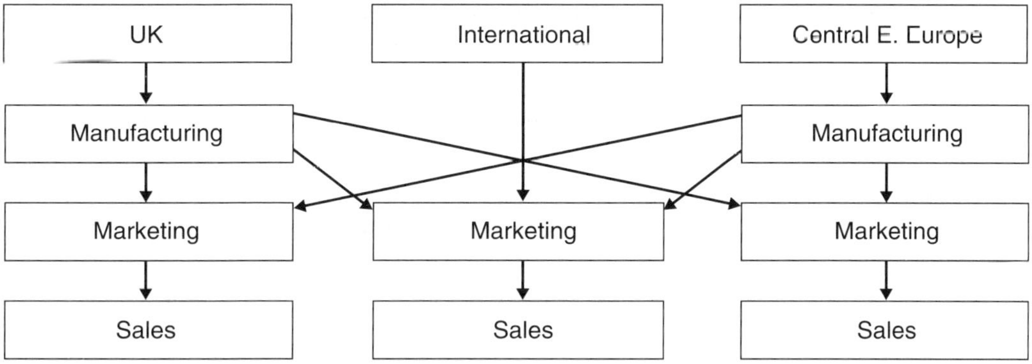

Fig. 40.1 New profit centre organisation

THE NEW ORGANISATION

Sales and marketing were incorporated into the autonomous sales and profit centres, each with a managing director and a small operating board. The emphasis was on creating clear profit objectives, with the report matching the authority for each manager, and with enhanced speed and accuracy of information. Management was committed to rebuilding profitability based on the strength of the existing business, products, and brands, but also on building for the future with new growth areas.

Sales

The account managers based in Thetford were responsible for selling all Jeyes product categories. Previously they had been mainly volume- and growth-oriented but now more attention was directed towards profitability. In order to create a more balanced approach, sales people were rewarded for both margin and volume performance.

Stephen had never been particularly happy with the fact that the account managers seemed to make some deals without first checking with the Wigan factory that they would actually be able to deliver on their promises. They certainly seemed to be chasing volume and did not really understand the complexity of product costs. Since he became factory manager, he had made a conscious decision to develop the account managers' knowledge of the wipes business, and make them understand the effects on manufacturing of their deals, and had tried to suggest appropriate selling prices. He began to get more feedback, and he felt that some signs of better co-operation were beginning to emerge. Although this all took time, persistence and energy, it seemed to have been worthwhile. But there were setbacks every week, and he had to keep on trying to help others understand the manufacturing point of view. He reflected on a recent conversation with one of the new account managers, who had proudly told him of a small, but high margin special canister order, he had just negotiated. Stephen had been persistent in his discussion:

'Do you know that it takes a whole day to make a set-up for this order, and that it is an extremely slow product on the lines. We can only make about 70 cases per hour, instead of around 250 cases per hour running normal canisters. If we could have actually run standard canisters instead, we would have been able to earn far more profit per hour for the company than for your small order, even though canisters are apparently lower margin products. It is not just a question of selling at a price or a margin . . . we should try to see how each product and order fits in with the others, before we can really predict the final benefit of an order to the business. This is because we have certain capacity bottlenecks. Depending on the mix of work, products have to be sequenced or run together to minimise set-up costs.'

Stephen had persisted with a lengthy and interesting discussion, but he knew this was time well spent, and he hoped it would result in more canister orders in the near future. He had sent the account manager one of his analyses, as shown in Appendix 40.1, in order to make him become more aware of which products were the most productive on the lines.

Purchasing

Purchasing was done centrally for the group, in order to be able to buy large quantities at the best prices from suppliers. Whereas all factories reported to the operations director, the purchasing function reported directly to the managing director. Unfortunately, sometimes the order quantities were totally unsuitable for the needs of the Wigan site, and the team had to work hard to change the views and objectives of the purchasing department at head office. Sometimes they had little use of large quantities, and they felt that unnecessary inventory had resulted.

Human Resources (HR)

There was a central HR function, but the factory was free to do much of its own hiring, to decide on rules of employment, shift times, and so on. For example, at Wigan a very flexible system was introduced in 1994 for 'seasonal working hours'. The company required employees to work longer hours at times of high demand, but credited these hours back in periods when the activity was lower. This was certainly a very market-orientated system, and helped in achieving management's objectives of improving service levels and reducing the excess accumulated inventories. However, the scheme did not actually meet with all-round approval, and was not repeated in 1995.

Technical Department

Overall, Wigan operated with considerable autonomy, but in co-operation with the group. Sometimes, as in the case of dealing with the central technical department, they were very dependent on getting answers in reasonable time. Stephen recalled what one customer had said recently:

> *'I really appreciate that you operate close to the market, and you always make an effort to provide us with what we want, on time . . . By the way, have you been thinking of what we discussed the other day? If you could arrange to provide me with those special red labels and lids on the baby canisters within three weeks, the next order is yours, but I have to know this week.'*

Stephen had been worried that if he was to put into action the 'correct' procedure using the technical department at the Thetford head office site, this would take at least six weeks. They were certainly very competent, but it usually took some time for enquiries of this type to be processed. Just the other day, he had received the latest official version of a customer enquiry flowchart, as shown in a simplified form in Fig. 40.2.

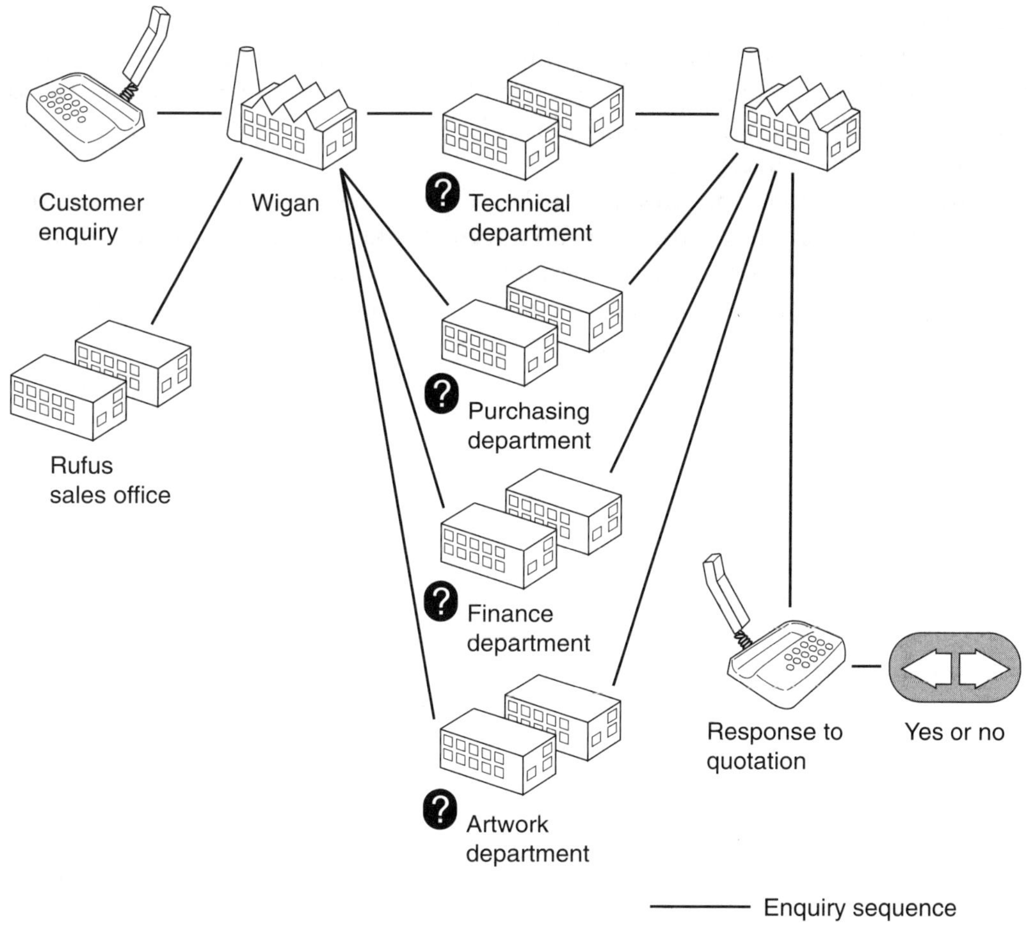

Fig. 40.2 Routine customer enquiries flowchart

The Wigan managers had recently taken more independent decisions on some easier technical matters, even though this was not always popular with everyone, because of the demands it put on them to take responsibility and adapt to change. They found no reason to bother the central department with most of the easier technical matters, and believed this should free up time in the central service to handle any more difficult issues.

SUMMER 1994

Stephen met many customers during his first year at Jeyes, and could relate well to the survey results that he was now reviewing for his work on the operations strategy. One thing that almost every customer wished to discuss was prices; but with the biggest retailers there was not ever really a meaningful discussion on this issue, as they seemed to have considerable power to dictate the prices they were prepared to pay.

Another performance factor often mentioned was delivery reliability, seeming to be especially important for the largest multiple retailers. At the request of the board, Stephen had recently increased finished goods inventory levels (from 6 to 12 weeks of sales cover) in an attempt to improve service levels, but without any measurable improvements in delivery reliability.

At the time of the completed survey in late 1993, it was widely felt that the answers had not revealed very much that they did not already know about the wipes business. However, Stephen believed that things had improved during the year, and that they could provide customers with benefits that were not easy to imitate. These went far beyond just conformity to standards and specifications demanded by customers. It seemed sometimes to consist of factors that were not really present in the survey.

His intuitive feeling was that they operated differently in some ways that really created a competitive advantage. They were certainly accommodating towards customers, and they tried to work in a way that promoted quick and desirable solutions for both the company and their customers. The team at Wigan constantly attacked old and poor working routines in a professional manner, in order to become more effective. All of this had been with the blessing of management, and every effort had been taken to contribute to the new structure and profit centre organisation. His thoughts went back to the survey. Surely, from what he knew of Jeyes, and from the results of this survey, he should be able to formulate an operations strategy.

Questions

1 What is Jeyes' corporate business strategy, and does this present any obstacles in establishing a local operations strategy?

2 What should be the main elements of the operations strategy for the Wigan site?

3 How should the other functions support the operations strategy, and what organisational problems does this create for the group?

4 Discuss potential threats and opportunities that should be considered in developing the operations strategy?

5 How does Wigan's approach to sales differ from the central Thetford view?

APPENDIX 40.1
ANALYSIS OF MANUFACTURING COSTS AND CONTRIBUTION FOR 25 REPRESENTATIVE PRODUCTS

Category	*Type*	*Product (disguised names)*	*Average output rate (cases/hr)*	*Units per case*	*Average selling price per unit*	*Direct manufacturing cost per unit*					*Gross margin*	
						Fabric	*Fluid*	*Packaging*	*Assembly line labour*	*Fabric prepn. labour*	*per unit*	*% of sales price*
Canisters	C	Babywipe 100s	238	12	46.80	19.70	0.75	8.80	7.60	2.30	7.65	16.35
	C	Babywipe 200s	202	6	82.70	39.40	1.50	15.00	9.00	4.60	13.20	15.96
	C	Adultwipe 100s	250	12	45.80	18.70	0.85	9.85	8.00	2.40	6.00	13.10
	B	Baba 40s	185	12	59.50	19.10	1.20	10.80	4.60	2.50	21.30	35.80
	B	Baba 80s	189	6	102.70	38.20	2.40	19.35	5.50	5.00	32.25	31.40
	B	Babex 75s	168	12	59.20	19.80	2.50	10.45	4.80	2.80	18.85	31.84
	B	Babex 150s	229	6	98.50	39.60	5.00	16.75	4.90	5.60	26.65	27.06
	B	New Baba 40s	165	6	80.00	16.40	1.50	7.42	4.80	2.50	47.38	59.22
Boxes	B	Boxies 40s	80	12	102.00	34.50	3.80	15.90	18.90	0.00	28.90	28.33
	B	Wiskaway 40s	72	12	99.80	33.00	3.80	17.50	19.50	0.00	26.00	26.05
	B	Easies 40s	90	12	81.70	23.90	2.10	17.00	19.00	0.00	19.70	24.11
	P	RinoStores 80s	115	6	109.20	42.23	5.25	18.81	18.54	0.00	24.37	22.32
	P	Saveco 40s	60	12	79.40	29.00	4.90	17.25	22.50	0.00	5.75	6.92

Category	*Type*	*Product (disguised names)*	*Average output rate (cases/hr)*	*Units per case*	*Average selling price per unit*	*Direct manufacturing cost per unit*					*Gross margin*	
						Fabric	*Fluid*	*Packaging*	*Assembly line labour*	*Fabric prepn. labour*	*per unit*	*% of sales price*
Refills	B Box	Boxies 40s	138	12	76.20	34.50	3.80	6.00	4.50	0.00	27.40	35.96
	B Box	Wiskaway 40s	138	12	73.90	33.00	3.80	5.80	4.20	0.00	27.10	36.67
	B Box	Boxies 80s	140	12	110.80	69.00	7.60	6.80	4.80	0.00	22.60	20.40
	B Can	Baba 40s	129	12	39.90	19.10	1.20	3.85	4.90	2.50	8.85	22.18
	B Can	Baba 80s	136	10	77.90	38.20	2.40	5.89	5.20	5.00	21.21	27.22
	P Can	Saveco canister R.	131	10	65.00	15.20	3.50	6.30	1.65	1.26	37.09	57.06
	P Box	Aldrose box R	108	8	94.00	32.50	5.40	7.55	8.70	0.00	39.85	42.39
Cosmetic Wipes	B	Wipeaway Lipstik	170	12	55.10	8.50	0.90	11.30	5.40	2.54	26.46	48.02
	B	Wipeaway Toner	182	12	48.30	9.70	1.50	11.45	5.70	0.00	19.95	41.31
	B	Wipeaway Travel	190	12	44.90	5.46	1.40	7.76	5.60	0.00	24.68	54.97
	B	Wipeaway Micro	185	16	34.50	6.50	0.95	8.75	5.20	0.00	13.10	37.97
	B	Wipeaway Valpac	116	6	95.00	15.64	3.55	10.79	7.85	0.00	57.17	60.18

Key: B = Branded P = Private Label C = Commodity (Generic)
All costs and prices in pence (£0.01 = 1 pence)

CASE 41

Indian Metals Corporation

Sara Mountney, Kenneth Work and Stuart Chambers

Case date 1996

INTRODUCTION

'The problem isn't the plant itself, it's the way it's being run.'

After four weeks in this remote part of north India, John Daley had seen at first hand the immense problems at the Lead and Zinc Processing Plant and was pleased to be heading home. He stared at the views from the taxi for the final time. The only signs of industrialisation in this isolated, mainly agricultural area were the makeshift sheds at the side of the road which had been put up by local villagers to service the trucks going to and from the plant.

John was part of a UN development team which had visited the site at the request of a team of European technical experts who were already on-site. The large processing plant and adjacent mine were owned by the Indian Metals Corporation (IMC). The complex had become operational in 1990.

THE REFINERY

The plant used a method known as the Dual Refinery Process (DRP) to extract lead and zinc from the mined ore. This method had been a new venture for IMC and John's UN agency had been involved in the development of the plant.

The mine was a great success. The refinery, however, was experiencing immense problems and it was hoped that the European team and the UN team could help to resolve them. Despite processing half the company's zinc output, the plant had only ever operated at a maximum of half its capacity level. The layout of the plant is shown in Fig. 41.1.

A mixture of the ore (from the mine) and other inputs are brought into the plant and processed into pre-product. Pre-product is a blend of inputs of a certain size and composition designed to enable the next stage, the furnace, to operate at maximum performance. The pre-product is broken down inside the furnace and both molten lead and molten zinc are tapped off and sent to the separate refineries

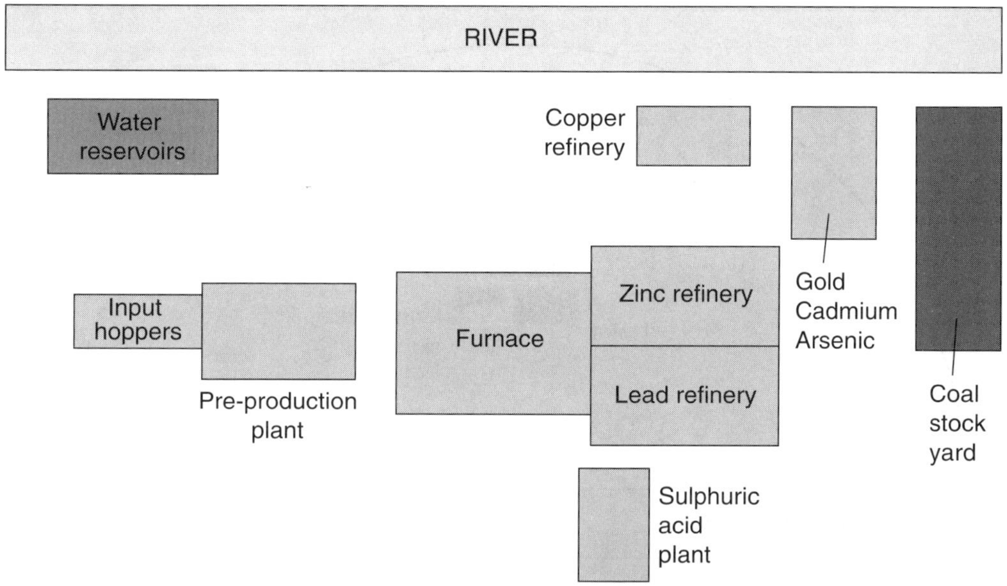

Fig. 41.1 The plant layout

for further processing. Lead processing is run in batches, but only when enough stock has built up to enable the refinery to run economically. Any contaminated or scrap lead can be recycled back into the furnace. The zinc refinery has to run continuously to prevent damage to the equipment. Large levels of buffer stock are needed to keep the refinery running because the furnace and pre-product units are unreliable and liable to shut down.

Other than zinc and lead, useful by-products produced are sulphuric acid, gold, cadmium and arsenic, all of which are processed and sold. A non-toxic black sand is also produced which is sold as land fill.

JOHN'S VISIT TO THE PLANT

John's taxi arrived back at *The Colony*, seven kilometres away, where the plant workers lived. A sketch of *The Colony* is shown in Fig. 41.2.

With the surrounding area being so isolated, the company had built it for staff at all levels. The houses, for staff and their families, ranged from fairly luxurious for senior management to communal barracks for contract workers, most of whom sent money home to their families. Basic living expenses and transport costs to and from work were paid for by the company. In all, the residents seemed satisfied with the amenities. John, however, did not like the surrounding barbed wire fence nor the look of the local militia who patrolled it. Back in the hotel, he began to think about

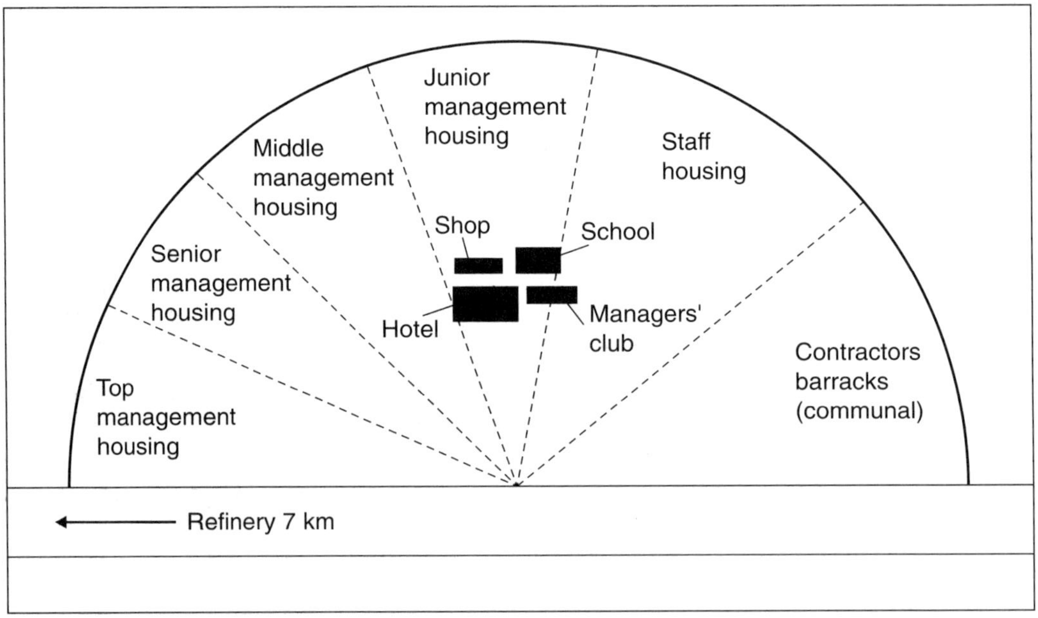

Fig. 41.2 The Colony

the main aspects of his visit to be included in a presentation to his superiors on his return.

Working conditions

He remembered how shocked the team had been at conditions inside the plant on their first visit. This visit had been the cause of some controversy – the team of European experts had been unhappy at the decision to allow the UN team inside as they thought it too dangerous. John and his team wore hard hats and masks, but had never received any safety briefing.

The first area they visited was the zinc refinery. The most obvious sight was the piles of lead and zinc dust everywhere. Zinc buffer stocks were also stored near equipment, and often across walkways and emergency exits. The team watched as a man stood on a 50mm girder over a conveyor belt from which hot zinc blocks (at around 250°C) were emerging. As each block appeared, he aligned it with the belt. This was repeated every ten seconds. The man was not wearing any protective clothing. Their guide told them that, as a contractor, he was not entitled to any. The team watched, impressed by the contractor's balance. If he had fallen down onto a block he would have burned to death before anyone could help him. The entire area was hazardous. As John had leaned back and put his hand out to support himself on what he thought was a horizontal sheet of aluminium, the guide swiftly stopped him. The aluminium sheet was in fact molten zinc.

The Staff

The next area he visited was the Pre-Product Plant, where the ore and inputs were crushed and processed for the furnace. Here, John talked to Mr Singh, the shift manager:

'I've worked here since the plant opened five years ago. As a shift manager, I work seven days a week, from 5.30 a.m. to 8 p.m. and I'm on call all night. The hours are excessive compared to other places, I must say. The pay here is low, but we do have some perks if we don't make waves and are liked by our managers. Perks include your own tea boy.

'Although I'm the shift manager, I'm not really too sure where my responsibilities lie, or sometimes even what I can and can't do. If there's a problem, I pass it on to my manager. That's how it is supposed to go – up the chain of command. Eventually, it comes down again. The management is very strict here and I prefer not to make a decision unless I really have to, because I could be punished.

'I had a situation only a few weeks ago. I was called in at night because that waste recycling machine over there wasn't working properly – it was making odd clanking noises. I didn't really know what to do about it – I wasn't going to close the plant down, that would be unthinkable, so I phoned my manager at home in The Colony. That took a bit of time because there's only one phone line. Anyway, he really didn't know what to do either so I left it with him. Nothing was done until about three hours later, when the general manager phoned me. In the meantime, the clanking noises had got louder and more frequent, but there was nothing I could do. As I spoke to the general manager, the machine literally fell to pieces in front of my eyes! Imagine having to tell that *to him! In the end we managed to repair the machine by stripping out parts from an older one. We managed to get it going again in three days. In order not to stop the plant operating, the waste that would normally be crushed by the machine and fed back into the process, was pumped into a wood at the back of the plant.*

'I live with my family on The Colony, where all the company workers live, about seven kilometres away. They pay for our house, our bills and transport. Our house is quite small, a bit crowded really, but we won't get a bigger one unless I'm promoted. I can only go up one more step because I have a higher education certificate and not a degree.'

The General Manager, Mr Paul, was quite unequivocal about his staff:

'My staff, unfortunately, are lazy, half-witted and useless! They should be whipped into doing some work! Unfortunately, I am stuck with them, as they cannot be dismissed. I have to make all the decisions in this company because I cannot trust anybody! You ask any worker here to think of the answer to a problem, even a trivial, simple one, and they cannot do it! They are all idiots!'

The organisational structure was extremely hierarchical. The team identified up to sixteen levels of management in some areas. A total of 2800 people worked in the plant. A comparable plant in Europe or the US would typically employ 800. Of the 2800, 800 were staff, identifiable by the company uniform, and the remainder were contractors, gangs of people who were hired casually.

The staff carried out the technical and administrative roles within the organisation, such as running and monitoring equipment, maintenance and repairs. Many members of staff were also employed as tea-makers, chair-setters and general helpers for management. These earned privileges could also be removed as punishment. Half of the staff had university degrees and the remainder had higher education certificates.

Contractors

The contractors were paid for non-technical manual labour, such as digging trenches, loading and unloading raw materials and cleaning. This was gruelling and dangerous work – two contractors had been killed since the plant opened. Half the contractors were female because they cost less, even though employment of women in lead mines and processing plants is illegal. Hans Schmidt, a member of the European team, commented:

'We'd heard that women were working in the plant but when we arrived we couldn't see any of them. It turned out that they'd been hidden from us as we toured the plant! A manager showed me an official letter he'd received from the general manager. It told him to say that no women were employed in the plant. The manager told us that the general manager hadn't said anything about showing us the letter!'

The staff were reluctant to criticise the plant at first, but they became more honest as the teams stayed. The head of the pre-product plant, Mr Chandra, told the team how the contractors had died:

'One woman was digging a trench and it collapsed in on her. The other, a man, was cleaning out a machine. It crushes the waste from the furnace into a fine powder, but debris does build up around the inside and this has to be knocked out with a stick. Normally this is done from outside the machine but the man's stick wasn't long enough so he climbed inside. When he hit the roof with the stick, all the debris fell down and crushed him. Of course, the company paid a reasonable pension to both of their families, but it wasn't really that much money.'

Chemical Poisoning

There was an exhibition on health and safety in one of the office blocks, with an example of a protective suit to be worn in dangerous and high temperature areas. Unfortunately, the staff did not know about the exhibition and the contractors were not allowed access to the building. The protective suit was also the only one in the whole of the plant.

The major health and safety issue within the plant was lead poisoning. Regulations were in place to protect employees, such as wearing respirators, but they were largely ignored. Most of the staff did not wear their respirators and the contractors were not issued with them. There were no safety posters within the plant itself, although some were pinned up in the office blocks. The posters were very dirty and neglected.

The UN team were concerned about the exposure of the employees to lead and were convinced that many were showing symptoms of lead poisoning, including dizziness and lethargy. Yet blood tests showed the levels to be acceptable. Paul Buchanan, a member of the UN team decided to investigate:

'The average reading from the plant's laboratories always showed less than 30 parts per million (PPM), but many of the staff tested had symptoms that you would relate to more than 55 PPM. We queried the levels with the laboratory officials, but their explanation was that lead was removed from the body far more quickly than in Europe because of the high levels of pulses in the Indian diet! This explanation was highly suspicious so we decided to carry out our own tests in the UK to check the plant's results. We took two blood samples each from six staff members and analysed them at the plant and at our testing centre in London. The plant tests revealed 30–35 PPM, an acceptable level, but the London results showed a 55–65 PPM – twice the Indian level. When we showed this to the IMC officials, we were bluntly told that there must be problems with the testing facilities at London.'

Another major health and safety concern was the transportation of sulphuric acid to the customer. The customer's tankers used were old and rusty and liable to spill. In fact, many spillages had occurred inside and outside the plant. The driver of the tank was often responsible for loading the acid and had not been issued with any protective clothing (except gloves) nor had he received training. The plant management were reluctant to do anything about this, seeing it as the customer's problem.

Despite these obvious health and safety breaches, the UN team discovered that the plant regularly passed all its inspections. These were carried out by a regional inspector.

Planning

Annual production targets for the plant were usually set in October for the following year and were reviewed every quarter. They were decided at a meeting at HQ which was attended by the general managers of the larger business units and the government, the plant's main customer. Junior management were not consulted, and the targets were generally fictitious – there was usually no possibility of them being achieved. Demand was theoretically steady, but in practice the plant produced as much zinc as it could. As the financial year progressed and successive monthly targets were missed, the production office reworked the production estimates. Mr Chandra commented:

'The production targets are seen as a joke which is not at all funny. We are all aware that they cannot be met but we have a conspiracy of silence. If you fail your target, which we always do, it is re-adjusted for the next month. There are no reprisals as long as the plant keeps running.'

There was no long-term planning within the company. The staff did not carry out short-term planning because their roles mainly involved minute-to-minute troubleshooting.

Maintenance

The policy at the plant was to always to continue operations until a breakdown. At this point, a combined repair and preventative maintenance team would carry out emergency repairs and maintenance work, where time allowed, simultaneously. The consequences were that the maintenance was only partially effective, there were frequent machine breakdowns and plant utilisation was as low as 50 per cent. Equipment which was expected to last ten years normally lasted just three.

A conventional approach for a plant of this type would be to have separate repair and maintenance teams. The repair team would carry out running repairs and fix plant breakdown, and the preventative maintenance team would work during scheduled plant downtimes, preparing equipment and spare parts while the plant was in operation. A plant using this strategy could expect to operate at 75 per cent–80 per cent utilisation. The mission of the preventative maintenance team would be to ensure that the repair team never had any work to do.

The plant was not shut down, even when serious problems developed, on the orders of the general manager. The heads of the pre-product, furnace and refinery units saw a plant breakdown elsewhere as an opportunity to carry out repairs on their own equipment. When a breakdown did occur, a witchhunt was carried out to find out who was to blame. Mr Chandra explained the consequences to the team:

'The general manager will record who is to blame every time the plant stops. Then, if it's your fault, you will be verbally berated and some of your privileges will be removed, or you will be demoted, or your promotion will be blocked. I have to say that we are frightened to stop the plant, even in the most extreme circumstances. The furnace manager stopped his area once because somebody's life was in danger. He was severely disciplined.'

Another problem had occurred in the furnace. It was noticed that the roof above the furnace was unsound but the general manager had refused to stop the plant. Three weeks later, the roof collapsed into the furnace, releasing carbon monoxide gas. Fortunately the area was clear at the time and nobody was killed or injured.

Modifications were carried out to the equipment and process in the pre-product unit to increase output. This was only partially successful because the pre-product produced was of such poor quality that the furnace took longer to process it into lead and zinc, leading to poor energy efficiency. The modifications to the pre-product plant also resulted in the release of sulphur dioxide into the atmosphere. This could be noticed by a foul sulphurous taste in the mouth up to half a mile away. With the wind in the right direction, the gas blew over local villages. Due to the inefficiency of the plant, traces of lead had been found in water samples from an outlet pipe which was fed into a nearbly river. This river was the source of the local water supply.

The plant drew its power supply from the public electricity supplier. Originally, the plant was supposed to have its own independent power station but this was never built. The electricity grid was unreliable and often the plant electricity supply failed or was reduced to a level where efficient operation was impossible. There were two back-up generators in the plant but neither of them worked.

The original machinery installed in the plant was of a high specification and from suppliers known to be world leaders. The equipment was controlled by basic electrical switching and was robust enough to deal with the fluctuating power supply. However, the quality of the equipment used in the plant had been affected by a process known as 'Indianisation'. The Indian government levies a 105 per cent tax on all imported industrial equipment. In order to reduce spares bills and to obtain them quickly, some equipment and spares were replaced by cheaper Indian goods. Unfortunately, these companies had not reached the same quality standards of the original suppliers and there were comfort stocks (long-lead time parts kept as duplicates in case of breakdown) in the warehouse which may not have worked when fitted to the equipment.

Quality

Product quality was fairly well monitored. The zinc and lead produced were regularly checked for conformance to specification, and feedback occurred to ensure that the equipment was adjusted if the products started to fail. However, if a product was produced out of specification it was still sent out and not re-processed. There were no reprisals for producing poor quality product as long as the plant was not stopped.

In the pre-product unit, John noticed several gangs of contractors clearing up a huge pile of ore and coal around a conveyor belt. A week earlier, a ten tonne hopper containing this pile had fallen off the steel girder which supported it and crashed down through a conveyor belt. Luckily, nobody was nearby at the time. It seemed that these 'near-misses' happened regularly yet nothing was done to prevent them.

The Kidnap

Outside the plant, a local village had decided that enough was enough. They told John how they had kidnapped a manager and held him hostage overnight. A man from the village commented:

'Since that plant opened a few years ago it's done nothing but spill out dangerous chemicals! We've had clouds of chemicals over the village. You couldn't see anything but you could taste it. I've also heard people say that there is lead in the water. I really worry about my health and my family's. We're all being slowly poisoned. We complain but they never listen, so we decided to do something to make them notice. As it was, it was useless. The manager said he'd be punished if he said anything.'

As he packed, John pondered over the problems at the plant. The staff themselves were highly skilled and very good at their jobs individually. They certainly did not need the European team to tell them how to run the plant. Yet they all said that they were unable to do their jobs properly. The problems at the plant were far more complex than was first thought. There was much more to be done than just replacing some machinery or installing a computer. John wondered, realistically, if the plant could ever be changed.

Questions

1 Evaluate the ethical issues concerned with the operations management decisions of the IMC plant.[1]

2 Comment on the maintenance strategy at the plant. Are there any alternative methods that would be suitable?

3 'John wondered, realistically, if the plant could ever be changed.' If you were to carry out improvements at the plant, what would your ethical priorities be?

Reference

1 You may find it useful to refer to Slack *et al.*, (1995), *Operations Management*, Pitman Publishing, pp. 858–9.

CASE 42

Singapore Airlines (SIA)

Robert Johnston

Case date 1996

INTRODUCTION

How does Singapore Airlines (SIA), an airline from a small country-state with a population of about three million inhabitants, on an island no larger than the Isle of Man, earn a reputation for being 'the most consistently profitable airline in the world, despite various world-wide recessions'?[1] How does SIA get voted, year after year, 'the best airline', 'the best for business travel', 'the best air cargo carrier', even 'Asia's most admired company'?[2] And, what puts this airline head and shoulders above the big players like British Airways, Royal Dutch KLM, American United Airlines, North West Airlines. Japanese JAL and Australian Qantas, in what must be one of the most ruthless and competitive of all international trades?

SIA's Managing Director, Dr Cheong Choong Kong, in a speech in 1994, accepting the Air Transport World's award for 20 years of excellence in international service, attributed the company's consistent success to recognising the importance of the passengers. He explained 'Our passengers . . . are our *raison d'être*, they are what this whole bewildering [airline] business is about. If SIA is successful, it is largely because we have never allowed ourselves to forget that important fact'.[3] Dr Cheong added a second reason to account for its success, the high level of motivation and teamwork among SIA's employees.

TAKING OFF AS IT MEANS TO GO ON

SIA's roots go back to 1947 when Malayan Airlines was formed (later becoming Malaysian Airways). In 1967 it became MSA – Malaysia-Singapore Airlines which, on 1 October, 1972, became two airlines, Malaysian Airlines System (more recently Malaysia Airlines) and Singapore Airlines. The newly formed airline took over a network of flights around much of south-east Asia and an expanding intercontinental network covering 22 cities in 18 countries. The Singapore government made it clear, right from the start, that it was not prepared to subsidise the airline and so twelve months later, with just ten aircraft and 6000 staff, SIA turned in an aftertax profit of S$12.5 millions.

Since its inception SIA has expanded progressively despite worldwide recessions. In 1978 the airline placed an order for over one billion Singapore dollars for thirteen B747s and six B727s. Over the following 25 years the company spent an additional S$30 billions on about 160 new aircraft. By 1993 SIA had the youngest fleet of any carrier (an average of just five years), with 58 planes serving 67 cities in 40 countries. By December 1995 SIA had 69 aircraft (29 Megatop B747s, six Big Top B747s, three B747 Combis, two B747-200, four B747s Mega Ark, one B747 Freighter, one DC8 Freighter, and 23 A310s). The company currently has seventy planes on order including 34 B777s.[4] SIA has also increased the number of destinations served to 73 cities in 41 countries, including two non-stop daily flights from Singapore to London and back.[5]

COMMITMENT TO INNOVATION AND DEVELOPMENT

Besides its bold aircraft acquisition and route development policies, SIA has been investing in many forms of technology and is an industry leader in product and service innovations. It has an ongoing research programme and is involved in a number of overseas ventures.

Mr B K Ong, the Senior Manager for Customer Service Affairs, explained 'We aim to stay ahead of the competitors in everything we do . . . When we have a big idea and see potential and big benefits, we put money into it.'

This is not a new policy. SIA was the first airline to introduce free drinks, a choice of meals and free headsets back in the 1970s. Dr Cheong explained 'At SIA we are committed to a constant process of refining and even, on occasions, reinventing our service. Among the many qualities that underpin our reputation for excellence is an innate urge to lead and also a passion for innovation. We were the first airline to offer passengers many products and services which have since become commonplace, such as choice of meals and complimentary drinks and headsets in economy class. More recently, we introduced the first global in-flight phone and fax service, "Celestel", on our Megatop 747s.'[6]

In 1995 SIA began a two-year programme to install 'KrisWorld', a new in-flight entertainment system, for passengers in all three classes of its Megatop B747s. KrisWorld offers 22 channels of video entertainment, twelve digital audio channels, ten Nintendo video games, destination information and a telephone at every seat. The installation takes about three weeks and costs about S$5 millions per aircraft.[7] KrisNews, a live teletext news service, is the most recent innovation and there are plans for the introduction of an interactive in-flight shopping service. Dr Cheong added 'As a major operator of intercontinental flights, we know that boredom is the scourge of the long-haul passenger, no matter how attentive the in-flight service, how comfortable the seat or how delicious the in-flight cuisine. On SIA, these problems are now a thing of the past . . . KrisWorld will bring to each passenger set an unprecedented quantity and variety of entertainment and information services via a personal in-seat video screen and a hand held remote control unit.'[8]

On another aspect of product development, SIA takes great care to provide its passengers with in-flight cuisine of the highest quality and the greatest variety. Menus change generally every three months, but this has increased to monthly and even weekly on heavily travelled routes to cater for frequent travellers. For flights out of Singapore, these meals are produced by SATS Catering, a wholly-owned subsidiary of SIA.

Assisting SIA's success is Singapore's Changi airport, often dubbed one of the world's greatest airports. This hub, conveniently situated for stop-offs and hub transfers for either intra-Asian or transhemispheric traffic, offers state-of-the-art facilities with plenty of capacity for expansion in the future. SIA has been developing many new facilities at Changi, and although this is a vital part of its expansion and innovation, these activities may be less obvious to its passengers than its developments in in-flight services.

In March 1995 SIA Engineering opened a new S$130m hangar, and an eight storey annex, which can accommodate up to two B747s (bringing its total hangar capacity to five). The new hangar has all the latest aircraft maintenance and servicing technology. SIA has also recently opened its new state-of-the-art SATS Superhub, its fifth airfreight terminal, greatly increasing its cargo handling capacity. SATS is a wholly-owned subsidiary of SIA which provides ground handling services. Twenty minutes drive from the airport the company has created a new supplies centre, opened in April 1995 by SIA Chairman J.Y. Pillay. This is a two storey block with 19 000 sq. metres of floor area with automatic storage and retrieval systems (a S$5.5m material handling system) to handle catering equipment, in-flight amenities, wines, spirits and stationery.

OVERSEAS VENTURES

For many years SIA was a stand alone operation but more recently it has been developing international partnerships and joint ventures. In 1989 SIA formed an alliance with Swissair and Delta Airlines to provide its Singapore-based passengers with a high quality and frequent service all around the world. This three continent link-up has led to better co-ordination of schedules, the sharing of airport lounges, and joint purchasing activities to try to create seamless world travel. SIA also maintains close links with its subsidiary SilkAir which flies leisure routes in the region. It has developed a frequent flyer programme in association with Cathay and Malaysia Airlines.

SIA Engineering Company (SIAEC), which was formed into a separate company in 1992, is a partner in a joint venture company called the Pan Asia Pacific Aviation Services (PAPAS) which is setting up an aircraft maintenance facility at Hong Hong's Chek Lap Kok airport. A joint venture company with Tata Consultancy will be set up shortly in Madras to develop and maintain computer software.[9]

REPUTATION FOR EXCELLENT SERVICE

'The service is excellent . . . not an obsequious, fawning service; just very attentive and responsive.'[10]

Central to SIA's customer service is the 'Singapore Girl' advertising campaign which has become synonymous with high quality in-flight service.[11] This must have been one of the most successful marketing campaigns in recent times, though there have been some murmurings about its correctness. The most famous Singapore Girl is stewardess Lim Suet Kwee who saw her waxwork double unveiled in Madame Tussaud's waxworks museum in London in 1993.

In the pursuit of excellent service, SIA never underestimates the importance of attention to detail. The company knows that this makes the difference between 'good' service and 'excellent' service; something even as simple as installing double castor wheels on the cabin carts which eases and speeds the service of meals. It has also developed a wide choice of menus and cuisines and keeps abreast of changing tastes, including meals to tempt those looking for lighter or healthier options. There are also special food events held to coincide with major festivals and celebrations. Flight attendants are instructed how to warm the meals for best results and they are even taught some of the finer points of wine appreciation.

Recent improvements to seats have been made including a greater seat pitch, improved lumbar support and increased leg room for passengers in Raffles Class.

PEOPLE-CENTRED APPROACH

SIA's people-centred approach starts at the top. Mr Ong said:

> *'The commitment of top managers is the driving force behind our success. At all levels we recruit the best people available. We like to inject new blood where and when we can to bring in fresh ideas. We also want to recruit people who can make an impression. We are also serious about training. We recently spent S$80m on our own training centre: training is a big business for us. At our centre we undertake three major types of training; functional, related to the job such as ticketing reservations, skills improvement, such as supervisory skills and management development where we run a range of management programmes.'*

Michael Tan, the company's deputy MD (commercial) stressed the importance of the front line staff:

> *'Ultimately our cabin crew, our service staff, make the difference. Underlying all of the other things is the service. That is hard to duplicate.'*[12]

SIA's stewardesses are employed on five-year renewable contracts. A stewardess can work up to 15 years (three contracts) without being promoted. If she is promoted to leading stewardess she is offered a three-year extension. Longer extensions are offered to those who rise further up the ladder, for example to chief stewardess or inflight supervisor. SIA looks to retain its crew members for about ten years though the average length of service is about four years only. Many crew members leave for further studies or a change of career. Dr Cheong added 'our problem is that our stewardesses leave too early, usually before the first contract is done. They meet someone interesting and get married'.[13]

SIA's pool of operating crew will almost double by the end of the century to keep in line with the airline's plans to expand at the rate of 8 to 10 per cent a year. The tight local labour market in Singapore cannot sustain this growth and, as the airline is not willing to lower recruitment standards, SIA has begun recruiting flight stewardesses from China and Indonesia. It already recruits from overseas, in particular from Japan, Taiwan and Korea to cater for the specific linguistic and cultural needs of passengers from these countries.

Mr Ong explained the company's approach to managing its staff and outlined one of its most recent initiatives in customer service:

'We believe in empowering our staff because it involves them more in their work, makes them more motivated, eases decision making and, of course, improves customer service. Our most recent initiative is called OSG – Outstanding Service on the Ground. We know cabin service is vital and we have put a lot of time and effort into it, but there is only so much you can do during a flight. The problems are not usually in the air where we have direct control over many of the factors but are away from the flight, such as service on the ground where we might be only one of many players. Outstanding service here is noticed by our customers, as is poor service, but it is more difficult to achieve because it often involves dealing with many other bodies, like handling agents for example. This is not a programme, it is a movement, led by the managing director. We are putting all of our ground staff through OSG courses now. We want people to first, show they care, second, dare to care, that is to go and make decisions, and thirdly, be a service entrepreneur, look for opportunities to impress. We are also running "take the lead" programmes for supervisors to carry through and support OSG.

'We try hard to quantify levels of service to help establish what is expected of staff, but they also have to be realistic. We have standards about how each task should be carried out, for example, time taken to serve a meal, telephone pick-up times, check-in times, times for bags to be delivered, punctuality targets, mishandling rates, complaint/compliment ratios, and deadlines to reply to complaints.'

INTERNAL COMMUNICATION

Service objectives and targets, new company developments, commitments to enhance passenger service and changes in the airline industry are just some of the features to be found in the companies in-house magazine, *Outlook*. This is a monthly magazine of between 20 and 24 pages aimed at all of SIA's 26 000 staff. It reports on the previous month's financial results together with productivity and service quality measures. Detailed information provided includes revenue, operating costs, profit, available freight and passenger capacities, on-time departures, on-time arrivals as well as number of complaints and compliments at each service delivery-point. It also includes extracts of complaint and compliment letters from passengers. The company's mission statement, on the first page of *Outlook*, serves to remind each employee about SIA's 'aim to provide services of the highest quality at reasonable prices for customers and at a profit for the company'. This magazine links together top management through the staff and middle-managerial functions down to the front-lines of ground services (ticketing, reservation and check-ins), in-flight services provided by cabin crews, the cockpit crews (pilots, co-pilots and flight engineers) and the rest of the SIA team (back-room baggage handling, logistics and office staff).[14]

SIA also produces newsletters for particular groups of staff. *Highpoint*, for example, is aimed at its in-flight crews, both cabin and cockpit, and *Higher Ground* is specifically for its ground service staff. *Highpoint* is produced monthly and contains between 12 and 16 pages of news and views. The objective of the newsletter is to keep its 8000 in-flight personnel informed about the airline's latest offerings and its commitments to passengers. The newsletter also focuses on teamwork, recent problems and their resolutions, as well as performance data for the previous month. The MD's quarterly service excellence award is also featured. Although the prize money is not large the award serves to encourage teamwork and high service levels. *Highpoint* also includes a regular features page with about eight or nine extracts from letters, half being compliments and the other half complaints. An example of a compliment received:

> *'I noticed the service, although in economy class, was professional and better than any flights I have ever been on. Miss Iris Lee was the most hardworking among all the crew. She came round distributing newspapers, drinks, postcards, playing cards, amenities etc. As a director of travel and tours, I fly often and I have never come across such an outstanding cabin hostess.'*[15]

An example of a complaint received:

> *'We were sitting close by the galleys and were able to observe the cabin crew at work throughout the flight, and the impression we gained was that they were unable to cope with a full load of passengers. There seemed also to be a lack of leadership and organisation – the cabin crew were rushing back and forth getting in each other's way and not the smooth activity which we have come to expect from Singapore Airlines.'*[16]

Valid comments and observations by passengers are taken very seriously by the company. A thorough investigation into the passenger's comments is conducted by Customer Affairs, together with the relevant departments. Passengers are accorded interim replies to assure them that the matter is being looked into, and a final response after the completion of the investigation is also sent to them.

Higher Ground is a bimonthly newsletter of between eight and twelve pages aimed at the ground services staff, including ticketing, reservations, check-in as well as baggage handling, logistics and transportation. This newsletter is similar to *Highpoint* but contains material pertinent to ground staff. One regular feature is the one page 'Service Tips' explaining that staff are the eyes and ears of the company and staff members have a responsibility to see and listen on its behalf as well as promoting its corporate image. There are regular features on service quality competitions and awards and, like *Highpoint*, *Higher Ground* contains extracts from letters, usually two complaints and one compliment. An example compliment printed in *Higher Ground* follows:

> *'I would like to pen a note of appreciation for the extra help your staff gave my aged parents when they took your SQ860 from Singapore to Hong Kong. They were told at the check-in counter to come back to see your staff. My brother accordingly brought them to the counter near the check-in time. Then one of your staff very kindly brought them into the restricted area, through immigration and right to the departure room. This was of great help to them as they do not understand the signs in English and may have had to look around or ask around for the directions to the departure room. Walking extra distance would also be troublesome for my mother who is recovering from a stroke. Thank you once again to your staff for going out of their way to assist my parents. I am indeed proud of our national airline.'*[17]

An example complaint was also printed:

> *'On 26th July we flew Singapore Airlines. Prior to the arrangement being made and also a few days before the actual flight, I reminded the airline that my mother would require a wheelchair for both embarkation and disembarkation . . . She had travelled last year by Singapore Airlines and had no trouble whatsoever. At embarkation, a wheelchair was provided and we boarded the plane with no problems . . . On arrival we were not docked at a bridge, but parked in the middle of the airfield. I was then asked if my mother could manage to get down two external steep flights of stairs and to walk to a bus which would then take her to the terminal. As she had got on the plane by wheelchair I would have thought it was patently obvious that this was totally impossible for her. We were told that it was our fault and that the airport had not been informed. I explained that I had done as much as I could in informing the station at departure, and they certainly knew she required a wheelchair to get on the plane and therefore, obviously, to get off the plane. It took an hour to get some means of transport to take her off the plane and into the airport terminal.'*[18]

There is also a monthly newsletter for technical and cockpit crews which features technical developments such as new avionics, and on-board hardware and software, air-safety, security and weather reports, and incidents and performance statistics on in-flight, fuel management, on-time arrivals and on-time departures.

EXTERNAL INFORMATION

SIA keeps its passengers informed through its in-flight magazine *Silver Kris*. This monthly publication includes a 'Message from the Managing Director' with a personal message from Dr Cheong outlining new and proposed services. There is also a regular page entitled 'Skylines' informing passengers of SIA's latest investments in hangars, pilot training facilities and joint-ventures into hotels in popular holiday resorts, for example.

LISTENING TO THE CUSTOMER

'We constantly monitor passenger feedback, re-examine service procedures and study new technologies to discover ways in which to further improve the service we provide', explains Dr Cheong Choong Kong.[19]

Mr Ong explained the details:

'We employ varied and systematic methods to obtain information from our passengers. We carry out quarterly passenger surveys and undertake focused group work with our frequent flyers. We do get some complaints and pride ourselves in being able to resolve them quickly. We analyse them and try to improve what we do and feed the information back to the people who can make it happen. We really value complaints and see them as opportunities to improve what we do and how we do it. We put a strong emphasis on service recovery, not damage control. We do have many contingency plans in place for when things go wrong and we have a philosophy of "making good"; trying to provide on the spot recovery and fair compensation for anything adverse that has happened.

'We sometimes use the Priority *magazine, a publication for frequent flyers, to get passengers' reactions to new ideas. We recently asked for feedback on the idea of installing a fax checking-in system to add to our telephone check-in system.*[20]

'We also check out the service for ourselves. We conduct on-site audits with test calls to reservations, for example, to see how service is being delivered. When any member of staff flies in our aircraft we ask them to submit reports of their travel experiences. Senior staff members must submit a comment sheet on each flight with their expense account.

'We even monitor our competitors and often go and check out their service. We monitor and assess their levels of service and their amenities.'

FINANCIAL SUCCESS

The company's financial performance is impressive. Describing the 1994/95 results Dr Cheong said, 'the improved performance in 1994/1995 is in line with the turnaround of the industry . . . Prevailing excess capacity and aggressive marketing by the competition will continue to tax the resourcefulness of our people.'[21] Table 42.1 summarises the company's recent financial performance.[22]

Table 42.1 Financial highlights

Year ending March	*1995*	*1994*	*1993*
Revenue (S$m)	6555	6236	5648
Net profit (S$m)	918	801	851
Earnings per share (cents)	72	63	67

SIA's commitment to a healthy bottom line is not achieved at the expense of quality. *Orient Aviation* in a special profile of SIA stated 'Singapore Airlines is proof that a fierce commitment to the financial bottom line is not in conflict with the production of a quality product. The quality product, in fact, is one of the keys to SIA's great bottom line success. SIA aimed to be the best and most successful airline in the world. And it succeeded.'[23]

INTERNATIONAL ACCOLADES

'Everything an airline should do well Singapore Airlines does excellently. Passenger service, financial planning, marketing, technical and fleet strategy and maintenance are all exemplary at Singapore Airlines.'[24]

SIA's success is demonstrated by the many international accolades and awards it receives, year after year. In 1995 SIA was voted Asia's Most Admired Company in a survey of 250 top companies conducted by *Asian Business* magazine. In the same survey it came first in the Best Managed Company category, second in Best Products and Services and Most Honest and Ethical Company and made it into the top ten in the Best Employer and Greatest Contribution to the Local Economy categories. In the same year SIA was voted the top airline for business travellers by *Asiamoney* and was honoured in the UK's *Decanter* magazine's Airline Wine Awards.[25]

In an annual poll of Britain's frequent travellers SIA was voted best carrier to the Far East in the 1995 Airline of the Year Awards. Its cabin crew and airport lounges scored top marks. The north American based *Business Traveler International* voted SIA Best airline for International Travel for the sixth year running.[26] Despite all of these accolades Dr Cheong is resolute that SIA cannot afford to be complacent. He explained 'its going to be much harder because . . . the worthy competition is getting better every year'.[27]

Questions

1 What makes SIA a world class service provider?

2 Describe SIA's operations strategy. Assess its effectiveness.

3 Use the Platts-Gregory procedure to help you consider how SIA might develop in the future.

References

[1] 'Superior, Innovative & Adept', *Air Transport World,* June 1994
[2] 'SIA – the pride of the Lion City', *Orient Aviation*, October 1993
[3] 'Superior, Innovative & Adept', *Air Transport World,* June 1994
[4] Company information
[5] Company information
[6] 'The SIA Story', *Silver Kris,* July 1995
[7] Company information
[8] 'The SIA Story', *Silver Kris,* July 1995
[9] Company information
[10] 'Superior, Innovative & Adept', *Air Transport World,* June 1994
[11] 'SIA – the pride of the Lion City', *Orient Aviation*, October 1993
[12] 'Superior, Innovative & Adept', *Air Transport World,* June 1994
[13] 'Superior, Innovative & Adept', *Air Transport World,* June 1994
[14] *Outlook,* May 1995
[15] 'Feedback', *Highpoint,* April 1994
[16] 'Feedback', *Highpoint,* April 1994
[17] 'Feedback', *Higher Ground,* November/December 1994
[18] 'Feedback', *Higher Ground,* September/October 1994
[19] 'The SIA Story', *Silver Kris,* July 1995
[20] *Silver Kris,* July 1995
[21] *The Straits Times*, 22 May 1995
[22] SIA group company accounts
[23] 'SIA – the pride of the Lion City', *Orient Aviation*, October 1993
[24] 'ATW Awards – 20 Years of Excellence, Singapore Airlines', *Air Transport World,* February 1994
[25] 'Skylines', *Silver Kris,* July 1995
[26] *Priority,* First Issue, 1995
[27] 'Superior, Innovative & Adept', *Air Transport World,* June 1994

CASE 43

Rover

Sara Mountney, Rob Lummis and Stuart Chambers

Case date 1996

INTRODUCTION

The Rover Group, owned by BMW, is the largest manufacturer of motor vehicles in the UK. It employs just under 40 000 people (known as associates) on sites in the West Midlands and Oxford. The company is continously improving by using Total Quality Management, employee empowerment and cellular manufacturing techniques. It also introduced its New Deal Programme in 1992 to facilitate a flexible labour force. These initiatives have developed as a consequence of benchmarking Japanese car manufacturers and a 15-year partnership with Honda which ended in 1994. Also in 1994, Rover was awarded the British section of the European Foundation of Quality Awards. The esteem in which the company is held may be illustrated by this quotation:

> *'Sir, let me reassure you that Sir Andrew Wood, Britain's ambassador in Moscow, does not merely "make do" with a Range Rover as opposed to a Rolls-Royce in that city. Anyone who has seen the gleaming green object in question outside the Foreign Office . . .would have no doubt this was not only the best vehicle for the job but also an outstanding achievement for Britain . . .'*[1]

However, this has not always been the case – a fact which makes Rover's achievements particularly inspiring. In the late 1970s, Rover, or British Leyland (BL) as it was then known, was on the point of bankrupcy.

SURVIVAL IN THE 1970S

> *'If British Leyland fails to succeed it will have the most dire effect on jobs and investment prospects, not to mention the reputation of Britain and British jobs overseas.*
>
> *'The question you will ask is "Can you really hope to influence such a situation?" I don't know. The task is enormous; some people would even say impossible. But I am going to try because I believe that British Leyland does have a future. It is a company which has talent at all levels. Talent that can and must be fully utilised. Given the right support from all in the company and government – and that could mean facing up to*

some tough decisions in the future – it is still possible to restore its growth and realise its full potential'[2]

(Sir Michael Edwardes, Chairman of BL 1977–1982, shortly after his appointment)

The British Leyland of the mid-1970s was a vast, centralised organisation of around 120 000 employees. It was largely a state-owned company formed from a number of motor manufacturers in 1968. The product range encompassed trucks (Leyland), cars (Austin, Morris, Triumph) and luxury cars (Jaguar, Rover). The problems which beset the company were numerous: the company was renowned for poor products, poor quality, and poor employee relations. For example, in 1977 a toolmakers' strike had cost the company 25 per cent of its annual production. Such events had made the company notorious in the business world.

In addition to its internal problems, a number of external factors were also threatening the future of the company. The industry itself was heavily unionised. Also, the 'second industrial revolution' of the 1980s was dawning, resulting in new technology such as robotics, new materials and new processes. This situation meant that the company had to change to survive.

Following the appointment of Sir Michael Edwardes as Chairman in 1977, a recovery plan was put into action to ensure the survival of the company. This included a joint enterprise with Honda, whom the company began benchmarking in 1979. This led to Honda cars being supplied in kit form and assembled at the Cowley (Oxford) plant as the Triumph Acclaim. This product was a suitable stopgap while BL began to develop the partnership with Honda. The partnership gave the company the ability to develop a full range of products something which previously it had been unable to do due to the lack of funds to support this type of work.

The management culture during that era is now seen, retrospectively, as being exceptionally confrontational and aggressive. Yet it was necessary at the time to ensure the company's survival.

IMPROVEMENT IN THE 1980S

Under the focused leadership of Sir Michael Edwardes and Harold Musgrove from 1982, BL made steps towards its survival. During the 1980s, various political changes also took place which helped to stabilise the industrial relations problems, such as the Industrial Relations Act which made Trade Unions more answerable to law.

Other initiatives were also taking place during this period. Total Quality Management was implemented from 1986, leading to greater employee involvement. At the same time, the results of an employee attitude survey also drew attention to the issue of employee involvement. Sir Graham Day, Chairman from 1986, instigated *Roverisation*, a process which aimed to introduce quality products aspiring to the perceived upmarket image of the Rover.

TQM (Total Quality Management)

Initial TQM training was carried out by consultants at board level, but from then on the initiative was wholly owned by the company. TQM training cascaded down through the whole organisational structure, a process which took five years. The main elements of the TQM programme were and continue to be as follows:

- concentration on prevention rather than detection of quality problems;
- right first time approach;
- everybody responsible;
- management led;
- company wide;
- measurement and reduction of cost of quality;
- continuous improvement.

Employee involvement

When the company began working with Honda in 1979, it initially concentrated its attention on the technical processes. However, it was soon realised that benefits could be gained by benchmarking Honda's relationship with its people as well. Honda was a demanding partner but also very valuable in terms of its business processes.

The breakthrough began in 1985 with a visit to a Honda plant in Marysville, Ohio. It was there that senior management saw at first hand Japanese techniques and employee relations transposed to a western culture. An employee attitude survey, *Viewpoint*, was launched in 1986 with 10 per cent random sample of the labour force participating. Some negative opinions were expressed:

- management is not leading its workforce correctly
- communication is poor
- there is little chance for involvement in the company
- there aren't opportunities to train and develop.

Rover's hypothesis was that people wanted to be respected, recognised, valued, treated individually, listened to, and be part of the same team. The employees also cared about the company – it was important to them. The challenge was to unleash this pent-up motivation. The reason why Rover decided to pursue the issue of employee involvement was because it was felt that people could be its competitive advantage. There were diminishing opportunities to strongly differentiate through the products as a new innovation would soon be followed by something similar from a competitor. In terms of technology, all car manufacturers used similar production techniques and all were reducing their cost-base. Rover thus concluded that their major competitive advantage lay with the labour force, a fact that the Japanese (the leading car manufacturers) clearly knew and utilised, as demonstrated by this famous quotation by Konosuke Matsushito in 1985[3]:

> *'We are going to win and the industrial West is going to lose out – there is nothing much you can do about it, because the reasons for your failure are within yourselves. For you, the essence of management is getting the ideas out of the heads of bosses into the hands of labour. For us, the core of management is precisely the art of mobilising and pulling together the intellectual resources of all employees in the service of the firm. Only by drawing on the combined brainpower of all its employees can a firm face up to the turbulence and constraints of today's environment.'*

The *Success Through People* initiative was launched in 1989, with the objective to create and sustain an environment in which everyone would willingly give their best contribution. The main areas of the initiative were to focus on individuals, instigate leadership from line management, ensure personal development and involve everybody. The aim was to move towards a more delegated environment and to empower employees within their range of skills, based on a motivational vision, shared values and common objectives. Rover's company vision was to be internationally renowned for delivering extraordinary customer satisfaction.

In early 1991, the company underwent a structural reorganisation to support it in to achieving these objectives. The culture and processes of the business were analysed, with the new structure resulting directly from this. The organisation was split into business units with individual managing directors. This emphasized the business aspects of the company and focused on the product and processes rather than functions. The structure itself was flat, with broader roles within the organisation.

THE NEW THREAT IN THE 1990S

The application of Total Quality principles began to change the style of the business and the company began to realise its potential. By 1988, the government had sold its shareholding to British Aerospace, developed a range of vehicles with Honda and sold the Jaguar and Leyland businesses. In 1991, George Simpson succeeded Sir Graham Day as Chairman and continued to consolidate the *Roverisation* programme.

However, a new threat was emerging which made Rover management realise that the transformation of the company over the past decade would not necessarily guarantee its survival. The new threat came from 'transplant' factories being built in the UK by competitors (Nissan, Toyota and Honda). A survey in the US[4] had shown that transplant factories there had provided extra capacity for 1.72 million units, and resulted in the closure of 1.82 million units of US-owned capacity. Rover carried out its own survey based in the UK and Europe and concluded that they faced a similar threat.

THE NEW DEAL

The New Deal (between management, employees and unions) was signed in April 1992 following six months of negotiations. The aim was to create a single status labour force which was flexible to adapt to future changes:

> *'We need a workforce distinguished only by individual or team contribution to the company.'*

These are the key issues involved in the New Deal:

- *Single status company.* The only distinction between people is their contribution. In practice, this was achieved by ending the artificial distinction between 'hourly paid' and 'staff' employees, such as removing the need for hourly staff to clock in and paying *all* employees by credit transfer. A common sick pay scheme, regular health checks and voluntary workwear were introduced. No employees were laid off, but transferred to other duties or involved in training and development.
- *Flexibility.* All employees were flexible in their job according to their skills. Teams became accountable for the quality of their work, becoming responsible for routine maintenance and housekeeping, waste disposal, plant or office layout and equipment, improvements to processes, cost reduction, work allocation, job rotation, training and materials control. This introduced Total Productive Maintenance (TPM) procedures.
- *Continuous improvement.* All company members were to participate in continuous improvement, by participating in suggestion schemes, discussion groups and quality action teams. The aim of this was to eliminate waste, increase efficiency and improve performance and quality.
- *Training.* All employees were given the opportunity to, and expected to participate in, training and development to increase their range of skills and knowledge.
- *Security of employment.* This was one of the major issues of the New Deal, as it was believed that security was needed to enable empowerment. All Rover employees have permanent employment providing they wish to stay with the company. In practice, this is only achievable if employees are prepared to be flexible and take up opportunities for retraining and development. Manpower reduction is achieved through retraining and redeployment, natural wastage, voluntary severence and early retirement.
- *Commitment to communication.* All employees receive and participate in open and honest two-way communication, with a greater emphasis on team briefings.
- *Rover and the unions.* A Joint Negotiating Committee was formed from the trade unions represented at the company – a move to 'single table' bargaining. Communication between Rover and the unions was enhanced to give the unions a greater view of company plans performance. The disputes procedure was strengthened to allow unresolved disputes to be transferred to arbitration, with no disputes to be recognised outside this procedure.

ROVER TODAY

The culture of the company has changed from a situation where management push for change to where change is supported by the people. As this evolves further, it is intended that the situation should arise where people push management for change. Associate involvement continues to be a key issue in the company.

To support the continuous improvement and empowerment initiatives, Rover Learning Business was launched in 1990 to provide an environment where people can develop their skills and change their attitudes. Rover Learning Business offered several initiatives at the launch. These have continued to develop and are ongoing. Some of them are detailed as follows:

- Rover Employee Assisted Learning (REAL), awards a bursary of £100 to each associate to undertake a non-vocational accredited course at an accredited institution. Examples of courses undertaken range from pottery to sports coaching. The philosophy behind this scheme was to encourage people back to learning. A tuition refund scheme also exists which allows the refund of fees on vocational courses.
- The personal development file is an optional file which forms a record of achievement which is used for personal development planning and reviewing with a supervisor.
- Performance and development review. This form replaced the old staff appraisal form and is used by all employees. It avoids rating scales and aims to be forward-looking instead, concentrating on objectives for the individual both personally and in the workplace.
- Training of Total Quality leaders, a continuation of the Total Quality initiatives.
- Educational courses at all levels run in conjunction with Warwick University.

Rover also recognised the need to attract young people into engineering in general and Rover specifically. Education partnerships were set up in the local community to give publicity to the industry. Some of the features of this scheme are teacher placements, rooms in local schools (Rover Rooms) and Skills Clubs for young people.

CONCLUSION

During the 1980s, Rover's vision was to be 'better than BMW'. In February 1994, Rover was bought by BMW. John Towers also became Chairman of Rover in 1994. The success of the initiatives, and indeed Rover's transformation, may be measured by these sample answers in the Viewpoint survey:

Table 43.1 Contrast of viewpoint survey results – 1988 and 1992

Opinion	*1988*	*1992*
Managers communicate effectively with employees	Disagree	Agree
Managers provide effective leadership	Disagree	Agree
My manager involves me in making Rover a better company	Disagree	Agree
Managers do not trust their people	Agree	Disagree
My work makes poor use of my abilities	Agree	Disagree
There are good opportunities to train for a better job	Disagree	Agree
What happens in my work is important to me	Agree	Agree

These quantitative results also reflect a more recent change:

	% Agree		
	1990	*1992*	*1994*
Rover a better place to work	48	54	61
Feel secure at Rover	36	41	67

Questions

1 Is it necessary to experience a crisis before major changes in working practices, such as in Rover, are possible?

2 To what extent and why has Rover exceeded its ethical obligations towards its workforce?

3 What were the most important elements of the 'New Deal' in terms of creating sustainable competitive advantages?

4 What could, or should, Rover do next?

References

[1] Letters to the Editor, *Financial Times*, 15 November 1995.
[2] Edwardes, M. E. (1983), *Back from the Brink*, Collins.
[3] Slack *et al.* (1998), *Operations Management* (2nd edn), Pitman Publishing.
[4] Womack, James, P. (1990), *The Machine that Changed the World*, Macmillan.

Index